A

NUMISMATIC MANUAL

A

NUMISMATIC MANUAL

BY

JOHN YONGE AKERMAN, F. S. A.

GYAN

Published by

Gyan Publishing House
5, Ansari Road
Daryaganj, New Delhi-110002
Phone: 011-47034999, 9811692060
E-mail: books@gyanbooks.com

Distribution Network
gyanbooks.com
India, USA, Canada, UK, Australia

ISBN: 978-81-212-8112-6 (HB)
First Published, 1832

2nd Impression 2024

Printed at: Gyan Press, Delhi.

A NUMISMATIC MANUAL
Author: JOHN YONGE AKERMAN

NUMISMATIC MANUAL.

" Les Médailles, qui sont les preuves de l'histoire, nous la font comprendre avec autant de plaisir que d'utilité, et l'histoire à son tour nous sert bien souvent de commentaires, pour découvrir le sens des inscriptions mystérieuses, que se rencontrent sur les médailles ; et ce secours reciproque oblige fort agréablement de joindre des cabinets d'antiquitéz au bibliothéques."

Patin, Hist. de Médailles.

A NUMISMATIC MANUAL

BY

JOHN YONGE AKERMAN, F. S. A.

CORRESPONDING MEMBER OF THE SOCIETY OF ANTIQUARIES OF SCOTLAND, HONORARY MEMBER OF THE SOCIETY OF ANTIQUARIES OF NEWCASTLE-UPON-TYNE, AND ONE OF THE HONORARY SECRETARIES OF THE NUMISMATIC SOCIETY OF LONDON.

LONDON:

TAYLOR & WALTON, 28, UPPER GOWER STREET,

BOOKSELLERS AND PUBLISHERS TO UNIVERSITY COLLEGE.

M.DCCC.XL.

TO

ALGERNON PERCY, BARON PRUDHOE,

OF PRUDHOE CASTLE IN THE COUNTY OF

NORTHUMBERLAND,

CAPTAIN, R.N., F.R.S., F.S.A.,

HONORARY MEMBER OF THE NUMISMATIC SOCIETY,

ETC., ETC., ETC.

THIS ATTEMPT TO FURNISH AN INTRODUCTION TO THE STUDY

OF

ANCIENT AND MODERN COINS

IS

MOST RESPECTFULLY

INSCRIBED.

PREFACE.

The ready sale of a small and very imperfect work bearing the same title as the present, not only proves that an elementary treatise is much wanted, but it also encourages the hope that a volume in an improved form, and of systematic arrangement, will be still more acceptable to the numismatic student.

The present work is divided into five parts. The First Part contains, together with elementary observations, a Geographical Classification, according to the system of Eckhel, of the *Greek Coins of Cities and Princes,* including those struck by various states while under the Roman dominion.

The Second Part treats of *Roman Coins,* and furnishes an accurate list of the Consular and Imperial Series, preceded by a concise introduction.

The Third Part comprises a summary account of our *English Coinage,* and a list of all the most remarkable examples.

The Fourth Part consists of a carefully arranged Catalogue of *Anglo-Gallic Coins;* and the Fifth contains brief notices of *Irish and Scotch Coins.*

With regard to the *Illustrations*, I earnestly hope that the method adopted will materially assist the younger student, and prove of some service to the more advanced numismatist.

I cannot dismiss this short notice, without expressing my acknowledgments to those kind friends upon whose indulgence and patience I have so largely drawn.

To Thomas Burgon, Esq., one of the Vice-Presidents of the Numismatic Society, I am greatly indebted for many valuable hints in the compilation of the list of Greek Coins of Cities and Princes, derived from his intimate acquaintance with that extensive and important series.

To John Brumell, Esq., my thanks are especially due for assistance in the estimations of the rarity of Roman Imperial Coins, which long experience and the possession of a most choice cabinet so well qualify him to give.

To James Dodsley Cuff, Esq., F.S.A., I am under many obligations, for much information relative to English Coins, which great practical experience and a rare and valuable collection of Saxon and English coins have enabled him to communicate, more particularly for the estimations of their rarity, a subject of much importance to those who are desirous of acquiring a collection.

To Count Maurice Von Dietrichstein, Prefect of the Imperial

Library of Vienna, my acknowledgements are due, for many marks of kindness with which he has honoured me, and especially for his recent present of a collection of casts of rare Imperial Greek Coins, preserved in that magnificent establishment.

From my friend, the Rev. J. B. Reade, F.R.S., I have at all times derived that information which good taste and scholarship are calculated to afford; and from his small but select cabinet of Roman coins, I have obtained drawings of several interesting reverses in that series.

My thanks are also due to M. Adrien de Longpérier, of the Bibliothéque du Roi, Paris, for his polite communication of several Notes on Anglo-Gallic Coins.

To John Lee, Esq., LL.D., F.R.S., of Hartwell House, Bucks, I am indebted for access, on all occasions, to his cabinet of Greek Coins, to his extensive collection of Numismatic works, and for that assistance which he is so well known to render to those who are engaged in the study of history and antiquity.

To Edward Hawkins, Esq., F.R.S., and Charles Frederick Barnewell, Esq., F.R.S., I return my acknowledgments for their attention to repeated applications at the British Museum, for examples of the Greek and Roman types, which will be found represented in the various Plates illustrating this volume.

To Professor H. H. Wilson, F.R.S., I am indebted for a list of the Coins of Bactrian Princes, and for a copy of the Bactrian and Old Sanscrit Alphabets, which will be found in the Plates.

In conclusion, I have merely to observe, that I have throughout endeavoured to render the work as concise as possible, and that, although there are many points on which I might have dilated, I have considered it advisable to confine the volume within its present limits.

CONTENTS.

SECTION I.

GREEK COINS.

SECTION II.

ROMAN COINS.

SECTION III.

ENGLISH COINS.

SECTION IV.

ANGLO-GALLIC COINS.

SECTION V.

IRISH AND SCOTCH COINS.

SECTION I.

GREEK COINS.

" Observandum deinde, non modo in Graecia, quam propriam appellamus, sed etiam in plerisque terris aliis, quas Graeci incoluere, hoc aevo operis monetarii artem fuisse absolutissimam. Omitto Graeciam Magnam, Siciliamque, felices, ut satis constat, artium omnium èxercitiorumque aemulas, quas Graecia propria mater invenit, excoluitque. At fuêre regiones, ut Thracia, Bithynia, Caria, Insulae Ægaei, &c., quarum ad artes liberales ingenium vix unquam a veteribus fuit celebratum, quin fuere etiam, et in ipsa quidem Graecia, populi, ut Boeoti et Arcades, quorum quidam stupor, et obstulior mentis acies in proverbium ivere. Tamen quanta fuerit has per terras, populosque artis pictoriæ perfectio, superstites eorum numi palam eloquuntur."—Eckhel, *Prol. General. Doct. Num. Vet.* Vol. I. p. cxxxix.

NUMISMATIC MANUAL.

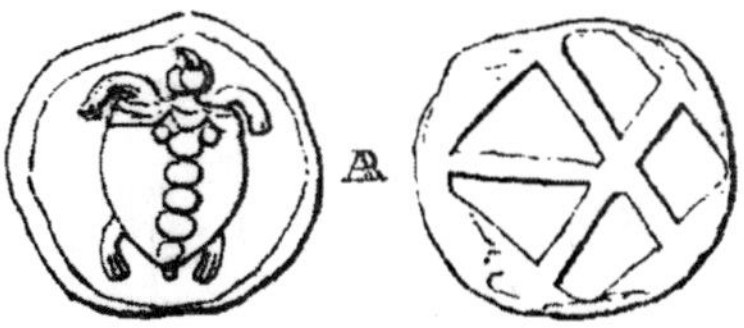

ORIGIN OF COINAGE.

ΑΦ ΟΥ Φ..ΔΩΝ Ο ΑΡΓΕΙΟΣ....ΕΣΚΕΥΑΣΕ ΚΑΙ ΝΟΜΙΣΜΑ ΑΡΓΥΡΟΥΝ ΕΝ ΑΙΓΙΝΗ ΕΠΟΙΗΣΕΝ ΕΝΔΕΚΑΤΟΣ ΩΝ ΑΦ ΗΡΑΚΛΕΟΥΣ.

Ex quo Phidon Argivus....apparavit, et numum argenteum in Aegina signavit, undecimus ab Hercule.

ECKHEL cannot suppress a sneer as he glances at the crude theories of some writers on the origin of coinage[1], which, notwithstanding the words of the Arundelian marble above quoted, is involved in much obscurity. Among the Greeks there existed a tradition, that Phidon, the Argive, was the inventor of weights and measures, and the first who stamped coins; but it is well known that certain ancient writers are not of this opinion. Herodotus[2] says, that the Lydians first coined money of gold and silver; and some of our modern numismatists are inclined to believe, that the money with the type of the tortoise is not the earliest. "Many cities of antiquity," observes M. Hennin, "claimed the honour of giving

[1] Prolegomena Generalia, part vi. cap. 3. [2] Lib. i. c. 94.

birth to Homer; and it was natural that the invention of coinage should also be disputed.[1]"

The coins which, by universal consent, are allowed to be most ancient, have on one side a cavity or indentation; and those assigned to the Island of Ægina are thus distinguished, and placed among the earliest examples. The type of these coins is a turtle or a tortoise, the reverse being merely an indented square divided into segments. Others of a later period have letters and symbols within the square.[2]

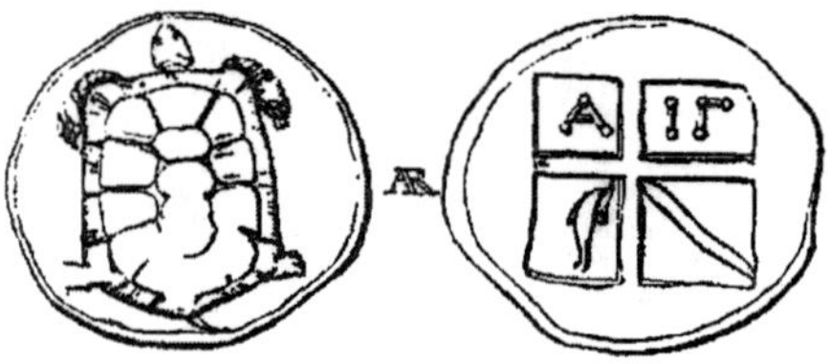

Those who have industriously sought for proofs of a stamped coinage before the times to which these coins may be referred, may, perhaps, have their doubts removed by the following observations of one our best informed and most sensible numismatists: "As the act of impressing a seal or signet was an understood sign of solemn compact, from the most early periods; and as engraved seals and signets were undoubtedly in general use long anterior to the invention of coinage, it appears highly probable, that the original idea of impressing a stamp on the uncoined lumps of gold and silver was derived from the common application of a seal to wax. The earliest coins may be therefore looked upon as pieces of *sealed metal;* which in fact they are, it being well known that, at first, coins were impressed only on one side. No device that could be imagined, was so well adapted to the peculiar necessity of the case, or so likely to satisfy the public mind, as the impress, by public authority, of the symbol of the tutelar divinity

[1] Manuel de Numismatique, tome i. p. 16.

[2] The Abbé Barthelemy's dissertation on a coin of Bœotia. bearing the magistrate's name ΦΙΔΟ, was a lamentable waste of time and learning. See the Memoirs of the French Academy, vol. xxvi. p. 543.

of their city; or some equally sacred and well-known emblem: and, even with respect to the inhabitants of distant cities to which the coin might be carried for purposes of commerce, the common reverence for the gods which was universally entertained, as well as for the sacred games and festivals instituted in their honour, would render sacred symbols not only grateful to their feelings, but would have the great additional advantage of speaking a language universally intelligible." [1]

The necessity of stamped coins in large empires was, perhaps, not experienced, as in the case of the Egyptians, whose circulating medium, as appears by the paintings which have descended to us, consisted of metal rings; but in smaller states, having commercial relations with each other, the want of an authorised and acknowledged currency was supplied by means at once natural and ample.

It may here be mentioned, that some writers have cited ancient coins bearing the heads of Homer, Pythagoras, Numa, Ancus, and other personages of antiquity, as proofs of the existence of a coinage in their time. Coins certainly exist with such portraits, and some of them in considerable numbers; for instance, that of Ancus on the denarii of the Marcia family, who boasted their descent from that prince. The people of Smyrna, and those of other cities, who claimed Homer as their countryman, placed his portrait on their coins: but this was done long after the age in which he is said to have flourished; a fact which is shown by the circumstance of the place of his birth being so much disputed. As none but the most sacred objects were depicted on the coins of the ancients, these portraits of their illustrious personages furnish interesting evidence of the high veneration in which they were held.

As regards the antiquity of Grecian coinage, we have the most certain evidence that it had attained some degree of excellence in the reign of Alexander I., King of Macedon, 497 to 454 B. C., of whom we have authentic coins,

[1] "An Inquiry into the Motive which influenced the Ancients in their Choice of the various Representations which we find stamped on their Money." By Thomas Burgon, Esq. Numismatic Journal, vol. i.

exhibiting the indented square;[1] a mark which does not disappear until the reign of Amyntas II., who reigned from 397 to 371 B. C. Of this monarch we have coins, both with and without the indented square.[2] Plutarch[3] informs us, that Lycurgus substituted copper money for that of gold and silver current in Lacedemonia; from which we learn, that gold and silver coins were current nine centuries before the Christian era. "This statement," observes M. Hennin,[4] "requires authentication, for, in a passage in the Eryxias, a dialogue attributed to Plato, the Lacedemonians are said to have used iron weights as money. M. Hennin justly supposes, that Plutarch meant uncoined gold and silver, and not stamped money.

Proceeding downward, we discover more authentic notices of a stamped currency among the Greeks. In the laws of Solon, six centuries B. C., the punishment of death is awarded to those who shall be found guilty of counterfeiting the public coin, a fact which justifies the remark of Neumann,[5] that the art of forging was almost coeval with the coining of money.

The coinage of the ancients has been classed under six epochs, as follows:—

I.—The earliest coinage, from the time of Phidon down to the reign of Alexander I. of Macedon, who died about the year 454 B. C., a period of two hundred years,[6] the invention of coinage being assigned to the seventh century B. C. These coins are characterised by an early style. M. Hennin remarks, that they are uncommon; but they have certainly descended to us in great numbers, particularly those of Ægina, a very surprising fact, considering their remote antiquity.[7]

II.—Coins struck from the reign of Alexander I., to that of Philip, father of Alexander the Great, a period of one

[1] Mionnet. Descrip., tome i. p. 505. [2] Ibid. p. 508. [3] In Lycurg.

[4] Manuel de Numismatique, tome i. p. 18.

[5] Romanorum Numi Anecdoti, p. 197.

[6] Eckhel Proleg. General. p. cxxxii.

[7] A naval friend, some years since, while at Rio, received, as the change of a Spanish dollar, several small pieces of silver, among which was one of these coins. A circumstance quite as singular, was related to me by the late Mr. Douce, who, when at Nismes (the ancient Nemausus), many years since, received, as sous pieces, on several occasions, the well-known coins of that city, with the type of the crocodile chained to a palm tree. These facts are mentioned, merely to show the imperishable nature of such records.

hundred years. A manifest improvement is visible in the coins included in this class.

III.—Coins struck from the last-mentioned period to the end of the Roman Republic, and the accession of Augustus.

IV.—Those which were struck from the time of Augustus to the end of the reign of Hadrian. It might be proper to add those of Antoninus Pius and his successors to this class.

V.—In the fifth class are included the coins struck from the time of the above-mentioned emperor to the reign of Gallienus. Considering the style of art during this period, this class should be subdivided.

VI.—Coins from Gallienus to the taking of Constantinople, and the extinction of the Empire of the East. This class, also, should be subdivided.

The coins of the first class are characterised by their early fabric, globulous shape,[1] and that certain mark of antiquity, the indented square in its primitive form.[2] Many are without legends; and when legends do occur, they are of the simplest description, retrograde, or boustrophedon, the characters partaking of the most ancient style.[3] The coins, the types of which, on one side, are indented, and on the other, in relief, are ranged with this class.[4]

In the coins of the second class, great improvement is evident, in the shape of the metal, and in the striking of the piece; but more especially in the workmanship of the type. The indented square gives place to a perfect reverse, except in some few instances, where it may have been retained in reverence for the ancient method. In this class are included the finest specimens of Greek art.

In those of the third class may be traced an improvement in the form of the characters; the legends are given at full length, with the addition of monograms and *dates*.

In the fourth class are comprised many varieties. To this

[1] The drachms of Ægina were called by the Greeks παχῖαι, or thick.

[2] See *Hunter*, tab. 66, and *Sestini* Descrizione Degli Stateri Antichi, tab. i. & ii. and iv. to viii.

[3] See Eckhel, Doct. Num. Vet. vol. i. p. xcvii. Plate 31 of Mionnet's Déscription de Médailles Antiques; and the plates to this volume.

[4] See those of Posidonia and Metapontum.

belong the extensive series termed *Greek Imperial* and *Colonial*, some of which are of fine execution, but the principal part indicate a melancholy decline in Greek art.[1] Many cities during this period yielded their rights to the Roman power, and the number of autonomous coins was considerably diminished. The Roman coins ranged in this class are of great interest, and many of them of considerable beauty.

In the fifth class may be observed a gradual declension, both in style and execution; although, in the coins of some reigns, workmanship of a superior character may occasionally be traced.[2]

In the sixth class are comprised the coins of nearly twelve hundred years. With few exceptions, their devices are rude, and, to many, uninteresting; and their legends of wearying sameness.[3] The greater part of this series bear on one side the seated figure of our Saviour; and on the other the barbarously executed figures of the emperors of the East, at full length, sometimes attended by their partners in the empire, and occasionally in company with their wives and children. Yet, to those who love to trace, by means of coeval monuments, the progress or decline of art, even the coins of this rude and uncouth series will not be without their interest; for the Byzantine style may be traced in the much later works of the artists of Italy. In the earliest paintings of the Italian school, it is easy to perceive the rigid outline in the human figure, and the elaborate arrangement of the draperies which characterise the age of the Paleologi.[4]

[1] These coins, however, in one respect, are of infinite value and interest, as will be noticed hereafter.

[2] It is remarkable that, among the numerous beautiful Greek coins, there is but one which we are certain bears the name of the artist, *Nevantus*, ΝΕΥΑΝΤΟΣ ΕΠΟΕΙ (the Doric for ΕΠΟΙΕΙ), namely, a coin of Cydonia in Crete. See *Eckhel, Doct. Num. Vet.*, vol. ii. page 309. Pliny has given the names of several engravers of gems, but mentions no engravers of dies for coins. The elegant silver medallions of Syracuse bear the name ΚΙΜΩΝ beneath the bust, which may possibly be that of the artist.

[3] These coins, notwithstanding their barbarous execution, served as models for several European states: in Venice and Sicily especially they were servilely imitated.

[4] The series of Byzantine coins has been ably illustrated by M. de Saulcy in his work entitled "*Essai de Classification de Suites Monetaires, Byzantine.*" 8vo. Metz, 1836, and a 4to. volume of Plates, executed with extraordinary fidelity and beauty.

MYTHOLOGICAL REPRESENTATIONS ON GREEK AND ROMAN COINS.

THE deities of the Greeks and Romans appear so frequently on their coins, that a description of some of them may be found useful to the tyro.

JUPITER. The head of this deity appears on many Greek coins, and may be recognized by the laurel-wreath,[1] venerable aspect, and flowing beard. On the reverse of many regal Greek coins, he is figured seated in a chair, holding the hasta-pura in his left hand, and an eagle in his right. Sometimes, instead of an eagle, he holds a small figure of Victory. On coins of Athens, he appears on foot, launching a thunderbolt. On coins of Seleucia, Jupiter is represented under the most ancient form, namely, a large stone or rock.[2]

SATURN is not often found on Greek coins. He appears on those of the Roman families, Calpurnia, Postumia, and Servilia. His attribute is a sickle; hence Ovid calls him *falcifer*.

NEPTUNE is figured on many Greek and Roman coins. On those of Posidonia he stands erect, and launches a trident. On a coin of Hadrian, he holds the acrostolium, and rests his foot on the prow of a vessel.

APOLLO. The head of this deity occurs on the gold coins of Philip of Macedon, and on the coins of numerous Greek

[1] Jupiter Dodonæus wears an *oaken* wreath on the coins of Alexander, King of Epirus.

[2] See a Dissertation on the Stone Worship of the Ancients in the second volume of the Numismatic Journal, p. 216.

cities. His face is beardless, and his head laureated. When represented as the Sun, as on the coins of Rhodes, his head is surrounded by rays. On some Roman coins, he appears in a female habit.

Mars occurs but seldom on Greek coins, though very frequently in the Roman series, where he is represented marching naked with a spear in his hand, and a trophy on his shoulder. On a coin of Corfinum, the Italian chiefs stand before an erect spear, the symbol of this deity.[1]

Mercury may be easily recognised by his attributes. He appears on an elegant coin of Marcus Aurelius in second brass, with the legend PIETATI · AVG.

Esculapius is generally figured at full length with a long bushy beard, and leaning on his club, round which a serpent is entwined. Sometimes he appears with Hygeia and Telesphorus. On a brass coin of Caracalla he is represented with the latter standing by his side enveloped in a mantle and peaked hood.

Bacchus may be known by the thyrsus and crown of ivy and vine leaves. His bust appears on many Greek coins. When figured at full-length, he holds the thyrsus and cantharus. On some imperial Greek coins, he appears in a chariot drawn by centaurs.

Serapis. The head of this deity is surmounted by the modius. It is found on some of the coins of Sicily, but more frequently on those of Alexandria in Egypt, upon some of which he appears as the Egyptian Pluto, in company with Cerberus.

Hercules appears on the coins of many Greek cities. His head, covered with the lion's skin, is found on most of the silver coins of Alexander the Great. When depicted as the young Hercules, he is without beard, and with short curly hair. Hercules Bibax is figured on the coins of Smyrna, holding the scyphus[2] in his right hand.

[1] Millingen, Sylloge, p. 7.

[2] *Scyphus* Herculis poculum est, ita ut Liberi Patris *cantharus*. Herculem vero fictores veteres non sine causa cum pocula fecerunt. *Macrobius*, Sat. lib. v. c. 21.

Harpocrates may be known by his finger placed on his mouth. He sometimes holds the sistrum, and sits on the lotus flower. His bust occurs on a small brass Egyptian coin of Hadrian, with the name of the Nome Prosopites.

Apis is represented as a bull, with a star above his head, on the brass coins of Julian the Apostate.

Canopus is represented on Egyptian coins as a vase, surmounted by a human head.[1]

Castor and Pollux appear, on both Greek and Roman coins, on horseback, with a star above the head of each. Their bonnets are often represented on coins, surmounted by the same symbols. On the consular series, they are figured on horseback, riding at full speed, with levelled lances.

Pan may always be recognised by his horns and ears. His head is found on the coins of the Vibia family.

Anubis is represented with a dog's head, on coins supposed to have been struck in the reign of Julian the Apostate.

Atis may be known by his Phrygian bonnet.

Cupid appears on the coins of Antiochus VII. of Syria.

Lunus. This deity is represented on a coin of Sept. Severus, struck in Antiochia. He wears the Phrygian bonnet; his head is backed by a crescent, and a cock stands at his feet.[2]

Vulcan is figured, with his attributes, on the coins of Lipara, Athens, and Aeserna.

Bonus Eventus is figured on several Roman coins as a youthful naked male figure, holding a patera and ears of corn.

Juno may be recognised by the peacock. She sometimes holds the hasta-pura. When represented as *Juno Pronuba*, as on the coins of Samos, she is covered with a long veil reaching to her feet. *Juno Sospita* has a buckler and spear; and her head is covered by a goat's skin. See the coins of the families Cornuficia and Mettia, and the brass of Antoninus.

Diana. This goddess may be known by her usual attributes. When represented as the Ephesian Diana, she appears like a *mummy case*, with her hands outstretched, each resting on a trident reversed.

[1] Zoega, tab. 3, fig. 8.

[2] Frölich, Quatuor Tent., p. 96.

MINERVA. The head of this goddess occurs on the gold coins of Alexander the Great. On numerous Roman coins she is represented with her well-known attributes.

VENUS is found on many Roman coins. On those of Faustina she is clothed; on those of Domna, naked, and leaning on a cippus, with the apple in her right hand. *Venus Victrix* sometimes appears holding a small figure of Victory and the hasta. On coins of Cyprus, Venus is represented under the figure of a cone-shaped stone, as on the coin the reverse of which is represented above.

CYBELE wears a turreted crown, and is sometimes drawn by lions. On coins of Greek cities, she appears riding on a lion,[1] and sometimes seated in a chair between two lions.

CERES may be recognised by her wheaten crown. She appears on the coins of Sicily.

VICTORY is most commonly represented winged, holding a palm-branch and a wreath; sometimes standing on the prow of a vessel; and often carrying, or crowning, a trophy.[2] She is figured on numerous Greek and Roman coins. Niké Apteros is without wings.

ISIS appears on many Greek coins, particularly on those of the Emperors, struck at Alexandria in Egypt. Her head is surmounted by the flower of the lotus. On several coins of Alexandria, *Isis Pharia* holds the sail of a vessel.

NEMESIS may be known by the wheel at her feet. She appears on many of the coins of Smyrna. Sometimes she is *veiled*, as on a coin of Caracalla struck at Samos.[3] A coin of Macrinus, struck at Cyzicus, has Nemesis with a turreted crown.

ASTARTE, an important deity in the cities of Phœnicia, appears on coins of Byblus, crowned with a mural crown, holding a long staff surmounted by a cross, and resting her foot on the prow of a galley. On coins of Tyre and Sidon, she is figured as a bust, with a radiated head, placed on a car.

There are also many other representations of ideal personages, such as *Security* in a chair, or leaning on a column;

[1] On denarii of Severus and his family, she is thus represented.
[2] Νίκη τροπαιοφόρος.
[3] Mionnet, tome v. p. 287.

Eternity, with a globe; *Justice* (Æquitas) with the scales; *Moneta* with scales and cornucopiæ; *Hope* walking, holding up her garments, and holding forth a bud; *Fortune*, with her rudder and cornucopiæ; *Liberty*, holding the freedman's cap, and the hasta; *Felicity*, with a long caduceus; *Peace* with an olive-branch; *Piety* sacrificing; *Abundantia* emptying a cornucopia; *Fecunditas* with her children; *Concord*, with patera and cornucopia, seated in a chair: *Pudicitia* veiled; and *Virtus* represented by an armed figure, with spear and shield.

River gods are generally figured seated on the ground, holding a bulrush, and supporting an urn, from which water escapes. On coins of Antioch, and other cities, the river is personified as a naked figure swimming at the feet of a female crowned with towers seated on a rock.

The consecration of an Emperor is generally denoted by the legend on the reverse, CONSECRATIO, the funeral pile, and the eagle. The coins with this type have the head of the Emperor bare, and the title *Divus*.

The Thensa, Carpentum, or divine car, denotes the consecration of an Empress, as on the coins of Agrippina. The peacock is also the symbol of consecration, and is sometimes represented bearing the Empress aloft. The ceremonies observed at the consecration of an emperor are detailed by Herodian.[1] The canonisation of saints, in after-times, is supposed to have been derived from this custom.[2]

This subject might be greatly enlarged upon, but enough has been said to answer the purpose intended.

[1] Lib. iv. [2] Num. Journal, Vol. I. p. 124.

GREEK COINS.

In the types of some of the earliest Greek coins, we find a spirit and boldness, both in design and execution, with which many of the more elaborate productions of modern times will not bear comparison. The rude, and often mis-shapen lump of silver upon which these types are impressed, contrasts most singularly with the wonderful freedom and spirit of the design. Armour, weapons, animals, plants, utensils, and the most graceful representations of the human figure, appear in infinite and astonishing variety within a space so circumscribed, that the artists of antiquity would seem to have sometimes vied with each other in the production of the most striking representations within the smallest possible limits.

Among the Greek coins most remarkable for their singularity and beauty, may be noticed those of Heraclea, upon which Hercules is represented destroying the Nemæan lion. A specimen of this beautiful piece, in the collection of the British Museum, is in singularly fine preservation. On the minute coins of Tarentum, the Infant Hercules is represented strangling the serpents; on another he is figured hugging the lion in his arms. The beauty of the Sicilian coins, and of the *Syracusan Medallion*, is acknowledged by all who are acquainted with ancient art. This charming work, though frequently to be found in collections of Greek coins, maintains a high price, and is justly valued as one of the finest medallic remains of the ancients.

Many coins of the Greek monarchs are of exquisite workmanship, particularly those of Macedon, Sicily, and Syria.[1]

That Greek coins as works of art, have been, and still are, the admiration of the most eminent artists, is a fact too well known to need further remark. But it is not in this respect alone that they are prized by the learned and curious. As records of the customs, ceremonies, and superstitions of a people, the very sites of whose cities are, in some instances, matters of doubt and dispute; as memorials of illustrious men, whose portraits are presented to us in a manner that forbids the most sceptical to gainsay their accuracy; as interesting and striking illustrations of ancient geography; and as indications of the wealth, magnitude, and importance of the numerous cities in which they were struck, the coins of Greece may take precedence of all other ancient monuments.

Geographical indications. Let us, however, by reference to a few particular examples, show that these are not mere assertions. On coins of Cæsarea in Cappadocia, we find the legend ΠΡ ΑΡΓ or Τ·ΠΡ·ΑΡΓΑΙΩΝ (των προς Αργαιων) i. e. Cæsarea *under Mount Argæus.* On those of Heliopolis, in Cœlesyria, ΠΡΟΣ ΛΙΒΑΝΟΝ, *under Mount Libanus.* On the coins of Antioch in Syria, ΤΩΝ · ΠΡΟΣ · ΔΑΦΝΗΙ. Those of Prusias in Bithynia, and Laodicæa in Syria, bear ΠΡΟΣ · ΘΑΛΑΣΣΗ, or ΘΑΛΑΣΣΑΝ, to distinguish them from other cities of the same name. Rivers and fountains, and sacred localities, are frequently mentioned on Greek coins; and, in some instances, serve to correct the errors of ancient writers.[2] Others denote the division of provinces by ΑΝΩ and ΚΑΤΩ. Many boast the proud title of ΝΕΩΚΟΡΟΣ, and record the celebration of games and festivals in honour of the emperors. We have, also, numerous examples of the concord existing between the cities of antiquity in the occurrence of the word ΟΜΟΝΟΙΑ, and

[1] Eckhel, Doct. Num. Vet., vol. iv., c. x. *De Mentione Situs, &c.*

[2] Take, as an example, the coins of Cæsarea in Commagene, with the legend ΚΑΙCΑΡΙΑC · ΓΕΡΜΑΝΙΚΗC. Stephanus, Ptolemy, and Theodoret, speak of Germanicia and Cæsarea as distinct cities; but these coins show that Germanicia is the distinguishing name. The greater part of these coins belong to the series termed "*Imperial Greek.*"

records of the various magistrates.[1] Several cities of Greece boasted the title ΝΑΥΑΡΧΙΔΟΣ, which is often found inscribed on their coins,[2] together with other distinctions, whether conferred upon them by the Emperors, or claimed by ancient right.[3] Besides these, there is much information to be derived from

THE NUMERALS ON GREEK COINS.

THE MONADES ARE:

Α	Β	Γ	Δ	Ε	ϛ	Ζ	Η	Θ
1.	2.	3.	4.	5.	6.	7.	8.	9.

THE DECADES:

Ι	Κ	Λ	Μ	Ν	Ξ	Ο	Π	ϟ
10.	20.	30.	40.	50.	60.	70.	80.	90.

THE CENTENARII:

Ρ	Σ	Τ	Υ	Φ	Χ	Ψ	Ω	ϡ
100.	200.	300.	400.	500.	600.	700.	800.	900.

Each character stands for itself, thus: ΔΚΧ signifies 624, which may be read either way. The Ψ, Ω, and ϡ are not found on coins, there being no epoch corresponding with so high a number. Χ occurs but rarely, and is found on the coins of Rhescuporis the Fifth, King of the Bosphorus.

Dates. } The era of Pontus and the Bosphorus, commences with the year of Rome 457, or 296 years before Christ.

The Egyptian era commences with the reign of Ptolemy I.

The Seleucidan era dates . . . 312 years B.C.
The Augustan or Actian era dates . 31 years B.C.
The Pompeian era dates . . . . 63 years B.C.
The Cæsarean era dates . . . 47 or 48 years B.C.

Sometimes the date is expressed thus: ΕΤΟΥΣ · ΛΖ (year 37), but more frequently in a contracted form, ΕΤ, or ΕΤΟ. On the coins of Alexandria, we find the word ΛΥΚΑΒΑΝΤΟΣ, instead of ΕΤΟΥΣ; *Λυκαβαντα* being an ancient term for year among the Greeks, as noticed by Macrobius.[4] On many

[1] Eckhel, Doct. Num. Vet., vol. iv. p. 157.
[2] Ibid. vol. iv. p. 309.
[3] See the list of Contractions on Greek Coins.
[4] Saturnalia, lib. i. c. 17.

coins, the initial letter only is given, which, instead of the Greek character Λ, is an L. Eckhel sagaciously accounts for this. He observes, that the Λ signifies as a numeral, 30, and that, placed before Σ thus, ΛΣ, the two characters would stand for the year 230. By using L, which is the more ancient form of the Greek Lambda, the possibility of any misinterpretation is at once removed.[1] Numerous coins of Alexandria in Egypt bear the date thus: L^Α, i. e. Λυκαβαντος Α (year one).

Denominations. Among the Greeks, the monetary unit was the *Drachma*. Its multiples and divisions were as follow:—

Multiples.		*Divisions.*	
The Didrachmum	2 drachms.	The Tetrobolus	4 Oboli.
Tridrachmum	3 „	Triobolus	3 „
Tetradrachmum	4 „	Diobolus	2 „
Pentadrachmum	5 „	Obolus.	
Decadrachmum	10 „	Hemiobolion, or Semiobolus	½ „
		Tetartobolus	¼ „

Of all these coins examples are extant. Of the copper of the Greeks, we have the Obolus, Diobolus, Triobolus, Tetrobolus, Hemiobolus, and Tetartobolus, besides the Chalcus,[2] and other minute pieces, probably of less denomination, being parts of the chalcus. Under the Roman yoke, the Greeks adopted the word Ασσαριον (*de assis*).

The gold coins of the Greeks were the Stater, the Double Stater, the Half Stater, and the Quarter Stater. The gold stater was equal in weight to two silver drachms, and in value to twenty. The silver stater contained four drachms, and was

[1] For the other, and less usual, method of placing the dates on coins, see Eckhel, Doct. Num. Vet., vol. iv. p. 395.

[2] The Chalcus was the earliest Greek copper coin, and is supposed to have been first struck in the time of the Peloponnesian war. Athenæus says, that the poet Dionysius was called the "the brazen orator," because he persuaded the Athenians to have brass money. That it was at the first a coin of small denomination, we may learn from Demosthenes, who, in speaking of a thing of little value, uses the phrase "not worth a chalcus." The information derived from Pollux, Hesychius, Suidas, and others, respecting the divisions of the chalcus, is most unsatisfactory.

equal in value to 3*s.* 3*d.* of our money. The learned Abbate Sestini has devoted one of his works to the subject of the staters of antiquity,[1] the existence of which, as actual coins, was questioned by Eckhel.[2]

Some Greek coins bear their denominations thus:—

ΔΙΔΡΑΧΜΟΝ or ΔΙΔΡΑΓΜΟΝ .	On a silver coin of Nero struck at Cæsarea in Cappadocia; also on the brass of Rhodes.
ΔΡΑΧΜΗ or ΔΡΑΓΜΗ . . .	On silver of Nero struck at Ephesus.
ΔΡΑΧΜΑ	On autonomous brass of Byzantium.
ACCAPIA (TPIA and ΔΥΩ) . .	On autonomous brass of Chios.
ACCAPION	On the same.
ΤΡΙΩΒΟΛΟ	On autonomous brass of Samothrace.
ΟΒΟΛΟΣ	On brass of Chios and Metapontum.
HMIOBЄΛIN (*sic*) AIΓION . .	On autonomous brass of Aegium in Achaia.
TЄTPAXAΛKON	On autonomous brass of Chios.
ΔΙΧΑΛΚΟΝ	On the same.
ΧΑΛ or ΧΑΛΚΟΥΣ	On autonomous brass of Antioch in Syria.

The Jewish Shekel,[3] and its divisions, bear their name and denominations in Samaritan characters, thus:—[Samaritan] *shekel of Israel;* [Samaritan], *half shekel;* [Samaritan] *quarter shekel.*[4]

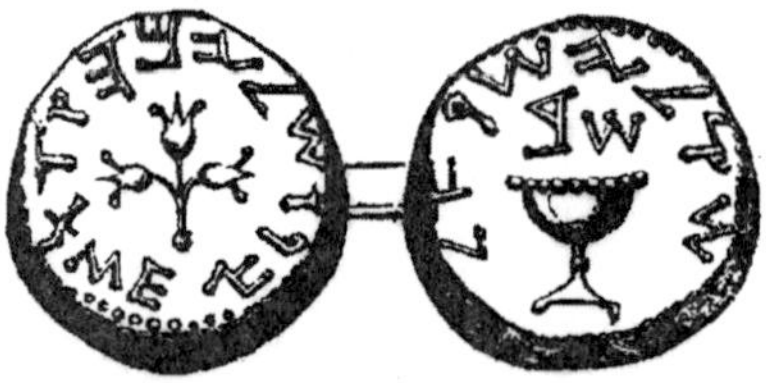

[1] Descrizione Degli Stateri Antichi, Illustrati con le Medaglie, *Firenze,* 4to. MDCCCXVII. [2] Doct. Num. Vet. vol. ii. p. 535.

[3] It may be proper to mention, that these shekels are of a much later period than is supposed by some of the early numismatic writers. They bear *Samaritan* characters: all those with *Hebrew letters* are modern forgeries. The genuine Hebrew shekel often bears the legend, [Samaritan] i. e. *Jerusalem the Holy,* of which our engraved specimen is an example. The characters of printed Samaritan, as may be observed, materially differ in figure from those on the coins, which are very irregularly formed.

[4] See Mionnet, Descript. de Médailles Antiques, tome vi. p. 560. The plates in the seventh volume of this work are most interesting and valuable.

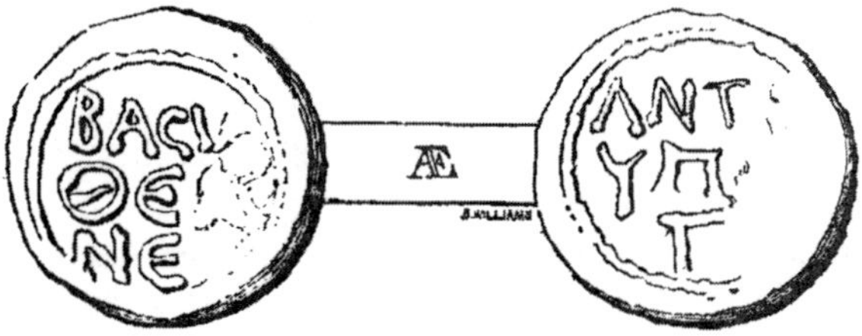

Titles. In the earlier times, the inscriptions on regal and civic coins were brief and modest; but, at a later period, the most extravagant titles were assumed and blazoned on the money of the Greeks: thus, the coins of Alexander the Great bear merely ΑΛΕΞΑΝΔΡΟΥ or ΑΛΕΞΑΝΔΡΟΥ · ΒΑΣΙΛΕΩΣ, while some of the Syrian monarchs assumed every high-sounding and vain-glorious title. Among these, the list on the coins of Antiochus XII. is the most extraordinary: ΒΑΣΙΛΕΩΣ ΑΝΤΙΟΧΟΥ · ΔΙΟΝΥΣΟΥ · ΕΠΙΦΑΝΟΥΣ · ΦΙΛΟΠΑΤΟΡΟΣ ΚΑΛΛΙΝΙΚΟΥ. On others we find, ΒΑΣΙΛΕΩΣ · ΒΑΣΙΛΕΩΝ; ΘΕΟΥ; and, on coins of Cleopatra, ΘΕΑ · ΝΕΩΤΕΡΑ. Some cities assumed high-sounding titles; we find, on coins of Ephesus, ЄΦЄCΙΩΝ · Δ · ΝЄΩΚΟΡων · Η · ΠΡΩΤΗ · ΠΑCΩΝ ΚΑΙ · ΜЄΓΙCΤΗ. The servile and degenerate Greeks, who, in the science of flattery, surpassed all other nations, showered the most fulsome compliments on several of the Roman tyrants, Commodus and Severus especially: on a coin of the latter is the inscription: CЄΟΥΗΡΟΥ · ΒΑCΙΛЄΥΟΝΤΟC · Ο ΚΟCΜΟC · ЄΥΤΥΧЄΙ.

The titles borne by various Greek Princes are as follow:—

ΑΥΤΟΚΡΑΤΩΡ...*Absolute Sovereign.* On coins of the Syrian monarch, Triphon, and the Parthian king, Arsaces IX.

ΚΑΛΛΙΝΙΚΟΣ ...*Conqueror.* By Demetrius III., Antiochus XII. and XIII., Mithridates, King of Armenia, &c. Hercules was thus styled.

ΘΕΟΣ ....*God.* By Demetrius II. & III., and Antiochus IV., and by the Ptolemies.

ΘΕΑ ....*Goddess.* By Cleopatra, whose coins, as before-mentioned, bear the title of ΘЄΑ · ΝЄѠΤЄΡΑ, *the new Goddess.*

ΔΙΚΑΙΟΣ ....*Just.* Common on the coins of the Parthian kings.

ΔΙΟΝΥΣΟΣ.......*Bacchus.* On coins of Antiochus VI. and XII. of Syria.

ΕΠΙΦΑΝΗΣ ......*Illustrious.* Borne by Nicomedes II. and IV., Ariarathes of Cappadocia; by the Syrian kings, Antiochus IV., VI., VIII., IX., XI., XII., and XIII., Alexander I., Seleucus VI., &c.

ΕΥΕΡΓΕΤΗΣ.....*Benefactor.* To this title our Lord alludes in his address to the apostles.[1] It is found on the coins of Mithridates V., of Pontus, Pylæmenes of Paphlagonia, Demetrius III., Antiochus VII., and Alexander I.; on those of the Parthian kings, and Ptolemy III.

ΕΥΠΑΤΩΡ ....*Nobly born.* By Mithridates VI., of Pontus, Antiochus V., and by the Parthian monarchs.

ΕΥΣΕΒΗΣ ....*Pious.* By Ariarathes and Ariobarzanes, kings of Cappadocia; and by Antiochus X. of Syria.

ΝΙΚΑΤΩΡ ....*Victor.* By Demetrius II. and Seleucus VI. of Syria, and by the Parthian kings.

ΝΙΚΗΦΟΡΟΣ ....*Gaining Victory.* By Antiochus IV. and Alexander I. of Syria, and by several of the Bactrian kings.[2]

ΦΙΛΑΔΕΛΦΟΣ...*Having fraternal affection.* By Ariarathes X., Demetrius II., Antiochus XI., and Philippus of Syria; Iotape of Commagene, and by Ptolemy II.

ΦΙΛΕΛΛΗΝ ......*Lover of the Greeks.* By Aretas of Damascus, and by the Parthian kings.

ΦΙΛΟΚΑΙΣΑΡ ...*Lover of Cæsar.* By Agrippa I. of Judæa.

ΦΙΛΟΚΛΑΥΔΙΟΣ...*Lover of Claudius.* By Herodes, king of Chalcedene.

ΦΙΛΟΜΗΤΩΡ....*Lover of his Mother.* By Ariarathes, king of Cappadocia, Demetrius III. of Syria, and by Ptolemy VI.

[1] Luke xxii. 25—καὶ οἱ ἐξουσιάζοντες αὐτῶν ΕΥΕΡΓΕΤΑΙ καλοῦνται.

[2] Numismatic Journal, Vol. II. p. 178-9.

ΦΙΛΟΠΑΤΡΙΣ ......*Lover of his Country.* By Archelaus, king of Cappadocia.

ΦΙΛΟΠΑΤΩΡ ......*Lover of his Father.* By Ariobarzanes II., Demetrius III., Seleucus IV., Antiochus IX., X., XII., and XIII., and by Arsaces IX., and Ptolemy IV.

ΦΙΛΟΡΩΜΑΙΟΣ ...*Lover of the Romans.* By Ariobarzanes I. & III., of Cappadocia, and by Mannus, king of Edessa.

ΣΩΤΗΡ..............*Saviour.* By Antiochus I. and III., by the kings of Bactriana,[1] and by the Egyptian monarchs, Ptolemy I. and VIII.

ΘΕΟΣΕΒΗΣ.........*Worshipper of the Gods.* By Sames, king of Armenia.

ΘΕΟΠΑΤΩΡ.........*Sprung from a Divine Parent.* By Alexander I. of Syria, and by the Parthian kings.[2]

Inscriptions. The form and style of the letters on early Greek coins are curious and interesting. On some, the legend is retrograde, ATƎM for Metapontum; OqϘ for Crotona; ƎΘA for Athenæ; NOIAMYꓘ for Cuma. On others it is boustrophedon, or *oxturning-wise*, thus:—

ΑΚΡΑϹ
ƸOTNA } Agrigentum in Sicily.

EИIOИ
ƧƧƎM } Messana in Sicily.

It is said that the laws of Solon were thus written; and Pausanias[3] describes the chest of Cypselius as bearing an inscription in the same style. The term *βουστροφεδον*, was given to it in consequence of the lines turning back like oxen at plough.

Dedicated coins. On some coins of the Greeks, struck under the Roman dominion, we find the word Ανεθηκε, implying that the piece was *offered-up*, or dedicated to the people, who

[1] Numismatic Journal, Vol. II., p. 178-9.
[2] Eckhel, Doct. Num. Vet., vol. iv., p. 460.
[3] Lib. v., c. 17. This author describes it as an *ancient* method of writing.

were commonly held sacred.[1] One of these pieces bears the head of Antinoüs, the infamous favourite of Hadrian, with the following legend:—ΟCΤΙΛΙΟC · ΜΑΡΚΕΛΛΟC · Ο · ΙΕΡΕΥC ΤΟΥ · ΑΝΤΙΝΟΟΥ · ΤΟΙΣ · ΑΧΑΙΟΙΣ · ΑΝΕΘΗΚΕΝ,[2] i. e. *Hostilius Marcellus, the Priest of Antinoüs, dedicates this to the Achaians.* Eckhel has illustrated these coins with his accustomed learning and sagacity, by reference to tabular inscriptions recording the liberality of private individuals to their fellow-citizens. He observes, that when an emperor bestowed presents, they were said to be *given*, because given by a superior to an inferior; but when the contrary happened, the Greeks made use of a more solemn word, namely, *offered-up*. He shows, too, that the word *ανατιθημι* (offer-up) was often used in this sense when money was presented to the people.[3]

Public games. The celebrations of the public games are often recorded on the coins of this period; of these, the most remarkable are—

ΚΑΒΕΙΡΙΑ ....Held at Thessalonica in honour of the Cabiri.

ΘΕΟΓΑΜΙΑ.........Celebrated in Sicily in honour of the marriage of Pluto and Proserpine.

CΕΟΥΗΡΕΙΑ ......Instituted by Septimius Severus.

ΚΟΜΟΔΕΙΑ ......Instituted by Commodus.

ΑΛΕΞΑΝΔΡΕΙΑ...In honour of Alexander the Great.

ΑΝΤΩΝΕΙΝΙΑ......In honour of Caracalla.

ΚΟΡΑΙΑ ....In honour of Proserpine, to whom the Greeks gave the name of *Κορα*.

ΔΙΔΥΜΕΙΑ ....In honour of Apollo Didymeus, worshipped at Miletus in Ionia.

ΔΙΟΝΥCΙΑ ....In honour of Bacchus, *Διονυσιος*, at Nicæa in Bithynia, of which he was the reputed founder.[4]

[1] This is shown by many Greek coins with ΙΕΡΟΣ · ΔΗΜΟΣ.

[2] Mionnet, Descript. tome ii. p. 160.

[3] Doct. Num. Vet. vol. iv. p. 373.

[4] On some coins he is styled *κτιστης*, or the founder.

ΟΙΚΟΥΜΕΝΙΚΑ....Or universal games, recorded on the coins of Attalia in Pamphilia, Ephesus, Nysa in Caria, Side in Pamphilia, Sidon, Tarsus, &c. &c.

ΟΛΥΜΠΙΑ..........Games common to all the cities of Greece, said to have been instituted by Hercules.

ΦΙΛΑΔΕΛΦΕΙΑ ...On coins of Caesarea in Cappadocia, Nicea in Bithynia, &c. &c.

ΠΡΩΤΑ ....On the coins of those cities which assumed the title of Πρωτα, or *prima*, i. e. Side, Perinthus, and Smyrna.

ΠΥΘΙΑ ....In honour of Apollo, celebrated in the cities of Emisa, Hierapolis, Laodicea in Phrygia, Miletus, Nicea, Nicomedia, Pergamus, &c. &c

ΑΥΓΟΥCΤΕΙΑ ... } ΣΕΒΑCΜΙΑ ..... } In honour of Augustus.

ΑΚΤΙΑ ....Triennial games, in honour of Apollo, in the cities of Hierapolis, Bostra, Damascus, Nicomedia, Pergamus, Tarsus, Tyrus, Thessalonica, &c.[1]

The coins bearing these inscriptions, generally have the representation of an urn, holding a palm-branch, the reward of the victor in the games.

On Roman coins, we have similar records. On a consular denarius of the family Memmia, the first festival in honour of Ceres is thus recorded:—MEMMIVS · AED · CERIALIA PREIMVS · FECIT. The celebration of the quinquennalian games is noticed on a beautiful coin of Nero, of the third size: CERTAMEN · QVINQ*uennale* · ROM*ae* · CO*nstitutum*. A Denarius of Domitian records the celebration of the Ludos Sæculares. And in the reign of Philip coins were struck with the legend, MILLIARIVM · SAECVLVM to commemorate the sæcular games held in honour of the thousandth year of Rome.

Archon. } On the imperial Greek coins, we have often very interesting legends, with the names of the Archon, or chief magistrate, during whose year of office the piece was

[1] See Eckhel, Doct. Num. Vet. vol. iv. cap. xxi. *De Festis ac Ludis.*

minted. One example will be sufficient. On a coin of Maeonia, we find ΕΠΙ · ΑΠΟΛΛΩΝΙΟΥ · ΑΡΧ · ΤΟ · Β · ΜΑΙΟΝΩΝ, viz. (money) *of the people of Mæonia, under Apollonius, Archon for the second time.* In Athens there were, as is well known, nine Archons, the first of whom gave the name to the year. These eponymous magistrates may be said to have represented the majesty of the state. By their name, the year of their magistracy was distinguished. They were the first in rank of the Archons at Athens, of the Ephori at Sparta, and of the Consuls at Rome. In some states, the eponymous officers had a sacerdotal as well as civil character. This appears to have been the case among the Magnetæ who appointed the high-priest to this rank; while at Smyrna it was sustained by the Stephanephori.

It is obviously necessary, in order to constitute a magistrate truly eponymous, *that the period of office should close with the year;* and it can be proved that this was the case, as well by inscriptions on marbles extant at this time, as by the united testimony of Plato, Diodorus, and Pausanias.[1] It was also necessary, in order to constitute a magistrate eponymous, *that his authority should extend over the whole state* and not be confined to particular and private bodies only.[2] Hence, when we read on the marble given by Spon, ΕΠΙ · ΑΡΧΟΝΤΟΣ · ΒΕΝΤΙΔΙΟΥ · ΣΩΤΑ · ΠΥΘΑΥΛΟΥ...... ΚΑΙ · ΓΡΑΜΜΑΤΕΩΣ · ΑΙΛΙΟΥ · ΑΓΑΘΕΜΕΡΟΥ · ΚΙΘΑΡΩΔΟΥ, &c., it is evident that the Archons and Scribes here alluded to, having but a limited authority, did not possess the high office in question. Attention to these *two rules* would have preserved many writers from error.

But there is yet a third and still more debatable point depending upon the signification of the particle ΕΠΙ. Eckhel enters into the matter with all his learning and discrimination,

[1] It is well known that at Rome the consul, or eponymous officer, was elected annually; hence Seneca takes occasion pretty smartly to rebuke the fickle ladies of his day, who made an annual transfer of their affections, by telling them that they had *eponymous husbands.*

[2] A friend observes, that limited societies at the present day have their eponymous honours, as may be perceived by reference to the "Senior Wrangler" at Cambridge. Thus we speak of *Herschel's year, Airey's year,* &c.

and shows very clearly, in opposition to Belleyus and others, that the use of this particle is not a certain indication of an eponymous magistrate. This he proves by a reference to the money of Antioch, Syracuse, and Smyrna, on all of which we find ΕΠΙ, applied to men who were in office several successive years, which is contrary to the first rule. He also shows that the second rule is violated by those who adduce the money of Smyrna and Byzantium, since ΕΠΙ is here applied to inferior officers, both of the colonies and of the state; and even, in one instance, to a woman, ΕΠΙ · ΘΕΑC · ΦΑΥCΤΕΙΝΗC. In these instances, the particle ΕΠΙ was used to signify, not a year, but the period when the money was issued; as, for example, ΕΠΙ ΙΚΕΤΑ implies that the coin was struck when Hicetas was Tyrant of Syracuse, and not that the office of Hicetas was eponymous. But, from all this, it is evident that the investigation of the subject of eponymous offices, by means of coins and ancient marbles, is a task of considerable difficulty.

Scribe. The office of Archon, as already shown, was frequently held more than once. It was the same with the Scribe (Γραμματευς), an officer who has been most appropriately termed, by the translators of the New Testament, "*Town Clerk.*" On coins of Apamea, we find ΕΠ · ΓΡΑΜ ΤΟ · Β; and on those of Nysa, in Caria, ΓΡΑΜ · ΤΟ · Β, *Scribe for the second time.* Vaillant states, that it was the custom to place the name of the scribe on the money, when the Archon died during the period of his holding office;[1] but Eckhel shows that many coins teach us to the contrary.[2]

Ephor. The name of the Ephor occurs on an autonomous brass coin of Lacedæmon, and on a coin of Poppæa, struck at Ancyra.

Prætor. The names of Prætors and Propraetors, ΣΤΡΑΤΗΓΟΣ and ΑΝΤΙΣΤΡΑΤΗΓΟΣ, are often placed on

[1] Num. Græca, p.313. [2] Doct Num. Vet. vol. iv., p. 197.
[3] Mionnet, Descript. tome iii. p. 190.

Greek coins. On one of Clazomene, Zosimus is styled Prætor for the fifth time.

Prytanis. The name of this officer appears on coins of Apamea, Cyme, Pergamus, Smyrna, Synnada, &c. On a gold autonomous coin of Smyrna, the title is given without the name of the person who held it:—ΣΜΥΡΝΑΙΩΝ ΠΡΥΤΑΝΕΙΣ.[3]

Quæstor. The title of Quæstor (ΤΑΜΙΑΣ) occurs but seldom. A coin of Pergamus, in Mysia, bears ЄΠΙ · ΤΑΜιε ΑΙΛ · ΘЄΟΦΙΛΙΑΝΟΥ.

High Priest. A coin of Eumenia, in Phrygia, bears ΙΟΥΛΙΟΣ ΚΛΕΩΝ · ΑΡΧΙΕΡΕΥΣ · ΑΣΙΑΣ.

Priest. The title of Ιερευς has already been noticed in the coin bearing the name of Hostilius Marcellus, the priest of Antinöus—ΙΕΡΕΥΣ · ΤΟΥ · ΑΝΤΙΝΟΟΥ.

Priestess. On a coin of Attuda, in Phrygia, the name of the priestess is given ΔΙΑ · ΦΛΑΒΙΑC · ΙЄΡΙΑC.

Asiarchus. The Asiarchi, or presidents of the games of Asia, often had their names inscribed on the public money. A coin of Otrus, in Phrygia, bears ΑΛΕΞΑΝΔΡΟC ΑCΙΑΡΧΗC · ΑΝЄΘΗΚЄΝ; another, of Smyrna, has ЄΠΙ ΤЄΡΤΙΟΥ · ΑCΙΑΡΧΟΥ, i. e. *under Tertius the Asiarch.*

Stephanephorus. This title[1] was given to a high order of priests who wore, in the public ceremonies, crowns, which were sometimes of gold. On coins of Mæonia, in Lydia, we find ΑΡΧ · Α · ΚΑΙ · CΤЄΦΑΝΗΦορυ, i. e. *Archon for the first time and Stephanephorus.*

[1] From Στέφανος, a crown, and φέρω, to bear.

Gymnasiarch. Panegyriarch. Agonothetos. The office of *Gymnasiarch* is recorded on a coin of Pergamus in Mysia. Μ · ΦΟΥΡΙΟΣ · ΓΥΜΝΑΣΙΑΡΧΗΣΑΣ. That of *Panegyriarch*, on money of Apamæa in Phrygia: ΠΑΥ · СТРАТОNΙΚΙΑΝΟΥ · ΠΑΝΗΓΥΡ; and that of *Agonothetus*, on a coin of the same city—ЄΠΙ · ΑΓΩΝΟΘЄΤΟΥ · ΑΡΤЄΜΑ · Γ.

Theologus. The name of this person, who was the interpreter of the sacred rites, occurs on a coin of Pergamus in Mysia: ЄΠΙ · СТР · ΤΙΒ · ΚΛ · ΑΛЄΞΑΝΔΡΟΥ ΘЄΟΛ. *Under the prætor Tiberius Claudius Alexander, Theologos.*

Hieromnemon. This title is found on a coin of Lucius Verus, struck in Byzantium: ΙЄΡΟΜΝΑμων[1] · ΑΙΛΙος СЄΟΥΗΡΟС · ΒΥΖΑΝΤΙΟΙС.

Amphictiones. A silver autonomous coin of Delphi bears the word ΑΜΦΙΚΤΙΟ, which has been illustrated by Eckhel.[2]

Curator. The title of Curator (Επιμεληταç) is found on a coin of Antiochia, in Caria, bearing the legend, ΕΠΙΜΕΛΗ · ΚΛ · ΑΓΛΑΟΥ.

Sophist. On a coin of Cidyessus, in Phrygia, we find the name of the Sophist (*omnis artifex*) inscribed thus: ЄΠ · ΑΡ · ΟΥΑΡΟΥ[3] · СΟΦΙСΤΟΥ.

The following titles and offices are recorded on coins struck by Greek cities while under the Roman dominion.

It has been shown, that, previous to their subjection, the Greeks had bestowed upon their kings the titles and honours of their deities. These were soon transferred to their conquerors: temples and altars were raised *to Rome and the*

[1] Doric for Ιερομνημων.
[2] Doct. Num. Vet., ii., p. 194. Mionnet, Descrip., ii., 96.
[3] i. e. *Varus*. The Greeks, having no V in their alphabet, thus spelled names commencing with that letter. Sometimes they used B, as on a coin of Lucius Verus: ΒΗΡΟС.

Emperor—ROMAE · ET · IMPERIO. This inscription is found on colonial coins of Corinth, while numerous others bear ΡΩΜΗ, or ΘΕΑ · ΡΩΜΗ. The senate and the people of Rome were honoured in a similar way by the legends, CΥΝΚΛΗΤΟC, or ΙΕΡΑ · CΥΝΚΛΗΤΟC, or ΙΕΡΑΝ · CΥΝΚΛΗΤΟΝ, or ΘΕΟΝ · CΥΝΚΛΗΤΟΝ, i. e. *The senate, the holy senate, the divine senate.*[1] The senate on these coins is personified, sometimes by a youthful head, bare, laureated, or wearing the diadem; and on a coin of Cydonia, in Creta, by a bearded male head. A coin of Nero, struck at Alexandria, bears the legend, ΔΗΜΟΣ · ΡΩΜΑΙΩΝ, and the figure of a man wearing the toga, and holding a cornucopia and the hasta.[2] The community of Elders was also honoured in a similar way, as we learn from a coin of Hierapolis, with the word ΓΕΡΟΥCΙΑ.[3] The Roman magistrates of the Equestrian order (Ιππικος) took care to record their rank on the numerous coins hearing their names. On a coin of Cotiæum, in Phrygia, we find ΕΠΙ · Π ΑΙΛ · ΔΗΜΗΤΡΙΑΝΟΥ · ΙΠΠΙΚ . ΑΡΧ.

Consul and Pro-consul. The Consulship is denoted by ΥΠΑΤΟΣ, or ΥΠΑΤΟC; and the number of times it was held, by the Greek numerals, Α · Β · Γ, &c. The Pro-consulship, by ΑΝΘΥΠΑΤΟΣ; but on colonial coins, by the Latin, PROCOS.

Procurator. The Procurator (Επιτροπος) is mentioned on a coin of Vespasian: ΕΠΙ · Λ · ΑΝΤΩΝΙΟΥ · ΝΑΣΩΝΟΣ ΕΠΙΤΡΟΠΟΥ · ΒΙΘΥΝΙΑ.

Neocoros. The most important title assumed by Greek cities, and so often recorded on their coins, is that of Neocoros, a name derived from νεως, a temple, and κωρεω, to sweep; and its primitive signification was nothing more than temple-sweeper. In process of time, however, it was assumed by particular cities, who considered themselves to be

[1] Eckhel shows, that by the word βουλη on coins, was meant the *Greek* senate, and that Συγκλητος signified the *Roman* senate.

[2] Eckhel, Doct. Num. Vet., iv., p. 224.

[3] Ibid., iv., p. 19.

the especial guardians of the temple of the deity supposed to preside over them: thus, the people of Ephesus called themselves the Neocori of the Great Diana, to which the "Town-Clerk" alludes, in his appeal to the mob, on the preaching of St. Paul in that city: *"Ανδρες 'Εφέσιοι, τίς γάρ ἐστιν ἄνθρωπος, ὅς οὐ γινώσκει τὴν 'Εφεσίων πόλιν* ΝΕΩΚΟΡΟΝ *οὖσαν τῆς μεγάλης θεᾶς 'Αρτέμιδος*, &c.[1] Sometimes the honour was conferred by the Emperor for the second and third, and even the fourth, time; and thus we find Β · ΝΕωΚΟΡΩΝ · Γ · ΝΕΩΚΟΡΩΝ, and Δ · ΝΕΩΚΟΡΩΝ · *δις, τρις, τετραχις, Νεωκορων*.[2] On the coins of Magnesia, in Ionia, we find ΜΑΓΝΗΤΩΝ · ΝЄΩΚΟΡΩΝ ΤΗC · ΑΡΤЄΜΙΔΟC; but the money of Ephesus bears the title most frequently, some pieces having, on the reverse, representations of four temples, three containing statues of Roman emperors; and the fourth the figure of Diana Polymamma.

Autonomous Cities. The frequent occurrence of the word ΑΥΤΟΝΟΜΟΥ on Greek coins, renders it necessary that we should say something of its signification. Several cities boasted this title; and it is frequently found at length on their money. Among these may be noted Antiochia, in Syria, Apamea, Laodicea, Samosata, Seleucia, Tripolis, &c. The title signifies that these cities were independent, and *enjoying their own laws*.[3]

Free Cities. A title almost as frequent is that of ЄΛЄΥΘЄΡΑC, or *Free* (i. e. exempt from tribute). It was borne by the cities of Thessalonica, Tarsus, Seleucia in Cilicia, Sebaste in Cilicia, the Island of Rhodes, Hippo in Zeugitania, Chersonesus Taurica, and Amisus. On the coins of Hippo we read LIBERA.

Immunes. The title of ΑΤЄΛЄЄC, *Immunes*, was also given to some cities, implying that they were free from taxes and imposts. A coin of Alabanda, in Caria, bears the legend ΑΤЄΛЄΙΑC · ΑΛΑΒΑΝΔЄΩΝ.

[1] Acts xix. 35.

[2] Eckhel, Doct. Num. Vet., iv., p. 288. Ancient marbles show that this title was sometimes conferred by decree of the senate.

[3] Ibid., iv., p. 262.

Concord between Cities. The friendship and alliance subsisting between many cities of antiquity, is recorded upon their coins. On one of Sagalassus, in Pisidia, is the legend, ΡΩΜΑΙΩΝ ϹΑΓΑΛΛΑϹϹΑΙΩΝ · ΠΡΩΤΗϹ · ΠΙϹΙΔΩΝ · ΚΑΙ · ΦΙΛΗϹ ϹΥΝΜΑΧΟΥ[1] (money) *of the Romans and Sagalassenses the first* (city) *of Pisidia and confederate ally.* The alliance between cities is, however, more commonly recorded by the word ΟΜΟΝΟΙΑ; and when it does not occur, it is sometimes denoted by two right hands joined, and the names of the friendly cities, as on coins of Nicæa and Sagalassus. On a coin of Marcus Aurelius, we find ΝЄΙΚΟΜΗΔЄΙΑ · ΒΟΥΛΗ ΔΗΜΟϹ · ΟΜΟΝΟΙΑ—*Concord of the senate and people of Nicomedia.*

Metropolis. The title *Metropolis* was assumed by many cities, and it appears on their coins, both in the Greek and Latin character; on those of Antiochia, in Syria, perpetually: ΑΝΤΙΟΧΕΩΝ · ΤΗΣ · ΜΗΤΡΟΠΟΛΕΩΣ; and on coins of Bostra, COL*onia* · METROPOLIS · BOSTRA; while those of Nicomedia bear ΡΩΜΗΝ · ΜΗΤΡΟΠΟΛΙΝ,[2] illustrating the line of Dionysius Periegetes, who styles Rome the mother of cities.[3]

Πρωτος, Protos. Many cities assumed the title of *Protos*, or first; among these, Ephesus, Nicæa, Nicomedia, and Smyrna, are most conspicuous. Both Ephesus and Smyrna style themselves ΠΡΩΤΩΝ · ΑϹΙΑϹ.

Asylum and Sacred. The right of *Asylum* was arrogated by many cities; by Tyre especially, on the coins of which it occurs with another title, namely, that of *Sacred* — ΙΕΡΑΣ · ΚΑΙ ΑΣΥΛΟΥ. An interesting account is given by Tacitus, of the cities which assumed the title of Inviolable.[4]

Navarchidus. Agæ in Cilicia, Carystus, Corycus, Dora, Nicopolis in Epirus, Sebaste, Sidon, Tomi and Tripolis, inscribed on their coins ΝΑΥΑΡΧΙΔΟϹ, implying that they had a seaport.

[1] Eckhel, Doct. Num. Vet., iv., p. 271.

[2] Rasche, Lexicon, vol. iii., pars i., p. 1445; and Haym, Tesoro Britannico vol. ii., p. 199; plate v., fig. 12.

[3] Μητερα πασαων πολεων.

[4] Annales, iv., p. 14.

Of the mention of sites and sacred localities, we have already spoken.

Demi-gods, Heroes, &c. The names and effigies of Deities, Demi-gods, and Heroes, sometimes appear on Greek coins.[1] To some of these the name of Κτιστης, or *Founder*, is given. On coins of Nicæa, in Bithynia, Hercules is honoured with this title;[2] while on others of the same city, the merit is given to Bacchus. Of the coins thus inscribed, the following are the most remarkable:—

Alexander the Great	ΑΛΕΞΑΝΔΡΟC · ΚΤΙCΤ	On coins of Apollonia in Caria.
Augustus .	ΚΤΙΣΤΗΣ	On the coins of Clazomena in Ionia.
—	CΕΒΑCΤΟΥ · ΚΤΙCΜΑ .	On the coins of Nicopolis in Epirus.
Bacchus .	ΤΟΝ · ΚΤΙCΤΗΝ ΝΙΚΑΙΕΙC[3].	On the coins of Nicæa in Bithynia.
Hadrian .	ΚΤΙCΤΗC	On the coins of Argos.
—	CONDitor · COLoniæ · AELiæ · CAPitolinæ.	
Hercules .	ΚΤΙCΤΗC	Callatia, Mœsia, Cyzicus, Nicæa, Perinthus, Prienes, &c.
—	ΤΟΝ · ΚΤΙCΤΑΝ	On the coins of Heraclea in Bithynia.
—	ΟΙΚΙΣΤΑΣ	On the coins of Bruttium.
Mercury .	ΕΡΜΗC · ΚΤΙCΑC . ΤΗΝ ΠΟΛΙΝ	On the coins of Amasea.
Menestheus	ΜΕΝΕCΘΕΟΥ · ΚΤΙCΤΗ	On the coins of Elea in Æolia.
Midas . .	ΤΟΝ · ΚΤΙCΤΗΝ	On the coins of Midæum in Phrygia.
Pergamus .	ΚΤΙCΤΗC	On the coins of Pergamus in Mysia.
Romulus .	ROMVLO · CONDITORI	On Roman coins of Hadrian.

[1] Eckhel, vol. iv., cap. xvii., p. 342. [2] Numismatic Journal, vol. i., p. 4.

[3] The legend is here given in the accusative case, which is often used in similar legends; thus, by ΟΥΕΣΠΑΣΙΑΝΟΝ · ΚΑΙΣΑΡΑ, we are to understand —*the people worship* Vespasianus Cæsar.

Tiberius	ΚΤΙϹΤΗΝ	On the coins of Magnesia in Lydia.
Tomus	ΤΟΜΟΥ · ΚΤΙϹΤΗϹ	On the coins of Tomi in Mœsia.

These personages were thus honoured, in consequence of their being the reputed founders of the cities: the names of others are recorded; and their portraits often figured on the coins of those cities which claimed the honour of having given them birth; among these are Homer, Anacreon, Pythagoras, Lycurgus, Hector, Hippocrates, Plato, Theseus, &c. The names of the Emperors and Empresses were frequently given to cities; and IVLIA · AVGVSTA and CAESAREA, often usurp the place of the original name on their money. The cities of Marcianopolis, Claudiopolis, and Adrianopolis, may be cited as examples of this practice.

Epithets. Among the remarkable epithets bestowed upon some cities, and placed by them on their coins, are the following:—

Plotinopolis in Thracia	ΑΔΕΛΦΙΑ · ΠΛΩΤΕΙΝΟΠΟΛΙϹ · ΔΟΜΗΝΟΠΟΛΙϹ	*The sisters, Plotinopolis and Domenopolis.*
Magnesia in Ionia	ΕΒΔΟΜΗ · ΤΗϹ · ΑϹΙΑϹ	*The seventh of Asia.*
Anazarbus, in Cilicia, and Side in Pamphilia	ΕΝΔΟΞΟϹ	*Illustrious.*
Syedra in Cilicia	ΕΝΔΟΞΟΤΕΡΑ	*More illustrious.*
Lalassis in Isauria	ΕΝΤΙΜος	*Honourable.*
Neapolis in Samaria	ΕΠΙϹΗΜΟϹ	*Renowned.*
Germanicopolis in Paphlagonia	ΕϹΤΙΑ · ΘΕΩΝ	*The house of the gods.*
Smyrna in Ionia	ΚΑΛΛΕΙ · ΚΑΙ ΜΕΓΕΘΕΙ	*For beauty and greatness.*
Side in Pamphilia	ΛΑΜΠΡΟΤΑΤΗ	*Most renowned.*
Nicæa in Bithynia	ΜΕΓΙϹΤΟΙ·ΑΡΙϹΤΟΙ	*Greatest, best.*
Syedra in Cilicia	ϹΕΜΝΗ	*Venerable.*
Carrhæ in Mesopotamia	ΦΙΛΟΡΩΜαιοι	*Lover of the Romans.*

Names of Cities changed. The ancient name of a city was sometimes abandoned for a new one. Examples are not unfrequent on coins. We find the following noted by Eckhel:—

Abonitichos . . .	changed to . .	Ionopolis.
Ace	— . .	Colonia Ptolemais.
Alexandria in Egypt	— . .	Rome herself.
Anthedon in Judæa	— . .	Agrippias.
Antiochia in Syria .	— . .	Theupolis.
Byzantium in Thracia	— . .	Constantinople.
Eleusa Insula . . .	— . .	Sebaste.
Jerusalem	— . .	Ælia Capitolina.
Soli	— . .	Pompeiopolis.
Sybaris	— . .	Thurium, and afterwards to Copia.
Zancle	— . .	Messana, and afterwards to Mamertinum.

The cities of Adana, Anazarbus, Anthedon, Bithynia, Cius, Edessa, Lugdunum, and Mantinea returned to their ancient names, whilst some retained both the old and the new. These latter are as follows:—

Apamea in Bithynia . .	anciently	Mylea . .	ΑΠΑΜΕΩΝ · ΤΩΝ ΜΥΡΑΕΑΝΩΝ.
Apamea in Phrygia . .	—	Cibotos .	ΚΙΒΩΤΟC · ΑΠΑΜΕΩΝ.
Cæsarea in Cappadocia	—	Eusebia .	ΕΥΣΕΒΕΙΑΣ·ΚΑΙΣΑΡΕΙΑΣ.
Crannon in Thessalia .	—	Ephyri .	ΚΡΑΝΝΟΥ · ΕΦΥΡ.
Flaviopolis in Bithynia .	—	Cretia . .	ΚΡΗΤΙΕΩΝ · ΦΛΑΟΥΟΠΟΛΕΙΤΩΝ.
Leucas Decapoleos . . .	—	Abila . .	ΛΕΥΚ · ΑΒΙΛΑ.
Patræ in Achaia	—	Aroe . . .	COL · *Augusta Aroe* PATRAE.
Scythopolis in Samaria .	—	Nysa . .	ΝΥCΑΙΕωΝ · ΤΩΝ ΚΑΙ · CΚΥΘΟΠΟΛΙΤΩΝ.[1]

[1] Eckhel, Doct. Num. Vet. vol. iv. p. 321.

Colonial Coins. A vast number of coins were struck by the Roman colonies. With few exceptions, they are of rude fabric. The ordinary types are, *a priest guiding two oxen yoked to a plough*, the usual mode of marking the boundaries of a town;[1] *one, two, or three military standards; the wolf and twins;* and a *bull*. The legends are in the Latin character, and are generally given in a contracted form.[2] Some of these colonies record the right of minting coins by the legend, PERM · AVG or, PERMISSV · CAESARIS · AVG.[3] A coin of Patrae bears INDVLGENTIAE · AVG · MONETA. Another of Carthago reads, PERMISSV · P · DOLABELLAE · PROCOS. The permission was also accorded by the senate, as we learn from a coin of Carteia, inscribed M · FALCIDIVS · IIIIVIR · EX S · C.[4]

The series of colonial coins have been described and illustrated by Vaillant,[5] in two folio volumes, containing numerous plates, a work of great learning, labour, and research: but in consulting it, it will be well to refer to Eckhel's *Doctrina*, which contains so many corrections of previous numismatic writers.

[1] The word *portal* is derived from the fact of the plough being *carried* over the space left for the *porta* or gate.—Eckhel, Doct. Num. Vet. vol. iv. 489.

[2] See the list of Abbreviations on Colonial Coins.

[3] See the coins of Cæsar Augusta in Spain.—Mionnet, Descrip. tom. i.

[4] Flores, Medallas de las Colonias, &c. tom. iii. p. 36. Eckel. Doct. Num. Vet. iv. p. 497. Bimard's note on Jobert, *Science de Medailles*, tom. ii. p. 68, *edit*. 1739.

[5] Numismata Ærea Imperatorum, &c. in coloniis percussa. Paris, 2 vols. folio.

LIST OF THE MORE COMMON ABBREVIATIONS ON GREEK COINS OF CITIES AND PRINCES.

N.B.—The names on coins of Greek Cities are generally given in the genitive case plural, thus: ΠΕΡΓΑΙΩΝ, i. e. [*money*] *of the people of Perga*. The names of kings occur perpetually in the genitive case, thus: ΒΑΣΙΛΕΩΣ ΠΤΟΛΕΜΑΙΟΥ, [*money*] *of King Ptolemy*. There are on Greek coins, however, examples of legends in the nominative and accusative cases, and the genitive case singular.

Α. Abassus, or Abdera, or Abydus, or *Αντιγονος*. Athens, Argos, Asylum, or Aulus, or *Ακτια*, or *Αλεξανδρος*: also *Primi*, or *first*: thus *Εφεσιων*, Α. *Ασιας* signifies [*of the*] *Ephesians, first* [*people*] *of Asia*.

ΑΒ. or ΑΒΥ. Abydus.

ΑΘ. or ΑΘΕ. Athens.

ΑΙΓ. or ΑΙ. Ægina.

ΑΙΓΟΣΠΟ. Aigospotamos.

ΑΙΛ. Ælius, or Ælia Capitolina.

ΑΙΝ. Ænos.

ΑΚ. or ΑΚΡΑΓΑΝ. Agrigentum.

ΑΚΙ. Acilium.

ΑΚΤ. Actium, or ΑΚ. in monograms.

ΑΛΕ. Alexandria.

ΑΜ. Amyntas.

ΑΜΒΡ. Ambracia.

ΑΜΦΙ. Amphilochia. Amphipolis.

ΑΝ. Ancyra. Andrus.

ΑΝΑ. Anactorium.

ΑΝΤ. Antoninus, or Antonius, or Antioch.

ΑΝΤΑΝ. Antandrus.

ΑΝΤΙ. Antium.

ΑΝΤΙΣ. Antissa.

ΑΝΘ. *Ανθυπατος*. Proconsul.

ΑΞ. Axus in Crete.

ΑΠ. Appius.

ΑΠΑ. Apamea.

ΑΠΟ. Apollonia.

ΑΠΤΑ. Aptera.

ΑΡ. Aradus, or Harma. Argos.

ΑΡΕΘΟ. Arethusa, in Mygdonia.

ΑRΙΜ. Ariminum

ΑΡΣΙ. Arsinoe.

ΑΡΥ. Aryca.

ΑΡΧ. *Αρχιερευς*, or *Αρχον*, High Priest or Magistrate.

ΑΣΙΑΡΧ. Asiarch, president of the games of Asia.

Α. Σ. *Προτοι Συριας*, the first of Syria.

ΑΣ. or ΑΣΥ· *Ασυλου*. Asylum.

ΑΣΚ. Ascalon.

ΑΤΑΡ. Atarnea.

ΑΥΓ. Augustus.

ΑΥ. or, oftener, ΑΥΤ. or ΑΥΤΟΚ· *Αυτοκρατωρ*, Emperor.[1]

ΑΥΤΟΝ. *Αυτονομος*, living under their own laws.

ΑΦΙ. Aphitis.

ΑΦΡ. Africanus.

ΑΧ. Achaia.

Β. Berytus, Bithynia, or *Βουλη*, Council. Β also supplies the place of V on Greek coins, where a Latin name is given: thus Verus is sometimes spelled ΒΕΡΟC: it is, however, more frequently given ΟΥΗΡΟC.

ΒΑΛ. Valerius.

ΒΑ. *Βασιλευς*.

ΒΗ. Berytus.

ΒΟΙ. Bœotia.

ΒΟΥΛ. *Βουλη*.

ΒΡΥΝ. or BRVN. Brundusium.

ΒΥ. Byzantium.

[1] On the Imperial Greek coins this title precedes the name, as IMP. on the Latin.

Γ. Γνωριμον. Illustrious, Renowned. Gaius, or Caius.
ΓΑ. Gallus, Galerius, or Gallienus.
ΓΕΛ. Gelas.
ΓΕΡ. Germanicus.
ΓΕΡΟΥ. Γερουσια.
ΓΝ. Gneius.
ΓΟΡΤΥ. Gortyna.
ΓΡΑΜ. Γραμματευς. Scribe.

Δ. Decimus, or Dymae.
ΔΑΚ. Dacicus (on coins of Trajan).
ΔΑΜ. Damascus.
ΔΑΡ. Dardanus.
ΔΗ. Δημος, the People; or Delos.
ΔΗΜΑΡΧ · ΕΞΟΥΣ, with Tribunician power.
ΔΕ. Decelia.
Δ. Ε. Δημος ευχαι. Vota publica.
ΔΕΚ. Decius.
ΔΙΟΠ. Diospolis.
ΔΥΡ. Dyrrhachium.

Ε. Eryce.
ΕΛΕΥ. Eleusis.
ΕΛΕΥΘ. Ελευθερας. Free.
ΕΠΙ. Epidaurus.
ΕΡΙ. Eriza in Caria.
ΕΡΥ. Erythræ.
ΕΡΧ. Erchomenus, or Orchomenus.
ΕΤ. or ΕΤΟ. Ετους. Year.
ΕΧ. Εχουσια. Power.
ΕΥ. or ΕΥΑ. Ευαγορας.
ΕΥ. or ΕΥΒΟ. Eubœa.
ΕΥΣ. Ευσεβης. Pious.
ΕΥΤ. Ευτυχης. Happy.
ΕΦ. or ΕΦΕ. Ephesus.
ΕΦ. Εφορος.

ΖΑ. Zacynthus.
ΖΑΝΚΛ. Zanclè in Sicilia, now Messana.

ΗΓ. Ἡγεμονος. President.
ΗΡΑ. Heraclea.

ΘΑ. Thasus.
ΘΕ. Thespiæ.
ΘΕ. or ΘΗΒ. Thebæ.
ΘΕΣ. Thessalonica. Thespiæ. Thessaly.

Ι. ΙΕΡ. Ιερας. Sacred.
ΙΕΡΑΠΥ. Hierapytna.
ΙΛΙ. Ilium.
ΙΟΥ. On coins of the city Julis, and often for Julius and Julia.
ΙΟΥΛ. Julia, or Julius.
ΙΡ. Irene Insula.
ΙΣ. Issa or Histiæa.

Κ. Caius, or Κουιντος. (Quintus).
Κ. Κ. Κοινον Κιλικιας. (The Community of Cilicia).
ΚΑΙ. Cælia in Peucetia. Cæsar.
ΚΑΙΛ. Cælius.
Κ. or ΚΑΙΣ. Cæsar.
ΚΑΛ. Chalcedon.
ΚΑΛΛΙ. Callipolis.
ΚΑΜΑ. Camara.
ΚΑΠ. Capua.
ΚΑΠΠ. Cappadocia.
ΚΑΡ. Carrhæ.
ΚΑΡΤ. Carthago.
ΚΑΡΘ. Carthea.
ΚΑΥ. Caulonia.
ΚΕ. Ceos.
ΚΙΛ. Cilbiani.
ΚΛ. Claudius.
ΚΛΑ. Clazomene.
ΚΛΗ. Cleone.
ΚΝΙ. Cnidus.
ΚΟ. Corinth.
ΚΟΙΝ. Κοινον. Community.
ΚΟΛ. Κολονιας. Colony, or Colophon.
ΚΟΜ. Commodus.
ΚΟΡ. Corcyra, or Corinth.
ΚΟΡΟ. or ΚΟ. Coronea in Bœotia.
ΚΡ. Cragus in Lycia.
ΚΡΑΝΟ. Crannon.
ΚΡΗ. Creta.
ΚΡΟ. Crotona.
ΚΟΣ. Cosa in Lucania. Cos Insula.
ΚΤΗ. Ctemenæ.
ΚΥ. Cyon, Cuma, or Cydonium.
ΚΥΘ. Cythnus.
ΚΥΠ. Cyprus.
ΚΥΡΑ. Cyrene.

Λ. or more commonly, L. Λυκαβαντος (Year.).
Λ. Lucius.
ΛΑ. Lacedæmon.
ΛΑΜ. Lamia, or Lampsacus.
ΛΑΡ. Larissa.
ΛΑΡΙ. Larinum.
ΛΕΒ. Lebadia in Bœotia.
ΛΕ. ΛΕΥ. Leucas.
ΛΕΟΝ. Leontium.
ΛΙΠ. Lipara.
Λ. ΛΟ. or ΛΩΚ. Locri.
ΛΟΓ. Longane.

Μ. Marcus, or Megalopolis.
ΜΑ. Maronea, Massilia, or Massicytes.
ΜΑΚΕ. Macedonia.
ΜΑΓ. Magnesia.
ΜΑΜ. Mamertini.
ΜΑΝ. Mantinea in Arcadia.
ΜΑΣΣ. Massilia.
ΜΕ. Metapontum. Messenia.
ΜΕ. or ΜΕΓ. Megara, Megalopolis, or Melita.
ΜΕΓ. Μεγαλος. Great.
ΜΕΣ. Messana.
ΜΕΤΑ. Metapontum.
Μ. or ΜΗΤΡΟ. Metropolis.
ΜΙ. Miletus.
ΜΥ. Mycalessus, Myconus, Myra, Myrina.
ΜΥΡ. Myrlea.
ΜΥΤΙ. Mytilene.

Ν. Naupactus.
ΝΑΞ. Naxos.
ΝΑΥΑΡΧ. Ναυαρχιδος. Having a sea-port.
ΝΕ. Νεωτερα.
Ν. ΝΕΩΚ. Νεωκοροι.
ΝΕΟΠ. Neapolis.
ΝΕΡ. Nerva.
ΝΙΚ. Nicæa, or Nicomedia.
ΝΥΣ. Nysa.

ΟΙ. Oetaei.
ΟΛ. ΟΛΒ. Olbiopolis, or Olbia.
ΟΜΟ. Ομονοια. Concord.
ΟΠΕΛ. Opelius.
ΟΡΧ. Orchomenus.
ΟΥΠ. or ΥΠ. Ουπατος, or Υπατος. Consul.
ΟΥΗ. or ΟΥΗΡ. Verus.[1]
ΟΥΕΣΠ. Vespasianus.
ΟΥΙΤΕΛ. Vitellius.
ΟΦΡΥ. Ophrynium.

Π. Παρα or Προς. Upon.
Π. ΠΑ. Paros, Parium, Paphos.
Π. ΠΟΠΛ. Publius.
ΠΑΙΣ. Pæstum.
ΠΑΛΕΙ. Palerios in Arcanania, *in a monogram.*
ΠΑΝ. Panormus, Panticapæum.
ΠΑΡΙ. Parium in Mysia.
ΠΑΡΘ. Parthicus.
ΠΕ. Perinthus.
ΠΕΛ. Pella.
ΠΕΡ. Perga, Pergamus, (in monogram).
ΠΕΡΤ. Pertinax.
ΠΕΣΚ. or ΠΕCΚ. Pescennius.
Π.ΠΗ. Pelusium.
ΠΛΑ. Platææ.
ΠΟ. Pontus.
ΠΟΛΥ. Polyrhenium.
ΠΟΣ. Posidonia.
ΠΡΑΣ. Prassus.
Π. ΠΡΥ. Πρυτανις. Præfect.
ΠΡ. ΠΡΕΣ. Πρεσβευς. Legate.
ΠΡΟ. Proconnesus.
ΠΡΟΔΙ. Προδικος. Curator.
Π. or ΠΡΩΤ. Πρωτος. First.
ΠΤ. Ptolemais.
ΠΥ. Byzantium, (in monogram).

ΡΟ. Rhodes.
ΡΥ. Rubi in Peucetia.

ΣΑ. Sala.
Σ. ΣΑ. Salamis; Syria; Samos, or Samosata.[2]
ΣΑΛΑΠ. Salapia.

[1] See the remark under letter B, page 33.
[2] It should be borne in mind, that on numerous Greek coins, the characters C Ϲ are often used for Σ.

ΣΑΡ. Sardis.
ΣΕ. Segeste, Seriphus, Sicyon.
ΣΕΒ. Σεβαστος. Augustus.
ΣΕΛ. Seleucia, or Selinus.
ΣΕΠΤ. Septimius.
ΣΙ. Siphnus, Sicyon.
ΣΙΔ. Side.
ΣΙΝΩ. Sinope.
ΣΚ. or ΣΚΙΑΘΙ. Sciathus Insula.
ΣΜΥ. Smyrna.
ΣΤΕΦ. Στεφανηφορος.
ΣΤΡ. or ΣΤΡΑ. or CΤΡΑΤ. Στρατηγος. Prætor.
ΣΥΒ. Sybaris.
ΣΥ. ΣΥΡΑ. Syracuse.
ΣΥΡ. Syria, Syrus.
ΣΩ. Soli.

Τ. Titus.
ΤΙ. or ΤΙΒ. Tiberius.
ΤΑ. ΤΑΝΑ. Tanagra, Temnus.[1]
ΤΑ. ΤΑΡ. ΤΑΡΑΣ. Tarentum.
ΤΑΡ. Tarsus.
ΤΑΥΡΟ. Tauromenium.
ΤΕ. Terone, or Torone, in Chalcidice.
ΤΕΡ. Terina.
ΤΗ. Tenus.
ΤΡΑ. Tralles.
ΤΡΙ. Tripolis.
ΤΡΟ. Trœzene, or Troade.
ΤΥΑΝ. Tyana.
ΤΥ. Tyndaris.
ΤΥΡ. Tyre, generally in a Monogram.

ΥΕ. or ΥΕΛ. Velia.
ΥΠ. or ΥΠΑΤ. Υπατος, Consul.

Φ, on Greek Coins, supplies the place of F in Latin names: thus, Faustina is spelled Φαυστεινα.
Φ. Philuntium Phœstus or Philippus.
ΦΑ. Phaselis.
ΦΑΡ. Pharsalus.
ΦΕ. Pheræ in Thessalia.
ΦΙ. Philippopolis, or Vibius.
ΦΛ. Flavius.
ΦΟΚ. Phocæa.
ΦΟΥΛ. Fulvia.

Χ. Chios Insula.
ΧΑΛ. Chalcis.
ΧΕΡ. Chersonesus.

[1] Aeolic for ΤΗ.

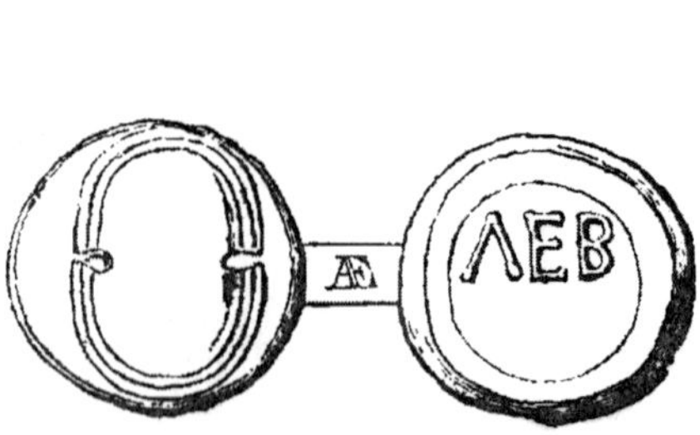

RIVERS AND FOUNTAINS, THE NAMES OF WHICH ARE FOUND ON GREEK COINS.*

ΑΙΣΑΡΟΣ. . . .	*Aesarus* . .	On coins of Crotona.
ΑΙCΗΠΟC . . .	*Aesepus* . . .	Cyzicus.
ΑΜΕΝΑΝΟΣ . .	*Amenanus*. . .	Catania.
ΑΝΓΗΟS . . .	*Anthos* . . .	Antiochia in Pisidia.
ΑΡΕΘΟΣΑ . . .	*Arethusa* . .	Syracuse.
ΑΣΣΙΝΟΣ. . . .	*Asines* . . .	Naxus.
ΑΥΛΙΝΔΗΝΟC . .	*Aulindenus*. .	Ceretape.
ΑΞΙΩ	*Axius*. . . .	Apamea in Syria
ΑΖΟC	*Axus*. . . .	Erythræ.
ΒΙΛΛΑΙΟC . . .	*Billaeus*. . .	Tius in Bithynia.
ΚΑΙΚΟC	*Caicus* . . .	Pergamus?
ΚΑΛΕΩΝ. . . .	*Caleon* . . .	Smyrna.
ΚΑΛΛΙΡΟΗΙ. . .	*Callirhoe* . .	Antiochia in Syria.
ΚΑΛΛΙΡΟΗ . . .	*Callirhoe* . .	Apamea in Phrygia.
ΚΑΛΥΚΑΔΝΩΙ . .	*Calycadnus* .	Seleucia in Cilicia.
ΚΑΠΡΟΝ. . . .	*Caper* . . .	Attusia in Phrygia.
ΚΑΟC	*Caus*. . . .	Eriza in Caria.
ΚΑΥCΤΡΟC . . .	*Cayster* . . .	Hypæpa in Lydia.
ΚΕΝΧΡΙΟC . . .	*Cenchrius* . .	Ephesus.
ΚΕCΤΡΟC . . .	*Cestrus* . . .	Sagalassus in Pisidia.
ΚΗΤΙΟC	*Cetius* . .	Pergamus in Mysia.
CRYSAS. . . .	*Chrysas*. . .	Assorus in Sicilia.
ΧΡΥCΟΡΟΑC . .	*Chrysorrhoas* .	Hierapolis in Phrygia, Damascus and Lucas in Cœlesyria.
ΚΟΡCΥΜΟC, or ΚΟΡCΥΝΟC . .	*Corsymus* . .	Aphrodisia.
ΚΥΔΝΟC	*Cydnus* . . .	Tarsus in Cilicia.
ΕΛΑΤΗΣ	*Elates* . . .	Midæum in Phrygia.
ΕΥΦΡΑΤΗΝ . . .	*Euphrates* . .	Antiochia in Commagene.

* The Greek names are given in the same cases as they actually occur on the coins. Sometimes the name of the river or fountain stands alone, but is more frequently coupled with the name of the city, thus, ΑΝΤΙΟΧΕΩΝ · ΠΡΟΣ · ΕΥΦΡΑΤΗΝ. The word ΠΗΓΗ (*fountain*), or ΠΗΓΑΙ, is of most rare occurrence. On some autonomous coins the personified head of the river appears, without legend, as on those of Oeniadae, with the head of the *Achelous*, Calydon with that of *Evenus*, &c. &c.

ΠΗΓΗ	(Anonymus)	Philadelphia in Lydia.
ΠΗΓΑΙ	(Anonymi)	Damascus in Cœlesyria.
ΓΑΛΛΟC	*Gallus*	Philomelium in Phrygia.
ΓΕΛΑΣ	*Gelas*	Gelas.
ΓΛΑΥΚΟC	*Glaucus*	Neocæsarea in Pontus and Eumenia in Phrygia.
ΑΛΥC	*Halys*	Germanicopolis in Paphlagonia.
ЄΡΜΟC	*Hermus*	Several cities of Aeolis, Lydia, and Phrygia.
ΙΠΠΑΡΙΣ	*Hipparis*	Camarina in Sicilia.
ΙΠΠΟΦΟΡΑC	*Hippophoras*	Apollonia in Pisidia.
ΙΠΠΟΥΡΙΟC	*Hippurius*	Blaundus in Lydia.
ΥΛΛΟC	*Hyllus*	Saetteni in Lydia.
ΥΠΙΟΥ	*Hypius*	Prusias in Bithynia.
ΗΥΨΑΣ	*Hypsas*	Selinus in Sicilia.
ΙCΤΡΟΝ	*Ister*	Nicopolis in Mœsia Inferior.
ΛΙΜΥΡΟC	*Limyrus*	Limyra in Lycia.
ΛΥΚΟC · ΚΑΠΡΟC	*Lycus & Caprus*	Laodicea in Phrygia.
ΜΑΙΑΝΔΡΟC	*Meander*	Antiochia and Tripolis in Caria, Apamea in Phrygia, and Magnesia in Ionia.
ΜΑΡΝΑΣ	*Marnas*	Ephesus.
ΜΑΡCΥΑC	*Marsyas*	Apamea in Phrygia.
ΜЄΛΗC	*Meles*	Amastris in Paphlagonia, and Smyrna in Ionia.
ΜЄCΤΩ	*Mestus*	Nicopolis in Thracia.
ΝΙΛΟΣ	*Nilus*	Alexandria in Egypt.
ΩΚЄΑΝΟC	*Oceanus*	Tyre.
Α · Π · Ο	Αντιοχεων Προς Ορόντη	Antiochia in Syria.
ΠΑΡΘЄΝΙΟC	*Parthenius*	Amastris in Paphlagonia.
ΠΙΤΝΑΙΟC	*Pitnaeus*	Agæ in Aeolis.
ΠΥΡΑΜΟC	*Pyramus*	Anazarbus, Hieropolis, Megarsus, Mopsus.
ΡΗΓΜΑ	*Regma*	Limyra in Lycia.
ΡΟΔΙΟC	*Rhodius*	Dardanus in Troade.
ΡΥΝΔΑΚΟC	*Rhyndacus*	Apollonia in Mysia.
CΑΓΑΡΙC	*Sagaris*	Nicæa in Bithynia.
CΑΝΓΑΡΙΟC CΚΟΠΑC	*Sangarius & Scopas*	Nicæa and Juliopolis.
CΑΡΔΟ	*Sardo*	Tius in Bithynia.

SARNINER (in Oscan characters) . .	*Sarnus* . . .	Nuceria in Campania.
ΣΑΡΟΝ	*Sarus* . . .	Antiochia in Cilicia.
CKAMANΔPOC . .	*Scamander* . .	Alexandria in Troade.
CЄΛINOC	*Selinus* . . .	Pergamus in Mysia.
CMAPΔ	*Smard* . . .	Phocaea in Ionia.
CTPYMΩN	*Strymon* . . .	Pautalia and Amphipolis.
COYNIAC	*Sunias* . . .	Pompeiopolis in Cilicia.
TЄPA	*Tera*	Phocaea.
TIBЄPIC	*Tiberis* . . .	Alexandria in Egypt.
TIΓPEI	*Tigris* . . .	Seleucia in Mesopotamia.
TIMЄΛHC	*Timeles* . . .	Aphrodisias in Caria.
TONZOC	*Tonzus* . . .	Hadrianopolis in Thracia.
ΞANΘOC	*Xanthus* . . .	Germanicopolis in Paphlagonia, and Cyme in Æolis.

GEOGRAPHICAL ARRANGEMENT OF GREEK COINS OF CITIES AND PRINCES,

ACCORDING TO THE SYSTEMS OF ECKHEL AND SESTINI, WITH THEIR DEGREES OF RARITY.

EUROPA.

HISPANIA in genere.

Autonomous, Æ. R.2.

LUSITANIA.

AMAIA (now *Portalegre*).—Aut. Æ. R.4.

The attribution of these coins is doubtful. The name is found on those of Coero.

BALSA (*Tavira*).—Aut. Æ. R.6.—Imperial of Caligula, Æ. R. 6.

COERE, vel Coero (*Coura*).—Aut. Æ. R.4.

COLIPPO (———).—Aut. Æ. R.4.

The attribution of these coins is doubtful.

EBORA (*Ebora*).—Imperial, Æ. R.4. to R.6., of Augustus.

EMERITA (*Merida*).—Imperial Colonial, AR. C., Æ. C. to R.6., of Augustus, Tiberius, and Julia.

MIROBRIGA[1] (———).—Æ. R.8.

MYRTILIS (*Mertola*).—Aut. Æ. R.4.

NORBA (*Brozas*).—Aut. Colonial, Æ. R.1.

Of doubtful attribution.

OSSONOBA (*Gibraleon*).—Aut. Æ. R.8.

PAX JULIA (*Badajoz*).—Imperial Colonial, Æ. R.6., of Augustus.

SALACIA (*Alcazar do Sal*).—Aut. Æ. R.8.

BAETICA.

ABDERA (*Adra*).—Aut. Æ. R.5. Phœnician legends. Imp. Col. Æ. R.5., of Tiberius.

ABRA (———).—Aut. Æ. R.4. (*doubtful*).

ACINIPO (*Ronda la Vieja*).—Aut. Æ. R.4.

AMBA (———).—Aut. Æ. R.4.

ANTIKARIA (*Antequera*).—Aut. Æ. R.4.

---

[1] Mionnet, Atlas de Géographie Numismatique. 4to. Paris, 1839.

ARIA or CUNBARIA (*La Maria*).—Aut. Æ. R.3.

ARVA (*Alcolea del Rey*).—Aut. Æ. R.5.

ASCUI or ASCUTA (———).—Aut. Æ. R.4. Imperial of

ASIDO (*Medina Sidonia*).—Aut. Æ. R.5. [Augustus, R.8.

ASPAVIA (———).—Aut. Æ. R.4.

ASTA (*Mesa d'Asta*).—Aut. Æ. R.6.

ASTAPA (*Estepa*).—Aut. Æ. R.8.

AUGURINA (*Santiago de la Higuera*).—Aut. Æ. R.2. (*doubtful*).

BAILO (*Balonia*).—Aut. Æ. R.8.

BAREA (*Vera*).—Aut. Æ. R.4.

CALLET (*Pruna*).—Aut. Æ. R.5.

CALPE (———).

The coins assigned to Calpe belong to Panormus in Sicily.

CANACA (*Alcocer*).—Aut. Æ. C. to R.6.

Some of these pieces bear the name of Odacisa, an unknown town in alliance.

CARBULA (*near Cordoba*).—Aut. Æ. R.4.

CARISA (*Cariza*).—Aut. Æ. R.4.

CARMO (*Carmona*).—Aut. Æ. R.4.

CARTEIA (*Rocadillo*).—Aut. Æ. C. to R.3.

Florez, Tom. I. p. 313. gives a coin of this city with the head of Julius Cæsar, but the head has been retouched.

CAURA (*Coria*).—Aut. Æ. R.6.

CELTI (*Puebla de los Infantes*).—Aut. Æ. R.6.

CORDUBA et PATRICIA[1] (*Cordoba*).—Aut. with the name of *Corduba*, Æ. R.4. Col. Imp. with the name of *Patricia*, Æ. R.2. to R.4. Coins of Augustus.

EPORA (*Montoro*).—Aut. Æ. R.4.

GADES (*Cadiz*).—Aut. AR. R.8. Æ. C. to R.8. Imp. Æ. R.3. to R.6. Augustus to Nero.

ILIBERIS (*Granada*).—Aut. Æ. R.6.

ILIPA, ILIPLA, ILUPLA, ILIPENSE (———).—Aut. Æ. R.2. to R.6.

ILITURGI (near *Andujar*).—Aut. Æ. R.6.

ILURCO (near *Grenada*).—Aut. Æ. R.6.

IPAGRO (*Aguilar*).—Aut. Æ. R.4.

IRIPPO (*Coripe*)..—Aut. Æ. R.3.

ITALICA. (*Sevilla la Vieja*).—Imperial Æ. C. to R.6. Augustus to Drusus.

Some of the coins of Italica bear the name of Bilbilis in alliance.

---

[1] The name given to Corduba on its becoming a Roman colony.

Ituci (*Castro del Rio el Leal*).—Aut. Æ. R.2. to R.4.

Julia (*Antequera et Lucena*).—Aut. Colonial Æ. R.8.

Lacippo (———).—Aut. Æ. R.8. Imperial Æ. R.8. of Augustus.

Laelia (*El Berrocal*).—Aut. Æ. R.4. to R.6. Imperial Æ. R.6. Augustus to Tiberius and Lucius Cæsar.

Lastigi (*Zahara?*).—Aut. Æ. R.6.

Luciferae (*San-Lucar-de Barrameda*).—Aut. Æ. R.2.

Of doubtful attribution.

Mirobriga (*Capilla*).—Aut. Æ. R.8.

Munda (*Monda*).—Aut. Æ. R.7.

Murgi (*Almeria*).—Aut. Æ. R.8.

Nabrissa or Nebrisa (*Lebrija*).—Aut. Æ. R.8. (*uncertain*).

Nema (———).—Aut. Æ. R.8.

Obulco (*Porcuna*).—Aut. Æ. C. to R.1.

Onuba (*Huelva*).—Aut. Æ. R.6.

Orippo (*Dos Hermanas*).—Aut. Æ. R.3. to R.6.

Oset, vel Osset (near *Romula*).—Aut. Æ. R.1. to R.3.

Romula (*Sevilla*).—Colonial Imperial, Æ. R.3. to R.7., from Augustus to Tiberius.

Sacili (*Acorrucer*).—Aut. Æ. R.6. to R.7.

Salpesa (near *Facialcazar*).—Aut. Æ. R.8.

Searo (———).—Aut. Æ. R.6.

Sisapo (*Guadalcanal*).—Aut. Æ. R.4.

Sisipo (*Almaden*).— Aut. Æ. R.6. Bearing *Detumo* or *Detumno*.

Tartessus (———).—Aut. Æ. R.8.

Traducta (*Algeciras*). Colonial Imperial, Æ. R.2. to R.7., from Augustus to Caius and Lucius Cæsar.

Tucci (*Martos*).—Aut. Æ. R.8.

Ventippo (*Casariche*).—Aut. Æ. R.8.

Ugia (*Los Cabezas de San Juan*).—Aut. Æ. R.6.

Of doubtful authority.

Ulia (*Montemayor*).— Aut. Æ. R.3. to R.4.

Urso (*Osuna*).—Aut. Æ. R.1. to R.4. Imperial, Æ. R.4. to R.7, of Augustus.

Some coins of Urso bear the name of Amba in alliance.

TARRACONENSIS.

Acci (*Guadex el Viejo*).—Aut. Æ. R 8. Colonial Imperial, Æ. R.2. to R.6., Augustus to Caligula.

Aesona et Orgia (*Isona*).—Aut. AR. R.2. Æ. R.2.

ARAE SESTIANAE (*Capo Turingas*).—Aut. AR. R.6. Æ. R.6. Imperial AR. R.8. Æ. R.8. Augustus.

ASTURICA (*Astorga*).—Colonial Imperial. Æ. R.8.

These coins bear the legend COL · AST · AVGVSTA. and may therefore belong to Asta, Astapa or Astigi, towns in Hispania Baetica.

AUSA (———).

Liebe has published a coin of Ausa which is pronounced false.

BEDESA (———).

See the coins of Rhoda, below.

BELEIA or BELITA (*Belchite*).—Aut. Æ. R.4.

BERSICAL (———).—Aut. AR. R4.

BILBILIS (*Calatayud*).—Aut. Æ C. to R.2. Imp. Æ. R.1. to R.3., Augustus to Caligula.

Some of these coins bear the name of *Italica* in alliance.

BURSADA (*Trillo*).—Aut. AR. R.2. Æ. R.4. (*doubtful*).

SALDUBA. CÆSARAUGUSTA (*Zaragoza*).—Imperial, Æ. C. to R6. Augustus to Caligula.

CALAGURRIS NASSICA (*Calahorra*).—Imperial, Æ.6. to R.4. Augustus to Caligula.

CALAGURRIS FIBULARIA (*Loarre*).—Aut. Æ. R.6.

CARTHAGO NOVA (*Cartagena*).—Aut. Æ. R.7. Colonial Imperial, Æ. R,1. to R.4. Augustus to Caligula.

CASCANTUM (*Cascante*).—Imperial, Æ. R.3. Tiberius.

CASTULO (*Cazlona*).—Aut. Æ. R.4

CELSA (*Vetillo de Ebro*).—Aut. Æ. C. to R.4. Colonial Imperial Æ. C. to R.6. of Augustus and Tiberius.

CISSA vel CISSUM (*Guissona*).—Aut. AR. R.4. Æ. R.1. (*doubtful*).

CLUNIA (*Coruna del Conde*).—Aut. Æ. R.4. Imperial Æ. R.2. to R.4. of Tiberius.

DERTOSA (*Tortosa*).—Colonial Imperial, Æ. R.6. Julius Cæsar to Tiberius.

There are coins of Dertosa bearing the name of *Ilercavonia* in alliance.

EMPORIAE (*Ampurias*).—Aut. AR. R.1. to R.6. Æ. C. to [R.3.

EQUAESI (———).—Aut. Æ. R.2.

ERGAVICA (*Milagro*).—Imperial, Æ. R.1. to R.3. Augustus to Caligula.

ETELESTA (———).—Aut. Æ. R.6. (*doubtful*).

GILI (———).—Aut. Æ. R.2.

Of doubtful attribution.

GLANDOMIRUM or GLANDIMIRUM (*Mondonnedo*).—Aut. Æ. [R.2.

Of doubtful attribution.

Graccurris (*Agreda*).—Imperial, Æ. R.2. Tiberius.

Helmantica (*Salamanca*).—Aut. AR. R.1. Æ. R.1.

Of doubtful attribution.

Hemeroscopium (*Denia* or *Artemus*).—Aut. AR. R.2. Æ. [R.2.

Of doubtful attribution.

Ibe (———).—Aut. Æ. R.2

Of doubtful attribution.

Ildum or Ilduni (———).—Aut. Æ. R.2.

Of doubtful attribution.

Ilercavonia (*Amposta*).— Aut. Æ. R.4. Imperial, Æ. R.4. Augustus to Tiberius.

There are coins of this town with Detorsa in alliance.

Ilerda (*Lerida*).—Aut. Æ. C. to R.4. Imperial, Æ. R.4. of Augustus.

Coins of this town bear the names of Cissa, Bedesa, and Sabenduno, (the last of which is unknown) in alliance.

Ilici (*Elche*).—Colonial Imperial, Æ. R.2. to R.4. Augustus [to Tiberius.

Libia (in *Murbogis*).—Aut. Æ. R.4.

Of doubtful attribution.

Libisosa (*Lezuza*).—Aut. Æ. R.4.

Of doubtful attribution.

Lobetum (*Albarracin*).—Aut. Æ. R.2.

Of doubtful attribution.

Meanenses (———).—Aut. AR. R.4. Æ. C.

Of doubtful attribution.

Merobriga (———).—Aut. AR. C. Æ. C.

Of doubtful attribution.

Nardinium (———).—Aut. Æ. R.2. to R.4.

Of doubtful attribution. Some of these coins bear the name of Rhoda in alliance.

Orospeda (———).—Aut. Æ. R.4.

Of doubtful attribution.

Osca (*Huesca*).—Aut. AR. R.2. to R.4. Imperial, Æ. R.2. to R.6. Augustus to Caligula.

Osicerda (*Cherta*).—Aut. AR. R.6. Æ. R.5. Imperial, Æ. R.5., of Tiberius.

Some bear the name of Sesaraca in alliance.

Ostur (———).—Aut. Æ. R.5.

Palantia (*Palencia*).—Aut. Æ. R.8.

Rhoda. (*Rosas*).—Aut. AR. R.5.

Some of these coins bear the names of Cissa, Ilerda, Taraeo, and Bedesa in alliance.

SAETABIS (*St. Felipe or Xativa*).—Aut. Æ. R.4.

SAGUNTUM et PERSEIANA (*Murviedro*).—Aut. Æ. R.2. to R.4. Imperial, Æ. R.2. to R.6., of Tiberius.

SEGOBRIGA (*Segorbe*).—Aut. Æ. R.3. Imperial, Æ. R.3. Augustus to Caligula.

SEGOVIA (*Segovia*).—Aut. Æ. R.6.

SEPONTIA (———).—Aut. Æ. R.6.

Of doubtful attribution.

SESARACA (———).—Aut. AR. R.6. Æ. R.4.

Of doubtful attribution.

SETELSIS (———).—Aut. Æ. R.4.

Of doubtful attribution.

SPALIO (———).—Aut. Æ. R.4.

Of doubtful attribution.

TAMARICI (———).— Aut Æ. R.4.

Of doubtful attribution.

TARRACO (*Tarragona*).—Colonial Aut. Æ. R.4. Colonial Imperial, Æ. R.2. to R.4. Augustus to Drusus.

TERMISUS (———).—Aut. Æ. R.4.

Of doubtful attribution.

THELORIS (*Torilla*).—Aut. Æ. R.6.

Of doubtful attribution.

TOLETUM (*Toledo*).—Aut. Æ. R.6.

TURIASO et SILBIS (*Tarazona*).—Aut. Æ. R.2. Imperial, Æ. C. to R.4. Augustus and Tiberius.

VALENTIA (*Valencia*).—Aut. Æ. R.4.

VIROVESCA (*Bribiesca*).—Aut. AR. R.4. Æ. R.6.

Of doubtful attribution.

URCESA (*Ucles*).—Aut. Æ. R.4.

TOWNS OF WHICH THE SITES ARE NOT KNOWN.

APORA—BORA—IPORA.—Aut. Æ. R.3.

ART (———).—Aut. Æ. R.3.

These pieces bear APT. which may not signify a town.

CERET (———).—Aut. Æ. R.6.

LONT—OLONT (———).—Aut. Æ. R.6.

TURRI (———).—Aut. Æ. R.6.

UNCERTAIN COINS OF SPAIN.

With Celtiberian Inscriptions.—Aut. Æ. C. to R.2.

With Latin and Celtiberian Inscriptions.—Aut. Æ. C. R.4.

With Latin and Phœnician Inscriptions.—Imperial, Æ. R.6., of Augustus and Agrippa.

With Latin Inscriptions.—Aut. Æ. C. to R.6. Imperial, Æ. R.2., of Tiberius.

EBUSSUS, *Insula* (*Ebiza.*)—Aut. Æ. R.8.

SPANISH CHIEFS.

These coins have Celtiberian legends, and generally bear a head on the obverse.—AR. C. to R.4. Æ. C. to R.2.

GALLIA.

GALLIA AQUITANICA.

AVARICUM (*Bourges*).—Aut. Æ. R.6.

PETROCORII (*Périgueux*).—Aut. AR. R.8. (*doubtful*).

SANTONES (*Saintes*).—Aut. AR. C. to R.2.

TURONES (*Tours*).—Aut. AR. R.8. Potin, R.8. Æ. R.1. [to R.6.

GALLIA NARBONENSIS.

ANTIPOLIS (*Antibes*).—Aut. AR. R.1. to R.4. Greek and Latin legends.

AVENIO (*Avignon*).—Aut. AR. R.7. Æ. R.7. Greek legends.

BETERRA (*Béziers*).—Aut. Æ. R.3. Greek legends.

CABELLIO (*Cavaillon*).—Aut. AR. R.6. Æ. R.2. to R.8. Colonial Imperial, AR. R.6. Æ. R.4., of Augustus.

GLANUM[1] (*Saint Remi*).—Aut. AR. R.8. Æ. R.8.

LACYDON (*the Port of Marseille*).—Aut. AR. R.6. Greek legends.

MASSILLIA (*Marseille*).—Aut. AR. C. to R.6. Æ. C. to R.6. Greek legends.

NEMAUSUS (*Nismes*).—Aut. Colonial, AR. R.4. to R.6. Æ. R.2. to R.6. Imperial Colonial, Æ. C. to R.4. Augustus and Agrippa.

RHODA or RHODANUSIA (———).—Aut. AR. R.7. Greek legends.

RUSCINO (*le Roussillon*).—Imperial Colonial, Æ. R.6. of Au- [gustus.

SEGUSIA (*Suze*).—Aut. AR. R.6.

VIENNA (*Vienne*).—Imperial Colonial, Æ. R.4. Julius Cæsar and Augustus, and Augustus and Agrippa.

VOLCÆ ARECOMICI.[2]—Aut. AR. R.5. Æ. R.3.

---

[1] See the Marquis Lagoy's "Description de Quelques Médailles inédites de Glanum," &c. 4to. *Aix*, 1834.

[2] The capital of the Volcæ Arecomici was Nemausus.

GALLIA LUGDUNENSIS.

ABALLO (*Avallon*).—Aut. Æ. R.8.

ANDEGAVI (*Angers*).—Aut. AR. R.4. Æ. R.4.

AULERCI EBUROVICES (*Evreux*).—Aut. Æ. R.4.

CABALLODUNUM (*Chalons sur Saone*).—Aut. AR. R.6.

CATALAUNUM (*Chalons sur Marne*).—Aut. Æ. R.4. Greek and Latin legends.

LUGDUNUM-COPIA (*Lyons*).—Aut. Colonial, AR. R.2. Imperial Colonial, Æ. C. to R.4. Augustus to Agrippa.

REMI (*Rheims*).—Aut. Æ. C. to R.2.

ROTOMAGUS (*Rouen*).—Aut. R.6.

SEQUANI.[1]—Aut. Æ. R.6.

GALLIA BELGICA.

AGRIPPINA (*Cologne*).—Imperial Colonial, Æ. R.8., of Postumus.

EBURONES (*District of Liege*).—Aut. AR. R.4.

MEDIOMATRICI (*Metz*).—Aut. Æ. R.6.

TORNACUM (*Tournay ?*)—Aut. C. to R.3.

VIRODUNUM (*Verdun*).—Aut. AR. R.4.

GAULISH CHIEFS.

AV. R.4. to R.8.—*Electrum*. R.4.—AR. C. to R.8.—*Potin*. —Æ. C. to R.8.

UNCERTAIN GAULISH COINS.

Aut. AV. C. to R.6.—*Electrum*, C. to R.4. AR. C. to R.6. *Potin*, C. to R.6. Æ. C. to R.4.

BRITANNIA.[2]

CAMULODUNUM (*Colchester*).—Aut. AV. R.6. to R.8.

VERULAMIUM (*Verulam*).—Aut. AV. R.6. to R.8. AR. R.6. to R.8. Æ. R.6. to R.8.

BRITISH CHIEFS.

SEGONAX.?—AV. R.8. (*doubtful appropriation*).

CUNOBELINUS.—AV. R.6. to R.8. AR. R.7. to R.8. Æ. R.6. to R.8.

UNCERTAIN COINS OF BRITANNIA.

AV. R.C. to R.8. AR. C. to R.8. Æ. C. to R.8.

---

[1] The Sequani inhabited the country between the Rhone and La Saone; their capital was Vesontio (*Besançon*.)

[2] See the remarks which precede the account of *English Coins*, Section III.

GERMANIA.

Of this country there exists no primitive money. See Eckhel, *Doctrina Num. Vet.* Vol. i. p. 81.

The coins of Hadrian bearing MET·NOR. (*Metallum Noricum*) are, of course, Roman.

ITALIA.

Italia Supera.

Aquileia (*Aquileia*).—Aut. Æ. R.8.

Ravenna (*Ravenna*).—Aut. Æ. R.1. to R.2.

Ticinum[1] (*Pavia*).—Aut. AR. R.8. Æ. R.7.

Etruria.

Camars (*Chiusi*).—Aut. Æ. R.8.

Cosæ (*Orbetello*).

See the coins of Cossea, in Thracia, to which they have been restored.

Faesulae (———).

The coin attributed to this town belongs to Telamon, in Etruria.

Faleria (———).

The coins supposed of this city, belong to Elis.

Felsuna (———).

The gold coin, supposed of Felsuna, is given by Sestini to Velia.

Graviscae[2] (———).

Attribution doubtful.

Luna (———).

The piece supposed of Luna belongs to Populonia.

Peithesa (———).

Restored to Veientum, in Etruria.

Populonia (*Populonia*).—Aut. AV. R.8. AR. R.4. to R.8. Æ. R.4. to R.6. Etruscan and Oscan legends.

Telamon (*Talamone*).—Aut. Æ. R.6. Etruscan legends.

Veientum? (———).—Aut. Æ. R.6. Etruscan legends.

Veterna (*Massa di Maremma*).—Aut. Æ. R.4. Etruscan legends.

Vetulonia (*Vetulonia*).—Aut. Æ. R.2.

These coins are also classed with those of Vettuna in Umbria.

Volaterrae (*Volterra*).—Aut. Æ. R.4. to R.8. Etruscan legends.

Uncertain Coins of Etruria.

Aut. Æ. C.

---

[1] Coins of Baduela, the Gothic King, bear the legend FELIX·TICINVS.

[2] These coins are attributed by Millingen to Crastus in Iapygia.

ISLANDS ADJACENT TO ETRURIA.

ILUA (*Elba*).

Lanzi gives a coin of this island, but it belongs to Tuder in Umbria.

UMBRIA.

ARIMINUM (*Rimini*).—Aut. Æ. R.4. to R.6.

FANUM (*Fano*).

Of doubtful attribution.

IGUVIUM (*Gubbio*).—Aut. Æ. R.8. Etruscan legends.

PISAURUM (*Pesaro*).—Aut. Æ. R.8. Greek and Latin legends.

PITNUM (———).—Aut. Æ. R.4. Etruscan legends.

TUDER (*Todi*).—Aut. AR. R.7. Æ. C. to R.6. Etruscan legends.

VETTUNA (*Bettona*).—Aut. Æ. R.4. Etruscan legends.

These coins are also attributed to Vetulonia, in Etruria.

PICENUM.

ANCONA (*Acona*).—Aut. Æ. R.6.

ASCULUM (*Ascoli*).—Aut. Æ. R.5. With *Hadria* in alliance.

HADRIA (*Atri*).—Aut. Æ. R.3. to R.6.

VESTINI.

The coins hitherto attributed to the Vestini are restored to Vescia in Latium.

MARRUCINI.

TEATE (*Chieti*).—Aut. Æ. R.1. to R.4., by some attributed to Teate in Apulia.

LATIUM.

ALBA (*Albano*).—Aut. AR. R.6. Pl. R.4.

AQUINUM (*Aquino*).—Aut. Æ. R.2. to R.4.

ARICIA (*Arricia*).—Aut. Pl. 8.

Doubtful if coins.

CORA (*Cora*).—Aut. AR. R.8. (see SORA).

MARUBIUM (———).—Aut. Æ. R.6.

MINTURNAE (———).—Aut. AR. R.8. Oscan legends.

PALACIUM (———).—Aut. Æ. R.8.

ROMA.

The coins bearing the inscription ROMA, were doubtless struck in Campania.

SIGNIA (*Segni*).—Aut. AR. R.7.

SORA (———).—Aut. AR. R.8.

LATIUM (*continued*).

TUSCULUM (*Frascati*).—Aut. Pl. R.8.

Doubtful if coins.

VELITURNUM (*Velletri*). Municipium.—Aut. Pl. R.8.

Doubtful if coins.

VERULAE (*Veruli*).—Aut. Pl. R.8.

Doubtful if coins.

VESCIA (———).—Aut. AR. R.8. Æ. R.4. to R.6.

SAMNIUM.

AESERNIA (*Isernia*).—Aut. Æ. R.2. to R.6.

ALLIPHA (———).—Aut. AR. R.4. to R.6.

Sestini gives this town to Campania. Millingen assigns the coins to Alliba in Campania.

AQUILONIA (*Lacedogna*).—Aut. Æ. R.7. Oscan legends.

BENEVENTUM (*Benevento*).—Aut. R.8.

CORFINIUM (———).—Aut. AR. R.2. to R.6. Oscan legends.

These coins are also arranged with the incerti of Samnium.

MELES (*Melisano*).—Aut. AR. R.8.

MURGANTIA (———).—Aut. Æ. R.8. Oscan legends.

PENTRI (———).

The coins given to this town belong to the Frentani.

The incerti of Samnium are of the style and module of the consular denarii, some of them bearing the inscription ITALIA, though many have Oscan legends. They are AR. R.2. to R.6.

FRENTANI in genere.

Aut. Æ. R.8. Oscan legends.

LARINUM (*Larino*).—Aut. Æ. R.4. to R.6.

They bear the retrograde inscription LADINOD, and uncial nobs, or globules.

CAMPANIA in genere.

Aut. AR. R.6. to R.8.

ACCERAE (*Acerra*).

These coins belong to Atella.

ATELLA (*Sant Arpino*).—Aut. Æ. R.4. to R.5. Oscan legends.

AURUNCI (———).—Aut. Æ. R.6.

CALATIA trans VULTURNUM or CAIATIA (*Galazze*).—Aut. Æ. R.8.

CALATIA cis VULTURNUM (*Caiazzo*).—Aut. Æ. R.8. Oscan legends.

CALES (*Calvi*).—Aut. AR. R.5. Æ. C. to R.3.

CAMPANIA (*continued*).

CAPUA (*Santa Maria di Capua*).—Aut. Æ. C. to R.4. Oscan legends.

COMPULTERIA or CUPELTERINI (———).—Aut. Æ. R.6. Oscan legends.

These coins were formerly attributed to Cumæ and Liternum.

COSSA (———).—Aut. Æ. R.2.

CUMAE (*Cuma*).—Aut. AV. R.8. Æ. R.2. to R.6.

HYRINA or HYRIUM (———).—Aut. AR. R.3. to R.5. Æ. R.8.

NEAPOLIS (*Naples*).—Aut. AV. R.8. AR. C. to R.8. Æ. C. to R.6.

NOLA (*Nola*).—Aut. AR. R.6. Æ. R.6.

NUCERIA ALTAFERNA (*Nocera dei Pagani*).—Aut. AR. R.6. Æ. R.2. to R.6. Greek and Oscan legends.

PHISTELIA or BISTELIA (*Puteoli?*).—Aut. AR. R.1. to R.6. Oscan legends.

PICENTIA (*Bicenza.*)—Aut. AR. R.8.

STABIAE (*Stabbia*).

The coin quoted by Eckhel is of Gelas.

SUESSA (*Sessa*).—Aut. AR. R.4. Æ. R.1. to R.6. Greek and Latin legends.

TEANUM (*Tiano*).—Aut. AR. R.6. Æ. R.2. to R.6. Greek, Latin, and Oscan legends.

VENAFRUM (*Venafro*).—Aut. Æ. R.7.

VISERIS? (Oscan characters).—Aut. AR. R.8. (*Millingen*).

UNCERTAIN COINS OF CAMPANIA.

These coins have Oscan legends. They are Æ. R.2.

There are also coins of Campania which are supposed to have been struck under the authority of the Romans. They bear the legends ROMA · ROMAN · ROMANO · ROMANOR in the Latin character. The gold pieces, with the numerals indicating their value, 20, 40, 60 sesterces, belong to this series.

Aut. AU. R.6. Æ. R.1. to R.4. Æ. C. to R.4.

APULIA.

ACHERONTIA (*Acerenza*).

The coins supposed of this town belong to Aquilonia.

ARPI (*Arpe*).—Aut. AR. R.7. Æ. R.1. to R.4.

ASCULUM (*Ascoli di Puglia*).—Aut. Æ. R.4.

BARIUM (*Bari*).—Aut. Æ. R.4.

CANUSIUM (*Canosa*).—Aut. Æ. R.4. to R.8.

CAELIA (———).—Aut. AR. R.8.

APULIA (*continued*).

GRUMUM (*Gruma*).

Sestini gives the coin of Grumentum to this town.

LUCERIA (*Lucera*).—Aut. Æ. R.2. to R.4. Latin legends.

MERINUM (*St. Maria di Merino*).

Sestini thinks the coins attributed to Merusium in Sicily belong to Merinum.

NATIOLUM? (———).—Aut. Æ. R.6. (*Millingen*).

NEAPOLIS (*Polignano*).—Aut. Æ. R.2.

RUBI VEL RYBASTINI (*Ruvo*).—Aut. AR. R.6. Æ. R.6.

SALAPIA (*Salpi*).—Aut. Æ. R.2. to R.6.

SIPONTUM (———).

The coins attributed to Sipontum are doubtful.

TEATES (*Pezza della Chiesa*).—Aut. AR. R.4. Æ. R.2.

Of doubtful attribution.

VENUSIA (*Venosa*).—Aut. Æ. R.2. to R.5. Latin legends.

Formerly attributed in error to Velia.

UREIUM (*Rodi*).—Aut. Æ. R.2.

CALABRIA.

AZETINI (———).—Aut. Æ. R.4.

Formerly attributed in error to a town of the same name in Attica.

BRUNDUSIUM (*Brindisi*).—Aut. Æ. C. to R.3. Latin legends.

BUTUNTUM (*Bitonto*).—Aut. Æ. R.4. to R.6.

CŒLIUM (*Ceglie*).—Aut. Æ. R.1. to R.4.

GRAIA GALLIPOLIS (*Gallipoli*).—Aut. Æ. R.4.

HYDRUNTUM (*Otranto*).—Aut. Æ. R.8.

LEUCA (———).

The coin supposed of Leuca belongs to Velia.

ORRA (*Uria*).—Aut. Æ. R.2. to R.4. Greek and Latin legends.

SALENTINI (———).

The coin supposed of Salentini is of Calacte.

STURNIUM (*Sternaccio*).—Aut. Æ. R.4.

TARENTUM (*Taranto*).—Aut. AV. R.4. to R.7. AR. C. to R.8. Æ. R.5.

UXENTUM (*Ogento*).—Aut. Æ. R.4. to R.6.

LUCANIA.

LUCANI in genere.—Aut. Æ. R.4.

ATINUM (*Atena*).—Aut. Æ. R.8.

BUXENTUM or PYXUS (*Policastro*).—Aut. AR. R.8.

These coins also bear the name of Siris in Lucania.

LUCANIA (*continued*).

COSA or COSSA (———).—Aut. Æ. R.8.

COSILYNAS (———).—Aut. Æ. R.6.

GRUMENTUM (*Armento*).—Aut. Æ. R.8.

HERACLEA (*Policoro*).—Aut. R.6. to R.8. AR. C. to R.8. Æ. R.4. to R.6.

On one coin of this city, the name of Metapontum is found in alliance.

LAUS (*Scalea*).—Aut. AR. R.8.

Some bear the name of Posidonia in alliance.

METAPONTUM (*Torre di Mare*).—Aut. AU. R.8. AR. C. to R.6. Æ. R.2. to R.6.

PALINURUS-MOLPIS (———).—Aut. AR. R.6.

POSIDONIA or PAESTUM (*Piesti* or *Pesto*).

With the name of *Posidonia*.—Aut AR. R.1. to R.6. Æ. R.3.

With the name of *Paestum*.—Aut. AR. R.8. Æ. R.2. to R.6.

Imperial of AUGUSTUS and of TIBERIUS.—Æ. R.4. With the legend Phistlus, or Phistulis.—Aut. AR. R.1. to R.6.

SIRIS (———).—Aut. AR. R.8. Æ. R.6.

A coin of this city in silver, bears the name of *Buxentum*.

SYBARIS
THURIUM } *Sibara Rovinata*.
COPIA

With the name of *Sybaris*.—Aut. AR. R.2. to R.7.

With the name of *Thurium*.—Aut. AV. R.8. AR. C. to R.4. Æ. R.2. to R.6.

With the name of *Copia*.—Aut. Æ. R.4.

VELIA (*near Castel a Mare della Bruca*).—Aut. AR. C. to R.6. Æ. R.1. to R.4.

(The gold coins of Velia are spurious). A coin of this city bears the name of Crotona in alliance.

URSENTUM (———).—Aut. Æ. R.8.

BRUTTII.

BRUTII in genere.—Aut. AV. R.4. AR. R.1. to R.5. Æ. C. to R.6.

CAULONIA (*Castel Vetere*).—Aut. AR. R.4. to R.8.

CROTON (*Crotone*).—Aut. AR. C. to R.8. Æ. R.2. to R.6.

Coins of this city, bear the names of Velia, Medama, and Pandosia. The gold coins given to Croton, belong to Cyrenaica.

BRUTTII (*continued*).

HIPPONIUM or VALENTIA } *Monteleone.*

With the name of *Hipponium.*—Aut. Æ. R.2. to R.4.

With the name of *Valentia.*—Aut. Æ. C. to R.4.

A coin of Valentia, bears also the name of ORRA, in alliance.

LOCRI (————).—Aut. AR. R.1. to R.5. Æ. R.1. to R.5.

MAMERTIUM (————).—These coins belong to Mamertini in Sicily.

MEDAMA and MESMA (*Mesima*).—Aut. Æ. R.8.

NUCERIA (*Nocera*).—Aut. Æ. R.6.

PANDOSIA (*Anglona*).—Aut. AR. R.8.

PERIPOLIUM PITANATA (*Limmana*).—Aut. AR. R.8.

PETELIA (*Strongoli*).—Aut. Æ. R.2. to R.4.

RHEGIUM (*Reggio di Calabria*).—Aut. AR. R.2. to R.6. Æ. C. to R.6.

TEMESA (*San Lucito*).—Aut. AR. R.8.

TERINA (*Nocera*).—Aut. AR. R.2. to R.8. Æ. R.2. to R.4.

UNCERTAIN COINS OF ITALY.

Aut. Æ. R.2. to R.4.

These coins have imperfect legends, or legends so contracted that they cannot be deciphered.

SICILIA.

SICILIA in genere.—Aut AR. R.8.

ABACAENUM (*Tripum*).—Aut. AR. R.2. to R.6. Æ. R.6.

ABOLLA (————).—Aut. Æ. R.8.

Of doubtful attribution.

ACRAE (*Pallazzolo*).—Aut. Æ. R.4.

ADRANUS (*Aderno*).—Aut. Æ. R.6.

SICILIA (*continued*).

AETNAEI (*San Maria di Licodia*).—Aut. AR. R.4. to R.8. Æ. R.2. to R.5.

AGATHYRNUS (*Agati*).—Aut. Æ. R.8.

With the name of Tyndaris in alliance.

AGRIGENTUM (*Girgenti*).—Aut. AV. R.8. AR. C. to R.8. Æ. C. to R.4.

Aut. Colonial AR. R.8. Æ. R.8.

Imp. Colonial Æ. R.6., of Augustus.

AGYRIUM (*San-Filippi d' Argiro*).—Aut. Æ. R.2. to R.6.

ALAESA (*Santa Maria delle Palate*).—Aut. Æ. R.2. to R.5.

The silver coins attributed to Alaesa belong to Allipha.

ALUNTIUM (*Alontio*).—Aut. Æ. R.4. to R.6.

AMESTRATUS (*Mistretta*).—Aut. Æ. R.8.

ASSORUS (*Asero*).—Aut. Æ. R.4. to R.5., Latin legends.

CAENA (———).—Aut. Æ. C. to R.4.

Formerly attributed to the Island of Caene.

CALACTE (*Caronia*).—Aut. Æ. R.4.

CAMARINA (*Torre di Camarana*).—Aut. AR. R.2. to R.8. Æ. C. to R.5.

CATANA (*Catania*).—Aut. AR. R.1. to R.6. Æ. C. to R.4.

CENTURIPAE (*Centorbi*).—Aut. Æ. C. to R.4.

CEPHALOEDIUM (*Cefalu*).—Aut. Æ. R.4. to R.7. Æ. R.3. to R.7.

Some bear the name of Heraclea in alliance.

ENNA (*Castro Giovanni*).—Aut. AR. R.8. Æ. R.4.

ENTELLA (*Antella* or *Roca di Antella*).—Aut. AR. R.6. Æ. R.2. to R.6.

ERBESSUS (———).—Aut. Æ. R.6.

ERYX (*Monte di San Giuliano* or *di Trapani*).—Aut. AR. R.5. to R.8. Æ. R.4.

EUBOEA (*Terra Nova*).—Aut. AR. R.8.

Bearing the name of Gelas in alliance.

GALARIA (*Gagliano*)—Aut. AR. R.8.

GELAS (*near Terra Nova*).—Aut. AU. R.8. AR. C. to R.6. Æ. C. to R.4.

Some bear the name of Euboea in alliance.

HERACLEA (*Capo Bianco*).—Aut. AR. R. 4. to R.7.

Some bear the name of Cephaloedium in alliance.

SICILIA (*continued*).

HIMERA or THERMAE } *Termini.*

With the name of *Himera.*—Aut. AR. R.2. to R.8. Æ. R.1. to R.4.

With the name of *Thermae.*—Aut. AR. R.4. to R.8. Æ. R.3. to R.5.

Some pieces bear both names.

HYBLA MAGNA (*Paterno*).—Aut. Æ. R.4.

HYCCARA? (*Maccari*).—Aut. Æ R.4.

Of doubtful attribution.

JAETA (*Jato* or *San Cosmano*).—Aut. Æ. R.6.

LEONTINI (*Lentini*).—Aut. AR. R.2. to R.6. Æ. R.1. to R.8.

Some bear the name of Megara in alliance.

LILYBAEUM (*Marsalla*).—Aut. Æ. C. to R.5.

LONGANE (———).—Aut. AR. R.8. (*Millingen*).

MACELLA? (*Monte Busamara*).—Aut. Æ. R.8.

Of doubtful attribution.

MAZARA (———).—Aut. AR. R.4. *Phœnician* legends.

MEGARA (*Monte Ibla*).—Aut. Æ. R.8.

Some bear the names of Leontini and Hybla in alliance.

MENAENUM (*Mines*).—Aut. Æ. R.2. to R.4.

MERUSIUM (———).—Aut. AR. R.8.

ZANCLES MESSANA or MAMERTINI } *Messina.*

With the name of *Zancles.*—Aut. AR. R.4. to R.8.

With the name of *Messana.*—Aut. AR. R.1. to R.8. Æ. C. to R.4.

With the name of *Mamertini.*—Aut. Æ. C. to R.6.

The coins of this city are highly interesting to the Numismatist, as the changes in the name throw much light upon, and fix the epochs in which the pieces were struck.

MORGANTIA (*Murgo*).—Aut. AR. R.8. Æ. R.3. to R.6. *Greek* and *Phœnician* legends.

MOTYA (———).—Aut. AR. R.6. to R.8.

NACONA (———).—Aut. Æ. R.6.

NAXUS (*Schiso*).—Aut. AR. R.2. to R.6.

NEETUM? (*Noto*).—Aut. Æ. R.8.

Of doubtful attribution.

SICILIA (*continued*).

PANORMUS (*Palermo*).

With *Phœnician* characters.—Aut. AV. R.2. to R.3. AR. R.3. to R.8. Æ. C. to R.6.

Phœnician without characters.—Aut. AV. R.1. to R.3. Electrum R.2. AR. R.1. to R.5. Æ. C. to R.2.

With *Greek* and *Phœnician* characters.—Aut. AR. R.8.

Greek.—Aut. AR. R.8. Æ. C. to R.4. Imperial. Æ. R.4., of Augustus and of Tiberius.

Latin.—Aut. Colonial Æ. R.4.

On some of the Latin coins the word HISPANORVM occurs.

PETRINI (*Petralia*).—Aut. Æ. R.6.

SEGESTA (*Pileri di Barbera*).—Aut. AR. R.2. to R.6. Æ. R.2. to R.4. Imperial Æ. R.4., of Augustus.

SELINUS (*Terra delli Pulci*).—Aut. AR. R.2. to R.6.

Some have the name of Syracuse in alliance.

SOLUS (*Monte Catalfano*).—Aut. Æ. R.4.

SYRACUSAE (*Siracusa*).—Aut. AV. C. to R.8. AR. C. to R.8. Æ. C. to R.6.

TAUROMENIUM (*Taormina*).—Aut. AV. R.1. to R.7. AR. R.6. to R.8. Æ. C. to R.4.

TRIOCALA? (———).—Aut. Æ. R.8.

TYNDARIS (*Il Tindaro*).—Aut. Æ. R.4. to R.6.

Some bear the name of Agathyrnus in alliance.

TYRACINA (———).—Aut. Æ. R.6.

ISLANDS ADJACENT TO SICILY.

CAENE (*Cani*).—See the coins of CAENA in Sicily.

CORSICA (*Corse*).—No coins known.

COSSURA (*Pantellaria*).—Aut. Æ. R.1. to R.2. *Phœnician* and *Latin* legends.

GAULOS (*Gozzo*).—Aut. Æ. C. to R.2. *Phœnician* and *Greek* legends.

LIPARA (*Lipari*).—Aut. Æ. C. to R.6.

LOPADUSA (*Lampedusa*).—Aut. Æ. R.8.

MELITA (*Malta*).—Aut. Æ. C. to R.4.

SARDINIA (*Sardegna*).—Aut. AR. R.4. Æ. R.2. *Latin*, *Greek*, and *Phœnician* legends.

The silver coins with Greek legends are of doubtful attribution. The brass coin with the Latin legend is one of the consular series, and bears SARD · PATER.

KINGS AND TYRANTS OF SICILY.

GELO. [B. C. 485 to 478].—Aut. AR. R.4. to R.6. Æ. C. to R.3.

With respect to the age of these coins, see Eckhel, Doct. Num. Vet. Tom. i. p. 251.

HIERO I. [B. C. 478 to 466].—Aut. AR. R.6. to R.7. Æ. C. to R.4.

See Eckhel, Doct. Num. Vet. Tom. i. p. 256.

DIONYSIUS I. [B. C. 405 to 365].—No coins known.

DIONYSIUS II. [B. C. 365 to 343].—Aut. AR. R.6.

Uncertain attribution.

AGATHOCLES. [B. C. 317 to 289].—Aut. AV. R.1. to R.8. AR. R.3. Æ. C. to R.2.

HICETAS II. [B C. 20 to——].—Aut. AV. R.2.

PYRRHUS.

The coins of this prince will be found under those of Epirus.

HIERO II. [B. C. 269 to 215].—Aut. AV. C. AR. R.8. Æ. C. to R.2.

HIERONYMUS. [B. C. 215 to 214].—Aut. AV. R.8. AR. R.4. to R.8. Æ. R.2. to R.8.

PHILISTIS.—Aut. AR. R.2. to R.6.

The beautiful silver coins attributed to Philistis, are, by some, supposed to have been struck in honour of Damareta, the wife of Gelo, the fabric being Sicilian and in the best style of Greek art. No mention is made of Philistis by ancient writers.

TYRANTS OF AGRIGENTUM.

THERO. [B. C. 476 to 472].—Aut. Æ. R.8.

Of doubtful authenticity.

PHINTIAS. [B. C. 280].—Aut. Æ. R.1. to R.2.

CHERSONESUS TAURICA.

CHERSONESUS in genere.—Aut. AV. R.8. AR. R.6. to R.7. Æ. R.5. to R.7. Imperial of Commodus Æ. R.6. to R.8.

HERACLEUM? (———).—Aut. Æ. R.3. to R.6.

PANTICAPAEUM (*Kertch*).—Aut. AV. R.8. AR. R.6. to R.8. Æ. R.2. to R.6.

THEUDOSIA? (*Caffa*).—Aut. Æ. R.8.

SARMATIA EUROPAEA.

OLBIA OLBIOPOLIS (*Stromohil*). — Aut. AR. R.8. Æ. R.4. to R.8. Imperial Æ. R.6. to R.8. Domitian to Severus Alexander.

TYRA (———).—Imperial Æ. R.4. to R.6. Vespasian to Geta.

ISLANDS ADJACENT TO SARMATIA EUROPAEA.

ACHILLEA (———).—Aut. AR. R.6. to R.8.

DACIA.

DACIA in genere.—Colonial Imperial Æ. C. to R.6. Philip to Gallienus.

PANNONIA.

The coins bearing METALLI · PANNONICI, are of Roman fabric, and are classed with the Roman series.

MOESIA SUPERIOR.

ALMUM (———).

Doubtful if any coins.

DARDANIA REGIO.

The coins bearing DARDANICI, belong to the Roman series.

PINCUM (*Gradisca*).

The coins bearing AELIANA · PINCENSIA, are of the Roman series.

VIMINACIUM (*Ram*). — Colonial Imperial Æ. C. to R.6. From Gordianus the Third to Gallienus.

MOESIA INFERIOR.

CALLATIA (*Mankalia. Kallati*).—Aut. AR. R.4. Æ. R.2. to R.5. Imperial Æ. R.4. to R.6. Marcus Aurelius to Philip, Jun.

DIONYSOPOLIS (———).—Aut. Æ. R.6. Imperial Æ. R.4. to R.6. Commodus to Gordian the Third.

ISTRUS (*Kargolik. Silistria*).—Aut. AR. R.1. to R.4. Æ. R.6. Imperial Æ. R.6. Hadrian to Tranquillina.

MARCIANOPOLIS (———).—Aut. Æ. R.6. Imperial Æ. C. to R.6. adrian to Philip, Jun.

NICOPOLIS AD ISTRUM (*Niebal Nigheboli*). — Aut. Æ. R.6. Imperial, Æ. C. to R.6. Trajan to Gordian.

Some of the Autonomous coins bear the name of Hadrianopolis in alliance.

TOMI (*Pangala*).—Aut. Æ. R.3. to R.4. Imperial Æ. C. to R.7. Tiberius to Philip, Jun.

THRACIA.

THRACIA in genere.—Æ. Imperial of Caracalla. R.2. to R.5.

GETAS, King of Edonis.—AR. R.8. (*Millingen*).

ABDERA (*Ghiumergin. Asperosa. Platystomon*).—Aut. AR. R.1. to R.8. Æ. R.1. to R.4. Imperial Æ. R.6. Nero to Faustina, Jun.

AENEIA (———).—Aut. AR. R.7. (*Millingen*).

This town may also be considered to belong to Macedonia.

AENUS (*Enes. Eno*).—Aut. AR. R.2. to R.6. Æ. R.2. to R.6. Imperial, Æ. R.6. Aurelius to Caracalla.

ANCHIALUS (*Akkiali, Tchienguene, Iskelessi*). — Aut. Æ. R.8. Imperial, Æ. C. to R.6. Domitian to Tranquillina.

APOLLONIA (*Sizepoli*).—Aut. Æ. R.8. Imperial, Æ. R.6. Domitian to Gallienus.

ARNAE? (———).—Aut. AR. R.8. (*Millingen*).

BISANTHE (*Tekir-Dagh, Rodosto*).—Aut. Æ. R.4.

BIZYA (———).—Aut. Æ. R.6. Imperial, Æ. R.2. to R.6. Hadrian to Philip, Jun.

BYZANTIUM, afterwards Constantinople (*Istambul*).—Aut. AR. R.6. Æ. C. to R.4. Imperial, Æ. C. to R.6. From Julius Cæsar to Macrianus.

Some have the name of Chalcedon in alliance.

COSSEA (———).—Aut. AU. R.4.

These gold coins which were formerly attributed to Cosae in Etruria, are supposed to have been struck by order of Marcus Junius Brutus.

CYPSELA (*Ipsala. Kipsela*).—Aut. Æ. R.8.

DEULTUM (*Derkon*).—Colonial Imperial, Æ. R.2. to R.6. From Trajan to Philip the younger. Latin legends.

DICAEA or DICAEOPOLIS (*Yakbeli*).—Aut. AR. R.8. Æ. R.8.

DIUM (———).—Aut. Æ. R.8. (*Millingen*).

HADRIANOPOLIS (*Edrene*).—Aut. Æ. R.6. Imperial, Æ. C. to R.7. Hadrian to Tranquillina.

MARONEA (*Marulia, Maronia, Marogna*).—Aut. AR. C. to R.7. Æ. R.1. to R.4. Imperial, Æ. R.6. Nero to Volusianus.

MESEMBRIA (*Misevria, Misimbria*).—Aut. AR. R.8. Æ. R.4. Imperial, Æ. R.2. to R.4. Hadrian to Philip the younger.

NICOPOLIS ad MESTUM (———). Imperial, Æ. R.3. to R.6. Commodus to Geta.

THRACIA (*continued*).

NYSA.

This city is restored to Paeonia.

ODESSUS (*Varna*).—Aut. AR. R.8. Æ. R.6. Imperial, Æ. C. to R.4. Trajan to Salonina.

ODRYSII (*Hedrine*).—Aut. AR. (*doubtful*). R.8. Æ. R.6.

ORESTIAS (———).—Aut. AR. R.8. (*Millingen*).

KINGS OF THE ODRYSAE.

AMADOCUS (*Period uncertain*).—Aut. Æ. R.8.

TERES II. (*Period uncertain*).—Aut. Æ. R.8.

SEUTHES IV. (*Period uncertain*).—Aut. Æ. R.6.

PASSA or PASSIA (———).—Aut. Æ. R.8. (*doubtful*).

PAUTALIA (———).—Imperial, Æ. C. to R.6. From Hadrian to Gordian.

The Autonomous pieces supposed of this city have been restored to Cnidus in Caria.

PERINTHUS (*Eraclia Erekli*).—Aut. Æ. R.2. to R.4. Imperial, Æ. C. to R.7. Claudius to Salonina.

PHILIPPOPOLIS (*Filibe*).—Aut. Æ. R.8. Imperial, Æ. C. to R.7. Domitian to Salonina.

PLOTINOPOLIS (*Demotica*).—Aut. Æ. R.8. Imperial, Æ. R.2. to R.8. Antoninus Pius to Caracalla.

SALA (———).—Aut. Æ. R.8. (*Millingen*).

SERDICA (*Sofia*).—Imperial, Æ. C. to R.5. Aurelius to Gallienus.

TEMPYRA ? (———).—Aut. AR. R.6.

TIRIDA (———).

The coin supposed of Tirida belongs to Tricca in Thessalia.

TOPIRUS (———).—Imperial, Æ. R.3. to R.4. Antoninus to Geta.

TRAJANOPOLIS or AUGUSTA TRAJANA (———).—Imperial, Æ. R.1. to R.4. Trajan to Gallienus.

CHERSONESUS THRACIA.

AEGOSPOTAMOS (———).—Aut. Æ. R.6.

AEOLIUM (———).—Aut. AR. R.8. Æ. R.8.

ALOPECONNESUS (———).—Aut. Æ. R.7.

CALLIPOLIS (*Gallipoli*).

The coins supposed of Callipolis have been restored to Apollonia in Caria.

CARDIA (*Karidia*).—Aut. AR. R.7. Æ. R.2. to R.6.

CHERRONESUS (———).—Aut. AR. C. to R.8. Æ. R.6.

CHERSONESUS THRACIA (*continued*).

COELA (*Municipium*).—Imperial, Æ. R.2. to R.5. Hadrian to Gallienus.

CRITHOSIUM or CRITHOTE (———).—Aut. Æ. R.8.

ELEUS (*Eles-Burun*).—Aut. AR. R.8. Æ. R.8.

LYSIMACHIA (*Hexamili*).—Aut. AR. R.2. to R.4. Æ. R.3. to R.5.

MADYTUS (———).—Aut. Æ. R.8. (*Millingen*).

SESTUS (*Zemenick*).—Aut. Æ. R.2. to R.6. Imperial, Æ. R.2. to R.8. From Augustus to Philip the younger.

ISLANDS ADJACENT TO THRACE.

IMBRUS (*Lambro*).—Aut. Æ. R.6.

LEMNUS (*Lemno*).—HEPHAESTIA Urbs Lemnia (*Paleopoli*). —Aut. Æ. R.4. to R.6.

MYRHINA Urbs Lemnia (*Palio-Castro*).—Aut. Æ. R.8.

NEA (———).

The coins supposed of Nea belong to Neontichos.

SAMOTHRACE (*Samotraki*).—Aut. Æ. R.5. to R.7. Imperial, Æ. R.8. Of Hadrian.

THASUS (*Tasso*).—Aut. AV. R.8. AR. C. to R.5. Æ. R.2. to R.6. Imperial, Æ. R.6. Hadrian to Geta.

KINGS OF THRACE.

SEUTHES III. [B. C. 324].

The coins supposed of this prince belong to Seuthes IV.

LYSIMACHUS. [B. C. 324 to 282].—Aut. AV. C. to R.8. AR. C. to R.8. Æ. C. to R.4.

AGATHOCLES LYSIMACHI FILIUS.

It is supposed that the head of this prince appears on some of the coins of his father.

SARIAS or ZARIAS [1] (*uncertain period*).—Aut. Æ. R.8.

CAVARUS. [B. C. 219 to 200].—Aut. Æ. R.7.

COTYS II. [B. C. 171].—Aut. AR. R.6. Æ. R.6. (*doubtful*).

COTYS III. Of the time of Pompey. Aut. Æ. R.8.

Some have the name of his son Sadales II.

SADALES II. Of the time of Pompey and Julius Cæsar.— Aut. Æ. R.7.

RHOEMETALCES I. Of the time of Augustus.—Aut. Æ. R.4. Imperial, Æ. R.1. to R.8., of Augustus, and Augustus and Livia.

[1] Vide Reges Illyrici.

KINGS OF THRACE (*continued*).

COTYS V., and RHASCUPORIS. Cotemporary with Augustus and Tiberius.—Aut. Æ. R.4. Imperial, AR. R.8., of Augustus.

RHOEMETALCES II. Cotemporary with Tiberius, Caligula, and Claudius.—Imperial, Æ. R.8., of Caligula.

COTYS —. (*uncertain period*).—Aut. Æ. R.8.

MOSTIS (*uncertain period*).—Aut. AR. R.8. Æ. R.6.

Formerly attributed in error to Mostis of Epirus.

LIBURNIA.

ALVONA (———). (*doubtful*).

DALMATIA.

No coins are known of Dalmatia. The pieces bearing METAL · DELM are of Roman origin.

ILLYRICUM.

ALLETA (———).—Aut. Æ. R.8. (*doubtful*).

AMANTIA (———).—Aut. Æ. R.4.

APOLLONIA (*Polina*).—Aut. AR. C. to R.8. Æ. R.1. to R.5. Imperial, Æ. R.1. to R.4. Augustus to Gallienus.

BILUDIUM (———).—Aut. Æ. R.8.

BYLLIS (———).—Aut. Æ. R.8.

DAORSI (———).—Aut. Æ. R.8.

DYRRACHIUM (*Durazzo*).—Aut. AR. C. to R.7. Æ. C. to R.5.

KING OF DYRRACHIUM.

MONUNIUS (*uncertain period*).—Aut. AR. R.8.

ENCHELIES OF ENCHELLII (———).—Aut. AR. R.8.

OLYMPE (———).—Aut. Æ. R.8.

SCODRA (*Scodra, Scuttari, Scutari*).—Aut. Æ. R.8.

ISLANDS ADJACENT TO ILLYRICUM.

DYSCELADAS (———).

The coins supposed of this Island, belong to Asculum in Apulia.

ISSA (*Lissa*).—Aut. Æ. R.2.

PHARUS (*Liesina*).—Aut. Æ. R.4.

ILLYRICUM (*continued*).

KINGS OF ILLYRICUM.

DEMETRIUS. [B. C. 220 ?].—Aut. AR. R.8.

GENTIUS. [B. C. 165].—Aut. Æ. R.8.

BALLAEUS (*uncertain period*).—Aut. Æ. R.2.

ZARIAS or SARIAS (*uncertain period*).—Aut. Æ. R.8.

GRAECIA.

PAEONIA.

PAEONIA in genere.—Aut. Æ. R.8.

NYSA (————).—Aut. Æ. R.8.

Formerly attributed in error to Nysa in Thracia.

KINGS OF PAEONIA.

AUDOLEON. [B. C. 340 to 330].—Aut. AR. R.3. to R.8. Æ. R.8.

EUPOLEMUS (*uncertain period*).—Aut. Æ. R.6.

It is not certain that this prince was of Paeonia.

LYCCEIUS (*uncertain period*).—Aut. AR. R.8.

PATRAUS (*uncertain period*).—Aut. AR. R.5.

MACEDONIA.

MACEDONIA in genere.—Aut. AR. C. to R.4. Æ. C. to R.2.

Aut. Roman, AR. R.2. to R.8. Æ. C. to R.2.

Aut. Roman, of the four provinces :—

First province.—AR. R.1. to R.8.

Second province.—AR. R.7. Æ. R.4.

Third province.—unknown.

Fourth province.—Æ. R.7. Imperial, Æ. C. to R.8. Augustus to Trebonianus.

ACANTHUS (*Erissos*).—Aut. AR. R.2. to R.8. Æ. R.4. to R.6.

AEGAE (————).—(*doubtful*).

AENIA or AENEA (————).—Aut. AR. R.7.

AMPHAXUS (————).—Aut. Æ. R.5.

MACEDONES AMPHAXII (————).—Aut. AR. R.8. (*Millingen*.

AMPHIPOLIS (*Jeni Kioj*).—Aut. AR. R.6. Æ. C. to R.6. Imperial, Æ. C. to R.6. Of Augustus to Salonina.

APHYTIS (*Afiti*).—Aut. Æ. R.5.

MACEDONIA (*continued*).

APOLLONIA (———).—Aut. Æ. R.4.

ARETHUSA (———).—Aut. Æ. R.8. (*Millingen*).

ARGILUS? (———).—Aut. Æ. R.8. (*Millingen*).

BERGA (———).—Aut. Æ. R.8.

BERHAEA (*Veria Beria* or *Kara-Beria*).—Aut. Æ. R.6.

BISALTAE (———).—Aut. AR. R.7.

BOTTIAEA (*Slanizza*).—Aut. AR. R.8. Æ. R.2. to R.6.

CASSANDREA (*Kassandria Capusi*).—Aut. Colonial, Æ. R.3. to R.5. Latin legends. Colonial Imperial, AR. R.6. *Potin*, R.6. Æ. C. to R.6. Claudius to Philip. Latin legends.

KING OF CASSANDREA.

APOLLODORUS (*uncertain period*).—Aut. R.8. (*doubtful*).

CASSERA (———).—Aut. AR. R.8.

CHALCIS (———).—Aut. AV. R.8. AR. R.1. to R.4. Æ. R.2.

Formerly attributed to Chalcis in Euboea.

DIUM (*Stan Dia*).—Colonial Imperial, Æ. C. to R.6. Of Augustus to Salonina. Latin legends.

EDESSA (*Edessa* or *Monglena*).—Imperial, Æ. C. to R.6. Augustus to Gallienus.

EURYDICEA (———).—Aut. Æ. R.5.

Formerly classed in error with those of Eurydicium.

HERACLIA? SINTICA (———).—Aut. AR. R.2. to R.3.

TYRANT OF HERACLEA.

ADAEUS (*uncertain period*).—Aut. Æ. R.5.

LETE (———).—Aut. AR. R.4. to R.8.

MENDE (*Calandra*).—Aut. AR. R.8. Æ. R.4.

NEAPOLIS (*La Cavalla*).—Aut. AR. C. to R.6. Æ. R.3.

The brass coins are supposed by some to belong to Neapolis in Ionia.

ORRESKIA (———).—Aut. AR. R.4. to R.8.

Some suppose these coins to be of Orestae.

OLYNTHUS (*Ayo-Mama*).—Aut. AR. R.8. Æ. R.8.

ORESTAE (———).—Aut. AR. R.4. to R.8.

See Orestias in Thrace.

ORTHAGORIA (*Stavro*).—Aut. AR. R.8. Æ. R.4. to R.7.

OSSA (*Bisaltarum*).—Aut. AR. R.8.

MACEDONIA (*continued*).

PELLA (*Ala Clissa. Pella* or *Palatisa*).—Aut. Æ. C. to R.2. Imperial, Æ. R.4. Mark Antony and Octavia. Colonial Imperial, Æ. C. to R.4. Trajan to Philip the younger. Latin legends.

PHILA (———).—Aut. Æ. R.8.

PHILIPPI (*Filippi*).—Aut. AV. R.8. AR. R.7. Æ. R.4. Colonial, Æ. R.1. Colonial Imperial, Æ. R.2. to R.6. Augustus to Gallienus.

POTIDAEA (———).—Aut. AR. R.7. (*Millingen*).

PYDNA (*Kitro*).—Aut. Æ. R.1. to R.6.

PYTHIUM (———).—Aut. Æ. R.8.

SCIONE (*Jeni-Kassandra*).—Aut. AR. R.8. Æ. R.8.

SCOTUSSA (———).—Aut. AR. R.8. Æ. R.8.

Query, if not of the Thessalian Scotussa?

STOBI MUNICIPIUM (*Stip*).—Aut. Æ. R.8. Imperial, Æ. C. to R.6. Vespasian to Elagabalus. Latin legends.

TERONE or TORONE (*Teroni*).—Aut. AR. R.8 Æ. R.7.

THESSALONICA (*Salonika, Salonicco*).—Aut. Æ. C. to R.4. Imperial, Æ. C. to R.6. Cæsar to Salonina.

TRAELIUM (———).—Aut. Æ. R.2.

TYRISSA? (———).—Aut. AR. R.6.

URANOPOLIS (*Castro*).—Aut. AR. R.2. to R.4.

KINGS OF MACEDONIA.

UNCERTAIN ANCIENT KINGS.—Aut. AR. R.2 to R.6.

ALEXANDER I. [B. C. 497 to 454].—Aut. AR. R.4. to R.8.

PERDICCAS II. [B. C. 454 to 413].—Aut. AR. R.8.

ARCHELAUS I. [B. C. 413 to 399].—Aut. AR. R.2. to R.7. Æ. R.4. to R.7.

AEROPUS III. [B. C. 399].—Aut. AR. R.8. Æ. R.8. Pl. R.8.

PAUSANIAS. [B. C. 398].—Aut. AR. R.8. Æ. R.6.

AMYNTAS II. [B. C. 397 to 371].—Aut. AR. R.4. to R.8. Æ. C. to R.5.

ALEXANDER II. [B. C. 371].—Aut. Æ. R.3. to R.6.

PERDICCAS III. [B. C. 366 to 359].—Aut. AR. R.8. Æ. R.3.

PHILIPPUS II. [B. C. 359 to 336].—Aut. AV. C. to R.2. AR. C. to R.6.

ALEXANDER III. (*Magnus*). [B. C. 336 to 324].—Aut. with ΑΛΕΞΑΝΔΡΟΥ only AV. C. to R.4. Æ. C. to R.6.

KINGS OF MACEDONIA (*continued*).

Coins of Alexander struck in different Cities.—AV. R.4. to R.8. AR. R.1. to R.8. Æ. R.3.

With Dates.—AR. R.2. to R.4.

With uncertain Symbols.—AR. C. to R.6.

With ΒΑΣΙΛΕΩΣ.—AV. C. to R.4. AR. C. to R.4. Æ. C. to R.4.

Coins struck after his Death.—AV. R.8. AR. C. to R.8. Æ. C. to R.6.

PHILIPPUS III. (*Aridaeus*). [B. C. 324 to 317].—Aut. AV. R.2. to R.7. AR. R.1. to R.6. Æ. C. to R.3.

CASSANDER. [B. C. 316 to 298].—Aut. Æ. C. to R.3.

PHILIPPUS IV. [B. C. 298 to 297].—Aut. Æ. R.3.

ANTIPATER.

The coins formerly attributed to Antipater have been restored to Antigonus Gonatas.

ALEXANDER IV. [B. C. 297 to 294].—Aut. Æ. C. to R.4.

ANTIGONUS, King of Asia. [B. C. 292].—Aut. AV. R.8. AR. R.4. Æ. R.4.

DEMETRIUS I. (*Poliorcetes*). [B. C. 294 to 287].—Aut. AV. R.8. AR. R.3. to R.8. Æ. R.6.

ANTIGONUS I. (*Gonatas*). [B. C. 276 to 243]. — Aut. AR. R.4. to R.7. Æ. C. to R.2.

DEMETRIUS II. [B. C. 243 to 232].—Aut. Æ. R.1. to R.6.

PHILIPPUS V. [B. C. 220 to 178].—Aut. AR. R.2. to R.7. Æ. C. to R.4.

PERSEUS. [B. C. 178 to 168].—Aut. AV. R.8. AR. R.4. to R.8. Æ. C. to R.3.

PHILIP VI. (*Andriscus*). [B. C. 149].

The coins supposed, by Visconti, of this prince, belong to Philippus V.

TITUS QUINCTIUS FLAMINIUS, *Consul*.—AV. R.8.

This piece is ranged with those of the Macedonian Princes. It is supposed to have been struck in honour of Flaminius, the Roman Consul, after the battle of Cynocephalus, in which he defeated Philip V. See *Mionnet's Description*, Supp. Tome iii. p. 260. It is engraved in the plates illustrating that volume.

THESSALIA.

THESSALIA in genere.—Aut. AR. C. to R.8. Æ. R.1. to R.6. Imperial, Æ. C. to R. 6. Augustus to Gallienus

AENIANES (———).—Aut. AR. R.4. Æ. R.5.

THESSALIA (*continued*).

ALOS (————).—Æ. R.7. (*Millingen*).

ARGESA (————).—Aut. AR. R.8. (*doubtful*).

ATRAX (*Boidanar*).—Aut. AR. R.6. Æ. R.8.

CIERIUM (————).—Aut. AR. R.8. Æ. R.8.

Sestini erroneously gives this city to Macedonia.

CRANNON (*Crania or Xeres*).—Aut. AR. R.8. Æ. R.7.

CRANNONII EPHYRI ? (————)—Aut. Æ. R.8.

CTEMENE (————).—Aut. AR. R.8. Æ. R.8.

DEMETRIAS (*Yeni-Sciehere. Volo*).—Aut. AR. R.8.

DEMETRIAS SACRA.

The coins supposed of this city belong to Demetrias in Phœnicia.

ELATEA OF ELATIA (————).—Aut. Æ. R.8.

ETHNESTAE. No certain coins.

GOMPHI (*Stagi, Kalem Pascia*)—Aut. Æ. R.7.

GYRTON (*Tacibolicati*).—Aut. Æ. R.4.

HERACLEA (*Trachin*).—Aut. AR. R.6. Æ. R.6.

HOMOLIUM (————).—Aut. AR. R.8. Æ. R.8.

LAMIA (*Demochi ?*).—Aut. AR. R.3. Æ. R.4.

LAPITHAE (————).—Aut. AR. R.7. Æ. R.8.

LARISSA (*Larisa*).—Aut. AR. C. to R.6. Æ. R.2 to R.7

LARISSA CREMASTE ? (————).—Aut. Æ. R.8.

MAGNESIA (*San Giorgio*).—Aut. AR. R.1. Æ. R.6. (*Cabinet of Mr. Burgon*).

MALIENSES POPULUS (————).—Aut. Æ. R.8.

METROPOLIS (*Mascoluri*).—Aut. AR. R.8. Æ. R.8. (*Cabinet of Mr. Burgon*).

MINYAE POPULUS ? (————).—Aut. Æ. R.8.

MOPSIUM (————).—Aut. Æ. R.8.

The silver coin described by Pellerin is of *Mende*.

OETAEI (————).—Aut. AR. R.8. Æ. R.5.

OTHRYTAE ? (————).—Aut. Æ. R.8.

PELINNA (————).—Aut. AR. R.6. Æ. R.7.

PERRHAEBIA (————).—Aut. AR. R.8.

PHACIUM (————).—Aut. Æ. R.8.

PHALANNA (————).—Aut. AR. R.8. Æ. R.4.

PHARCADON (————).—Aut. AR. R.7.

PHARSALUS (*Tzatalze Fersala*).—Aut. AR. R.2. to R.6. Æ. R.4.

THESSALIA (*continued*).

PHERAE (———).—Aut. AR. R.7. Æ. R.6. to R.8.

TYRANT OF PHERAE.

ALEXANDER. [B.C. 369 to 359].—Aut. AR. R.8. Æ R.8. (*Cabinet of Mr. Burgon*).

PHILIPPOPOLIS QUÆ ET GOMPHI (———).—Aut. AR. R.8. (*Millingen*).

PROANA OR PROERNA (———).—Aut. AR. R.8.

SCOTUSSA (———).—Aut. AR. R.8. Æ. R.8.

THIBROS? (———).—Aut. Æ. R.8. (*doubtful*).

TRICCA (*Tricala, Trikki*).—Aut. AR. R.5. Æ. R.8.

TYRANT OF THESSALIA.

TISIPHON. Contemporary with Philip II. and Alexander the Great.—Aut. AR. R.8. Æ. R.8.

ISLANDS ADJACENT TO MACEDONIA AND THESSALIA.

HALONESUS (*Pelagnisi*).—Aut. Æ. R.8.

IRRHESIA? (———).—Aut. Æ. R.8. (*doubtful*).

PEPARETHUS (*Piperi*).—Aut. Æ. R.4. to R.6. Imperial, Æ. R.8. Augustus and Commodus.

SCIATHUS (*Schiatti*).—Aut. Æ. R.7.

EPIRUS.

EPIRUS in genere.—Aut. AR. R.2. to R.6. Æ. R.1. to R.4.

AMBRACIA (*Ambrakia*).—Aut. AR. R.1. to R.7. Æ. R.1. to R.2.

BUTHROTUM (*Butronto, Butrinto*).—Aut. Æ. R.8. Aut. Colonial, Æ. R.6. Imperial Colonial, Æ. R.6. to R.8. Augustus and Tiberius.

CASSOPE (———).—Aut. AR. R.6. Æ. R.3. to R.5.

DAMASTIUM (———).—Aut. AR. R.6. Æ. R.2.

HORRHEUM? (———).—Aut. Æ. R.4. (*doubtful*).

MOLOSSI (———).—Aut. Æ. R.8.

MOLOSSI CASSOPAEI (———).—Aut. Æ. R.8.

NICOPOLIS (*Prevesa Vecchia*).—Aut. Æ. R.6. Imperial, Æ. R.1. to R.7. From Augustus to Salonina.

ORICUS (———).—Aut. Æ. R.8.

Oricus might be considered in Illyria.

PANDOSIA (———).—Aut. Æ. R.2. to R.3.

PHOENICE OR PHOENICAPE (*Sopoto*).—Aut. Æ. R.6. Imperial, Æ. R.6., of Nero and Trajan.

EPIRUS (*continued*).

THESPROTIA EPIRI REGIO.

THESPROTIA in Genere.—Aut. Æ. R.8., with the name of Pyrrhus.

CELTAE AIDONITES (*Aidonia*).—Aut. Æ. R.8. (*doubtful*).

KINGS OF EPIRUS.

ARISBAS. [B. C. 351 to 342].—No certain coins.

NEOPTOLEMUS. [B. C. 350].—Aut. Æ. R.7.

ALEXANDER I. [B. C. 342 to 326].—Aut. AV. R.8. AR. R.6. to R.8. Æ. R.3.

PHTHIA, Mother of Pyrrhus. [Aut. Æ. R.2., with the name of Pyrrhus also.

PYRRHUS. [B. C. 294 to 271].—Aut. AV. R.3. to R.6. AR. R.3. to R.8. Æ. R.1. to R.4.

ALEXANDER II.? [B. C. 272].—Aut. AR. R.4. to R.6. Æ. R.3.

PTOLEMAEUS? (*period unknown*).—Aut. Æ. R.3.

MOSTIS.

The coins supposed of this prince have been restored to Mostis of Thrace.

ISLANDS ADJACENT TO EPIRUS.

CORCYRA.

CORCYRA in genere (*Corfu*).—Aut. AR. R.1. to R.6. Æ. C. to R.4. Imperial, Æ. C. to R.6. From Trajanus to Gordianus Africanus.

CASSOPE CORCYRAE (*Cassopo*).—Aut. Æ. R.4.

ACARNANIA.

ACARNANIA in genere.—Aut. AV. R.8. AR. R.4. to R.6. Æ. R.1. to R.4.

ALYZIA (*Aelias*).—Aut. AR. R.5. to R.8. Æ. R.8.

ANACTORIUM (*Bonitza*).—Aut. AR. R.2. to R.8, Æ. R.4. to R.8.

AMPHILOCHIUM and ARGOS AMPHILOCHIUM (*Filokia*).—Aut. *with the name of Argos*, AR. R.2. to R.4. Aut. *with the name of Amphilochium*, Aut. R.2. to R.4.

HERACLEA (———).—Aut. AR. R.3. to R.7. Æ. C. to R.4.

LEUCAS or LEUCADIA. (*Leucadia or Santo Maura*).—Aut. AR. R.2. to R.5. Æ. R.2. to R.4. Imperial, Æ. R.8. Commodus.

METROPOLIS? (———).—Aut. AR. R.8.

OENIADAE (———).—Aut. Æ. C. to R.4.

ACARNANIA (*continued*).

STRATOS (*Conopina*).—Aut. AR. R.8.

TAPHIAS (———).

The coin supposed of this town belongs to Tarentum in Calabria.

THYRREUM (———).—Aut. AR. C. to R.6. Æ. R.8.

AETOLIA.

AETOLIA in genere—Aut. AV. R.8. AR. R.4. to R.6. Æ. R.2. to R.4.

AEGAE (———).—No coins known.

APOLLONIA (———).—Aut. Æ. R.8.

ATHAMANES (———).—Aut. Æ. R.8.

CALYDON (*Galata*).—Aut. Æ. R.8. Imperial, Æ. R.8. Severus.

LYSIMACHIA ? (———).—Aut. AR. R.4.

NAUPACTUS (*Lepanto*).—Aut. AR. R.2. Æ. R4.

LOCRIS.

AMPHISSA (*Salona* or *Lampeni*).—Aut. Æ. R.6.

AXIA ? (———).—Aut. Æ. R.2.

LOCRI (———).—Aut. AR. R.2. to R.4. Æ. R.3.

LOCRI EPICNEMIDII (———).—Aut. Æ. R.2. to R.8.

LOCRI OPUNTII (———).—Aut. AR. R.3. to R.6. Æ. R.2. to R.4.

LOCRI OPUNTII EPICNEMIDII ? (———).—Aut. Æ. R.6.

LOCRI INCERTI (———).—Aut. AR. R.3. Æ. R.2. to R.4.

THRONIUM (*Paleocastro*).—Aut. Æ. R.8.

PHOCIS.

PHOCIS in genere.—Aut. AV. R.8. AR. R.2. to R.8. Æ. R.2. to R.4.

AMPHICAEA ? (———).—Aut. Æ. R.8.

CYPARISSUS (———).—Aut. Æ. R.8. (*doubtful*).

DELPHI (*Castri* or *Castro*).—Aut. AR. R.4. to R.8. Æ. R.4. to R.7. Imperial, Æ. R.4. to R.6. From Hadrian to Caracalla.

ELATEA (*Eleuta*).—Aut. Æ. R.6.

MEDEON or MODEON (———).—Aut. AR. R.7.

ΜΩΔΑΙΩΝ. Of doubtful attribution.

TITHOREA.—No certain coins.

BOEOTIA.

BOEOTIA in genere.—Aut. AR. C. to R.8. Æ. C. to R.5.

ANTHEDON ? (*Lukisi* or *Talandi*).—Aut. R.8. (*doubtful*).

ARIARTUS or HALIARTUS (———).—No coins.

ASPLEDON (———).—Aut. AR. R.8. Æ. R.8. (*doubtful*).

CHERONEA (*Capurna*).—Aut. AR. R.6. (*doubtful*).

COPAE (———).—Aut. AR. R.8. Imperial, Æ. R.6. Vespasian.

CORONEA (*Camari*).—Aut. AR. R.6. to R.8.

DELIUM (*Delis*).—Aut. AR. R.8. Æ. R.8.

ERYTHRAE (———).—Aut. AR. R.4. to R.7. Æ. R.4. to R.8. (*doubtful*).

HYLA ? (———).—Aut. Æ. R.8. (*doubtful*).

ISMENE (———).—Aut. Æ. R.8. (*doubtful*).

LARYMNA. No coins.

The piece attributed to this town belongs to Salamis.

LEBADIA (———).—Aut. Æ. *unique*.[1]

MYCALESSUS (———).—Aut. AR. R.8.

ORCHOMENUS (*Skripu*).—Aut. AR. R.8. Æ. R.8.

PELECANIA ? (———).—Aut. Æ. R.4. (*doubtful*).

PHARAE or PHERAE (———).—Aut. Æ R.8.

PLATAEAE (*Cocla*).—Aut. AR. R.8. Æ. R.7.

POTNIAE ? (———).—Aut. Æ. R.8. (*doubtful*).

TANAGRA (*Gremata*).—Aut. AR. R.4. to R.8. Æ. R.5. Imperial, Æ. R.4. to R.8. Augustus to Faustina junior.

THEBAE (*Stives, Thiva, Thiba*).—Aut. AV. R.8. AR. R.2. to R.8. Æ. R.2. to R.6.

THESPIAE (———).—Aut. AR. R.6. to R.8. Æ. R.4. Imperial, Æ. R.4. Vespasian to Domitian.

THISBE ? (*Halike, Gianikki, Langia*).—Aut. Æ. R.3.

The coins supposed of this town are of Thebes.

ATTICA.

ANAPHLYSTUS (———).—Aut. Æ. R.8.

ATHENAE (*Satines, Atini*).—Aut. AV. R.8. AR. C. to R.8. Æ. R.6. to R.8.

There are no authentic imperial coins.

---

[1] See the cut at p. 36, and the "Numismatic Chronicle," Vol. I. p. 248.

ATTICA (*continued*).

AZETINI (———).

Sestini gives the coins supposed of this town to Azetini in Calabria.

DECELIA (———).—Aut. Æ. R.8. (*doubtful*).

ELEUSIS (*Lefsina*).—Aut. Æ. C. to R.4. Imperial, Æ. R.8. Of Commodus.

MEGARA (*Megra, Megara*).—Aut. AR. R.6. Æ. C. to R.6. Imperial, from Antoninus to Geta.—Æ. R.2. to R.5.

NISAEA ?—No coins.

Those formerly given to this town are of Nysa in Caria.

OROPUS (*Ropo*).—Aut. Æ. R.7.

PAGAE (*Libadostani*).—Imperial, Æ. R.4. to R.5. From Antoninus Pius to Septimius Severus.

ISLANDS ADJACENT TO ATTICA.

AEGINA (*Eghina, Eugia*).—Aut. AR. R.2. to R.8. Æ. R.2. to R.6. Imperial, Æ. R.5. to R.8. From Severus to Plautilla.

HELENA or CRANAE (*Macronisi*).—Aut. Æ. R.6. (*doubtful*). Imperial, Æ. R.4. to R.7. Julia to Otacilia.

SALAMIS (*Koluri*).—Aut. Æ. R.2. to R.8. Imperial, Æ. R.8. Of Severus to Caracalla.

PELOPONNESUS.

ACHAIA.

ACHAIA in genere.—Aut. AR. C. Æ. R.2. to R.8. Imperial, Æ. R.5. to R.8. Of Antinous, Verus, and Severus.—Aut., of the Achæan league,[1] AR. C. to R.8. Æ. R.4. to R 8.

AEGIALUS (———).

The coins supposed of this town belong to Aegialus in Paphlagonia.

AEGIRA (———).—Aut. Æ. R.8. Imperial, Æ. R.6. Of Severus, Domna, and Plautilla.

AEGIUM (*Vostitza*).—Aut. AR. R.4. Æ. R.4. to R.6. Imperial, Æ. R.4. Antoninus to Geta.

BURA (———).—Imperial, Æ. R.6. Of Septimius Severus and his family.

CARINAEA ? (———).—Aut. Æ. R.8. (*doubtful*).

---

[1] *Vide* Cousinery's "Essai Historique, &c., sur les Monnaies d'Argent de la Ligue Achéenne," &c., 4to,; and Sestini, "Sopra Le Medaglie Antiche relative alla confederazione degli Achei." 4to. Milano, 1817.

ACHAIA (*continued*).

CORINTHUS (*Korito, Corinto*).—Aut. AR. C. to R.7. Æ. R.8. Aut. Colonial, Æ. C. to R.8. Imperial Colonial, Æ. C. to R.7. From Julius Cæsar to Gordianus.

PATRAE (*Patra, Patrasso*).—Aut. AR. R.4. Æ. R.2. to R.3. Aut. Colonial, Æ. R.4. Imperial Colonial, Æ. C. to R.6. From Augustus to Gordian.

PELLENE (———).—Aut. AR. R.6. Æ. R.4. Imperial, Æ. R.6. Commodus, to Severus and his family.

PHLIUS (*Santa Flica*).—Aut. AR. R.6. Æ. R.2. Imperial, Æ. R.4. to R.6. Of the family of Severus.

RHYPAE (———).—Aut. Æ. R.4.

Sestini doubts the appropriation.

SICYON (*Basilica, Vasiliko*).—Aut. AR. R.1. to R.6. Æ. C. to R.6. Imperial, Æ. R.5. Of the family of Severus.

ELIS.

ELIS in genere.—Aut. AR. R.2. to R.6. Æ. R.4. Imperial, Æ. R.4. to R.6. Hadrian to Caracalla.

EURYDICIUM.

The coins supposed of this city, belong to Erydicium in Macedonia.

PHEA (———).

Sestini doubts the existence of any coins.

PHIALA? (———).—Aut. Æ. R.7.

PHIGALEA (———).—Aut. Æ. R.7.

PYLUS (———).

The coins supposed of Pylus are of doubtful attribution, or rather, of Byzantium in Thrace.

ISLANDS ADJACENT TO ELIS.

ASTERIA? (———).—Aut. Æ. R.8.

CEPHALLENIA (*Cefalonia*).

CEPHALLENIA in genere.—Aut. AR. R.6. Æ. R.4.

CRANIUM CEPHALLENIAE (*Crania*).—Aut. AR. R.6. Æ. R.4. to R.6. Imperial, Æ. R.6. Maximinus to Otacilia.

PALLENSES CEPHALLENIAE (*Palliki, Lixuri*).—Aut. AR. R.6. Æ. R.1. to R.4.

PRONI CEPHALLENIAE (———).—Aut. AR. R.8. Æ. R.4.

SAME CEPHALLENIAE (———).—Aut. AR. R.4. Æ. R.4.

ELIS (*continued*).

ZACYNTHUS (*Zakintos, Zante*).—Aut. AR. R.2. to R.8. Æ. R.2. to R.4. Imperial, Æ. R.3. to R.5. From Antoninus to Elagabalus.

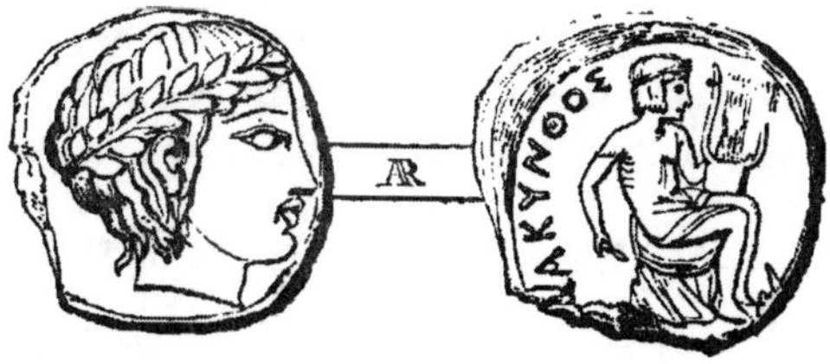

ITHACA (*Tiaki*).—Aut. Æ. R.6.

MESSENIA.

MESSENIA in genere.—Aut. AR. R.4. to R.8. Æ. C. to R.4. Imperial, Æ. R.4. to R.7. Of Severus and his family.

AMPHEA (———).

Sestini doubts the existence of any coins.

COLONE (———).—Aut. Æ. R.6. Imperial, Æ. R.8. Of Severus.

CORONE (*Koroni, Corone*).—Aut. Æ. R.6.

CYPARISSIA (*Castel Rampano*).—Aut. Æ., unique. (*Cabinet of Mr. Burgon*). Imperial, Æ. R.4. Of Severus and his family.

MOTHONE (*Modoni, Modone*).—Imperial, Æ. R.5. Of Severus and his family.

PYLUS (*Yavarino, Navarino*).—Aut. AR. R.6. Æ. R.3. Imperial, Æ. R.2. to R.6. Of Severus.

See the note to Pylus in Elis, which equally applies here to the autonomous coins.

THURIA (———).—Aut. Æ. R.6. Imperial, Æ. R.4. Of Severus and his family.

LACONIA.

ASOPUS (*Esapo*).—Imp. Æ. R.5. Of the family of Severus.

BOEA (———).—Imperial, Æ. R.6. Of the family of Severus.

GYTHIUM (*Kolokithia*).—Imperial, Æ. R.2. to R.6. Of the family of Severus.

LACEDAEMON (*Misitra*).—Aut. AR. R.4. to R.8. Æ. C. to R.5. Imp. Æ. C. to R.4. From Augustus to Salonina.

LACONIA (*continued*).

KINGS OF LACEDEMONIA.

AGESILAUS (*uncertain period*).—Aut. AR. R.8.

POLYDORUS.

Goltizius gives a coin of this king, but it is not authenticated.

AREUS. [B. C. 309 to 265].—Aut. AR. R.8.

CLEOMENES III. [B. C. 230 to 220].—Aut. AR. R.8.

LAS (———).—Imperial. Of the family of Severus. Æ. R.7.

PIRRICHOS (———).—Aut. Æ. R.8.

TALETUM ? (———).—Aut. Æ. R.2. (*doubtful*).

ARGOLIS.

ARGOS (*Planizza*).—Aut. AR. C. to R.4. Æ. C. to R.4. Imperial, Æ. R.2. to R.4. From Hadrian to Salonina.

ASINE (*Furnos*).—Aut. Æ. R.8. Imperial, Æ. R.6. Of the family of Severus.

CLEONE (*Clegna*).—Aut. Æ. R.7. Imperial, Æ. R.6. Of Commodus and the family of Severus.

EPIDAURUS (*Pedauro, Napoli di Malvasia*).—Aut. AR. R.8. Æ. R.1. to R.4. Imperial, Æ. R.4. to R.6. From Antoninus to Severus Alexander.

HERMIONE (*Kastri*).—Aut. Æ. R.6. Imperial, Æ. R.6. Of the family of Severus.

METHANA (*Metana*).—Aut. Æ. R.6. Imperial, Æ. R.7. to R.8. Of the family of Severus.

THYREA (———).—Aut. Æ. R.3.

The attribution of certain coins to this town does not rest on a sure foundation.

TROEZEN (*Damala*).—Aut. AR. R.7. Æ. R.5. Imperial, Æ. R.4. to R.6. Of Commodus and the family of Severus.

ISLAND ADJACENT TO ARGOLIS.

IRENE (———).—Aut. AR. R.4. Æ. R.4. (*doubtful*).

ARCADIA.

ARCADIA in genere.—Aut. AR. C. to R.6. Æ. R.2. to R.6. Imperial, Æ. R.4. Of Antinous only.

ALEA (———).—Aut. Æ.? Imperial, Æ. R.8. Of Marciana, but doubtful if authentic.

The Autonomous coins are of Alos, in Thessaly. The Imperial are of dubious authenticity.

ARCADIA (*continued*).

ALIPHEIRA (———).—Aut. Æ. R.8. Of the Achæan League.

ASEA (———).—Aut. Æ. R.6. Of the Achæan League.

BASILIS (———).—Aut. AR. R.8.

This attribution is not certain.

CAPHYA (———).—Aut. Æ. R.6. Imperial, Æ. R.4. Of the family of Severus.

CHARISIA ? (———).—Aut. Æ. R.2.

CLITORIUM (———).—Imperial, of Julia Domna, Æ. R.8.

EVA (———).—Aut. Æ. R.6. Of the Achæan League. (*doubtful*).

HERAEA (———).—Aut. AR. R.8.—(*Cabinet of Mr. Burgon*). Imperial, Æ. R.6. Of the family of Severus.

MANTINEA ANTIGONIA (———).—Aut. AR. R.8. (*Cabinet of Mr. Burgon*). Æ. R.7. Imperial, Æ. R.4. to R.6. Of the family of Severus.

MEGALOPOLIS (*Sinano*).—Aut. AR. R.2. to R.4. Æ. R.6. Imperial, Æ. R.4. to R.6. Of the family of Severus.

METHYDRIUM (———).—Aut. Æ. R.8. (*doubtful*).

ORCHOMENUS (*Kalpaki*).—Imperial, Æ. R.4. to R.6. Of the family of Severus.

PALLANTEUM (*Tripolizza*).—Aut. Æ. R.6. Of the Achæan League.

PHENEUS (*Phonia*).—Aut. AR. R.4. to R.7. Æ. R.4. Imperial, Æ. R.4. Of the family of Severus.

PHIGALEA or PHIALEA (———).—Aut. Æ. R.6. Imperial, Æ. R.3. Of the family of Severus.

PSOPHIS (———).—Imperial, Æ. R.6. Of the family of Severus.

STYMPALUS (*Vussi*).—Aut. AR. R.7. to R.8. Æ. R.6.

TEGEA (*Moklia ?*).—Aut. AR. R.7. Æ. R.3. to R.6. Imperial, Æ. R.6. Of the family of Severus.

ALEUS, King of Tegea.—Aut. Æ. R.6. (*uncertain period*).

THELPUSA (———).—Aut. Æ. R.4. Imperial, Æ. R.6. Of Commodus and the family of Severus.

THISOA (———).—Aut. Æ. R.6. Of the Achæan league.

CRETA INSULA.

CRETA in genere (*Kriti, Ghirit, Adassi, Candia*).—Imperial, AR. R.5. to R.8. Æ. C. to R.6. From Augustus to Caracalla.

CRETA INSULA (*continued*).

ALLARIA (———).—Aut. AR. R.6.

APOLLONIA? (———).—Aut. AR. R.4.

APTERA (*Paleo Castro*).—Aut. AR. R.4. to R.6. Æ. R.1. to R.2.

ARCADIA? (*Capo Arcadi*).—Aut. AR. R.6.

ARGOS? (———).—Aut. AR. R.6.

ARSINOE (———).—Aut. Æ. R.6.

AXUS or OAXUS or SAXUS? (———).—Aut. Æ. R.2.

CERAITE (———).—Aut. AR. R.6. Æ. R.6.

CHERSONESUS (*Spina Longa*).—Aut. AR. R.4. to R.6. Æ. R.7.

CNOSSUS (———).—Aut. AR. R.1. to R.7. Æ. R.2. Imperial, Æ. C. to R.7. Of Augustus and Tiberius.

CYDONIA (*La Canea*).—Aut. AR. R.2. to R.8. Æ. R.1. to R.3. Imperial, AR. R.4. to R.7. Æ. R.1. to R.6. Of Augustus to Julia Domna.

CYPARISSUS (———).—Imperial of Antoninus Pius. Æ. R.4. (*doubtful*).

ELEUTHERNAE (———).—Aut. AR. R.4. to R.6. Æ. R.2. Imperial of Tiberius, Æ. R.7.

ELYRUS (———).—Aut. AR. R.4. Æ. R.4.

GORTYNA (*Kortina*).—Aut. AV. R.8. AR. R.2. to R.8. Æ. C. to R.2. Imperial of Caligula to Hadrian, AR. R.8. Æ. R.5.

HIERAPYTNA (*Ierapietra, Gerapetra*).—Aut. AR. R.4. Æ, R.4. to R.6. Imperial of Augustus to Caracalla, AR. R.8. Æ. R.5.

HYRTACUS or HYRTACINUS.—Aut. AR. R.6.

ITANUS (———).—Aut. AR. R.4. Imperial, AR. R.8. Of Augustus.

LAMPA or LAPPA (———).—Aut. AR. R.4. Æ. R.4. Imperial of Augustus to Commodus, Æ. R.4. to R.6.

LASOS (———).—Aut. Æ. R.8.

LISSUS (———).—Aut. Æ. R.7.

LYTTUS (———).—Aut. AR. R.2. to R.4. Æ. R.2. Imperial of Caligula and of Germanicus, Æ. R.8.

OLUS (———).—Aut. AR. R.7. Æ. R.8.

PETRA (———).—Aut. Æ. R.6.

PHAESTUS (———).—Aut. AR. R.3. to R.5. Æ. R.1. to R.3.

PHALANNA (———).—Aut. AR. R.8.

PHALASARNA (———).—Aut. AR. R.4. Æ. R.8.

CRETA INSULA (*continued*).

POLYRHENIUM (———).—Aut. AR. R.3. to R.8. Æ. R.2. Imperial, AR. R.8. Æ. R.6. Of Augustus to Trajan.

PRAESUS (———).—Aut. AR. R.5. Æ. R.4.

PRIANSUS (———).—Aut. AR. R.4. Æ. R.5. Imperial, Æ. R.8. Of Hadrian.

RHAUCUS (———).—Aut. AR. R.4. Æ. R.4.

RHITHYMNA (*Retimo*).—Aut. AR. R.8. Æ. R.3.

SYBRITIA (———).—Aut. AR. R.7. Æ. R.4.

TANOS (———).—Aut. AR. R.8. Æ. R.8.

TEGEA (———).—Aut. AR. R.4. Æ. R.4.

Probably of Tegea in Arcadia.

THALASSA (*Kalo Limno*).—Aut. Æ. R.4. Imperial of Augustus to Trajan, AR. R.2. Æ. C. to R.2.

TYLISSUS (———).—Aut. AR. R.4.

EUBOEA INSULA.

EUBOEA in genere (*Eiriboss Adassi, Negroponte*).—Aut. AR. R.2. to R.4. Æ. C. to R.4.

ARTEMISIUM? (———).—Aut. AR. R.7. Æ. R.6. (*doubtful*).

CARYSTUS (*Karisto, Castel Rosso*).—Aut. AV. R.8. AR. R.4. to R.5. Æ. R.4. Imperial of Nero to Antoninus, Æ. R.6.

CERINTHUS? (———).—Aut. Æ. R.8. (*doubtful*).

CHALCIS (*Egripos Negroponte*).—Aut. AR. C. to R 4. Æ. R.4. Imperial of Augustus to Caracalla, Æ. R.4.

Some of these coins were formerly confounded with those of Chalcis in Macedonia. The coins of Chalcis in Macedonia have the head of Apollo and the lyre.

ERETRIA (———).—Aut. AR. R.4. to R.6. Æ. C. to R.6.

HISTIAEA (*Orio*).—Aut. AR. C. to R.8. Æ. R.3.

SMALLER ISLANDS OF THE EUROPEAN AEGAEAN.

AMORGUS (*Amorgo*).—Aut. Æ. R.8.

AEGIALE AMORGI (*Hyali*).—Aut. Æ. R.7.

ANAPHE (*Naufio*).—Aut. Æ. R.6.

ANDRUS (*Andro*).—Aut. AR. R.8. Æ. R.2. Imperial, Æ. R.6., of Antoninus to L. Verus. (*doubtful*).

CEOS or CEA (*Murtad Adassi, Zea*).—Aut. AR. R.8. Æ. R.3.

CARTHAEA CEAE (———).—Aut. AR. R.8. Æ. R.3.

EUBOEA INSULA (*continued*).

CORESIA or CORISIA CEAE (———).—Aut. AR. R.8. Æ. R.4.

JULIS CEAE (———).—Aut. Æ. R.2.

POEESA CEAE (———).—Aut. Æ. R.6.

CIMOLIS (*Kimoli, L' Argentiera*).—Aut. Æ. R.7.

CYTHNUS (*Thermia*).—Aut. Æ. R.6.

DELUS (*Istille, Stile*).—Aut. AR. R.8. Æ. R.4.

GYAROS (*Yura*).—Aut. Æ. R.8.

IOS (*Nio*).—Aut. Æ. R.4. Imperial, of Faustina and Lucilla, Æ. R.7.

MELOS (*Deyrmen Adassi, Milo*).—Aut. AR. R.6. to R.8. Æ. C. to R.6. Imperial, Æ. R.5. to R.7. Of Nero to Caracalla.

MYCONUS (*Miconi*).—Aut. AR. R.6. Æ. R.4. Imperial, Æ. R.8. Of Augustus and of Domitian.

NAXUS (*Naxia*).—Aut. AR. R.6. Æ. R.3. Imperial, Æ. R.4. to R.6. Of Severus and his family.

PAROS (*Paros, Naucsa*).—Aut. AR. R.8. Æ. R.4. Imperial, Æ. R.7. Of Aurelius and of Faustina, Jun.

PHOLEGANDRUS (*Policandro*).—Aut. Æ. R.8.

SERIPHUS (*Serfanto*).—Aut. Æ. R.8.

SICINUS (*Sikino*).—Aut. Æ. R.6.

SIPHNUS (*Sifanto*).—Aut. AR. R.6. Æ. C. to R.4. Imperial, Æ. R.4. to R.6. Of Severus to Gordian.

SYRUS (*Sira*).—Aut. Æ. R.6. Imperial, Titus to Severus Alexander, R.4. to R.7.

TENUS (*Tine, Tino, Istindil*).—Aut. AR. R.6. Æ. C. to R.3. Imperial, of Sabina to Maximus, Æ. R.4.

THERA (*Santorini*).—Aut. Æ. R.3. to R.8. Imperial, Æ. R.4. to R.6. Of Aurelius to Severus.

ASIA.

BOSPHORUS CIMMERIUS.

GORGIPPIA (———).—Aut. AR. R.8. Æ. R.6.

PHANAGORIA (*Taman*).—Aut. AR. R.8. Æ. R.6.

The Kings of the Cimmerian Bosphorus, are ranged with those of Pontus, which see.

COLCHI.

DIOSCURIAS (*Iscuriah*).—Aut. Æ. R.4.

PONTUS.

PONTUS in genere. Imperial, Æ. R.6., of Marcus Aurelius.

AMASIA (*Amassia*).—Aut. Æ. R.4. Imperial, Æ. R.2. to R.8. Of Domitian to Mamea.

AMERIA? (———).—Aut. (*doubtful*). Æ. R.8.

AMISUS ANTEA PIRAEA (*Himiso Samsun*).—Aut. AR. R.4. Æ. C. to R.6. Imperial, AR. R.2. to R.4. Æ. R.3. to R.5. Of Trajan to Salonina.

ASIBA? (———).—Imperial, Æ. R.8. Of Gordian (*doubtful*).

CABIRA (*Turkal*)—Aut. Æ. R.6.

CERASUS (*Chrixonda, Ghirecin, Keresun*).—Imperial, Æ. R.6. Of Antoninus, of Aurelius, and of Elagabalus.

CHABACTA (———).—Aut. Æ. R.4.

COMANA (*Mermer Klissa, Gomanak*).—Aut. Æ. R.4. Imperial, Æ. R.4. Of Nerva to Elagabalus.

The colonial coins supposed of this town, are of Comana in Cappadocia.

GAZIURA (*Azurnis*).—Aut. Æ. R.6.

LAODICEA (*Ladik*).—Aut. Æ. R.7.

MARIANDYNI.—Aut. AR. R.8.

NEOCÆSAREA (*Niksar, Nixaria*).—Aut. Æ. R.8. Imperial, Æ. R.2. to R.6. Of Tiberius to Gallienus.

PHARNACIA (———).—Aut. Æ. R.5.

PIMOLISA (*Osmangik*).—Aut. Æ. R.6.

SARBANISSA (———).—Aut. Æ. R.8. Of Polemon II.

PONTUS (*continued*).

SEBASTOPOLIS (———).—Aut. Æ. R.7. Imperial. Of A. Pius and J. Domna. Æ. R.7.

TRAPEZUS (*Trabisan, Trebisonda*).—Imperial, Æ. R.4. Of Trajan to Philip.

ZELA (*Zile*).—Imperial, Æ. R.5. Of Julia Domna to Geta.

KINGS OF PONTUS, AND THE CIMMERIAN BOSPHORUS.

PAERISADES II. (supposed the son of Spartacus IV.) King of Bosphorus. [B. C. 289 to —].—Aut. AV. R.8.

LEUCO II.—Æ. R.7.

SPARTOCUS.—AR. (*unique*).

MITHRIDATES III., King of Pontus. [B. C. 297 to 266]. Aut. AR. R.7. to R.8.

PHARNACES I. (son of Mithridates IV.), King of Pontus. [B. C. 184 to 157].—Aut. AR. R.8.

The gold pieces are modern fabrications.

MITHRIDATES V. (*Evergetes*), (son of Pharnaces I.), King of Pontus. Aut. AR. R.8. (*doubtful*).

MITHRIDATES VI. (*Eupator Dionysius*), King of Pontus, afterwards of the Bosphorus. [B. C. 123 to 62].—Aut. AV. R.7. to R.8. AR. R.4. to 8.

This is the great Mithridates.

PHARNACES II., King of the Bosphorus, afterwards of Pontus. [B. C. 62 to 47].—Aut. AV. R.7. to R.8. AR. R.8.

ASANDER, ARCHON, afterwards King of the Bosphorus. [B. C. 46 to 13]. Aut. AV. R.6. AR. R.7. Æ. R.8.? Plumb. R.8.

POLEMO I. King of Pontus, and afterwards of Bosphorus. [B. C. 13. to the commencement of the Christian era.]—Imperial, AR. R.8. (*doubtful.*) Æ. R.8. Of Antony and Augustus.

PYTHODORIS, wife of Polemo I.—Imperial, AR. R.7. Of Augustus and of Tiberius.

POLEMO II. King of Pontus and the Bosphorus.—[A.D. 38 to 63]. Imperial, AR. R.4. to R.8. Æ. R.8. of Claudius, Agrippina Jun. and of Nero.

TRYPHAENE, wife of Polemo II.—Aut. AR. R.8. (*without her head.*)

KINGS OF THE BOSPHORUS ONLY.

SAUROMATES I.—Aut. AV. R8. The cotemporary of Augustus and Tiberius. Æ. R.4. to R.6. Imperial, Æ. R.6. of Augustus and of Tiberius.

SAUROMATES II.—[A. D. 13—16.] Æ. R.4. to R.7.

PONTUS (*continued*).

RHESCUPORIS I. Cotemporary of Augustus, Tiberius, and Caligula.—Aut. Æ. R.6. Imperial, AV. R.8. Æ. R.4. to R.6. of Augustus, Tiberius and Caligula.

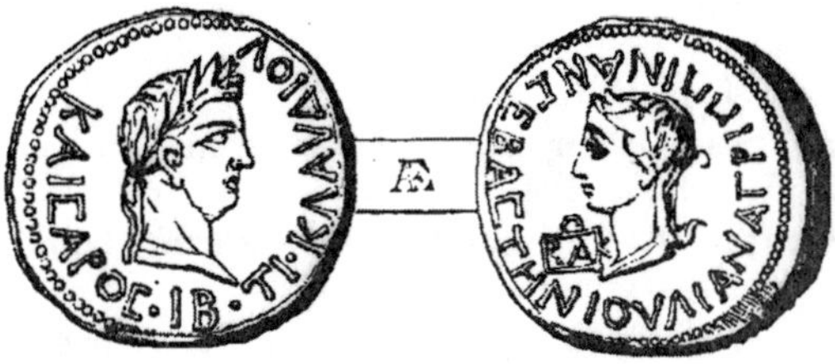

RHESCUPORIS II. Cotemporary of Tiberius and Caligula.—Imperial, AV. R.8. Æ. R.5.

MITHRIDATES, Cotemporary of Claudius.—Aut. Æ. R.6.

GEPAEPIRIS, wife of Mithridates.—Æ. R.8.

COTYS I. Cotemporary of Claudius and Nero.—Imperial, AV. R.6. Æ. R.4. of Claudius, Agrippina Junior, and Nero; with the head of Britannicus unique.[1]

RHESCUPORIS III. Cotemporary of Domitian.—Imperial, AV. R.8. Aut. Æ. R.4.

SAUROMATES III. Cotemporary of Trajan and Hadrian.—Aut. Æ. R.4. to R.6. Imperial of the above Emperors, AV. R.4. to R.8.

COTYS II. Cotemporary of Hadrian.—Aut. Æ. R.6. Imperial of Hadrian, AV. R.5.

RHOEMETALCES, Cotemporary of Hadrian and Antoninus.—Aut. Æ. R.6. Imperial of Hadrian and Antoninus, AV. R.4. to R.5.

EUPATOR, Cotemporary of Antoninus and Aurelius.—Aut. Æ. R.6. Imperial of the above Emperors, AV. R.4. to R.5.

SAUROMATES IV. Cotemporary of Aurelius. Commodus, and Severus.—Aut. Æ. R.6. Imperial of Aurelius, Commodus, Severus, and Caracalla, AV. R.4. to R.8. Electrum, R.4. AR. R.6.

RHESCUPORIS IV. Cotemporary of Caracalla, Elagabalus, and Severus Alexander.—Aut. Æ. R.6. Imperial of the above Emperors, AV. R.6. *Electrum.* R.6. to R.8. AR. R.6.

COTYS III. Cotemporary of Sev. Alexander.—Imperial, AV. R.6. *Electrum.* R.6. AR. R.6.

COTYS IV. Cotemporary of Sev. Alexander.—Imperial. AR. R.4. Æ. R.6.

[1] See "Coins of the Romans relating to Britain," p. 12.

PONTUS (*continued*).

SAUROMATES V. Cotemporary of Sev. Alexander.—Imperial, AR. R.8.

SAUROMATES V. Cotemporary of Sev. Alexander.—Imperial, AR. R.8.

RHESCUPORIS V.—Imperial, AR. R.4. *Potin.* R.4. to R.8. Æ. R.4. to R.8.

ININTHIMEUUS, Cotemporary of Maximinus and Gordian.—Aut. Æ. R.6. Imperial. AR. R.6. Æ. R.6. to R.8.

RHESCUPORIS VI. Cotemporary of Gordian, Trebonian, and T. Decius.—Imperial, *Potin.* R.3.

AREANSES, Cotemporary of Aemilianus, Valerianus, and Gallienus.—Imperial, *Potin.* R.8.

RHESCUPORIS VII. Cotemporary of Valerianus? and Gallienus.—Imperial, Æ. R.5. to R.8.

SAUROMATES VI. Cotemporary of Tacitus or Probus.—Imperial, Æ. R.8.

TIERANES, Cotemporary of Probus.—Imperial, Æ. R.8.

THOTHORSES, Cotemporary of Diocletian.—Imperial, Æ. R.5. to R.6.

RHADAMSES, or RHADAMSADES, Cotemporary of Constantine the Great.—Imperial, Æ. R.8.

RHESCUPORIS VIII. Cotemporary of Constantine the Great.—Imperial, Æ. R.3. to R.8.

SAUROMATES VII.—No coins.

PAPHLAGONIA.

ABONI-TICHOS, IONOPOLIS (*Aineh-Boli, Ynebolu*).—With the name of Aboni-Tichos.—Aut. Æ. R.7. Imperial of Antoninus and M. Aurelius, Æ. R.6.

With the name Ionopolis.—Imperial of L. Verus, Æ. R.6.

AEGIALUS (*Do Castelli. Calla de Gide*).—Imperial of Domna and of Caracalla, Æ. R.6.

AMASTRIS (*Amassreh, Amastra, Amarsa, Amassera, Samatro*).—Aut. AR. R.8. Æ. R.2. to R.6. Imperial of Domitian to Gordian III., Æ. C. to R.8. With the name of *Sebasta* and of *Amisus* in alliance.

AULARI (———).—Aut. Æ. R.8.

CROMNA (*Cromena, Calle de Caragat*).—Aut. AR. R.4.

GANGRA, GERMANICOPOLIS (*Ghiengari, Ghiengra*).—Imperial of M. Aurelius, Faustina, Jun., and of the family of Severus, Æ. R.4. to R.7.

MASTIA? (———).—Aut. Æ. R.6. (*doubtful*).

PAPHLAGONIA (*continued*).

NEOCLAUDIOPOLIS (———).—Imperial, Æ. R.6. Of Antoninus to Caracalla.

POMPEIOPOLIS (*Tache Kupru*).—Imperial, Æ. R.6. Of Aurelius and Faustina, Jun.

SEBASTE (*Sivas*).—Aut. Æ. R.8.[2] Imperial of Trajan, Aurelius, and Verus, Æ. R.6.

SESAMUS (———).—Aut. Æ. R.6.

SINOPE (*Sinub, Sinab, Sinope*).—Aut. AR. C. to R.8. Æ. C. to R.4. Aut. Colonial, Æ. R.8. Imperial Colonial of Cæsar to Gallienus, Æ. C. to R.8.

KINGS OF PAPHLAGONIA.

PYLAEMENES (*uncertain period*).—Aut. Æ. R.6.

The name of Pylaemenes was common to the kings of Paphlagonia.

BITHYNIA.

BITHYNIA in genere.—Imperial of Vespasianus to Salonina, AR. R.3. to R.6. Æ. R.3. to R.8.

ALYATTA? (———).—Aut. Æ. R.6.

APAMEA. MYRLEA (*Medaniah, Madagna*).—Aut. Æ. R.4. to R.6. Aut. Colonial, Æ. R.8. Imperial Colonial, Æ. R.3. to R.6. Of Augustus to Gallienus.

ASTACUS? (———).—Aut. AR. R.8. (*Millingen*).

BITHYNIUM, CLAUDIOPOLIS (*Bastan*).—Aut. with the name of Bithynium, Æ. R.6. Imperial, with the name of Claudiopolis, Æ. R.4. Of Claudius to Hadrian. Imperial, with the name of Bithynium, Æ. R.4. to R.7. Of Antinous to Gallienus.

CAESAREA (———).

The coins supposed of Bithynium Caesarea belong to Tralles in Lydia.

CHALCEDON (*Kadi-Kioy*).—Aut. AR. R.4. to R.7. Æ. R.4. Imperial, Æ. R.2. to R.6. Of Agrippina the younger to Tranquillina.

CIUS, PRUSIAS AD MARE (*Kio. Kiemlik*).—With the name of Cius, AR. R.4. Æ. R.5. With the name of Prusias, Aut. Æ. R.6. Imperial, Æ. R.5. Of Domitian. With the name of Cius restored, Aut. Æ. R.5. Imperial, Æ. R.2. to R.8. Of Claudius to Salonina.

CRATIA. FLAVIOPOLIS (*Bayndir*).—With the name of Cratia.—Aut. Æ. R.6. With the name of Fluviopolis.—Aut. Æ. R.8. Imperial, Æ. R.4. to R.8. Of Antoninus Pius to Gallienus.

---

[2] This coin bears the name of Amastris in alliance.

BITHYNIA (*continued*).

DIA (———).—Aut. Æ. R.6.

EREBOEA? (———).—Imperial, Æ. R.6. Of Commodus. (*doubtful*).

HADRIANI (*Edrenes*).—Aut. Æ. R.6. Imperial, Æ. R.4. to R.8. Of Hadrian to Salonina.

HADRIANOPOLIS (*Boli*).—Aut. Æ. R.6. Imperial, Æ. R.3. to R.8. From Hadrian to Philip.

HADRIANOTHERAE (———) Aut. Æ. R.6. Imperial, Æ. R.4. to R.6. Of Hadrian to Philip.

HERACLEA (*Rachia, Elegri, Ereyli, Penderaski*).—Aut. AR. R.4. to R.8. Æ. R.4. to R.6. Imperial, Æ. R.2. to R.6. Of Vespasian to Salonina.

KINGS OF HERACLEA.

TIMOTHEUS AND DIONYSIUS. Cotemporary with Philip II., King of Macedon.—Aut. AR. R.6.

DIONYSIUS *only*. Cotemporary of Alexander the Great.—Aut. AR. R.6.

AMASTRIS, *Wife of Dionysius*.—Aut. AR. R.7. Æ. R.8.

JULIOPOLIS (*Bey Bazar*).—Aut. Æ. R.8. Imperial, Æ. R.2. to R.7. Of Trajan to Gallienus.

METROUM? (———).—Aut. Æ. R.8. (*doubtful*).

NICAEA (*Isnik*).—Aut. Æ. R.3. to R.6. Imperial, Æ. C. to R.8. From Julius Cæsar to Quietus.

NICOMEDIA (*Isnid, Isnimid, Nicomedia*).—Aut. Æ. R.2. Imperial, Æ. C. to R.8. Augustus to Salonina.

PRUSA AD OLYMPUM (*Brusa*).—Aut. Æ. R.6. Imperial, Æ. R.1. to R.6. Of Nero to Salonina.

PRUSIAS AD HYPIUM (*Uskubi*).—Aut. Æ. R.8. Imperial, Æ. R.2. to R.6. Of Vespasian to Gallienus.

PRUSIAS AD MARE.—See CIUS.

PYTHOPOLIS (———). No certain coins.

See Note to Pylus in Elis.

TIMAEA.—Aut. Æ. R.8.

TIUM (*Thios, Tillios, Filios, Falios*).—Aut. Æ. R.6. Imperial, Æ. R.2. to R.6. Of Domitian to Gallienus.

KINGS OF BITHYNIA.

NICOMEDES I. [B. C. 276 to 250].—Aut. AR. R.8. Æ. R.4.

No coins are known of his son Zelas.

PRUSIAS I. [B. C. —— to 187].—Aut. AR. R.6. Æ. C. to R.4. Of Prusias I. or Prusias II.

There are false coins, both in gold and silver.

BITHYNIA (*continued*).

PRUSIAS II. [B. C. —— to 149].—Aut. AR. R.5. Æ. C. to R.4.

NICOMEDES II., EPIPHANES. [B. C. 149 to 93].—Aut. AV. R.8. AR. R.6.

NICOMEDES III. Epiphanes. [B. C. 93 to 73]. Aut. AR. R.8.

ORADALTIS, Queen of Bithynia (*uncertain period*).—Aut. Æ. R.6.

MUSA ORSOBARIS, Queen of Bithynia (*uncertain period.*— Aut. Æ. R.6.

MYSIA.

MYSIA in genere.—Imperial, Æ. R.8. Of Domitian.

ABBAETI, MYSI.

These coins belong to Aba in Caria.

ADRAMYTIUM (*Edremit, Adramitti*).—Aut. AR. R.8. Æ. R.4. to R.6. Imperial, Æ. R.3. to R.6. Of Domitian to Gallienus.

ANTANDRUS (*Atandro*).—Aut. AR. R.7. Æ. R.6. Imperial, Æ. R.6. to R.8. Of Titus to Julia Paula.

APOLLONIA AD RHYNDACUM (*Abullona*).—Aut. Æ. R.8. Imperial, Æ. R.2. to R.6. Of Domitian to Gallienus.

ASSUS (*Asso*).—Aut. AR. R.7. Æ. R.4. Imperial, Æ. R.4. to R.8. Of Augustus to Severus Alexander.

ASTYRA (————).—Aut. AR. R.6. Æ. R.8.

The *Imperial* coins supposed of this city belong, it is imagined, to Antandrus.

ATARNEA (————). Aut. EL. R.8. Æ. R.4. Imperial, Æ. R.6. Of Marcus Aurelius to Gordianus.

CAME, or CANA, or CAMENA (*Coloni*).—Imperial, Æ. R.7. Of Hadrian, Commodus, and Severus.

CISTHENE (————).—Aut. Æ. R.7.

CYZICUS (————).—Aut. AV. R.4. to R.8. EL. R.3. AR. R.4. to R.8. Æ. C. to R.4. Imperial, Æ. C. to R.6. Of Augustus to Claudius Gothicus.

GARGARA (*Ine-Kioy*).—Aut. AR. R.7. Æ. R.4. Imperial, Æ. R.8. Of Commodus.

GERGITHUS (*Gergiti*).—Aut. Æ. R.6.

GERME, HIERA-GERME (————).—Aut. Æ. R.3. to R.6. Imperial, Æ. R.2. to R.6. Of Trajanus to Philip Jun.

LAMPSACUS (*Lapseki, Lamsaki*).—Aut. AV. R.6. AR. R.3. to R.8. Æ. R.2. to R.4. Imperial, Æ. R.3. to R.5. Of Augustus to Gallienus.

MYSIA (*continued*).

MILETOPOLIS (*Melte*).—Aut. Æ. R.6. Imperial, Æ. R.4. to R.6. Of Tiberius to Otacilia.

PARIUM (*Kiemer, Kamares, Porto Camera*).—Aut. AV. R.8. AR. R.2. to R.6. Æ. R.2. to R.4. Aut. Colonial, Æ. R.2. to R.8. Imperial, Colonial, Æ. R.2. to R.8. Of Julius Cæsar to Salonina.

PERGAMUS (*Bergam, Pergamo*).—Aut. AV. R.8. EL. R.6. AR. R.2. to R.8. Æ. C. to R.4. Imperial, Æ. C. to R.8. Of Augustus to Saloninus.

KING OF PERGAMUS.

PHILETAIRUS [reigned in the third and second centuries B. C.]—Aut. AR. R.4. to R.7. Æ. R.2. to R.4.

Philetairus was the common name of the Kings of Pergamus, and the coins of particular monarchs cannot, in consequence, be distinguished readily. But see "Viconti Iconographie Grecque."

PERPERENE (———).—Aut. Æ. R.8. Imperial, Æ. R.4. to R.7. Of Nero to Otacilia.

PIONIA (———).—Aut. Æ. R.8. Imperial, Æ. R.7. Of Severus and his family.

PITANE (———). — Aut. Æ. R.4. Imperial, Æ. R.6. Caius and Lucius Cæsar to Sev. Alexander.

POEMANENI (———).—Aut. Æ. R.6. Imperial, Æ. R.7. Trajan.

POROSELENE (*Musco Nisi*).—Aut. Æ. R.7. Imperial, Æ. R.7. Ant. Pius to Valerian.

PRIAPUS (*Karaboa*).—Aut. Æ. R.4. to R.6. Imperial, Æ. R.6. Augustus.

TRIMENOTHYREI (———).—Aut. Æ. R.6. Imperial, Æ. R.4. to R.6.

These coins have often been confounded with those of Temenothyræ in Lydia.

ISLAND ADJACENT TO MYSIA.

PROCONNESUS (*Mermer-Adassi, Marmara*).—Aut. AR. R.8. Æ. R.6.

TROAS.

ABYDOS (*Aidos, Nagara*).—Aut. AV. R.8. El. R.8. AR. R.2. to R.8. Æ. R.2. to R.4. Imperial, Æ. R.4. to R.6. Augustus to Maximinus.

ALEXANDRIA-TROAS (*Eski-Stambul*).—Aut. El. R.8. AR. R.6. Æ. C. to R.2. Colonial, Aut. Æ. C. to R.6. Colonial, Imperial, Æ. C. to R.8. Trajan to Salonina.

TROAS (*continued*).

AMAXITUS, see HAMAXITUS.

ARISBA (*Mussa-Kioy*).—Aut. Æ. R.6. Imperial, Æ. R.8. Trajan to Pescennius Niger.

The Coin of Pescennius Niger is doubted.

BERYTIS (———).—Aut Æ. R.8. (*Millingen*).

DARDANUS (*Burnu Punta del Barbieri*).—Aut. AR. R.7. Æ. R.3. to R.4. Imperial, Æ. R.4. to R.7. Augustus to Geta.

HAMAXITUS (———).—Aut. Æ. R.8. (*Millingen*).

GENTINOS (———).—Aut. Æ. R.8.

ILIUM (*Bunar-Bachi*).—Aut. AR. R.4. to R.7. Æ. R 3. to R.6. Imperial, Æ. R.2. to R.6. Augustus to Salonina.

NEANDRIA (———).—Aut. Æ. R.7.

OPHRYNIUM (———).—Aut. AR. R.8. Æ. R.5.

SCEPSIS (———).—Aut. AR. R.7. Æ. R.5. to R.7. Imperial, Æ. R.4. to R.7. M. Aurelius to Maximin.

SIGEUM (*Yeni-Cheher*)—Aut. Æ. R.3. to R.6.

THEBE (———).—Aut. Æ. R.8. (*Millingen*).

The name of this town is also found on an autonomous coin of Adramytium in Mysia, with which it was in alliance.

ZELEIA ? (———).—Aut. Æ. R.8.

Dumersan, Descr. des Med. du Cab. d'A. de Hauteroche, pl. xiii.

ISLAND ADJACENT TO TROAS.

TENEDUS (*Bozgia, Boghce-Adassi, Tenedos, Tenedo*).—Aut. AV. R.8. AR. R.3. to R.6. Æ. R.6.

AEOLIS.

AEOLIS in genere.

The coins hitherto attributed to this country, have been restored to Aeolium in the Thracian Chersonesus.

AEGAE (*Ghiusel-Hyssar*).—Aut. AR. R.4. to R.8. Æ. R.3. to R.5. Imperial, Æ. R.4. to R.6. Claudius to Trajan Decius.

CYME (*Sanderli, Nemurt*).—Aut. AR. R.4. to R.6. Æ. R.2. to R.6. Imperial, Æ. R.2. to R.8. Drusus to Saloninus.

ELAEA (*Ialea*).—Aut. AR. R.7. Æ. R.3. to R.7. Imperial, Æ. R.4. to R.6. Augustus to Hostilian.

LARISSA ? (———).—Aut. Æ. R.7.

AEOLIS (*continued*).

MYRHINA (———).—Aut. AR. R.4. Æ. R.2. to R.4. Imperial, Æ. R.4. to R.5. Domitian to Tranquillina.

NEONTICHOS (———).—Aut. Æ. R.6.

TEMNUS (*Melemen*).—Aut. Æ. R.3. to R.6. Imperial, Æ. R.2. to R.6. Augustus to Philip the younger.

ISLANDS ADJACENT TO AEOLIS.

LESBUS (*Metelen*), in genere.—Imperial, Æ. R.3. to R.6. Marcus Aurelius to Commodus.

ANTISSA (*Petra*).—Aut. Æ. R.4.

ERESUS (*Eresso*).—Aut. AR. R.6. Æ. R.2. to R.6. Imperial, Æ. R.7. Adrian to Sev. Alexander.

METHYMNA (———).—Aut. AR. R.6. to R.7. Æ. R.2. to R.4. Imperial, Æ. R.4. to R.6. Augustus to Severus Alexander.

MYTILENE (*Midilli, Castro*).—Aut. AR. R.4. to R.6. Æ. C. to R.6. Imperial, Æ. R.2. to R.7. Augustus to Salonina.

The autonomous coins of Mytilene, often bear the names of Ephesus, Pergamus, and Smyrna, in alliance; the imperial, those of Adramytium and Pergamus.

NAPE? (———).—Aut. R.8. Æ. R.8. (*doubtful*).

IONIA.

IONIA in genere.—Imperial Æ. R.6. Antoninus and M. Aurelius.

APOLLONIA (———).—Aut? Æ. R.3. Imperial, Æ. R.8. Marcus Aurelius and Severus Alexander.

CADME, PRIENE (———).—With the name of *Cadme*. Aut. Æ. R.8. With the name of *Priene*.—Aut. AR. R.5. Æ. R.3. to R.5. Imperial, Æ. R.7. Augustus to Valerian.

CLAZOMENE (*Klisma*).—Aut. AV. R.8. AR. R.5. to R.8. Æ. C. to R.4. Imperial, AR. R.8. Æ. R.4. to R.8. Augustus to Gallienus.

Some have the name of *Smyrna* in alliance.

COLOPHON (———).—Aut. AV. R.6. AR. R.5. Æ. R.2. to R.4. Imperial, Æ. R.2. to R.6. Nero to Saloninus.

On an autonomous coin the name of *Teos* is found in alliance; and on the Imperial, *Pergamus*.

EPHESUS (*Ayasuluk Efeso*).—Aut. AV. R.8. AR.* R.1. to R.6. Æ. R.1. to R.6. Imperial, AR. R.6. Æ. C. to R.6. From the time of the Triumvirs to Saloninus.

Many coins of Ephesus bear the names of other cities in alliance.

---

* See a Notice of the Coins of Ephesus, while called *Arsinoe*, in the Numismatic Chronicle, Vol. II. p. 171.

IONIA (*continued*).

ERAE? (———).—Imperial, Æ. R.8. Of Augustus. (*doubtful*).

ERYTHRAE (*Eritra*).—Aut. AV. R.8. AR. R.1. to R.6. Æ. R.1. to R.4. Imperial, Æ. R.4. to R.7. Augustus to Valerian.

On the autonomous coins the name of *Chios* is found in alliance.

GAMBRIUM (———).—Aut. Æ. R.4.

HERACLEA (———).—Aut. AR.? R.4. Æ. R.3. to R.5. Imperial, Æ. R.5. Augustus to Geta.

LEBEDUS (*Sivri-Hyssar*).—Aut. AV. R.8. AR. R.7. Æ. R.3. to R.5. Imperial, Æ. R.4. to R.7. Vespasian to Geta.

MAGNESIA (*Aidin Ghiusel. Hyssar*).—Aut. AR. R.4. to R.6. Æ. R.1. to R.4. Imperial, Æ. R.1. to R.6. Livia to Gallienus.

METROPOLIS (*Turbali*).—Aut? Æ. R.5. Imperial, Æ. R.1. to R.6. Trajan to Gallienus.

On these the name of Ephesus occurs in alliance.

MILETUS (*Balat, Palaisca, Milet*).—Aut. AR. R.2. to R.4. Æ. C. to R.4. Imperial, Æ. R.2. to R.6. Augustus to Salonina.

On these the names of *Ephesus, Smyrna, Cos,* and *Amisus,* are found.

NEAPOLIS (*Kuche-Adassi, Neapoli, Scalanuova*).—Aut. Æ. R.7. Imperial, Æ. R.6. Of Domna, Gordian, and Trebonian.

The name of *Harpasa* in Caria is found on an imperial coin.

PHOCEA (*Foya, Foggia, Fokia, Vecchia, Le Foglieri*).—Aut. AV. R.7. Electrum, R.7. Æ. R.2. to R.4. Imperial, Æ. R.2. to R.7. Claudius to Philip, Junior.

PHYGELA (———).—Aut. Æ. R.4.

SMYRNA (*Ismir, Smirne, Le Smirnea, Smyrne*).—Aut. AV. R.7. Electrum, R.7. AR. R.1. to R.8. Æ. C. to R.6. Imperial, Æ. C. to R.7. Of Augustus to Saloninus.

The coins of Smyrna, Teos, Chios, and Samos, often bear the names of other cities in alliance.

TEOS (*Sigagik*).—Aut. AV. R.6. to R.8. AR. R.4. to R.6. Æ. R.1. to R.6. Imperial, Æ. R.2. to R.7. Augustus to Saloninus.

ISLANDS ADJACENT TO IONIA.

CHIOS (*Sakiss, Adassi, Chio, Scio*). — Aut. AV. R.8. Electrum, R.8. AR. R.2. to R.6. Æ. C. to R.6. Imperial, AR. R.5. Of Augustus.

IONIA (*continued*).

ICARIA (*Nakaria*).—Aut. Æ. R.6. Imperial, Æ. R.8. Of Commodus?

PATMOS (*Patmos, Palmosa*).—Aut. Æ. R.8. Imperial, Æ. R.8.? Of Septimius Severus.

SAMOS (*Susam, Adassi, Samo*).—Aut. AV. R.6. Electrum, R.6. AR. R.5. to R.7. Æ. R.2. to R.6. Imperial, Æ. C. to R.5. Of Augustus to the younger Valerian.

CARIA.

ABA (———).—Aut. Æ. R.4. Imperial, Æ. R.7. Marcus Aurelius, Lucius Verus, and Severus Alexander.

ALABANDA (———).—Aut. AR. R.6. Æ. R.4. to R.6. Imperial, Æ. R.2. to R.6. Augustus to Gordian.

ALINDA (*Mugla*).—Aut. Æ. R.4. Imperial, Æ. R 6. Augustus to Annia Faustina.

ANTIOCHIA (*Yeni-Chiehere*).—Aut. AR. R.6. Æ. R.2. to R.5. Imperial, Æ. R.3. to R.8. Augustus to Salonina.

On the Imperial Coins, the name of *Laodicea* occurs.

APHRODISIAS (———).—Aut. AR. R.4. Æ. R.2. to R.4. Imperial, Æ. R.3. to R.6. Augustus to Salonina.

On the autonomous coins, we find the name of *Plarasa* in Caria, and on the Imperial, *Hierapolis* and *Ephesus*.

APOLLONIA (———).—Aut. Æ. R.2. to R.8. Imperial, Æ. R.6. Augustus to Salonina.

BARGASA (*Arab-Hyssar*).—Aut. Æ. R.5. to R.6. Imperial, Æ. R.5. to R.6. Nero to Salonina.

BARGYLIA (———).—Aut. AR. R.6. Æ. R.7. Imperial, Æ. R.4. to R.6. Titus to Geta.

CALYNDA? (———).—Aut. Æ. R.8.

CERAMUS (*Keramo*).—Aut. AR. R.8. Æ. R.8. Imperial, R.8. Antoninus Pius.

CNIDUS (*Porto Crio*).—Aut. AR. R.1. to R.5. Æ. R.1. to R.5. Imperial, Æ. R.4. to R.6. Nerva to Caracalla and Plautilla.

CYON (———).—Aut. Æ. R.5. Imperial, Æ. R.8. Julia Domna.

DAEDALA (———).—Imperial of Caracalla only, Æ. R.8.

EIRIZA (———).—Aut. Æ. R.8.

EURALIUM (———).—Imperial of Caracalla, Æ. R.8.

CARIA (*continued*).

EVIPPE (———).—Imperial, Æ. R.8. Lucilla and Domna,

EUROMUS (———).—Aut. Æ. R.6. Imperial, Æ. R.7. Severus and Caracalla.

HALICARNASSUS (*Budrun, Bodroni, San Pedro*).—Aut. AR. R.7. Æ. R.6. Imperial, Æ. R.3. to R.6. Agrippina Claudii to Gordian.

Some of these coins bear the name of Cos and Samos in alliance.

HARPASA (*Arpache-Kallessi*).—Aut. Æ. R.6. Imperial, Æ. R.6. Antoninus Pius to Gordian.

Some have the name of Neapolis in Ionia in alliance.

HERACLEA (———).—Aut. Æ. R.6. (*doubtful*).

HYLLARIMENE (———).—Aut. Æ. R.8. (*Millingen*).

HYDRELA (*Denisli*).—Aut. Æ. R.8.

IASUS (*Askein-Kalessi*).—Aut. Æ. R.4. Imperial, Æ. R.4. to R.5. Augustus to Gordian.

IMBRUS (———).—Aut. Æ. R.6. (*doubtful*).

MEDMASA (———).—Aut. AR. R.7.

MYLASA (*Meless, Mylaso, Marmora*).—Aut. Æ. R.4. Imperial, Æ. R.3. to R.6. Augustus to Valerian and his son.

MYNDUS (*Menteche, Mimdes*).—Aut. AR. R.7. Æ. R.3. to R.4. Imperial, Æ. R.6. Antoninus to Septimius Severus, and Domna.

NEAPOLIS (———).

The coins supposed of Neapolis in Caria, belong to Neapolis in Ionia.

NYSA (*Nazely, Nozly*).—Aut. AR. R.8. Æ. R.4. to R.6. Imperial, Æ. R.2. to R.6. Augustus to Gallienus.

Some bear the name of *Ephesus* and *Ancyra* in alliance.

ORTHOSIA (———).—Aut. Æ. R.3. to R.5. Imperial, Æ. R.4. to R.6. Augustus to Maximinus.

PLARASA (———).—Aut. Æ. R.4. to R.7.

Some bear the name of Aphrodisias in Caria, in alliance.

PRENASSUS or PRINASSUS (———).—Aut. Æ. R.4.

PYRNUS (———).—Aut. Æ. R.6.

SEBASTOPOLIS (———).—Aut. Æ. R.6. Imperial, Æ. R.4. to R.6. (*Millingen*).

STRATONICEA (*Eski-Chiehere*).—Aut. AR. R.7. Æ. R.4. to R.6. Imperial, AR. R.8. Æ. R.3. to R.7. Antoninus Pius to Saloninus.

TABA (*Dava-su, Tabas*).—Aut. AR. R.7. Æ. R.4. to R.5. Imperial, Æ. R.4. to R.7. Drusus to Salonina.

TELEMISSUS (———).—Aut. Æ. R.8.

CARIA (*continued*).

TRAPEZOPOLIS (*Karagia-Su*).—Aut. Æ. R.4. to R.6. Imperial, Æ. R.6. Augustus, Commodus, and Domna.

TRIPOLIS (*Tribul*).—Aut. Æ. R.3. to R.5. Imperial, Æ. R.3. R.6. Augustus to Salonina.

KINGS OF CARIA.

HECATOMNUS. [Died about the year B. C. 381].—Aut. AR. R.8.

MAUSSOLUS. [Died in the year B. C. 353].—Aut. AR. R.5. to R.6.

ARTEMISIA, wife of Maussolus.—No coins.

HIDRIEUS. [Died in the year B. C. 344].—Aut. AR. R.6. to R.7.

ADA, wife of Hidrieus.—No coins.

PIXODARUS. [Died in the year B. C. 336].—Aut. AV. R.8. AR. R.6.

OTHONTOPATES. [Died in the year B. C. 334].—Aut. AR. R.8.

ISLANDS ADJACENT TO CARIA.

ASTYPALAEA (*Stimfalia*).—Aut. ? Æ. R.4. Imperial, Æ. R.7. Of Livia and Tiberius.

CALYMNA (*Calmine, Calymnium, Calymnæ*).—Aut. AR. R.6.

COS (*Istanko, Lango*).—Aut. AR. R.1. to R.8. Æ. C. to R.8. Imperial, Æ. R.1. to R.5. Augustus to Philip.

The Imperial coins sometimes bear the name of *Miletus*, in Ionia, in alliance.

MEGISTE ? (———).—Aut. AR. R.8. (*Millingen*).

Erroneously given by Sestini " Lett. Num. Tom. vi," to Medmasa in Caria.

NISYROS (*Nisari, Nicero*).—Aut. AR. R.8. Æ. R.4.

RHODUS (*Rodus, Rodi*).—Aut. AV. R.8. AR. C. to R.4. Æ. C. to R.3. Imperial, Æ. R.3. to R.6. Tiberius to Commodus.

ASTYRA RHODI (———).—Aut. Æ. R.8.

CAMIRUS RHODI (———).—Aut. AR. R.6.

TELOS (*Elleci, Tillos, Episcopi*).—Aut. Æ. R.8.

LYCIA.

LYCIA in genere.—Imperial, AR. R.3. Claudius to Trajan.

Some bear the name of Apollonia in Pisidia in alliance.

LYCIA (*continued*).

ANTIPHELLUS (———).—Imperial, Æ. R.8. Of Gordianus.

APERRAE (———).—Imperial, Æ. R.6. Of Gordianus.

APOLLONIA (———).—Aut.? Æ. R.6. Imperial, Æ. R.6. Marcus Aurelius, Geta, and Gallienus.

ARAXA (———).—Aut. Æ. R.8.

ARYCANDA (———).—Imperial, Æ. R.7. Of Gordianus and Tranquillina.

CABALIS? (———).—Aut. AR. R.8. (*Millingen*).

CORYDALLUS (———).—Aut. Æ. R.6. Imperial, Æ. R.6. Of Gordianus and Tranquillina.

CRAGUS (———).—Aut. AR. R.4. Imperial, Æ. R.6. Of Augustus and Julia.

CYANEAE (———).—Aut. AR. R.6. Æ. R.6. Imperial, Æ. R.5. Gordianus.

CYDNA? (———).—Aut. AR. R.8.

LIMYRA (———).—Aut. AR. R.6. Imperial, Æ. R.6. Gordianus.

MASSICYTES (———).—Aut. AR. R.3. to R.6. Æ. R.4. Imperial, AR. R.4 Æ. R.8. Of Augustus.

MYRA (*Mira*).—Aut. Æ. R.7. Imperial, Æ. R.4. to R.6. Antoninus Pius to Valerian.

The names of *Patara* and *Side* are found on the Imperial coins.

OLYMPUS (*Porto Venetico*).—Aut. AR. R.6.

PATARA (*Patera*).—Aut. AR. R.7. Æ. R.8. Imperial, Æ. R.4. to R.5. Of Gordianus.

The name of *Myra* occurs on the imperial coins.

PHASELIS (*Fionda*).—Aut. AR. R.6. Æ. R.3. to R.5. Imperial, Æ. R.7. Of Gordianus.

PHELLUS (———).—Imperial, Æ. R.8. Of Gordian.

PODALIA (———).—Aut. Æ. R.8. Imperial, Æ. R.8. Of Tranquillina.

RHODIA, RHODIOPOLIS (———).—Aut. AR. R.8.

TITYASSA (———).—Imperial, Æ., of Geta, R.8.

TLOS (———).—Aut. AR. R.7. Æ. R.7. Imperial Æ. R.8. Of Gordianus.

TRABALA (———).—Aut. Æ. R.8.

XANTUS (*Eksenide*).—Aut. AR. R.8.

PAMPHYLIA.

ARIASSUS (———).—Imperial, Æ. R.6. Of Lucilla to Geta.

ASPENDUS (*Menugat, Aspindus*).—Aut. AR. R.7. Æ. R.6. Imperial, Æ. R.4. to R.5. Of Augustus, and from Julia Soæmias to Saloninus.

ATTALIA (*Palea-Attalia*).—Aut. Æ. R.4. Imperial, Æ. R.2. to R.5. Augustus to Saloninus.

Some have the name of *Side*, in Pamphylia, in alliance.

CASA (———).—Imperial, Æ. R.6. Of Gordian, Etrucilla, and Herennius.

ETENNA (———).—Aut. Æ. R.4. Imperial, Æ. R.6. Faustina Junior to Severus Alexander.

ILOEA (———).—Imperial, Æ. R.8. Of Gordian III.

ISINDUS (———).—Aut. Æ. R.3. to R.5. Imperial, Æ. R.6. to R.7. Lucius Verus to Valerian.

MAGYDUS (———).—Aut. Æ. R.8. Imperial, Æ. R.6. Augustus to Julia Domna.

PANEMOTICHOS (———).—Imperial, Æ. R.8. Of Julia Domna.

PERGA (*Kara, Hyssar, Tekie-si*).—Aut. AR. R.5. Æ. R.2. to R.4. Imperial, AR. R.6. Æ. R.1. to R.5. Augustus to Salonina, Aurelian and Tacitus.

Some bear the name of Apollonia in Pisidia.

POGLA (———).—Imperial, Æ. R.7. Of Geta and Trajan Decius.

SIDE (*Candeloro*).—Aut. AR. R.1. to R.8. Æ. R.1. to R.4. Imperial, Æ. R.1. to R.6. Augustus to Saloninus.

Some have the names of *Myra*, in Lycia, and *Attalia* and *Perga*, in Pamphylia, in alliance.

SILLYUM (———).—Aut. Æ. R.6. Imperial, Æ. R.4. to R.6. Of Augustus, and from Antoninus Pius to Saloninus.

PISIDIA.

ADADA (———).—Aut. Æ. R.8. (*Millingen*). Imperial, Æ. R.8. Valerian? and Gallienus?

AMBLADA (———).—Imperial, Æ. R.6. Marcus Aurelius to Severus Alexander.

PISIDIA (*continued*).

ANDEDA (———).—Imperial, Æ. R.8.

See an article by Mr. Borrell, in "The Numismatic Chronicle," Vol. II. p. 1—4. The existence of coins of *Andeda* does not, however, prove that there are none of Adada, as Mr. Borrell supposes, since coins of the latter city are given on the authority of Mr. Millingen.

ANTIOCHIA (*Ak-Chichere*).—Colonial, Aut. Æ. R.6. Colonial Imperial, Æ. C. to R.5. Tiberius to Claudius Gothicus.

APOLLONIA (———).—Aut. Æ. R.6. Imperial, R.8.

See a very interesting notice of the coins of this city by Mr. Borrell. Numismatic Chronicle, Vol. II. p. 182.

BARIS (———).—Imperial, Æ. R.8. Of Severus Alexander.

CONANE (———).—Aut. Æ. R.8. Imperial, Æ. R.7. Of Marcus Aurelius, Plautilla, and Philip Junior.

CREMNA (*Krebinaz*).—Colonial Imperial, Æ. R.4. to R.6. Of Caracalla to Trebonianus Gallus. Latin legends.

CRETOPOLIS? (———).—Aut. Æ. R.—.

HADRIANOPOLIS (———).—Imperial, Æ. R.8. Of S. Severus.

LAODICEA COMBUSTA (———).—Imperial, Æ. R.8.

LYRBE (———).—Imperial, Æ. R.4. to R.5. Severus Alexander to Saloninus.

LYSINIA (———).—Imperial of Caracalla, Æ. R.8.

MYLIAS (———).—Aut. AV. Of Alexander the Great, R.1. AR. R.8.

OLBASA (———).—Colonial Imperial, Æ. R.8. Of J. Mæsa and Gordianus.

OROANDA? (———).—Aut. Æ. R.8.

PEDNELISSUS (———).—Imperial, Æ. R.8. Of Commodus and Maximus.

PROSTANNA (———).—Aut. Æ. R.8. Imperial, Æ. R.6. Of Claudius Gothicus.

SAGALASSUS (*Sadyaklu*).—Aut. AR. R.6. Æ. R.4. Imperial, Æ. R.4. to R.8. Augustus to Claudius Gothicus.

The name of *Lacedæmon* in Laconia, is found on these coins.

SANDALIUM (———).—Aut. Æ. R.8.

SELEUCIA (*Selefke*).—Imperial, Æ. R.5. to R.6. Hadrian to Claudicus Gothius.

SELGE (———).—Aut. AR. R.2. to R 8. Æ. R.3. Imperial, Æ. R.4. to R.6. Hadrian to Salonina.

The name of *Lacedæmon* in Laconia, is found on these coins.

PISIDIA (*continued*).

TERMESSUS (*Estenaz?*).—Aut. Æ. R.2. to R.5. Imperial, Æ. R.7. Augustus to Severus Alexander.

TITYASSUS (———).—Imperial, Æ. R.6. Of Hadrian, Antoninus Pius, and Geta.

ISAURIA.

CARALLIA (———).—Imperial, Æ. R.6. to R.7. Marcus Aurelius to Maximin.

CLAUDIOPOLIS? (———).—Colonial, Aut. Æ. R.8.

ISAURUS (*Rey-Chiehere*).—Imperial, Æ. R.8. Of Geta and Elagabalus.

LALASSIS (———).—Aut. AR. R.6. Æ. R.6.

LACAONIA.

LACAONIA in genere.—Aut. Æ. R.6. With the head of Antiochus IV. king of Commagene.

COROPISSUS (*Ku-Hyssar*).—Imperial, Æ. R.7. Of Hadrian, Faustina Junior, and Maximin.

ICONIUM (*Kunyah, Konyeh, Cogni*).—Aut. Æ. R.5. Imperial, Æ. R.6. Of Nero and Poppæa, Hadrian, Marcus Aurelius, and Faustina Junior. Colonial Imperial, Æ. R.3. to R.4. Of Gordian, Valerian, and Gallienus. Latin legends.

PARLAIS (———).—Colonial Imperial, Æ. R.4. to R.5. Marcus Aurelius to Maximin. Imperial, Æ. R.6. Of Gallienus.

LARANDA (———).—Imperial, Æ. Medallion of Philip the Younger, R.8.

SAVATRA (———).—Imperial, Æ. R.8. Of Antoninus Pius.

CILICIA.

CILICIA in genere.

The coins formerly supposed of Cilicia belong to Creta Insula.

AEGAE (*Aias-Kale*).—Aut. Æ. R.4. Imperial, AR. R.8. Æ. R.2. to R.8. Augustus to Salonina.

ALAE (———).—Imperial, Æ. R.8. Of Hadrian.

CILICIA (*continued*).

ALEXANDRIA ad ISSUM (*Iskanderona, Alessandretta*).—Aut. Æ. R.7. to R.8. Imperial, Æ. R.6. Of Trajan, Hadrian, and Caracalla.

Some of the coins of this city bear the head of Antiochus IV. king of Commagene.

AMANIENSES (———).—Aut. Æ. R.8.

ANAZARBUS, CAESAREA ad ANAZARBUM (*Aynzarba*).—Aut. Æ. R.7. Imperial, Æ. R.3. to R.8. Claudius to Gallienus.

ANCHIALE (———).—Aut. Æ. R.8. With the head of Anchialus, the founder.

ANEMURIUM (*Anamur, Scalemura*).—Aut. Æ. R.8. Imperial, Æ. R.3. to R.7. Domitian to Valerian.

Some of the coins of this city bear the head of Antiochus IV. king of Commagene.

ANTIOCHIA ad SARUM, ADANA (*Edene, Adana*).—With the name of Antiochia. Aut. Æ. R.6. to R.8. Imperial, Æ. R.8. Of M. Aurelius.—With the name of Adana. Aut. AR. R.8. Æ. R.5. to R.8. Imperial, Æ. R.4. to R.8. Marcus Aurelius to Gallienus.

Some of the autonomous coins bear the head of Antiochus IV.

ANTIOCHIA MARITIMA (———).—Imperial, Æ. R.6. Of Philip and Valerian.

ANTIOCHIA incerta CILICIAE (———).—Aut. Æ. R.8.

ARGOS (———).—Imperial, Æ. R.4. to R.5. Of Valerian, Gallienus, and Salonina.

AUGUSTA (———).—Aut. Æ. R.8. Imperial, Æ. R.4. to R.6. Augustus to Valerian.

CELENDERIS (*Kelnar*).—Aut. AR. R.4. to R.5. Æ. R.4. to R.8. Imperial, Æ. R.8. Lucius Verus to Etruscilla.

Some of the autonomous coins bear the head of Antiochus IV.

CENNATI (———).

The name of the *Cennati* is found on the coins of Olba and of Diocaesarea.

CODRIGAE (———).

The name of this town is found on coins of Tarsus in Cilicia.

COLYBRASSUS (———).—Imperial, Æ. R.6. M. Aurelius to Saloninus.

CORACESIUM (*Castel Ubaldo*).—Imperial, Æ. R.7. Trajan to Salonina.

CORYCUS (*Korkum, Korcu, Korigos*).—Aut. Æ. R.4. Imperial, Æ. R.3. to R.6. Trajan to Gallienus.

CILICIA (*continued*).

DIOSCAESAREA (———).—Imperial, Æ. R.6. Severus to Philip.

DORON (———).—Imperial, Æ. R.8. Marcus Aurelius.

OENIANDOS. EPIPHANEA (———).—Aut. Æ. R.8. Imperial, Æ. R.8. Hadrian to Gordian.

FLAVIOPOLIS (———).—Imperial, Æ. R.4. to R.6. Domitian to Valerian.

GERMANICOPOLIS? (———).—Aut. Æ. R.8.

HAMAXIA? (———).—Aut. Æ. R.8.

HIEROPOLIS (———).—Aut. Æ. R.5. to R.7. Imperial, Æ. R.4. to R.6. M. Aurelius to Caracalla.

Some of the autonomous coins bear the head of Antiochus IV. Those bearing the name of Castabala, formerly attributed to this town, have been restored to Castabala in Cappadocia.

IOTAPE (———).—Imperial, Æ. R.7. Philip Junior to Valerian.

IRENOPOLIS (———).—Aut. Æ. R.6. Domitian to Gallienus.

Some bear the name of Zephyrium in alliance.

LACANATIS, REGIO (———).—Imperial, Æ. R.4. to R.8. With the name or the head of Antiochus IV.

LAERTE (———).—Aut. With head of Antiochus. Æ. R.8. Imperial, Æ. R.6. Trajanus to Saloninus.

MALLUS (*Mallo*).—Aut. AR. R.7. Æ. R.7. Imperial, Æ. R.7. Augustus to M. Aurelius.

MEGARSUS (———).—Aut. Æ. R.8.

MOPSUS, MOPSUESTIA (*Messis*).—Aut. With head of Antiochus IV. Æ. R.5. to R.7. Imperial, Æ. R.5. to R.7. Domitian to Gallienus.

NAGIDIS (———).—Aut. AR. R.4. to R.8. Æ.? R.8.

NEPHELIS NEPHELIDDA (———).—Aut. AR. R.6. Æ. R.8.

OLBA (———).—Colonial Imperial, Æ. R.8. Sept. Severus.

PRIESTS AND PRINCES OF OLBA.

POLEMON, Cotemporary of M. Antony.—Imperial, Æ. R.7.

These coins bear the name of the *Cennati*.

AIAX, Cotemporary of Augustus.—Aut. Æ. R.7. Imperial, Æ. R.8.

SELEUCIA ad CALYCADNUM (*Selefke*).—Aut. Æ. R.2. to R.3. Imperial, AR. R.8. Æ. R.1. to R.6. Tiberius to Gallienus.

CILICIA (*continued*).

SELINUS, TRAJANOPOLIS (*Selenti*).—Aut. AR. R.8. Æ. R.8. Imperial, Æ. R.8. Of Lucilla.

SOLI, SOLOPOLIS, POMPEIOPOLIS (*Lamuzo*)—With the name of Soli. Aut. AR. R.3. to R.5. Æ. R.4.—With the name of Solopolis. Imperial, Æ. R.8. Of Pompey the Great.—With the name of Pompeiopolis. Aut. Æ. R.4. to R.6. Imperial, Æ. R.4. to R.8. Pompey the Great to Trebonianus.

SYEDRA (———).—Imperial, Æ. R.1. to R.4. Nero to Salonina.

TARSUS (*Tarsus, Tersine, Tarso, Tersus*).—Aut. AR. R.7. Æ. C. to R.6. Imperial, AR. R.4. to R.8. Æ. C. to R.7. Augustus to Salonina.

ZEPHYRIUM (———).—Aut. Æ. R.6. Imperial, Æ. R.6. Of Hadrian and Trebonian.

On a coin of Trebonian the name of Irenopolis is found in alliance.

UNCERTAIN COINS OF CILICIA.—Aut. AV. R.5. AR. R.3. to R.8. With Phœnician and unknown characters.

ISLANDS ADJACENT TO CILICIA.

ELAEUSA, SEBASTE (*La Piccola Isola di Curco*).—With the name of Alaeusa. Aut. Æ. R.4. to R. 6.—With the name of Sebaste. Aut. Æ. R.6. to R.7. Imperial, Æ. R.4. to R.5. Augustus to Valerian.

On the autonomous coins the heads of Antiochus IV. and Iotape are found.

KINGS OF CILICIA.

TARCONDIMOTUS I., Cotemporary of J. Caesar and Augustus.—Aut. Æ. R.8.

PHILOPATOR I. or II., Cotemporary of Augustus.—Aut. Æ. R.8.

CYPRUS INSULA.

CYPRUS INSULA (*Kipri, Cipri, Cipro, Kipru-Adassi*).

CYPRUS in genere.—Aut? Æ. R.8. Imperial, AR. R.3. Æ. R.2. to R.8. Augustus to Macrinus.

IDALIUM? (*Dalin*).—Aut?

MARIUM (———).—Aut. AR. R.6.

PAPHUS (*Baffo*).—Aut. AR. R.8.

SALAMIS (*Costanza*).—Aut. AR. R.8.

CYPRUS INSULA (*continued*).

ISLANDS ADJACENT TO CYPRUS.

CLIDES? (———).—Aut. Æ. R.8. ?

KINGS OF CYPRUS.

These coins were for a long time ranged with those of Cyrene, but have been rightly assigned by Mr. H. P. Borrell, in a work entitled "Notice sur quelques Médailles Grecques des Rois de Chypre." 4to. Paris, 1836.

EVAGORUS I. [B. C. 350].—AV. R.8.

NICOCLES, King of Paphos.—AR. R.6. to R.8.

EVAGORUS II.—AV. R.7. AR. R.7.

PYTHAGORAS.—AR. R.7.

PNYTAGORUS.—AV. R.8. AR. R.7.

MENELAUS —AV. R.8.

LYDIA.

LYDIA in genere.

A coin of Blaundos bears the legend, KOINON·ΠΡΩ·ΛΥΔΙΑC.

ACRASSUS (———).—Aut. Æ. R.5. Imperial, Æ. R.3. to R.6. Trajan to Sev. Alexander.

ANINESUM (———).—Aut. Æ. R.7.

ANOLUS? (———).—Aut? Æ. R.8.

APOLLONIA (———).—Imperial, Æ. R.6.

APOLLONIS or APOLLONIDEA (———).—Aut. Æ. R.4. Imperial, Æ. R.5. to R.8. Domitian to Sev. Alexander.

APOLLONOSHIERON (———).—Aut. Æ. R.6. Imperial, Æ. R.6. Tiberius, Nero, Hostilian.

ASIA (———).—Aut. Æ. R.8. Imperial, Æ. R.4. Trajan to Gordian.

A coin of the latter emperor bears the name of Smyrna in alliance.

ATTALIA (———).—Aut. Æ. R.4. to R.6. Imperial, Æ. R.4. to R.6. Trajan to Geta.

AURELIOPOLIS (———).—Aut. Æ. R.8. Imperial, Æ. R.6. Of Commodus and Gordian.

BAGAE (———).—Aut. Æ. R.4. to R.5. Imperial, AR. R.8. Æ. R.4. to R.6. Nero to Saloninus.

The site of Bagae is not known, but a coin of Gallienus bears the name of *Temenothyræ* in Lydia in alliance.

LYDIA (*continued*).

BLAUNDOS (———).—Aut. Æ. R.3. to R.6. Imperial, Æ. R.3. to R.5. Nero to Volusian.

BRIULA (———).—Aut. Æ. R.7. Imperial, Æ. R.7. Trajan, Antoninus and M. Aurelius.

CHARACA? (———).—Imperial of Drusus, Æ. R.8. (*Millingen*).

CAYSTRIANI (———).—Aut. Æ. R.6.

CILBIANI in genere.—Aut. Æ. R.8.

CILBIANI inferiores.—Aut. Æ. R.7. Imperial, Æ. R.7. Of Augustus.

CILBIANI superiores.—Aut. Æ. R.8. Imperial, Æ. R.4. to R.5. Augustus to Geta.

CILBIANI Nicaeenses.—Aut. Æ. R.8. Imperial, R.4. to R.7. Of Caius and Lucius Caesar to Geta.

CILBIANI Pergameni.—Imperial R.5. to R.7. Of Domitian.

CILBIANI Nicaeenses Pergameni.—Imperial, Æ. R.4. to R.7. Domitian to Caracalla.

CILBIANI Ceaetei.—Aut. Æ. R.8.

DALDIS (———).—Aut. Æ. R.4. to R.6. Imperial, Æ. R.3. to R.6. Augustus to Philip Junior.

DIOSHIERON (———).—Aut. Æ. R.6. Imperial, Æ. R.4. to R.6. Augustus to Sev. Alexander.

GORDUS-JULIA (*Gordu*).—Aut. Æ. R.3. Imperial, Æ. R.2. to R.4. Trajan to Gallienus.

HERACLEA (———).—Imperial, Æ. R.4. Hadrian to Maximin.

HERMOCAPELIA (———).—Aut. Æ. R.4. Imperial, Æ. R.4. to R.6. Hadrian to Hostilian.

HERMUPOLIS (———).—Aut. Æ. R.6. Imperial, Æ. R.6. Trebonianus.

HIEROCAESAREA (———).—Aut. Æ. R.4. to R.5. Imperial, Æ. R.5. to R.6. Vespasian to Caracalla.

HYPAEPA (*Pyrge, Birge*).—Aut. Æ. R.4. Imperial, Æ. R.2. to R.7. Augustus to Salonina.

HYRCANIA (———).—Aut. Æ. R.4. Imperial, Æ. R.4. to R.6. Hadrian to Philip Jun.

MAEONIA (———).—Aut. Æ. R.3. to R.4. Imperial, Æ. R.3. to R.6. Nero to Etruscilla.

LYDIA (*continued*).

MAGNESIA ad SIPYLUM (*Manassie*).—Aut. Æ. R.3. to R.5. Imperial, Æ. R.2. to R.8. Augustus to Salonina.

On a coin of Valerian the name of Smyrna is found in alliance.

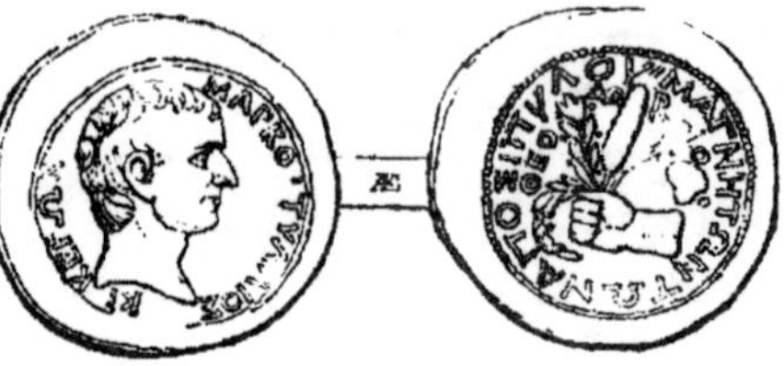

MASTAURA (*Tiria*).—Aut. Æ. R.7. Imperial, Æ. R.4. to R.6. Tiberius to Saloninus.

MOSSINA or MOSSINUS (———).—Aut. Æ. R.6.

MOSTENE (———).—Aut. Æ. R.7. Imperial, Æ. R.3. to R.6. Claudius to Salonina.

NACRASA (———).—Aut. Æ. R.4. Imperial, Æ. R 3. to R.5. Domitian to Geta.

ORESTEI ? (———).—Imperial. Of Commodus. Æ. R.8. In alliance with Philadelphia.

PACTOLUS (———).—Aut. Æ. R.8.

This town is not noticed by the ancient geographers.

PHILADELPHIA (*Ala-Chiehere*).—Aut ? AR. R.8. Æ. C. to R.4. Imperial, Æ. R.2. to R.6. Augustus to Valerian.

Both the autonomous and imperial coins have the name of Smyrna in alliance; that of Ephesus is also found on the latter.

SAETTENI (———).—Aut. Æ. R.3. to R.4. Imperial, Æ. R.3. to R.5. Hadrian to Salonina.

SARDES (*Sarde, Sard, Sart*).—Aut. AR. Cistophori. R.6. Æ. C. to R.4. Imperial, Æ. C. to R.8. Augustus to Valerian Jun.

The imperial coins bear the names of *Pergamus* in Mysia, *Ephesus*, *Smyrna*, and *Hypæpa* in alliance.

SILANDUS (———).—Aut. Æ. R.6. Imperial, Æ. R.5. to R.7. Domitian to Caracalla.

TABALA (———).—Aut. Æ. R.6. Imperial, Æ. R.6. to R.7. Trajan to Gordian and Tranquillina.

TEMENOTHYRAE (———).—Aut. Æ. R.4. to R.6. Imperial, Æ. R.4. to R.6. Mamaea to Saloninus.

The imperial have sometimes the name of *Bagae* in alliance.

LYDIA (*continued*).

THYATIRA (*Ak-Hyssar*).—Aut. Æ. R.1. to R.4. Imperial, Æ. C. to R.8. Augustus to Saloninus.

The Autonomous coins bear the name of ***Smyrna*** in alliance.

THYESSUS (———).—Aut. Æ. R.8.

TMOLUS (*Buz-Daghi*).—Aut. Æ. R.7. Imperial, Æ. R.7. Sabina and Faustina.

TOMARENA (———).—Aut. Æ. R.7.

TRALLES-SELEUCIA (*Sultan-Hyssar*).—Aut. (Cistophori) AR. R.5. to R.7. Æ. R.2. to R.5. Imperial, AV. R.8. Æ. R.1. to R.7. Augustus to Valerian Jun.

On the Imperial coins the names of ***Amorium, Ephesus, Laodicea, Pergamus, Smyrna***, and ***Synnada*** are found in alliance.

PHRYGIA.

PHRYGIA in genere.—Imperial, Æ. R.4. to R.6. Of Nero, Vespasian, and Caracalla and Plautilla. (*Struck at Apamea.*)

ACMONIA (———).—Aut. Æ. R.4. Imperial, Æ. R.3. to R.6. Tiberius to Saloninus.

ACCILLEA (———).—Imperial, Æ. R.7. Of Gordian III.

AEZANIS (———).—Aut. Æ. R.3. to R.5. Imperial, Æ. C. to R.7. Julius Cæsar to Gallienus.

ALIA (———).—Aut. Æ. R.7. Imperial, Æ. R.5. Of Gordianus.

AMORIUM (*Hergian, Amoria*).—Aut. Æ. R.5. Imperial, Æ. R.5. to R.6. Augustus to Gallienus.

On the Imperial coins we find the name of ***Tralles*** in alliance.

ANCYRA (*Angur*).—Aut. Æ. R.4. to R.5. Imperial, Æ. R.4. to R.6. Nero to Gallienus.

APAMEA (*Afiun-Kara-Hyssar*).—Aut. (Cistophori) AR. R.4. to R.7. Æ. C. to R.4. Imperial, Æ. R.2. to R.6. Augustus to Saloninus.

A coin of Trebonian bears the name of ***Ephesus*** in alliance.

ATTAEA (———).—Aut. Æ. R.5. Imperial, Æ. R.4. to R.6. Augustus to Geta.

ATTUDA (———).—Aut. Æ. R.4. to R.5. Imperial, Æ. R.4. to R.5. Augustus to Saloninus.

ATTUSIA, or ATUSIA (———)—Aut. Æ. R.8.

BRIANA (———).—Aut. Æ. R.8. Imperial, Æ. R.8. Of J. Domna.

PHRYGIA (*continued*).

BRUZUS (———).—Imperial, Æ. R.3. to R.6. Antoninus to Gordian.

CADI (*Kedus*).—Aut. Æ. R.3. to R.8. Imperial, Æ. R.3. to R.7. Claudius to Gallienus.

An autonomous coin bears the head of *Midas*. Some of the Imperial have the name of *Gordus-Julia*, in Lydia, in alliance.

CERETAPE (———).—Aut. Æ. R.6. Imperial, Æ. R.5. to R.6. Plotina to Sept. Severus.

Some bear the name of *Hierapolis* in alliance.

CIBYRA (*Buruz, Buras*).—Aut. AR. R.4. to R.7. Æ. R.4. Imperial, Æ. R.4. to R.6. Hadrian to Etruscilla.

Some bear the name of *Hierapolis* in alliance.

KINGS OF CIBYRA.

MOGETES (B. C. —— ?).—Aut. Æ. R.4. to R.6.

AMINTAS (B. C. —— ?).—Aut. Æ. R.6.

CHOTIS (B. C. —— ?).—Aut. AR. R.8.

CIDRAMUS (———).—Aut. Æ. R.8. Imperial, Æ. R.6. M. Aurelius to Jul. Maesa.

CIDYESSUS (———).—Imperial, Æ. R.6. Domitian, Caracalla, and Philip Senior and Junior.

COLOSSAE (*Kolos*).—Aut. Æ. R.5. to R.6. Imperial, Æ. R.5. to R.7. Agrippina the Elder, Commodus, and Gordian.

COTIAEUM (*Kutaye-Cutaya*).—Aut. Æ. R.4. to R.5. Imperial, R.2. to R.7. Tiberius to Salonina.

On a coin of Caracalla the name of *Ephesus* is found in alliance.

DIOCOCLIA (———).—Imperial, Æ. R.8. Of Gordian.

DIONYSOPOLIS (———).—Aut. Æ. R.7. Imperial, Æ. R.8. Augustus to Annia Faustina.

DOCIMEUM (*Kara-Chiehere*).—Aut. Æ. R.4. to R.5. Imperial, Æ. R.4. to R.7. Nero to Gordian.

DORYLAEUM (*Eski-Chiehere*).—Imperial, Æ. R.4. to R.7. Augustus to Philip Junior.

EPICTETUS (———).—Aut Æ. R.2. to R.4.

EUCARPIA (———).—Aut. Æ. R.3. to R.5. Imperial, Æ. R.3. to R.6. Augustus to Trebonianus.

EUMENIA (———).—Aut. Æ. R.4. to R.6. Imperial, Æ. R.4. to R.7. Augustus to Gallienus.

On the imperial the name of *Attuda* in Phrygia and *Trapezopolis* in Caria are found in alliance.

PHRYGIA (*continued*).

HIERAPOLIS (*Pambuk-Kalessi*).—Aut. Æ. R.2. to R.4. Imperial, Æ. R.2. to R.6. Augustus to Gallienus.

The names of several other cities are found on these coins in alliance; among them Smyrna and Ephesus.

HYRGALEA (————).—Aut. Æ. R.7 Imperial, Æ. R.7. Domna to Caracalla.

IPSUS (————).—Aut. Æ. R.8.

JULIA (————).—Imperial, Æ. R.4. to R.7. Agrippina Junior to Valerian Junior.

LAODICEA (*Eski-Hyssar*).—Aut. (Cistophori) AR. R.6. Æ. R.4. to R.6. Imperial, Æ. R.1. to R.7. Augustus to Saloninus.

The names of several other cities are found on these coins in alliance; among them Smyrna and Ephesus.

LYSIAS (————).—Aut. Æ. R.7. Imperial, Æ. R.8. Of Gordian.

An autonomous coin bears the name of *Apollonia* in Pisidia.

METROPOLIS (*Tireh*).—Aut. Æ. R.4. Imperial, Æ. R.1. to R.4. Nero to Saloninus.

MIDAEUM (*Seid-Gazi*).—Imperial, Æ. R.3. to R.6. Caligula to Philip Junior.

The head of *Midas* is found on a coin of Gordian.

MOCOCLIA.

See *Diococlia*, to which place the coins bearing this name are assigned.

NACOLEA (————).—Aut. Æ. R.8. Imperial, Æ. R.4. to R.7. Titus to Gordian.

OTRUS (————).—Aut. Æ. R.7. Imperial, Æ. R.6. to R.7. Domna and Geta.

PELTAE (————).—Aut. Æ. R.6. Imperial, Æ. R.8. A. Pius and S. Alexander.

PHILOMELIUM (*Ilgun*).—Aut. Æ. R.3. to R.4. Imperial, Æ. R.3. to R.4. Augustus to Trebonian.

PRYMNESSUS (————).—Aut. Æ. R.6. Imperial, Æ. R.3. to R.5. Augustus to Gallienus.

The coins of King *Midas* bear the name of this city.

SALA (————).—Aut. Æ. R.4. to R.6. Imperial, Æ. R.3. to R.7. Domitia to H. Etruscus.

SEBASTE (————).—Aut. Æ. R.6. Imperial, Æ. R.6. Domna to Gordian.

SIBIDUNDA (*Sibildi*).—Imperial, Æ. R.4. Of Caracalla.

Phrygia (*continued*).

Siblia (———).—Aut. Æ. R.8.

Stectorium (———).—Aut. Æ. R.6. Imperial, Æ. R.4. to R.7. Faustina Junior, Philip, and Philip Junior.

Synaos (———).—Aut. Æ. R.5. to R.6. Imperial, Æ. R.5. to R.8. Nero, Agrippina the Younger, M. Aurelius, and L. Verus.

Synnada (*Sandakli*).—Aut. Æ. R.3. to R.6. Imperial, Æ. R.4. to R.6. Augustus to Gallienus.

Themisonium (*Teseni*).—Aut. R.8. Imperial, Æ. R.5. to R.6. Antoninus to Philip Junior.

Tiberiopolis (———).—Aut. Æ. R.4. Imperial, Æ. R.4. to R.7. Trajan to Caracalla.

Timbrias (———).—Imperial, R.8. Hadrian.

Trajanopolis (———).—Aut. Æ. R.3. to R.6. Imperial, Æ. R.7. Trajan to Gordian.

Trimenothyrae (———).—Aut. Æ. R.7.

Kings of Phrygia.

Midas (B. C. — ?).—Aut. (with the name of the city *Prymnessus*) Æ. R.6. to R.7.

GALATIA.

Galatia in genere.—Imperial, Æ. R.2. to R.6. Nero to Trajan.

Ancyra (*Enguri, Angora*).—Imperial, Æ. C. to R.4. Nero to Salonina.

Germe (*Ghermesti*).—Colonial, Imperial, Æ. R.7. Domitian to Etruscilla. (Latin legends.)

Pessinus (*Uchiache-Kioy*).—Aut. Æ. R.7. Imperial, R.2. to R.7. Augustus to Geta.

Sebaste (———).—Aut. Æ. R.6. Imperial, Æ. R.4. to R.7. Claudius to Gordian.

Tavium (———).—Imperial, Æ. R.4. to R.7. M. Aurelius to Elagabalus.

Tectosages (———)

See the coins of *Sebaste* in Galatia.

Tolistobogi (———).—Imperial, Æ. R.6. Of Nero.

This name is also found on an imperial coin of *Pessinus* in Galatia.

GALATIA (*continued*).

TROCMI (———).—Aut. Æ. R.8. Imperial, Æ. R.6. Domitian to A. Pius.

The name of *Trocmi* is also found on an imperial coin of *Tavium* in Galatia.

KINGS OF GALATIA.

BITOVIUS (*period unknown*).—Aut. Æ. R.4.

BITOVIOGOGUS (*idem*).—Aut. Æ. R.7.

BITUCUS (*idem*).—Aut. Æ. R.6.

CAEANTOLUS (*idem*).—Aut. Æ. R.6.

PSAMYTES (*idem*).—Aut. Æ. R.6.

RIGANTICUS (*idem*).—Aut. Æ. R.8.

See the *Revue Numismatique*, Vol. I.

AETOLOBUS (*idem*).—Aut. Æ. R.6.

BROGITARUS (B. C. 56).—Aut. AR. R.8.

DEIOTARUS (Cotemporary of Pompey and Julius Cæsar).—Aut. Æ. R.8.

AMYNTAS (Cotemporary of M. Antony and Augustus).—Aut. Æ. R.3.

CAPPADOCIA.

CASTABALA (*Kalat-Masman*).—Aut. Æ. R.7. Imperial, Æ. R.6. Of Faustina Sen., Macrinus and Son, and Elagabalus.

COMANA (*Al-Bostan*).—Colonial Imperial (*Latin legends*), Æ. R.6. A. Pius and Caracalla.

CYBISTRA (*Bustereh*).—Aut. Æ. R.6.

EUSEBIA, CAESAREA (*Kayserie*).—With the name of Eusebia. Aut. Æ. R.4. to R.8.—With the name of Eusebia and Caesarea. Aut. Æ. R.6.—With the name of Caesarea only. Aut. Æ. R.8. Imperial, AV. R.8. AR. R.2 to R.7. Pot. R.4. to R.6. Æ. C to R.6. Tiberius to Gordian.

On some of the imperial coins the name of Smyrna is found in alliance.

SARICHA (———).—Aut. Æ. R.8

TYANA (*Tiana*).—Aut. Æ. R.6. Imperial, Æ.3. to R.6. Nero to Severus. Colonial Imperial, Æ. R.3. to R.6. Of Caracalla.

KINGS OF CAPPADOCIA.

ARIARATHES IV. [From —— to 220 B.C.]—Aut. AR. R.8.

CAPPADOCIA (*continued*).

ARIARATHES V., EUSEBES [From 220 to 166 B. C.]—Aut. Æ. R.2. to R.3.

ARIARATHES VI., PHILOPATOR [From 166 to 132 B. C.]—Aut. AR. R.3. to R.7.

ARIARATHES VII., EPIPHANES [From 132 to 117 B. C.]—Aut. AR. R.2.

ARIARATHES VIII., PHILOMETOR [From 117 to 105 B. C.]—Aut. AR. R.3.

ARIOBARZANES I., PHILOROMAEUS [From 91 to 58 B. C.]—Aut. AR. R.2.

ARIOBARZANES II., PHILOPATOR [From 66 to 52 B. C.]—Aut. AR. R.6.

This king reigned jointly with his father the first eight years.

ARIOBARZANES III., PHILOROMAEUS, EUSEBES [From 52 to 42 B. C.]—Aut. AR. R.4. to R.6.

ARIARATHES X., EUSEBES, PHILADELPHUS [From 42 to 36 B. C.]—Aut. AR. R.6.

ARCHELAUS [From 36 B. C. to 17 A. D.]—Aut. AR. R.7.

ARMENIA.

ARMENIA in genere (no coins.)

There are no civic coins of *Armenia*. The *Imperial Greek* and *Roman* coins of Trajan, bearing the name of *Armenia*, were struck in commemoration of his victories in that country.

KINGS OF ARMENIA.

ARSAMES [about 245 B. C.]—Aut. Æ. R.8.

SAMES (uncertain period.)—Aut. Æ. R.7. With his Queen Pythadoris on the reverse.

XERSES [about 148 B. C.]—Aut. Æ. R.8.

The silver coin is a forgery.

ABDISSARUS (uncertain period.)—Aut. Æ. R.8.

MITHRIDATES [about 148 B. C.]—Aut. Æ. R.8.

TIGRANES.

Classed with those of the kings of Syria.

ARTAVASDES [61 to 34 B. C.]—Aut. Æ. R.8.

TIGRANES IV. and his Queen ERATO [——— B. C.]—Aut. Æ. R.7.

ARISTOBULUS and his Queen SALOME [——— B. C.?]—Aut. Æ. R.8.

ARMENIA (*continued*).

ARTAXIAS with the head of GERMANICUS [——— B. C.]—AR. unique?

Numismatic Chronicle, Vol. II., p. 4.

SYRIA.

SYRIA in genere.—Æ. C. to R.2. Trajan, Domna, and Caracalla.

KINGS OF SYRIA.

SELEUCUS I., NICATOR [312 to 282 B. C.]—AV. R.7. AR. R.3. to R.5. Æ. C. to R.2.

ANTIOCHUS I., SOTER [282 to 262 B. C.]—AV. R.8. AR. R.2. to R.4. Æ. C. to R.2.

ANTIOCHUS II., DEUS [262 to 247 B. C.]—AV. R.8. AR. R.4. to R.8.

SELEUCUS II., CALLINICUS, POGON [247 to 226 B. C. —AV. R.8. AR. R.6. Æ. C. to R.4.

ANTIOCHUS, HIERAX [226 B. C.]—AR. R.5. to R.7.

SELEUCUS III., CERAUNUS [about 227 to 224 B. C.]—AR. R.4.

ANTIOCHUS III., MAGNUS [223 to 187 B. C.]—AR. R.4. to R.6. Æ. C. to R.3.

ACHAEUS ——— [about 227 B. C.]—AV. R.8. Æ. R.6.

SELEUCUS IV., PHILOPATER [187 to 176 B. C.]—AR. R.4. Æ. R.3.

ANTIOCHUS IV., DEUS, EPIPHANES, NICEPHORUS [176 to 164 B. C.]—AV. R.8. AR. R.4. to R.8. Æ. C. to R.8.

ANTIOCHUS V. EUPATOR [164 to 163 B. C.].—AR. R.5. Æ. R.6.

DEMETRIUS I. SOTER [163 to 151 B. C.].—AV. R.8. AR. R.2. to R.6. Æ. C. to R.3.

The silver coins bear the name of *Laodice* his Queen.

ALEXANDER I. BALA, THEOPATOR, EVERGETES, EPIPHANES, NICEPHORUS [151 to 146 B. C.].—AR. R.3. to R.4. Æ. C. to R.6.

DEMETRIUS II. DEUS, PHILADELPHUS, NICATOR [146 to 126 B. C.].—AR. R.4. to R.6. Æ. C. to R.5.

ANTIOCHUS VI. EPIPHANES, DIONYSUS [146 to 143 B. C.]. AR. R.4. to R.6. Æ. C. to R.2.

SYRIA (*continued*).

TRYPHON, AUTOCRATOR [143 to 138 B. C.].—AR. R.8. Æ. R.1. to R.6.

ANTIOCHUS VII. SIDETES, EVERGETES [138 to 127 B. C.].—AR. R.3. to R.6. Æ. C. to R.2.

ALEXANDER II. ZEBINA [129 to 123 B. C.].—AR. R.3. to R.5. Æ. C. to R.6.

SELEUCUS V. [about 120 B. C.]

As there were several kings of the name of Seleucus, many of their brass coins are confounded with each other. The coins of Seleucus V. cannot be identified. This is also the case with some of the brass coins of the *Antiochi* and Demetrii.

CLEOPATRA, DIVA, CERES.—AR. R.7. Æ. R.1. to R.4.

Mother of Antiochus VIII.

ANTIOCHUS VIII. GRYPHUS EPIPHANES [123 to 97 B. C.].—AR. R.5. to R.7. Æ. R.1. to R.6.

ANTIOCHUS IX. CYZICENUS PHILOPATOR [113 to 96 B. C.].—AR. R.5. to R.6. Æ. C. to R.3.

SELEUCUS VI. EPIPHANES NICATOR [96 to 95 B. C.].—AR. R.5. to R.6. Æ. R.2.

ANTIOCHUS X. EUSEBES PHILOPATOR [about 95 B. C.].—AR. R.6. Æ. R.2.

ANTIOCHUS XI. EPIPHANES, PHILADELPHUS [about 95 B. C.].—Æ. R.4.

PHILIPPUS EPIPHANES, PHILADELPHUS [about 95 B. C.].—AR. R.2.

DEMETRIUS III. DEUS, PHILOPATOR, SOTER, PHILOMETOR, EUSEBES, CALLINICUS, EVERGETES [95 to 89 B. C.].—AR. R.7. Æ. R.1. to R.3.

ANTIOCHUS XII. DIONYSUS, EPIPHANES, PHILOPATOR, CALLINICUS [89 to — B. C.].—Æ. R.2. to R.4.

TIGRANES, REX REGUM, DEUS, MAGNUS [83 to 66 B. C.].—AR. R.6. Æ. R.2. to R.4.

King of *Armenia* and *Syria*.

ANTIOCHUS XIII. ASIATICUS, EPIPHANES, PHILOPATOR, CALLINICUS [about 60 B. C.].—Æ. R.4.

COMMAGENE.

COMMAGENE in genere.—Aut. Æ. R.2.

ANTIOCHIA ad EUPHRATEM (*Anteb*).—Imperial, Æ. R.5. Of Aurelius and Verus.

COMMAGENE (*continued*).

ANTIOCHIA sub TAURO (———).—Imperial, Æ. R.7. Faustina Junior.

DOLICHE (*Deluk*).—Imperial, Æ. R.1. to R.4. Aurelius, Verus, and Commodus.

GERMANICIA CAESAREA (*Germanigh*).—Imperial, Æ. R.1. to R.8. Hadrian to Valerian.

SAMOSATA (*Samosata, Chiamsat, Samsat*).—Aut. Æ. R.2. to R.6. Imperial, Æ. C. to R.4. Hadrian to Tr. Decius.

ZEUGMA (*Zekme*).—Aut. Æ. R.8. Imperial, Æ. C. to R.4. Antoninus Pius to Philip Junior.

KINGS OF COMMAGENE.

ANTIOCHUS IV. EPIPHANES, MAGNUS, DEUS [40 to 70 B. C.]. —Aut. Æ. R.2. to R.6.

Some of these coins bear the name of *Iotape*, his queen.

IOTAPE, wife of Antiochus IV.—Aut. Æ. R.3. to R.6.

EPIPHANES and CALLINICUS, sons of Antiochus IV. [about 70 B. C.].—Aut. Æ. R.1. to R.4.

Some of these coins bear the name of their father.

CYRRHESTICA.

CYRRHESTICA in genere (no coins).

The coins formerly supposed of *Cyrrhestica* in genere have been restored to *Cyrrhus* as below.

BEROEA (*Halep, Aleppo*).—Imperial, Æ. C. to R.1. Trajan to Antoninus.

CYRRHUS (*Korus*).—Aut. (with the names of Syrian kings), Æ. R.3. Imperial, Æ. C. to R.2. Trajan to Philip Junior.

HIEROPOLIS (*Membrik, Bambuk*).—Aut. Æ. R.4. to R.6. Imperial. C. to R.4. Trajan to Philip Junior.

CHALCIDENE.

CHALCIS (———).—Aut. Æ. R.4. Imperial, Æ. C. to R.3. Trajan to Commodus.

KINGS AND TETRARCHS OF CHALCIDENE.

PTOLEMAEUS, TETRARCH [—— to 60 B. C.].—Aut. Æ. R.6.

CHALCIDENE (*continued*).

LYSANIAS, TETRARCH, son of PTOLEMAEUS [—— to 60 B. C.].—Aut. Æ. R.6.

HERODES III., KING.—See the Kings of Judaea.

AGRIPPA II., KING.—See the Kings of Judaea.

PALMYRENE.

PALMYRA (*Tadmur*).—Aut. Æ. R.8.

The coins of the Princes of *Palmyra* are ranged with the imperial Greek struck in Egypt.

SELEUCIS, PIERIA.

SELEUCIS, PIERIA, FRATRES POPULI in genere.—Aut. Æ. R.2. to R.4.

ANTIOCHIA ad ORONTEM (*Antak, Antakie*).—Aut. of the Seleucidan era. Æ. C. to R.4.—Aut. uncertain era. Æ. C. to R.2.—Aut. Actian era. Æ. C. to R.2.—Imperial, Actian era. AR. R.1. to R.4. Æ. C. to R.2. Of Augustus and Tiberius.—Aut. Caesarean era. Æ. C. to R.4.—Imperial, Caesarean era. Æ. R.1. to R.4. Augustus to Titus.—Imperial, without dates. AR. R.2. to R.8. Potin. C. to R.2. Galba to Volusian.—Imperial, with S. C. on reverse. Æ. C. to R.8. Augustus to Valerian.—Colonial Imperial, with S. C. on reverse. Æ. C. to R.2. Antoninus to Valerian Senior.

ANTIOCHENI ad DAPHNEM.—Aut. Æ. R.1. to R.2.

ANTIOCHENI, PTOLEMAIDIS.—Aut. Æ. R.2. to R.6.

ANTIOCHENI ad CALLIRHOEN.—Aut. Æ. R.1.

APAMEA (*Famiah*).—Aut. Æ. R.1. to R.2. Imperial, Æ. R.4. Of Augustus.

ARETHUSA (*Al-Rustan*).—Aut.? Æ. R.8. Imperial, Æ. R.7. Severus and Diadumenian.

BALANEA (————).—Aut. Æ. R.8. Imperial, Æ. R.7. Antony and Augustus.

EMISA (*Hams*).—Imperial, Æ. R.1. to R.4. Domitian and Antoninus.—Colonial Imperial, Potin. R.8. Æ. R.1. to R.8. Domna to Sulpicius Antoninus.

See Haym's *Tesoro Britannico*.

EPIPHANIA (*Hamah*).—Aut. Æ. R.6. to R.8. Imperial, Æ. R.3. to R.6. Tiberius to Gordian.

SELEUCIS, PIERIA (*continued*).

GABALA (*Gebele*).—Aut. Æ. R.7. Imperial, Æ. R.2. to R.6. Augustus to Julia Soaemias.

HERACLEA ? (———).—Imperial, Æ. R.4. Of Caracalla.

LAODICEA (*Latakie, Latakkia*).—Aut. AR. R.6. Æ. C. to R.4. Imperial, AR. R.7. Æ. C. to R.7. Augustus to Caracalla.—Colonial Imperial (Latin legends), Æ. C. to R.6. Severus to Valerian Senior.

On a coin of Hadrian the name of *Aradus* is found in alliance.

LARISSA (*Chizar*).—Aut. Æ. R.6.

MYRIANDRUS (———).—Imperial, Æ. R.6. to R.7. Antoninus and M. Aurelius.

NICOPOLIS SELEUCIDIS (———).—Imperial, Æ. R.4. Commodus, Sev. Alexander and Philip Senior.

PALTOS (*Boldo*).—Imperial, Æ. R.4. to R.6. Commodus to Julia Paula.

REPHANEA (———).—Imperial, Æ. R.4. Elagabus to Sev. Alexander.

RHOSUS (*Rosos*).—Aut. Æ. R.5. Imperial, Æ. R.7. Commodus to Severus.

SELEUCIA (*Suveidieh*).—Aut. AR. R.4. to R.6. Æ. R.1. to R.4. Imperial, AR. R.8. Æ. C. to R.4. Augustus to Sev. Alexander.

COELESYRIA.

CAPITOLIAS (———).—Imperial, Æ. R.6. Aurelius to Macrinus.

DAMASCUS (*Chiam, Damich, Damasco*).—Aut. Æ. R.4. to R.6. Imperial, Æ. R.1. to R.6. Augustus to Sev. Alexander. Colonial Imperial, Æ. R.1. to R.5. Sev. Alexander to Saloninus.

KING OF DAMASCUS.

ARETAS (*uncertain period*).—Aut. Æ. R.6.

HELIOPOLIS (*Baalbeck*).—Colonial Imperial, Æ. R.1. to R.5. Nerva to Gallienus.

LAODICEA ad LIBANUM (———).—Imperial, Æ. R.4. to R.6. Antoninus to Trajan Decius.

LEUCAS (———).—Aut. Æ. R.6. Imperial, Æ. R.4. to R.6. Claudius to Gordian.

TRACHONITIS ITURAEA.

CAESAREA-PANIAS, (*Baniass, Panaas*).—Aut. Æ. R.8. Imperial (Latin legends), Æ. R.1. to R.6. Augustus to Aquilia Severa.

The autonomous coins bear the name of *Agrippa* I., king of Judaea.

GABA (———).—Imperial, Æ. R.3. to R.7. Titus to Caracalla.

NERONIAS (———).—Imperial, Æ. R.5. Of Nero and Agrippa II.

DECAPOLIS.

ABILA-LEUCAS (———).—Imperial, Æ. R.6. Faustina Junior to Elagabalus.

ANTIOCHIA ad HIPPUM (———).—Imperial, Æ. R.4. to R.8. Nero, and Antoninus to Commodus.

CANATHA (———).—Imperial, Æ. R.4. Claudius to Domitian.

DIUM (———).—Imperial, Æ. R.6. Caracalla to Geta.

GADARA (———).—Imperial, Æ. R.2. to R.7. Augustus to Gordian.

GERASA (*Gerrach*).—Imperial, Æ. R.4. to R.6. Hadrian to Sev. Alexander.

PELLA (———).—Imperial, Æ. R.7. Commodus to Elagabalus.

PHILADELPHIA (*Amman*).—Aut. Æ. R.8. Imperial, Æ. R.4. to R.8. Agrippina Junior to Sev. Alexander.

PHOENICE.

PHOENICE in Genere.—Aut. Æ. R.6. Imperial, Æ. R.6. Caracalla.

BERYTUS (*Beyrat, Beyrout, Barati*).—Aut. AR. R.8. Æ. R.2. to R.5. Colonial Aut. Æ. R.6. Colonial Imperial, Æ. C. to R.7. Julius Caesar to Saloninus.

BOTRYS (*Botrun*).—Imperial, Æ. R.6. Aurelius to Soaemias.

BYBLUS (*Gebail*).—Imperial, Æ. R.3. to R.5. Augustus to Valerian Junior.

CAESAREA (ARCA) ad Libanum (*Arka, Archis, Areche*).—Imperial, Æ. R.4. Antoninus and Aurelius.—Colonial Imperial, Æ. R.5. Caracalla to Sev. Alexander.

PHOENICE (*continued*).

DEMETRIAS (———).—Aut. Æ. R.4. Imperial, Æ. R.8. Augustus to Tiberius.

The coins of this city were formerly attributed to Demetrias in Thessalia.

DORA (*Tartura*).—Aut. Æ. R.4. to R.7. Imperial, R.4. to R.6. Vespasian to Aquilia Severa.

MARATHUS (———).—Aut. Æ. R.1. to R.4. (Phoenician legends).

ORTHOSIA (———).—Aut. Æ. R.4. to R.6. Imperial, Æ. R.4. to R.6. Tiberius to Severus Alexander.

SIDON (*Seida*).—Aut. AR. R.4. to R.6. Æ. R.1. to R.4. Imperial, Æ. R.1. to R.4. Augustus to Hadrian. Colonial Imperial (Latin legends), Æ. C. to R.7. Elagabalus to Severus Alexander.

The autonomous coins bear the heads of several of the Syrian kings.

TRIPOLIS (*Tripoli di Soria, Chiam-Tarabulus*).—Aut. AR. R.6. to R.8. Æ. R.1. to R.6. Imperial, Æ. C. to R.6. M. Antony to Maximus.

KING OF TRIPOLIS.

DIONYSIUS (Cotemporary with Pompey).—Aut. Æ. R.8.

TYRUS (*Tiro, Tur*).—Aut. AR. R.2. to R.8. Æ. C. to R.4. Colonial Imperial, Æ. C. to R.8. Severus to Salonina.

ISLAND ADJACENT TO PHOENICE.

ARADUS (*Avret-Adassi, Rovad*).—Aut. C. to R.4. Æ. C. to R.3. Imperial, Æ. C. to R.8. M. Antony to Elagabalus.

UNCERTAIN COINS OF PHOENICE.

Aut. AR. R.6. Æ. C. to R.6.

GALILAEA.

ACE, PTOLEMAIS (*St. Giovanni d'Acri, Ake, Akka, Acri*).—With the name of Ace. Aut. Æ. R.8.—With Phoenician legends. Aut. AV. R.4. AR. R.4. Æ. R.6.—With the name of Ptolemais. Aut. Æ. R.4. to R.6. Imperial, Æ. R.8. Of Claudius. Colonial Imperial (Latin legends), Æ. C. to R.5. Claudius to Salonina.

SEPPHORIS, DIOSCAESAREA (*Sefuri, Safurie*).—With the name of Sepphoris. Imperial, Æ. R.2. Of Trajan.—With the name of Dioscaesarea. Aut. Æ. R.6. Imperial, Æ. R.4. to R.6. Antoninus, Commodus, and Caracalla.

GALILAEA (*continued*).

TIBERIAS (*Tabariah*).—Aut. with the name of Herod. Æ. R.4. to R.6. Imperial, Æ. R.1. to R.6. Tiberius to Antoninus.

SAMARIA.

CAESAREA (*Kayserie*).—Imperial, Æ. R.1. to R.6. Nero and Caligula. Colonial Imperial (Latin legends), Æ. C. to R.4. Domitian to Gallienus.

A coin of *Caligula* bears the name of Agrippa I. king of Judæa.

DIOSPOLIS (*Lud*).—Imperial, Æ. R.4. to R.6. Of Severus and his family.

JOPPE (*Jaffa, Giaffa*).—Aut. Æ. R.8.

NEAPOLIS (*Nabolos, Napulosa*).—Imp. Æ. R.1. to R.4. Titus to Volusian. Colonial Imperial, Æ. C. to R.4. Philip Senior to Volusian.

NYSA, SCYTHOPOLIS (*Bethsan, Beysan*).—Imperial, Æ. R.3. to R.6. Nero to Gordian.

SEBASAE (*Chiemrum*).—Aut. Æ. R.8. Imperial, Æ. R.2. to R.4. Nero to Caracalla. Colonial Imperial, Æ. R.4. Domna, Caracalla, and Geta.

JUDAEA.

JUDAEA in genere.

The coins bearing IVDAEA · CAPTA and IVDAEA · DEVICTA, as well as those with ΙΟΥΔΑΙΑΣ · ΕΑΛΩΚΥΙΑΣ (*Judaeae Captae*) were struck to celebrate the Roman conquest of that country.

AELIA CAPITOLINA (*Hierosolyma, Gerusalemme, Ilia, Kud-el Cherif*).—Colonial Imperial (Latin legends). Æ. C. to R.6. Hadrian to Hostilian.

AGRIPPIAS, ANTHEDON (———).—With the name of Agrippias. Aut. Æ. R.7.—With the name of Anthedon. Aut. Æ. R.8. Imperial, Æ. R.8. Of Caracalla.

The autonomous coins with the names of Agrippa I. and II., kings of Judaea.

ASCALON (*Askalon, Ascalona*).—Aut. AR. R.8. Æ. R.1. to R.4. Imperial, AR. R.8. Æ. R.4. Augustus to Severus Alexander.

AZOTUS (*Azud, Ezdod*).—Imperial, Æ. R.6. Severus and Domna.

ELEUTHEROPOLIS (———).—Imperial, Æ. R.6. Domna and Caracalla.

GAZA (*Gaza, Gazza*).—Aut. Æ. R.4. Imperial, Æ. R.1. to R.7. Augustus to Gordian.

JUDAEA (*continued*).

NICOPOLIS (*Amoas*).—Imperial, Æ. R.7. Trajan to Faustina Senior.

RAPHIA (———).—Imperial, Æ. R.5. to R.7. Commodus to Philip Senior.

UNCERTAIN COINS OF JUDAEA.—Imperial, Æ. R.1. to R.4. Augustus to Nero.

KINGS AND PRINCES OF JUDAEA.

SIMEON, Prince [144 to 135 B. C.].—Aut. AR. R.4. to R.8. Æ. R.1. to R.3. Aut. (Samaritan legends). AR. R.8. Struck in the time of Trajan and Hadrian.

ALEXANDER, JANNAEUS, and JONATAN, Kings [105 to 79 B. C.].—Aut. Æ. R.3. to R.5.

ANTIGONUS, King [40 to 38 B. C.].—Aut. Æ. R.5.

HERODES MAGNUS, Tetrarch and afterwards King [40 to 4 B. C.].—Aut. Æ. R.4. to R.5.

ARCHELAUS, Ethnarch of Judaea [4 B. C. to ———].—Aut. Æ. R.8.

HERODES ANTIPAS, Tetrarch of Galilaea [4 B. C. to 39 A. C.]. —Aut. Æ. R.4. to R.6. Imperial, Æ. R 7. Caligula.

PHILIPPUS, Tetrarch of Traconitis [4 B. C. to 34 A. C.].—Imperial, Æ. R.5. Of Augustus.

AGRIPPA I., MAGNUS, King [A. D. 37 to 44].—Aut. Æ. R.8. Imperial, Æ. R.5. Caligula and Claudius.

HERODES III., King of Chalcidene (Cotemporary of Claudius). —Imperial, Æ. R.7. Of Claudius.

AGRIPPA II., King of Chalcidene [48 to 99 A. D.].—Aut. Æ. R.1. to R.3. Imperial, Æ. R.1. to R.6. Nero, Vespasian, Titus, and Domitian.

ZENODORUS, Tetrarch and High Priest (Cotemporary of Augustus).—Imperial, Æ. R.5. Of Augustus.

ARABIA.

ARABIA in genere.—Imperial of Hadrian, Æ. R.5.

ADRAA (*Edrai*).—Imperial, Æ. R.7. Aurelius to Aemilian.

BOSTRA (*Bostra*).—Imperial, Æ. R.4. to R.6. Antoninus to Caracalla. Colonial Imperial (Latin legends), Æ. R.2. to R.5. Elagabalus to Trajan Decius.

ESBUS (*Esebon*).—Imperial, Æ. R.7. Of Caracalla.

MOCA (———).—Imperial, Æ. R.8. Antoninus and Septimius Severus.

ARABIA (*continued*).

PETRA (*Petra*).—Imperial, Æ. R.3. to R.5. Hadrian to Geta.

PHILIPPOPOLIS (————).—Colonial Imperial, Æ. C. to R.6. Marinus, Philip Senior, and Otacilia.

RABOTHMOBA (————).—Imperial, Æ. R.5. to R.6. S. Severus to Gordian.

MESOPOTAMIA, Diarbek.

ANTIOCHIA IN MYGDONIA (————).—Æ. Of Antiochus IV., Epiphanes. R.8. (*Millingen*).

ANTHEMUSIA (————).—Imperial Potin. R.8. Æ. R.6. to R.7. Of Domitian, Caracalla, and Maximinus.

CARRHAE (————).—Aut. Æ. R.8. Imperial, Æ. R.4. Aurelius and Verus. Colonial Imperial, Æ. R.1. to R.6. Aurelius to Tranquillina.

EDESSA (*Roha, Ursa*).—Imperial, Æ. C. to R.6. Commodus to Trajan Decius.

KINGS OF EDESSA or OSRHOENI.

The kingdom of Edessa was founded in the year 136 B.C. It was conquered by Caracalla, but was probably not a Roman province before the time of Constantine. The names of *Abgarus* and *Mannus* appear to have been common to the kings of this country, but as their coins bear the portraits of the Roman Emperors, with whom they were cotemporary, several of them are therefore thus distinguished.

MANNUS (Cotemporary with Hadrian).—No coins.

ABGARUS (Cotemporary with Aurelius and Verus).—No coins.

MANNUS (Cotemporary with Aurelius and Verus).—Imperial, Æ. R.4. to R.6. Of Aurelius, Faustina Junior, Verus, and Lucilla.

ABGARUS (Cotemporary of Commodus).—Imperial, Æ. R.3. Of Commodus.

ABGARUS (Cotemporary with Septimius Severus).—Aut. With head of Mannus, Æ. R.6. Imperial, C. to R.4. Septimius Severus.

MANNUS, Son of Abgarus (Cotemporary of Caracalla).—Aut. Æ. R.6. Imperial, Æ. R.8. Of Caracalla.

ABGARUS (Cotemporary of Gordian).—Imperial, C. to R.3. Of Gordian.

MAIOZAMALCHA (————).—Colonial Aut. Æ. R.8. (Latin legends).

MESOPOTAMIA (*continued*).

NICEPHORIUM (———).—Imperial, Æ. R.6. Gordian and Gallienus.

NISIBI (*Nisbin*).—Colonial Imperial, Æ. R.1. to R.8. Elagabalus to Trajan Decius (Latin legends).

RHESAENA (*Ras-Ayn*).—Imperial, Æ. R.4. Of Caracalla. Colonial Imperial, Æ. C. to R.5. Severus Alexander to Herennius.

SELEUCIA ad TIGRIM (*Suleiman-Pak*).—Aut. Æ. R.8.

SINGARA (*Sengiar*).—Imperial, Æ. R.1. to R.4. Severus Alexander to Philip Senior.

ZAYTA (———).—Imperial, Æ. R.8. Trajan and Septimius Severus.

UNCERTAIN COINS OF MESOPOTAMIA.—Imperial, AR. R.2. to R 6. Æ. R.2. M. Aurelius to Commodus.

BABYLONIA.

BABYLONIA in genere.—No coins.

KINGS OF BABYLONIA.

TIMARCHUS [about 160 B. C.].—Aut. Æ. R.8.

Cotemporary with Antiochus IV. of Syria.

ASSYRIA.

ATUSIA (———).—Aut. Æ. R.8. (*Millingen*).

DEMETRIAS (———).—Aut. Æ. R.8. (*Millingen*).

NINIVA, CLAUDIOPOLIS (———).—Colonial Imperial, Æ. R.7. Trajan to Gordian.

PARTHIA.

PARTHIA in genere (no coins).

The coins bearing the name of Parthia were struck by Trajan to commemorate his victories in that country.

TAMBRAX (———).—Aut. AR. R.8. Of Arsaces XI., King of Parthia.

KINGS OF PARTHIA.

ARSACES I. (*uncertain period*).—Aut. Æ. R.6.

PARTHIA (*continued*).

ARSACES II. (*idem*).—Aut. AR. R.6.

ARSACES III., ARTABANUS I. (*idem*).—No coins

ARSACES IV., PRIAPATIUS (*idem*).—Aut. AR. R.6.

ARSACES V., PHRAATES I. [190 to 165 B. C.].—Aut. AR. R.5. Æ. R.8.

ARSACES VI., MITHRIDATES I. [155 to 140 B. C.].—Aut. AR. R.5. Æ. R.6.

ARSACES VII., PHRAATES II. [140 to 126 B. C.].—Aut. AR. R.2. to R.5.

ARSACES VIII., ARTABANUS II. [about 100 B. C.].—Aut. AR. R.4.

ARSACES IX., MITHRIDATES II. [95 to 90 B.C.].—Aut. AR. R.4.

ARSACES X., MNASKYRES? (*uncertain period*).—No coins.

ARSACES XI., SANATROECES [77 to 70 B. C.].—Aut. AR. R.5.

ARSACES XII., PHRAATES III. [70 to 60 B. C.].—Aut. AR. R.4. to R.5.

ARSACES XIII., MITHRIDATES III. (*uncertain period*).—No coins.

ARSACES XIV., ORODES I. [——— to 37 B. C.].—Aut. AR. R.1. to R.8.

ARSACES XV., PHRAATES IV. (*uncertain period*).—Aut. AR. R2. to R.7.

THERMUSA, Queen of Arsaces XV.—Aut. AR. R.7.

MNASKYRES, King of Apolloniatis, (*uncertain period*).—Aut. AR. R.8. With Phraates IV.

ARSACES XVI., PHRAATACES (*idem*).—No coins.

ARSACES XVII., ORODES II. (*idem*).—No coins.

ARSACES XVIII., VONONES, or ONONES I. (Cotemporary of Augustus and Tiberius).—Aut. AR. R.8.

ARSACES XIX., ARTABANUS III. [——— to 41 A. C.].—Aut. AR. R.8.

ARSACES XX., BARDANES [——— to 47 A. C.].—Aut. AR. R.8.

ARSACES XXI., GOTARES [——— to 50 A. C.].—Aut. AR. R.1. to R.8.

MEHERDATES, Son of Arsaces XVIII. [about 49 A. C.].—Aut. AR. R.8.

ARSACES XXII., VONONES or ONONES II. (*uncertain period*).—No coins.

ARSACES XXIII., VOLAGESES I. (*idem*).—Aut. AR. R.7.

PARTHIA (*continued*).

ARSACES XXIV., ——— (*idem*).—No coins.

ARSACES XXV., PACORUS [about 84 to ——— A. C.].—Aut. AR. R.8.

ARSACES XXVI., CHOSROES [———to 122 A. C.].—Aut. Æ. R.8.

ARSACES XXVII., VOLAGESES II. [——— to 148 A. C.]. —Aut. AR. R.8.

ARSACES XXVIII., VOLAGESES III. [——— to 190 A. C.]. —Aut. AR. R.4. to R.6. Pot. R.2. to R.4. Æ. R.4.

ARSACES XXIX., VOLAGESES IV. [——— to 196 A. C.].—Aut. Potin. R.6.

ARSACES XXX., VOLAGESES V. [——— to 219 A. C.].—Aut. Potin. R.3. to R.6.

UNCERTAIN COINS OF PARTHIAN KINGS.—Aut. AR. R.1. to R.6. Æ. R.1. to R.6.

PERSIA.

No civic coins of Persia are known.

ANCIENT KINGS OF PERSIA.—Aut. AV. R.7. AR. R.2. to R.8. Æ. R.2. to R.6.

The empire of the Persians extended from the year 560 B. C., when it was formed by *Cyrus*, and ceased with Darius *Codoman*, who was subdued by Alexander the Great.

PARTHIAN KINGS OF THE RACE OF ARSACES.—ARSACIDAE.

See the preceding list.

PERSIAN KINGS OF THE RACE OF SASSAN.—SASSANIDAE.

Sassan was the grandfather of *Artaxerxes*. All these coins have Sassanian legends.

ARTAXERXES, or ARDECHIR I. [226 to 240 B. C.].—Aut. AR. R.8. Potin. R.7.

SAPOR I. [240 to 271 B. C.].—Aut. AR. R.4.

HORMUS, or HORMISDAS I. [271 to 273 B. C.].—Aut. AR. R.8.

VARARANES, or BAHRAM I. [272 to 276 B. C.].—Aut. AR. R.8.

VARARANES II. [276 to 293 B. C.].—AV. R.8. AR. R.8.

VARARANES III. [293 to 297 B. C.].—AV. R.8. AR. R.8.

NARSES [297 to 302 B. C.].—AV. R.8. AR. R.8.

SAPOR II. [309 to 397 B. C.].—AR. R.2. to R.5.

PERSIA (*continued*).

SAPOR III. [383 to 388 B. C.].—Aut. AR. R.4.

UNCERTAIN COINS OF THE SASSANIDAE.—Aut. AR. R.2. to R.4. Æ. R.2. to R.4.

BACTRIANA.

No *civic* coins of Bactriana are known.

KINGS OF BACTRIANA.*

BACTRIAN PRINCES.

DIODOTUS.—AV. Unique?

EUTHYDEMUS.—AV. Unique. AR. R.6. Æ. R.8.

DEMETRIUS.—AR. R.8.

ARKEBIAS.—AR. R.8.

But two coins are known, and these differ in the reverse. One reads *Arkelius*.

LYSIAS.—AR. Unique. Æ. R.8.

ANTIALKIDAS.—AR. R.8. Æ. R.8.

ANTIMACHUS.—AR. R.8. Æ. R.8.

AMYNTAS.—Æ. Unique?

A second coin is described in the *Journal des Savans, Fevrier*, 1839.

PHILOXENES.—AR. Unique? Æ. R.8.

BACTRO-INDIAN PRINCES.

EUKRATIDES.—AR. R.8. Æ. R.6.

HELIOCLES.—AR. R.8. Æ. Unique?

A second coin is described in the *Journal des Savans, Dec.*, 1838.

---

* For this list I am indebted to Professor H. H. Wilson, who likewise kindly furnished me with the degrees of rarity. This gentleman observes, "that it is not to be supposed that all the princes are consecutive, and that it is yet unsafe to speculate upon their classification; but they belong to collateral dynasties, of which possibly the founders are:—1. Diodotus. 2. Euthydemus. 3. Eucratides. 4. Menander. 5. Undapherres. 6. Agathocles. The last monarch is certainly one of the latest of the purely Greek kings, and reigned more in India than in Bactria, and his coins, and those of Pantaleon, bear for the local legend Indian characters, not Bactrian." It will be seen that this arrangement differs entirely from that of M. Mionnet, in the eighth Supplementary Volume of his *Descrip. de Med. Grecques*. Accounts of these singular coins, the discovery of which forms a new epoch in Numismatic research, may be found in the following works: *Journal of the Asiatic Society of Bengal* for 1834 and following years; *Numismatic Journal*, Vol. II; *Journal des Savans*, 1834, 1835, 1836, and 1839; *Journal Asiatique*, February, 1836; in several of the literary periodicals of Germany, and in the work of Professor Lassen, *Zur Geschichte der Griechischen und Indo-skythischen Könige in Baktrien*. Bonn, 1838; and that of Grotefend on *Die Münzen der Griechischen, Parthischen, und Indo-skythischen Könieg von Baktrien*. Hannover. 1839.

BACTRIANA (*continued*).

HELIOCLES and LAODIKE.—AR. Unique.

DIOMEDES.—Æ. Unique.

MENANDER.—AR. R.6. Æ. R.6.

APOLLODOTUS.—AR. R.7. Æ. R.6.

HERMAEUS.—AR. R.8. Æ. R.6.

HERMAEUS and KALLIOPE.—AR. Unique.

GRAECO-BARBARIC, BACTRO-INDIAN.

UNDAPHERRES.—AR. R.8. Æ. R.6.

VONONES.—AR. R.8.

MAYES.—Æ. R.8.

AZES.—AR. R.8. Æ. R.6.

AZILISES.—AR. R.8.

SPALIRIS.—Æ. R.7.

INDO-GREEK.

AGATHOCLES.—AR. R.8. Æ. R.8.

AGATHOKLEIA.—Æ. Unique.

PANTALEON.—Æ. R.8.

CHARACENE.

No *civic* coins are known of this country.

KINGS OF CHARACENE.

TIRAEUS (Cotemporary of Seleucus II., King of Syria).—Aut. AR. R.8.

ARTABAZES (Cotemporary of the last of the Seleucidae and Arsaces XII.).—Aut. AR. R.8.

ATTAMBILUS (Cotemporary of Augustus).—Aut. Potin. R.7.

ADINNIGAUS (Cotemporary of Tiberius).—Aut. Potin. R.8.

MONNESES (Cotemporary of Trajan).—Aut. Æ. R.8.

ARTAPANUS, or ERTAPANUS [beginning of the third century, A. D.].—Aut. Potin. R.8. Æ. R.8.

MEREDATES and UIPHOBA his Queen (*uncertain period and country, presumed of Characene*).—Æ. R.8. (*Millingen*).

AFRICA.

AEGYPTUS.

Kings of Aegypt.

Ptolemaeus I., Soter [300 to 285 B. C.].—Aut. AV. R.4. to R.6. AR. R.2. to R.5. Æ. C. to R.4.

Berenice, Wife of Soter.—Aut. Æ. C. to R.8.

Ptolemaeus II., Philadelphus [285 to 246 B. C.].—Aut. AR. R.1. to R.3. Æ. R.2. to R.4.

Arsinoe, Wife of Philadelphus.—Aut. AV. R.3. to R.8. AR. R.6. Æ. R.4.

Ptolemaeus III., Evergetes I. [246 to 221 B. C.].—Aut. AR. R.4. Æ. R.2. to R.6.—Aut. with the legend ΘΕΩΝ · ΑΔΕΛΦΩΝ restored by this king. R.4. to R.8.

Berenice, Wife of Evergetes.—Aut. AV. R.6. to R.8. AR. R.7. Æ. R.6.

Ptolemaeus IV., Philopator [221 to 204 B. C.].—Aut. AV. R.8. AR. R.8.

Arsinoe, Wife of Philopator.—Aut. AV. R.8.

Ptolemaeus V., Epiphanes [204 to 181 B. C.].—Aut. AV. R.8. AR. R.7.

Ptolemaeus VI., Philometor [181 to 146 B.C.].—Aut. AR. R.8. Potin. R.1. Æ. R.4.

Ptolemaeus VII., Evergetes II., Physcon [146 to 116 B. C.].—Aut. AR. R.2. to R.4. Æ. R.1. to R.3.

Cleopatra, Wife of Evergetes.—Aut. Æ. C. to R.4.

Ptolemaeus VIII., Soter II., Deus, Lathyrus [116 to 81 B. C.].—Aut. AV. R.8. Æ. R.1. to R.2.

Cleopatra Selene, Wife of Ptolemaeus VIII.—Aut. Æ. R.6.

Ptolemaeus IX., Alexander I. [106 to 88 B. C.].—Aut. Æ. C. to R.2.

Ptolemaeus X., Alexander II. [about 81 B. C.].—No certain coins.

He died in exile 65 B. C.

Ptolemaeus XI., Auletes, Neos, Dionysos [59 to 50 B. C.].—Aut. Æ. R.3.

Ptolemaeus XII., Dionysos [50 to 47 B. C.].—Aut. AR. R.8.

Ptolemaeus XIII. [47 to 42 B. C.].—No certain coins.

AEGYPTUS (*continued*).

CLEOPATRA, Queen [50 to 30 B. C.].—Aut. AR. R.8. Æ. R.4. to R.5. Imperial, AR. R.6. Æ. R.2. to R.5. Of M. Antonius.

UNCERTAIN COINS OF EGYPTIAN KINGS.—Aut. AR. R.1. to R.5. Æ. C. to R.4.

Numerous brass coins bear the head of Jupiter Ammon, reverse, an eagle standing on a thunderbolt, with the legend, ΒΑΣΙΛΕΩΣ ΠΤΟΛΕΜΑΙΟΥ, and from their uniformity of type and legend, cannot be appropriated. Among these are pieces of very large size, the great number of which negative M. Hennin's idea that they were not current money. They must have been minted in immense numbers, as they are extremely common. We have examined many hundreds of these coins.

COINS OF THE ROMAN EMPERORS STRUCK IN EGYPT.

The coins of the Roman emperors struck in Egypt may be distinguished by their fabric from any others issued in the provinces during the Roman dominion. Many of them are of the mixed metal termed by the French Numismatists *Potin*, but the greater number are of brittle brass, generally of the first and third sizes. Of the latter size, those of Probus, Diocletian, and Maximian are common to excess, the type of the reverse being generally an eagle, with the Greek numerals denoting the date (see page 15), but there are other reverses of much interest. Those of some of the large coins are very curious. Vide Zöega, "Numi Ægyptii Imperatorii in musco Borgiano Velitris," Romæ, 4to, 1787, and Mionnet, "Descrip." Tome VI. where a very extensive list is given.

MARCUS ANTONIUS?—Æ. R.5.

AUGUSTUS.—Æ. C. to R.4.

LIVIA.—Æ. R.2. to R.5.

CAIUS CAESAR.—Æ. R.6.

LUCIUS CAESAR.—Æ. R.6.

TIBERIUS.—Potin. R.3. Æ. R.1. to R.3.

ANTONIA.—Potin. R.4. With Claudius.

CLAUDIUS.—Potin. R.1. to R.6. Æ. C. to R.4.

MESSALINA.—Potin. R.1. With Claudius.

AGRIPPINA Junior.—Potin. R.5. Æ. C. to R.5. With and without Nero.

NERO.—Potin. C. to R.3. Æ. C. to R.5.

OCTAVIA.—Potin. R.4. With Nero.

POPPAEA.—Potin. R.3. to R.4. Æ. R.4. With Nero.

GALBA.—Potin. R.2. to R.4. Æ. R.2. to R.5.

OTHO.—Potin. R.6. Æ. R.5. to R.8.

VITELLIUS.—Potin. R.6. Æ. R.7.

VESPASIANUS.—Potin. R.3. Æ. C. to R.4. Sometimes with Titus.

AEGYPTUS (*continued*).

DOMITILLA.—Æ. R 8.

TITUS.—Potin. R.1. Æ. C. to R.4. Sometimes with Vespasian.

DOMITIANUS.—Potin. R.5. Æ. C. to R.3.

DOMITIA.—Æ. R.8. With Domitian.

NERVA.—Potin. R.4.

TRAJANUS.—Potin. R.1. to R.4. Æ. C. to R.4.

HADRIANUS.—Potin. C. to R.2. Æ. C. to R.4. Some bear the head of Antinous.

SABINA.—Potin. R.5. Æ. R.2. to R.4. Some have the head of Hadrian.

ANTINOUS.—Æ. R.4. to R.6. Some with the head of Hadrian.

AELIUS CAESAR.—Potin. R.1. Æ. R.1. to R.4.

ANTONINUS PIUS.—Potin. R.1. to R.2. Æ. C. to R.6. Pl. R.4. Sometimes with Faustina the elder.

FAUSTINA Senior.—Potin. R.2. Æ. R.4. With Antoninus.

MARCUS AURELIUS.—Potin. C. to R.4. Æ. C. to R.5. Pl. R.4. Sometimes with Faustina Junior or L. Verus.

FAUSTINA Junior.—Potin. R.2. to R.4. Æ. R.1. to R.4. Sometimes with M. Aurelius.

LUCIUS VERUS.—Potin. R.1. to R.3. Æ. C. to R.5. Sometimes with M. Aurelius.

LUCILLA.—Potin. R.5. Æ. R.5.

COMMODUS.—Potin. C. to R.2. Æ. R.1. to R.4.

CRISPINA.—Potin. R.5. Æ. R.4. to R.5.

PERTINAX.—Æ. R.8.

TITIANA.—Potin. R.7.

SEPTIMIUS SEVERUS.—Potin. R.5. Æ. R.5. to R.7.

JULIA DOMNA.—AR. R.8. Potin. R.4. Æ. R.4. Sometimes with her sons.

CARACALLA.—Potin. R.5. Æ. R.5. Sometimes with J. Domna.

GETA.—Potin. R.8. Sometimes with Julia Domna.

MACRINUS.—Potin. R.6. Æ. R.7.

DIADUMENIANUS?

ELAGABALUS.—Potin. C. to R.2. Sometimes with Julia Paula.

JULIA PAULA.—Potin. R.1. to R.3. Sometimes with Elagabalus.

AQUILIA SEVERA.—Potin. R.3.

ANNIA FAUSTINA.—Potin. R.5.

AEGYPTUS (*continued*).

JULIA SOEMIAS.—Potin. R.2. to R.4.

JULIA MAESA.—Potin. R.4.

SEVERUS ALEXANDER.—Potin. C. to R.4. Æ. R.1. to R.5.

ORBIANA.—Potin. R.5.

MAMAEA.—Potin. R.1. to R.5. Æ. R.1. to R.3.

MAXIMINUS.—Potin. R.1. to R.2.

MAXIMUS, CAESAR.—Potin. R.3.

GORDIANUS I., AFRICANUS.—Potin. R.6.

GORDIANUS II., AFRICANUS.—Potin. R.7.

BALBINUS.—Potin. R.6.

PUPIENUS.—Potin. R.6.

GORDIANUS III.—Potin. C. to R.3. Æ. R.5. Sometimes with Tranquillina.

TRANQUILLINA.—Potin. R.5.

PHILIPPUS.—Potin. C. to R.2. Æ. R.1. to R.4.

OTACILIA.—Potin. R.1. to R.2. Æ. R.2.

PHILIPPUS Junior.—Potin. R.1. to R.6. Æ. R.2. to R.4.

TRAJANUS DECIUS.—Potin. R.1. to R.2. Æ. R.4.

ETRUSCILLA.—Potin. R.5.

HERENNIUS ETRUSCUS.—Potin. R.6.

HOSTILIANUS.—Potin. R.7.

TREBONIANUS GALLUS.—Potin. R.2.

VOLUSIANUS.—Potin. R.3.

AEMILIANUS.—Potin. R.7.

CORNELIA SUPERA.—Potin. R.8.?

VALERIANUS.—Potin. C. to R.1.

GALLIENUS.—Potin. C. to R.6. Æ. R.4.

SALONINA.—Potin. C. to R.2. Æ. R.4.

SALONINUS.—Potin. R.3.

MACRIANUS Junior.—Potin. R.5.

QUIETUS.—Potin. R.6.

DOMITIUS DOMITIANUS.—Potin. R.7.

CLAUDIUS GOTHICUS.—Potin. C. to R.2. Æ. R.7.

QUINTILLUS.—Potin. R.3.

AURELIANUS.—Potin. C. to R.2. Sometimes with *Vabalathus* or *Zenobia*.

SEVERINA.—Potin. R.1.

ZENOBIA.—Potin. R.6. to R.7. Sometimes with Aurelianus.

VABALATHUS, ATHENODORUS.—Potin. R.1. to R.7. Sometimes with Aurelianus.

AEGYPTUS (*continued*).

TACITUS.—Potin. R.1. to R.2.

PROBUS.—Potin. C. to R.1.

CARUS.—Potin. R.1. to R.2.

NUMERIANUS.—Potin. C. to R.2.

CARINUS.—Potin. C. to R.2.

DIOCLETIANUS.—Potin. C. to R.1.

MAXIMIANUS HERCULES.—Potin. C. to R.2.

CONSTANTIUS CHLORUS.—Potin. R.2. to R.3.

GALERIUS MAXIMIANUS.—Potin. R.3.

EGYPTIAN NOMES OR PREFECTURES.

Vide Tóchon d'Annecy's "Recherches Hist. et Géograph. sur les Médailles des Nomes," &c. 4to.; a work in which these singular coins are very ably illustrated.

ALEXANDRIA (*Rakoti, Iskenderie, Alessandria d'Egitto*).—Imperial, Æ. R.7. Of Hadrian.

ANTAEOPOLITES (*Tkoou, Kaou, El-Kharab*).—Imperial, Æ. R.6. to R.8. Trajan and Hadrian.

APHRODITOPOLITES (*Tpih, Athfihh, Asphoun, Asfun*).—Imperial, Æ. R.6. to R.7. Trajan and Hadrian.

APOLLONOPOLITES (*Atbo, Odfou, Edfou*).—Imperial, Æ. R.7. to R.8. Hadrian and Antoninus Pius.

ARABIA (*Tiarabia*).—Imperial, Æ. R.7. Trajan and Hadrian.

ARSINOITES (*Piom, Fayyoum*).—Imperial, Æ. R.4. to R.5. Trajan and Hadrian.

ATHRIBITES (*Atrib, Athribi*).—Imperial, Æ. R.6. to R.7. Trajan and Hadrian.

BUBASTITES (*Phelbes, Belbeis, Tall-Bastah*).—Imperial, Æ. R.8. Of Hadrian.

BUSIRITES (*Pousiri, Aboussir*).—Imperial, Æ. R.7. Hadrian and A. Pius.

CABASITES (*Chbehs, Kabas*).—Imperial, Æ. R.5. Of Hadrian.

CANOPUS (*Kahi-Annoub, Abou-Kir*).—Imperial, Æ. R.8. Hadrian. (*Doubtful if genuine*).

COPTITES (*Keft, Quift, Qefth*).—Imperial, Æ. R.4. to R.6. Trajan and Hadrian.

CYNOPOLITES (*Kais, El-Gis*).—Imperial, Æ. R.6. to R.8. Hadrian.

DIOSPOLIS MAGNA (*Tape, Medineh-Tabou*).—Imperial, Æ. R.7. to R.8. Of Hadrian.

DIOSPOLIS PARVA (*Ho, Hou*).—Imperial, Æ. R.8. Hadrian and Antoninus.

AEGYPTUS (*continued*).

GYNAECOPOLITES (———).—Imperial, Æ. R.8. Of Hadrian.

HELIOPOLITES (*On, Mathariah*).—Imperial, Æ. R.8. Of Hadrian.

HEPTANOMIS (———).—Imperial, Æ. R.8. Of Hadrian. (*Doubtful if genuine*).

HERACLEOPOLITES (*Knes, Anhas*).—Imperial, Æ. R.4. to R.7. Of Hadrian.

HERMONTHITES (*Ermont, Erment, Arment, Balad-Mousa*).—Imperial, Æ. R.6. Of Hadrian.

HERMOPOLITES (*Chmoun, Ochmounein*).—Imperial, Æ. R.5. to R.6. Hadrian and Ant. Pius.

HEROOPOLITES (———).—Imperial, Æ. R.7. Of Hadrian. (*Doubtful if genuine*).

HYPSELIOTES (*Scholp*).—Imperial, Æ. R.8. Of Hadrian.

LATOPOLITES (*Sne, Esne, Asna*).—Imperial, Æ. R.8. Of Hadrian.

LEONTOPOLITES (*Thamoui, Tel-Essabe*).—Imperial, Æ. R.4. to R.6. Hadrian and A. Pius.

LETOPOLITES (*Derote*).—Imperial, Æ. R.8. Of Hadrian.

LIBYA (*Niphaiat*).—Imperial, Æ. R.8. Of Hadrian.

LYCOPOLITES (*Sioout, Aiouth, Osiouth*).—Imperial, Æ. R.7. Hadrian.

MAREOTES (*Mariouth*).—Imperial, Æ. R.8. Hadrian and Ant. Pius.

MEMPHITES (*Mesi, Memfi, Massr-el-Gadimah*).—Imperial, Æ. R.6. to R.8. Trajan, Hadrian, and Antoninus.

MENDESIUS (*Chmoun-an-Erman, Ochmoum*).—Imperial, Æ. R.4. to R.6. Hadrian, Antoninus, and Aurelius.

MENELAITES (———).—Imperial, Æ. R.4. to R.6. Trajan, Hadrian, Antoninus, and Aurelius.

METELITES (*Damalidi*).—Imperial, Æ. R.8. Hadrian.

NAUCRATIS (*Samocrat*).—Imperial, Æ. R.7. Trajan, Hadrian, and Aurelius.

NEOUT (———).—Imperial, Æ. R.8. Of Hadrian.

NICOPOLITES (———).—Imperial, Æ. R.8. Antoninus. (*Doubtful if genuine*).

OASIS MAGNA (*Ouahhat*).—Imperial, Æ. R.8. Of Trajan. (*Doubtful if genuine*).

OMBITES (*Ambo*).—Imperial, Æ. R.8. Of Hadrian.

ONUPHITES (*Nuf*).—Imperial, Æ. R.6. Of Hadrian.

OXYRYNCHITES (*Pemsye, Behnese, Bahnasa*).—Imperial, Æ. R.3. to R.4. Hadrian and Antoninus.

AEGYPTUS (*continued*).

PANOPOLITES (*Chmin, Chmim, Akhmim*).—Aut. Æ. R.4. Imperial, Æ. R.6. Of Hadrian.

PELUSIUM (*Peremoun, Alfarama*).—Imperial, Æ. R.3. to R.5. Of Hadrian.

PHARBAETHITES (*Pharbait, Horbait*).—Imperial, Æ. R.8. Hadrian.

PHTHEMPHITES (———).—Imperial, Æ. R.8. Hadrian.

PHTHENEOTES (*Pteneto*).—Imperial, Æ. R.8. Of Hadrian.

PINAMYS (———).—Imperial, Æ. R.6. Of Hadrian. (*Doubtful if genuine*).

PROSOPITES (*Pchati Abchadi*).—Imperial, Æ. R.4. to R.5. Hadrian, Antoninus, and Aurelius.

SAITES (*Sai, Ssa*).—Imperial, Æ. R.4. to R.6. Hadrian and Antoninus.

SEBENNYTES (*Syemnouti, Semenoud, Samannoud*).—Imperial, Æ. R.4. Trajan, Hadrian, and Antoninus.

SETHROITES (*Psariom*).—Imperial, Æ. R.4. to R.6. Trajan and Antoninus.

TANITES (*Syani, Tzan, Ssan*).—Imperial, Æ. R.8. Hadrian.

TENTYRITES (*Nitenthory, Dendera*).—Imperial, Æ. R.5. Of Hadrian and Antoninus.

THINITES (*Tunah*).—Imperial, Æ. R.6. Of Hadrian.

XOITES (*Skoou, Sakha*).—Imperial, Æ. R.6. Of Hadrian.

UNCERTAIN COINS OF EGYPT.—Aut. Æ. R.2. to R.5.

LIBYA.

LIBYA in genere.—Aut. AR. R.5. to R.8.

MARMARICA.

PETRA.—Aut. Æ. R.8. (*Doubtful*).

CYRENAICA.

CYRENAICA in genere.—Aut. AR. R.6. Æ. C. to R.1.

Proconsular of the family PORCIA.—Æ. R.1. to R.3.

Those of Augustus and Agrippa are R.2.

——————— OPPIA.—Æ. R.8.

——————— PUPIA.—Æ. R.1. to R.3.

CYRENAICA (*continued*).

Proconsular of the family LOLLIA.—Æ. R.1. to R.4. Imperial, Æ. R.2. to R.8. Augustus, Tiberius, Drusus, and Titus.

ARSINOE.—Aut. AR. R.6. Æ. R.4. to R.7.

AUTOMALA? (———).—Aut. Æ. R.2. (*Doubtful*).

BARCE (*Berke*).—Aut. AR. R.3. to R.7.

CAENOPOLIS (———).—Aut. AR. R.8. Æ. R.8.

CYRENE (*Curin*).—Aut. AV. C. to R.6. AR. C. to R.8. Æ. C. to R.4.

ENESSIPHIRA (———).—Aut. AR. R.8.

HERACLEA (———).—Aut. Æ. R.8.

LIBYA (———).

PHYCUS (———).—No coins.

PTOLEMAIS (———).—Aut. Æ. R.6.

ISLAND ADJACENT TO CYRENAICA.

LAEA (———).—Aut. Æ. R.6.

KINGS OF CYRENAICA.

OPHILON,* Tyrant of Barce? (*uncertain period*).—Aut. AR. R.8.

MAGAS, King [—— to 256 B. C.].—Aut. Æ. R.5.

PTOLEMAEUS, APION [—— to 96 B. C.].—Aut. AR. R.7. Æ. R.6.

SYRTICA.

AEA (———).—Aut. Æ. R.8. (*Doubtful*).

LEPTIS MAGNA (*Lebida*).—Colonial Aut. Æ. R.1. to R.2. Imperial, Æ. R.6. Augustus, Tiberius, and Agrippina Germanici.

OCEA (———).—Imperial, Æ. R.8. Of Antoninus Pius.

BYZACENE.

ACHULLA (*Elalia*).—Imperial, Æ. R.4. to R.6. Julius Caesar and family of Augustus. (Latin legends).

HADRUMETUM (*Herkla*).—Aut. Æ. R.8. Imperial, Æ. R.4. to R.6. Julius Caesar and Augustus. (Latin legends).

THAPSUM (*Demass*).—Imperial, Æ. R.8. Of Tiberius.

---

* Millingen retracts his former opinion, that this coin, inscribed *Ophilon*, might belong to Ophellas, tyrant of the Cyrenaica—it being probably the name of a magistrate (*Sylloge*, p. 87).

ZEUGITANA.

The coins of the Pro-Praetor Clodius Macer, struck in Zeugitana, were executed on the model of the Denarius, and are ranged with the Roman series, as are also those of the Vandal kings in the fifth and sixth centuries.

CARTHAGO.—Aut. AV. C. to R.3.—Electrum. R.2. AR. R.1. to R.4. Æ. C. to R.6.—Colonial Aut. Æ. C. to R.4. (Latin legends).

CLUPEA (———).—Imperial, Æ. R.4. Of Tiberius and Drusus. (Latin legends).

HIPPO-LIBERA (*Bizerta*).—Aut. Æ. R.7. Imperial, Æ. R.8. Tiberius, Julia, and Drusus. (Latin legends).

UTICA (*Buchiatter*).—Imperial, Æ. C. to R.1. Augustus, Tiberius, and Julia. (Latin legends).

MAURETANIA.

IOL, CAESAREA (*Chierchiell*).—Aut. (with African legends), Æ. R.6. Imperial (with bilingual legends—Latin and African), Æ. R.1. to R.5. Augustus, Tiberius, and Julia.

BABBA (———).—Colonial Imperial, Æ. R.3. to R.6. Claudius to Galba.

CISSA (———).—Aut. Æ. R.6.

NUMIDIA.

TABRACA (———).—Aut. Æ. R.8.

Formerly given erroneously to Abdera in Baetica.

KINGS OF NUMIDIA AND MAURETANIA.

BOCCHUS (*uncertain period*).—Aut. AR. R.8.

JUBA I. [—— to 46 B. C.].—Aut. AV.? R.8. AR. R.1. to R.4. Potin. R.4. Æ. R.2.

JUBA II. [30 B. C. to 19 A. C.].—Aut. AR. R.4. to R.8. Æ. R.3. to R.6.

CLEOPATRA, Wife of Juba II.—Aut. AR. R.6. to R.8. Æ. R.5. to R.8.

PTOLEMAEUS, Son of Juba II.—Aut. AR. R.6. Æ. R.4. to R.6. Imperial, Æ. R.4. to R.7. Of Augustus and Tiberius.

UNCERTAIN COINS OF AFRICA.—Aut. AR. R.6. Æ. R.2. to R.4. Imperial, Æ. R.2. to R.8. Of Augustus. (With African legends).

SECTION II.

ROMAN COINS.

"Ecce, Cæsar, quibus successisti! Ecce quos imitari studeas, et mirari; ad quorum formulam, et imaginem te componas: quos præter te unum, nulli hominum daturus eram; tua me movit authoritas. Licet enim horum mores et nomina, horum ego res gestas norim, tuum est, non modum nosse sed sequi. Tibi itaque debebantur."

Petrarch to the Emperor Charles IV., with a present of Roman coins.

ROMAN COINS.

IF reliance may be placed on the account of Pliny, the origin of Roman money must be referred to the time of Servius Tullius, nearly seven centuries before the Christian era.[1] According to that historian, it consisted of brass only, and was called *pecunia,* from the figure of a *pecus* which it bore. The earliest piece was the As Libralis, of twelve ounces, which continued of that weight down to the first Punic war. This author also informs us, that the coinage of silver at Rome commenced five years before the reduction in the weight of the As; the Denarius then struck being, as its name implies, equal in value to ten Ases. During the first Punic war, the As was reduced to two ounces; and subsequently, about the year B. C. 216, to one ounce, the value of the Denarius being raised to sixteen Ases. We are further informed, that the As dwindled to half an ounce at the time of the passing of the Papirian law.

The accuracy of this account has been much questioned by modern writers. The sudden and extensive reduction of the As has been considered too dangerous a measure in the times it is stated to have taken place. Leaving, however, this question to be weighed and considered by the learned, we shall proceed to notice the pieces which have descended to us. Of these we have many varieties, differing in type and module.

The As, its parts and multiples.

1. The *Decussis,* or piece of ten Ases, bearing the head of Minerva, or Victory, in a biga; reverse, the prow of a vessel.

[1] " Servius Rex primus signavit aes." *Hist. Nat.* lib. xxxiii. 13. Cassiodorus says, " Servius rex monetam in ære primum impressisse perhibetur."

2. The *Quadrussis*, or piece of four Ases, of various types, the most common of which is a bull.
3. The *Tripondius*, or piece of three Ases, with the head of Minerva and prow.
4. The *Dupondius*, or piece of two Ases. Some of these pieces are of Italian origin, and bear the word FELATHRI in retrograde Etruscan characters.[1]
5. The *As*, or piece of twelve unciæ, which, besides its type, often bears its value, I. These pieces, after the reduction of the As, bear the names of Roman families.
6. The *Semis*, or half As, marked S.
7. The *Quincunx*,[2] or piece of five unciæ, marked ●●●●●
8. The *Triens*, or third of the As, marked ●●●●
9. The *Quadrans*, or fourth ,, ●●●
10. The *Sextans*, or sixth ,, ●●
11. The *Uncia*, or twelfth ,, ●

Coinage of Silver. The earliest type of the Roman silver, which according to Pliny was first struck in the year of Rome, 485 (B. C. 269), appears to have been the double head of Janus; reverse, a figure guiding a biga. In later times, the Denarius bore this type, while its half, the Quinarius, was impressed with the figure of Victory, so that *Bigati* and *Victoriati* were the terms generally used to denote these coins. Numerous denarii exist at this day with the common type of the biga. Of these, the pieces of large module, having the word ROMA on a tablet beneath the biga in incuse or indented letters, are without doubt the most ancient.

Many consular coins bear the indications of their value thus:—the *Denarius*, X, or ✕, or XVI. The *Quinarius*, V, or Q. The *Sestertius*, IIS, or HS. The marks on the Dena-

[1] See the *Numismatic Alphabets*, Pl. iii.

[2] The *Roman* Quincunx bears a cross on each side, and is uncommon: that with the type of the Dioscuri is of great rarity. The five globules, marking the Quincunx, are found on the very common Italian coins of Teate, Larinum, &c.

rius have reference to its original value, ten Ases, and subsequently sixteen Ases. The brass Decussis, or piece of ten Ases, bears the numeral X. The Q on the Quinarius is the initial of its name; the V marks its original value, five Ases. The HS denotes two Ases and a half, the original value of the Sestertius. With few exceptions, the Quinarius and Sestertius are not of common occurrence, from which it may be inferred their issue was not abundant. The legends on consular coins are often given in a contracted form, or with braced letters, of which examples will be found in the plates.

Coinage of Gold. Pliny states that gold was first coined in Rome, in the year of that city, 548 (B. C. 206). The pieces supposed by some writers to be of this coinage, bear on one side a helmed bearded head; reverse, an eagle with expanded wings, and ROMA:[1] they are of three sizes, and their value is indicated by the numerals ↓X, for sixty Sesterces; XXXX, forty Sesterces; and XX, twenty Sesterces. There is, however, every reason to believe that these coins were not minted in Rome, but in some of the cities of Campania under the Roman authority.[2] They are all rare.

Types of Consular Denarii. The greater part of the series denominated consular coins bear the biga type, but there are many denarii of great interest, some of which are sufficiently common to be within the reach of every collector. Of the types in question we may notice that of a denarius of the Æmilia family, upon which M. LEPIDUS is represented placing a crown on the head of the young king Ptolemy Epiphanes, with the title TVTOR REGIS (*the king's guardian*). Another coin of this family, with the legend L · BVCA, represents the dream of Sylla, as described by Plutarch. A third coin records the youthful valour of M. Lepidus, who is represented, on horseback, bearing a trophy; legend, M · LEPIDVS · AN · XV · PR · H · O · C · S (*Marcus Lepidus annorum* XV. *Prætextatus hostem occidit civem servavit*). A fourth

[1] Several cities of Campania struck silver coins with the word ROMA, ROMANO, or ROMANOM; see page 49.

[2] Eckhel, Doct. Num. Vet. vol. v. p. 44.

coin, of the Æmilia family, represents Aretas, king of Arabia, submitting himself to Marcus Scaurus. This is beautifully typified by a figure kneeling by the side of a camel, presenting an olive branch, from which depends a fillet or ancient diadem.

On denarii of the Antonia family we find the names of the egions who served under the Triumvir. On those of the Cæcilia family we have records of the victory obtained over the Carthaginians in the first Punic war, and also over the Macedonians. A coin of Calpurnia records the purchase of corn by Piso and Cæpio in time of scarcity. The investigation of Q. Cassius is perpetuated on a denarius of the family, Cassia. Hostilia has two interesting types. Mamilia, who boasted their descent from Ulysses, has left us a type, the interest of which redeems its rudeness. Marcia presents us with a portrait of Ancus. Memmia commemorates the first festival of the Cerealia, a type considered by Trajan, in after times, worthy of restoration. Numonia records the heroism of a member of that family. Papia has a type illustrating a fable of Dionysius Halicarnassus.[1] Plautia has handed down an interesting memorial of the capture of Privernum by Hypsæus. Sergia's one-armed hero is represented riding at full speed, with his enemy's head in his remaining hand,[2] and Titurja commemorates the perfidy of Tarpeia and the rape of the Sabines. Several interesting portraits also occur on these coins, among which may be noticed, those of the elder Brutus, Numa, Sylla, Ahala, &c.

Types and Legends of the Imperial series.

Such are the illustrations to be found in the series of coins denominated *Consular*. To notice in detail those of the imperial series would require a volume much larger than the present. Of the numerous authentic portraits which they bear, it will scarcely be necessary to speak, except that on some we have likenesses of personages who have escaped the notice of historians.[3] The

[1] Lib. i. c. 51.

[2] Liv. lib. vii. c. 28.

[3] See the coins of Barbia Orbiana, wife of Severus Alexander, Paulina, wife of Maximinus, Cornelia Supera, wife of Valerianus, Magnia Urbica, wife of Carinus, &c.

devices and legends of the reverses are in numerous instances of singular interest; witness those of Augustus, with AEGYPTO CAPTA; the large brass of Tiberius, recording his munificence to the twelve cities of Asia; the gold and silver of Claudius, with DE · BRITANNIS. The memorials of the conquest of Judea on the coins of Vespasian and Titus, IVDAEA · CAPTA and IVDAEA · DEVICTA. The coins of Trajan and Hadrian record the principal acts of their reigns: among these the legends, VIA · TRAIANA. — PARTHIA · CAPTA.—AQVA · TRAIANA. — REX PARTHIS · DATVS.—and the names of the various provinces visited by the last-mentioned emperor, claim especial notice.

The series of first or large brass coins extends to the reign of Gallienus, but by far the most elegant are those of the first fifteen emperors. After the reigns of the Antonines, the large brass coin decreases in size, as well as in interest of design and beauty of fabric, and disappears entirely in the reign of Gallienus.

The Roman silver and gold coins (aurei and denarii) have descended to our times in immense numbers, and fine collections have been formed in each metal. The copper is of three sizes, which are termed by numismatists *large*, *middle*, and *small brass*. Of each of the two former sizes a nearly perfect series may be formed. Of the small brass a complete series cannot be made; and it is doubtful if any coins exist of some of the earlier emperors. On the disappearance of the large brass, in the reign of Gallienus, the coinage of small brass recommenced, and much of it is extremely common, as the extensive lists in the elaborate work of Bandurius testify.[1] In the reign of Diocletian appeared a copper coin, termed the *Follis*, of the module of the middle brass of the first thirteen emperors, but much thinner. The coinage of these pieces appears to have been extensive, as they are at this day very common, both of Diocletian, and his colleague, Maximian, as also of Constantius-Chlorus, Severus Cæsar, and Maxentius.

[1] The small brass of Gallienus, Claudius Gothicus, Prolus, Victorinus, Tetricus Diocletianus, Maximianus, and the family of Constantine exist in prodigious numbers, every year bringing to light fresh hoards.

Of Romulus, the son of the latter, pieces were struck of this denomination; but these last are uncommon.

Restored Coins. Some Roman coins were *restored* by succeeding emperors. On these we find the word, RESTITVIT, or its abbreviation. Trajan restored many of the Consular series, as well as those of his predecessors.[1]

Portraits. In the earliest and more simple days of Rome, the portraits of no living personage appeared on the public money; the heads were those of their deities, or of some person who had received divine honours. Julius Cæsar was the first who obtained the express permission of the senate to place his portrait on the coins; and the example was soon followed by others. The heads of Lepidus and of Antony appear on their denarii, and even the money of Brutus, with the two daggers and cap of Liberty, bears, on the obverse, the head of the man who killed his friend, because he had assumed the regal power and authority. We have no evidence, however, that this money, which is of great rarity, was struck with the knowledge and sanction of Brutus; and it is possible that it is a posthumous coin.

Surnames and Titles. Like the Greek monarchs, the Roman emperors were at first satisfied with simple titles. Julius Cæsar was content with those of *Imperator*, *Perpetual Dictator*, and *Pater Patriæ;* and here it should be observed, that the title, Imperator, *following* the name, has a very different signification than when it is placed *before* it. The military title of Imperator was given by Sylla to Pompey, and victorious generals were often thus saluted by their troops after a battle:[2] it was only in later times, when the people had become fami-

[1] See an article in the Numismatic Journal, Vol. i. p. 243, "*On the Coins denominated Restored.*" Most of the restored coins are of considerable rarity, although the original types are generally those with which every numismatist is familiar.

[2] Suetonius observes of Claudius "prænomine Imperatoris abstinuit," which is confirmed by the coins of that emperor, upon which it never appears as a *prænomen*, though we find even IMP · XVI. *following* the title.

liarised with sovereignty, that we find IMP*erator* used as a prænomen. Augustus added to his titles those of *Tribune*, and *Pontifex Maximus;* Claudius styled himself *Censor*. Antoninus received from the senate the title of *Pius*, which was also borne by several of his unworthy successors; for we find "Antoninus Pius" on the coins of Caracalla and Elagabalus. Commodus added *Felix* to his other unmerited epithets: D. Julian was styled *Rector Orbis*, and Niger was surnamed *Justus*. Tetricus, as well as his son, was styled *Invictus*, and this title is found on some of the coins of Carausius. In the time of Constantine the style *Nobilis Cæsar*, or *Nobilissimus Cæsar*, is common.[1] *Perpetuus Augustus* and *Semper Augustus* are also found among other titles. On coins of Diocletian and Maximian, the epithets *Beatissimus* and *Felicissimus* sometimes occur, while on those of the former emperor we find *Senior* and *Æternus*.[2] The second Justinianus called himself *Servus Christi* and *Multus Augustus*. At a later period of the empire, the letters D · N., signifying *Dominus Noster*, usurp the place of IMP*erator*, and the Byzantine tyrants rejoiced in the title of *Despot* (δεσποτης).[3] Surnames were often adopted by the emperors, and recorded on their money: thus Trajan gloried in those of *Dacicus*, *Parthicus*, and *Germanicus*, while the senate, on the numerous coins struck in his honour, style him OPTIMVS PRINCEPS. Commodus took the surname of *Britannicus*, as did also Severus and his sons;[4] and the second Claudius is sometimes distinguished from the earlier emperor of that name by the surname of *Gothicus*.

The empresses were also honoured with titles by the senate;

[1] It first appears on the coins of Carinus.

[2] The coins on which Diocletian is styled *Eternus* are conjectured to have been struck after his abdication.

[3] The Empress Theodora is called δεσποινα. Père Jobert observes of *Despotes*, (*Science de Médailles, Tome* 1er, *p.* 244), "C'est un mot Grec, qui dans sa première origine signifie ce que marque en Latin le mot *Herus*, et en François celui de maître, par rapport aux serviteurs. On en fit à peu près ce que les Latins avoient fait du nom de Cæsar comparé à celui d'Auguste, βασιλευς répondant à *Augustus*, et δεσποτης à Cæsar." In the days of Johannes Zimisces, the imperial effigy and titles gave place for a time to uncouth representations of the Saviour, with the legend, IC · XC · BACIΛEVC · BACIΛEωN (*Jesus Christus, King of kings*), in the angles of a large cross on the reverse.

[4] In allusion to the surnames of Caracalla, the younger Pertinax observed that he had not blazoned that of *Geticus*. The joke cost him his life.

among these are *Genetrix Orbis*, *Mater Castrorum*, *Mater Senatus*, and *Mater Patriæ*.[1]

The Consular Office. The subject of the consulship has been discussed at considerable length by Eckhel[2]; and from him we take all that can be said on this important office, which is perpetually mentioned on Roman coins, generally by the abbreviation COS. After the subjugation of the Roman empire by Julius Cæsar, he and his successors not only allowed the annual elections of the consuls to proceed as usual, although nothing but a nominal dignity remained to them, but the emperors often took upon themselves the consular office, in conjunction with private individuals.

As among the Romans, the calendar and every calculation of dates depended on the succession of consuls on the calends of January; and as from this arose the custom which prevailed from the time of Julius Cæsar to the period of the lower empire, of princes inscribing their own consulates and the repetitions of them on their coins, a knowledge of the Cæsarean consulates is important to the clear understanding of the chronology of Roman history, and especially of that of the emperors.

After noticing the errors of Page[3] and other writers on the consulship, the learned author of the *Doctrina* proceeds to say, that, contrary to the opinions entertained by many, the emperors subjected themselves to no rules in taking upon themselves the consulship, but that, as in most other things, they followed their own caprice alone. He then arranges his own argument under different heads, as follows:—

§ I. Under the first head occur the perpetual consulships, either spontaneously conferred on generals, or arbitrarily assumed by them. By a very ancient decree of the people it was provided, that no one should serve the office of consul until after an interval of ten years from the period of his first

[1] Coins of Plautilla bear the singular legend, PROPAGO · IMPERI.

[2] Doct. Num. Vet. vol. viii., cap. i. *De Consulibus Cæsaribus.*

[3] Dissertatio Hypatica, &c. Lyons, 1682.

election.[1] But, towards the close of the Republic, when the laws no longer ruled, but were subjected to the rule of others, the old regulation was infringed. The seven consulships of Marius are notorious: immediately afterwards, Sylla, in an interval of not more than eight years, was not only again made consul, but also *dictator* at the same time. His example was followed by Julius Cæsar, who *received the perpetual consulship and the perpetual dictatorship*. This is confirmed by the coins of Cæsar.

After the reduction of Artaxata by Corbulo, in the year of Rome 811, the senate decreed the perpetual consulship to Nero,[2] an honour, however, which, according to the annals and his coins, he does not appear to have accepted. Vitellius intended himself for perpetual consul, but did not effect his purpose. In the reigns of some of the emperors, the consulships differed but little from perpetual ones. Vespasian, during a reign of about ten years, renewed this office eight times. Titus was proud of the honour, and his brother and successor, Domitian, served the office of consul seventeen times. Elagabalus may be cited as another instance, and the coins of Theodosius the younger, quoted by Mediobarba and Banduri,[3] shew that he held the office of consul eighteen times.

§ II. The history of the age of the emperors shews that they had the power of nominating the consuls; nor can it be questioned that that power was unlimited; hence Mamertinus[4] wittily observed of Julian, when that emperor was engaged in nominating the consuls, "He began to revolve the consulship *in the comitium of his sacred breast*;" as if, in truth, he alone represented the ancient *comitia* in which the consuls were elected[5]. But the emperors, though the consular office was always combined with the imperial power, took upon themselves the consulship, either that they might leave some

[1] Liv. lib. vii. c. 42.; lib. x. c. 13.
[2] Tacit. Annales, xiii. c. 41.
[3] These coins are, however, not known at this time.
[4] Gratiar. Act. ad Julian. c. xv.
[5] The inclosure of the *Comitium* is figured on the denarii of the families Antonia, Mussidia, and Silia.

appearance of the old form of the republic to its more stern admirers (a plan, as Appian[1] thinks, derived from Sylla), or that they might render the year intended for some remarkable festivities distinguished by their consulship, or from vanity, or from an unwillingness to advance the reputation of others, which Ausonius elegantly satirizes in Domitian, or from any other cause : at any rate, it may clearly be inferred, that the office was an agreeable one, as even the least ostentatious of the emperors served it several times.

§ III. Rome, in her freedom, was unacquainted with the *consules suffecti*, or substituted consuls, except when one of the consuls died while serving the office; and it became necessary to appoint another in his stead for the remainder of the year. Julius Cæsar gave the precedent of *consules suffecti* independent of this cause. Dio, on the year U. C. 709,[2] states, "He forthwith, and before his arrival into the city, entered on the consulship, which, however, he did not serve the whole year, but after his arrival at Rome he abdicated, and entrusted it to Q. Fabius and C. Trebonius; and, as Fabius had died on the last day of the consulate, he appointed in his stead for the remaining hours C. Caninius." Cicero,[3] in relating the same fact, humourously adds, "Know, then, that no one dined while Caninius was consul. Yet no mischief was committed in his consulship, for he was a man of wonderful vigilance, as he knew not what sleep was during the whole of his consulate." The precedent, once established, it subsequently was of rare occurrence, that those consuls who were appointed on the calends of January remained in office during the whole year; for the emperors, as a reward to those who had done them service, appointed others to share this honour; and there was a time when this license exceeded all bounds, as when Cleander, the all-powerful chamberlain of the emperor Commodus, who had once been a slave, is said to have appointed twenty-five consuls for one year! Caligula and Elagabalus obtained their first *consulatus suffectus* by previously depriving the legitimate consuls of their power.

[1] Bell. Civ. lib. i. c. 103.
[2] Lib. xliii. 46.
[3] L. vii. Famil. Epist. 30.

The consuls who were created on the calends of January were called *ordinarii*, and gave the name to the year.[1] They were consequently in greater authority than the *suffecti*, who were almost unknown out of Rome and Italy, and were on that account called *minores*. As the consuls *suffecti* occasionally obtained the ordinary consulate, they were accustomed to reckon the *consulatus suffectus* with it. Octavius, A. U. C. 711, was *suffectus* appointed in the place of the consuls who had been slain in battle; when he was subsequently created consul, A. U. C. 721, he was styled in all the monuments ITERVM CONSVL, *a second time consul.* Caligula, consul *suffectus* from the calends of July, A. U. C. 790, was created *consul iterum* on the calends of January, A. U. C. 792. Domitian added to the list *the five consulatus suffectus which he had served before he succeeded to the empire:* on one coin, however, no reference is made to these five times of his holding the office of *suffectus.*

§ IV. During the integrity of the republic, the consuls were *designated* only for the following year; but this practice yielded to innovation. Under the rule of the Triumviri, A. U. C. 715, for the sake of the republic, the consuls for eight years were designated, among whom Marc Antony was selected for the years 720 and 723. Therefore, from the year U. C. 710, in which he was first appointed consul, until the above-mentioned 715, COS. only is found on his coins; but subsequently to the year 720, COS · DES · ITER · ET · TER (*consul elect for the second and third time*); then, from the year 723, in which he entered on his third consulship, *consul a third time.* Octavianus also observed the same rules, being in the same year, U. C. 715, designated consul for the years 721 and 723. Augustus designated Caius and Lucius, his grandsons, as consuls, so that they should enter on the office after five years. Nero was designated consul at the age of fourteen, which office he was to undertake at the age of twenty; for this reason we find on his coins, COS · DESIGN (*consul elect*).

The emperors, when they wished to appoint themselves consuls, did not neglect to add this designation on public

[1] See the Eponymous Consul "Greek Coins," page 22.

monuments, whence it is common, for example, to find in them COS · III · DES · IIII (*consul for the third time; elect for the fourth*). Page has attempted to shew that it was the practice of the emperors to inscribe on monuments the consulship elect, *leaving out* the word implying *elect;* thus, instead of COS · III · DES · IIII, he supposes they inscribed COS · IIII. This opinion is founded on error, and is of course opposed by Eckhel, who, however, observes, that his remarks apply only to the healthier times of the empire; and that the notation of time, from the reign of Gallienus downward, is evidently spurious and absurd. But, if we have no example to be depended on of the omission of DES in similar inscriptions, because it would have confused the dates, still the number of the consulate which preceded the DES could with safety be omitted. Thus, for example, whether they had written COS · III · DES · IIII, or simply COS · DES · IIII · it would have been the same; for in either case it is understood that the third consulship has been entered upon. This number has been sometimes omitted,[1] and Maffei, not aware of the fact, pronounced as spurious the Tergestini marble bearing the following inscription:—

IMP · CAESAR · COS · DESIG · TERT
III · VIR · R · P · C · ITERVM
MVRVM · TVRRESQ · FECIT

because the COS was unaccompanied by any numeral, although DESIG · TERT follows.

§ V. The consular ornaments, or honours (*ornamenta consularia*), were a sort of image of the consulship, decreed to any one by the emperors. Dio states, that while the republic still existed, C. Carbo, although he had only as yet served the office of tribune of the people, was adorned with the *consular honours;* but we do not discover in what these honours consisted. Their true origin may without doubt be traced from Julius Cæsar, who, to grant favours to many, as he could not confer the consulate *ordinarius*, or *suffectus*, on all, invented this specious honour of the consulship. " He," says Dio, " added many to the number of the patricians and consular

[1] See the coin of Antony, struck A. U. C. 720, inscribed merely COS · DES · III.

men, εἰς τους ὑπατευκοτας;" and Suetonius remarks, "He granted consular honour to the prætorian men." When Octavius was a candidate for the consulship, on the death of the consuls Hirtius and Pansa, the senate, unwilling that so eminent an honour should be conferred on a boy, gave him, instead of the consulate, merely the consular honours. After that period many examples may be found of this dignity being conferred, and that, indeed, even on strangers, as when Claudius wished Agrippa, grandson of Herod the Great, to be adorned with it, when the Roman senate had previously, under the rule of Caligula, decreed to him prætorian ornaments or honours. Dio[1] has negatived the supposition, that those who received the consular honours increased the number of their consulship, on their being afterwards created consuls. Severus was the first to change this custom; for when he had presented Plautianus first with these *honours*, and afterwards with the consulship itself, he ordered him to be announced as consul for the second time. The Emperor Macrinus was opposed to this new regulation.

§ VI. It has been already shewn (§ II.) why the emperors took upon themselves the office of consul, and why they renewed it frequently. Among the hypatic rules drawn up by Page, the first is, that the emperors were accustomed to come forth as consuls in the first calends of January after their accession to the empire. This rule is fallacious: the custom was derived from Nero, but his successors, down to Nerva, entered on the consulship on the *next* calend of January. When Trajan did not think proper to do this, Pliny[2] said, "*In the beginning of your rule you refused the consulship, which, although it was destined for others, new emperors were wont to transfer to themselves.*"

It was also a practice of the emperors to assume the consulship on account of various solemnities. Suetonius[3] says of Augustus, that he assumed his thirteenth and last consulship that he might attend, or be the *deductor* of, his sons Caius and Lucius into the forum on the occasion of their changing the

[1] In Octavian.
[2] Paneg. c. 57.
[3] In. Aug. cap. 26.

toga virilis, while he himself was holding the highest office of the magistracy. The rulers of the lower empire, at least those who were called the consuls of the east, says Themistius, thought that they ought always to avoid conceding the office by which the year is denoted to any one on the recurrence of either the quinquennial or decennial period. "Wherefore," says he, "it seemed evidently unusual that Theodosius the Great yielded this honour to Saturninus, a private individual, on the occurrence of the quinquennalia."

§ VII. When the emperors had subjected all power to their will, the consular office became unimportant. No longer leading the armies of the Romans nor providing for the state, and conspicuous at Rome by their Trabea only, instead of conducting the affairs of the empire, they were obliged to pass their lives in ignoble ease. Mamertinus, therefore, rightly observes of the consuls in the Imperial age, "In administrations labour is connected with the honour; in the consulship the honour is received without the labour." Cassiodorus alludes more severely to the inactivity of the consuls, and remarks, that of the innumerable proofs of madness manifested by Caligula, the most pardonable was that of deeming his horse capable of performing the duties of a consul. What, therefore, was the advantage of that office the Emperor Julian has explained, viz: "It is to private individuals a sort of reward or recompense for virtue, or good faith, or good will towards the emperors, or for any illustrious action; but to the emperors themselves it is, as it were, an accession of honour and dignity to those advantages which they already possess."

§ VIII. The *half consulship* (*consulatus dimidius*) consisted of one consul only, without any colleague. Such, though the first example of the kind, was the third consulate of Pompey the Great, A. U. C. 702. He was elected in the *comitium* sole consul, without colleague. The dissension among the people at that period was the cause of this unusual election, and the disunion among many in command in the reign of Constantine the Great led to the same thing. The annals of the ancients mark the years 310 and 312 after Christ as distinguished by the consulship of Maxentius only.

The Oriental & Occidental Consul. On the division of the empire into eastern and western, Constantine determined that one of the consuls should be appointed at Rome and the other at Constantinople. This practice was commenced A. D. 338, on the calends of January, of which year, as Constantine the Great had lately died, and in accordance with his wish, the rule being divided between his three sons, the first consuls of the kind were appointed, Ursus in the West, Polemius in the East. Whence it arose, that if it were not known who was the consul of the other quarter of the globe, it was recorded in the public acts, "the consuls being . . . . . . , and whoever shall have been announced," or "the consuls, of whom one is Aristænetus, for I know not his colleague." Similar examples are given by Page.

The formula after the Consulship. Post Consulatum. When, either on account of the discord of the rulers, or wars, or the murders of princes, or other causes, the year had not its consuls, at least, certain and recognised ones, it frequently occurred that this one year which was vacant, received its name from the recognised consul of the preceding year: for example, the years 541, 542, 543 after Christ are designated as follows: "In the year of the city when Basilius was consul. In the second year after the consulship of Basilius. In the third year after the consulship of Basilius." This formula is read for the first time A. D. 307, when the consuls of the preceding year had been Constantius, Chlorus VI., and Galerius Maximianus VI.

§ IX. Although the consulates were recorded by the ancients on monuments of various kinds, and in private documents, especially when they wished to secure credit, still, on their numismatic records they were neglected at an early period. It occurs for the last time on the coins of Heraclius, the second son of Heraclius the First, on one of whose coins we read, in the mixed characters of the period, ERACAIO · CONSVAI. At length, this venerable magistracy, divested of its former splendour, was held so cheap, that Leo VI. *Sapiens*, who came to the empire A. D. 886, ordered "*Novella CV.*" of Justinian, which treats of the consulship, and contains a law no longer relating to the government of the state, to be, with other useless ones, erased from the code. Subsequently, in the East, they reckoned the date of the year from the epoch of the creation of the world, which, according to the computation of the seventy interpreters, was created in the 5508th year, 3rd month, and 25th day, before the birth of Christ.

The Consular Insignia. § X. With regard to the insignia of the consuls, we have the following. Florus says of Tarquinius Priscus, "For he subdued the people of Tuscany by frequent arms, and from them were derived the fasces, the trabeæ, the curules, the rings, the trappings, the paludamenta, and the prætexta; thence the custom was introduced, that the general in a triumphal procession was drawn in a golden car by four horses; thence the embroidered togas and tunicæ palmatæ, in fine, all the ornaments and insignia by which the dignity of authority is made conspicuous." Dionysius Halicarnassus, among the insignia of rule which Priscus then introduced at Rome, mentions a golden crown, and a staff surmounted by the figure of an eagle, a purple tunic diversified with gold, and a purple embroidered toga. He adds, that these insignia were permitted to the consuls after the expulsion of the kings, with the exception of the crown and embroidered toga; although they even made use of these when they triumphed. The consular coins afford but little information as to the use of these insignia while Rome yet enjoyed freedom. On the coins of the family *Junia*, the elder Brutus, first consul after the expulsion of the kings, is represented marching between two lictors, each bearing the fasces and axe;[1] but we know from other sources that twelve fasces were carried before the consul. On the denarii of Sylla, which represent the two consuls, Sylla and Rufus, as also on the denarius of V. Messalla, inscribed PATRE · COS, the *sella curulis* is assigned to the consul; but even other and inferior magistrates had this in common with the consuls. On the denarius of Augustus, struck A. U. C. 752, are represented the staff with the eagle,

[1] See Descrip. Cat. of Roman Coins, Plate 2, No. 4; and the Numismatic Journal, Vol. I., where this very common though interesting type is illustrated.

the embroidered toga, and laurel wreath; but these are considered by Eckhel rather as triumphal ornaments than consular insignia. At a later period more information is afforded. In Vopiscus, the Emperor Valerian addresses Aurelian in these among other words: "Take, then, to thyself, for thy great deeds, the prætexta, the tunica palmata, the embroidered toga, the subarmalis profundus, the ivory seat; for I this day appoint thee consul, and shall write to the senate, that they assign thee a staff and also the fasces." Cassiodorus writes to the same effect, while he inveighs severely against those whom the emperors adorned with consular insignia, although not entitled to them by their merits. "But now," says he, "you take these with greater good fortune, since we have the labours of the consuls, and you the pleasure of the dignity. Depict the broad shoulders with the varied colour of the palmata, the powerful hand with the renowned staff of victory, even go out of your own house with gilded shoes, mount with difficulty the sella curulis with many steps by reason of its height, that, lying at your ease, you may gain what we in command acquire by the greatest labours."

On the coins of the emperors, from the time of the decline of the empire, there often occurs a bust of the emperor, robed in the palmata, and bearing a sceptre in his hand surmounted by an eagle, from which we may infer that the emperor is a consul. The whole dress of the consul is, however, illustrated by Ducange, who, in his dissertation on the coins of the lower empire, has given an ivory diptych with a consular figure.[1]

The consular Procession. The consuls were said to proceed (*procedere*) or make their procession, when those designated for the consulship in the preceding year entered on the office, on the 1st of January, with the customary pomp and attendance of the magistrates; and this annual practice was usually called the "consular procession," as may be learned from coins inscribed, FELIX · PROCESS*us* · CONSVL · AVG · N. Eckhel refers to examples of ancient authors who have expressed the

[1] Tab. i. s. iv.

consular procession solely by the word *processus*, omitting even the name of the consul. Juvenal thus reproaches those who from lowly origin arrived at the greatest honours by depraved and tortuous paths :—

> " Cum te summoveant, qui testamenta merentur
> Noctibus, in cœlum quos evehit, optima *summi*
> Nunc via *processus*, vetulæ vesica beatæ."

The word *summoveant* employed in this passage makes the intention of the poet sufficiently clear, as the consul's lictors walked before him in the procession, and cleared the way through the crowd. In reference to this practice, Horace appropriately says, " Neither wealth, nor the consular Lictor removes the wretched torments of the mind, and cares flitting around vaulted roofs." [1]

It is sometimes difficult to determine when an emperor is represented on coins as carried in the Quadriga, either of horses or elephants, and bearing the sceptre with the eagle, whether a triumph or consular procession is denoted by this type, because, as has been shewn, the eagle is common both to those who triumphed, and to the consuls. However, the coins not unfrequently afford the means whereby we may distinguish each of these solemnities. Where there is a similar representation on a coin of any year, in which it is certain that the emperor made this procession, and especially if history makes no mention of any triumph in that year, it cannot be doubted that it is a consular procession, and that it has been represented on the coins after the manner in which all illustrious deeds were wont to be represented. Coins of Commodus with the type in question are inscribed, TR · P XV · IMP · VIII · COS · VI (*Tribunitia Potestate decimum quintum, Imperator octavum, Consul sextum*), which are sure marks of the year 943 U. C. on the calends of January of which year this emperor made the procession as consul for the sixth time. Coins of Caracalla bear TR · P · XI and XVI, denoting the years 961 and 966 U. C. in which years respectively, he was consul

[1] Carm. L. ii., 16.

for the third and fourth time. On a remarkable coin of Gordian, the emperor is figured with the *toga picta*, or *palmata*, and bearing in the hand the sceptre with the eagle: on the reverse, PONTIFEX · MAX · TR · P · IIII · COS · II · P · P. The emperor in a quadriga, in his right hand an olive branch, in his left an eagle, Victory standing behind the emperor, and a soldier, with other figures preceding him bearing palms. This coin is of the year 994 U. C. in which year Gordian entered on his second consulship. Coins of Caracalla with COS · II, and of Geta with COS only and a similar type, are well known. Both are of the year of Rome 958; in which Caracalla was consul for the second, and Geta for the first time. Two coins of large brass of Trebonianus Gallus and Volusianus bear COS · II · ET · COS with a similar type.[1] These emperors were consuls together 1007 U. C. the father for the second, the son for the first time. Eckhel shews that the remarkable gold coin of Diocletian and Maximian may be subjected to the same rule:—

IMPP · DIOCLETIANO · ET · MAXIMIANO · AVGG. Laureated busts of the emperors, clad in the consular trabæa, and holding the sceptre surmounted by an eagle.

Rev.—IMPP · DIOCLETIANO · III · ET · MAXIMIANO · COSS. The emperors in a quadriga of elephants, their rulers bearing palms; Victory flying above the emperors.

A coin of Maxentius bears: FELIX · PROCESS · CONSVL (or CONSVLAT) AVG · N. The emperor in a quadriga of elephants (or drawn by six horses), holding a branch and a sceptre. It is plainly shewn that the consular procession is exhibited on the former coin, but it is much more clear in the latter, on which we find the *processus consulatus* recorded. Noris, however, in a learned dissertation attempted to shew that this was not the case, and that the coin of Diocletian commemorated a triumph. The same writer recognises a triumph on a coin of Alexander Severus, on which that emperor appears in a

[1] Though Victory is represented flying above the emperor, we must regard this type as implying that they were *always attended by this important deity*, and not as denoting a triumph. It is in fact a graphic illustration of a common title on the coins of the lower empire, VICTORIOSVS · SEMPER.

quadriga; legend, TR · P · VIII · COS · III. But Eckhel, however, observes that this type affords undeniable testimony of a consular procession, for Alexander, in his eighth tribunitial power, was consul for the third time. He admits that the quadriga of elephants gives the most weight to the opinion of Noris, as the emperors not unfrequently triumphed in quadrigæ of this animal, a practice of which Pompey was the first to give an example, after his African triumph, as related by Pliny. Lampridius says that Alex. Severus, after his return from the Persian expedition, was drawn to the capital in a triumphal car by six elephants. When the victory of Gordian over the Persians was announced at Rome, the senate decreed quadrigæ of elephants to the victor. On this account, Pacatus[1] calls them triumphal beasts. Nevertheless, we often see on coins that elephants were attached to the cars of emperors and empresses, and Suetonius informs us that Claudius ordered that there should be decreed to his grandmother, Livia, divine honours, and a chariot drawn by elephants, similar to that of Augustus in the procession of the Circus. Eckhel shews that the triumphs were sometimes celebrated with horses, and sometimes with elephants, but generally with the former. Apuleius[2] says, "The quadrigæ of white horses, and the toga palmata, are proper for those who celebrate a triumph." When similar representations are found on coins, the event intended to be commemorated may be ascertained by our enquiring whether a triumph or a consular procession was celebrated in that year. A coin of Tiberius, struck A. U. C. 766, furnishes an example of this kind, for in this year he entered on the consulship, but history mentions no triumph. Among the coins of Aurelius is one struck in the year U. C. 898. In that year he entered on the consulship; but there was not even war at that time, so that a triumph could not have been intended. With regard to the olive branch, which the emperors often bear in their hand on these coins, Eckhel has shewn, that though appropriate to the celebration of a triumph, it was equally so to that of the consulship.

[1] Paneg. Theod. c. 22. [2] Apolog. p. m. 270.

The Proconsulates. There were three kinds of proconsulates among the Romans, namely, the *ordinary* one of those who were sent out under the usual regulations to govern the provinces of the empire;[1] another, *extraordinary*, as was that of those who received an enlarged but temporary authority over many provinces; the third, *perpetual*, which extended over all provinces, and which from the time of Augustus was decreed to all the emperors, and by them not unfrequently to the Cæsars, their successors.

The title, PROCOS, is inscribed on the coins of Diocletian, Maximianus Hercules, Constantius Chlorus, Licinius the Elder, and Constantine the Great; and it is a singular fact, that the numbers, ITERVM · III · IV, &c. are sometimes attached to these imperial proconsulates; but even the sagacious Eckhel cannot suggest a sufficient cause for this *renewal* of a *perpetual office*.[2]

It must be carefully borne in mind that the title, *Proconsul*, was not derived from the title, *Imperator*. The latter indicated the emperor's supreme direction, both of foreign and domestic affairs, but the former expressively signified that the *provinces of the people*, though under the rule of the ordinary proconsulate, were, nevertheless, so administered under the emperor's auspices, as to establish the pre-eminence of Cæsarean proconsular authority.

The Tribunitian Power. Records of the tribunitian power are very frequent on the coins of the earlier emperors, and are generally given in the abbreviations TRIB · POT. It is important to distinguish between the old *tribunes of the people* and the emperors endued with the tribunitian power. Augustus and his successors did not bear the title of tribune of the people, but only the title of the tribunitian power. Under the republic, no tribune of the people could at the same time hold the

[1] Records of the *ordinary* proconsulship are found on numerous consular coins. The coins of Pompey bear, PROCOS.

[2] It is about as significant as the titles, "Semper Augustus," and "Multus Augustus," on the coins of the lower empire.

office of consul, or be invested with any magisterial power; neither could he be absent from the city, or exercise his authority beyond it. The emperors, as is well known, were unfettered by such restrictions; and, further, the old tribuneship was, according to the ordinary law, only of a year's duration, and entered upon on the 10th of December, whereas the tribunitian power of the emperors was perpetual, and decreed at any period of the year.

As the tribunitian power, together with the title of emperor, was, as it were, a basis of authority, and he who bore it was either a prince, or destined for that honour, particular princes thought proper to form a sort of epoch of the day on which this power was conferred, and, as Dio says, "to reckon the preceding years of their rule from that date, as if they received it yearly with the tribunes of the people."[1] Hence the inscription of the tribunitian power, and its number on coins and other monuments as early as the time of Augustus; for Augustus himself, on the celebrated monument of Ancyra, on which he records a series of his exploits, has marked out the periods, not only by consulships, but also by the tribunitian power, when he relates, that largesses were distributed *the 12th year of the tribunitian power*, and, soon afterwards, *the 18th of the tribunitian power, the 12th consulate.* Thus, also, at his death, his last tribunitian power was the xxxviith. From this it is obvious, that a knowledge of the manner of inscribing the tribunitian power must conduce to the right understanding of the chronology of the emperors, and of their acts, under the proper dates.

Many authors have attempted to explain the difficulties with which this subject is beset; but, instead of reciting their opinions for the mere purpose of confuting them, it will suffice to refer to the more satisfactory explanation of Eckhel. This great numismatic luminary lays down the following concise rules:—

"The tribunitian power of the emperors was repeated in such manner, that, from the time of Augustus to the time of

[1] Lib. liii. 17.

Antoninus Pius, it was renewed every year on the same day as that on which it was received; and from the time of Antoninus Pius to Gallienus, every first of January." The former part of this opinion is easily understood; the other is to be interpreted thus:—on whatever day of the Julian year any one was presented with the tribunitian power, on the next first of January he commenced the second tribunitiate, although the time of his receiving that honour might precede the said calends, or first of January, by only a few months or even days. This doctrine, being in opposition to the opinion of other writers, is confirmed by the following rules:—

Rule I. The tribuneships, when compared with the consulships, indubitably shew whether the emperors renewed the tribunitian power on any day, after the first of January, within the same Julian year. Numerous coins of Domitian are extant, some of which unite the *sixth* tribunitian power, others the *seventh*, with the thirteenth consulship; but the coins inscribed in either of these years are of one and the same Julian year, that of Rome, 840. They cannot be of the preceding year, 839, for it was then the 12th consulship of that emperor, nor of the following year, 841, for it was then his 14th consulship. Therefore Domitian renewed the tribuneship within the same Julian year and the calends of January; that is to say, he renewed it on the very same day as that on which it was received. This is further established by the coins of Caligula, Titus, and others. Nevertheless, these excellent auxiliaries very often fail us, as some princes, among whom are Vespasian, Trajan, and Hadrian, generally neglected to add the proper number of their tribunitian power; and, indeed, from the time of Philip and his son, the consulships are not numbered on coins.

Rule II. As the tribunitian power never varies on the coins of any emperor within one and the same Julian year, it is clear that it was renewed on the first of January. If from the circumstance that a second tribuneship occurs within the same Julian year, it follows of itself that the tribunitian power of the emperor to whom these coins belong was repeated within the year, it will likewise necessarily follow, if in the coins of an emperor two different tribuneships never occur within the same Julian year, but always one and the same, that the tribunitian power was wont to be renewed by that emperor on the first of January. Examples are to be met with on the coins of princes who held the empire from the time of Antoninus Pius; but after the time of Gallienus the numbers of the tribuneship are so confused, that they contribute scarcely anything to be depended on for the service of history and chronology.[1]

Princeps Juventutis. The title of Prince of the Roman Youth occurs on the coins of the Cæsars, or heirs apparent, from the time of Augustus to a late period of the empire. Caius and Lucius Cæsar were thus designated,[2] and on a common second brass coin are represented on horseback, with the legend C · L · CAESARES · PRINC · IVVENTVTIS.[3] This title is found perpetually on the reverses of the coins of Diadumenian, Maximus, Philip the Younger, Herennius, Hostilian, Volusian, Saloninus, and down to Constantius the Second. On these the prince is represented bare-headed, holding a spear and a baton of command, and standing near two ensigns.[4]

Coins inscribed VOTIS. It is well known that the jurisdiction and privileges of the chief officers of the state, though granted to Augustus by degrees, was afterwards conferred upon his successors *at once*, by one single instrument, and despotic monarchy established by a law called afterwards "*lex regia.*" Thus Augustus *consented* to receive the sovereign power for ten years. When the ten years expired, he was *prevailed upon* to accept it for ten more, and in this manner kept it all his life. His successors, in imitation of this example, although they had the empire settled upon them without

[1] Doct. Num. Vet. vol. viii. *De Tribunitia Potestate.*
[2] Tacit. Ann. lib. i. 3.
[3] A coin of Nero bears EQVESTER · ORDO · PRINCIPI · IVVENT., and the same is found on a marble in Gruter.
[4] See the plate of Reverses of Roman Coins.

any limitation of time, nevertheless, at the end of every ten years, celebrated solemn feasts as for a renewal or continuation of the sovereignty in their persons. On these occasions the *numi votorum* were struck by them, and were designed to indicate both the discharge and the repetition of their votive engagements. Accordingly we meet with the following inscriptions: PRIMI · DECENNALES—VOTA · SVSCEPTA · XX · VOTA SOLVTA · DEC—VOT · XX · MVLT · XXX. Had this decennial issue been confined to the calends of January at the commencement of each period, we should possess a valuable test of the accuracy of important dates; but, unfortunately, the caprice of the emperors introduced so much irregularity into the solemnities connected with the renewal of their authority, that, in spite of the laboured essays of Page, Noris, and Mazzoleni, we must acknowledge, with the more learned and more accurate Eckhel, that the votive coins, in a *chronological* point of view, are absolutely useless. We find, for instance, on the coins of Antoninus Pius, VOTA · SVSCEP · DECENN · III. joined with TR · P · XXI · XXII and XXIII; and, again, on the coins of Commodus, VOTA · DECENN · SVSC. with TR · P · VI · IX and X. With these facts before us, it is sufficient to have pointed out the origin of a curious and very frequent legend.[1]

S · C. } Everything appears to indicate that the coinage of brass was under the direction and controul of the senate, while that of gold and silver was at the disposal of the emperor. Hence we perpetually find on the former the letters S · C (*Senatus Consulto*). These letters generally appear in the field of the coin, but are sometimes placed in the exergue.[2] When they appear on gold and silver coins, which is very rarely, their signification admits of another interpretation, and may be referred to some act performed by the senate in honour of the emperor, and not as implying that the piece was struck by decree of the "Conscript Fathers."

[1] On the coins of the Lower Empire the inscriptions VOT · XX · MVLT · XXX. &c., occur perpetually within a garland, as shewn in the plate of Roman Types.

[2] The *exergue* is the space below the line on which the figures of the reverse are placed.

Exergual Letters. The custom of inserting letters in the exergue, to denote the place of mintage, was resorted to at a late period of the empire, and in the reign of Diocletian became general. Thus, ANT stood for Antioch, SIS for Siscia, LVG for Lugdunum, and the number of the mint was denoted by a Greek numeral, ANTΓ (*Antioch, in the third mint*). Sometimes, instead of the numeral, a small symbol appears, a star or a crescent, probably the badge or mark of the mint master.[1] An explanation of the exergual letters will be found in the following lists.

[1] It was probably this crescent following the letters LON that caused Camden to read, in the exergue of a coin of Constantine, LOND. We are acquainted with a collector who was once led into the same error.

LIST OF THE PRINCIPAL ABBREVIATIONS ON ROMAN COINS.

A. in the exergue denotes the first mint, as ANT. A. coined at Antioch in the first mint.

A. A. A. F. F. Auro, Argento, Aere, Flando, Feriundo.

A. or AN. Annus.

A. A. Apollo Augusti.

A. F. A. N. Auli Filius, Auli Nepos.

ABN. Abnepos.

ACT. Actiacus, or Actium.

AD.FRV.EMV. Ad Fruges Emundas.

ADIAB. Adiabenicus.

ADOP. Adoptatus.

ADQ. Adquisata.

ADV. Adventus.

AED. Ædes.

AED. P. Ædilitia Potestate.

AED. S. Ædes Sacræ.

AED. CVR. Ædilis Curulis.

AED. PL. Ædilis Plebis.

AEL. Ælius.

AEM. or AIMIL. Æmilius.

AET. Æternitas.

AFR. Africa, or Africanus.

ALBIN. Albinus.

ALIM. ITAL. Alimenta Italiæ.

ALVIT. Alvitius.

ANN. AVG. Annona Augusti.

A. N. F. F. Annum Novum Faustum Felicem.

ANIC. Anicius.

ANN. DCCCLXIIII. NAT. VRB. P. CIR. CON. Anno 864, Natali Urbis Populo Circenses Constituti.

ANT. Antonius, or Antoninus.

ANT. AVG. Antonius Augur.

AP. Appius.

A. P. F. Argento Publico Feriundo.

A. POP. FRVG. AC. A Populo Fruges Acceptæ.

AQ. or AQL. Aquilius.

AQVA. MAR. Aqua Martia.

ARAB. ADQ. Arabia Adquisita.

ARAB. Arabicus.

ARR. Arrius.

AVG. Augur, Augustus, Augusta.

AVG. D. F. Augustus Divi Filius.

AVGG. Two Augusti.

AVGGG. Three Augusti.

AVR. or AVREL. Aurelius.

B. the mark of the second mint in any city.

BAEB. Baebius.

BALB. Balbus.

BARB. Barbatus, Barbula.

B. or BEAT. Beatissimus.

BROC. Brocchus.

BON. EVENT. Bonus Eventus.

B. R. P. NAT. Bono Reipublicæ Nato.

BRIT. Britannicus.

BRVT. Brutus.

C. Caius, Colonia.

C. A. Cæsarea Augusta.

C. CAE. or CAES. Cæsar.

CAE. or COE. Cælius.

CAE. Cæcina, Cæcilia.

CAL. Calpurnius, or Calidius, or Calvinus.

CAM. Camillus.

CAP. Capito, Capitolinus.

C. CVP. Caius Cupiennius.

C. C. Cæsares.

C. F. Caius Fabius.

C. F. C. N. Caii Filius, Caii Nepos.

C. F. L. R. Q. M. Caius Furius Lucius Rupilius Quintus Marcius.

CAESS. Cæsares.

CARTH. Carthaginem.

CASTROR. Castrorum.

CEN. Censor.

CENS. P. Censor Perpetuus.

CEST. Cestius, or Cestianus, or Cestia.

CIR. CON. Circum Condidit, or Circenses Concessit.

CIVIB. ET. SIGN. MILIT. A. PARTH. RECVP. Civibus et Signis Militaribus a Parthis Recuperatis.

CL. Claudius, or Claudia.

C. L. AVG. F. Caius Lucius Augusti Filius.

C. L. CAESS. Caius and Lucius Cæsares.

C. MAL. Caius Malleolus.

CN. DOM. AMP. Cnaeus Domitius Amplus.

CN. Cneius.

COEL. Cœlius.

CON. OB. Constantinopoli Obsignata, or Constantinopoli Officina Secunda.

COL. Colonia.

CONS. SVO. Conservatori suo.

CONSERVAT. PIETAT. Conservator Pietatis.

CONCORD. Concordia.

CL. V. Clypeus Votivus.

COMM. Commodus.

CLOD. Clodius.

CL. or CLAVD. Claudius.

COGN. or COGNAT. Cognatus.

COS. Consul.

COSS. Consules.

CORN. Cornelius.

C PAET. Caius Paetus.

CRAS. Crassus.

C. VET. LANG. Caius Vettius Languido.

CVR. X. F. Curavit Denarium Faciendum.

D. Decimus Divus, Designatus.

DAC. Dacicus.

D. C. A. Divus Cæsar Augusti.

D. D. Decreto Decuriorum.

DEC. Decius.

D. F. D. N. Decii Filius Decii Nepos.

D. F. Dacia Felix.

D. M. Diis Manibus.

DES. or DESIG. Designatus.

DICT. Dictator.

DOMIT. Domitianus.

D. N. Dominus noster.

DID. Didius.

D. P. Dii Penates.

DR. CAES. Q PR. Drusus Cæsar Quinquennalis Præfectus.

DOS. Dossenus.

DV. Divus.

EID. MAR. Idus Martiæ.

EX. CONS. D. Ex Consensu Decuriorum.

EX. S. C. Ex Senatus Consulto.

EQ. ORDIN. Equestris Ordinis.

EX. A. PV. Ex Argento, or Auctoritate Publica.

EXER. Exercitus.

ETR. Etruscus.

F. Filius, or Filia, or Felix, or Faciundum, or Fecit, or Fabius.

F. or FAB. Fabius.

FAD. Fadius.

FEL. Felix.

FELIC. Felicitas.

FL. Flavius.

FLAM. Flamen.

FAN. Fannius.

FORT. RED. Fortunæ Reduci.

FOR. Fortissimus (*Maximianus*).

FORT. or FOR. (*Decentius*).

FOVRI. Fourius, for Furius.

FONT. Fonteius.

FRVGIF. (Cereri) Frugiferæ.

FVL. Fulvius.

FVLG. Fulgerator.

G. Gneius, Genius, Gaudium.

GA. Gaditanus.

GAL. Galerius.

G. D. Germanicus Daccius.

G. Galendicus (Surname of Volusian)

GRA. Gracchus.

GEN. Genius.

GERM. Germanicus.

GL. E. R. Gloria Exercitus Romani.

GL. P. R. Gloria Populi Romani.

GOTH. Gothicus.

G. P. R. Genio Populi Romani.

G. T. A. Genius Tutelaris Ægypti, or Africæ.

HEL. Helvius.

HEL. Heliopolis.

HER. Herennius, or Herennia.

HIP. Hippius.

HO. Honos.

IIS. Sestertius.

I. Imperator, Jovi, Julius.

IAN.CLV. Janum Clusit (for Clausit).

IMP. Imperator.

IMPP. Imperatores.

I. or INVICT. Invictus.

I. S. M. R. Juno Sospita, Mater (or Magna), Regina.

IT. Italia, Iterum.

ITE. Iterum.

IVL. Julius, or Julia.

IVST. Justus.

I-IS. Sestertius.

I. O. M. SACR. Jovi Optimo, Maximo, Sacrum.

II. VIR. Duumvir.

III. VIR. R. P. C. Triumvir Reipublicæ Constituendæ.

IIII. VIR. A. P. F. Quatuorvir, or Quatuorviri, Auro, or (Argento, or Ære), Publico Feriundo.

IVN. Junior.

K. Kaeso.

KAN. Kanninius.

L. Lucius.

LAT. Latinus.

L. CAN. Lucius Canninius.

L. COE. Lucius Cœlius.

LEG. PROPR. Legatus Proprætoris.

LEG. I. &c. Legio Prima, &c.

LEP. Lepidus.

LENT. CVR. X. F. Lentulus Curavit Denarium Faciundum.

L. F. L. N. Lucii Filius, Lucii Nepos.

L. H. T. Lucius Hostilius Tubero.

L. M. RVF. P. C. Q. Lucio Mescinio Rufo Publio Carisio Quinquennalibus.

LON. Longus.

L. P. D. AE. P. Lucius Papirius Desig. Ædilis Plebis.

L. R. Lucius Rubrius, or Roscius, or Rutilius, or Rupilius.

LIBERO. P. Libero Patri.

LIBERO. CONS. AVG. Libero Conservatori Augusti.

LIB. PVB. Libertas Publica.

LIB. Liberator.

LIC. Licinius.

L. S. DEN. Lucius Sicinius Dentatus.

LVC. Lucifera.

LVD. CIR. Ludi Circenses.

LVD. EQ. Ludi Equestres.

LVD. SAEC. F. Ludos Sæculares Fecit.

LVP. Lupercus.

MA. Manius.

M. AB. M. F. Marcus Aburius, Marcus Fannius.

M. AEM. Marcus Æmilius.

MA. CANI. Manius Caninius.

M. ANN. Marcus Annius.

MAR. or MR. Marcus.

M. AVF. or AF. Marcus Aufidius.

M. Marcus, or Marius.

M. C. Mater Castrorum.

MAR. CL. Marcellus Clodius.

M. F. Marci Filius.

M. OTACIL. Marcia Otacilia.

MAG. or MAGN. Magnus, or Magister.

MAC. Macellum.

MAX. Maximus.

MAR. Martia (aqua).

MAR. VLT. Marti Ultori.

MEDI. Medicus.

MES. Messius.

METOE. Mœticus.

M. MAR. Marcus Marcellus.

METAL. Metallum.

MINAT. Minatius.

MINER. Minerva.

M. M. I. V. Municipes Municipii Julii Uticensis.

MON. or MONET. Moneta.

M. POP. Marcus Popilius.

MV. Mucius Munacius.

N. Nepos, or Noster.

N. Numerius.

NV. Numa.

N. C. Nobilissimus Cæsar.

NAT. VRB. Natalis Urbis.

NEP. Nepos.

NEP. RED. Neptuno Reduci.

NOB. or NOBIL. Nobilissimus.

N. F. N. N. Numerii Filius, Numerii Nepos.

NICER. Nicerius.

O. Optimo.

OB. C. S. Ob Cives Servatos.

OF. Officina.

OGVL. Ogulnius.

OLY. Olympius.

OPEI. Opimius.

OPEL. Opelius.

ORB. TERR. Orbis Terrarum.

P. or POT. Potestate.

PAC. ORB. TER. Pacatori Orbis Terrarum.
PÆ. PÆT. Pætus.
PIV. PIVES. Pivesuvius (Tetricus).
PLAN. Plancus.
PLAE. TRAN. Plaetorius Tranquillinus.
P. AV. CO. PA. Publius Aurelius Catelius Patiscus.
PAPI. Papius or Papirius.
PART. or PARTH. Parthicus.
PER. or PERP. Perpetuus.
PERS. Persicus (*Carus*).
PERT. or PERTIN. Pertinax.
PESC. Pescennius.
P. F. Pius Felix.
PLAET. Plætorius.
P. M. or PONT. MAX. Pontifex Maximus.
POL. Pollio.
POMP. Pompeius.
P. P. Pater Patriæ.
PR. Prætor.
P. R. Populus Romanus.
PR. H. O. C. S. Praetextatus Hostem Occidit Civem Servavit.
PRAEF. CLAS. ET. OR. MARIT. Præfectus Classis et Oræ Maritimæ.
PRINC. IVVENT. Princeps Juventutis.
PRIV. Privernum.
PROC. Proconsul.
PRON. Pronepos.
PROP. Proprætor.
PROQ. Proquæstor.
PROV. DEOR. Providentia Deorum.
PVPIEN. or PVPIE. Pupienus.
PVR. Purpureus.

Q. Quintus, or Quæstor.
Q. CAS. Quintus Cassius.
Q. C. M. P. I. Quintus Cæcilius Metellus Pius Imperator.
Q. DESIG. Quæstor Designatus.
Q. M. Quintus Marcius.
Q. O. C. F. Quinto Ogulnio et Caio Fabio.
Q. PAPIR. CAR. Q. TER. MON. Quinto Papirio Carbone et Quinto Terentia Montana.
QUAD. Quadrans.
Q. P. Quæstor Prætorius.
Q. PR. Quæstor Provincialis.

R. Roma, or Restituit.
RECEP. Receptis, or Receptus.
RES. Restius, or Restitutus.
REST. Restituit.
ROM. ET. AVG. Romæ et Augusto.
R. P. C. Rei Publicæ Constituendæ.

SAEC. AVR. Sæculum Aureum.
SAEC. FEL. Sæculi Felicitas.
SAL. Salus.
SALL. Sallustia.
SARM. Sarmaticus.
SAVF. or SAF. Saffeius.
S. C. Senatus Consulto.
SCIP. ASIA. Scipio Asiaticus.
SCR. Scribonius.
SENTI. Sentia.
SEMP. Semper.
SIL. Silius.
SEC. ORB. Securitas Orbis.
SEC. PERP. Securitas Perpetua.
SEC. TEMP. Securitas Temporum.
SEN. Senior.
SEPT. Septimius.

SER. Servius.
SEV. Severus,
SEX. Sextus.
SIC V. SIC X. Sicut Quinquennalia, Sic Decennalia.
SIG. Signis.
S. M. Signata Moneta.
S. P. Q. R. Senatus Populusque Romanus.
SP. Spurius.
STABIL. Stabilita (terra).
SVL. Sulla.

T. Titus, Tribunus.
TER. Terentius, or Tertium.
TEMP. Temporum.
TI. Tiberius.
TF. Titus Flavius.
T. M. AP. CL. Titus Manlius et Appius Claudius.
TREB. Trebonianus.
TRAN. Tranquillus.
TREBAN. Trebanius.
TVL. H. Tullius Hostilius.
TR. MIL. Tribunes Militaris.
TR. P. or TRIB. POT. Tribunicia Potestate.

V. Quintum.
VAR. RVF. Varius Rufus.
V. C. Vir Clarissimus.
VENT. Ventidius.
VET. LANG. Vettius Languidus.
VESP. Vespasianus.
VIB. Vibius.
VICT. Victoria.
VII. VIR. EPVL. Septemvir Epulonum.
VIL. PVB. Villa Publica.
VIRT. Virtus.
VOL. Volusius.
VOLER. Volero.
VIN. Vinicius.
VOC. Voconius.
VARG. Varganteius.
VL. or VLP. Ulpius.
VN. MR. Venerandæ Memoriæ.
VOT. X. MVLT. XX. Votis Decennalibus Multiplicatis Vicennalibus.

X. Decem, Denarius.
XV. VIR. SACR. FAC. Quindecim Vir Sacris Faciundis.

ABBREVIATIONS IN THE EXERGUE.*

A. (OFFICINA) Prima.
ALE. Alexandria.
AMB. Antiochensis Moneta Secundæ Officinæ.
AN. ANT. ANTI. Antiochia.
ANB. Antiochiæ Secunda Officina; or, ANH. Antiochæ Octava Officina.
AP. L. Prima Percussa Lugduni.
AQ. AQVL. Aquileiæ.
AQ. O. B. F. Aquileiæ Officinæ Secundæ Fabrica.
AQ. P. S. Aquileiæ Pecunia Signata.

* The exergue of a coin is that part which is divided from the field by a line upon which the figures of the reverse stand. Vide Eckhel, D. N. Vet. vol. viii. p. 518.

AQ. S. Aquileiæ Signata.
A. AR. ARL. Arelate.
A. SISC. Prima (in Officina) Sisciæ.

B. SIRM. Secunda Sirmii.

CON. Constantinopoli.
CONS. Constantinopoli.

KAR. KART. Carthago.
K. O. Carthaginensis Officina.

L. LC. LVC. LVG. Lucduni, Lugduni.
L. LON. Londini.
L. P. Lugdunensis vel Londinensis Pecunia.
LVG. P. S. Lugduni Pecunia Signata.

MDPS. Mediolani Pecunia Signata.
M. K. V. T. Moneta Kartaginensis Urbis (in officina) Tertia.
M. L. Moneta Lugdunensis vel Londinensis.
MOSTT. Moneta Officinæ Secundæ Treverorum.
MSTR. Moneta Signata Treveris.

O. Officina.
OFF. III. CONST. Officina Tertia Constantinopoli.

PARL. Percussa, or Pecunia Arelate.
PLON. Pecunia Londinensis.
PLVG. Pecunia Lugdunensis.
P. R. Pecunia Romana, or Percussa Romæ.
P. T. Pecunia Treverensis.

Q. AR. Quincta Arelatensis (officina).

R. RO. ROM. Romæ.
RA. Ravennæ.
ROPS. Romæ Pecunia Signata.

S. AR. Signata Arelate.
S. CONST. Signata Constantinopoli.
SIS. Sisciæ.
SS. P. Sisciensis Pecunia.
SISC. V. Siscia Urbis.
SMA. Signata Moneta Antiochiæ.
S. M. HER. Signata Moneta Heracleæ.
S. M. N. Signata Moneta Nicomediæ.
S. M. R. Signata Moneta Romæ.
S. T. Signata Treveris.

TESOB. Tessalonicæ Officina Secunda.
THEOPO. Theopoli.
THEVP. Theupoli.
TR. Treveris.
TROB. Treveris Officina Secunda.

THE ROMAN AS,

ITS DIVISIONS AND MULTIPLES, WITH THEIR DEGREES OF RARITY.*

Decussis (ten Ases).—Æ. R.8.
Quincussis (five Ases).—No pieces known.
Quadrussis (four Ases).—Æ. R.6. to R.8.
Tripondius (three Ases).—Æ. R.4.
Dupondius (two Ases).—Æ. R.3.
As (12 unciæ).—Æ. C. to R.4.
Semis (half As).—Æ. C. to R.4.
Quincunx (five unciæ).—Æ. R.1. to R.6.
Triens (one-third of the As).—Æ. C. to R.8.
Quadrans (one-fourth As).—Æ. C. to R.4.
Sextans (one-sixth As).—Æ. C. to R.2.
Uncia (one-twelfth As).—Æ. C. to R.4.

COINS OF ROMAN FAMILIES,

WITH THEIR DEGREES OF RARITY.

Aburia (a plebeian family).—AR. C. to R.1. Third brass, parts of the Roman As.

Accoleia (known only by their coins).—AR. R.1.

Acilia (plebeian rank).—AR. C. Brass, see the parts of the As.

Aebutia (unknown rank).—Colonial brass only.

Aelia and Allia (plebeian rank).—AR. C. First brass, moneyers of Augustus, C. Second brass, Colonial, R.1.

Aemilia (patrician rank). — AV. R.8. AR. C. *Restored by Trajan*, R.6. Second brass, Colonial, C.

Afrania (plebeian rank).—AR. R.1. First and third brass, parts of the As.

Allienus (a surname).—AR. R.5.

---

* Vide "Descriptive Catalogue," vol. i.

Annia (plebeian rank). — AR. R.1. Third brass, moneyers of Augustus.

Antestia, or Antistia (plebeian rank). — AV. R.8. AR. C. First and third brass, parts of the As.

Antia (plebeian rank).—AR. R.2.

Antonia (patrician rank). — AV. R.8. AR. C. *Quinarii.* R.1.

Appuleia (plebeian rank).—Brass, see the As.

Apronia (plebeian rank).—Brass, of the Colonies, and of the moneyers of Augustus.

Aquillia (plebeian and patrician). AR. R.1.

Arria (plebeian family).—AV. R.6. AR. R.6. Brass, Colonial.

Asinia (plebeian family).—Brass, of the moneyers of Augustus.

Atia (plebeian family).—AV. R.8. AR. R.8. Æ. R.2.

Atilia (patrician and plebeian).—AR. C. Brass, see the parts of the As.

Aufidia (plebeian family).—AR. R.2.

Aurelia (plebeian family).—AR. C.

Autronia (unknown rank).—AR. R.4.

Axia (plebeian rank).—AR. R.2. Third brass, see the As.

Baebia (plebeian rank). — AR. R.1. Brass, Colonial, and parts of the As.

Betelienus (a surname).—Third brass, of the moneyers of Augustus, C.

Caecilia (plebeian rank). — AV. R.6. AR. C. Restored by Trajan, R.6. Cistophori of Pergamus, R.5. Brass, see the As.

Caecina (a surname).—Brass, see the As.

Caesia (plebeian rank).—AR. R.2.

Calidia (plebeian rank).—AR. R.1.

Calpurnia (plebeian rank). — AV. (A quinarius). Unique? AR. C. Sestertii, R.4. Brass, moneyers of Augustus and Antonius.

Canidia (plebeian rank). — First brass, R.5. Second brass, R.3.

Caninia (plebeian rank). — AR. Moneyers of Augustus, R.1. Third brass, Colonial, of Corinth, R.5.

Carisia (plebeian rank).—AR. C. to R.2. Restored by Trajan, R.6. Quinarii, moneyers of Augustus, R.1. Sestertii, R.8. AR. Colonial, C. Brass Colonial, R.1.

Carvilia (plebeian family).—AR. C. Second brass, see the As.

Cassia (plebeian and patrician).—AR. C. Restored by Trajan, R.6. First and second brass, see the As and its parts, R.2. Second and third brass of Antioch, R.3. Second brass, moneyers of Augustus, C.

CESTIA (plebeian rank). — AV. R.4. Second and third brass, of Enna, in Sicily, R.5. Second and third brass, of Nero, of Antioch, R.1.

CIPIA (plebeian rank).—AR. R.1. Second brass, see the semis. R.2.

CLAUDIA (a Sabine patrician family).—AV. R.4. AR. C. Restored by Trajan, R.6. Cistophori, R.6. Third brass, moneyers of Augustus, C.

CLOVIA (plebeian rank).—Second brass, moneyers of J. Cæsar, C.

CLOULIA (patrician rank).—AR. Denarii and quinarii, C.

COCCEIA (unknown rank).—AR. R.4.

COELIA (plebeian rank).—AV. R.8. AR. C.

CONSIDIA (plebeian rank).—AR. Denarii, C. Quinarii, R.2. Sestertii, R.5.

COPONIA (unknown rank).—AR. R.2.

CORDIA (unknown rank).—AR. C. Quinarii and sestertii, R.8.

CORNELIA (patrician and plebeian rank). — AV. R.4. AR. C. Quinarii, R.1. Cistophori, R.5. First and second brass, see the As and its parts, R.1. Third brass, moneyers of Augustus, C.

CORNUFICIA (plebeian rank).—AV. R.8. AR. R.6. Restored by Trajan, R.7.

COSCONIA (plebeian rank).—AR. C.

COSSUTIA (of the equestrian rank).—AR. R.2.

CREPEREIA (of the equestrian rank).—AR. C. to R.4.

CREPUSIA (unknown rank).—AR. C.

CRITONIA (plebeian rank).—AR. R.4.

CUPIENNIA (unknown rank).—AR. R.1. Second and third brass, see the semis, R.3.

CURIATIA (plebeian rank).—AR. R.1. to R.2. Second and third brass, see the parts of the As, R.1.

CURTIA (plebeian rank).—AR. R.1. Second and third brass, R.1.

DIDIA (plebeian rank).—AR. R.1. to R.2.

DOMITIA (plebeian, raised to patrician rank).—AV. R.6. AR. C. Second and third brass, see the semis and quadrans, C.

DURMIA (unknown rank). — AV. R.4. AR. C. Both of the moneyers of Augustus.

EGNATIA (plebeian rank).—AR. R.2.

EGNATULEIA (unknown rank).—AR. Quinarii only, C.

EPPIA (unknown rank).—AR. R.2. Brass, see the As, R.4.

FABIA (patrician rank).—AR. C. Brass, see the As, R.2. Brass, Colonial, C.

FABRICIA (plebeian rank).—Second brass, R.4.

FABRINIA (unknown rank).—Second and third brass, triens and sextans, C.

FANNIA (plebeian rank).—AR. R.1. Cistophori, of Tralles, R.7.

The type of the *Cistophori* will be found among the plates in this volume. A very common quinarius of Augustus bears on the reverse a figure of Victory standing on the *Cistus*; legend, ASIA · RECEPTA.

FARSULEIA (plebeian rank).—AR. C.

FLAMINIA (plebeian rank).—AR. R.1.

FLAVIA (plebeian rank). AR. C.

FONTEIA (plebeian rank).—AR. C. Brass, see the As and its parts, R.1. Brass, of the moneyers of Antony, R.4.

FUFIA (plebeian rank).—AR. R.1.

FULVIA (plebeian rank).—AR. C.

FUNDANIA (plebeian rank).—AR. C.

FURIA (patrician rank).—AV. R.8. AR. C. Second brass, R.6. First and second brass, see the As, R.2.

GALLIA (plebeian rank).—First and second brass, moneyers of Augustus.

GELLIA (unknown rank).—AR. R.1. to R.2.

HERENNIA (plebeian rank).—AR. C.

HIRTIA (plebeian rank).—AV. R.1.

HORATIA (patrician rank).—AR. R.8.

This very rare coin was restored by Trajan. The type is the usual head of Minerva; reverse the *Dioscuri* on horseback; but the obverse bears the name COCLES.

HOSIDIA (uncertain rank).—AR. R.1.

HOSTILIA (patrician rank).—AR. R.1. Third brass, R.4.

ITIA (unknown rank).—AR. R.3.

JULIA (patrician rank).—AV. R.4. AR. C. Of the moneyers of J. Cæsar, R.2.

JUNIA (patrician and plebeian rank).—AR. C. Restored by Trajan, R.7. First brass, see the As, R.2.

LICINIA (plebeian rank).—AR. R.1. First brass, R.1. First and second brass, see the As and its parts, C. First and second brass, moneyers of Augustus, C.

LIVINEIA (plebeian rank).—AV. R.7. AR. C. to R.1. Restored by Trajan, R.6. Third brass, moneyers of Augustus.

LOLLIA (plebeian rank).—AR. R.2. Brass of the Colony of Cyrenaica, R.1.

LUCILIA (plebeian rank).—AR. R.1.

LUCRETIA (patrician and plebeian rank).—AR. C. Restored by Trajan, R.6.

LURIA (unknown rank).—First and second brass, moneyers of Augustus.

LUTATIA (plebeian rank).—AR. R.1. First brass, moneyers of Augustus.

MAECILIA (plebeian rank).—First and second brass, moneyers of Augustus, C.

MAENIA (plebeian rank).—AR. R.1. Third brass, R.3.

MAIANIA (unknown rank).—AR. R.1. First brass, see the As, C. Third brass, moneyers of Augustus, R.6.

MAMILIA (a noble Tuscan family, of plebeian rank in Rome).—AR. C. Restored by Trajan, R.7.

MANLIA (patrician rank).—AV. R.6. AR. C.

MARCIA (patrician and plebeian family).—AR. C. Restored by Trajan, R.6. First and second brass, moneyers of Augustus, C. First brass, see the As, R.2. Second brass, R.1. to R.2. Third brass, C. to R.3. First brass, with heads of Ancus and Numa, R.2.

MARIA (plebeian rank).—AV. Moneyers of Augustus, R.8. Silver, R.1. Restored by Trajan, R.6. Of the moneyers of Augustus, R.1.

MEMMIA (plebeian rank).—AR. C. Restored by Trajan, R.6. Second brass (semis), R.3.

MESCINIA (plebeian rank).—AV. Moneyers of Augustus, R.8. AR. R.2.

METTIA (unknown rank).—AV. Moneyers of J. Cæsar, R.5. AR. R.1. AR. Quinarii, R.4.

MINATIA (plebeian rank).—AR. Of Cnæius Pompey, the son, R.6.

MINEIA (unknown rank).—Third brass. R.3.

MINUCIA (plebeian rank).—AV. R.4. AR. C. Restored by Trajan, R.7. Second and third brass, C. to R.1.

MITREIA (unknown rank).—Third brass, moneyers of Augustus, R.2.

MUCIA (plebeian rank).—AR. R.1. See family Fufia.

MUNATIA (plebeian rank).—AV. See the coins of Antony, R.1. AR. R.4.

MUSSIDIA (plebeian rank).—AV. Moneyers of Antony Octavius and Lepidus, R.2. AR. R.2. Of the moneyers of J. Cæsar and Lepidus, R.2. First, second, and third brass, moneyers of Augustus, C.

NAEVIA (plebeian rank).—AR. C. First, second, and third brass, moneyers of Augustus, C.

NASIDIA (plebeian rank).—AR. See the coins of S. Pompey, R.2.

NERIA (plebeian rank).—AR. R.2.

NONIA (plebeian rank).—AR. R.1. First and second brass, moneyers of Augustus, C.

NORBANUS (a surname).—AV. R.6. AR. C. Restored by Trajan, R.6.

NUMITORIA (plebeian rank).—AR. R.4. Second and third brass, semis and quadrans, C.

NUMONIA (plebeian rank).—AV. R.8. AR. R.7. Restored by Trajan, R.8.

OGULNIA (plebeian rank).—AR. R.4. Second brass, see the As, R.1.

OPEIMIA (plebeian rank).—AR. R.1. First, second, and third brass, see the As and its divisions, R.1.

OPPIA (plebeian rank).—Second brass, C. Second brass, see the As, R.1.

PACUVIA, or PAQUIA (unknown rank).—Second and third brass, R.2.

PAPIA (plebeian rank).—AR. C. to R.4. Denarii and quinarii.

PAPIRIA (plebeian rank).—AR. C. First, second, and third brass, see the As and its divisions, R.1.

PEDANIA (plebeian rank).—AR. R.2.

PETILLIA (plebeian rank).—AR. R.2.

PETRONIA (plebeian rank).—AV. Moneyers of Augustus, R.2. AR. R.2.

PINARIA (patrician rank).—AR. C. First brass, see the As, R.1. First brass, with heads of Antony and Cleopatra, R.6. Third brass, quadrans, R.1.

PLAETORIA (plebeian rank).—AR. C. AR. coins of Brutus, R.6.

PLANCIA (plebeian rank).—AR. R.1.

PLAUTIA, or PLUTIA (plebeian rank).—AR. C.

PLOTIA (plebeian rank).—First and second brass, moneyers of Augustus, C.

POBLICIA (plebeian rank).—AR. C.

POMPEIA (plebeian rank).—AV. R.8. AR. C. AR. of Cnæius Pompey, the son, R.6. First brass, R.2. Second and third brass, As and quadrans, C.

POMPONIA (plebeian rank).—AR. R.1.

PORCIA (plebeian rank).—AR. C.

POSTUMIA (patrician rank).—AR. C.

PROCILIA (plebeian rank).—AR. R.1.

PROCULEIA (plebeian rank).—Third brass, R.3.

PUPIA (unknown rank).—Brass, struck in Cyrenaica.

QUINCTIA (plebeian, afterwards patrician).—AV. R.8. AR. R.1. First, and second brass, moneyers of Augustus, C. Second brass, semis, R.4.

RENIA (rank unknown).—AR. C.

ROSCIA (plebeian rank).—AR. C.

RUBELLIA (of the equestrian order).—Third brass, moneyers of Augustus, C.

RUBRIA (plebeian rank).—AR. C. Restored by Trajan, R.6. Quinarii, R.3. First brass, see the As, R.2.

RUSTIA (unknown rank).—AV. R.8. AR. R.1.

RUTILIA (plebeian rank).—AR. R.1.

SALVIA (plebeian rank).—AR. Moneyers of Octavius, R.1 First and second brass, moneyers of Augustus, C.

SANQUINIA (unknown rank).—AR. Moneyers of Augustus, R.1. First and second brass, moneyers of Augustus, C.

SATRIENUS (a surname).—AR. C.

SAUFEIA (plebeian rank).—AR. R.1. First brass, see the As, C. Second brass, semis and triens, R.1.

SCRIBONIA (plebeian rank). — AV. R.8. Silver, C. Restored by Trajan, R.6. First brass, As, R.1. Third brass, triens, C.

SEMPRONIA (unknown rank).—AV. Moneyers of Augustus, R.5. AR. C. AR. Moneyers of J. Cæsar and Augustus, R.2. First brass, As, R.2. First and second brass, moneyers of Augustus, C. First brass, with the head of Antony, R.4.

SENTIA (plebeian rank).—AR. C.

SEPULLIA (unknown rank). — AR. R.2. Quinarii and sestertii, R.8.

SERGIA (patrician rank).—AR. R.1.

SERVILIA (of plebeian and afterwards of patrician rank).—AV. R.4. AR. C. Third brass, quadrans, R.3.

SESTIA (of patrician and afterwards of plebeian rank). — AR. R.2. Quinarii, R.5.

SICINIA (of patrician and afterwards of plebeian rank).—AR. R.1.

SILIA (plebeian rank). — AV. R.7. AR. R.1. First brass, moneyers of Augustus, C.

SOSIA (plebeian rank).—Second and third brass, with head of Antony, R.6. Third brass, with head of Bacchus, R.8.

SPURILIA (unknown rank).—AR. R.1.

STATIA (plebeian rank).—AR. R.7. Third brass, R.6.

STATILIA (unknown rank). — Second brass, (Spanish), R.6. Third brass, moneyers of Augustus, C.

SULPICIA (patrician and plebeian rank). — AV. R.8. AR. C. Restored by Trajan, R.6. Second and third brass, R.4.

TARQUITIA (patrician and plebeian rank).—AR. R.2.

TERENTIA (plebeian rank).—AR. C. First brass, As, R.1. Second and third brass, semis and quadrans, R.1. First brass, moneyers of Augustus, R.4.

THORIA (plebeian rank).—AR. C.

TITIA (plebeian rank). —AR. C. Restored by Trajan, R.6. Quinarii, R.1. First brass, As, C.

TITINIA (patrician and plebeian).—AR. R.1. Second brass, As, C.

TITURIA (unknown rank).—AR. C.

TREBANIA (unknown rank).—AR. R.1. Second and third brass, divisions of the As, R.1.

TULLIA (patrician and plebeian).—AR. R.1. Restored by Trajan, R.6. Cistophori, R.6. Second brass, Colonial.*

VALERIA (patrician and plebeian).—AV. Moneyers of M. Antony, R.8. AR. C. Quinarii, R.4. Restored by Trajan, R.6. Second and third brass, moneyers of Augustus, C.

VARGUNTEIA (unknown rank). — AR. R.1. Second and third brass, divisions of the As, C.

VENTIDIA (plebeian rank).—AR. Moneyers of Antony, R.6.

VETTIA (unknown rank).—AR. R.2.

VETURIA (patrician rank). — AV. Denarii and quinarii, R.6. AR. R. 2.

VIBIA (plebeian rank).—AV. R.7. AR. C. First brass, As, R.1.

VINICIA (plebeian rank).—AR. R.2.

VOCONIA (plebeian rank). — AV. Moneyers of Octavius, R.4. AR. Moneyers of J. Cæsar, R.2.

VOLTEIA (unknown rank).—AR. C.

UNCERTAIN COINS.—AV. C. to R.8. AR. C. to R.8.

---

* These coins bear the head of Cicero, and were struck at Magnesia, in Lydia. A specimen is engraved at page 104.

COINS OF ROMAN EMPERORS, EMPRESSES, CAESARS, & USURPERS,

FROM CNAEIUS POMPEIUS TO CONSTANTINUS PALEOLOGUS; WITH THEIR DEGREES OF RARITY.

CNAEIUS POMPEIUS Magnus.—Born A.C. 106. Killed A.C. 48.
AV. R.6. AR. R.1. to R.2. Restored by Trajan, R.8. First and second brass, R.1.

CAIUS JULIUS CAESAR.—Born A.C. 100. Made Perpetual Dictator and killed, 44 A.C.

AV. Without his head, C. With his head, R.6. Restored by Trajan, R.5. to R.8. AR. Without his head, C. With his head, R.1. to R.4. First brass, R.1 to R.3. Second brass, C. to R.4.

CNAEIUS POMPEIUS, son of Pompeius Magnus.—Born, A.C. — Killed, 45 A.C.
AR. R.1. to R.6.

SEXTUS POMPEIUS, son of Pompeius Magnus.—Born, 65 A.C. Killed, 35 A.C.

AV. R.6. AR. Without head, R.1. With head, R.5.

MARCUS JUNIUS BRUTUS.—Born, 85 A.C. Killed himself, 42 A.C.
AV. R.8. AR. R.4. to R.6. Restored by Trajan, R.7.

CAIUS CASSIUS LONGINUS.—Born, — A.C. Killed himself, 42 A.C.
AV. R.4. AR. R.1. to R.2. (Without his head).

MARCUS AEMILIUS LEPIDUS.—Born, — A.C. Died, A.D. 13.
AV. R.8. AR. With head of Augustus, R.3. Of Antonius, R.5.

His silver is generally ill struck and much worn.

MARCUS ANTONIUS.—Born, 83 A.C. Killed himself, 30 A.C.
AV. R.3. to R.8. AR. Legions, C. to R.6. With head, R.1. to R.4. Second brass, R.1. to R.4.

OCTAVIA, wife of Antonius.—Born, — A.C. Died, 11 or 10 A.C.
AV. R.8. With M. Antonius.

Pinkerton gives a gold coin of this lady in his text and plate, but excludes her from his estimate; and another aureus, differing a little in the legend, but with a similar portrait, may be found in the *Gentleman's Magazine* for 1768 (p. 56). This is said to belong to Mr. Lefroy, of Leghorn, and is probably now in the collection made by him, which is believed to be still entire, but the weight, as Mr. Brumell, who communicates this note, observes, militates against the supposition of its being an aureus, if a genuine coin. The weight is 164 grains.

MARCUS ANTONIUS, son of M. Antonius.—Born, — A.C. Killed, 30. A.C.
AV. R.8. With his father.

CLEOPATRA, queen of Egypt.—Born,—A.C. Reigned from A.C. 51 to A.C. 30, when she destroyed herself.
AV. R.8. AR. R.4. Second and third brass, R.4.

Her coins in silver are rarely fine, or even in good condition.

CAIUS ANTONIUS, brother of the Triumvir.—Born, —A.C. Died, — A.C.
AR. R.6. Without his head.

LUCIUS ANTONIUS, brother of the Triumvir. — Born, — A.C. Died, — A.C.
AV. R.8. AR. R.4. With his brother, M. Antonius.

AUGUSTUS. Caius Octavius Caepius Augustus.—Born, A.C. 63. Died, 14 A.D.
AV. C. to R.4. Restored by Trajan, R.8. AR. C. to R.3. Restored by Trajan, R.6. First brass, R.1. to R.4. Reverse, of Agrippa, R.7. Second brass, C. to R.3. Restored by Claudius, Nero, Titus, Domitian, Nerva, and Trajan, R.2. to R.6.

Towards the end of this emperor's reign, the gold and silver coins are very beautiful, and the standard of great purity.

LIVIA, wife of Augustus.—Born, A.C. 57. Died, 29 A.D.
First brass, Representing Justitia, R.4. Second brass, As Justitia, Pietas, or Salus, C. *Justitia* and *Salus Augusta* restored by Titus, R.3. *Pietas*, restored by Titus and Domitianus, R.2.

MARCUS AGRIPPA.—Born, A.C. 63. Died, 12 A.D.
AV. R.8. AR. R.6. to R.7. Second brass, C. to R.4. Third brass, R.4.

JULIA, daughter of Augustus.—Born, A.C. 39. Starved to death by order of Tiberius her husband, A.D. 14. First brass (Greek), R.5. Second brass, R.1.

CAIUS and LUCIUS CAESARES, sons of M. Agrippa and Julia.—Caius born, A.C. 20. Died, A.D. 4. Lucius born, A.C. 17. Died, A.D. 2.

AV. C. AR. C. On Reverses, of Augustus.

Caius alone is AV. R.1. AR. R.1. In the Cat. d'Ennery a second brass coin is described with laureated head of Augustus; reverse, PONT · COS., head of Caius; but it is without the S · C. It is R.5.

AGRIPPA POSTUMUS, son of Agrippa and Julia.—Born, A.C. 12. Killed, A.D. 14. Greek and Colonial coins only.

TIBERIUS.—Born, A.C. 42. Killed, A.D. 37.

AV. C. Restored by Titus or Trajan, R.8. AR. C. Reverse, of Augustus, R.4. Of Drusus, R.8. First brass, R.1. to R.4. Restored by Trajan (Morell), R.6. Second brass, C. to R.4. Restored by Titus and Domitian, R.2. Third brass, C.

Half aurei occur of Augustus and of Tiberius, which are R.2. Those of subsequent reigns, when they do occur, are of considerable rarity.

DRUSUS JUNIOR, son of Tiberius.—Born, about 13 A.C. Poisoned, A.D. 23.

AR. (Reverse, of Tiberius), R.6. First brass, R.6. Without his head, R.1. Second brass, C. to R.3.

NERO CLAUDIUS DRUSUS (Drusus, senior), brother of Tiberius.—Born, A.C. 38. Died, A.D. 9.

AV. R.4. AR. R.4. First brass, R.3. to R.5. Restored by Titus or Domitian, R.6.

ANTONIA, wife of Drusus, senior.—Born, about 39 A.C. Poisoned, 38 A.D.

AV. R.4. AR. R.4. Second brass, C.

GERMANICUS, son of Drusus and Antonia.—Born, A.C. 15. Poisoned, 19 A.D.

AV. R.4. to R.6. AR. R.3. Reverse, of Augustus, R.6. First brass, R.8. Second brass, C. restored by Titus or Domitian, R.2.

AGRIPPINA, SENIOR, wife of Germanicus.—Born, A.C. 15. Starved to death, A.D. 33.

AV. R.4. to R.8. AR. R.4. First brass, R.2. Restored by Titus, R.6.

NERO and DRUSUS CAESARES.—Nero born, about A.D. 7. Starved to death, A.D. 31.—Drusus, born about A.D. 8. Starved to death, A.D. 33.

Second brass, C. With the brothers on horseback.

CAIUS CALIGULA*.—Born, A.D. 12. Killed, A.D. 41.

AV. R.4. With heads of Agrippina and Julia (if genuine). R.8. AR. R.2 to R.4. First brass, R.2. Second brass, C.

See also the silver and gold coins of Augustus, on some of which his head appears.

CLAUDIA, wife of Caligula.—The coins supposed of this Empress are pronounced false.

ORESTILLA, second wife of Caligula.—The same.

PAULINA, third wife of Caligula.—The same.

CAESONIA, fourth wife of Caligula.—The same.

DRUSILLA, daughter of Caesonia.—The same.

DRUSILLA, sister of Caligula.—Born, A.D. 17. Died, A.D. 38.

There are only Greek coins of Drusilla, but she appears on the reverse of a large brass Latin coin of Caligula, in company with her sisters.

JULIA LIVILLA, sister of Caligula.—Born, A.D. 18. Killed, A.D. 41.

CLAUDIUS.—Born, A.C. 10. Poisoned, A.D. 54.

AV. R.1, to R.3. Restored by Trajan, R.8. AR. R.1. to R.3. First brass, C. With "De Germanis," R.5. Restored by Titus, R.2. Second brass, C. Restored by Titus, Domitian, and Nerva, R.1. to R.3.

VALERIA MESSALINA, third wife of Claudius.—Born, —. Killed, A.D. 48.

Only Greek and Colonial coins.

AGRIPPINA, JUNIOR, fourth wife of Claudius, sister of Caligula.—Born, A.D. 16. Killed, A.D. 59.

AV. R.3. AR. R.2. Reverse, head of Nero, R.6. First brass, R.8.

CLAUDIA, daughter of Claudius and Plautia Urgulanilla.—Born, —. Killed, A.D. 65.

Only Greek and Colonial coins.

BRITANNICUS CAESAR, son of Claudius and Messalina.—Born, A.D. 42. Poisoned, A.D. 55.

First brass, R.8. ?

---

* It may be proper to remind the Tyro that *Caligula* was merely *an epithet* bestowed on the emperor, and that it is consequently not found on his coins. The same remark applies to the money of *Caracalla*, who on coins is styled *Antoninus Pius*. This caution may scarcely be deemed necessary, but we have lately seen an historical work, in which a coin of Caracalla is assigned to Antoninus, merely because it is inscribed ANTONINUS PIUS. Elagabalus also took the name of Antoninus Pius, as will be noticed hereafter.

NERO.—Born, A.D. 37. Killed himself, A.D. 68.

AV. C. to R.3. AR. C. to R.3. First, second, and third brass, C. to R.4.

OCTAVIA, first wife of Nero.—Born, about A.D. 42. Put to death, A.D. 62.

Only Greek and Colonial coins.

POPPAEA, second wife of Nero.—Born, —. Died, 66 A.D.

Only Greek and Colonial coins.

STATILIA MESSALINA, third wife of Nero.—Born, —. Died, —.

No Latin coins.

CLAUDIA, daughter of Nero and Poppaea.—Born, A.D. 64.

Died young. PL. R.8.

CLODIUS MACER, Propraetor in Africa.—Born, —. Killed, A.D. 68.

AR. R.6. to R.8.

GALBA.—Born, 3 A.C. Killed, A.D. 69.

AV. R.2 to R.4. Restored by Trajan, R.8. AR. C. to R.4. First brass, R.1. Restored by Titus, R.6. Second brass, C. Restored by Titus, Domitian, Nerva, or Trajan, R.2. to R.4.

OTHO.—Born, A.D. 32. Began to reign, A.D. 69. Killed in the same year.

AV. R.4. AR. R.1. to R.3.

There are no Latin brass coins of Otho, but there is a second brass coin of Otho, *restored by Titus*, in the Cat. d'Ennery.

VITELLIUS.—Born, A.D. 15. Began to reign, A.D. 69. Killed in the same year.

AV. R.4. With Reverse of his father, R.8. AR. C. to R.3. With Reverse of his father, R.6. First brass, R.3. to R.6. Second brass, R.2. to 6.

LUCIUS VITELLIUS, father of the emperor.—Born, —. Died, 48 or 49 A.D.

AV. R.8. AR. R.6. On the Reverse of his son's coins.

VESPASIANUS.—Born, A.D. 9. Began to reign, A.D. 69. Died, A.D. 79.

AV. C. to R.5. With *Triump. Aug.* or restored by Trajan, R.8. AR. C. to R.2. First brass, C. to R.4. Second brass, C. to R. 3. Third brass, R.3.

FLAVIA DOMITILLA, wife of Vespasian.—Died the year previous to Vespasian's succession.

AV. R.8. AR. R.6. to R.8. First brass, R.2.

DOMITILLA, daughter of Vespasian and Domitilla. — Born, —. Died before her father's succession.

First brass, R.2. Without her head.

POLLA, mother of Vespasian.

No authentic coins.

TITUS, son of Vespasianus and Domitilla.—Born, A.D. 41. Cæsar, A.D. 69. Joint Emperor with his father, A.D. 71. Sole Emperor, A.D. 79. Died, A.D. 81.

AV. C. With head of Julia, R.8. Restored by Trajan, R.6. AR. C. to R.4. First brass, C. to R.8. Second brass, C. to R.4. Third brass, R.3.

JULIA, daughter of Titus and Furnilla his second wife.—Born, A.D. —. Died in the reign of Domitian.

AV. R.8. AR. R.4. to R.6. Second brass, R.2.

DOMITIANUS, son of Vespasianus and Domitilla.—Born, A.D. 51. Cæsar, A.D. 69. Emperor, A.D. 81. Killed, A.D. 96.

AV. C. to R.3. With Domitia, R.8. AR. C. to R.2. With bare head, as Cæsar, R.4. With head of Domitia, R.6. First brass, C. to R.5. Second brass, C. With head of his father, R.3.

DOMITIA, wife of Domitian.—Born, —. Died, A.D. 140.?

AV. R.6. to R.8. AR. R.4. to R.6. First brass, R.8. Second brass, R.6.

VESPASIANUS, JUNIOR.

Only Greek coins.

NERVA—Born, A.D. 32. Emperor, A.D. 96. Died, A.D. 98.

AV. R.2. to R.3. With biga of elephants, R.8. AR. C. to R.5. First brass, C. to R.4. Second brass, C. to R.2. Third brass, C.

TRAJANUS.—Born, A.D. 53. Cæsar and Emperor, A.D. 97. Sole Emperor, A.D. 98. Died, A.D. 117.

AV. C. to R.6. AR. C. to R. 2. With head of Plotina, R.8. Restored by Hadrian (if genuine). R.8. First brass, C. to R.6. Second brass, C. to R.3. Third brass, R.1. to R.4.

Trajan restored the gold coins of J. Cæsar, Augustus, Agrippa, Tiberius, Claudius, Galba, Vespasian, and Titus, omitting those of Nero, Otho, Vitellius, and Domitian. He also restored denarii of the following families:—Aemilia, Caecilia, Carisia, Cassia, Claudia, Cornelia, Cornuficia, Horatia, Julia, Junia, Livineia, Lucilia, Mamilia, Marcia, Memmia, Minucia, Norbana, Numonia, Pompeia, Rubria, Scribonia, Sulpicia, Titia, Tullia, Valeria, and Vipsania. They are R.5. to R.8.

PLOTINA, wife of Trajan.—Born, —. Died, 129 A.D.

AV. R.6. to R.8. AR. R.6. Reverse of Trajan, R.8. First brass, R.6.

TRAJANUS, father of the Emperor.—Born, —. Died, A.D. 100.?

AV. R.4. First brass, R.4.

MARCIANA, sister of Trajan.—Born, —. Died, A.D. 114.?
AV. R.6. AR. R.6. First brass, R.6.

MATIDIA, daughter of Marciana.—Born, —. Died, probably in the reign of Antoninus.
AV. R.6. AR. R.6. First brass, R.8.

HADRIANUS.—Born, A.D. 76. Adopted by Trajan, A.D. 117. Emperor the same year. Died, A.D. 138.

AV. C. to R.6. AR. C. to R.6. First brass, C. to R.6. Second brass, C. to R.5. Third brass, R.1. to R.4.

In the reign of this emperor the imperial mintage evidently reached its acme. The gold and silver of Augustus affords many fine specimens of art, but his brass coins are of inferior execution and of low relief. Of Nero we have many fine brass coins, while his gold and silver is of indifferent workmanship; but the brass coins of Hadrian are of surprising beauty, and particular care appears to have been taken in their mintage.

SABINA, wife of Hadrian.—Born, —. Killed herself, A.D. 137.

AV. R.3. to R.5. AR. C. to R.3. First brass, C. to R.4. Second brass, C. to R.3.

AELIUS.—Born, —. Adopted and created Cæsar by Hadrian, 135 or 136 A.D. Died, 138 A.D.

AV. R.4. to R.5. AR. R.3. First brass, C. to R.3. Second brass, C.

The gold and silver coins of Aelius surpass in beauty even those of Hadrian; nevertheless many of the denarii are plated on copper.

ANTINÖUS, favourite of Hadrian.—Born, —. Destroyed himself, A.D. 130.

There are only Greek coins of Antinöus.

ANTONINUS PIUS.—Born, A.D. 86. Adopted and created Cæsar, A.D. 138. Emperor the same year. Died, A.D. 161.*

AV. C. to R.3. AR. C. to R.3. With the head of Faustina, R.8. First brass, C. to R.4. Second brass, C. to R.6. Third brass, R.2.

FAUSTINA, SENIOR, wife of Antoninus.—Born, A.D. 105. Died, A.D. 141.

AV. C. to R.4. With *Puellae Faustinianae*, R.8. AR. C. to R.3. With *Puellae Faustinianae*, R.6. First brass, C. to R.5. Second brass, C. to R.4.

The veiled portrait and the coins struck in her lifetime are rarer than the others in all metals.

---

* There is an obvious change in the workmanship of the coins in the reign of this emperor, and the *complexion of the metal* is also altered, although assays shew that no considerable reduction in the standard had yet taken place. See the Assay of Roman Denarii prefixed to "A Descriptive Catalogue of Roman Coins," 2 vols. 8vo. 1834.

Galerius Antoninus, son of A. Pius and Faustina.—Born, —. Died before his father's succession.

Greek coins only.

Marcus Aurelius, son-in-law of Antoninus Pius.—Born, A.D. 121. Adopted by A. Pius, A.D. 138, and named Cæsar. Emperor, A.D. 161. Died, A.D. 180.

AV. C. to R.2. AR. C. to R.5. Reverse, of Commodus. R.8. First brass, C. to R.4. With head of Verus. R.7. Second brass. C. to R.4. Third brass. R.2.

The third brass ceases after this reign, until the time of Trajan Decius, with the exception of Caracalla; but query if his are really third brass coins?

Faustina, Junior, wife of Aurelius.—Born, —. Died, A.D. 175.

AV. C. to R.5. AR. C. to R.2. First brass, C. to R.4. Second brass, C. to R.4.

Annius Verus, son of M. Aurelius and Faustina.—Born, A.D. 163. Created Cæsar, A.D. 166. Died, A.D. 170.

Brass medallions, R.6. to R.8. With Commodus.

Lucius Verus, son of Lucius Aelius and son-in-law of M. Aurelius.—Born, A.D. 130. Adopted by Antoninus, A.D. 137, but without the title of Cæsar. Associated in the empire with Aurelius, A.D. 161. Poisoned, A.D. 169.

AV. C. to R.3. AR. C. to R.6. First brass, C. to R.4. With head of Aurelius, R.6. Second brass, C. to R.2.

It is a remarkable fact, that the coins of Verus are generally of much finer execution than those of his colleague. He and his father, L. Aelius, appear to have worn wigs, and to have been very vain of them. A very fine bust of Verus may be seen in the Gallery of Antiquities in the British Museum, and will be recognised in a moment by those who are familiar with his portrait on coins.

Lucilla, daughter of M. Aurelius and Faustina, wife of L. Verus.—Born, A.D. 147. Exiled to Capreæ, A.D. 183, and killed shortly afterwards.

AV. R.1. to R.2. AR. C. to R.2. First brass, C. to R.4., Second brass, C. to R.1.

Commodus, eldest son of M. Aurelius and Faustina.—Born, A.D. 161. Created Cæsar, A.D. 166. Associated in the Empire, but without the title of Augustus, A.D. 176. Sole Emperor, A.D. 180. Killed, A.D. 192.

AV. R.5. to R.8. AR. C. to R.4. First brass, C. to R.5. with Annius Verus, R.8. Second brass, C. to R.4. With sacrifice of eight figures, R.6.

The standard and shape of his silver coins are alike bad. A round denarius is seldom met with, whilst his gold is badly rounded, though of fine workmanship. Commodus appears to have had a taste for numismatics, as medallions in bronze abound of his reign. Upwards of one hundred and fifty varieties are known, and some of them are of great beauty. Winckelmann bears testimony to their excellence as works of art.

CRISPINA, wife of Commodus.—Born, —. Killed, A.D. 183.
AV. R.6. AR. C. to R.1. First brass, C. to R.2. Second brass, C. to R.2.

PERTINAX.—Born, A.D. 126. Emperor, A.D. 193, and killed in the same year.
AV. R.3. to R.6. AR. R.4. to R.6. First brass, R.6. Second brass, R.5.

TITIANA, wife of Pertinax.[1]
Greek coins only.

DIDIUS JULIANUS.— Born, A.D. 133. Emperor, 193. Killed in in the same year.
AV. R.6. AR. R.6. First brass, R.3. Second brass, R.6.

MANLIA SCANTILLA,[2] wife of D. Julian.
AV. R.8. AR. R.6. First brass, R.3. Second brass, R.6.

DIDIA CLARA, daughter of D. Julianus and Scantilla.—Born, A.D. 153. Died, —.
AV. R.8. AR. R.6. First brass, R.4.

PESCENNIUS NIGER.—Born, —. Emperor in Syria, A.D. 193. Killed, A.D. 194.
AV. R.8. AR. R.5. to R.7.[3] Brass (Greek only), R.8.

CLODIUS ALBINUS.—Born, —. Named Cæsar by S. Severus, A.D. 193. Emperor in Britain, A.D. 196. Killed in battle against Severus, A.D. 197.
AV. R.8. AR. R.2. to R.4. First brass, R.2. Second brass, R.3.

"The name of Eckhel," observes Mr. Brumell," has given weight to the supposition that the coins of Albinus were minted at Rome only, with the exception of such as are said to have been struck at Lyons (Lugdunum). I cannot assent to this opinion. Whoever examines the coins in question cannot fail to be struck with the character of the fabric of many of them, so different from that of the Roman mint."

SEPTIMIUS SEVERUS.—Born, A.D. 146. Emperor, A.D. 193. Sole Emperor, A.D. 197. Died, A.D. 211.
AV. R.2. to R.6. With heads of his family, R.5. to R.7.[4] AR. C. to R.5. With heads of his family, R.3. to R.5.[5] First brass, R.1.[6] Second brass, C. to R 5.

Two gold coins of this emperor bear the types of the Legions, and are very rare. The Legionary silver of Severus is very base, and of bad workmanship. Mr. Brumell remarks, that a gold legionary coin in his cabinet appears to be much alloyed with silver.

---

[1] This lady retired to private life on the death of her husband.
[2] Idem.
[3] These coins are not of Latin fabric, but more probably were minted at Antioch.
[4] About fifteen varieties. [5] About twenty-two varieties. [6] Rather than C.

JULIA DOMNA, wife of Severus.—Born, —. Starved or poisoned herself, A.D. 217.

AV. R.2. to R.7. AR. C. to R.5. First brass, C. Second brass, C. to R.4.

MARCUS AURELIUS ANTONINUS, *vulgo* CARACALLA.[1]—Born, A.D. 188. Cæsar, A.D. 196. Augustus, A.D. 198. Joint Emperor with Geta, A.D. 211. Sole Emperor, A.D. 212. Killed, A.D. 217.

AV. R.3. to R.6. With Plautilla, R.8. AR. C. to R.6. With Plautilla, R.8. First brass, C. to R.6. Second brass, C. to R.5. Third brass, R.6.

FULVIA PLAUTILLA, wife of Caracalla.—Born, —. Put to death, A.D. 212.

AV. R.6. to R.8. AR. C. to R.1. With Caracalla, R.8. First brass, R.6. to R.8. Second brass, R.1 to R.6.

GETA, son of Severus and Domna.—Born, A.D. 189. Cæsar, A.D. 198. Augustus, A.D. 209. Joint emperor with his brother Caracalla, A.D. 211, by whom he was killed, A.D. 212.

AV. R.4. to R.6. AR. C. to R.4. First brass, R.2. to R.6. Second brass, C. to R.5.

MACRINUS.—Born, A.D. 164. Emperor, A.D. 217. Killed, A.D. 218.

AV. R.6. to R.8. AR. R.1. to R.5. First brass, R.2 to R.5. Second brass, R.1. to R.3.

DIADUMENIANUS, son of Macrinus. — Born, A.D. 208. Cæsar and Augustus, A.D. 217. Killed, A.D. 218.

AV. R.8. AR. R.3. to R.6. First brass, R.4. to R.6. Second brass, R.2. to R.4.

Mr. Brumell observes, that the late Mr. Miles, a dealer in coins, shewed him a denarius of Diadumenian, with *laureated head*, which is probably unique. He sold it to a Russian gentleman for ten guineas. Mr. Brumell says he considered it a genuine coin, but it should be remarked, that history does not acquaint us that Macrinus conferred the imperial dignity on his son, which the laureated head would seem to indicate.

MARCUS AURELIUS ANTONINUS, *vulgo* ELAGABALUS, *vel* HELIOGABALUS[2].—Born, A.D. 205. Emperor, A.D. 218. Killed, A.D. 222.

AV. R.2. to R.4. With head of A. Faustina, *unique*. Of Aq. Severa, R.8. AR. C. to R.5. With head of I. Soaemias, R.7. First brass, R.2. to R.4. Second brass, C. to R.3.

---

[1] Denarii of a larger size appear in the reign of this emperor. They have the radiated portrait, and were, it is supposed, struck after the death of Geta. These coins are more scarce than those of the smaller size, until the reign of Gordian III., with whom the small size becomes scarce, and ends with Philip.

[2] See the remarks under page 181.

JULIA CORNELIA PAULA, first wife of Elagabalus. — Born, —. Repudiated, A.D. 220. Died in obscurity.

AV. R.6. to R.8. AR. R.1, to R.2. First brass, R.3. to R.5. Second brass, R.3.

The name of *Cornelia* is found only on Greek Coins.

AQUILIA SEVERA, second wife of Elagabalus.—Born,—. Died, —, after Elagabalus.

AV. R.8. AR. R.2. to R.4. First brass, R.4. to R.6. Second brass, R.2. to R.3.

ANNIA FAUSTINA, third wife of Elagabalus. — Born, —. Repudiated by Elagabalus.

AV. R.8. AR. R.8. First brass, R.8.

JULIA SOAEMIAS, mother of Elagabalus.—Born, —. Killed, A.D. 222.

AV. R.7. AR. C. to R.1. Reverse of Elagabalus, R.7. First brass, R.2. to R.5. Second brass, C. to R.2.

JULIA MAESA, sister of Julia Domna, and grandmother of Elagabalus.—Born, —. Died, A.D. 223.

AV. R.7. AR. C. to R.1. "Consecratio," R.6. First brass, C. to R.6. Second brass, C.

SEVERUS ALEXANDER, cousin of Elagabalus.—Born, A.D. 205. Adopted by Elagabalus, and made Cæsar, A.D. 221. Emperor, A.D. 222. Killed, A.D. 235.

AV. R.1. to R.5. With the heads of Orbiana, Mammæa, or with the "*Thermæ Alexandrinæ*," R.8. AR. C. to R.5. With the before-mentioned reverses, R.8. First brass, C. to R.6. Second brass, C. to R.6. Third brass?[1]

MEMMIA, second wife of Severus Alexander.

No authentic coins. Nothing is known of this lady.

ORBIANA, third wife of Severus Alexander.

Known only by her coins.[2]

AV. R.8. AR. R.1. to 4. First brass, R.2. to R.3. Second brass, R.2. With Alexander, R.8.

JULIA MAMAEA, sister of Soaemias, and mother of Alexander Severus. Born, —. Killed, A.D. 235.

AV. R.6. to R.8. AR. C. to R.3. First brass, C. to R.6. Second brass, C. to R.6.

---

[1] See the remarks under M. Aurelius, p. 185.

[2] Orbiana was formerly supposed to have been the wife of Trajan Decius, until the discovery of coins which represent her with her husband Alexander.

URANIUS ANTONINUS.—Assumed the Purple, and proclaimed himself emperor at Emisa, in the reign of Severus Alexander.

AV. R.8.

MAXIMINUS.—Born, A.D. 173. Emperor, A.D. 235. Killed A.D. 238.

AV. R.6. to R.8. AR. C. to R.4. First brass, C. to R.6. Second brass, C. to R.6.

PAULINA, wife of Maximinus.[1]—Known only by her coins.

AR. R.4. First brass, R.2. to R.5.

MAXIMUS, son of Maximinus. — Born, —. Cæsar, A.D. 235. Killed, A.D. 238.

AV.? if genuine, R.8. AR. R.3. First brass, R.1. to R.6. Second brass, R.1. to R.2.

JUNIA FADILLA.—No authentic coins.

TITUS QUARTINUS.—No coins.[2]

GORDIANUS AFRICANUS, SENIOR.—Born, A.D. 158. Proclaimed emperor, in Africa, A.D. 238, and killed himself shortly afterwards.

AR. R.5. to R.6. First brass, R.4.

GORDIANUS AFRICANUS, JUNIOR, son of the Elder Gordianus.—Born, A.D. 192. Elected Emperor with his father, A.D. 238, and killed a short time after.

AR. R.6. First brass, R.4. to R.5.

BALBINUS.—Born, A.D. 178. Emperor with Pupienus, A.D. 238, and killed three months afterwards.

AV. R.8. AR. R.2. to R.4. First brass, R.2. to R.5. Second brass, R.6.

PUPIENUS.—Born, A.D. 164. Emperor with Balbinus, A.D. 238, and killed three months afterwards.

AV. R.8. AR. R.2. to R.4. First brass, R.2. to R.5. Second brass, R.5.

GORDIANUS PIUS, nephew of Gordianus Africanus, Sen. — Born, A.D. 222. Cæsar, A.D. 238. Emperor in the same year. Killed, A.D. 244.

AV. R.1. to R.8. AR. C. to R.4. First brass, C. to R.4. Second brass, C. to R.6.

TRANQUILLINA, wife of Gordianus Pius.—Born, —. Died after her husband.

AR. R.8. First brass, R.8. Second brass, R.8.

---

[1] Paulina is considered to be the wife of Maximinus, from the resemblance of her coins to those of that emperor and his son. They bear the consecration type, from which it may be inferred that she died before her husband.

[2] See the note under T. Decius, p. 190.

PHILIPPUS, SENIOR. — Born, A.D. 204. Emperor, A.D. 244. Killed, 249.

AV. R.6. With portrait of Otacilia, R.8. AR. C. to R.2. With portrait of Otacilia and Philip, Jun. R.6. to R.8. First brass, C. to R.4. With Adlocution type, R.6. Second brass, C. to R.3. With Octacilia, R.6.

MARCIA OTACILIA SEVERA, wife of Philippus, Sen. — Born, — Died after her husband.

AV. R.5. to R.8. AR. C. to R.8. First brass, C. to R.3. Second brass, C. to R.3. With her husband and son, R.6.

PHILIPPUS, JUNIOR, son of Philippus, Sen. — Born, A.D. 237. Cæsar, A.D. 244. Augustus, A.D. 247. Killed, A.D. 249.

AV. R.4. to R.5. AR. C. to R.4. First brass, C. to R.3. Second brass, C. to R.6.

MARINUS.—No authentic coins.*

IOTAPIANUS. — Proclaimed emperor in Syria, A.D. 248. Killed shortly afterwards.

AR. R.8.

PACATIANUS.—Known only by coins.

AR. R.8.

SPONSIANUS.—Known only by coins.

AV. R.7.

TRAJANUS DECIUS. — Born, A.D. 201. Emperor, A.D. 249. Perished in a swamp, A.D. 251.

AV. R.4. to R.5. AR. C. to R.3. First brass, C. to R.5. Second brass, C. to R.2. Third brass, R.2.

A set of Billon coins of this period have usually been attributed to Gallienus, but their workmanship and general appearance rather indicate that they were struck by Decius, in imitation of the restorations of his namesake, Trajanus. They bear the radiated portraits of the following emperors, with the legends of the obverse in the dative case, DIVO AVGVSTO, &c.; reverse, CONSECRATIO, with the usual type. Augustus, Vespasian, Titus, Nerva, Trajan, Hadrian, Antoninus Pius, Commodus, Severus, and Alexander. These coins are R.1. The coin of Titus belonging to this series was formerly given by the early numismatic writers to *Titus Quartinus*.

ETRUSCILLA, wife of Trajanus Decius.—Known only by coins and an inscription.

AV. R.6. AR. C. to R.1. First brass, R.1. Second brass, R.1.

HERENNIUS ETRUSCUS, son of Trajan Decius and Etruscilla.— Born, A.D. —. Cæsar, A.D. 249. Augustus, A.D. 251. Killed in the same year.

AV. R.8. AR. C. to R.4. First brass, R.1. to R.5. Second brass, R.1.

---

* The coins bearing ΘΕΩ ΜΑΡΙΝΩ are Greek, and their appropriation to this usurper is doubtful.

HOSTILIANUS, son of Trajan Decius and Etruscilla.—Born, A.D. —. Cæsar, A.D. 249. Associated with T. Gallus, A.D. 251. Died in the same year.

AV. R.8. AR. C. to R.2. First brass, R.2. to R 4. Second brass, R.1. to R.3.

TREBONIANUS GALLUS.—Born about 207, A.D. Emperor, A.D. 251. Killed, A.D. 254.

AV. R.4. to R.6. AR. C. to R.8. First brass, C. to R.2. Second brass, C. to R.1.

VOLUSIANUS, son of Trebonianus Gallus. —Born, A.D. —. Cæsar, A.D. 251. Associated in the empire with his father, A.D. 252. Killed, 254.

AV. R.5. to R.6. AR.* C. to R.6. First brass, C. to R.2. Second brass, C. to R.1.

AEMILIANUS.—Born, A.D. 208. ? Proclaimed emperor in Moesia, A.D. 253. Killed three months afterwards.

AV. R.8. AR. R.1. to R.2. . First brass, R.6. to R.7. Second brass, R.6.

CORNELIA SUPERA, wife of Aemilian.—Known only by her coins.

AV. R.8. AR. R.8.

VALERIANUS, SENIOR. — Born, A.D. 190. Emperor, A.D. 253. Taken prisoner by the Persians, A.D. 260. Died in captivity, A.D. 263.

AV. R.6. AR.C. to R.2. First brass, R.1. to R.4. With *Felicit. Augustorum*, R.6. Second brass, C. to R.3. Third brass, R.4.

MARINIANA, supposed second wife of Valerianus.—Known only by her coins.

AR. R.1. to R.3. First brass, R.2 to R.4. Second brass, R.2. to R.3. Third brass, R.2.

GALLIENUS, son of Gallienus by his first wife. — Born, A.D. 218. Associated in the empire, A.D. 253. Emperor, A.D. 260. Killed, A.D. 268.

AV. R.2. to R.5. With *Gallienæ Augustæ*, R.7. AR. (Billon), C. to R.3. With *Gallienæ Augustæ*, R.8. First brass, R.1. to R.8. Second brass, C. to R.4. Third brass, C. to R.2.

The third brass is common to excess.

---

* The silver coin, which for the preceding fifteen years gradually degenerates in standard, now becomes extremely base, and has been designated by the French Numismatists *Billon*. The series of silver coins is, however, continued by collectors, with the third brass washed with silver or tin, which is exceedingly common. In the reign of Diocletian good silver reappears, and is found of succeeding emperors down to the extinction of the empire, the *weight* declining but the standard being good (see the Weights of Denarii, Descriptive Catalogue, vol. i.).

SALONINA, wife of Gallienus.—Born, A.D. —. Killed, A.D. 268.

AV. R.4. to R.6. AR. ? R.6. Bil. C. to R.2. First brass, R.1. to R.3. Second brass, R.1. Third brass, C.

SALONINUS, son of Gallienus and Salonina. — Born, A.D. 242. Cæsar, A.D. 253. Augustus, A.D. —. Killed, A.D. 259.

AV. R.6. AR.? R.8. Bil. C. to R.4. First brass, R 4. to R.6. Second brass, R.2. Third brass, C. to R.2.

QUINTUS JULIUS GALLIENUS, son of Gallienus and Salonina—No coins.

VALERIANUS, JUNIOR, brother of Gallienus. — Born, A.D. —. Killed, A.D. 268.

The coins formerly attributed to this prince belong to Saloninus.

LICINIA GALLIENA.—No authentic coins.

POSTUMUS,[1] SENIOR. — Proclaimed emperor, in Gaul, A.D. 258. Killed, A.D. 267.

AV. R.3. to R.6. Bil. C. to R.2. With heads of Postumus and Hercules, R.6. First brass, R.1. to R.4. Second brass, C. to R.3. Third brass, C. to R.2.

The third brass of Postumus is extremely common.

JUNIA DONATA, supposed wife of Postumus.

Nothing is known of this lady, and the coins which have been published are false.

POSTUMUS, JUNIOR, son of Postumus, Senior. — Born, A.D. —. Cæsar and Augustus, in Gaul, A.D. 258. Killed, A.D. 267. No authentic coins.[2]

LAELIANUS.—Usurper in Gaul in the time of Gallienus.

AV. R.8. Bil. R.2. to R.5. Third brass, R.2. to R.5.

LOLLIANUS. ?—Usurper in the reign of Gallienus. ?

Third brass, R.8.

Tanini gives this coin in third brass, but Eckhel doubts the existence of money of this usurper. Mr. Brumell, however, says, that a coin appeared in the sale of the late Mr. Bentham's cabinet, with the legend IMP. VL. C. LO●IANVS. PF. AVG. (with a perforation after the letter O); reverse, VICTORIA AVG., Victory marching. The profile strongly resembled that of Pupienus, and the coin was mixed with two of that emperor's denarii, and included in lot 356. Mr. Brumell adds, that though its authenticity was doubted by some, it was assuredly a struck, and not a cast coin, and that the portrait was not like that of Laelianus (upon whose coins those attributed to Lollianus are said to be cast), the nose being decidedly aquiline, while the nose of Laelianus is, like that of Postumus, *vulgo*, " pug-shaped."

---

[1] With Postumus the series of Roman large brass closes.

[2] M. Mionnet has given a coin of Postumus the elder with a head on the reverse, which he supposes to be that of his son, but it is doubtless the head of some deity. Vide " Descriptive Catalogue of Rare and Unedited Roman Coins," vol. ii. p. 62.

QUINTUS VALENS AELIANUS. ?—Usurper in Gaul, in the reign of Galienus. ?

Third brass, ? R.8.

VICTORINUS, SENIOR.—Born, A.D. —. Associated in the empire by Postumus, in Gaul, A.D. 265. Killed, A.D. 267.

AV. R.6. to R.8. Bil. R.3. to R.5. Third brass, C. to R.8.

VICTORINUS, JUNIOR.—Born, A.D. — Cæsar, in Gaul, A.D. 267, and killed shortly after.—No authentic coins.

VICTORINA, mother of Victorinus, Senior.—Born, A.D. —. Died, A.D. 268. ?

No authentic coins. The piece attributed to her is no doubt a blundered coin of Victorinus, and ought never to have been produced as a coin of his mother.

MARIUS.—Born, A.D. —. Usurped the Purple, in Gaul, A.D. 267, and killed, as is supposed, three days afterwards.

AV. R.8. Bil. R.3. to R.4. Third brass, R.2. to R.6.

Although the third brass of Marius are scarce, they are occasionally dug up in this country. Eckhel supposed that he held the sovereignty longer on account of the number of his coins, but it is very probable these pieces were prepared previous to his assuming the Purple.

TETRICUS, SENIOR.—Born, A.D. —. Assumed the Purple, in Gaul, A.D. 267. Resigned the province to Aurelian, A.D. 273. Died, A.D. —.

AV. R.4. to R.6. Bil. R.2. Third brass, C. to R.2. With his son, R.4. to R.8.

The third brass of Tetricus are common to excess, and are yearly found in great numbers in this country and in France.

TETRICUS, JUNIOR.—Born, A.D. —. Cæsar, in Gaul, A.D. 267. Retired to private life, A.D. 273.

AV. R.6. to R.8. Bil. R.2. Third brass, C. to R.6.

CYRIADES.—Usurper in Asia, A.D. 257. Killed in the following year.—No authentic coins.

MACRIANUS, SENIOR.—Born, A.D. —. Proclaimed emperor in the East, A.D. 261. Killed in the following year.

No authentic coins. Those which were formerly attributed to this usurper belong to his son.

MACRIANUS, JUNIOR, son of Macrianus, Senior.—Born, A.D. —. Assumed the Purple with his father, A.D. 261. Killed, A.D. 262.

Bil. R.3. to R.4.

QUIETUS, son of Macrianus, Senior.—Born, A.D. —. Assumed the Purple with his father and brother, A D. 261. Put to death at Emisa, A.D. 262.

AV.? R.8. Bil. R.3. to R.4. Second brass, R.8.

The second brass is in the Cabinet of Vienna.

BALISTA.—Born, A.D. —. Assumed the Purple, in Syria, A.D. 262. Killed, A.D. 264.—No authentic coins.

INGENUUS.—Born, A.D. —. Assumed the Purple, in Moesia, and Pannonia, A.D. 261, and killed shortly afterwards.—No authentic coins.

REGALIANUS.—Born, A.D. —. Usurped the Purple, in Moesia, A.D. 261. Killed, A.D. 263.?

AR. R.8.? Doubtful.

DRYANTILLA, supposed wife of Regalianus.

AR. R.8. ? (*doubtful*).

VALENS.—Born, A.D. —. Assumed the Purple, in Achaia, A.D. 261, and killed shortly afterwards.—No authentic coins.

PISO FRUGI.—Born, A.D. —. Assumed the purple, in Thessaly, A.D. 261, and killed shortly afterwards. No authentic coins.

ALEXANDER AEMILIANUS.—Born, A.D. —. Assumed the Purple, in Egypt, A.D. 262 or 263, and strangled in the same year.—No authentic coins.

SATURNINUS I.—Born, A.D. —. Proclaimed emperor in one of the Provinces, A.D. —, and killed shortly after.—No authentic coins.

TREBELLIANUS.—Born, A.D. —. Assumed the Purple, in Isauria, about A.D. 264, and killed shortly after.—No authentic coins.

CELSUS. — Born, A.D. —. Assumed the Purple, at Carthage, A.D. 265, and killed seven days after.—No authentic coins.

AUREOLUS.—Born, A.D. —. Assumed the Purple, in Illyria or Rhætia, about A.D. 267. Killed, A. D. 268.

AV. R.8. Third brass, R.8.

SULPICIUS ANTONINUS.—Born, A.D. —. Assumed the Purple, in Syria, about A.D. 267, and killed shortly afterwards.

The only coins known of this tyrant are Greek, struck at Emisa.

CLAUDIUS GOTHICUS.—Born, A D. 214 or 215. Emperor, A.D. 268. Died of the plague, A.D. 270.

AV. R.6. to R.8. Billon, R.8.* Third brass, C. to R.4.

CENSORINUS.—Born, A.D. —. Assumed the Purple, at Bologna, A.D. 270, and killed seven days after.

No authentic coins. Those given by Goltzius are spurious.

---

* The coins described as of *silver* by various writers are neither *silver* nor even *billon*, but *third brass washed with silver or tin.* Mionnet informs us, that the coins described in the Catalogue d'Ennery as silver are merely washed; but Mr. Brumell has an undoubted Billon coin of this emperor. There are gold *quinarii* of Claudius, which are of the first rarity.

QUINTILLUS, brother of Claudius Gothicus.—Born, A.D. —. Proclaimed emperor, A.D. 270. Destroyed himself shortly after.

AV. R.8. Bil.? Third brass, C. to R.4.

Third brass coins of Quintillus are sometimes discovered in England.

AURELIANUS.—Born, about A.D. 207. Emperor, A.D. 270. Killed, A.D. 275.

AV. R.3. to R.5. Second brass, R.1. to R.4. Third brass, C. to R.3.

A coin of Aurelian bears the legend, DEVS ET DOMINVS NOSTER AVRELIANVS AVG. Small gold medallions exist of this emperor and of some of his successors.

SEVERINA, wife of Aurelianus.

AV. R.4. to R.6. Second brass, R.1. to R.4. Third brass, C. to R.2.

Nothing is known of this lady except her coins.

SEPTIMIUS ODENATHUS, king of Palmyra, and associate in the empire with Gallienus.—No authentic coins.

ZENOBIA, second wife of Odenathus.

No Latin coins. There are pieces of Egyptian brass of the third size. See "Greek Coins," page 129.

HERODES, son of Odenathus by his first wife.—No coins.

HERENNIANUS and TIMOLAUS, son of Odenathus and Zenobia.—Only Greek coins.

VABALATHUS ATHENODORUS,[1] son of Zenobia.—Born, A.D. —. Emperor, in Syria and Egypt, A.D. 266 or 267. Captured by Aurelian, A.D. 273. Died, A.D. —.

Third brass, R.2. to R.6. (Often with Aurelianus).

MAEONIUS, cousin of Odenathus.—Born, A.D. —. Assumed the Purple, in Syria, A.D. 266 or 267, and killed soon after.—No authentic coins.

FIRMUS.—Born, A.D. —. Assumed the Purple, in Egypt, A.D. 273. Vanquished and killed in the same year.

Coins have been given of this usurper, but they are not properly authenticated.[2]

TACITUS.—Born, A.D. —. Emperor, A.D, 275. Killed,? A.D. 276.

AV. R.3. to R.5. Billon, R.3. Second brass, R.6. Third brass, C. to R.6.

Vabalathus is a Syriac word, and *Athenodorus* is its Greek signification, namely, *given of Minerva*.

[2] Vopiscus says he coined money at Alexandria, and it is not unlikely that an example may some day be discovered.

FLORIANUS, brother of Tacitus. — Born, A.D. —. Proclaimed emperor by the legions of Cilicia, A.D. 276, and killed soon after by his own troops.

AV. R.4. to R.6. Second brass, R.2. to R.4. Third brass, R.1. to R.3.

PROBUS.—Born, A.D. 232. Emperor, A.D. 276. Killed, A.D. 282.

AV. R.4. to R.6. AR. R.8. Third brass,[1] C. to R.6.

BONOSUS, SATURNINUS, PROCULUS. } The coins given of these tyrants by the early numismatic writers are false.

CARUS.—Born about 230, A.D. Emperor, A.D. 282. Killed by lightning, A.D. 283.

AV. R.4. to R.6. Second brass, R.3. to R.6. Third brass, C. to R.6.

NUMERIANUS, youngest son of Carus. — Born about A.D. 254. Cæsar, A.D. 282. Emperor with his brother Carinus, A.D. 283. Killed, A.D. 284.

AV. R.4. to R.6. Second brass, R.4. Third brass, C. to R.5.

CARINUS, eldest son of Carus.—Born, A.D. 249. Cæsar, A.D. 282. Emperor with his brother, A.D. 283. Killed, A.D. 285.

AV. R.4. to R.6. Second brass, R.3. Third brass, C. to R.2.

MAGNIA URBICA, wife of Carinus.—Known only by her coins.

AV. R.8. Third brass, R.2. to R.6.

NIGRINIANUS, supposed son of Carinus.—Known only by his coins.

AV. R. 8. Third brass, R.5.

M. A. JULIANUS.—Born, A.D. —. Proclaimed Emperor, in Pannonia, A.D. 284. Killed, A.D. 285.

AV. R.8. Third brass, R.6. to R.8.

DIOCLETIANUS.—Born, A.D. 245. Emperor, A.D. 284. Associated with Maximianus, A.D. 286. Abdicated, A.D. 305. Died, A.D. 313.

AV. R.4. to R.7. Bil. R.3. AR.[2] R.1. to R.4. Second brass, C. to R.6. Third brass, C. to R.2.

In the reign of this emperor a new coin appears, of the size of the second brass of the earlier emperors, but much thinner, and of low relief. Those

---

[1] The small brass of Probus are common to excess, and the reverses are very numerous. The Abbé Rothelin possessed more than two thousand varieties, and the late Mr. Douce collected about 800. The number at present known amounts to 2500! There are gold and silver medallions of Probus of small size. There is also brass of the size of the quinarius, which is R.1. Pieces of this size are found of Carus, Numerianus, Carinus, and some of the succeeding emperors, R.1. to R.3.

[2] Diocletian restored the coinage of fine silver, although the washed third brass was still used.

with the reverse, GENIO POPVLI ROMANI; Genius standing, holding a patera and a cornucopia, are exceedingly common. It is a common reverse also of the same coins of Maximianus, Constantius Chlorus, and Flavius Severus.

MAXIMIANUS HERCULES.—Born, A.D. 250. Associated with Diocletianus, A.D. 286. Abdicated in favour of Constantius Chlorus, A.D. 305. Resumed the imperial power, A.D. 306. Abdicated a second time, A.D. 308. Proclaimed himself emperor, at Arles, for the third time, A.D. 309. Deprived of the Purple, A.D. 310, when he strangled himself.

AV. R.1. to R.6. AR. R.1. to R.4. Second brass, C. to R.6. Third brass, C. to R.5.

EUTROPIA, wife of Maximianus Hercules.—No authentic coins.

AMANDUS.—Born, A.D. —. Assumed the Purple, in Gaul, A.D. 285. Killed, A.D. 287.—No authentic coins.

AELIANUS.—Born, A.D. —. Assumed the Purple, in Gaul, A.D. 285. Killed, A.D. 287.—No authentic coins.

CARAUSIUS.—Born, A.D. —. Assumed the Purple, in Britain, A.D. 287. Killed by Allectus, A.D. 293.

AV. R.8. AR. R.6. to R.8. Third brass, R.1. to R.8.[1]

ALLECTUS.—Born, A.D. —. Assumed the Purple after his assassination of Carausius, A.D. 293. Killed in battle, A.D. 296.

AV.[2] R.7. to R.8. AR. R.8. Third brass, R.1. to R.8.

ACHILLEUS.—Born, A.D. —. Assumed the Purple, in Egypt, about A.D. 292, and was killed shortly after. No authentic coins.

DOMITIUS DOMITIANUS.—Born, A.D. —. Assumed the Purple, in Egypt, about 305, A.D. Died, —.

Second brass, R.4.[3] One type only, GENIO POPVLI ROMANI.

CONSTANTIUS I. CHLORUS.—Born, about 250, A.D. Created Cæsar by Maximianus, A.D. 292. Augustus and emperor, A.D. 305. Died, A.D. 306.

AV. R.4. to R.6. AR. R.2. to R.4. Second brass, C. to R.4. Third brass, C. to R.2.

HELENA, first wife of Constantius Chlorus.—Born, about A.D. 248. Died about A.D. 328.

Third brass, C. to R.5.

THEODORA, second wife of Constantius Chlorus.—Born, A.D. —. Died, A.D. —.

AR. R.6. Third brass, C.

---

[1] A very long list of the coins of Carausius will be found in the second vol. of "A Descriptive Catalogue of Rare and Unedited Roman Coins," p. 155, 2 vols. 8vo. London, 1834.

[2] The gold coins of Allectus are by no means so rare as those of Carausius.

[3] This coin resembles those of Diocletianus and Maximianus, and bears the exergual letters, ALE, for Alexandria, where they were doubtless minted.

Galerius Maximianus.—Born, A.D. —. Created Cæsar by Diocletianus. A.D. 292. Augustus and emperor, A.D. 305. Died, A.D. 311.

AV. R.4. to R.6. AR. R.3. to R.5. Second brass, C. to R.3. Third brass, C. to R.3.

Valeria, second wife of Galerius Maximianus.—Born, A.D. —. Put to death, A.D. 315.

AV. R.6. AR. R.6. Second brass, R.1. Third brass, R. to R.4.

Flavius Severus.—Born, A.D. —. Created Cæsar by Maximianus Hercules, A.D. 305. Augustus and emperor, A.D. 306. Put to death, A.D. 307.

AV. R.5. to R.7. AR.? Second brass, C. to R.1. Third brass, R.2. to R.3.

Maximinus Daza, nephew of Galerius Maximianus.—Born, A.D. —. Created Cæsar by Diocletianus, A.D. 305. *Son of the Augusti*, A.D, 307. Assumed the Purple, A.D. 308. Poisoned himself, A.D. 313.

AV. R.5. to R.6. AR. R.4. to R.6. Second brass, C. to R. Third brass, C. to R.3.

The silver of Maximinus is extremely base.

Maxentius.—Born about A.D. 282. Assumed the Purple, at Rome, A.D. 306. Drowned in the Tiber, A.D. 312.

AV. R.8. AR. R.7. Second and third brass, C. to R.1.

Romulus, son of Maxentius.—Born about A.D. 306. Cæsar, A.D. 307. Augustus soon after. Died, A.D. 309.

AV. R.6. to R.8. AR.? R.8. Second brass, R.3. to R.6. Third brass, R.1. to R.3.

Alexander.—Born, A.D. —. Assumed the Purple, at Carthage, A.D. 308. Defeated and killed, A.D. 311.

AR. R.8. Second brass, R.8. Third brass, R.6.

Licinius, Senior.—Born, A.D. 263. Created Cæsar and Augustus and associated in the empire by Galerius Maximianus, A.D. 307. Defeated and taken prisoner by Constantine, and afterwards strangled, A.D. 323.

AV. R.4. to R.6. AR.? R.8. Bil. R.2. Second brass, C. to R.5. Third brass, C. to R.4.

The silver of Licinius, father and son, is very base.

Constantia, wife of Licinius, Senior.—Born, A.D. —. Died about A.D. 330.—No authentic coins.

Licinius, Junior.—Born, A.D. 315. Cæsar, A.D. 317. Deprived of his title, A.D. 323. Killed, A.D. 326.

AV. R.4. to R.6. AR. R.3. Third brass, C. to R.5.

AURELIUS VALERIUS VALENS.—Born, A.D. —. Created Cæsar by Licinius, A.D. 314. Deposed and killed, A.D. —.

The coin described in the Catalogue d'Ennery, No. 4660, is doubted.

MARTINIANUS.—Born, A.D. —. Created Cæsar and Augustus by Licinius, A.D. 323. Killed two months afterwards.

Third brass, R.6. *With the legend in the dative case,* R.8.

CONSTANTINUS MAXIMUS, son of Constantius Chlorus and Helena.—Born, A.D. 274. Cæsar and Augustus, A.D. 306. Baptized, A.D. 311. Sole emperor, A.D. 323. Removed the seat of empire from Rome to Byzantium, which he named Constantinople, A.D. 330. Died, A.D. 337.

AV. R.1. to R.6. AR. R.3. to R.6. Second brass, C. to R.3. Third brass, C. to R.5.*

FAUSTA, wife of Constantinus Maximus.—Born, A.D. —. Killed, A.D. 326.

AV. R.8. AR. R.4. Third brass, C. to R.5.

CRISPUS, son of Constantinus and Minervina. — Born, A.D. 300. Cæsar, A.D. 317. Killed by order of his father, A.D. 326.

AV. R.4. to R.6. Third brass, C. to R.3.

HELENA, supposed wife of Crispus.

Third brass, R.6.

DELMATIUS, or DALMATIUS, nephew of Constantinus Maximus.—Born, A.D. —. Cæsar, A.D. 335. Killed, A.D. 337.

AV. R.6. to R.8. AR. R.6. Third brass, R.1. to R.3.

HANNIBALIANUS, brother of Delmatius.—Born, A.D. —. Created king by Constantinus his uncle, and appointed governor of Pontus, Cappadocia, and Armenia, A.D. 335. Killed, A.D. 337.

AV. *none.* Third brass, R.6.

CONSTANTINUS II., eldest son of Constantinus Maximus and Fausta.—Born, A.D. 316. Cæsar, A.D. 317. Emperor and Augustus, A.D. 337. Defeated and killed, A.D. 340.

AV. R.3. to R.5. AR. R.3. to R.4. Third brass, C.

CONSTANS, son of Constantinus Maximus and Fausta. — Born about A.D. 320. Cæsar, A.D. 333. Emperor and Augustus, A.D. 337. Killed, A.D. 350.

AV. C. to R.3. AR. R.1. to R.3. Second brass, R.2. Third brass, C. to R.3.

---

* The brass coins of Constantine, and his sons, Constantine, Jun., and Crispus, are perhaps the most common in the Roman series. Immense numbers exist at this day, and more are almost daily discovered.

SATURNINUS III.—Proclaimed emperor in the reigns of Constantius I. or Constantius II.—No authentic coins.

CONSTANTIUS II. son of Constantinus Maximus and Fausta.—Born, A.D. 317. Cæsar, A.D. 323. Augustus, A.D. 337. Sole emperor, A.D. 350. Died, A.D. 351.

AV. C. to R.5. AR. C. to R.4. Second brass, C. to R.2. Third brass, C. to R.2.

FAUSTA, supposed wife of Constantius II. — Known only by her coins.

Third brass, R.6.

NEPOTIANUS, nephew of Constantinus Maximus.—Born, A.D. —. Proclaimed emperor, at Rome, A.D. 350, and killed about a month afterwards.

Second brass, R.6.

VETRANIO.—Born, A.D. —. Assumed the Purple, in Pannonia, A.D. 350, and relinquished it at the end of ten months. Died, A.D. 356.

AV. R.8. AR. R.8. Second brass, R.5. Third brass, R.6.

NONIUS. ?

It is doubtful whether such a personage existed as Nonius, although coins are given by Goltzius.

MAGNENTIUS. — Born about A.D. 303. Assumed the Purple, A.D. 350. Killed himself, A.D. 353.

AV. R.1. to R.3. AR. R.4. to R.7. Second brass, R.2. Third brass, C.

DECENTIUS, brother of Magnentius.—Born, A.D. —. Cæsar, A.D. 351. Strangled himself, A.D. 353.

AV. R.4. to R.7. AR. R.4. to R.7. Second brass, R.1. to R.2. Third brass, R.1. to R.2.

DESIDERIUS, brother of Magnentius. — Born, A.D. —. Cæsar, A.D. 351. Stabbed by Magnentius, A.D. 353.

The coins given by Goltzius are not authenticated.

CONSTANTIUS GALLUS, nephew of Constantinus Maximus.—Born, A.D. 325. Cæsar, A D. 351. Put to death, A.D. 354.

AV. R.3. to R.5. AR. R.2. to R.5. Second brass, R.1. Third brass, C. to —.

CONSTANTIA, wife of Hanniballianus, and afterwards of Constantius Gallus. — Born, A.D. —. Died, A.D. 354. — No authentic coins.

SYLVANUS.—Born, A.D. —. Assumed the Purple, at Cologne, A.D. 355. Killed shortly after by his own troops.—No authentic coins.

JULIANUS II. (the apostate), nephew of Constantinus Maximus.—Born, A.D. 331. Cæsar, A.D. 355. Emperor, A.D. 360. Sole emperor, A.D. 361. Killed in battle against the Persians, A.D. 363.

AV. R.2. to R.3. AR. C. to R.4. Second brass, C. to R.3. Third brass, R.1. to R.3.

HELENA, wife of Julianus II.—Born, A.D. —. Died, A.D. 360.

AV. R.8. Third brass, C.

JOVIANUS.—Born, A.D. 331. Emperor, A.D. 363. Died, A.D. 364.

AV. R.3. to R.6. AR. R.2. to R.5. Second brass, R.1. to R.3. Third brass, R.1. to R.3.

VALENTINIANUS I.—Born, A.D. 321. Emperor, A.D. 364. Died, A.D. 375.

AV. C. to R.4. AR. C. to R.2. Second brass, C. Third brass, C. to R.3.

VALERIA SEVERA, first wife of Valentinianus.— Born, A.D. —. Supposed to have died in the reign of Gratian.— No authentic coins.

JUSTINA, second wife of Valentinianus.— Born, A.D. —. Died, A.D. 387.—No authentic coins.

FLAVIUS VALENS, brother of Valentinianus.— Born, A.D. 328. Associated in the empire, A.D. 364. Burned alive, A.D. 378.

AV. C. to R.2. AR. C. to R.3. Second brass, C. Third brass, C. to R.3.

DOMINICA, wife of Valens.—Born, A.D. —. Died in the time of Theodosius the Great.—No authentic coins.

PROCOPIUS.—Born about A.D. 334. Assumed the Purple, A.D. 365. Put to death, A.D. 366.

AV. R.7. AR. R.5. Second brass, R.8. Third brass, R.6. to R.8.

GRATIANUS, son of Valentinianus I. and Valeria Severa.—Born, A.D. 359. Augustus, A.D. 367. Emperor, A.D. 375. Killed in battle with Magnus Maximus, A.D. 383.

AV. C. to R.3. AR. C. to R.3. Second brass, C. Third brass, C. to R.3.

CONSTANTIA, wife of Gratianus.—Born, A.D. 362. Died, A.D. 383.—No authentic coins.

VALENTINIANUS II., son of Valentinianus I.— Born, A.D. 371. Augustus, A.D. 375. Emperor of the East, A.D. 383. Killed, A.D. 392.

AV. C. to R.2. AR. C. to R.4. Second brass, R.3. Third brass, R2.

THEODOSIUS MAGNUS.—Born, A.D. 346. Augustus, A.D. 379. Died, A.D. 395.

AV. C. to R.1. AR. C. to R.2. Second brass, C. Third brass, C.

FLACILLA, wife of Theodosius.—Born, A.D. —. Died, A.D. 388.

AV. R.5. AR. R.5. Second brass, R.1. Third brass, R.1.

MAGNUS MAXIMUS.—Born, A.D. —. Augustus, in Britain, A.D. 383. Killed, A.D. 388.

AV. R.1. to R.2. AR. C. to R.6. Second brass, R.1. Third brass, R.1.

FLAVIUS VICTOR, son of Magnus Maximus. — Born, A.D. —. Augustus, A.D. 383. Killed, A.D. 388.

AV. R.5. AR. R.1. to R.5. Third brass, R.2.

EUGENIUS. — Born, A.D. —. Augustus, at Vienna, A.D. 392. Killed, A.D. 394.

AV. R.3. to R.5. AR. R.1. to R.3. Third brass, R.7.

ARCADIUS, son of Theodosius Magnus.—Born, A.D. 377. Augustus, A.D. 383. Emperor of the East, A.D. 395. Died, A.D. 408.

AV. C. to R.2. AR. C. to R.1. Second brass, R.1. Third brass, C. to R.3.

EUDOCIA, wife of Arcadius.—Born, A.D. —. Died, A.D. 404.

Eckhel restores the coins assigned to this lady to Eudoxia, wife of Theodosius II.

HONORIUS, son of Theodosius and Flaccilla. — Born, A.D. 384. Augustus, A.D. 393. Emperor of the West, A.D. 395. Died, A.D. 423.

AV. C. to R.1. AR. C. to R.3. Second brass, R.1. Third brass, C. to R.3.

CONSTANTIUS III., brother-in-law of Honorius.—Born, A.D. — Augustus, A.D. 421. Died in the same year.

AV. R.6. to R.7. AR. R.7.

GALLA PLACIDIA, wife of Constantius III.—Born, A.D. —. Died, A.D. 450.

AV. R.5. to R.7. AR. R.4. to R.5. Second and third brass, R.5. to R.7.

CONSTANTINUS III.—Born, A.D. —. Augustus, A.D. 407. Killed, A.D. 411.

AV. R.2. AR. R.2. Third brass, R.2.

CONSTANS, son of Constantinus III. — Born, A.D. —. Augustus, A.D. 408. Killed, A.D. 411.

AR. R.5.

MAXIMUS.—Born, A.D. —. Emperor, in Spain, A.D. 409. Retired to private life, A.D. 411.

AR. R.5.

JOVINUS.—Born, A.D. —. Emperor, A.D. 411. Killed, A.D. 413.

AV. R.4. AR. R.2. Third brass, R.8.

SEBASTIANUS, brother of Jovinus.—Born, A.D. —. Emperor with his brother, A.D. 412. Killed, A.D. 413.

AR. R.5.

PRISCUS ATTALUS.—Born, A.D. —. Proclaimed emperor of Rome by Alaric, A.D. 409. Died in exile.

AV. R.4. AR. R.5. to R.8. Third brass, R.6.

THEODOSIUS II., son of Arcadius.—Born, A.D. 401. Augustus, A.D. 402. Emperor of the East, A.D. 408. Died, A.D. 450.

AV. C. to R.2. AR. R.3. to R.5. Third brass, R.4. to R.6.

EUDOXIA, wife of Theodosius II. Born about A.D. 393. Died, A.D. 460.

AV. R.3. to R.5. AR. R.4. Third brass, R.4.

JOHANNES.—Born about A.D. 380. Emperor, A.D. 423. Killed, A.D. 425.

AV. R.3. to R.6. AR. R.5. Third brass, R.8.

VALENTINIANUS III., son of Constantius.— Born in Rome, A.D. 419. Cæsar, A.D. 424. Augustus, A.D. 425. Killed, A.D. 455.

AV. C. to R.5. AR. R.2. to R.4. Third brass, R.2. to R.3.

LICINIA EUDOXIA, wife of Valentinianus III.— Born, A.D. 423. Died, A.D. —.

AV. R.5.

HONORIA, sister of Valentinianus III. Born, A.D. 417. Augusta, A.D. 433.? Died, A.D. 454.?

AV. R.5. to R.6. AR. R.6.

ATTILA, king of the Huns.

No coins known. Some Gaulish pieces were at one time absurdly attributed to this king.

PETRONIUS MAXIMUS.— Born, A.D. 395. Emperor, A.D. 455. Killed soon after his election.

AV. R.4. AR. R.4. Third brass, R.8.

MARCIANUS, brother-in-law of Theodosius II.—Born, A.D. 391. Emperor, A.D. 450. Died, A.D. 457.

AV. R.2. to R.6. AR. R.4. Third brass, R.6.

PULCHERIA, sister of Theodosius and wife of Marcianus.—Born, A.D. 399. Augusta, A.D. 414. Died, A.D. 453.

AV. R.6. AR. R.4. Third brass, R.6.

AVITUS.—Born, A.D. —. Augustus, A.D. 455. Abdicated, and became priest, A.D. 456.

AV. R.4. AR. R.4. Third brass, R.6.

LEO I.—Born, A.D. —. Emperor of the East, A.D. 457. Died, A.D. 474.

AV. C. to R.1. Third brass, R.5.

VERINA, wife of Leo I.—Born, A.D. —. Died, A.D. 484.

AV. R.6.

MAJORIANUS.—Born, A.D. —. Augustus, A.D. 457. Killed, A.D. 461.

AV. R.2. to R.4. AR. R.5. Third brass, R.5.

LIBIUS SEVERUS. — Born, A.D. —. Emperor, A.D. 461. Poisoned, A.D. 465.

AV. R.2. AR. R.5. Third brass, R.6.

ANTHEMIUS.—Born, A.D. —. Augustus, A.D. 467. Killed, A.D. 472.

AV. R.2. AR. R.7. brass. ?

EUPHEMIA, wife of Anthemius. Born, A.D. —. Died, A.D. —.

AV. R.6.

OLYBRIUS.—Born, A.D. —. Emperor, A.D. 472, and died the same year.

AV. R.5. to R.6. AR. R.6. PL. R.8.

PLACIDIA, wife of Olybrius.—Born, A.D. —. Died, A.D. —.

AV. R.8*

On a piece in lead she is represented with her husband.

GLYCERIUS.—Born, A.D. —. Emperor, A.D. 473. Dethroned, A.D. 474. Died, A,D. 480. ?

AV. R.4. AR. R.7.

LEO II.—Born, A.D. 459. ? Emperor of the East, A.D. 474. Died the same year.

AV. R.4. With Zeno.

ZENO, father of Leo II. —Born, A.D. 426. Associated with his son, A.D. 474. Dethroned, A.D. 476. Regained the throne, A.D. 477. Died, A.D. 491.

AV. C. AR. R.2. Second brass, R.4. Third brass, R.3.

BASILISCUS, brother-in-law of Leo I.—Born, A.D. —. Emperor, A.D. 476. Dethroned and died of hunger, A.D. 477.

AV. R.2. to R.3. AR. R.4. Third brass, R.8.

AELIA, wife of Basiliscus. — Born, A.D. —. Perished with her husband, A.D. 477.

AV. R.5.

---

* See Descrip. Catal. vol. ii., p. 377.

MARCUS, son of Basiliscus.—Born, A.D. —. Associated with his father, A.D. 476. Perished with his parents, A.D. 477.

He appears on coins of his father only.

LEONTIUS I.—Born, A.D. —. Augustus, A.D. 482. Killed, A.D. 488.

AV. R.3.

JULIUS NEPOS.—Born, A.D. —. Emperor of the West, A.D. 474. Dethroned, A.D. 475. Killed, A.D. 480.

AV. R.1. to R.3. AR. R.4. Third brass, R.7.

ROMULUS AUGUSTUS.—Born, A.D. —. Emperor of the West, A.D. 475. Dethroned by Odoacer, A.D. 476.

AV. R.4. Third brass, R.8.

END OF THE ROMAN EMPIRE IN THE WEST.

EMPERORS OF THE EAST.

[The following List is compiled from a very admirable work by M. de Saulcy, entitled "Essai de Classification des Suites Monetaires Byzantines," Metz, 1836, to which the student is referred for a more extended account of this rude though very remarkable series. It is proper to remark, that this intelligent numismatist uses no less than ten degrees of rarity, but these have been thought unnecessary in the present list. The Byzantine series is also described in the second volume of "A Descriptive Catalogue of Rare and Unedited Roman Coins," 2 vols. 1834.]

ANASTASIUS.—AV. C. AR. R.4. Æ. C.

VITALIANUS.—AV. R.8.

JUSTINUS I.—AV. R.1. AR. R.3. Æ. C.

JUSTINUS I. and EUPHEMIA.—Æ. R.1. ?

JUSTINUS I. and JUSTINIANUS I.—AV. R.8.

Justinianus I., alone.—AV. C. AR. R.2. Æ. C.
Justinus II.—AV. R.6. AR. R.5. Æ. R.2.
Justinus II. and Sophia.—Æ. C.
Tiberius-Constantinus.—AV. R.2. AR. R.6. Æ. R.1.
Tiberius and Anastasia.—Æ. R.4.
Mauricius Tiberius.—AV. R.2. AR. R.5. Æ. C.
Mauricius, Constantina, and Theodosius.—Æ. R.6.
Focas.—AV. R.2. AR. R.5. Æ. R.1.
Focas and Leontia.—Æ. R.2.
Heraclius, Præfect of Africa.—AR. R.8. Æ. R.5.
Heraclius I.—AV. R.1. AR. R.5. Æ. R.2.
Heraclius I., Eudocia, and Heraclius II.—AR. R.6.
Heraclius I. and Heraclius II.—AV. R.1. AR. R.4. Æ. C.
Heraclius I., Martina, and Heraclius II.—Æ. R.3.
Heraclius I., Heraclius II., and Heracleonas.—AV. R.4. Æ. R.6.
Heraclius II. and Heracleonas.—AR. R.8. Æ. R.2.
Heracleonas, alone.—Æ. R.8. ?
Heracleonas, Tiberius III. and Constans II.—Æ. R.3.
Constans II., alone.—AV. R.3. AR. R.7. Æ. R.3.
Constans II. and Constantinus Pogonatus.—AV. R.3. AR. R.5. Æ. R.2.
Constans II., Constantinus, Heraclius, and Tiberius.—AV. R.4. AR. R.8. Æ. R.2.
Constantinus IV., Pogonatus, Heraclius, and Tiberius.—AV. R.2. AR. R.6. Æ. R.2.
Constantinus IV., Pogonatus, alone.—AV. R.2. AR. R.6. Æ. R.3.
Justinianus II., Rhinometus, alone.—AV. R.3. AR. R.8. Æ. R.6.
Leontius II., alone.—AV. R.8.
Tiberius V., Absimarus.—AV. R.5. AR. R.7. Æ. R.8.
Justinianus II. and Tiberius IV.—AV. R.5. Æ. R.8.
Filepicus-Bardanes, alone.—AV. R.5. AR. R.8.
Anastasius II., alone.—AV. R.5.
Theodosius III., alone.—AV. R.6. AR. R.8.
Theodosius III. and family.—AR. R.10.
Leo III., the Isaurian.—AV. R.3. AR. R.5.
Leo III. and Constantinus V., Copronymus.—AV. R.1. AR R.5. Æ. R.2.
Constantinus V. Copronymus, alone.—AV. R.3. AR. R.6. ?

Artavasdus and Nicephorus.—AV. R.8. AR. R.8.

Artavasdus and Constantinus V.—AV. R.8.

Constantinus V. and Leo IV., Chazarus.—AV. R.3. Æ. R.4.?

Leo IV., Chazarus, alone. Æ. R.7.

Leo IV., Chazarus, and Constantinus VI.—AV. R.6. Æ. R.5.

Constantinus VI. and Irene.—AV. R.8. AR. R.8. Æ. R.8.

Constantinus VI., alone.—No coins.?

Irene, alone.—AV. R.6.

Nicephorus I., Logotheta.—Æ. R.8.

Nicephorus I. and Stauracius.—AV. R.4. Æ. R.7.

Michael I., Rhangabe, alone.—Æ. R.8.

Michael I. and Theophylactus.—AR. R.6. Æ. R.6.

Leo V., Armenius and Constantinus VII.—AV. R.5. Æ. R.3.

Michael II., Balbus, alone.—No coins.?

Michael II. and Theophilus.—AV. R.4. AR. R.8. Æ. R.1.

Theophilus, alone.—AV. R.4. AR. R.8. Æ. R.1.

Theophilus and Michael III.—No coins.?

Theophilus and Constantinus.—Æ. R.8.?

Michael III. and Theodora.—AV. R.8.

Michael III., Theodora, and Thecla.—AV. R.8. AR. R.8.

Michael III.—AV. R.2. Æ. R.3.

Michael III. and Basilius-Macedo.—AV. R.6. Æ. R.8.

Michael III. and Constantinus Filius.—AV. R.5. Æ. R.4.

Basilius I., Macedo, alone.—AV. R.5. AR. R.8. Æ. R.2.

Basilius I. and Constantinus VIII.—AV. R.5. AR. R.6.? Æ. R.4.

Basilius I., Constantinus VIII., and Leo VI.—Æ. R.4.

Basilius I., Leo VI., and Alexander.—AV. R.8. Æ. R.8.

Leo VI., Philosophus, alone.—AV. R.8. AR. R.5. Æ. C.

Leo VI. and Alexander.—Æ. R.4.

Leo VI. and Constantinus X.—AR. R.5.

Constantinus X. and Zoe-Carbonopsina.—Æ. R.2.

Constantinus X. and Romanus Lacapenus.—AV. R.8.

Constantinus X., Romanus I. and Christophorus.—AV. R.8. AR. R.6.

Constantinus X., Romanus I., Stephanus, and Constantinus.—AR. R.8.

Constantinus X., alone.—AV. R.5. AR. R.8. Æ. R.2.

Constantinus X. and Romanus II., Junior.—AV. R.5. AR. R.8. Æ. R 5.

ROMANUS I., LACAPENUS, alone.—Æ. R.3. ?
ROMANUS I. and CHRISTOPHORUS.—AV. R.5.
ROMANUS I., CHRISTOPHORUS, STEPHANUS, CONSTANTINUS, and SOPHIA.—AV. R.8.
ROMANUS II., JUNIOR, alone.—Æ. R.3. ?
THEOPHANO, alone.—Æ. R.8.
NICEPHORUS II., FOCAS, and BASILIUS II.—AV. R.8.
NICEPHORUS II., FOCAS, alone.—AV. R.5. AR. R.8. Æ. R.5.
JOHANNES I., ZIMISCES, BASILIUS II., and CONSTANTINUS XI.—AR. R.8.
JOHANNES I., ZIMISCES, alone.—AV. R.5. AR. R.7. Æ. C.
BASILIUS II. and CONSTANTINUS XI.—AV. R.5. AR. R.7.
CONSTANTINUS XI., alone.—AV. R.8. AR. ?
ROMANUS III., ARGYRUS, alone.—AV. R.5.
MICHAEL IV., PAPHLAGO.—No coins.
MICHAEL V., CALAPHATES.—No coins.
CONSTANTINUS XII., MONOMACHUS.—AV. R.6. AR. R.8.
THEODORA, alone.—AV. R.8. ?
MICHAEL STRATIOTICUS, alone. AV. R.8. ?
ISAACIUS I., COMNENUS.—AV. R.8.
CONSTANTINUS XIII. — DUCAS, alone. — AV. R.4. AR. R.8. Æ. R.5.
CONSTANTINUS XIII. and EUDOCIA DALASSENA.—Æ. R.4.
EUDOCIA and ROMANUS IV., DIOGENES.—AV. R.5. Æ. R.8.
EUDOCIA, ROMANUS IV., MICHAEL, ANDRONICUS, and CONSTANTINUS.—AV. R.8.
EUDOCIA, MICHAEL, and CONSTANTINUS.—AV. R.8.
ROMANUS IV. DIOGENES, alone.—Æ. R.3.
MICHAEL VII., DUCAS, alone.—AV. R.5. AR. R.8. Æ. R.6.
MICHAEL VII. and MARIA.—AV. R.6. AR. R.8.
NICEPHORUS III. BOTONIATES, alone. — AV. R.6. AR. R.8. Æ. R.3.
ALEXIUS I., COMNENUS, alone.—AV. R.6. AR. R.8. Æ. R.2.
ALEXIUS I. and CONSTANTINUS PORPHYROGENETUS.—AV ? Æ. ?
ALEXIUS I. and JOHANNES II., COMNENUS.—AV. ? Æ. ?
JOHANNES II., COMNENUS, alone.—AV. R.5. AR. R.7. Æ. R.3.
JOHANNES II. and ALEXIUS FILIUS,—AV. ? Æ. R. ?
MANUEL I., COMNENUS, alone.—AV. R.5. AR. R.6. Æ. R.3.
ALEXIUS II., COMNENUS, alone.—AR. R.8.
ALEXIUS II. and ANDRONICUS I., COMNENUS,—AV. ?

ANDRONICUS I., COMNENUS, alone.—AV. R.6. AR. R.8. Æ. R.5.
ISAACIUS II., ANGELUS, alone.—AV. R.5. AR. R.5. Æ. R.3.
ALEXIUS III., ANGELUS-COMNENUS, alone.—AR. R.8. Æ. R.4.
ALEXIUS IV. and ISAACIUS II., ANGELUS.—AV. ? Æ. ?
ALEXIUS V., DUCAS-MURTZUPHLUS.—Æ. R.7. ?

LATIN EMPERORS AT CONSTANTINOPLE.

BALDWIN I. of Flanders.—Æ. R.8.
HENRY of Flanders.—Æ. R.4. ?
PETER DE COURTENAI.—Æ. R.4. ?
ROBERT DE COURTENAI.—Æ. R.4. ?
BALDWIN II. DE COURTENAI.—Æ. R.8.

GREEK EMPERORS AT NICÆA.

THEODORUS I., LASCARIS.—Æ. R.8.
JOHANNES III., DUCAS-VATATZES.—AR. R.8. Æ. R.7.
THEODORUS II., DUCAS-VATATZES.—AR. R.8. Æ. R.9.

GREEK EMPERORS AT THESSALONICA.

THEODORUS ANGELUS, alone.—Æ. R.8.
MANUEL ANGELUS, alone.—Æ. R.8.
JOHANNES ANGELUS, alone.—Æ. R.6.

GREEK EMPERORS AT CONSTANTINOPLE AFTER THE EXPULSION OF THE LATINS.

MICHAEL VIII., PALEOLOGUS, alone.—AV. R.8. Æ. R.8. ?
MICHAEL VIII. and ANDRONICUS II., PALEOLOGUS.—AV. R.8.
ANDRONICUS II., PALEOLOGUS II., alone.—AV. R.6. AR. R.8.

ANDRONICUS II. and MICHAEL IX.—AV. R.6. AR. R.6. Æ. R.6.

ANDRONICUS II. and ANDRONICUS III.—AR. R.8.? Æ. R.8.

ANDRONICUS III. PALEOLOGUS, alone.—Æ. R.8.

JOHANNES V., PALEOLOGUS, alone.—Æ. R.8.

ANDRONICUS IV., PALEOLOGUS, alone.—AR. R.8.

MANUEL II., PALEOLOGUS, alone.—AR. R.8.

MANUEL II., JOHANNES VII., and IRENE.—Æ. R.8.

JOHANNES PALEOLOGUS VIII., alone.—AR. R.8. Æ. R.8.?

MAHOMET II., conqueror of Constantinople.—Æ. R.8.*

---

* This remarkable coin, which closes the Byzantine series, bears the legend—ΟΜ ΜΗΛΗΚΙC ΠΑCΗC ΡωΜΑC ΚΑΙ ΑΝΑΤΟΛΗC ΜΑΧΑΜΑΤΗC; i. e. *The sovereign of all Greece and Anatolia—Mahomet !*

SECTION III.

ENGLISH COINS.

"The interest which naturally attaches itself to the correct classification of uncertain coins, ought to be heightened in us by national feeling for those *found in our own country;* and it must be confessed to be high time that we should begin to furnish our successors with *gradually accumulating data concerning the finding of these coins*, so that in time they may arrive at some satisfactory conclusions as to the places to which they belong."—MR. BURGON, "On a Mode of ascertaining the Places to which British Coins belong." (*Numismatic Chronicle*, Vol. I. p. 38).

ANCIENT BRITISH COINS.

THE doubt expressed by Eckhel[1] of the existence of primitive British coins has led many numismatists to deny to our rude ancestors the knowledge and use of a stamped currency. Among these are Sestini and Mionnet. The former hesitates to admit them in his Geographical List,[2] while in the lists of the latter they are found mingled with Gaulish coins,[3] though in many instances they are tacitly taken solely from English works! Eckhel's unbelief is founded on the well-known passage in Cæsar[4]—"Utuntur (Britanni) aut aere, aut taleis ferreis, ad certum pondus examinatis pro numo." It appears that some anonymous English numismatist endeavoured to convince this learned man of his error, but, though he notices the remonstrance in the Addenda to the *Doctrina*,[5] he nevertheless refuses to allow that the Britons, before the arrival of Cæsar, had a coinage of their own.[6]

---

[1] Doct. Num. Vet. vol. i. p. 80.
[2] Classes Generales, p. 10.
[3] Descrip. de Méd. Grecques, tome 1, and supp. tome 1.
[4] De Bell. Gall., lib. v.
[5] Addenda ad Eckhelii, ed. A. Steinbüchel. Vindob., 4to., 1826.
[6] It should be observed, that, in a MS. of the 10th century, in the British Museum, the reading is "Utuntur *aut aere, aut nummo aureo*, aut annulis ferreis ad certum pondus examinatis, pro nummo." The reading of many other MSS. is very similar. (See Num. Chron., Vol. I., p. 17).

It is evident, however, that the rude coins discovered in this country are not of Gaulish origin, and it is equally certain that they are not formed on the Roman model. A perusal of several papers in the *Numismatic Journal*[1] and *Numismatic Chronicle*[2] will convince the most sceptical that the Britons struck money previous to the arrival of Cæsar. Mr. Hawkins, in one of these papers, observes—"The British types seem to be taken principally from those of Philip of Macedon, barbarous imitations of which abounded in Europe. The resemblance to the original would be more or less correct, according to circumstances, being affected by distance of time and place, the greater or less degree of skill of the artists employed, the wish to modify the original type, and accommodate it to the tastes or feelings of the people for whose use it was made. The imitation, too, appears to have depended upon memory; for, though there is a general resemblance to the original type, it is evidently not executed with the ancient coin before the eye of the artist. The coin is clearly not a coarse copy of a fine original, but is itself the original work of an artist, who retains no more than a very general idea of the device he is to execute. From tradition he learns that he is to put a head on one side, and a chariot or a horseman on the other; and, as he has not skill, he executes the device according to his want of power, aided a little by the less rude imitation of his predecessors, each succeeding coinage being worse than the other, till the more frequent intercourse with the Romans improved the skill of the native artists; for it will be observed that the rudest coins are entirely without any letters, and that the introduction of Roman letters upon the coins is coincident with the improvement of the workmanship, till it attained its highest perfection under Cunobeline; immediately after which I imagine the genuine British coinage to have ceased, and to have been superseded by that of Rome."[3]

This view of the ancient British coins is perfectly in accord-

---

[1] Vol. I., pp. 91, 209.
[2] Vol. I., pp. 13, 36, and 73. Vol. II., pp. 71, 191, and 231.
[3] Observations upon British Coins, Numismatic Chronicle, Vol. I. p. 25.

ance with that of all our practical numismatists, and we feel assured that any other explanation of their types will lead to endless confusion and misrepresentation, and embarrass the studies of those who may undertake the task of illustrating this rude series.

Many of these pieces exhibit what may probably be an attempt, as Mr. Hawkins supposes, to accommodate the type to the peculiar fancy of the people for whose use they were intended; but, although we cannot be certain of this in the ancient British series, it is manifest on many Gaulish coins, on which we find the androcephalous horse,[1] an eagle holding the reins of a horse, or an equestrian figure, as on this silver coin, which is one of those copied by the Gauls from the Tetradrachms of Philip of Macedon.[2]

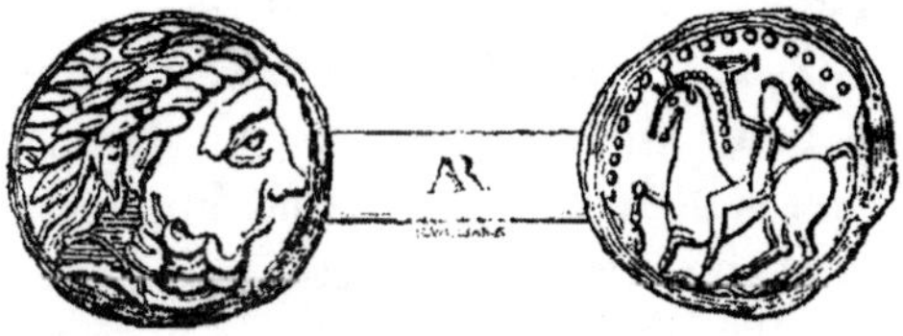

The types of some of the British coins are so utterly barbarous, that it is only by comparing them with other pieces less rude that we can be assured of the meaning of the object intended to be represented. For example, it will scarcely be believed that figures 9 and 10, in Ruding's 1st Plate, bear what is intended for a *laureated head*, with a *horse* on the reverse, until they are compared with Nos. 13, 14, and 15, in the same plate; and it is only by viewing them collectively that we can trace on others the origin of *the wreath placed between two crescents*,[3] when it becomes apparent that the original was a laureated head!

Admitting that the passage in Cæsar may have been inter-

---

[1] It is remarkable that the horse with a human head does not occur on ancient British coins; while it is repeatedly found on those of Gaulish origin.

[2] This singular piece is now in the cabinet of Mr. John Huxtable, who for some years past has collected Gaulish and British coins.

[3] See more especially the plate of British coins discovered at Ashdown Forest, in the Numismatic Chronicle, Vol. II. Figures 35 to 39, and even 40 to 42, in

polated, and it must be confessed that the various readings of MSS. quoted by Mr. Hawkins favour such a supposition, it may be urged that too much reliance has been placed by learned men on the accuracy of the statement it contains, especially when it is considered that the Roman general's visit was a hostile one, and that he was actively engaged in military operations during his brief stay in the island. The various accounts which ancient writers have given of Britain are worthy of notice. Cicero[1] says to his brother—"In Britanniâ nihil esse audio *neque auri neque argenti.*" To Atticus[2] he observes—"Illud jam cognitum est, neque *argenti scrupulum ullum* esse in illâ insulâ, neque ullam spem prædæ, nisi ex mancipiis."[3] On the other hand Tacitus[4] says—"Fert Britannia aurum, argentum, et alia metalla, pretium victoriæ;" and Strabo[5]—*Φέρει δὲ σῖτον καὶ βοσκήματα, καὶ χρυσὸν, καὶ, ἄργυρον, καὶ σίδηρον.* Further examples might be quoted, both from Suetonius and Pliny, as to the British pearls, but the foregoing are sufficient to prove that implicit credit should not be yielded to the account of Cæsar.

The earliest British coins, as before observed, generally bear on one side the rude figure of a horse; in some instances of such barbarous execution, that we can only be assured of the fact that the representation of that animal is intended, by comparing it with more successful representations.[6] Other figures and symbols often occur; and, while some pieces are stamped on one side only, others bear on what, for the sake of distinction, must be called the reverse, rude ornaments of various kinds, the meaning of which cannot be readily ex-

---

Ruding's 2nd plate, may be referred to the same origin. It is proper to remark, that many of the coins engraved by Ruding are Gaulish, but little attention having been paid to these pieces at the time of the publication of that work.

[1] Epist. ad Famil. lib. vii., ep. 7.

[2] Lib. iv., ep. 16.

[3] The whole of this sentence is highly characteristic of a people whose rapacity had no bounds:—

Si qua fert tellus quæ fulvum mitteret aurum,
Hostis erat.

[4] Vita Agricolæ, c. 12.

[5] Lib. iv., c. 5.

[6] Vide Ruding, Pl. 1., Nos. 9—15; the Numismatic Journal, Vol. I., Pl. I., No. 9; Numismatic Chronicle, Vol. I., Nos. 2, 6, 14.

plained, though in all probability they had their origin in rude attempts to imitate more perfect representations. The *wheel* is the most common of the accessory symbols; but it is extremely probable that even this formed part of the chariot of the prototype, of which the British artists were perhaps no longer capable of giving a perfect or intelligible copy. M. de Saulcy, a very able correspondent of the *Revue Numismatique*, and the author of an excellent work on the Byzantine Series, supposes he has discovered the origin of the type of the wheel in certain relics dug up in France; of which representations are here given:[1]

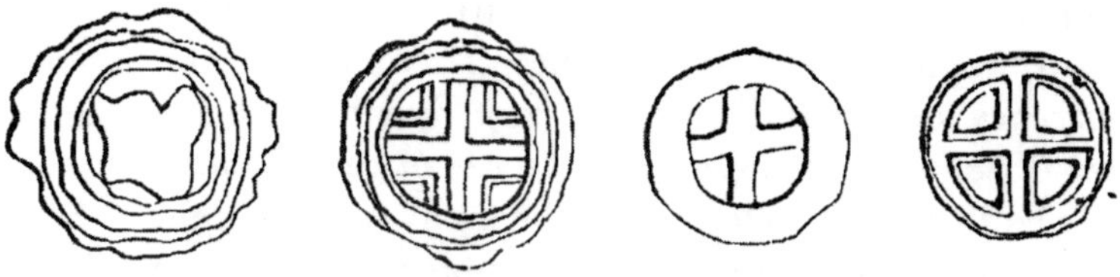

but, as the wheel forms a conspicuous object on the coins of Massilia, the modern Marseilles,[2] it appears more probable that it was derived from that source, if really intended as a distinct symbol; but of this we cannot be assured.

With regard to the iron rings mentioned by Cæsar, it is somewhat remarkable that nothing of the kind is known to have been discovered with British coins in England, while in Ireland rings of gold and of brass, of the form hereafter represented, have been dug up in great numbers. Enough to load a cart were found in a tumulus, in Monaghan, a few years since; and this fact proves, that though these rings might *occasionally* have been applied to the purposes of money, they were originally intended for *fibulæ*, or some such personal ornaments.

---

[1] Revue de la Numismatique Françoise, tome i., p. 162; Numismatic Journal, Vol. I., p. 218.

[2] See a very interesting Tract by the Marquis Lagoy, entitled "Description de quelques Médailles de Massilia," &c., 4to. Aix, 1834.

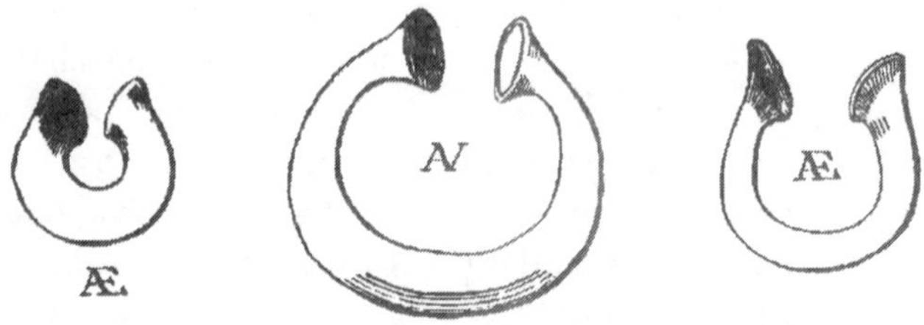

Rings of precious metal are repeatedly mentioned in Holy Writ, and are found figured as money on Egyptian monuments; but there is nothing to warrant the belief that those above represented were originally intended as the metallic currency of Ireland, whose primitive inhabitants appear to have been unacquainted with the use of coined money.

The list which follows contains many singular coins. Several of them may be regarded as unique, and the remainder, with very few exceptions, of the greatest rarity. Those of Cunobeline are particularly interesting, many of them bearing types which are obvious copies of Roman denarii of the time of Augustus.

LIST OF BRITISH COINS.[1]

SEGONAX.?

1. TASCIO. On a tablet, across the field; above and below a wheel, between two annulets and pellets.

   SEGO. A horseman to the right; his right arm elevated: below an annulet, with a pellet in the centre. Ruding, Pl. 4.—AV. R.8.

The appropriation of this and the following coin to Segonax is not certain.

2. SEGO. On a tablet, across the field, surrounded by a double twisted line.

   No legend. A horseman, to the right. Ruding, Appendix, Pl. 29. No. 5.—AR. R.8.

COINS ATTRIBUTED TO BOADICEA.[2]

1. BODVOC. Across the field.

   No legend. The barbarously drawn figure of a horse, with other symbols.—AV. R.8.?

2. BODVOC. Beardless head to the right.

   No legend. A horse galloping, to the right, with various symbols in the field.—AR. R.8.

---

[1] The coins here described are for the most part of better execution than those without inscriptions, of which there are many varieties. To attempt to describe the latter would be useless; and the reader is therefore referred to the plates in *Ruding*, as well as to those in the *Numismatic Journal* and *Numismatic Chronicle*. Many engravings of uninscribed British coins will be found in the latter works, with occasional notices of the places of their discovery. Those coins which have imperfect or illegible legends are also purposely omitted, as any certain interpretation of their signification must for the present be suspended. It is much more safe to wait the discovery of pieces with legends which may be read with certainty, than to speculate and indulge in theories upon the signification of what may after all be a barbarous imitation of some Greek legend. The word ΦΙΛΙΠΠΟΥ is often rudely imitated on Gaulish coins, and it is not unlikely that the British coins afford in some instances evidence of the same practice, though others might be discovered to bear the names of towns or chiefs.

[2] The appropriation of these coins to Boadicea rests upon very slight authority, and it is by no means certain that they are of British origin. Pieces of this type are of great rarity.

COINS INSCRIBED "TASCIO" OR "TASCIA" ONLY.

1. TASC. On a square tablet, across the coin; the field filled with various unknown ornaments.

No legend. Pegasus; (?) below, a star.—Ruding, Appendix, Pl. 29. No. 8.—AR. R.4.

2. No legend. Rude bearded head, the hair and beard formed of dots or beads: before, a cluster of five pellets.

TASCIA. An equestrian figure: a star and other symbols in the field.—AR.*

The workmanship of this coin is very peculiar.

3. No legend. Bearded head to the right.—Æ.

TASC. A horse; ? two clusters of pellets in the field.

4. TASCIA VA. Bare youthful male head, to the right.—Æ.

TA. Pegasus, standing, to the left.

5. TASCIA I. Bare bearded male head, to the right.—Æ.

No legend. A Centaur to the right, playing on the double flute: above, a crescent and a pellet.

6. No legend. An ornament occupying the whole of the field, probably suggested by the Macedonian shield.

TASCIO? A horse galloping, to the left. Ruding, Pl. 5. No. 5.—Æ. R.7.

COINS INSCRIBED "VER," ETC.

1. TASC. An equestrian figure, to the right, brandishing a club: ? in the field, a star of five points, within a circle.

VER. In the compartments of various ornaments, which occupy the whole of the field, (see cut, p. 218).—AV.

We know of no other than the one figured. There are many varieties of these coins, some having merely the letter V, others a T in the *centre* of the reverse. They are all convex and concave. Others occur without any letter on the convex side: those with letters are R.6. and R.7.; without, R.4.

2. VER. Across the field, within a beaded circle.

TASCIA. A horse galloping, to the right.—Æ.

3.—Similar type and legend.

No legend. An equestrian figure, to the right.—Æ.

4. VERLAMIO. Around what is probably imperfectly imitated from a shield.

No legend. A bull.—Æ. R.7.

5. Similar types and legend on a smaller flan of metal.—Æ. R.7.

---

* Those pieces without the estimations may be considered generally of the highest degree of rarity.

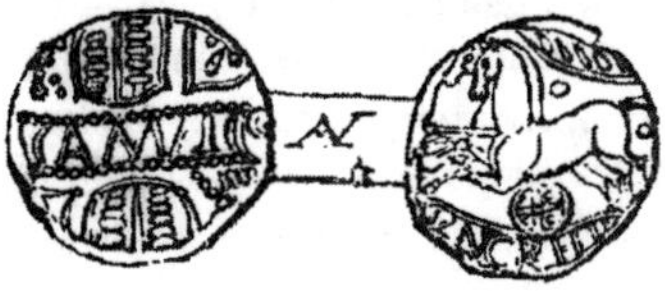

COINS OF CUNOBELINE.

1. CVNOBELI. Two horses galloping, to the right: below, a wheel.
   CAMV. On a tablet, across the field, which is nearly filled by a kind of ornamented cross, with heart-shaped ornaments in the angles.—AV. R.7.

2. CVNO. A horse, unbridled, galloping, to the right: above, a branch.
   CAMV. An ear of barley, placed perpendicular to the legend.—AV.

   There are varieties of this type differing in minute particulars, or by the addition of a subordinate symbol in the field.

3. Similar type and legend, half the size of the preceding.—AV. R.6.

   The types of these pieces are after those of the earlier Greek coins, and are utterly dissimilar from those of the Romans.

4. CVNO. Winged bust of Cupid (or Victory ?), to the right.
   TASCIO. A sphinx, squatting, to the right.—AR. R.6.

   The obverse type appears to have been derived from a consular denarius. The piece itself is of the module of a quinarius.

5. TASC. Beardless bust, to the right.
   CVNOBEII. Figure half naked, seated, holding a lyre: behind, a branch, which rises from the ground.—AR. R.8.

6. CVNOBELINI. Bare, beardless head, to the right.
   No legend. A horse galloping to the right.—AR. R.6.

7. CAMVI. Rude bare head, without beard, to the left.
   CVNO. Victory, seated in a chair, to the right, wearing a cap with border. (?)—AR.

8. CVNOBEL. In two compartments, across the field of the coin.—AR.
   CVN. An equestrian figure, to the right.

   There are varieties of this type: some have a star above and below the compartments.

9. ᴉꞀƎꓭONAƆ. (Retrograde), in two compartments,* across the field: above and below, a star.

No legend. An equestrian figure brandishing a spear. (?)—AR.

10. No legend. Bearded head to the right, the hair and beard formed of dots or beads: in the field two clusters of five pellets each.

TASCIO. A naked horseman, to the right, the right arm elevated: above, two clusters of pellets.—AR.

11. TASCIA. Laureated male beardless head to the right.

No legend. A horse? grazing: above, a branch, and a star of five points.—AR.

12. TASC. On a tablet across the field, which is encircled by a beaded line.

No legend. A horseman galloping, to the left, bearing a large oval shield.—AR.

13. TAS. Pegasus to the left.

No legend. Pegasus galloping, to the right, within a beaded circle, between two lines.—AR.

14. ᴉꞀƎꓭONAƆ. (Retrograde), in the compartments of a tablet: above, and below, a star.

No legend. A naked horseman, to the right, wearing a cap like the Macedonian *causia*, and poising a spear. (?)—AR.

15. CVNO. Across the field. Hercules, naked, leaning on his club.

TASCIIOVA. Europa on the bull.—AR.

This remarkable and very elegant coin is formed on the Greek model.

16. CVN. On a tablet across the field.

No legend. An unknown animal preparing to spring, to the left.—AR.

17. CVN. Naked figure with the pallium, holding the hasta and —?

SOLIDO. Within a circle formed of two twisted lines.—AR.

18. CVNOBELINI. Bare beardless head to the right.—AR.

TASCIO. A horse galloping, to the right: above, a crescent.

19. CVNOBELIN. Laureated head, like that on the denarii of Augustus.

TASCIOVANI. A Centaur winding a horn.—Æ.

20. CVNOBELIN. Winged beardless head.

TASCIO. Vulcan, seated, forging a helmet.?—Æ.

---

* The Marquis Lagoy, in his Essay on the Coins of Cunobelinus, observes that this style of inscription is not found on Gaulish coins.

21. CVNOBELINVS REX. Bare head without beard.

TASC. A bull butting, as on the denarius of Augustus, inscribed IMP. X.—Æ.

22. CVNOB. The head of Jupiter Ammon.

CAM. A lion? crouching, to the right: above, a branch.—Æ.

23. CVNO. Male bearded head, with the horn of Ammon.

CAM. A horse galloping, to the right: above, the figure of the driver.—Æ.

24. CVNO. Bare beardless head.

No legend. A hog, with its mane erect, like that on the Gaulish coins: above, a branch?: below, an annulet, with a point in the centre.—Æ.

25. CVNOBELINI. Male beardless head, with a kind of helmet.

TASCIOVANIT. A hog, to the right.—Æ.

26. CVNO. On a tablet: below, a double beardless head, like that of Janus.

CAMV. On a tablet; a hog couchant.—Æ. R.4.

27. CVNO. A sphinx squatting.—Æ.

CAM. Bacchus? standing before an altar, holding a bunch of grapes and the thyrsus, as on the coins of Maronea.*

28. CVNOBELINI. In two compartments, across the field: above and below, an annulet, with a pellet in the centre.

No legend. Victory seated, holding a garland.—Æ.

29. CVNO. On a tablet, placed perpendicularly in the centre of a wheaten crown.

CAMV. A horse, unbridled, to the right.—Æ.

The obverse type was probably borrowed from a denarius of the Postumia family.

30. CVNO. On a tablet, across the field.

CAM. A horse, unbridled, caracoling to the right.—Æ.

31. CVN. A naked figure on horseback, to the right, brandishing a short staff or baton.

TASCIIOVA. A helmed military figure, standing, wearing the *pallium*, and holding a staff or spear in his right hand.—Æ.

32. CVNO. Across the field. Victory, standing, holding with both hands a wreath.

CAMV. Pegasus, to the left.—Æ.

33. CVN. A horseman, to the right.

No legend. Victory, walking to the right, holding a wreath.—Æ. *Unique*.

---

* Ruding's artist has made a human head, with all the features, of the object held in the right hand of the figure. Vide Numismatic Journal, Vol. I. p. 218.

34. CVNO. Pegasus to the right.

TASCI. Winged figure, overpowering a bull.—Æ.

This type is evidently borrowed from that of a gold coin of Augustus, with the legend ARMENIA CAPTA. The same representation occurs on an unique medallion of Antoninus Pius.

35. CVNO. A horse, unbridled, galloping, to the right: above, a star of four points. (?)

No legend. A griffin walking, to the right.—Æ.

ROMAN COINS RELATING TO BRITAIN.

THIS series has been described in a work published by the Author in 1836, under the title of "*Coins of the Romans Relating to Britain, Described and Illustrated.*" The following emperors struck coins to commemorate their victories in this country:—

CLAUDIUS	AV. and AR.
HADRIANUS	Æ. only.
ANTONINUS PIUS	AV.? Æ.
COMMODUS	Æ. only.*
SEVERUS	AV. AR. Æ.
CARACALLA	AV. AR. Æ.
GETA	AV. AR. Æ.

USURPERS IN BRITAIN.

CARAUSIUS	AV. AR. Æ.
ALLECTUS	AV. AR. Æ.

Besides the foregoing, there are small brass coins of the family of Constantine, with the exergual letters, PLON., which were doubtless struck in London. Many of the coins of Clodius Albinus, with the title of Cæsar, should, perhaps, be classed with this series, together with those of the Usurpers who assumed the Purple in Britain in the decline of the empire.

---

* There is a fine *medallion* of this emperor, with Victory holding a buckler, inscribed, VICT. BRIT. See "Coins of the Romans," &c. p. 26.

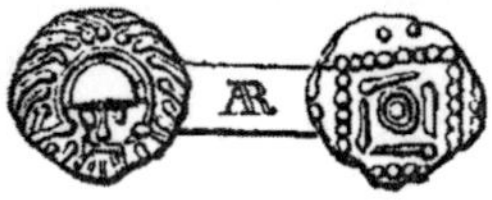

SAXON COINS.

RUDING commences his account of the Saxon coinage with the following observations: * — "Those who deny that the Saxons possessed any knowledge of the art of coinage before they landed in Britain, will find it extremely difficult to point out the source from whence they derived it after their arrival; for the Anglo-Saxon money bears not either in form, type, or weight, the least resemblance to those coins which at that time were the current specie of the island. This must necessarily have been composed of Roman money, with possibly a small intermixture of the British, neither of which could have been the prototype of the Saxon. That the barbarous workmanship of the British coins should not have excited their imitation is not surprising; but that they should have continued their own rude mode of coining, in preference to the beautiful specimens of Roman art which were constantly before their eyes, must be ascribed to a rooted detestation of that people, whose oppression they had experienced, and whose manners and customs they therefore abhorred to follow."

A careful examination of the imperial series, struck after the Romans had quitted Britain, would have satisfied our author that the moneyers of the Saxons *were* indebted to that people. It was evidently not a "rooted detestation" of the Romans which led them to adopt the great variety of crosses, and other totally uninteresting objects, which we find on the reverses of their money; for the obverses and reverses in many

* Annals of the Coinage, vol. i. 4to edition.

instances indicate an attempt to imitate the coins of the lower empire. Our author had forgotten that the best specimens of the Roman coinage, if really in circulation at the time of the arrival of the Saxons, must have been too much defaced and obliterated to furnish copies to their rude artists. He admits, however, that two pieces [1] are evident copies from a Roman model, but does not attempt to account for its adoption by the Saxon moneyers. These pieces are, in fact, imitations of the very common little brass coin of the time of Constantine, with the wolf on the reverse, which no doubt circulated in this country long after the Romans had quitted it.[2] Ruding appears to think it impossible that a vanquished people should imitate the arts of their conquerors, and therefore concludes, either that the Saxons invented their own style of coinage, or endeavoured to render it as little as possible like that of the Romans.

The reason of the dissimilarity (and it must be admitted that many Saxon coins are not in any respect like those of the Romans) appears to be this:—The Saxon artists were incapable of executing more perfect pieces, and evidently stamped their dies upon circular pieces of silver, previously punched out. When they attempted a portrait, the effigies on the coins of the lower empire served them for copies, which they travestied in a most barbarous manner. The thinness of the flan of metal rendered it impossible to produce a bold relief, and this gave to many specimens of the Saxon money an appearance wholly dissimilar to that of the former occupiers of Britain. As regards the *weight* of the Saxon money, it would be difficult to shew that it does not assimilate to that of the lower empire after the abandonment of Britain by the Romans. The denarius of the time of Honorius weighs, on an average, 48 grains; and its half, the quinarius, if we may judge

---

[1] It should be observed that the genuineness of the penny of Ethilbert in the Museum is doubted.

[2] If we are to allow, with Ruding, that the Saxons entertained so violent a hatred of the Romans, in what manner can we possibly account for the adoption of a type so peculiarly Roman, in two instances?

from its being by no means uncommon at this day, must have been in very common use. From this latter coin the Saxons in all probability adopted their penny, which, as shewn in the authorities quoted by Ruding, should weigh 24 grains.[1]

The question, whether the Saxons coined *gold*, has been often warmly discussed by numismatic writers. Pegge, who, like his brother enthusiast, Stukeley, viewed everything through a false medium, having met with a small gold coin, said to have been discovered at Hull, pronounces it to be a piece of Saxon mintage.[2] Ruding deems this opinion worthy of debate and refutation, and devotes several pages to shew, that the worthy but mistaken old antiquary was dealing with a subject of which he was profoundly ignorant. It is certain that, at present, we have no proof that the Saxons had a gold coinage, although a piece, with the name of Edward the Confessor, has lately been produced.[3] To those who are desirous of making themselves acquainted with the arguments adduced in proof that the Saxons really coined gold, a perusal of Clarke's "Connexion" is recommended.[4] Ruding has noticed at some length the extraordinary speculations of this writer, many of which betray a most singular ignorance of coins.

Sceatta. The *sceatta*, or *skeatta*, is the earliest Saxon coin, and, as some of them are without the symbol of christianity, they have been assigned to the Pagan princes previous to the arrival of St. Augustine. The first of these pieces which exhibits the cross is that of Ecgberht, king of Kent.

The word *sceatta* is by some derived from ꞅceaꞇ, a *part*, or *portion*. Professor White, in a paper read to the Ashmolean Society, remarks, that it is of Mæso-Gothic origin, *scatt* signifying

---

[1] Hence the term *pennyweight*.

[2] "Undoubtedly an Anglo-Saxon of the Northumbrian kingdom, being struck at York in the beginning of the 10th century!"—*Dissertation on some Anglo-Saxon Remains*, &c. A reference to Bouterouе will convince the reader that the Doctor's coin was one of those struck by the Merovingian princes.

[3] See Numismatic Journal, Vol. I. p. 54, and Ruding (new edition), Pl. H., 44.

[4] "Connexion of the Roman, Saxon, and English Coins," 4to. London, 1767.

in the Gospels of Ulphilus, *a pound, a penny*, and, indeed, money in general. This gentleman rationally concludes, that the term was used for money generally, as well as a distinct coin; as *getymbrian* signified *to build*, either of timber, stone, or other materials. Ruding observes, that "whatever might have been the precise value of the *sceatta*, it was undoubtedly the smallest coin known among the Saxons at the latter end of the seventh century, as appears from its forming part of a proverb:—Ne Sceat ne Scilling, *from the least to the greatest*.

Penny. } The *penny* is the next in antiquity. It is first mentioned in the laws of Ina. The term has been derived by various writers from almost every European language; but the conjecture of Wachter, as noticed by Lye, seems the most reasonable. This writer derives it from the Celtic word *pen*, head—the heads of the Saxon princes being stamped on the earliest pennies. The fact of the *testoon* of later times having been so named, certainly adds weight to the opinion of Wachter.

Halfpenny and Farthing. } Besides the penny, the Saxons had the *halfpenny* and *farthing* (Halpenige and Feorðling or Feorðung). Examples of the former are known, but no specimen of the farthing has come down to us. Both the farthing and the halfpenny are mentioned in the Saxon Gospels. In the twelfth law of Canute, the latter is stated to be the value of the wax charged on every hide of land for church lights.

Styca. } The *styca*[1] was of *copper*, and appears to have been struck only in the Northumbrian mints, and by the Archbishops of York. The mention of its value inci-

---

[1] Lye derives this word from Stýcce, *minuta pars*. Ruding does not attach much credit to this derivation: he finds, however, "that these coins seem to be the same as that which occurs in Domesday Book (vol. i. fol. 268), under the term *minuta*, from whence comes our mite."

dentally occurs in the Gospel of St. Mark, where the two mites, which make one farthing, are termed *stycas.*[1]

Pound, Mancus, Mark, Ora, Thrymsa, Shilling.

Some writers have contended that the *pound*, the *mancus*, the *mark*, the *ora*, the *thrymsa*, and the *shilling*, were current coin, and not money of account. Ruding has carefully reviewed each argument in favour of such supposition, but without discovering anything in support of it. He has also considered the derivation of the various terms; and the result is certainly not in favour of those who contend that there were actual coins of the above denominations. The mention of the purchase of an estate by a Bishop of Durham for 120 *mancuses* of the purest gold, is not, in our opinion, evidence of such pieces of money having been in circulation. We think, with a correspondent of the *Gentleman's Magazine*,[2] that the word *mancus* meant originally a manica, manicle, or bracelet for the wrist. The bracelets of an earlier period are of excellent gold, and, being adjusted to a certain weight, occasionally served the purposes of coined money. In the Saxon times, bracelets or other personal ornaments may have been similarly substituted; the *name* and value at least may have been retained, as in the case of our guinea at the present day. Elfric, Archbishop of Canterbury, gives to Ceolric "V. punðan and L mancuſan ᵹolðeſ;" i. e. five pounds and fifty *mancuses* of gold. In the ninth century, *mancuses* of silver, as well as of gold, are mentioned in payments. Tho *mark* would appear to have derived its name from some continental coin of general circulation at this period, bearing the effigy of Saint Mark.

Passing to the coins which have descended to us, we find pieces denominated *sceattas*, of Ecgberht, who reigned, in Kent, from A.D. 665 to A.D. 674.[3] In design and execution these coins are barbarous. A *penny* of Ethilbert the Second follows. This piece is remarkable for its singular reverse, which bears

---

[1] ꞇþeᵹen ſꞇẏcaſ, ꝥ ıſ, ꝼeoꞃðunᵹ penınᵹeſ. Mark xii. 42.

[2] Page 373, year 1837. The writer, however, confounds *mark* and *mancus*, which is a palpable error, as shewn by Ruding, p. 225.

[3] According to Ruding; but see the remarks hereafter.

an imitation of the small brass coin of the Constantine family, as before observed. The pennies of Beldred, king of Kent, bear on the reverse the abbreviation of DOROVERNIA CIVITAS.

The first coin of the kingdom of Mercia is of Eadvald, whose reign commenced A.D. 716. Of Offa we have a great variety of types, many of which are of singularly good execution, a circumstance attributable to this monarch having visited Rome, and brought with him to England Italian artists. Ruding aptly observes, that, as Offa's journey was undertaken about two years previous to his death, the best executed pieces should be placed last in arranging this monarch's coins.[1] Coins exist of Cenethreth, the queen of Offa. On the accession of Ecgberht, his son, who struck coins, the foreign artists appear to have been sent home, as the money of this reign is of rude execution. Of Coenvulf we have a great variety of types, some of which appear to be rude imitations of the coins of Offa. Of Ciolvulf, one coin is remarkable for its evident imitation of the obverse of the coins of Arcadius and Honorius. Those of Beornvulf, Ludica, Berhtulf, and Burgred, are of the most barbarous execution. The latter monarch's coins are of various types, amounting to nearly thirty varieties.

Of the kings of the East Angles, the earliest coins known are of Beonna, whose reign commenced about A.D. 690. These resemble the *skeattas* in size and design. We have pennies of Eadmund, whose reign commenced in A.D. 855; and there are also pennies of Ethelward and Ethelstan.

The next in antiquity are the *stycas* of the Northumbrian mints, the only brass coinage of the Anglo-Saxons. The earliest are of Ecgfrith, whose reign commenced A.D. 670, and extended to A.D. 685; and the latest are those of Osbert, who reigned from A.D. 848 to A.D. 867.

On the pennies of Regnald, and on some of those of Anlaf, we find the Saxon CVNVNC, instead of the Latin REX. These coins are without the heads of those monarchs. Those of Eric, or Yric, sometimes bear on the obverse the rude figure of a sword. The pennies inscribed SI PETRI MO, resemble the coins

[1] Annals, Vol. I. p. 236.

of Eric, and are therefore placed next in succession. Pennies of Saint Martin are also similarly stamped with a sword, and evidently belong to the same period, as do those of Saint Edmund, which, though without the sword, resemble those of Saint Peter and Saint Martin in style and fabric. Pennies of the Archbishops of Canterbury, commencing with Jaenberht, date from the time of Offa, whose name they bear. The pennies of Aethilheard also bear the name of Offa; one has the name of the archbishop, with that of Coenvulf. Those of Vulfred, Ceolnoth, and Plegmund, are without the monarch's name. Of the Archbishops of York, we have *stycas* with the names of Eanbald, Vigmund, and Vulfhere.

The pennies of the sole monarchs differ but little from those of the Heptarchic period. Examples of Ecgbeorht and Ethelvulf bear the word SAXONIORVM, or its abbreviation; and the latter, in addition, OCCIDENTALIVM. On the money of the great Alfred, the monogram of London occurs, and occupies the whole field of the reverse.[1] Coins occur of this prince both with and without the head.

There are some peculiarities in the coins of Edward the First which are deserving of notice. On some appears a flower, on others an ornament, which it would be difficult to describe and name, while several bear the representations of what may be conjectured to be Saxon edifices. One of these coins, however, bears an imitation of the gate of the prætorian camp, as it appears on the very common small brass coins of Constantine, and furnishes another proof that the Saxons did not disdain to imitate the coins of the Romans. On some of the pennies of this king the hand of Providence appears, as it is represented on the coins of the Byzantine princes. Of this king *halfpennies* have been found, resembling in type his pennies without the head. There is reason to suppose that halfpennies were struck by the Saxon princes, his predecessors, but none have descended to these times. Of Athelstan's pennies, in whose reign there was evidently an extensive coinage, we have upwards of thirty types. The

---

[1] See the Plate of Reverses of Saxon Coins.

obverse often bears REX SAXORVM, or REX TOTIVS BRITANNIÆ, although the whole of England was not under his sway. In his charters he styles himself as "Regnum totius Albionis." On some of the pennies of Ethelred the Second, the word CRVX occurs within the angles of a cross, and on others the hand of Providence appears between the letters Alpha and Omega.[1] Numerous coins of Canute remain: they are all pennies, and differ but slightly from those of the preceding kings. The pennies of Edward the Confessor offer a great variety of types, some of which differ entirely from any of the Saxon coinage.[2] Those on which the king is represented at full length, seated in a chair of state and holding the globe and sceptre, are more particularly referred to. The coins of his successor, Harold the Second, are imitations of one of the types of the preceding king.

---

[1] See the Plates of Reverses of Saxon Coins.

[2] A halfpenny of this king has been discovered recently. See Num. Chronicle, Vol. II. p. 35.

LIST OF SAXON COINS.[1]

KINGS OF KENT.

ETHILBERHT.

A.D. 561 TO A.D. 616.

SCEATTA.—R.8.

Obv.—EÐILIREX (?) in two lines across the field: the whole within three circles of pearls.

℞—A rude attempt to represent some figure, supposed of a bird, in a manner similar to that of some of the earlier uninscribed sceattas.

The legend of the obverse appears to be a mixture of Saxon and Runic letters, and to present the name of *Ethilred* rather than that of *Ethilberht*. The above is Ruding's reading, but it is certainly not satisfactory.

ECGBERHT

A.D. 665 TO A.D. 674.

SCEATTA.—R.2. to R.6.

Obv.—ECGBERHT. A male figure standing, holding in each hand a long cross.

℞—E◻TBEREHTVL. In the centre of the coin a cross.

Other skeattas of Ecgberht have a dragon on the obverse. Ruding has engraved ten specimens. It is doubtful, however, whether these coins belong to Kent. It is the general opinion that they are of Northumbrian origin, and that these skeattas are of Eadbert and his brother Egbert, Archbishop of York. (See a Note in the *Numismatic Journal*, Vol. I. p. 78, and a paper by Mr. Hawkins in the *Numismatic Chronicle*, Vol. I. p. 1).

---

[1] This List is given as examples of Saxon coins, and is not intended to include all the known varieties.

ETHILBERT THE SECOND.

A.D. 749 TO A.D. 760.

PENNY. (?)

Obv.—ETHILBERHTII. The bare head of the king, to the right.

℞—REX, placed above the figures of two children, suckled by a wolf, as on the Roman coins. *Ruding, Plate* 3.

This coin is considered by some to be a modern fabrication. It belongs to the collection of the British Museum.

EADBEARHT.

A.D. 794 TO A.D. 797.

PENNY.—R.8.

Obv.—EADBEARHT. REX., in three lines across the field.

℞—TIDHEAH, in two lines.

CUTHRED.

A.D. 797 TO A.D. 805.

PENNY.—R.1. to R.5.

1. *Obv.*—+CVÐRED REX CANT. The head of Cuthred with the diadem of pearls, as on the portraits of the Roman emperors.

℞—SIGEBERHTI MONETA. In the centre a cross.

Ruding gives two varieties of these coins.

2. *Obv.*—+CVÐRED REX. In the centre a cross.

℞—+ DVDA, between the angles of an ornamented figure, resembling the letter Y.

Two varieties of his coins are known without the head.

BELDRED.

A.D. 805 TO A.D. 823.

PENNY.—R.8.

1. *Obv.*—+BALDRED REX CANT. Bearded head to the right.

℞—+DIORMOD MONETA. In the field DO VR / CI TS. (*Dorovernia Civitas*).

2. *Obv.*—+BELDRED REX CANT. In the centre a cross with a pellet in each of the angles.

℞—+OBA. In the centre a similar cross.

Another has a cross crosslet in the centre, and a plain cross in the centre of the reverse.

SOUTH SAXONS.

No coins of the South Saxons are known.

KINGS OF THE WEST SAXONS.

AETHELWARD.[1]

A.D. 726 TO A.D. 740.

PENNY.—R.2. to R.4.

Obv.—EÐELƿARD REX. In the centre a cross, with a crescent in each angle.

℞—AEÐELHELM. A cross, with a pellet in each angle.

Others have an A in the centre.

BEORHTRIC.

A.D. 784 TO A.D. —.

PENNY.—R.8.

Obv.—+BEORHTRIC REX. In the centre, A.

℞—ECCHARDI. With two crosses, having pellets in the angles, and a similar cross in the centre.

KINGS OF MERCIA.

EADVALD.

A.D. 716.

PENNY.—R.8.

Obv.—EADVALD REX. In three lines, the ALD being the first.

℞—EADNOT, in the compartments of a kind of quartfoil.

There are two varieties of the coins of Eadvald.

OFFA.

A.D. 757 TO A.D. 796.

PENNY.—R.2. to R.8.

1. *Obv.*—+OFFA REX X. Male bust, with bare head.

℞—+LVLLA, between four double circles. In the centre a star.

---

[1] See, however, the coins of Aethelweard, p. 239.

2. *Obv.*—OFFA REX MERCIOR∴ Bust to the right, with bare head, the hair arranged in large curls.

℞—EADMVN between the angles of an ornamented cross.

3. *Obv.*—OFFA REX M, in two lines, between two rows of beads.

℞—BEANEARD, in two lines, with a division across the centre of the coin.

4. *Obv.*—OFFA REX. Bare male head to the right, with short curls.

℞—ALHMVND, in three lines, within a wreath.

5. *Obv.*—IBBA. Bust to the right with diadem of pearls, as on the Roman coins of the Lower Empire.

℞—OFRM, in the compartments of a kind of quartfoil.

The moneyers of Offa are numerous.

CENETHRETH, OR QUINDRED,

Wife of Offa.

PENNY.—R.8.

1. *Obv.*—EOBA. Bust to the right.

℞—+CENEÞREÞ REGINA. In the centre, ɣ.

2. *Obv.*—EOBA. Bust to the right.

℞—Similar to that of the preceding coin.

3. *Obv.*—+CENÞREÞ REGINA. In the centre of the coin, ɣ

℞—OBA M.

EGCBERHT.

A.D. 796 TO A.D. —.

PENNY.—R.8.

1. *Obv.*—+ECCBERHT. In the centre of the coin, R.

℞—BABBA, in the angles of an ornamented cross.

2. *Obv.*—Similar to that of the preceding coin.

℞—VDD. across the field; above and below various ornaments.

COENVULF.

A.D. 796 TO A.D. 819.?

PENNY.—R.2. to R.6.

1. *Obv.*—COENVVLF REX M. A rude head, with the diadem of pearls.

℞—+DVN MONETA. In the centre, a cross crosslet.

2. *Obv.*—A similar type and legend.

℞—+TIDBEARHT MONETA. In the centre four C's placed back to back, and a pellet.

3. *Obv.*—A similar type and legend.

℞—LVL+, in the angles of an ornamented cross, each letter encircled by a string of beads.

4. *Obv.*—+COENVVLF REX. In the centre, Y̅.

℞—+EOBA, in the angles of a large ornamented Y.

5. *Obv.*—COENVVLF REX F Y̅, in three lines.

℞—LVD◇MAN, in two lines, with various ornaments.

His moneyers' names are numerous.

CIOLVULF THE FIRST.

About A.D. 819 to A.D. 819. (?)

Penny.—R.7. to R.8.

1. *Obv.*—CIOLVVLF REX M̅. A rude head, with the diadem of pearls. No inner circle.

℞—+EALH·TAN MONETA. In the centre, a small cross, four crescents back to back, and four small diamonds.

2. *Obv.*—+CIOLVVLE (*sic*) REX.·. Bust with diadem of pearls. No inner circle.

℞—DEALINC MON, between the angles of an ornamented cross.

BEORNWULF.

About A.D. 819 to A.D. 824.

Penny.—R.8.

Obv.—BEORNPVLF REX. An *attempt* to represent a human head with the diadem.

℞—EVLGA MONETA. In the centre, a cross crosslet.

LUDICA.

A.D. 824 to A.D. 826. ?

Penny.—R.8.

Obv.—+LVDICA REX ME. A rude head, with the diadem of pearls.

℞—PERCALD MOHE, in three lines across the field, which is entirely without ornament.

BERHTULF.

A.D. 839 to A.D. 852.?

Penny.—R. 2. to R.4.

1. *Obv.* BERHTVLF REX. A rude head.

   ℞—+ÐENEHEAN. An ornamented cross.

2. *Obv.*—Similar head and legend.

   ℞—+ZIGEHEAH. In the centre a cross, with an annulet in each angle.

BURGRED.

A.D. — to A.D. 874.

Penny.—C. to R.1.

1. *Obv.*—+BVRGRED REX. A rude attempt at the regal portrait.

   ℞—+TATA MONETA, in three lines.

There are slight varieties of this type; but the coins of Burgred are very similar to each other.

CEOLVULF.

AD. 874 to —.

Penny.—R.6. to R.8.

1. *Obv.*—+CEOLVVLF REX ꝶ. The regal portrait.

   ℞—+OBA MONETA, in three lines.

The coins of Ceolvulf resemble those of his predecessor.

KINGS OF THE EAST ANGLES.

BEONNA.

A.D. 690 to AD. —.

Penny.—R.8.

1. *Obv.*—+BEOᛋNA REX. In the field a circle, with a pellet in the centre.

   ℞—+EᛏE (*sic*). In the centre a cross, within a square composed of beads or pellets.

2. *Obv.*—+BEOXX≋ REX (*sic*). In the centre a pellet, within a circle of beads or pellets.

   ℞—Similar to the preceding coin.

These coins resemble the *skeattas*.

EADMUND.

About A.D. 855 to —.

Penny.—R.2. to R.7.

1. *Obv.*—+EADMVND REX AN. In the centre, A.

℞—+EADMVND MONE. In the centre, a cross with a pellet in each angle.

2. *Obv.*—+ADMVND REX AN. In the centre, a cross with a small crescent in each angle.

℞—+EÐEΓNEΓ (*sic*). MMO. *pro.* Ethilhelm. In the centre, a cross with a pellet in each angle.

Ruding gives nine varieties of these coins, which differ but slightly from each other: they are without the head.

AETHELWEARD.

A.D. — to A.D. —.?

Penny.—R.2. to R.4.

1. *Obv.*—AEÐELVVEARD REX. In the centre, A.

℞—As Eadmund, No. 1.

The other pennies of Aethelweard so closely resemble those of Eadmund, that this king is supposed to have reigned over the East Angles about the same period, and not over the West Saxons as was at first conjectured.

ETHELSTAN.

Raised to the Throne of East Anglia by Alfred, A.D. 870; baptized, A.D. 878; died, A.D. 890.

Penny.—R.3. to R.6.

1. *Obv.*—+EÞELSTAN. In the centre, A.

℞.—+RERNHER. In the centre, a pellet within a circle.

Ruding gives ten varieties of the coins of Ethelstan, all of which are without the head.

KINGS OF NORTHUMBERLAND.

ECGFRID.

A.D. 670 TO A.D. 685.

STYCAS.—R.6. Brass.

ALDFRID.

A.D. 685 TO A.D. 705.

SCEATTAS.—R.8.

Only two known; one of fine silver, the other of brass. See the above cut.

EADBERT.

A.D. 737 TO A.D. 758.

SCEATTAS.—R.8. Base silver.

ALCHRED.

A.D. 765 TO A.D. 774.

SCEATTAS.—R.8. Silver.

ELFWALD.

A.D. 779 TO A.D. 788.

SCEATTAS.—R.8. Silver.

HEARDULF.

A.D. 794 TO A.D. 806.

STYCAS.?—R.8. Brass.

EANRED.?

A.D. 808 TO A.D. 840.

PENNY.—R.8.

1. *Obv.*—+EANRED REX. The regal bust, to the right.

R—DES MONETA ω̄ (*sic*). In the centre, a cross; two of the limbs terminating in crosses and two in Y's.

STYCA.—C.

1. *Obv.*—+EANRED REX. In the centre, a cross.
   ℞.—+MONNE. In the centre a cross.
2. *Obv.*—+EANHEDHEX (*sic*). In the centre a cross, with a pellet in the first quarter.
   ℞.—+VVLFHEARD. In the centre a cross, with a pellet in the second quarter. (*Ruding, No.* 3).
3. *Obv.*—+EANRED REX. In the centre a cross.
   ℞.—+BRODR (*sic*). In the centre, a pellet within an annulet.

ETHELRED.

A.D. 840 TO A.D. 848.

STYCAS.—C. to R.4. Brass. One is known of fine silver.

REDULF.

A.D. 844 TO —.

STYCAS.—R.3. Brass.

OSBERCHT.

A.D. 848 TO A.D. 867.

STYCAS.—R.2. Brass.

REGNALD.

A.D. — TO A.D. 944.

PENNY.—R.8.

Obv.—+REGNALD CVNVC. In the centre a cross fleury.
℞.—+AVRA MONIT RE (*sic*). In the centre a small cross.

ANLAF.

A.D. — TO A.D. 944.

PENNY.—R.6. to R.8.

1. *Obv.*—+ANLAF CVNVNCI. A rude figure of a raven.
   ℞.—+ÆELFERDMINETI (*sic*). In the centre a small cross.

2. *Obv.*—+ANLAF CVNNVNC. An unknown object.
   ℞.—+FARMAN MONETA. In the centre the sacred standard of the Danes?

Ruding gives other types.

ERIC.

A.D. 952 TO —.

PENNY.—R.6. to R.7.

1. *Obv.*—ERIC REX, in two lines across the field; between them, a sword.
   ℞.—+INCÆLCAR. In the centre a cross, with a pellet in each quarter.

There are two varieties of this type.

2. *Obv.*—+ERIC REX N, and two crescents. In the centre a small cross.
   ℞.—INCELCAR̄M, in two lines; between them, three small crosses.

SAINTS.

SAINT PETER.

(*York*).

PENNY.—R.1.

1. *Obv.*—S̄CIPETRIMO, in two lines.
   ℞.—EBORACECI (*sic*). In the centre a cross within a circle of pearls. (*Ruding, No.* 10).
2. *Obv.*—SCIPETRIIO, in two lines; between them, a sword like that on the coins of Eric; below, an object probably intended for the head of a spear, with the point downwards.

SAINT MARTIN.

(*Lincoln*).

PENNY.—R.7.

1. *Obv.*—S̄CIMARTI, in two lines; between them a sword; below, ⊥.
   ℞.—+LINCOIACIVIT (*sic*). An open plain cross, with another cross in the centre.

SAINT EDMUND.

(*Bury Saint Edmunds*).

PENNY.—R.1.

1. *Obv.*—+SCEÆDMVNE. In the centre, Æ.
   ℞—+ELISMVSAAO (*sic*). In the centre, a plain cross.

There are several varieties of these pennies, but they do not differ materially from each other.

ARCHBISHOPS OF CANTERBURY.[1]

JAENBERHT.

A.D. 763 TO A.D. 790.

PENNY.—R.8.

1. *Obv.*—IÆENBRHT AREP. In the centre, a star.
   ℞ .—OFFA REX, in two lines, within an ornamented area.

AETHILHEARD.

A.D. 790 TO A.D. 803.

PENNY.—R.8.

1. *Obv.*—∴ÆEDILHEÆRD PONT T. In the centre a cross crosslet.
   ℞ . —OFFA REX M. In three lines.
2. *Obv.*—+ÆEDILHEÆRD ǢR. In the centre ĒP̄.
   ℞ .—CENVLF REX T̄, between the angles of a large figure resembling the letter Y.
3. *Obv.*—+ÆEDILHEARD ÆR. In the centre ep̄.
   ℞ .—+COENVVLF REX. In the centre, M̄.

No. 1 bears the title of *Pontifex* only. The others that of Archiepiscopus.

VULFRED.

A.D. 803 TO A.D. 830.

PENNY.—R.3. to R.7.

1. *Obv.*—+VVLFRED ÆRCHIEP T. A rude full-faced bust.
   ℞ .—SAEBERHT MONETA. In the centre the monogram of Dorovernia.

---

[1] See a paper " On the Arrangement of the Coins of the Archbishops of Canterbury." Num. Chronicle, Vol. II., p. 209.

2. *Obv.*—+VVLFREDI ARCHIEPISCOP. A rude full faced bust.

℞.—+DOROVERNIA CIVITATIS. In the centre a cross crosslet.

3. Another with a similar obverse, but with +DOROVERNIA CIVITAS, in four lines across the field.

CEOLNOTH.

A.D. 830 TO A.D. 870.

PENNY.—R.1. to R.8.

1. *Obv.*—+CEOLNOÐ ARCHIEP̄. A rude full-faced head, as on the coins of Wulfred.

℞.—+HEBECA MONETA, within a large cross extending to the edge of the coin, the letters NETA being in the angles.

2. *Obv.*—+CIALNOÐ ARCEPIS. A rude full-faced bust.

℞.—+VVNERE MONETA. In the centre the monogram, composed of the Greek letters X and P, as on the coins of the Lower Empire.

3. *Obv.*— +CEOLNOÐ ARCHIEP̄. A rude bust to the right, with a fillet round the head, ornamented with a crescent.

℞.—+TOCFA MONETA, in three lines across the field.

Ruding gives eight varieties of the coins of Ceolnoth.

ETHERED.

A.D. 871 TO A.D. 891.

Obv.—+ EÐERED ARCHIEPI. The bust of Coenvulf (?)

℞.— EÐERED MONETA.

PLEGMUND.

A.D. 891 TO A.D. 923.

PENNY.—R.7. to R.8.

1. *Obv.*—+PLECMVND ARCHIEP. In the centre ♆

℞.—ÆÐELVLF MO., in two lines across the field, divided by three small crosses.

There are four varieties of the coins of Plegmund.

UNCERTAIN.

Supposed to be Archiepiscopal.

PENNY.—R.4.

1. *Obv.*—+SVVEFNERD MONETA. Diademed head to the right.

   ℞—DOROBERNIA CIVITAS, in three lines across the field.

2. *Obv.*—Same legend. Diademed head to the right.

   ℞—SVVEFNERD MONETA. In the centre DR CI VR TZ

ARCHBISHOPS OF YORK.

EANBALD.

STYCA.—R.1.

1. *Obv.*—+EANBALD. In the centre, a small cross.

   ℞—+EDILVEARD. In the centre, a small cross.

VIGMUND.

STYCA.—R.

1. *Obv.*—+VIGMVND AR. In the centre a cross, with a pellet in each angle.

   ℞—+HVNLAF. In the centre, a plain cross.

2. *Obv.*—+VIGMVND IREP. In the centre, a plain cross.

   ℞—+FROINNE. In the centre, a cross, composed of pellets or studs.

VULFHERE.

STYCA.—R.2.

1. *Obv.*—VVLFHERE REP. (*retrograde*). round a wheel with four spokes. ?

   ℞.—+VVLFRED. In the centre four crescents, placed back to back.

SOLE MONARCHS.

ECGBEORHT.

About A.D. 800? to A.D. 837.

Penny.—R.4. to R.8.

1. *Obv.*—+ECGBEORHT REX. A rude head to the right.

   ℞—+SIGESTEF. In the centre, a cross crosslet.

2. *Obv.*—+ECGBEVRHT R. A rude head to the right.

   ℞—+SVEFNVRD MON. In the centre a monogram, probably intended for Canterbury.

Ruding gives five varieties with the head, and four without it.

3. *Obv.*—ECBEORHT REX. In the centre a monogram, and letters composing part of the word SAXONIORVM.

   ℞—+TIDEMAN MONE. In the centre a plain cross.

ETHELVULF.

A.D. 837 to A.D. 857.

Penny.—R.2. to R.5.

1. *Obv.*—EÐELVVLF REX. A rude head with the diadem, to the right.

   ℞—+BIARNNOÐ. In the centre an ornamented A.

2. *Obv.*—Similar legend and type.

   ℞—HVNRED MONETA, disposed as on the coin of Archbp. Ceolnoth, No. 1, p. 244.

3 *Obv.*—+EDELVVLF REX. In the centre a cross, with a triangular point in each angle.

   ℞—+BEAHꝏVVND (*sic*). In the centre a cross crosslet.

4 *Obv.*—+EÐELVVLF REX. In the centre the letters DORIBI.

   ℞—+EALGMVND MONETA. In the centre CAN

5 *Obv.*—EÐELVVLF REX. In the centre, as No. 3.

   ℞—+OSMVND MONETA. In the centre, SAXONIORVM in three lines.

6. *Obv.*—A similar type, with OCCIDENTALIVM in the place of the moneyer's name.

AETHEBALD.

A.D. 857 TO A.D. 862.

No coins are known of this monarch.

AETHELBEARHT.

A.D. 862 TO 867.

PENNY.—C. to R.5.

1. *Obv.*—+AEÐELBEARHT REX. A rude bust with bare head.
   ℞.—DELBEARHT MONETA, disposed upon and within the angles of a large cross, occupying the whole field of the coin.
2. *Obv.*—Same legend. Rude bust with diadem.
   ℞—CENVEALD MONETA. In the centre an ornamented cross.

Two hundred and forty-nine coins of the type of No. 1 were found at Dorking in the year 1817. But few specimens of his money were previously known.

AETHELRED.

A.D. 867 TO A.D. 872.

PENNY.—R.2.

1. *Obv.*—+AÐELRED (*or* AEÐELRED) REX. Rude bust with diadem.
   ℞—DENEVALD MONETA, in three lines, within compartments.
2. *Obv.*—+EÐELRED REX SAXORV. In the centre, a small cross.
   ℞ —

AELFRED.

A.D. 872 TO A.D. 901.

PENNY.—R.1. to R.8.

1. *Obv.*—+AELBRED REX +. Rude bust with diadem.
   ℞.—+IARNRED MONETA, in three lines within compartments.
2. *Obv.*—ELFRED REX. Diademed bust. No inner circle.
   ℞—The large monogram of LONDONIA.
3. *Obv.*—AELFRED REX. In the centre a small cross.
   ℞—ÆÐELVLF MO (*neta*), in two lines.
4. *Obv.*—+ELFRED M+-+. Rude head.
   ℞—+DVDD MONETA, in three lines.

EADWEARD THE FIRST.

A.D. 901 TO A.D. 924.

PENNY.—C. to R.8.

1. *Obv.*—XƎЯ ᗡЯAƎVVᗡAƎ (*sic*). Rude bust to the right.
   ℞—II ZIVVMAЯƎ (*sic*), in two lines.
2. *Obv.*—EADVVEARD REX. Diademed bust to the left.
   ℞—EᴀLSTAN MO, in two lines.
3. *Obv.*—Similar legend. In the centre a small cross.
   ℞—VVALEMAN MO. In two lines.
4. *Obv.*—Similar legend. In the centre a small cross.
   ℞—VVLFSIΓE, in two lines. A building with round arches.
5. *Obv.*—Similar legend and type.
   ℞—ΓVDBERHT, in two lines. A building surmounted by a star.*
6. *Obv.*—Similar legend and type.
   ℞—VVLFΓAR, across the field, divided by a line, on which is the representation of a building with wings; below, a cross.
7. *Obv.*—Similar legend and type.
   ℞—ALHSTAN MO, in three lines; a hand descending from the clouds, as on the Byzantine money, backed by a nimbus encircling a cross.

HALFPENNY.—R.8.

8. *Obv.*—Similar legend and type.
   ℞—BIORNVVALD, in two lines.
9. *Obv.*—Similar legend and type.
   ℞—CIOLVLF MO, in two lines.

ATHELSTAN.

A.D. 924 TO A.D. 940.

PENNY.—C. to R.8.

1. *Obv.*—+ÆÐELSTAN REX. A *crowned* bust, to the right.
   ℞—+DRVHTVALD MON. In the centre a small cross.
2. *Obv.* Similar legend. A small cross in the centre.
   ℞—ABBA MON̄, in two lines.

---

* The object on the reverse is copied from that on the very common coin of the time of Constantine the Great, generally called the gate of the Prætorian Camp.

3. *Obv.*—Similar legend and type.

℞—REGNALD MON EBoRAC AC, in four lines from the bottom, the field of the coin divided by a line, upon which stands a tower, or some such edifice.

4. *Obv.*—+EÐEΓSTAN RE SAXORVM. In the centre, a cross.

℞—+BOIGA MOT. CT. DEORABVI. Small cross.

5. *Obv. only.*—+ÆÐELSTAN REX TOT. BRIT. In the centre, a small cross.

EADMUND.

A.D. 940 TO A.D. 946.

PENNY.—C. to R.8.

1. *Obv.*—EADMVND REX. A rude bust, to the right, with a kind of helmet.

℞—+BESE MONETA. A cross crosslet in the centre.

2. *Obv.*—EADMVND REX. A *crowned* bust, to the right.

℞—ELERED MONETA, in two lines.

3. *Obv.*—+EADMVND REX, in the centre, a small cross.

℞—BACIAΓER, in two lines.

The pennies with his head are extremely rare.

EADRED.

A.D. 946 TO A.D. 955.

PENNY.—C. to R.3.

1. *Obv.*—+EADRED REX. A crowned bust, to the right.

℞—+FREDRED MONETA. In the centre, a small cross.

2. *Obv.*—+EADRED REX. In the centre, a small cross.

℞—+LIFINC MO, in two lines.

EADWIG.

A.D. 955 TO A.D. 959.

PENNY.—R.1. to R.8.

1. *Obv.*—+EADVVIG REX. A crowned bust, to the right.

℞—ÆÐVLF MONETA LVND. In the centre, a small cross.

2. *Obv.*—+EADPIG REX. In the centre, a small cross.

℞—HERIGER MO. In two lines across the field.

3. *Obv.*—+EADVVIC REX. In the centre, a small cross.
   ℞—CRIM, on a tablet or compartment across the field of the coin.
4. *Obv.*—Similar legend. In the centre, a small cross.
   ℞—OSPALD. A grotesque ornament.

Only one penny is known with his head.

EADGAR.

A.D. 959 TO A.D. 975.

PENNY.—R.1. to R.6.

1. *Obv.*—+EADCAR REX. A crowned bust, to the right.
   ℞—+AÐVLF MONETA LVND (*London*). In the centre, a small cross, and a still smaller cross near the inner circle.
2. *Obv.*—+EADCAR REX ANCLORVM. In the centre, a small cross.
   ℞—+PVNSICE MONETA PINTO (*Winchester*). In the centre, a small cross.

EADWEARD THE SECOND.

A.D. 975 TO A.D. 979.

PENNY.—R.1.

1. *Obv.*—+EADPEARD REX A. Diademed bust, to the left.
   ℞—+DVN MO EOFORPIC (*York*). In the centre, a small cross.
2. *Obv.*—+EADPARD REX ANGL̄. Diademed bust, to the left.
   ℞—+ESCMAN M O. STANF (*Stamford*). In the centre, a small cross.

AETHELRED THE SECOND.

A.D. 797 TO —

PENNY.—R.1. to R.6.

1. *Obv.*—+ÆÐELRED REX ANGLO. Diademed head, to the right.
   ℞—+LEOFSTAN ON CANT. In the centre, a small cross.
2. *Obv.*—+ÆÐELRED REX ANGLO. Diademed bust, to the right.
   ℞—+VALTFERÐ M̄O GIP (*Ipswich*). In the centre, the hand of Providence between Ā. ω̄.

3. *Obv.*—ÆÐELRED REX ANGLO. A rude bust with bare head, to the right, without the inner circle.

R—+TOGA MO MELVD (*Maldon*). A voided cross, to the edge of the coin, without the inner circle.

4. *Obv.*—ÆÐELRÆD REX ANGLO. Armed bust, to the left, with radiated crown. No inner circle.

R—+DRENG MO. LINC (*Lincoln*). A large voided cross, reaching to the edge of the coin, over a lozenge with three pellets at each corner.

5 *Obv.*—+ÆÐELRÆD REX ANGLOR. Bust with bare head, to the left; a sceptre in front.

R—+ÆLFPINE MO. NA. In the centre, a voided cross, in the angles of which are the letters CRVX.

SUEIN.

A.D. 1013.

The penny engraved by Ruding is a Danish coin.

CNUT.

A.D. 1017 to —

Penny.—C. to R.8.

1. *Obv.*—+CNVT REX ANGLOR. Diademed bust, within a quatrefoil.

R—ÆCELPINE ON BRI (*Bristol*). A voided cross, reaching to the edge of the coin.

2. *Obv.*—CNVT REX AN. Diademed bust, to the left, with a sceptre surmounted by a kind of *fleur de lis;* no inner circle.

R—+PVLMOÐ ON EOFER (*York*). A voided cross, reaching to the inner circle, with an annulet in the centre.

3. *Obv.*—CNVT REX ANGLORV. A crowned bust, to the left.

R—+ƿVLFRED ON LVNDEN. A voided cross, reaching to the edge of the coin, over a quatrefoil.

4. *Obv.*—CNVT REX ANG. Bust to the left, with a conical-shaped cap; before, a sceptre.

R—+EÐLSTAN ON BAÐA (*Bath*). A voided cross, reaching to the inner circle, &c.

5. *Obv. only.*—+VLF ON LINCOLN C. A voided cross, with PAX in the angles.*

---

* An extremely rare type.

HAROLD THE FIRST.

A.D. 1036.

PENNY.—R.2. to R.8.

1. *Obv.*—+HAROLD R. Bust to the left, with diadem.

   R—+EDPINE ON DOFR ∴ (*Dover*). In the centre, a kind of voided cross; no inner circle.

2. *Obv.*—+HAROLD RECX A. Bust with sceptre. No inner circle.

   R—+ELFPINE ON ÐEOD (*Thetford*). A voided cross, reaching to the edge of the coin. In each angle, a kind of *fleur de lis*.

HARTHACNUT.

A.D. 1040.

PENNY.—R.6. to R.8.

1. *Obv.*—+HARÐACNVT REX. Diademed bust, to the right. No inner circle.

   R—ELFPINE ON PICE (*Worcester*). A kind of voided cross, as Harold, No. 1. No inner circle.

2. *Obv.*—A similar legend. Diademed bust, holding a sceptre, to the left.

   R—+CODRIC ON CLEPECE (*Gloster*). A voided cross; a mascle in the centre.

3. *Obv.*—+HARÐCNVT RE. A similar bust.

   R—+LEFENOOÐ ON HERE (*Hereford*). A similar cross to that on No. 2.

EDWARD THE CONFESSOR.

A.D. 1042 TO 1066.

PENNY.—C. to R.7.

HALFPENNY.—R.8.*

1. *Obv.*—+EDPERD REX. Diademed bust, to the left, with sceptre. No inner circle.

   R—+SCVLA ON EOFERPIC (*York*). A kind of voided cross, reaching to the inner circle; in the second quarter an annulet.

2. *Obv.*—EADPARD REX. Crowned bearded bust, to the right, with sceptre; no inner circle.

---

* See Numismatic Chronicle, Vol. II. p. 35, and Numismatic Journal, Vol. II. p 253.

℞—SENEBRN ON EOFR. Across the field, a tablet reaching to the inner circle, inscribed PAX.

3. *Obv.*—+EDPERD REX. Diademed bust, to the left, with sceptre.

℞—+LITLIL ONN (*sic*) EOFERP. No inner circle. A voided cross reaching to the letters of the legend; in the angles, the letters P. A. L. X.

4. *Obv.*—EADPÆRD REX ANLLORV. A robed and crowned male bearded figure, seated on a chair of state, holding in his right hand a staff surmounted by a cross, and in his left outstretched, a globe, surmounted by a cross. No inner circle.

℞+DEORMAN ON LVNDE∴ (*London*). A voided cross, reaching to the inner circle; in each quarter, a martlet.

5. *Obv.*—EADPARD RX (*sic*) ANLLO. A crowned beardless figure, seated in a chair of state, holding the same insignia as the figure on the preceding coin. No inner circle.

℞—Type as No. 4.

6 *Obv.*—EDPEARD REX. Full faced crowned bust, holding a sceptre in the right hand. No inner circle.

℞—MANPINE ON DOPER (*Dover*). A voided cross, reaching to the inner circle; in the angles, an ornament.

7. *Obv.*—+EDPARDE REX. A full-faced bearded bust, with a round cap, surmounted by a cross, formed of five pellets.

℞—+NOLTEL ON EORP (*York*). In the centre, a small cross; above, an annulet.

8. *Obv.*—+EDPARD RE.⁻ Diademed bust, to the left.

℞—+SPOTA ON BEDE (*Bedford*). A voided cross, reaching to the letters of the legend; no inner circle.

There are upwards of five hundred varieties of the coins of this king.

HAROLD THE SECOND.

A.D 1066.

PENNY.—R.2.

1. *Obv.*—HAROLD REX ANLL. Bearded bust with a kind of ducal cap, to the left; before, a sceptre.

℞—+SNAEBEORN ON EON (*Exeter*)? and across the field, a tablet inscribed PAX. The inner circle and the tablet composed of rows of dots or pellets.

A TABLE OF THE WEIGHTS OF ENGLISH SILVER COINS IN TROY GRAINS, FROM WILLIAM THE FIRST TO ELIZABETH.

	A. D.	Farthing	Half-penny.	Penny.	Half-groat.	Groat.	Quarter-Shilling.	Half-Shilling.	Shilling.	Half-Crown	Crown.
William I.	1066	...	...	22½							
28th of Edward I.	1300	5½	11	22							
18th Edward III.	1344	5	10	20¼							
20th ,,	1346	5	10	20							
27th ,,	1353	4½	9	18	36	72					
13th Henry IV.	1412	3¾	7½	15	30	60					
4th Edward IV.	1464	3	6	12	24	48					
18th Henry VII.	1504	3	6	12	24	48	...	...	144		
18th Henry VIII.	1527	2½	5	10½	21¼	42½					
34th ,,	1543	2½	5	10	20	40	...	...	120		
36th ,,	1545	2½	5	10	20	40	...	...	120		
1st Edward VI.	1547	2½	5	10	20	40	...	...	120		
3rd ,,	1549	...	...	...	...	...	...	...	80		
5th ,,	1551	...	...	...	...	...	...	...	80		
6th ,,	1553	5½	11	8	...	...	24	48	96	240	480
1st Mary	1553	6	12	8	16	32	...	...	96	240	480
2nd Elizabeth	1560	...	4	8	16	32	24	48	96		
43rd ,,	1601	...	3¾	7¾	15½	31	22¼	46¼	92¾	232¼	464½

*** The weight of Elizabeth's *three-farthing piece* is 6 grains. Her *three-halfpenny piece* weighs 12 grains. The *ten-shilling piece* of Charles I. should weigh 929 grains, or 1 oz. 18 dwts. 17 grains. His *twenty-shilling piece*, 1858 grains, or 3 oz. 17 dwts. 10 grains.

WEIGHTS OF ENGLISH GOLD COINS, FROM HENRY THE THIRD TO ELIZABETH.

	Gold Penny.	Florin.	Noble.	Angel.	Sovereign or Double Rial.	George Noble.	Crown.
Henry III. . . .	45, 45·2, 45·2*						
18th Edward III. .	....	108·	136·7				
20th ,, .	....	...	128·6				
27th ,, .	....	...	120·				
1st Richard II. .	....	...	120·				
13th Henry IV. .	....	...	108·				
5th Edward IV. .	....	...	120·	80·			
1st Henry VII. .	....	...	...	...	240·		
18th Henry VIII.	....	...	...	...	....	71·1	57.3
34th ,, .	....	...	...	80·	200·		
36th ,, .	....	...	...	...	192·		
3rd Edward VI. .	....	...	...	...	169·4		
4th ,, .	....	...	...	80·	240·		
6th ,, .	....	...	...	...	174·5		
43rd Elizabeth . .	....	...	...	79·3	171·9		

* These are the respective weights of the three pieces known.

A TABLE OF THE STANDARD FINENESS OF SILVER MONEY, FROM THE 28TH OF EDWARD THE FIRST TO THE 43RD OF ELIZABETH.

	Fine.		Allay.			Fine.		Allay.	
	oz.	dwt.	oz.	dwt.		oz.	dwt.	oz.	dwt.
28th Edward I. . .	11	2	0	18	1st Richard III. .	11	2	0	18
18th Edward III .	11	2	0	18	19th Henry VII. .	11	2	0	18
19th ,, .	11	2	0	18	29th ,, ,, .	11	2	0	18
20th ,, .	11	2	0	18	18th ,, VIII. .	11	2	0	18
27th ,, .	11	2	0	18	23th ,, ,, .	11	2	0	18
30th ,, .	11	2	0	18	34th ,, ,, .	10	0	2	0
18th Richard II. .	11	2	0	18	36th ,, ,, .	6	6	6	0
3rd Henry IV. . .	11	2	0	18	37th ,, ,, .	4	0	8	0
9th ,, V. . .	11	2	0	18	1st Edward VI. .	4	0	8	0
1st ,, VI. . .	11	2	0	18	2nd ,, .	4	0	8	0
4th ,, ,, . .	11	2	0	18	3rd ,, .	6	0	6	0
24th ,, ,, . .	11	2	0	18	4th ,, .	3	0	9	0
49th ,, ,, . .	11	2	0	18	5th ,, .	3	0	9	0
4th Edward IV. .	11	2	0	18	6th ,, .	11	1	0	19
5th ,, . .	11	2	0	18	1st Mary	11	1	0	19
7th ,, . .	11	2	0	18	1st Elizabeth . .	11	2	0	18
8th ,, . .	11	2	0	18	2nd ,, . .	11	2	0	18
11th ,, . .	11	2	0	18	19th ,, . .	11	2	0	18
16th ,, . .	11	2	0	18	25th ,, . .	11	2	0	18
22nd ,, . .	11	2	0	18	43th ,, . .	11	2	0	18

A TABLE OF THE STANDARD FINENESS OF GOLD MONEY, FROM THE 41ST OF HENRY THE THIRD TO THE 43RD OF ELIZABETH.

	1.		2.		3.		4.	
	Fine.	Allay.	Fine.	Allay.	Fine.	Allay.	Fine.	Allay.
	car. gr.	car. gr	car. gr.	car. gr.	car. gr.	car. gr.	car. gr.	car. gr.
41th Henry III.								
18th Edward III.								
19th ,,								
20th ,,								
23rd ,,								
27th ,,								
30th ,,								
18th Richard II.								
3rd Henry IV.								
13th ,,								
9th Henry V.								
1st Henry VI.	23 3½	0 0½						
4th ,,								
24th ,,								
49th ,,								
4th Edward IV.								
5th ,,								
8th ,,								
11th ,,								
16th ,,								
22nd ,,								
1st Richard III.								
19th Henry VII.								
29th ,,								
18th Henry VIII.	....	....	....	....	22 0	2 0		
22nd ,,	23 3½	0 0½	....	....	22 0	2 0		
23rd ,,								
34th ,,	....	....	23 0	1 0				
36th ,,	....	....	....	....	22 0	2 0		
37th ,,	....	....	....	....	....	....	20 0	4 0
1st Edward VI.	....	....	....	....	....	....	20 0	4 0
2nd ,,								
3rd ,,	....	....	....	....	22 0	2 0		
4th ,,	23 3½	0 0½						
6th ,,	23 3½	0 0½	....	....	22 0	2 0		
1st Mary	23 3½	0 0½						
1st Elizabeth	23 3½	0 0½	....	....	22 0	2 0		
2nd ,,								
19th ,,								
25th ,,	23 3½	0 0½						
26th ,,								
27th ,,	....	....	....	....	22 0	2 0		
35th ,,								
43th ,,	23 3½	0 0½	....	....	22 0	2 0		

ENGLISH COINS.

FROM THE REIGN OF WILLIAM THE FIRST TO THAT OF ANNE.

A.D. 1066. Although it has been deemed advisable to place the English Coins struck after the death of Harold in a separate section, it will be seen that no material alteration took place on the accession of William the First, who, anxious to make his new subjects believe that he had obtained the crown by right of inheritance, and not by force of arms, not only solemnly ratified the laws of Edward the Confessor, but caused his coins to be struck in imitation of those of the Saxon Princes. We accordingly find some of the pennies of William resembling those of Harold in every respect, except in the name; the Saxon Ƿ being used instead of the Roman W, which, though found on his great seal, never appears on his coins.

From this period down to the reign of Henry III., no remarkable change was made in the English coinage. The old chroniclers speak of the coinage of half-pence and farthings in the reign of Henry I. Ruding thinks that, if really issued, these small pieces were disliked by the people, and called in. None of them are at present known.

A.D. 1222. In the sixth year of the reign of Henry the Third a writ was issued, commanding proclamation to be made that no halfpenny or farthing should be current unless it were round.[1] This alludes to the practice of

[1] Ruding, vol. i. p. 349.

dividing the penny into halves and quarters, of which examples have been found in recent discoveries of English pennies.

Grafton says that about the year 1227, a parliament was held in London which ordained that a *groat* should be coined, having on one side the king's effigy; and on the other, a cross reaching to the edge, "to avoyd clippyng." None of these groats are to be seen in the cabinets of our collectors. If really coined, the issue was probably very limited.

A.D. 1247. In the year 1247, the crime of forging and clipping increased to such a degree, that both in France and England the most rigorous measures were adopted against the offenders. Shortly after, a new coinage was issued by Henry. This is minutely described both in the Annals of Waverly and by Matthew Paris. The "new money differed from the old in two respects," says Ruding; "namely, that the double cross was extended to the outside of the circle which contained the legend, and that it was distinguished either by Roman numerals, or by TERCI, from the money of the two preceding monarchs of the same name; but in weight and type it remained nearly as before." He then adds in a note: "It is extraordinary that both the author of these Annals and also Matthew Paris should have omitted to state the most remarkable particular in which these coins differed from all which had preceded them—I mean the distinction of numerals, or words equivalent, to shew to which king of the name of Henry they belonged."

The coin here engraved, shews, however, that *some* of the early coinage of Henry the Third had that distinction which the author of the "Annals of the Coinage," considered wanting.

This penny reads HENRICVS . REX.; the type being similar to the early coinage of Henry III. The reverse reads TER . RI . ON . LVND; *i. e.*, TERCI . RICHARD . ON . LVND. Ruding gives TERIRI as one of the moneyers of Henry III., having probably seen an imperfect or ill-struck coin, and mistaken the dot after the word TER. for an I.[1]

Grafton's mention of a groat, ordered by the Parliament to be coined in the year 1227, has already been noticed. The same chronicler informs us that in 1249 "the king summoned a parliament at London, in which it was enacted that a coyne of a certeine weight of silver called a grote should be stamped, and that it should have on the one syde the picture of the Kinges face; and on the other, a crosse extended in length to the extreme parts thereof, to the entent there should be no deceyt used by diminishing or clipping the same." None of these groats have yet come to light.

A.D. 1257. Gold Penny. In the forty-first year of this king's reign (A.D. 1257), the "*gold penny*" appeared. It appears by a MS. Chronicle, preserved in the archives of the city of London, that this piece weighed two sterlings, and was current for twenty-pence. It was made current by proclamation; but the Londoners having entered a remonstrance against it, it was called in. It continued current, however, for several years after;[2] and in Henry's forty-ninth year its value was raised to twenty-four pence. "This piece," says Ruding, "was properly a Ryal, and the first of the sort coined in Europe: the petit Ryal of Philip le Belle being much in imitation of it, and he was the first king of France who coined Ryals."[3]

A.D. 1270. In the year 1270, a general proof and assay of the coins was ordered to be made throughout the

---

[1] See the Numismatic Journal, Vol. I. p. 39, where this coin is noticed. The engraving is made from a specimen in the author's cabinet.
[2] Ruding's Annals, vol. i. p. 358. Snelling's View of the gold coin of England, p. 11.
[3] Ruding, vol. i. p. 359.

kingdom, and the base money to be seized and applied to the king's use.

A particular description of the coins of Henry III. will be found in the list which follows these remarks.[1]

Forging, clipping, and the importation of foreign coins of inferior standard, prevailed to such an extent on the accession of Edward the First, that one of his earliest acts after his return to England was the reforming of that great abuse.[2] The offenders, among whom as usual were numbers of Jews, were seized; and many of that persecuted people, as well as Christians, met the cruel death awarded to those who were found guilty of debasing the public money. If the author of the Annals of Waverly may be credited, the Jews were really guilty; an immense quantity of clippings having actually been found in their houses. At any rate, their great wealth, under continued exactions, was calculated to excite suspicion. This base practice, it must be confessed, was not confined to the Jews. Guy, Prior of Montacute, was twice found guilty both of clipping and forging, and heavily fined.

A.D. 1279. Indenture with William de Turnemire.

In 1279, William de Turnemire was appointed Master of the Mint; and Mints were established in London, Canterbury, York, and Bristol. Dies for a new coinage were delivered on the 17th of May, 1280, to Gregory de Rokesley, Lord Mayor of London, and Rolandine de Podio, the keepers of the Mint; and pennies, halfpennies, and farthings were coined.[3]

---

[1] The pieces commonly called "Pennies of St. Paul," noticed by Ruding under this reign, and supposed by him to be of English origin, belong to Münster in Westphalia. They were conjectured to be English from the circumstance of their bearing the voided cross and pellets, in imitation of the money of Henry III.; but our collectors should have borne in mind that the English money was imitated by continental states at a much earlier period than this. Even the money of Bohemia was struck on the type and model of the Anglo-Saxon coins.

[2] Ruding, vol. i. p. 367, quoting the Annals of Waverly, observes that the Pope's Nuncio had authority to enquire into—de falsariis et de falso convictis.

[3] In one of the registers of the Dean and Chapter of Saint Paul's, the name of an engraver of dies occurs. Theobald de Lyleston is described as a goldsmith, and the engraver of the dies for coinage throughout England:—"Aurifaber et insculptor cuneorum monetæ totius Angliæ."—*See a Communication of Sir Henry Ellis to the Numismatic Society, printed in the Numismatic Journal*, Vol. II. p. 254.

As a proof of the little reliance that can be placed on the statements of the chroniclers respecting the coinage of this country, it may be mentioned that Hollinshed, more minute and less fanciful than some of his brethren, gravely tells us that the English coins before the time of Edward the First were *square*.[1]

Langtoft, after noticing the punishment inflicted upon the forgers and clippers, thus describes the new coinage:—

> " Eduard did smyte rounde peny, halfpeny, ferthyng,
> Þe croice passed þe bounde of all þorghout þe ryng,
> Þe kynges side salle be þe hede, and his name writen.
> Þe croyce side what cite it was in coyned and smyten."

Ruding observes, that it is remarkable that Robert de Brunne, of whose translation the above lines are a specimen, omits that part of the original which speaks of the *groats* coined by Edward—" Gros Tournais Englays qe valent verayment quartre esterlinges en achate & vent."[2] In the uncouth rhyme of Harding, he speaks of

> " The grote, halfgrote, all in new coine."

No specimen of the half-groat is, however, to be found in the cabinets of our collectors, the half-groat mentioned in the introduction to Anderson's *Diplomata Scotiæ* having, as Ruding informs us, been looked for in vain in the Advocates' library at Edinburgh.[3]

The author of the " Annals of the Coinage " considers it necessary to notice an event in the tenth year of this king, which is in some manner connected with his subject; namely, the total subjugation of Wales, and the defeat and death of Prince Lewellyn, who, by a pretended prophecy of Merlin, had been led to believe that he should be crowned in London *when the English money should be coined round!* The head of the unfortunate prince was crowned with ivy, and fixed upon

---

[1] Description of England, p 218. Query, might not the idea of square money have originated—by a *lucus a non lucendo* inference—from the words of the writ of Henry III., already mentioned; namely, that no "penny, halfpenny, or farthing should be current *unless it were round?*"

[2] Ruding, vol. i. p. 373. Hearne's Langtoft, vol. ii. p. 238.

[3] Ibid. vol. i. p. 374, *note*.

the Tower, and thus the prediction was fulfilled. As there are several versions of this story, it is highly probable that it was invented long after the execution of the unfortunate chief; and the mention of round money encourages the suspicion that the tale was fabricated by those from whom Hollinshed obtained his information, that before the reign of Edward the First the English money was square.[1]

A.D. 1283. In the year 1283, loud complaints were made of the state of the coinage. Clipping, forging, and the introduction of counterfeit money from the continent, increased to such a degree, that the most rigorous measures were adopted against the offenders. Three hundred persons were convicted, and many suffered the horrible punishment of the time.

Counterfeit Sterlings. Among the numerous frauds then practised, was one which was well calculated to deceive all but the most wary: namely, the importation of a silver coin, very closely resembling the pennies of Edward, but bearing on the obverse EDW ROBERTVS COMES, so that if not carefully examined, it might easily be mistaken for a genuine sterling. There were also pieces with types closely imitated from the English penny, struck at Luxemburg,[2] to which Chaucer, in the Monk's Prologue, alludes:—

> "This maketh that our wives wol assaye
> Religious folk, for they moun better paye
> Of Venus payementes than mowen we:
> God wote, no *Lussheburghes* payen ye."

Piers Plowman also refers to the Luxemburgh introduction:

---

[1] It may here be mentioned as a remarkable fact, that no coins of the Welch princes are known to exist, although their exclusive right to coin money is mentioned in the Welch laws. Edward Lluyd is said to have been told by the then Bishop of Bangor, that a relation of the prelate had possessed for many years a coin of Lhywelyn ap Jorweth, who reigned in the time of our Richard the First and his successor John. Accounts have from time to time been given of triangular pieces of silver, with a hole in the centre, and a circular inscription, but they cannot be relied on. See Ruding's Annals, vol. i. p. 375, and *note*, p. 376.

[2] Some of these pieces have been recently engraved by Dr. Gröte in the *Blätter für Münzkunde*.

"As in Lushburth is a luther alay, yet lokith like sterling.
The *marke* of the money is *good* and the *metel feble;*
So fareth it by some folk now," &c. &c.

It is easy to conceive the magnitude of the evil in an age when but very few of the humbler classes could read or write, and when, consequently, these spurious coins could be circulated with little hazard of detection.

A. D. 1290. In this year the Jews were banished the kingdom, but subsequent acts of the Parliament shew, that with their departure the crime of forgery had not ceased. Pollards, Crokards, Scaldings, Brabants, Eagles, Leonines, Sleepings, and many others of different denominations still continued to be imported in great numbers. These, for a short time, were allowed to pass at the rate of two for a penny, or sterling, but were soon prohibited, and then five or six were exchanged for one English penny.[1]

"Abbey Pieces." To the foregoing list of base coins, may be added Abbey Pieces, or Rosaries, which North, in his remarks on Clarke's conjectures, supposes to have been so designated on account of their bearing the legend AVE MARIA, &c., being probably not intended for money, but as *Tesseræ Sacræ*, for the use of monks and pilgrims who travelled from one religious house to another. These pieces being often found in old ruins, are mistaken for money by persons ignorant of the coinage of the period.[2]

"From the conquest," observes Ruding, "to the 28th of Edward, the penny weighed twenty-four grains Tower, or one penny weight, so that a pound of silver money was a pound both in weight and tale. But now the first variation from this rule took place, and the penny was reduced to 23.7073 grains

---

[1] Ruding, on the authority of Hemingford, says, that shortly afterwards a method of refining the foreign coin with lead was discovered, when two of them were found to be equal to a sterling, whereby many became rich who had obtained them in exchange when they were thought to be of so base a quality. The king, however fined these persons heavily for having exchanged or bought money without special licence. Annals, vol. i. p. 387.

[2] They are generally of brass, or mixed metal, and of the size of the groats of the time, with the types of a globe and cross, a dolphin, fleurs de lis, &c. &c.

Tower. This appears from an indenture in Lowndes' report, which recites that an indented trial piece of the goodness of old sterling was lodged in the exchequer, and every pound weight of such silver was to be shorn at twenty shillings and three pence. According to this, the value of the silver in the coin was one shilling and eightpence farthing an ounce, and the debasement amounted to $1\frac{1}{80}$ per cent."[1]

A.D. 1303. The statute of Edward's 31st year (A.D. 1303) ordains that the penny should weigh thirty-two grains of wheat, taken from the middle of the ear, being the same terms as those prescribed in the 51st year of Henry III.[2] About three years previously an extensive coinage took place, mints being established in London, Canterbury, Kingston-upon-Hull, Newcastle-upon-Tyne, Bristol, and Exeter. Pennies struck in all these places still exist, and those of London and Canterbury in immense numbers.

The pennies of the three Edwards closely resemble each other, and for a long time were not properly distinguished. Archbishop Sharp, in his observations on the coins of England, was the first to attempt their appropriation, and he is followed by Leake,[3] except in the case of the Irish penny, which he shews is not to be distinguished; those of Edward I. and Edward II. having each EDW.

Mr. Bartlett paid much attention to these coins.[4] This gentleman, by examining the pennies struck by the Bishops in the reigns of the Edwards, found the names and mint-marks to be as follows:—

Edward I.	EDW.	cross moline.	Anthony Beck.
Edward II.	EDWAR.	———	
	EDWAR.	crosier *to the left.*	Richard Kellow.
	EDWAR.	Lion & Fleur de lis.	Lodowic Beaumont.
Edward III.	EDWARDVS.	crosier *to the right.*	Thomas Hatfield.

[1] Ruding, vol. i. p. 388.

[2] Ruding is in doubt as to which of these two kings it originated with, and observes that the Roman weights were derived from the seed of the lentil.

[3] Historical Account of English Money, *sub anno.*

[4] Archæologia, vol. v. page 335.

The legends on the reverse of those coins which from their bearing EDW. are assigned to Edward the First, are—

VILLA BEREVICI, or BERVICI—*Berwick.*
VILLA BRISTOLLIE—*Bristol.*
CIVITAS CANTOR—*Canterbury.*
CIVITAS CESTRIE—*Chester.*
CIVITAS DVREME—*Durham.*
CIVITAS EBORACI—*York.*
CIVITAS EXONIE—*Exeter.*
VILL. KYNGESTON—*Kingston-upon-Hull.*
CIVITAS LINCOL—*Lincoln.*
CIVITAS LONDON; CIVI LONDONIA[1]—*London.*
LONDRIENSIS[2]—LONDONIENSIS.
VIL. NOVI CASTRI, or NOVICASTRI[3]—*Newcastle.*
VILLA RADINGI—*Reading.*
VIL. SCIEDMVNDI, and VILLA SEDMVNDI—*Saint Edmundbury.*

In the reign of Edward the First the custom of placing the moneyer's name on the coins was discontinued. But one name appears on the money of this king; namely, Robert of Hadley, inscribed—ROBERT DE HADELEIE, or, ROBERTVS DE HADL.[4]

It may be here mentioned that the heavy piece termed the groat, which has been by some writers attributed to this prince, belongs in all probability, to Edward the Third. Folkes, in his tables of English coins, notices those weighing 92, 116, and 138 grains respectively; a circumstance which serves to shew that they were rather trial pieces than coins. Ruding thinks that the style "Dei gratia," shews that they belong to the third Edward.[5]

---

[1] On the piece called a groat.
[2] On a farthing in the collection of Mr. Cuff. This explains the term "*Londrenses,*" which occurs in the indenture with William de Turnemire, in 1279.
[3] On a half-penny. The same legend occurs on a halfpenny of Edward II.
[4] Snelling has erroneously given Hadelie as a *mint,* and not a moneyer's name.
[5] Annals, vol. i. p. 397. Ruding, in this place thinks the statement of an old writer respecting a leather coinage worthy of notice. The author in question says that Edward the First had coins "bearing his name, stamp, and picture, which he used in the building of Carnarvon Castle, &c., to spare better bullion." These pieces, if really issued, must, as Ruding observes, be considered as counters or tokens.

The reign of Edward the Second offers nothing remarkable to the student of English coins. The parliament held at Northampton a short time after his accession, ordained that the money current in the previous reign should still be considered as the lawful coin. Some writers do not hesitate to charge this monarch with forcing his subjects to receive even the base coin current in the reign of his father.

A.D. 1310. The alteration and subsequent crying down of the pieces termed Pollards and Crocards, in the year 1310, appears to have created some discontent, especially in the provinces. In the same year a proclamation was issued commanding that the money should be current at the same value as in the reign of Edward the First. Ruding observes that at this time, it appears from the articles delivered to the King by the Commons, that the money was depreciated more than one half.[1] About this time another proclamation was issued, forbidding the importation of false money on pain of forfeiture. Clipping, and the coinage of base money, appears to have increased in this reign, since we find that in 1321, commissioners were appointed to inquire into these offences.

Edward the Third, by several acts endeavoured to prevent the introduction of foreign coin, which being much lighter was secretly conveyed into England from abroad. "Black money" of every description was denounced, and the melting-down of the authorised coin was forbidden on pain of forfeiture of the molten money. The exportation of money and plate was also prohibited.[2]

"From 1257 [the forty-first of Henry the Third] to the beginning of the year 1343," observes Ruding, "a period of little less than ninety years, no notices of any coinages of gold have occurred, nor have any coins been hitherto discovered, although three specimens of the coinage of 1257 are known to exist."[3] This author accounts for the non-coinage of gold during the period alluded to by supposing that it was not

---

[1] Annals, vol. i. p. 399. [2] Ibid. vol. i. p. 406. [3] Ibid. vol. i. p. 417.

required; the price of the necessary articles of life being within the reach of an inferior metal.

A.D. 1343. Gold Florin & its divisions. Be this as it may, the first coinage of gold in the reign of this monarch was in his seventeenth year, as shewn by an indenture of that date. This indenture specifies that three monies of gold shall be made; one to be current at six shillings, and the half and quarter to be in proportion. They are all to be of fine gold,[1] and fifty are to be made out of the pound Tower. The first is to be of the weight of two petit florins of Florence. Ruding is inclined to believe that this coinage was deferred until the following year, when a new indenture for making gold and silver coins was made between the king and Walter Dunfleurs, then master and worker of the Mint. The obverse type of these coins is described in a proclamation of the year 1343; three sorts of gold money are mentioned:—"One coin with two leopards, each piece to be current for six shillings, &c.; another piece of one leopard; and another piece of one helm."[2] This new money was soon found to be too highly valued in proportion to the silver coin; and a proclamation, promulgated in the same year, ordained that it should not be taken in payment without the consent of the party to whom it was tendered. In the following month it was declared no longer current without the consent of the party to whom offered.

Gold Noble & its divisions. A new gold coinage was immediately ordered and made current by proclamation. It is described as consisting of Noble, Maille Nobles, and Ferling Nobles; and their exportation was prohibited under pain of forfeiture.

The device on these coins was entirely novel, and is supposed by most writers to commemorate the victory obtained by Edward over the French fleet in the year 1340, with trifling loss

---

[1] Twenty-three carats, three grains and a half fine gold.

[2] Annals, vol. i. p. 420. Ruding observes that though termed leopards, the animals were really *lions;* and refers to Nisbet in a note.

to the English. Selden supposes this type to denote the English naval superiority, and to record Edward's claim to the sovereignty of the seas, supported by a navy of eleven hundred ships; but Ruding shows that it could not have been at the period in question, which was fifteen years subsequent to the first issue of these coins.[1] It is these pieces which are thus spoken of in the ancient rhyme:—

> "Four things our noble sheweth unto me,
> King, ship, and swerd, and power of the sea."

Strange stories were circulated, and to a late period believed, respecting these fine coins. Camden says, "our alchymists do affirm (as an unwritten verity) that the gold was made by projection or multiplication alchymical of Raymund Lully, in the Tower of London."[2] Ruding, however, shows that, unfortunately for this story, Lully died about twenty years before this coinage took place.

A.D. 1344. In the year 1344, the weight of the noble was reduced nearly ten grains, and the penny to twenty grains.

On the taking of Calais by Edward, he endeavoured to people it with English, and appointed thirty English burgesses to establish themselves there. A mint was also set up, and it was ordained that the white money therein struck should be the same as that coined in England. Ruding observes, that in the year 1349, some alteration in the standard of this money was commanded, but it is doubtful if it were carried into effect.

A.D. 1351. In the year 1351, an important alteration was made in the coin, which had been of so much better quality than that of other states, that notwithstanding the ordinances against its exportation, it continued to be sent out of the kingdom, while base money was constantly imported. A new coinage of the noble was therefore ordered, which, though of less weight than the former coinage, was to pass for six

---

[1] Annals, vol. i. p. 423.

[2] Remains, Art. Money.

shillings and eightpence, and its parts in due proportion. A new groat and half groat were also coined. Ruding shows that the date of this indenture has been incorrectly given by Lowndes. Folkes and Snelling also consider it to have been two years later. This reduction of the weight of the coin is said to have been adopted at the suggestion of William Edington, Bishop of Winchester, Treasurer of England, and, as may be supposed, was exceedingly unpopular. In 1354, by a writ directed to the Mayor of Bayonne, the English groats and half groats were made current in the Duchy of Aquitaine at their respective values.

Hitherto the coins of Scotland were of the same weight and fineness as the English,[1] but about this time, they were diminished in weight and fineness. Proclamation was consequently made, condemning these new coins, and threatening with heavy penalties those who should presume to take them. Those coins of Scotland which had formerly been current in England were allowed to remain in circulation.

A.D. 1358. Knyghton says, that in the year 1358, David, king of Scotland, came to London, and intreated Edward that the coins of England and Scotland might be current in both kingdoms on equal terms, and that, in consideration of the great humility of the Scottish monarch, his petition was allowed.

It is proper to notice, that in the treaty of peace with John, king of France, in the year 1360, Edward renounced his claim to that kingdom. He resumed it, however, in 1369. During the interval, the title of Edward, as king of France, does not appear on his coins.

A.D. 1361. In this year the fineness of the coins was made the subject of special inquiry. The occasion of the inquiry appears to be the conduct of King John of France, who had been taken prisoner at the battle of Poictiers in 1356.

---

[1] Scottish coins are often discovered mixed with English pennies.

The sum proposed for his ransom was three millions of crowns of gold, "in Florins de Scutor, or D' Escu, of which two were equal in value to the Florin de Noble of England." The French are said to have taken advantage of this, and debased their coins both in weight and alloy, alleging that the English money was of inferior standard to that required by the indenture. The assay of the English money was made in the following year, and proved satisfactory.[1]

Among the reasons for summoning the Parliament in the following year, are mentioned the unlawful exchanges of money, and "the feebleness of the coins." The Commons petitioned the king for an issue of plenty of gold and silver, and that a gold piece of smaller denomination, to be current for ten or twelve pence, should be coined. The gracious answer to this request was, "Le Roi voet q'il soit fait p' bon Conseil."[2] No gold coins of this description are mentioned in the indentures of the time.

A. D. 1364. In the year 1364, the severe laws against the exportation of English money were mitigated to those who were engaged in the supply of salt obtained at La Baye, in Britany. Fourscore pounds of sterlings were allowed to be exported by each person, but security was taken from them, that they should bring into the port of Harwich salt to that amount. In the April of this year, John king of France died at the Savoy palace in London. He had, during his imprisonment in England, employed agents, who secretly collected the picked gold money of the realm, besides military weapons. On his death-bed he confessed this to the king of England, who pardoned him, but severely punished the agents. Ruding gives this account from Knyghton, and, remarking on the secretion of the best gold coins (electum aurum Regni), supposes them to have been Edward's nobles of the first and second coinage, which are at this day so much scarcer than those of the third coinage.[3] Much of the col-

[1] Ruding, vol. i. p. 444. [2] Ibid. vol. i. p. 444-5. [3] Ibid. vol. i. p. 427.

lected gold was seized, and no doubt recoined. Ruding observes, that this story "but ill agrees with that noble maxim of the French monarch, that if good faith should be totally abandoned by the rest of mankind, it ought still to be found in the breast of princes." He, however, adds that there are reasons for believing it to be authentic.

A.D. 1366. In Edward's fortieth year the payment of Peter's Pence was abolished. It was nevertheless not entirely suppressed, since Fabian in his Chronicle informs us, that in some of the counties of England it was collected in his time. It was finally stopped by the statute of the 25th Henry VIII.[1] (1533.)

In the year 1367, all foreign and Scottish coins were put down. In 1369, Edward again took the title of King of France, and the seals on which that title had been omitted were called in, and others ordered including it; the French King, Charles, having broken the peace made between Edward and his father. Two priests were about this time charged with offences against the statutes relating to the coinage.

It is worthy of observation that the words DEI GRATIA, which occur in the introduction to the laws of Ina, King of the West Saxons, and are found on all the great seals of our English monarchs after William the First, appear on English coins for the first time in the reign of Edward the Third. They are only found on the larger pieces.

The mints on the coins assigned to this king are—

VILLA BERVICI—*Berwick.*
CIVITAS CANTOR—*Canterbury.*
CIVITAS DVNELMIE—*Durham.*
—— DVNOLM ,,
—— DVREME ,,
VILLA DVREMMIE ,,

---

[1] Fabian's Chronicle, 40th of Edward IV. Ruding remarks that "this tax was one principal drain by which the coins were carried out of the realm."—*Annals*, vol. i. p. 449.

CIVITAS EBORACI—*York.*
CIVITAS LONDON—*London.*
LONDONIENSIS „
VILLA RADINGY—*Reading.*

A.D. 1377. Richard the Second ascended the throne when eleven years of age. Fortune frowned upon the youthful monarch; the French and Scotch threatened his dominions; and to resist them, heavy taxes were found necessary. These events at once rendered him unpopular. "Among other expedients to procure money," says Ruding, "a writ was issued for the discovering of *black money*, and other subterraneous treasure hidden of old in the county of Southampton, in whosesoever hands it might be, and to seize it to the King's use. He afterwards claimed black money to the amount of 150 lb. of full weight, which had been found in that county, as belonging to him in right of his crown."[1]

A petition of the Commons, in this reign, prays that small money may be coined, and that halfpence[2] and farthings may be struck for small purchases and charity. The King promised that this should be done as soon as he was provided with bullion. In 1381 another petition of the Commons sets forth in woful terms the wretched condition of the people, from the state of the coin. Clipping, and the exportation of the coin, were the grievances most loudly complained of. This petition received no answer at the time, but subsequently a proclamation was issued forbidding the exportation of English money without license. In the year 1387, July 30th, a writ was issued to all the sheriffs in England, commanding them to make proclamation every week until the Michaelmas ensuing, that Scottish money should be paid and received at the following rates; namely—the penny for three farthings, and the halfpenny for a farthing and a half of the current English money. Ruding mentions an artful method of falsifying the gold coin at this period, which was practised by seven coiners

---

[1] Annals, vol. i. p. 457. [2] Halfpence are now the most common of his coins.

at Lincoln, who were drawn and hanged for the offence. The practice of these men was to melt down a genuine noble, and recoin it into six quarter nobles. In 1390 the Commons petitioned for the total abolition of all the Scottish coins. This prayer was not granted; but it was ordained that the groat, half groat, penny, and halfpenny should be current for no more than half their value in English money. Three years afterwards the Commons again petitioned for a coinage of halfpence and farthings, alleging that often when a poor man would buy his victuals, &c., and had only a penny, for which he ought to receive a halfpenny, he many times did spoil his penny. The words are, "*Il perdra son Denier.*" Ruding supposes this to mean either that he was forced to give the whole for want of change, or that he spoiled it by dividing it in order to make a halfpenny.[1] The answer to the petition was, that halfpennies and farthings should be made.

At this time the Sergeants-at-Arms were directed to take into custody Henry Goldsmyth, of Eton, in Bedfordshire, who was suspected of counterfeiting the coin of the realm in that village.

A.D. 1398. The proclamation commanding the Scottish groat and half groat to be taken for half their value in English money, appears to have had but little effect, since it was repeated in the year 1398. In the following year the Pope's agents were required to make oath that they would not take out of the kingdom any money they had collected without special license from the king.

The money of this monarch appears to have been struck only in the following mints, thus designated:—

CIVITAS DVNELM—*Durham.*
CIVITAS DVNOL "
CIVITAS EBORACI—*York.*
CIVITAS LONDON—*London.*

A.D. 1399. Shortly after the accession of Henry the Fourth a proclamation was issued, and repeated in the

[1] Annals, vol. i. p. 474.

following year, against certain silver halfpennies, said to have been brought from Venice, of so light a weight that three or four of them were no heavier than an English penny. The petition of the Commons in 1402, for a coinage of halfpennies and farthings, was complied with, and coins of that denomination were issued. False money, of various descriptions, appears to have been still conveyed into England. In the year 1411, a new regulation of the money occurs: it was ordained that fifty nobles should be coined from the pound of gold; and that from the pound of silver there should be struck thirty shillings in pennies; thereby reducing the groat to sixty grains, and the penny to fifteen grains; and their divisions in proportion.

The gold coins of Henry IV., struck previous to his thirteenth year, are of the same weight as those of his predecessor, and may thus be distinguished from those of Henry V. and VI. On the coins of Henry IV. the arms of France are "*semè*," of *fleurs-de-lis*. Those of Henry V. have the shield with *three fleurs-de-lis* only. His silver coinage cannot be distinguished from that of Henry V. previous to his ninth year.

Stowe, in his Survey of London, says that in the reign of Henry V. silver money had become so scarce that it could not be obtained in exchange for gold. The gold and silver coins of this king cannot be distinguished from those of Henry VI. previous to his forty-ninth year.

In 1422 Henry VI. succeeded to the crown of England; and shortly after an indenture was made between the king and Bartholomew Goldbeter, who was authorised to coin money at York and Bristol, as well as at London and Calais. About the same time John Bernes was appointed to make weights for the Noble and its divisions. The parliament, in the second year of this king, ordained that Galley halfpence, Suskins and Dodeykins, and all kinds of Scottish silver money, should no longer be current in England. The ordinance was but little regarded, since it was found necessary to put a stop to the circulation of these coins in the ninth year of Henry VIII.

In 1444-5 the Commons petitioned for a supply of the smaller denominations of silver coin, which was granted, the king reserving to himself the power of revoking the ordinance whenever he pleased. Henry was taken prisoner at the battle of Hexham, in 1464, and recovered his kingdom in 1470, in in which year an indenture was made with Sir Richard Tunstall, the master of the mint. By this indenture the weight of the coin was reduced. The pound weight Tower of gold was ordained to be coined into twenty-two pounds ten shillings by tale, or sixty-seven angels and a half at six shillings and eightpence each; and the pound weight of silver into one hundred and twelve groats and a half. Folkes, in his table of English silver coins, supposes the groats with an open crown and the mint mark of a fleur-de-lis to be of this coinage, but Ruding shews that they may with greater probability be assigned to Henry the Seventh, who coined groats of the same weight. The coins struck at York and Bristol are supposed to be this king's, as in the reigns of Henry IV. and V. money was not struck in those mints.

Edward IV. obtained the sovereignty in 1460-1. An old writer quoted by Ruding says that he caused the money of the three Henries to be called in, and melted down and recoined, but the number of coins of those princes which remain to this day shews that little reliance can be given to the story. In 1464, Edward's fourth year, a new coinage of gold was ordered. The gold coins, says Ruding, were then reduced to twenty pounds sixteen shillings and eightpence in the pound weight by tale; that is to say, there were to be made out of each pound of gold fifty nobles, to be current at eight shillings and fourpence. The silver was àlso reduced to thirty-seven shillings and sixpence the pound weight by tale. All the chroniclers, with the exception of Stowe, have confounded this coinage with that of the succeeding year. In the following year an indenture was made with Lord Hastings, and the gold coins were further reduced, forty-five nobles being made to the pound, and passing at ten shillings, and *angels* at six shillings and eightpence. The new nobles were termed *ryals*, a name given by the French to their gold coins impressed with the figure of the sovereign in his royal robes, and by no means applicable to the pieces in question, which bore the same type as those of the other English kings. Ruding observes that the name of Ryal was perhaps intended to obviate the inconvenience which might have been experienced from the nobles in currency and the nobles in account being of different value, and that the new money called the *angel*, being of the same value as the noble, was called the *noble angel!*[1]

In 1483 there was another coinage, which, however, did not differ from that of Edward's fifth year.

It has been supposed by some antiquaries that during the wars of York and Lancaster there were no fixed places of mintage, and that the dies were carried about from place to place as necessity might arise. This notion has been entertained in consequence of some of Edward's coins being found impressed with initial letters on the breast of the bust; thus a groat of the Coventry mint has a B on the breast, which has been supposed to signify that the piece was struck at Bristol.

Besides the Irish mints, Edward's coins were struck in the following places:—

Bristol:	*Durham:*
VILLA BRESTOLL.	CIVITAS DONOLI.
„ BRESTOW.	„ DVNELME.
„ BRISTOL.	„ DVNELMIE.
„ BRISTOLL.	„ DVNOL.
„ BRISTOW.	„ DVNOLI.
Canterbury:	„ DVNOLM.
CIVITAS CANTOR.	*York:*
Coventry:	CIVITAS EBORACE.
CIVITAS COVETRE.	„ EBORACI.
„ COVETRIE.	*London:*
Durham:	CIVITAS LONDON.
CIVITAS DERAM.	*Norwich:*
„ DERAME.	CIVITAS NORVIC.
„ DERHAM.	„ NORWIC.

On the death of Edward IV. his son, then in his thirteenth year, was proclaimed king, by the title of Edward V. In the month following, Sir William Hastings was appointed master and worker of the mint. Ruding thinks it probable

---

[1] Annals, vol. ii. p. 34.

that the execution of this indenture was prevented by the usurpation of the Duke of Gloster, but quotes Ross of Warwick's "Historia Regum Angliæ," wherein this king is said to have coined money[1]—"moneta tunc facta sub ejus nomine est percussa et formata," &c.

Richard III. in the first year of his reign endeavoured, by an act passed by the parliament at Westminster, to stop the exportation of the coin by Italian merchants.

The coins of this king differ but in mint marks and other trifling distinctions from those of his brother. They were struck in—

Durham:	*York:*
CIVITAS DIRHAM.	CIVITAS EBORACI.
„ DVNOLM.	*London:*
	CIVITAS LONDON.

A.D. 1485. Henry VII. succeeded to the throne in 1485, and in the same year an indenture was made with Sir Giles Dawbeny and Bartholomew Reed, joint masters and workers of the mint. No alteration was made in the standard of the coins. The statute of 1487 made it treason to counterfeit the foreign gold and silver coins, a crime of which many persons had been guilty.[2] In 1489, Henry's fifth year, a new coin made its appearance, namely, the sovereign, a term revived in our own times. The coin in the indenture is to have course for twenty shillings, to be of the standard of the gold money of the realm, and to be double the weight of the royal; twenty-two and a half of such pieces to be coined out of the pound Tower.[3] In every pound weight of gold coined within the Tower, two pieces of this denomination to be coined and no more, unless by permission or command of the king. In the year 1498 a proclamation was issued by Henry, commanding his subjects to receive in payment all small thin and old pennies, upon pain of imprisonment. Ruding thinks that the coins

---

[1] Ruding refers to a French MS. in the British Museum, in which drawings are given of a groat and penny of this king, but which he considers to belong to Edward III. An angel is known with the *rose* for a mint mark on one side, and the *boar's head* on the other, which may have been struck for this king.

[2] Ruding, vol. ii. p. 56. [3] Ibid. vol. ii. p. 57.

alluded to were never struck of the proper weight, and that this is another instance of that king's detestable avarice, such money having been authorised or connived at by him.[1]

At this period, clipping and false coining appear to have prevailed. In a MS. account of the building the steeple and repairing the church of Louth, in Lincolnshire, mention is often made of bad money, and one entry is of a gift of sundry clipped groats. In 1504, Henry's nineteenth year, an act was passed that the sovereign, half-sovereign, ryal, half-ryal, quarter-ryal, angel, and half-angel, should pass current for the sums at which they were coined. The silver coins of England, and also those of other countries, were to be received in the same manner, if not clipped or otherwise materially diminished. Groats and half-groats were ordered to be coined at this time, and it was ordained that every piece should have "a circle about the utter part thereof;" and that the gold pieces should have "the whole scripture about every piece of the same gold, without lacking of any part thereof, to the intent that the king's subjects might hereafter have perfect knowledge by that circle or scripture when the same coins were clipped or impaired."[2]

Side-faced Portrait. Fabian, in his chronicle, informs us that the parliament ordered a new coinage of silver, namely groats, half-groats, and *shillings* "with half faces." These shillings are, as Leake observes, "great rarities." It has been supposed by some writers that they were only struck as trial or pattern pieces; but Ruding, quoting the account of Lord Bacon,[3] whose words imply a considerable coinage of these new pieces, is of opinion that the extensive issues of base coin in the reign of Henry VIII. were a strong temptation to the dishonest to melt down the larger pieces of standard coin, and that to this their scarcity at the present day may be attributed.

Arched Crown. No change was made by Henry VII. in the standard of the coins, but the variations in the types deserve especial notice. First is the *arched crown*, which distin-

---

[1] Ruding, vol. ii. p. 59. [2] Ibid. vol. ii. p. 61. [3] Life of Henry VII.

guishes his money from that of his predecessors. The coins of his nineteenth year have the portrait *side-faced*, and a dotted line instead of the double tressure on the obverse of the groats and half-groats; the inner circle of the reverse is omitted, and instead of the pellets in each quarter of the cross the royal arms appear, a barbarous device continued to the present day.

Some of his coins are also distinguished by the word SEPTIMVS, or the equivalent letters or numerals. On the coins struck by the Archbishops during his reign, the king is represented seated on a throne holding the globe and sceptre. The types of his gold money are not materially varied from those of his predecessors, except that of the sovereign, as before noticed. This coin bore on the obverse the king seated in his royal robes, and on the reverse the double rose, in allusion to the union of the rival houses, with the royal arms in the centre. Ruding says—"I have not been able to discover in what part of his reign these coins were first struck. They are not mentioned in any record I have seen before the statute of his nineteenth year; but a MS. note by Browne Willis, in the margin of Leake's Historical Account of English Money, says, they 'were first struck anno 5 Henry VII., as I remember the date of the indenture for coining them.'"[1]

A rose ryal is remarkable in having the arms of France in the centre of the double rose on the reverse, a type considered by Leake as indicating Henry's claim to the crown of France. This writer says it was struck by the king in the year 1492, when he laid siege to Boulogne.

The English mints of this monarch were—

Canterbury:
CIVITAS CANTOR.

Durham:
CIVITAS DIRHAM.
,, DVRRAM.

York:
CIVITAS EBORACI.

London:
CIVITAS LONDON.

Henry VIII. succeeded to the English throne in 1509. His first coinage resembles his father's, and is only distinguished from it by the addition of the numerals VIII. About

---

[1] Annals, vol ii. p. 67.

this time private tokens were struck in lead, to supply the want of silver coins. In 1519, the circulation of galley halfpence was prohibited by the statute. In 1523 it was enacted, that twenty pounds in half angels should be made of every hundred pounds worth of gold, and of every hundred pounds worth of silver as many groats as should amount to fifty pounds sterling, twenty pounds in half groats, ten marks in halfpennies, and five marks in farthings. As the farthings and halfpennies were struck from one die, it was ordained, that for the future the farthings should bear on one side a portcullis, and on the other side a rose. In the year 1526, a writ was issued to Thomas, Cardinal-Archbishop of York, commanding him to effect at once the reduction of the English money to the standard of the foreign coins. One of the reasons alleged for this infamous proceeding is, that the king had failed in his attempt to persuade foreign princes to reform their coin!

George Noble. The value of the English gold coins was now raised, and a new piece, called the *George Noble*, was ordered to be coined.[1] A half George Noble was also struck. In addition to these, a gold *crown* was minted. This piece received the name of the *crown of the rose:* it was of the same weight and quality as the French *couronnes du soleil.* New coins of silver were also ordered, "sterling, like the others, but differing in weight." At this period the pound Troy was established in the mint, and the pound Tower abolished.

In the year 1529, among other articles exhibited against Cardinal Wolsey, was one charging him with having "enterprised to join and imprint the cardinal's hat" upon his "coin of groats." Ruding considers that the fault here laid to the Cardinal's charge was not merely the placing of the hat upon his money, but the striking of coins of a larger denomination and value than the penny, he being the only prelate who struck groats and half-groats: but this conjecture is groundless, as there are half-groats of the other prelates with their initials. It was clearly the *hat* which gave the offence.

---

[1] The Angel Noble was raised to 7*s.* 6*d.* and the George Noble was to pass current for 6*s.* 8*d.*

[2] Annals, vol. ii. p. 77.

By an indenture of the year 1543, both the gold and silver coin was debased. The gold was to be of twenty-three carats fine and one carat allay; the silver ten ounces fine and two ounces allay, to be coined into forty-eight shillings by tale, viz. testoons (or shillings), groats, half-groats, pennies, half-pennies, and farthings. Ruding remarks, in reference to the new name given to the shilling, that it must have been mere caprice. The name Testoon had been given to the new coins of Louis XII. of France, because they bore the head of that prince; but it was unnecessary in the case of the English coin, since nearly all the money of this country bore the head of the sovereign. In 1544, Henry's 36th year, by an indenture made with Sir Martin Bowes, the gold coin was reduced to twenty-two carats and two carats allay, and the silver to six ounces fine and six ounces allay. In the following year a still further reduction was made, to the eternal infamy of the English Herod. The gold coin was now made twenty carats fine and four carats allay, and the silver four ounces fine and eight ounces allay.

This king had mints at Bristol, Canterbury, Durham, York, London, and Southwark. A more particular account of the pieces struck by him will be found in the list of English coins which follows this introduction.

A.D. 1546-7. Henry died in January 1546-7, and was succeeded by his son, Edward VI. Indentures were made in the first year of the youthful king with the Mint Masters of the Tower, Southwark, and Canterbury, the money to be of the same debased character as that of his father's thirty-seventh year. Other indentures were made in his second year, but with no alteration in the quality of the coins. In 1548, the pieces called testoons were called in by proclamation, all persons being forbidden to utter or receive them in payment. "But all persons possessing them might bring them to the mints, there to receive the just value as they were then current, either in groats, or in other his highness' coins."

About this time some of the officers of the Mint were convicted of corrupting the public money. The principal offender was Sir Edward Sharington, who confessed that he had counterfeited in the mint at Bristol twelve thousand pounds of coins, resembling the testoon, without any authority from the king, besides clipping and shearing to the amount of four thousand pounds, and the falsifying the indentures and accounts. This was supposed to have been done at the instigation of the king's uncle, Sir Thomas Seymour, Lord High Admiral, to enable him to carry on his traitorous designs.[1] Sharington was found guilty, and his whole possessions forfeited; but he was afterwards pardoned and restored. The proclamation for the calling in of the testoons was repeated in the following year, but not with the desired effect. The officers of the mint were ordered to receive them at the rate of twelve pence for every piece. Subsequently, the testoons of Henry VIII. were to be received as bullion only. In 1549, the coins were slightly improved in quality, but reduced considerably in weight. The pound of gold of twenty-two carats fine and two carats allay, to be coined into thirty-four pounds by tale. The silver was to be six ounces fine and six ounces allay. Ruding thinks that it is the shillings of this coinage to which Bishop Latimer alluded in his sermon before the king. "We have now," says the preacher, "a prety little shyllyng; indeed a very pretty one. I have but one, I thynke in my purse: and the last day I had put it away almost for an old grote, and so, I trust, some will take them. The finesse of the silver I cannot see, but therein is printed a fine sentence, that is '*Timor domini fons vitæ et sapientiæ.*'—The feare of the Lord is the fountayne of lyfe and wisdome. I would God this sentence were always printed in the hart of the king, in chosing his wyfe, and in all his officers." Folkes supposes, however, that the bishop referred to the small shilling of fine silver, with the date 1547, which it could not be, as shewn by Ruding.[2] Latimer's sermon gave great offence, and he was charged with disloyalty; an accusation which he ingeniously repelled in another sermon, delivered at

---

[1] Annals, vol. ii. p. 97,

[2] Ibid. note, vol. ii. p. 101.

the end of the month. The style is so singular and characteristic that we cannot pass it without a quotation:—

"Thus they burdened me ever with sedition. And wot ye what? I chaunced in my last sermon to speake a mery word of the new shillyng (to refresh my auditorie), how I was like to have put away my new shillyng for an olde groat. I was herein noted to speake seditiously. Yet I can comfort myself in one thing, that I am not alone, and that I have a fellow—a companion of sedition; and wot ye who is my fellow? Esay, the prophet. I spake but of a little preaty shillyng, but he speaketh to Hierusalem after another sort, and was so bold as to meddele with their coine. Thou proude, thou covetous, thou hautie citie of Hierusalem, *argentum tuum versum est in scoriam*, thy silver is turned into what? Into Testions? *Scoriam*, into dross. Ah, seditious wretch! what had he to doe with the Minte? Why should not he have left that matter to some master of policie to reprove," &c.

At this time the French crowns of the sun were made current by proclamation. In the year 1550, the old standard of the gold coin was restored; namely, to twenty-three carats, three grains and a half fine, and half a grain allay. In the following year, an extraordinary entry is made in the King's Journal:—"Also it was appointed to make 20,000 pound weight for necessity somewhat baser, to get gains £160,000 clear; by which the debt of the realm might be paid, the country defended from any sudden attempt, *and the coin amended*."[1] "Absurd as it may seem," observes Ruding, "to prepare for the expense of a future amendment of the coins, by abasing them in the present time, yet such was undoubtedly the intention of this plan, as may be seen in another extract from the Journal, under the 30th of May, in this year."

In 1551, a commission was given to Sir Edward Peckham, by which the pound weight of silver, of three ounces fine and nine ounces allay, was coined into seventy-two shillings, at twelve pence a piece. A proclamation was issued, with a view to the quieting of the public mind on the reduction of the coin; but it produced no good effect: and shortly after, the

---

[1] Annals, note, p. 107, vol. ii.

testoon was reduced from nine-pence to six-pence; the groat, from three-pence to two-pence; the half groat to a penny; the penny to a halfpenny; and the halfpenny to a farthing; an act which shews that the people had just cause for doubt and alarm. Ruding remarks, that the smaller pieces under the groat are now for the first time mentioned; and he questions whether they were not reduced in value before. On the 12th of September, in this year, the nine-penny and six-penny testoons were forbidden to be melted down. An entry in the King's Journal at this time runs thus:—"Agreed that the stamp of the shilling and six-pence should be on one side a king, painted to the shoulders in parliament robes, with a chain of the order. Five shillings of silver, and half five shillings, should be a king on horseback, armed with a naked sword hard to his breast." The commission for the making[1] of these coins, as well as groats and six-pences, eleven ounces fine; and pennies, and halfpennies, and farthings, four ounces fine, was signed on the first day of October following. To Edward, therefore, the merit is due of reforming the English coinage, which he had nearly completed, when his death, on the 6th July, 1553, left it to be completely effected by his sister Elizabeth. The English mints of this king were at Bristol, Canterbury, York, London, and Southwark.

A.D. 1553. Mary succeeded to the English throne upon the death of her brother. On her arrival in London, she issued a proclamation, from which the people were led to expect it was her intention to restore the silver coin to the old standard. An indenture of this year, however, shews to the contrary, and that it was her intention even to debase it. On the 25th of July in the following year, her marriage with Philip, king of Spain, was solemnised. His name accordingly appears on some of her coins, bearing only the head of the queen, in consequence, it is supposed, of the new dies not being ready. Coins of the same year have, however, the heads of the king and queen face to face, while others have them on opposite sides of the piece. Lowndes says, that in this year there was

---

[1] Ruding, vol. ii. p. 115.

an indenture, by which both the gold and silver coins were to be minted of the old standard; but Ruding thinks this coinage extended only to the shillings, half shillings, and groats: and that it was at this time the pieces with the heads of the king and queen were struck, out of the quantity of bullion which the Spanish monarch brought with him to England. This writer also remarks, that no mention is made of an indenture for these coins; and that even Stowe, so exact in his account of the money of the period, does not mention them. The parliament of this year enacted that it should be high treason to bring into the country from abroad forged and counterfeit money, "like to the coin of foreign realms." At the close of the year, a commission was granted to Thomas Egerton and others to make shillings, half shillings, half and quarter shillings, and halfpennies, under the covenants of the 20th August of the queen's first year. Also to make two kinds of base coins, three ounces fine and nine allay, called *rose-pence;* and halfpence, four hundred and eighty to the pound—the pound-weight to make forty shillings in current money.[1] In November 1555, Thomas Egerton and others were authorised to make seven thousand pounds of pence, according to the standard of the first and second years of the king and queen. In the following year, the merchants adventurers were permitted to carry money out of the realm for their expences. The melting down of the coin was about this time forbidden by proclamation. In 1556, rumours had been circulated that the testoons would be decried; but the effect was checked by a proclamation commanding every one to receive them in payment as heretofore.

Mary died in 1558. Her English pennies only bear the name of the mint; namely, LONDON.

A.D. 1558. Elizabeth, soon after her accession to the throne in 1558, issued a commission to Sir Edmund Peckham and others, authorising them to make "sovereigns at thirty shillings, twenty-four to the pound-weight; angels at ten shillings, seventy-two to the pound; and angelets, of the fineness of

[1] Annals, vol. ii. p. 126.

twenty-three carats, ten grains and a half fine gold, and one grain and a half allay;[1] and of crown gold, twenty-two carats fine; sovereigns at twenty shillings, thirty-three to the pound; half-sovereigns, crowns, and half-crowns. By proclamation in the year 1560, the base penny was reduced in current value to three farthings; the half-groat to three halfpence; and the testoon of six-pence to four-pence halfpenny; "excepting the testoons, marked in the uppermost part in the border thereof with one of the following four marks; namely, a lion, a rose, a harp, or a *fleur-de-luce;* which were not above a sixth part of the said base testoons, but which were so base and full of copper (as was easy to be seen and understood), and differed so much in value from all the rest of the base testoons," &c.

On the 8th of November in this year, an indenture was made with Thomas Stanley and others for coining gold and silver of the old standard, by which a pound weight of gold of twenty-three carats, three grains and a half, fine, was ordered to be coined into thirty-six pounds by tale, namely, into twenty-four sovereigns at thirty shillings a piece, or forty-eight rials at fifteen shillings a piece, or seventy-two angels at ten shillings a piece, or one hundred and forty-four half-angels at five shillings a piece. A pound weight of crown gold, of twenty-two carats fine and two carats allay, to be coined into thirty-three pounds by tale, or into thirty-three sovereigns at twenty shillings a piece, or sixty-six half-sovereigns at ten shillings, or one hundred and thirty-two crowns at five shillings. A pound weight of the old standard silver, of eleven ounces two penny-weights fine, and eighteen penny-weights alloy, was to be coined into three pounds by tale, or into one hundred and twenty half-shillings, or the proportionate number of groats, quarter-shillings, half-groats, three-halfpenny pieces, pennies, and *three-farthing* pieces. Ruding thinks that this coinage did not take place immediately, "as the indentures for receiving the base monies, out of which it seems that this coinage was formed, bore date upon the 9th of December

---

[1] Ruding remarks, that it stands thus in the record, instead of three grains and a half fine, and half a grain allay.

following."[1] It appears that there was a separate mint in the Tower, for the purpose of converting the base money into sterling. The treasurer, Burleigh, and Sir Thomas Smith were the advisers of this measure. The medal given by Snelling, Plate V. No. 3, records the event.

A.D. 1560. { In 1560-1, the base coins were called in, and in 1561, their circulation was prohibited by proclamation; the greater part of the base testoons had, however, been brought in to the mint within nine months after the issue of the ordinance which lowered their current value. At this time, the queen paid a public visit to the Tower, when she inspected the mints, and coined several pieces of gold, which she presented to those who attended her.

About this time, the complaints of the scarcity of small coins became loud and urgent, whereupon her majesty commanded an issue of half-shillings and quarter-shillings, and pieces of *three-halfpence.* A *three-farthing piece* was also ordered to be struck. All these pieces were to be coined of sterling silver. The sixpence, the threepence, three-halfpenny and three-farthing pieces of this coinage bear the date 1561 above the shield, and are distinguished by the full-blown rose placed behind the queen's bust. A passage in Beaumont and Fletcher's "Scornful Lady," alludes to a piece of roguery common in those days. *Lovelass*, speaking of *Morecraft* the usurer, says—

> "He had a bastard, his own toward issue,
> Whipp'd, and then cropp'd, for *washing out the roses*
> *In three farthings, to make them pence.*"

Martin Folkes says, he had seen a groat upon which some knave had attempted to stamp a rose, to make it resemble a sixpence of this coinage. Ruding, quoting from a MS. proclamation in the library of the Society of Antiquaries, says that a foreign piece of gold circulated at this time in England for ten shillings, though not worth nine shillings and threepence. A print of the English angel of the coinage of Henry

---

[1] Annals, vol. ii. p. 146.

the Eighth, with H. and a rose under the arms of the cross on the reverse, is given in the proclamation in question. The counterfeit angels are one of Tournay with M.B., the other of Holland with W.B.[1] In this year, coining by the mill and screw was first introduced into the English mint by a Frenchman, said by some writers to have been Philip Mestrelle, who was executed at Tyburn in 1569, having been found guilty of illegal coining; but it appears that the Christian name of Mastrelle was Eloye. To quiet the alarm which the rumour of a decry of money had raised in the public mind, a proclamation was issued, by which the value of the gold coins was thus fixed:—

		formerly current for	to pass for
Fine gold.	The Sovereign,	30s.	20s.
	Ryal,	15s.	10s.
	Angel,	10s.	6s. 8d.
	Half-Angel,	5s.	3s. 4d.
Crown gold.	Sovereign,	20s.	13s. 4d.
	Half-sovereign,	10s.	6s. 8d.
	Crown,	5s.	3s. 4d.
	Half-crown,	2s. 6d.	1s. 8d.
Silver, fine sterling.	Shilling,	12d.	8d.
	Half-shilling,	6d.	4d.
	Quarter-shilling,	3d.	2d.
	Three-halfpence,	1d. ob.	1d.
	Three-farthings,	ob. q.	ob.

And as the groats, half-groats, and pennies could not be reduced in value one by one, it was ordered that three groats should be current for eightpence, and the others in proportion.

In 1562-3, the parliament at Westminster passed an act for the prevention of offences against the coinage, by which it was made treason to file, clip, or otherwise diminish the current money. The chroniclers inform us that, in 1568, Philippe Mestrelle and two Englishmen were executed at Tyburn. The Frenchman had coined false gold; the Englishmen had made imitations of the silver coins in *tin*. In 1572, an indenture was made with John Lonison for the coinage of angels,

[1] Annals, vol. ii. 153.

angelets, and quarter-angels, also half-shillings, three-pence, three-halfpence, and three-farthing pieces. At this time the mill and screw, which had been introduced into the mint by Mestrelle, was objected to as imperfect; an objection arising, as Ruding thinks, from the prejudice of the mint wardens.[1] Two years afterwards Lonison was directed to coin pennies of eleven ounces and two penny-weights, fine; ten pounds weight to be struck annually. At this time the abundance of private tokens issued by tavern-keepers and tradesmen was the subject of repeated complaints, although the abuse must have existed long previous to this reign. These pieces were composed either of lead, or latten, and sometimes of leather;—proposals were accordingly made to the queen for the striking of small coins of base silver. It was also suggested to her majesty that a coinage of copper pledges for farthings and halfpence would obviate the evil. To the first proposal the queen strongly objected; but to the latter her majesty's assent was obtained, and a proclamation was prepared for the purpose of rendering the copper pledges current. The proclamation is supposed to have been never published, and the coinage itself did not take place. A few pieces in copper and silver, from the die of the halfpenny only are known: they are of great rarity, and were doubtless patterns. At this period a licence was granted to the city of Bristol to coin tokens of copper, with the figures of a ship on one side, and the letters C. B. (*Civitas Bristol*) on the other. In 1576, the payment of one penny for the exchange of every noble, "both by the deliverer and taker," was reduced to one farthing. In the following year, and by indenture with Lonison, gold and silver was coined of the same standard as that of Elizabeth's fourteenth year. Clipping and coining was at this time much practised, and several persons suffered for the crime. A commission of this year directs Lonison to coin pennies, in addition to the other pieces. Commissions were also issued, in 1582-3, for the coining of money as heretofore; and in the last year the halfpenny was first struck in this reign. In 1584, a commission authorised a new

[1] Some have the date as late as 1601.

coinage of gold, the pound troy to be coined into forty-eight nobles, or twenty-four double nobles. In 1586, the Earl of Leicester was sent into Holland to assist the Dutch; on which occasion it is supposed gold and silver coins of Elizabeth were counter-marked with the arms of Zealand, to give them currency in the Low Countries. There is an angel of Henry VI., in the collection of the British Museum, thus marked. A commission was granted to Sir Richard Martyn, in 1598, to coin sovereigns, half-sovereigns, crowns, and half-crowns in gold.

In her forty-third year she contracted for the coining of angels, halfangels, pieces of an angel and a half, and of three angels of the finest angel gold; and (of a coarser crown gold) pieces of twenty, ten, and five shillings. The former sort had the legend, A DOMINO FACTVM EST ISTVD, ET EST MIRABILE, on their reverse; and the latter, SCVTVM FIDEI PROTEGIT EAM.[1] This contract is supposed not to have been completed, as the pieces of an angel, halfangel, and three angels are not known.

In the same year, a novel description of coin was struck, by law allowed to be exportable, and minted for the especial use of the East India Company. The pieces of this coinage are the crown, halfcrown, shilling, and six-pence;[2] and they are distinguished by their type from her English coins, having on one side the shield of arms; and on the other a portcullis.

On the 29th of July, 1601, by commission granted to Sir Richard Martyn and his son, the weight of the English gold and silver was reduced in a trifling degree. Elizabeth died on the 24th of March, 1602-3. She assumed to herself the sole merit of having restored the coins to their original standard; but, as has been already shewn, the good work had been commenced by her brother. She however, on every occasion, boasted, in allusion to such reformation, "that she had conquered now that monster which had so long devoured her people." Ruding justly observes that her conduct in suffering

[1] Ruding, vol. ii. p. 177.

[2] The weights were, however, regulated by those of the Spanish piastre, or piece of eight reas; the queen having refused to allow the carrying of the Spanish coins to the East Indies.

the master of the mint to depart from the terms of his indentures, for the express purpose of coining the money of less weight and fineness, is most reprehensible, and "that instead of entirely reforming the base coins, she only transferred them to Ireland, for the use of her wretched subjects in that kingdom; where four thousand pounds of these coins, only three ounces fine, were coined into eight thousand pounds of Irish currency."[1] The only mint worked in the reign of Elizabeth was that in the Tower of London.

A.D. 1603. James the First succeeded to the throne of England, and was proclaimed king on the same day as Elizabeth died. Before his arrival in England, a proclamation was issued declaring the rate at which Scottish coins should be current in England; a measure intended for the convenience of the Scotch noblemen, who followed in his train, and who were not able to furnish themselves in time with English money. On the 21st of the following month of May, indentures were made with Sir Richard Martyn for a new coinage, which was directed to be of the same fineness as that of the 43rd of Elizabeth. The title of King of Scotland was of course added to the style, and the second quarter of the shield was charged with the arms of that kingdom. James, in his second year, assumed the title of King of Great Britain, France, and Ireland, which was subsequently by proclamation ordered to be placed on his coins. In 1604, the following pieces were coined: 1. The *unit* of gold, having on one side the king's bust, with the legend, JACOBVS D.G. MAG. BRIT. FRANC & HIB. REX.; and on the reverse, the royal arms, and FACIAM EOS IN GENTEM VNAM. 2. The double crown of ten shillings; and, 3. The crown of five shillings, with legend, HENRICVS ROSAS REGNA JACOBVS[2] on the reverse. A halfcrown was also to be coined of gold, with the legend, J.D.G. ROSA SINE SPINA: and his arms on the reverse. The silver coins were the crown, half-

---

[1] Annals, vol. ii. p. 189.
[2] In allusion to the union of the two roses by Henry VII., and the wished-for union of the two kingdoms by James.

crown, two-pence, and penny. By indenture of the year 1605, the pound-weight of gold was to be coined into forty pounds ten shillings by tale; or twenty-seven rose rials, at thirty shillings each; or fifty-four spur rials, at fifteen shillings each; or eighty-one angels, at ten shillings each. It is said that in or about the year 1608, the king sent Walter Basbee, the assay-master of the Goldsmith's Company, to the Emperor of Russia, for the purpose of making for that country a standard of gold and silver, equivalent to that of the Tower of London.[1]

In 1611, complaints having been made against the exportation of gold, which even the heavy penalties could not entirely check, the unit being valued abroad at twenty-two shillings; a proclamation was published on the 23rd of November, by which the unit was made current in England at twenty-two shillings. In the following year the complaints of the want of a small coinage were renewed; tradesmen and others having still continued to issue tokens of lead and other base metal. Accordingly, in May, 1613, these tokens were abolished by royal proclamation; and his majesty and council discussed the necessity of issuing a smaller coin. A proclamation shortly after declared that John Harrington, Baron, of Exeter, his executors, &c., were authorised and empowered to make "a competent quantity of farthing tokens of copper." They were declared not to be monies, but merely pledges of monies, and the people were not compelled to take them in payment. In Drunken Barnaby's "Itinerarie," allusion is made to these tokens, which were very unpopular at the time: the people in several counties refusing to take them.

> Thence to *Harrington*, be it spoken,
> For *name-sake* I gave a token
> To a beggar that did crave it,
> And as cheerfully receive it;
> More, he need not me importune,
> For 't was the utmost of my fortune."

By proclamation of the 1st July, 1618, a piece of fine angel gold, of the value of thirty shillings sterling, was ordered to be

---

[1] Ruding, vol. ii. p. 201.

coined. It was to bear on one side his majesty's picture crowned and robed, seated in a chair, with a portcullis at his feet, &c. Also, a piece of gold, of half the value of the former, bearing a lion crowned, holding a sceptre in one paw, and a shield in the other, with the numerals xv. Also another piece, of the value of ten shillings, with "the figure of an angel striking a serpent," and the numeral x.; the reverse to bear a ship with one sail displayed, and charged with the royal arms. Gold pieces, of the value of twenty shillings, with his majesty's bust laureated, and coins of half their value with the same type, were also ordered to be struck. These last two coins were vulgarly termed "laurels." On the 17th of July, 1623, an indenture was made with Randal Cranfield, for making rose rials, spur rials, and angels of the old standard, and of crown gold; units, double crowns, and Britain crowns. Also, silver monies of five shillings, half five shillings, half shillings, two-pences, pence, and halfpence.

James died on the 27th of March, 1625. During his reign a considerable quantity of silver coin was minted from silver obtained from the lead of the mines in Wales: it is distinguished by the feathers above the arms. His only English mint was that of the Tower of London.

A.D. 1625. Charles I. was proclaimed king the day after the death of his father. On the first of April in this year, a special commission directed the using the dies of the former sovereign in the mint until others should be provided. On the 30th of May a proclamation was published, prohibiting the circulation of all farthing tokens except those authorised by government. On the 11th July, letters patent were granted to the Duchess of Richmond and Sir Francis Crane, conferring on them the sole right of making farthing tokens for seventeen years. These were directed to be made of copper, of the same type as those of the former king, and to weigh six grains each, or more, at the discretion of the patentees.[1] For this privilege the king was to receive annually a rent of one hundred marks.

[1] Ruding, vol. ii. p. 235.

In the year 1628, the workmanship of the coins was greatly improved by a French artist named Nicholas Briot, who had quitted his native country in disgust. The king, whose taste for the arts was allowed even by his enemies, readily afforded the foreign artist employment. He was at once naturalised, and by letters patent, dated 26th December, was authorised to engrave a new set of coins, which were to be "of a more perfect roundness, weight, figure, and impression, and with less charge than by the ordinary way of hammering then used." A mint is said to have been set up at York in the year 1629, where, as Ruding supposes, some coins were struck while the king was sojourning there on his way into Scotland, in 1633. It is known that Briot accompanied him in his progress, as a medal was executed by that artist at Edinburgh.[1] About this period gold was so plentiful, and silver so scarce, that a premium was often paid to obtain twenty shillings in silver for a piece of gold of the value of twenty shillings, which caused great complaints among tradesmen and dealers. In the autumn of this year the fabricators of false farthing tokens were rendered liable to a fine of one hundred pounds, to stand in the pillory, to be whipped and imprisoned in Bridewell, and to find security for their future good behaviour. The reader will find in Ruding many particulars relating to this coinage, which continued to be very unpopular, and was often forged. In March 1635-6, the farthing token was ordered to be made with a small piece of brass in the centre.

On the 30th of July, 1637, a mint was established in the castle of Aberystwith, for the purpose of refining and coining the silver obtained from mines in the principality of Wales. The coins, which were half-crowns, shillings, half-shillings, two-penny pieces, and pennies, were to be of the same value as those minted in the Tower, but with the distinction in type of the badge termed the Prince of Wales' feathers. A subsequent commission empowered Mr. Bushell, the master and warden, to add groats, three-penny pieces, and halfpennies to this coinage. In 1640, the king gave orders to seize the bullion in the

---

[1] Medallic History of England, Plate xv. No. 19.

mint of the Tower, a measure which necessarily occasioned much surprise and alarm. This was afterwards compromised for 40,000*l.* A large quantity of pepper was bought up by the king, and immediately afterwards sold at a low price; but even these measures were found unavailing, and a debasing of the coin was contemplated by the government. This was prevented by the manly remonstrance of Sir Thomas Roe, whose advice and opinion were consulted on the occasion. At this period, the king was reduced to great extremity, in consequence of the scarcity of bullion; plate was subscribed and melted down, and recoined at Shrewsbury, at York, and at Oxford. On the 12th of April the coinage and issue of farthing tokens was forbidden. About this time, the parliament is supposed to have coined money in the king's mint; but the pieces with a P. for mint-mark cannot, as Leake supposes, be those which were then struck, as others of this reign have an R. In 1644, the citizens of London, but especially the poor, complained loudly of the farthing tokens, for which it was alleged "there was no rechange, to their great damage, even to their utter undoing." The Common Council, who were consulted on the subject, among other things stated—"that there were 1500*l.* in farthings in the hands of the patentees, which, if melted, would go a good way to satisfy the poor; besides, the estate of the patentees might contribute to the same. That the poor were in great straits, not knowing what to trust unto; and therefore if the tokens were decried, they desired that course might be taken for the coinage of new farthings, according to the intrinsic value; and that, in the Tower, pennies, two-pences, and small monies might be coined." It seems that in order to circulate these obnoxious pieces, the patentees allowed one shilling in twenty to those who purchased them, and who forced them upon all descriptions of persons. Ruding has given an interesting account of these farthing tokens,[1] which, together with the forgeries of them, occasioned great loss and inconvenience to the people.

Of the various coins struck during the turbulent reign of

---

[1] Annals, vol. ii. p. 278-9.

this unfortunate monarch, examples will be found in the list which follows these remarks. Besides other places unknown, money was coined by him at Aberystwith, Carlisle, Chester, Colchester, Cork, Dublin, Edinburgh, Exeter, London, Newark, Oxford, Pontefract, Scarborough, Shrewsbury, Worcester, and York.

The commonwealth, as has been observed, struck money during the lifetime of the king, with his name and titles; but after his death new dies were ordered to be made by Thomas Simon. These coins are distinguished from all others in the English series, and will be particularly described hereafter. The types furnished the cavaliers with a subject for much joke and ribaldry. The double shield on the reverse was called "The Breeches for the Rump." In allusion to the legends, God and the Commonwealth were said to be on opposite sides. A wag launched the following epigram at them:—

> "May their success like to their coin appear,
> Send double crosses for their single cheer."

The witty Fuller says, "I hope hereafter, when the question is asked of our coiners, Whose image and superscription is this? it will be returned, The *Cæsars* of England."[1]

A copper coinage was contemplated about this time. Patterns of these pieces have been preserved to this day: some of them are dated 1649, and others 1651, and, as Ruding observes,[2] are remarkable from the circumstance of their bearing the effigy and titles of Cromwell, as Protector of England, Ireland, and Scotland, although he was not publicly invested with these titles until the end of the year 1653. The council of state and parliament had it represented to them that the coins of the government might be greatly improved by means of a screw press and mill, and resolved to send for Peter Blondeau, a foreign artist then at Paris. He arrived in London in the month of September, and encountered so much opposition from the moneyers, that it was some time before he could commence work. He produced some fine pattern pieces,

---

[1] Worthies of England, p. 193. [2] Annals, p. 300.

and the moneyers in turn produced other patterns by one of their body, David Ramage. Examples of both are still existing, and are much valued by collectors.[1]

During the Protectorate, silver was coined in New England, namely, the shilling, half, and quarter. They were of rude execution, and bore the legend MASATHUSETS IN NEW ENGLAND, AN. DOM. 1652.[2] The pieces with N.E. near the edge, and XII. or VI. on the reverse, are supposed to be of the same origin, and to have preceded the first-mentioned coins. Lord Baltimore, lord-proprietor of Maryland, is supposed to have struck about this time silver and copper in that province, with his name and title. Ruding observes that all these coins want better than two pennies in a shilling of the weight of the English money, which adds to the probability that the pieces with N.E. just spoken of were of American origin, and not struck at Newcastle.

In the year 1656, the Protector struck money with his name and titles. These coins were the work of Thomas Simon, who had been appointed chief engraver of the mint and medal maker. They were executed with the mill and screw. It does not appear that they were in circulation at any time, and the circumstance of their not being mentioned in the proclamation issued in September 1661, forbidding the currency of the money of the commonwealth, is considered as evidence that they were never considered current money. Coins of the Commonwealth occur with the date 1659, in which year Richard Cromwell resigned the Protectorship.

It is conjectured that Charles II. struck some crowns and half-crowns, in the interval between his father's death and his own restoration in 1660. These pieces bear on the obverse an imperial crown, and on the reverse the numerals indicating their value, and are supposed to have been struck for Charles in Ireland, by the Marquis of Ormond, who caused this monarch to be proclaimed king in all those places which

---

[1] Num. Chron., Vol. I. p. 169.

[2] "Musket balls full bore" were a legal tender in Massachusetts in 1656, and were "current for a farthing a piece, provided that no man be compelled to take above twelve at a time of them."

remained true to the royal cause, immediately after the death of his father. The coins struck at Pontefract Castle by Colonel John Morris, the Governor, are, of course, previous to the restoration, as the castle surrendered about seven weeks after King Charles the First was beheaded.

Soon after the restoration, an order was issued for the preparation of dies for new coins of gold and silver. The indenture for the coinage with Sir Ralph Freeman was dated the 20th July, 1660. The money was therein stated to be of the same denomination and value as that of the late king. Crown pieces are mentioned, but none were coined.[1]

A warrant dated 28th November, 1661, directs, that the values of the several pieces to be coined by virtue of the indenture of last year are to be stamped upon them; and a commission of subsequent date orders that groats and quarter shillings shall be added. "It was now thought proper," observes Ruding, "that the coins which were struck during the usurpation should be called in." Pepys in his Diary, under the date 30th November, 1661, observes, "this is the last day for the old states coyne to pass in common payments; but they say it is to pass in public payments to the king three months still."[2]

An order of Council dated January 1761-2, directs the payment to Sir William Parkhurst and others of fourteen hundred pounds, towards defraying the expenses of erecting houses, mills, engines, &c., for the coining of money by the mill. By an order of the Privy Council, at which the king was present, it was expressly decreed that all engraving of irons, &c., for coinage, should be performed in the Tower, and no where else. The same order required Thomas Simon to deliver to the officers of the Mint all tools and engines he might have in his possession. Vertue, in his account of the works of this artist, says, that after this time his connexion with the Mint appears to have ceased; but Ruding observes that mention is made of Simon at a later period.

---

[1] Ruding, Annals, vol. ii. p. 319.

[2] Diary, vol. i. p. 124.

In April 1662, the Council discussed the subject of coining money by "the mill and press:" the result was the appointment of Peter Blondeau to a place in the Mint. The officers of that establishment stated to the Council, that they had offered to "Thomas Simon and John Roetier, gravers of the Mint, to accept of certain *præmia* therein specified, for the furnishing the Mint with stamps for coining in the new way, but that, by reason of a contest in art between them, they had found it difficult to bring them to any agreement."[1] Roetier, it appears, was a native of Antwerp, and having been presented to Charles, when abroad, came over to England after the restoration, when he was appointed one of the engravers of the Mint. Simon and Roetier were competitors for the designs of new money, which being shown to the king at court, his majesty preferred those of the Dutch artist, to the mortification of Simon, who soon after quitted the mint, as is supposed, in disgust at the treatment he had experienced. Nevertheless, it appears that Simon made puncheons for the Scotch coinage, which was delivered in January 1662-3.

In 1663, the twenty-shilling pieces received the name of *guineas*, being made from gold brought from Guinea by the African Company. In order to encourage the company to import gold, they were permitted by charter to have the figure of an elephant stamped on these pieces. The units, or pound pieces, of the reign of James I., Charles I., and the Commonwealth were now termed broads, or broad-pieces. In this year Simon produced his beautiful pattern piece, known as the *petition crown;* but good taste and feeling were strangers to the heart of the licentious Charles, and the prayer of this eminent artist was unheeded.

In 1665, there was a coinage of half-pence and farthings in copper. The former were without date; the farthing had 1665 under the bust. The obverse of both these pieces had the laureated bust of the king, with CAROLVS A CAROLO, reverse, QVATVOR MARIA VINDICO; in the exergue, BRITANNIA. Ruding supposes they were never current. The

---

[1] Ruding, Annals, vol. ii. p. 331.

legend of the reverse was changed on a subsequent coinage, which took place in 1672, and the word BRITANNIA only was retained. These coins were intended to supersede the tokens issued by tradesmen in town and country, the circulation of which it was found very difficult to check, notwithstanding the penalties with which the utterers and receivers were threatened.[1] Ruding supposes that they were finally suppressed in 1674.[2]

In the year 1678, the East India merchants were permitted to strike money for the use of the factory at Bombaim, a settlement of the Portuguese yielded to Charles, upon his marriage with the Infanta in 1662. The period when this licence was granted is not known, but some of these pieces bear the date 1678.

In the following year, a coinage of pewter farthings was contemplated; and in 1684, coins in this metal were issued. They bore the same type as those of copper, having a piece of that metal through the centre, and the words NUMMORUM FAMULUS, 1684, in order to prevent forgeries of them; a precaution which proved unavailing, as they were counterfeited in great numbers.

The English money of James II. offers nothing remarkable; but that struck by him in Ireland deserves especial notice, and will be described under the head of Irish coins.

In the third year of William and Mary (1690), there was a considerable coinage of tin farthings, with a piece of copper in the centre, and the legend of the reverse resembling that on the tin farthings of Charles II. Half-pennies and farthings of copper and pewter were coined in this year. In 1693, Andrew Corbet, Esq. obtained a patent for coining farthings for a term of nine years, at the annual rent of one thousand pounds; but upon the representation of the master of the mint, the patent was transferred to other hands in the following year. A petition of the tradesmen of London, in 1693-4,

[1] For an account of these tokens see Snelling; also a paper "On Tradesmen's Tokens" in the first volume of the Numismatic Journal.

[2] Annals, vol. ii. p. 347. The proclamation was issued on the 5th of December, not the 15th, as stated by Ruding. See Numismatic Journal, Vol. II. p. 254.

complains of the number of forgeries of these half-pence and farthings, and prays that in future all such coins may be struck in his majesty's mint. Clipping and false coining had for some time been carried on to an alarming extent, and at length roused the attention of parliament, who appointed a committee to inquire into the abuse. The committee recommended a general recoinage as a remedy for the evil, when the recommendation was debated in the house and finally adopted. The great recoinage occupied nearly four years, and was completed in 1699. The total amount[1] of silver coined was:—

In the Tower Mint, . . .	£5,091,121	7	7
In the Country Mints, . .	1,791,787	12	0
	£6,882,908	19	7

The mint charges amounted to 179,431*l.* 6*s.*, and the charges and consequent losses are supposed to have been equal to 2,700,000*l.* The letters B. C. E. N. and Y. on the obverse of these coins denote the various mints in which they were struck, namely, Bristol, Chester, Exeter, Norwich, and York.

In the reign of Queen Anne much attention was paid to the coinage of the United Kingdom, and her money forms a striking contrast to that of her successors. In 1702 the town of Vigo was taken from the Spaniards, and the silver found therein was coined with the word VIGO under the queen's bust. These pieces bear the date 1702 and 1703. In 1707 the royal arms on the reverse of the coins were differently arranged. England and Scotland occupied the first and third quarterings, France was placed in the second, and Ireland in the fourth.

About the year 1712, Dean Swift proposed to the Lord Treasurer a plan for improving the coins, as follows: "1. That the English farthings and halfpence be recoined upon the union of the two nations. 2. That they bear devices and inscriptions alluding to all the most remarkable parts of her Majesty's reign. 3. That there be a society established for

[1] In our own times, the extensive coinages in the Royal Mint, from the year 1816 to 1822, amounted to £7,402,236:11:7.

the finding out of proper subjects, inscriptions and devices. 4. That no subject, inscription, or device, be stamped without the approbation of this society, nor, if it be thought proper, without the authority of Privy Council."—"By this means," he continues, "medals, that are at present only a dead treasure, or mere curiosities, will be of use in the ordinary commerce of life, and at the same time perpetuate the glories of her Majesty's reign, reward the labours of her greatest subjects, keep alive in the people a gratitude for public services, and excite the emulation of posterity."

Ruding thinks the Dean's proposition met with but little encouragement; and the result would seem to shew that his conjecture is well founded; nevertheless, some patterns for halfpence and farthings were struck. The halfpenny has Britannia holding a rose and thistle growing upon the same stalk; and one of the farthings has, on the reverse, peace in a car, and the legend, PAX MISSA PER ORBEM. Another pattern for a farthing, has a female figure, holding an olive branch and a spear, with the legend, BELLO ET PACE, 1715, although Queen Anne, died in August 1714. The designs and execution of these pieces are sufficient to show that at that time the English artists were not equal to the tasks which the Dean would have set them; and if Swift himself designed these subjects, they furnish but little proof of his taste or invention, the designs being trite and commonplace in the extreme. The idea was, however, a noble one, and though in our own time, while the skill and talent of our artists are admitted, good taste is outraged by the unmeaning and gothic coat of arms on the reverses of our coin, we yet indulge the hope that we shall at some very early period be emancipated from this barbarity.[1]

"Oh, when shall Britain, conscious of her claim,
Stand emulous of Greek and Roman fame?
In living medals see her wars enrolled,
And vanquished realms supply recording gold?"—*Pope.*

---

[1] On the accession of her Majesty Victoria, it was gravely queried in several of the newspapers, whether the queen's arms on her coins—shades of Camden and Gwillim hear it!—*would be placed on a lozenge.*

Of the common farthing of Queen Anne, it will be necessary to speak, as there is a singular error respecting it, which cannot be too generally known and corrected. Among the vulgar, to whom, however, the idea is not confined, an opinion prevails that there were but three farthings of Queen Anne struck.[1] The officers of the British Museum are consequently frequently intruded upon by individuals possessing an example of this supposed rare coin; whose astonishment, disappointment, and chagrin, may be conceived upon being shewn many specimens in the national collection. The truth is that a Queen Anne's farthing may be purchased of any dealer in coins; and even the scarce patterns before alluded to, may be obtained without much difficulty.

Of the coins of the succeeding monarchs, it will scarcely be necessary to speak; except to notice their utter insignificance both in design and execution: the same stiff, formal, and inelegant figure of Britannia appears on the copper,[2] while the reverses of the gold and silver provoke a smile, and almost tempt us to exclaim, with the gentle Pinkerton, that a nation which could retain such a device has not yet emerged from barbarism!

---

[1] In the Numismatic Journal, Vol. I., is an account of a curious trial of one George Hone, for the detention of a Queen Anne farthing.

[2] We do not admire the present figure of Britannia. Why does she wear a Grecian helmet? and, indeed, why is her head covered at all? The figure who meets and welcomes Carausius, on the silver coin of that usurper, is evidently intended for the genius of Britain; but although she holds a trident, her head is bare.

ENGLISH COINS.

FROM WILLIAM THE FIRST TO ANNE.

WILLIAM THE FIRST.

A.D. 1066 TO A.D. 1087.

PENNIES only.—C. to R.8.

1. *Obv.*—+[1] PILLEMVS REX. A full-faced crowned head, under a canopy or pavilion.

   ℞—+BRINTRED ON OXEN[2] (*Oxford*).

2. *Obv.*—+PILLEMV REX. A full-faced crowned head, with fillets pendent on each side the face.

   ℞—+ODNOTH ON PICE (*Winchester*).

3. *Obv.*—+PILLEM. . . . A full-faced crowned bust, holding in the right hand a sword.

   ℞—+ORGAR ON LVND (*London*).

4. *Obv.*—+PILLELM REX. A full-faced crowned bust, with a sceptre in the right hand.

   ℞—SEPINE ON IEXEC (*Exeter*). In the field, a cross reaching to the inner circle; in the angles of the cross, the letters P A X S.

5. *Obv.*—+PILLEM REX ANGLOI. Full-faced crowned bust, with two sceptres; that on the right surmounted by a cross *patée*, and that on the left by four pearls.

   ℞—+COLSPEGEN ON LVND (*London*).

---

[1] The Saxon Ƿ is used on the coins of this king instead of the W; but it has the form of the Roman P.

[2] The coins of this period have generally some kind of ornamented cross on the reverse, of which it is scarcely possible to give a description. See the Plates of Reverses of English Coins.

6. *Obv.*—PILLE REX I. Full-faced crowned bust, with a sceptre in the right hand.

℞—OSMVND ON SVÐI (*Southwark*), within the angles of a plain cross, reaching to the inner circle; the letters, P.A.X.S. each within a circle.

The PAXS type was of great rarity, until the discovery of a large hoard at Beaworth, in Hampshire, in 1833.

WILLIAM THE SECOND.[1]

A.D. 1087 TO A.D. 1100.

PENNIES ONLY.—R.2. to R.6.

1. *Obv.*—PILLEEM RE. Crowned full-faced bust; on each side, a star within a circle.

℞—+ITHELSTAN ON ROFF (*Rochester*). The letters THEL braced together.

2. *Obv.*—+PILLEM REX ANI. Crowned full-faced bust; on each side, a star of six points.

℞—+MVNPINE ON DOF (*Dover*).

3. *Obv.*—+PILLELM RE. Full-faced crowned bust; in the right hand a sceptre fleury; in the field, to the left of the bust, a star of six points.

℞—+ORDPI ON IRFRD (*Hereford*)?

4. *Obv.*—LVILLEM DVO (*sic*). A full-faced bust, with a crown composed of two rows of pearls; a star on each side the neck.

℞—WILLEM ON RST.

5. *Obv.*—WILLELMVS. A full-faced bust, with a pellet on each side.

℞—V . . . . ON WIS.

This and the preceding coin are remarkable for the Roman W, which here supplants the usual Saxon ƿ. No. 4 for the word DVO.

HENRY THE FIRST.

A.D. 1100 TO A.D. 1135.

PENNIES ONLY.—R.2. to R.8.

1. *Obv.*—+HENRI REX. Side face, crowned, to the right; before, a sceptre, with cross of pearls.

℞—+ SEWINE ON SVT (*Southwark*)?

---

[1] The coins of the two Williams cannot positively be distinguished from each other, and those here assigned to Rufus may belong to William the First. See a paper on the coins found at Beaworth, in 1833, in the *Archæologia*, vol. xxvi.

2. *Obv.*—+ HENRI REX I. Crowned full-faced bust; above each shoulder, a pellet; on each side the head, an annulet.

℞—+ ORDGAR ON LVND (*London*).

STEPHEN.

A.D. 1135 TO A.D. 1154.

PENNIES ONLY.—R.2. to R.8.

1. *Obv.*—+ STIEFN . . E. Bust crowned, three-quarter face; a sceptre fleury in the right hand.

℞—+ AELEM . . . LEG (*Leicester*).

2. *Obv.*— + S . . EFNERE. Side face, to the left; the crown and sceptre as on the preceding.

℞—. . .·. ME ON CA (*Canterbury*)?

3. *Obv.*—+STEFNE. As No. 1.

℞—+HERMER ON NOR (*Norwich.*)

4. *Obv.*—+STIEN. Side-faced portrait to the left, crowned with a diadem of three *fleurs de lis*.

℞— Flowers, and other ornaments, occupying the place of the legend.

5. *Obv.*— STE FN. Crowned side-faced bust to the left, holding a horseman's mace. *Snelling, Plate* 1, *No.* 28.

6. *Obv.*— STIEFNEI. Profile bust in armour to the left, crowned with a crown fleury, the right hand on a staff surmounted by a *fleur de lis*, having a banner charged with a cross fitchée, under which is a mullet of six points.

℞—SPTIDETS ON LV.

ROBERT, EARL OF GLOSTER.

ILLEGITIMATE SON OF HENRY THE FIRST.

PENNIES ONLY.—R.8.

1. *Obv.*—+RODBERTVS IV. An equestrian figure with a pointed helmet, and a drawn sword in the right hand.

℞—The same as that of Stephen, No. 4.

HENRY, BISHOP OF WINCHESTER.?

PENNIES ONLY.—R 8.

1. *Obv.*—+HENRICVS EPC. Head of Stephen, similar to that on the penny of that king, No. 4.

℞—STEPHANVS REX.

It seems probable that this is an ill-struck and blundered penny of Stephen.

EUSTACE.

(SON OF STEPHEN.)

PENNIES ONLY.—R.6.

1. *Obv.*—+EVSTACIVS. An armed figure with a pointed helmet, represented as far as the knees.

   ℞—+EBORACI EDOTS.

2.—*Obv.*+EISTAOHIVS *(sic)*. A lion passant to the left; under his feet, two double shackle bolts with a bar in the middle; between the fore-legs, a cross patée; above it a lozenge, over that a pellet, and at the back a curved figure like a crosier.

   ℞—Various ornaments in the place of the legend. In the centre of the field, an ornamented cross.

STEPHEN AND HENRY.?

PENNIES ONLY.—R.7.

1. *Obv.*—+STIEFNER. Two human figures, face to face, joining hands. Between them a kind of cross, surmounted by a *fleur de.lis.*

   ℞—Various ornaments in the place of the legend.

Much has been said and written about this coin, and it has brought high prices at public sales, *but query if it be an English penny?* See the *Revue Numismatique, Tome I. p.* 284.

There is a coin of the size of the English penny, said to have been found near Salisbury, and supposed to have been struck by some of the turbulent Barons in defiance of Stephen. It bears on the obverse an armed profile to the right, with a large sword of the period erect in the right hand; behind the head is a rose.[1] The type of the reverse is similar to some of the coins of Stephen, and the letters of the legend are SI . . . . SA.

HENRY THE SECOND.

A.D. 1154 TO A.D. 1189.

PENNIES ONLY.—C. TO R.6.

1. *Obv.*—+HENRI REX ANGL. Full-faced crowned bearded bust; in the right hand a sceptre, surmounted by a cross patée.

   ℞— WIT: ON: LVNDE *(London.)*

---

[1] A rose is placed *before* the bust on a penny of Stephen.

2. *Obv.*—+HENRICVS R. Crowned beardless bust in profile to the right, holding a sceptre fleury.

℞— GODRIC: ON . . . . . .

This penny, from the youthful bust, is supposed of Henry's son.

3. *Obv.*—+HENRICVS. Crowned bust, three-quarters face, holding a sceptre fleury.

℞—+OC: ON: NORWIC (*Norwich.*)

4. *Obv.*—+HENRI RE. Crowned bust, three-quarter faced; in the field, before, three pellets.

℞—+SIGAR. ON LVNDENE (*London.*)

Among the coins of Henry the Second, found at Tealby, and now in the British Museum, are two struck at Wilton, bearing the names of Achetil and Lantier, as moneyers. In the record called "The Chancellor's Roll," of the 11th of Henry II., in the British Museum, Anschetil and Lantier, unquestionably the same persons, occur as moneyers at Wilton, a circumstance which leaves no doubt as to the correct appropriation by Combe and Ruding of the coins of Henry II. See the communication of Sir Henry Ellis to the Numismatic Society, November 1837. Numismatic Journal, Vol. II. p. 254.

The pennies of this king are of very rude execution, and so ill-struck that the name can scarcely ever be read. They are never round, but appear to have been shaped hastily with the shears, and not punched out.

RICHARD THE FIRST.

A.D. 1189 TO A.D. 1199.

Of this king no English coins have been discovered. The specimens which have been engraved were fabrications of a dealer in coins named White. Collectors fill up the hiatus with the Poitou or Aquitaine penny, described under the head of Anglo-Gallic Coins.[1]

JOHN.

A.D. 1199 TO 1216.

All the money at present known of this king was coined in Ireland. The following are examples:—

PENNY.—R.2.

Obv.—+IOHANNES REX. Full-faced crowned bust, within a triangle; a sceptre in the right hand.

℞—ROBERD. ON DIVE (*Dublin.*) Within a triangle, a crescent surmounted by a blazing star; a small star in each angle of the triangle.

---

[1] See "Anglo-Gallic Coins," Section iv.

HALFPENNY.—R.2.

Obv.—+IOHANNES DOM. A full face, bounded by the inner circle.

℞—+TOMAS ON DW (*Dublin.*) Voided cross reaching to the inner circle; a pellet in each angle.

FARTHING.—R.6.

Obv.—WILLEN. ON. Type as the penny, but without the hand and sceptre.

℞—IOHANES DW. A blazing star within a triangle.

HENRY THE THIRD.

A.D. 1216 TO A.D. 1272.

GOLD PENNY.—R.8.

Obv.—HENRIC. REX III. The king crowned with an open crown, sitting on a chair of state. The sceptre passes under the right arm, and the orb is held in his left hand, both being surmounted by a cross of pearls.

℞—WILLEM ON LVND (or LVNDE or LVNDEN). A cross moline voided throughout and pierced in the centre; in each quarter of the cross a rose between three pellets.

Three specimens only of this rae coin are known. The types differ merely in minute particulars.

SILVER PENNY.—C. to R.4.

1. *Obv.*—HENRICVS REX. Full-faced crowned bust, with a sceptre in the right hand, surmounted by a cross of pearls.

   ℞— ADAM. ON. WINC. A double cross, extending only to the inner circle; in each angle, three pellets.

2. *Obv.*—HENRICVS REX III. Full-faced crowned head, the crown consisting of a fillet or band surmounted by a cross of pearls.

   ℞—WILLEM. ON. WINC. A double cross extending to the edge of the coin; in each angle, three pellets.

3. HENRICVS REX ANG. A similar type, with the star preceding the legend of the obverse placed within a crescent.[1]

---

[1] Sir Henry Ellis, in a communication to the Numismatic Society, November 1837, observes, that in the reign of John an entry upon the Rolls of Parliament directs that the star and crescent, called the king's livery, shall be worn only by menials of his household. See also a paper in the Numismatic Chronicle, Vol. II. p. 187, "On the types of the Irish Coins of King John."

4. *Obv.*—HENRICVS REX. TERCI. A similar type to that of No. 2.

℞—NICOLE ON LVND. A similar type to that of No. 2.

PENNIES OF SAINT PAUL.

These coins, from their resemblance to the money of Henry III., were supposed to have been struck during his reign; but they belong to Munster, in Westphalia. See page 260.

EDWARD THE FIRST.

A.D. 1272 TO A.D. 1307.

PENNY.—C. to R.6.[1]

1. *Obv.*—+EDW. R. ANGL. DNS. HYB. Full-faced, head with an open crown fleury, the hair extending on each side the face.

℞—ROBERT DE HADELEIE (or DE HADL'). A plain cross extending to the edge of the coin.

2. *Obv.*—+EDW. R. ANGL. DNS. HYB. Full-faced head as on the preceding coin.

℞—CIVITAS LONDON. A plain cross and pellets, as on the preceding coin.

HALFPENNY.—C. to R.4.

3. *Obv.*—+EDW. R. ANGL. DNS. HYB. Full-faced head, as on No. 1.

℞—CIVITAS LONDON. A plain cross and pellets.

FARTHING.—R.2.

4. *Obv.*—+E. R. ANGLIE. No inner circle, full-faced head.

℞—CIVITAS LONDON. A plain cross and pellets.

5. *Obv.*—EDWARDVS D. G. R. Full-faced head.

℞—VILLA BERVICI. A boar's head in two of the quarters of the cross.

On the coins of the preceding monarchs the *sceptre* often appears, but on those of Edward I. it is omitted, and does not occur again in the same manner. The style of the portrait which is now found on our English coins was continued until the reign of Henry VII., who introduced the arched crown, and subsequently the profile likeness. Much has been written and said about the supposed likenesses on our English coins, but the first attempt to represent the sovereign as he really appeared was in the reign of Henry VII. Some writers have remarked upon the *ugliness* of the portraits on the coins of Edward IV., who, according to our historians, was possessed of much beauty; but we have seen groats of this prince with very comely busts, though they were perhaps not intended for a *likeness;* in fact, the *ugliness* alluded to is clearly not the result of design, but owing to the artist's want of skill or care.

---

[1] The penny of the Reading mint is very rare.

EDWARD THE SECOND.

A.D. 1307 TO A.D. 1327.

GROATS. ?

PENNIES.—C.

HALFPENNIES.—C.

FARTHINGS.[1]

The coins of this prince resemble those of his father in nearly every respect.

The type of the heavy pieces termed groats, will be found among the plates. Though noticed here, they doubtless belong to the succeeding king. They are R.8.

EDWARD THE THIRD.

A.D. 1327 TO A.D. 1377.

HALF-FLORIN.—R.8.

Obv.—EDWAR. D. GRA. REX ANGL. Z. FRANC. DNS. HIB. A leopard crowned, with a banner, charged with the arms of England, fastened to his neck and flowing over the shoulder.

℞—DOMINE NE IN FVRORE TVO ARGVAS ME. In a tressure of four curves, with a lion of England at every outward angle, a cross fleury having a quatrefoil opening in the centre, and at the extremity of each arm.

QUARTER-FLORIN.—R.8.

Obv.—EDWR. R. ANGL. Z. FRANC. D. HIB. In a field semée de Lys, a helmet with lambrequins; crest, a lion passant guardant crowned.

℞—EXALTABITVR IN GLORIA. A cross fleury with a rose in the centre.

NOBLE.—C to R.8.[2]

Obv.—EDWARD DEI GRA. REX ANGL. Z. FRANC. D. HYB. The king, armed and crowned, standing full-faced in a ship with a streamer at the mast-head, charged with the cross of Saint George. His right hand holding a sword; in his left, a shield bearing the arms of France and England quarterly; on the bulwarks of the ship, a row of lions passant guardant to the right; below, two tiers of ports.

---

[1] The farthing cannot be identified.

[2] The noble of the London mint, with an L. in the centre, is extremely rare.

HALF-NOBLE.—C. to R.8. Types as the noble.

QUARTER-NOBLE.—C. to R.8.

Obv.—EDWARD DEI GRA. REX ANGL. The royal arms within a tressure of eight arches pointed with trefoils.

℞—EXALTABITVR IN GLORIA. In a double tressure, with *fleurs de lis* and lions in the arches; a cross fleury, with trefoils in the angles, and four pellets in the centre.

(Silver).

GROAT.—C.

Obv.—+EDWARD DEI G. REX ANGL. DNS. HYB. Z. AQT. Full-faced head, crowned with an open crown fleury, within a double tressure of nine arches.

℞—POSVI DEVM ADIVTOREM MEV, in the outer circle; in the inner circle, CIVITAS LONDON, cross and pellets.

HALF GROAT.—C.

Obv.—+EDWARDVS REX ANGLI Z FRANCI. Head as No. 1.

℞—POSVI DEV. ADIVTOREM. In the inner circle, CIVITAS LONDON. Type as No. 1.

PENNY.—C. to R.8.

Obv.—+EDWARD ANGL. R DNS. HYB. Crowned head.

℞—CIVITAS LONDON. Cross and pellets.

HALFPENNY.—C. to R.8.

Obv.—+EDWARDVS REX A. Crowned head.

℞—CIVITAS LONDON. Cross and pellets.

FARTHING C. to R.4.

Obv.—+EDWARDVS REX A. Crowned head.

℞—As the preceding.

RICHARD THE SECOND.

A.D. 1377 TO A.D. 1399.

NOBLE.—C.

Obv.—RICARD DI GRA. REX ANGL. Z. FRANC. DNS. HIB. Z. AQT. Type similar to that of the noble of Edward III.

℞—IHC. AVTEM, &c., as on the noble of Edward III., but with an R. for Ricardus, in the centre.

HALF-NOBLE.—R.4.

Obv.—RICARD DEI GRA. REX ANGL. DNS. HIB. Z. AQ. Similar type and inscription on the Reverse to those of the half noble of his predecessor, with an R. in the centre.

QUARTER-NOBLE.—R.2.

Obv.—RICARD. DI GRA. REX ANG. Similar type and inscription on the Reverse to that on the quarter-nobles of his predecessor, with an annulet in the centre.

GROAT.—R.3.

1. *Obv.*—+RICARD. DI. GRA. REX. ANGL. Z. FRANCIE. Full-faced head, with open crown.

℞—+POSVI DEVM ADIVTOREM MEV'., in the outer circle. In the inner circle, CIVITAS LONDON.

HALF GROAT.—R.5.

2. *Obv.*—+RICARD. DI. G. REX. ANGL. Z. FRANC. Full-faced head.

℞—Legend and type as the preceding.

3. *Obv.*—RICARD. DI. GRA. REX ANGLIE. Full-faced head.

℞—As the preceding.

PENNY.—R.1.[1]

4. *Obv.*—+RICARD. REX ANGL. Z. FRAC. Full-faced head.

℞—CIVITAS LONDON. Cross and pellets.

5. *Obv.*—+RICARD. REX ANGL. Z FRAN. Full-faced head, with pearls between the *fleurs de lis* on the crown.

℞—CIVITAS EBORACI. Cross and pellets; a double rose in the centre of the cross.

HALFPENNY.—C.

6. *Obv.*—+RICARD. REX ANGL. Full-faced head.

℞—CIVITAS LONDON. Cross and pellets.

FARTHING.—R.8.

7.—Obverse and reverse as the preceding.

HENRY THE FOURTH.

A.D. 1399 TO A.D. 1413.

The first coinage of this king was of the same weight as that of the preceding monarchs, but none are at present known. He reduced the weight of the groat to sixty grains in his 13th year. Henry V. coined at London and at Calais, and his successor at both these places, and also at York and Bristol. The coins of Henry the IVth, Vth, and VIth, are therefore in several instances not to be distinguished from each other.

NOBLE.—C.

1. *Obv.*—HENRIC. DI. GRA. REX ANGL. Z. FRANC. DNS. HIB. Z. AQ. Type similar to that of the noble of Richard II., but without the flag at the mast head; in the centre of the cross, H.

---

[1] If in fine preservation, R.8.

QUARTER NOBLE.

2. *Obv.*—HENRICVS DI. GRA. ANGL. Z. FR. AN. Similar type and inscription on the Reverse to that of the quarter noble of Richard II.

See the observations at page 268.

(*Silver.*)

GROAT.—C.[1]

3. *Obv.*—HENRI. D. G. REX ANGL. Z. FRANC. D. HY.

℞—POSVI DEVM ADIVTOREM MEVM, in the outer circle. In the inner circle, CIVITAS LONDON. Cross and pellets, the latter in two of the quarters conjoined by an annulet.

HENRY THE FIFTH.[2]

A.D. 1413 TO A.D. 1422.

NOBLE.—C.

1. *Obv.*—HENRIC. DI. GRA. REX ANGL. Z. FRANC. DNS. HYB. The king standing in a ship, which has two ropes only instead of three; no flag at the mast; under the right elbow, an annulet; in the quarters of the shield three *fleurs de lis.*[3]

℞—Same legend and type as the nobles of his predecessors. Mint mark, a *fleur de lis.*

Others have the flag at the mast.

HALF NOBLE.—C.

2 *Obv.*—HENRIC. DI. GRA. REX ANGL. Z. FRANC. A similar type to the preceding, but with the flag at the stern.

℞—Similar type and legends as the Reverse of his predecessors, but with an H in the centre.

QUARTER NOBLE.—C.

3. *Obv.*—HENRIC. REX ANGL. Z. FRANC. The royal arms between a crescent and a rose; above, a *fleur de lis.*

℞—Similar type and legend to the quarter noble of Richard II., but with a *fleur de lis* in the centre.

(*Silver.*)

GROAT.—C.

4. *Obv.*—+HENRIC. DI. GRA. REX ANGL. Z. FRANC. Full-faced head: an annulet on each side the neck.

℞—+POSVI DEVM ADIVTORĒ MEVM, in the outer circle; in the inner circle, CIVITAS LONDON. Mint mark, a cross pierced.

---

[1] With the Roman N. R.6. The "heavy groat" is unknown.

[2] For a description of the money of this king, struck at Calais, see the account of "Anglo-Gallic Coins," Sect. IV.

[3] Sandford is of opinion that Henry IV. first reduced the *fleurs de lis* to three.

HALF GROAT.—C.

5. *Obv.*—Legend and type as the preceding.

℞—Legend and type as the preceding.

See the observations under Henry IV. as to the other coins.

HENRY THE SIXTH.

A.D. 1422 TO A.D. 1461.

NOBLE.—C.

1. *Obv.*—HENRIC. DI. GRA. REX ANGL. Z. FRANC. DNS. HYB. Type similar to that of his predecessors. Three ropes to the ship, and a *fleur de lis* under the king's elbow.

℞—The usual type and legend. *Fleur de lis* for mint mark.

HALF NOBLE.—C.

2. Similar type and legend.

QUARTER NOBLE.—C.

3. *Obv.*—HENRIC. DI. GRA. REX ANGL. The usual type, with a *fleur de lis* over the arms, and a *fleur de lis* for mint mark.

℞—The usual type and legend.

ANGEL.—C.

4. *Obv.*—HENRIC. DI. GRA. REX ANGL. Z. FRANC. The Archangel Saint Michael trampling on the dragon, and thrusting into his mouth a staff, the upper end of which terminates in a cross crosslet.

℞—PER CRVSE' TVA' SALVA NOS XPE. REDE' TOR. A ship, with a cross for the mast; on the right side, the letter H; on the left, a *fleur de lis*; mint mark, a cross crosslet.

ANGELET.—R.8.

5. *Obv.*—HENRIC. DEI GRA. REX ANGL. Z. FR. Similar type.

℞—O CRVX. AVE SPES VNICA. Similar type.

(*Silver.*)

GROAT.—C.

6. *Obv.*—+HENRIC. DI. GRA. REX ANGL. Z. FRANC. Full-faced head, &c. Mint mark, a cross crosslet.

℞—POSVI DEVM ADIVTOREM MEVM, in the outer circle; in the inner circle, CIVITAS LONDON; after "civitas" a lozenge, after "London," a leaf.

GROAT.[1]—R.2.

7. *Obv.*—Legend as the preceding. An E on the breast of the bust for *Eboracum*. Mint mark, *fleur de lis*.

℞—POSVI DEVM ADIVTOREM MEVM, in the outer circle; in the inner circle, CIVITAS EBORACI. Mint mark, a *fleur de lis*.

HALF-GROAT.—C. to R.6.

8. *Obv.*—+HENRICV. DI. GRA. REX. ANGL. Z. FR. Type as the preceding.

℞—Legend and type as the preceding.

PENNY.—C.

9. *Obv.*—HENRIC. REX ANGLI. Full-faced head, between a mullet of five points, and a trefoil.

℞—CIVITAS EBORACI. Cross and pellets.

HALFPENNY.—C.

10.—HENRIC. DEI GRA. REX ANG. Full-faced bust, with a trefoil on each side the neck ; mint mark, rose.

℞—CIVITAS EBORACI. Cross with a rose in the centre, and pellets.

FARTHING.—R.6.

11. *Obv.*—HENRIC. REX ANGL. Full-faced head; mint mark, *fleur de lis*.

℞—CIVITAS LONDON. Cross and pellets.[2]

12. *Obv.*—HENRIC. DI. GRA. REX AN. Under the bust, a key.

℞—CIVITAS EBORACI. Cross and pellets.

---

[1] There is another groat with a rose for a mint mark, and the legend HENRIC. DI. GR. REX ANGL. FRANC., weighing 48 grains. See the observations at p. 269.

[2] The appropriation of this farthing is doubtful: it may belong to Henry IV. V. or VI.

EDWARD THE FOURTH.

A.D. 1461 TO A.D. 1483.

(Gold.)

RIAL, or ROSE NOBLE.—C. to R.3.

1. *Obv.*—EDWARD. DI. GRA. REX. ANGL. Z. FRANC. DNS. 'IB. The usual type of the noble, with a full-blown rose on the side of the ship, and a square flag at the stern charged with the letter E.

   ℞—IHC AVTEM, &c. Within the usual tressure of arches, a large sun of sixteen rays (in the place of the cross); in the centre, a rose. Mint mark, a coronet.[1]

HALF-RIAL.—C. to R.4.

2. *Obv.*—EDWARD. DI. GRA. REX ANGL. Z. FRANC. Similar types and legends, with B. or E. under the rose. Mint mark, a sun.

QUARTER-RIAL.—R.2.

3. *Obv.*—EDWARD. DI. GRA. REX ANGL. The Royal arms within a tressure of four arches, within which are the letter E, a *rose*, a *fleur de lis*, and a *sun*. Mint mark, the *sun*.

   ℞—Type same as half-rial.

ANGEL.—C.

4. *Obv.*—EDWARD. DEI GRA. REX ANGL. Z. FRANC. A similar type to that of the angel of Henry VI.

   ℞—PER CRVCEM TVA' SALVA NOS XPE REDEMPT. A similar type to that of the angel of Henry VI., but with E on the right side of the cross, and a rose on the left.

Angels of the country mints are very rare.

ANGELET.—R.4.

5. *Obv.*—EDWARD. DEI GRA. REX ANGL. Type as the preceding.

   ℞—O CRVX AVE SPES VNICA. Type as the preceding.

---

[1] Others have C. under the rose, for Canterbury. The letters E. and B., for Eboracum (York) and Bristol, are found on the half-rial.

(*Silver.*)

GROAT.—C. to R.3.[1]

6. *Obv.*—EDWARD. DI. GRA. REX ANGL. Z. FRAN. Full-faced bust, with a *fleur de lis* on the neck. Mint mark, cross crosslet.

℞—POSVI, &c. In the inner circle, CIVITAS LONDON. Mint mark, *fleur de lis*.

HALF-GROAT.—C. to R.6.

7. *Obv.*—EDWARD. DI. GRA. REX ANGL. Z. FRA. Full-faced bust with the letter C on the breast. Mint mark, rose.

℞—POSVI DEVM, &c. in the outer circle; in the inner circle, CIVITAS CANTOR. Mint mark, rose.

PENNY.—R.1.

8. *Obv.*—EDWARD. DI. GRA. REX ANGL. Full-faced bust, with a *fleur de lis* on each side of the neck. Mint mark, *crown*.

℞—CIVITAS LONDON. Cross and pellets.

PENNY.—R.1. to R.4.

9. *Obv.*—EDWARD. DI. GRA. REX. ANG. Full-faced bust; on the right side of the neck, B; on the left, a key.[2]

℞—CIVITAS DERAME. In the centre of the cross D.

HALFPENNY.—R.1.

10. *Obv.*—EDWARD. DI. GRA. REX. Full-faced bust. Mint mark, rose.

℞—CIVITAS LONDON. Cross and pellets.

11. Another with a pellet on each side the bust.

FARTHING.—R.8.

12. *Obv.*—EDWARD....EX ANGL. Full-faced bust.

℞—CIVITAS LONDON. Cross and pellets. Weight 2⅓ grains. (*Cab. of Mr. Cuff.*)

EDWARD THE FIFTH.
A.D. 1483.

There are no certain coins of this prince. See the Notice under this reign in the Introductory Account, p. 271.

---

[1] Other groats have a rose on each side the neck, and a sun for mint mark. One has a sun on the obverse and reverse. The groats of the provincial mints differ but slightly in type, with the legends VILLA BRISTOW, or BRISTOLL—CIVITAS EBORACI—CIVITAS NORWIC—CIVITAS COVETRE.

[2] The cognisance of Laurence Booth, bishop of Durham.

RICHARD THE THIRD.

A.D. 1483 TO 1485.

(*Gold.*)

ANGEL.—R.3.

1. *Obv.*—RICARD. DI. GRA. REX ANGL. Z. FRANC. Type the same as the angel of Edward IV. Mint mark, a *boar's head* on both sides.[1]

   ℞—PER CRVSEM, &c. The letter R on the right side of the cross, and a rose on the left.

HALF-ANGEL.—R.8.

2. *Obv.*—RICARD. DI. GRA. REX ANGL. The usual type.

   ℞—O CRVX AVE, &c. The usual type.

(*Silver.*)

GROAT.—R.1.

3. *Obv.*—RICARD. DI. GRA. REX. ANGL. Z. FRANC. The usual bust of the period. Mint mark, a rose.

   ℞—POSVI DEVM, &c. In the inner circle, CIVITAS LONDON. Mint mark, rose.

GROAT.—R.6.

4. Similar type on obverse and reverse, with CIVITAS EBORACI.

5. Another, with the boar's head for mint mark on obverse and reverse.

HALF-GROAT.—R.8.

6. *Obv.*—RICARD. DI. GRA. REX. ANGL. Z. FRA. Full-faced bust. Mint mark, a boar's head.

   ℞—As the groat, but the pellets united and resembling a trefoil.

PENNY.—R.8.

7. *Obv.*—+RICARD...... ANGL. Full-faced bust.

   ℞—........... A rose of four leaves in the centre of the usual cross. (*Cabinet of Mr. Cuff.*)

The place of mintage is illegible; but the type of the reverse shews it to be of this king's mint at York. It is the only *regal* penny known.

HALFPENNY.—R.8.

8. *Obv.*—RICARDVS REX ANGL. Full-faced bust.

   ℞—CIVITAS LONDON. Cross and pellets.

FARTHING.

Not known.

---

[1] Others have a rose for mint mark.

HENRY THE SEVENTH.

A.D. 1485 TO A.D. 1509.

(Gold.)

SOVEREIGN, OF DOUBLE-RIAL.—R.7.

1. *Obv.*—HENRICVS DI. GRACIA REX ANGLIE ET FRANC. DNS. IBAR. The king, crowned and clad in royal robes, seated on a throne: in his right hand, a sceptre fleury, in his left the orb; the back ground powdered with *fleurs de lis.*

   ℞—IHS. AVTEM TRANSIENS PER MEDIVM ILLORVM IBAT HE. Within a double tressure of ten arches with trefoils in the outer angles, the English lion and *fleur de lis* alternately within a double rose; in the centre, a plain escutcheon of France and England quarterly.

There is another type, differing from this, with the throne surmounted by a canopy, and the sceptre surmounted by a cross, instead of being fleury. Another type has the king on a different throne, with a dragon on a pedestal on each side, and a dragon for mint mark.

SOVEREIGN.—R.7.

2. *Obv.*—HENRIC. DI. GRA. REX ANGL. FRANC. Z. &c. The king on a throne, &c., but differing from the preceding. Mint mark, a rose.

   ℞—IHS AVTE TRANSIENS PER MEDIV ILLORV IBAT. Double rose, with large shield of arms crowned. Mint mark, rose.

ROSE RIAL.—R.8.

3. *Obv.*—HENRIC. DI. GRA. REX ANGL. FRANC. DNS IBAR. The crowned figure of the king armed and standing in a ship, with sword and shield. English roses on the side of the vessel, and at the head a banner, charged with the letter H.; at the stern, another banner, charged with a dragon.

   ℞—IHC. AVTEM, &c. The double rose, with the arms of France alone, in the centre. A cross fitchée for mint mark.

ANGEL.—C.

4. Usual type of this coin, with additional ropes to the ship. Mint mark, on both sides, a greyhound's head.
5. Another, with the angel standing with both feet on the dragon. Mint mark, on both sides, a pheon.

ANGELET.—R.2.

6. Types similar to the angel.

(*Silver.*)

SHILLING.—R.8.

1. *Obv.*—HENRIC. SEPTIM. DI. GRA. REX ANGL. Z. FR. Profile crowned bust. Mint mark, *fleur de lis.*

℞—POSVI DEVM, &c. The arms of England and France quarterly on a cross fourchy at the ends.[1] Mint mark, *fleur de lis.*

GROAT.—C.

2. *Obv.*—HENRIC. DI. GRA. REX AGL. Z. FR. Full-faced bust crowned with a crown of four arches, surmounted by a globe and cross. Mint mark, anchor.

℞—POSVI DEVM, &c. In the inner circle, CIVITAS LONDON. The cross fourchy at the ends. Mint mark, anchor.

3. *Obv.*—HENRIC. VII. DI. GRA. REX AGL. Z. FR. Profile crowned bust. Mint mark, pheon.

℞—POSVI DEVM, &c. Arms on a cross fourchy, as on the shilling. Mint mark, pheon.

4. Another, slightly differing in the legend of the obverse, with the mint mark[2] of a greyhound's head on each side.

GROAT.—R.8.

5. *Obv.*—HENRIC. SEPTIM. DI. GRA. REX ANGL. Z. FR. Side-faced bust, crowned with an arched crown. Mint mark, *fleur de lis* on each side.

℞—POSVI DEVM, &c. Cross and shield of arms.

HALF-GROAT.—C.

6. *Obv.*—HENRIC DI. GRA. REX AGL. Z. F.

℞—POSVI DEVM, &c. In the inner circle, CIVITAS LONDON.

The half-groat of Canterbury, CIVITAS CANTOR, has a *Tun* on each side for mint mark. That of York, CIVITAS EBORACI, a *martlet* on each side for mint mark.

---

[1] Until this period the cross which divides the pellets and extends to the edges of the reverse of the coin is patée at the ends. On the coins of this king the crosses are patée fourchée.

[2] The other mint marks on the groats of this king are a rose, an escalop shell, a cinquefoil, and a *fleur de lis.*

7. *Obv.*—HENRIC. VII.[1] DI. GRA. REX AGL. Z. F. Profile bust of the king to the left, with a crown of one arch only. Mint mark, a *fleur de lis.*

℞—POSVI DEV. ADIVTORE. MEV. The arms of France and England quarterly on a cross patée fourchée. Mint mark, a *fleur de lis.*

Another half-groat reads HENRIC, and is without the Z. F., and has for mint mark, on each side, a cross patée.

PENNY.—C.

8. *Obv.*—HENRIC. DI. GRA. REX. The king seated on his throne holding the sceptre and globe. Mint mark, pheon.

℞—CIVITAS LONDON. The arms of France and England quarterly on a cross fourchy. Mint mark, pheon.

FULL-FACED PENNY.—R.7.

9. *Obv.*—HENRIC. DI. GRA. REX ANG. Full-face, with arched crown without the tressure. Mint mark, on both sides, a tun.

℞—CIVITAS CANTOR. Cross fourchy and pellets.

HALFPENNY.—R.4.

10. *Obv.*—HENRIC. DI. GRA. REX A. Full face, with an arched crown.

℞—CIVITAS EBORACI. A cross fourchy and pellets.

11. *Obv.*—H. D. G. REX ANGLIE. Z. FRA. Full face, with arched crown.

℞—CIVITAS LONDON. Cross and pellets.

12. Another with *open* crown.

HENRY THE EIGHTH.

A.D. 1509 TO A.D. 1546-7.

(*Gold.*)

DOUBLE-SOVEREIGN.—R.8.

1. *Obv.*—HENRICVS DEI GRACIA REX ANGLIE ET FRANC. DNS. HIB. The king crowned, sitting in a chair of state, within the inner circle, engrailed and pointed. On each arm of the chair a cross *patonce,* as on the sceptre; at his feet a portcullis. Mint mark, *fleur de lis.*

℞—IHESVS AVTEM TRANSIENS PER MEDIVM ILLORVM IBAT. The double rose and shield of arms within a foliage. Mint mark, cross crosslet.

SOVEREIGN.—R.1. to R.4.

2. *Obv.* & ℞—As the double sovereign, but with pellets between the *fleurs de lis* on the obverse, and an arrow on the reverse.

---

[1] The numerals distinguishing the monarch by whom the coin was struck, now appear for the first time since the reign of Henry the Third.

3. *Obv.*—HENRIC. 8 DI. GRA. ANGLIE. FRANCIE ET HIB'E REX. Type as the preceding, but a double rose under the feet of the king,[1] instead of the portcullis, and the sceptre fleury. Mint mark, *fleur de lis* on both sides.

℞—IHESVS AVTEM TRANCIENS PER MEDIVM ILLORV. IBAT. The royal arms crowned, supported by a crowned lion and a dragon; below, the letters H. R.

HALF-SOVEREIGN.—C. to R.2.

4. *Obv.*—HENRIC. 8 DEI GRA. AGL. FRA. Z. HIB. REX. The king in a chair of state, with angels on the arms of it; a double rose at his feet.

℞—IHS. AVTEM, &c. Type as No. 3.

GEORGE NOBLE.—R.8.

5. *Obv.*—TALI DICAT SIG°. MES FLVCTVARI NEQT'. St. George, on horseback, in armour of this period, attacking the dragon with his spear. Mint mark, rose on both sides.

℞—HENRIC. D. G. R. AGL. Z. FRANC. DNS. HIBER. Type as the angel; a double rose on the mast, which is between the letters H. R.

ANGEL.—C.

6. *Obv.*—HENRIC. VIII. DI. GRA. REX AGL. Z. FRA. Usual type of St. Michael and the dragon. Mint mark, a portcullis crowned.

℞—PER CRVCE, &c. Usual type.

ANGELET.—R.2.

7. *Obv.*—HENRIC. VIII. DI. GRA. REX AN. Type as No. 6.

℞—O CRVX AVE. SPES. VNICA. Type as No. 6.

QUARTER ANGEL.—R.2.

8. *Obv.*—HENRICVS VIII. DI. GRA. AGLIC. Type, &c. as the angel and angelet, but without the annulet on the ship.

CROWN.—C.

9. *Obv.*—HENRIC. 8. DEI GRA. REX ANGL. Z. FRA. Royal arms crowned.

℞—HENRIC VIII. RVTILANS ROSA SINE SPIN. Cross fleury, with large rose in the centre. In the angles, the letter H crowned and English lion alternately. Mint mark, a lion.

---

[1] Did the artist intend to satirize this rapacious and bloody tyrant, by representing him with the English rose beneath his feet, or was the type adopted by Henry in sheer arrogance?

CROWN.—C.

10. *Obv.*—HENRIC. 8 ROSA SINE SPINE. Type as preceding, but the letters crowned. Mint mark, plain cross or quartrefoil.

℞—D. G. ANGLIE. FRA. Z HIB. REX. Royal arms crowned. Mint mark, VY, with a plain cross or quartrefoil.

HALF-CROWN.—R.2.

11. *Obv.*—RVTILANS ROSA SINE SPINA. Double rose crowned, between the letters H. K. Mint mark, *fleur de lis.*

℞—HENRIC. 8 DI. GRA. AGL. Z FRA. Arms crowned, between H. K.[1]

(*Silver.*)

CROWN?—R.8.

12. *Obv.*—HENRIC. 8 DEI GRACIA ANGLIE FRANCIE Z. HIBERN REX. Full-faced bust to the waist, with a crown of *fleurs de lis* and plain crosses. In the right hand a sword, in the left a mound. On each side a *fleur de lis*, as mint mark.

℞—ANGLICE Z HIBERNICE ECCLESIE SVPREMVM CAPVT. The royal arms crowned, with supporters, a lion and dragon; the letters H. R. beneath the shield.

This piece is considered by some to be a *medal*, struck on Henry's assumption of the supremacy in 1530.

SHILLING or TESTOON.—R.4.

13. *Obv.*—HENRIC. VIII. DI. GRA. AGL. FRA. Z. HIB. REX. The full-faced crowned bust of the king in the royal mantle. Mint mark, on each side, a *fleur de lis.*

℞—POSVI DEVM ADIVTOR, &c. A double rose crowned, between the letters H. and R., likewise crowned.

Scarcely ever fine.

GROAT.—C.

14. *Obv.*—HENRIC. 8 D. G. AGL. FRA. Z. HIB. REX. Three-quarter-faced bust. Mint mark, Bolt.

℞—POSVI, &c. Arms on a cross fourchy.

GROAT.—R.4.

15. *Obv.*—Legend and type as No. 14.

℞—REDDE CVIQVE QVOD SVVM EST. As No. 14, with a small *fleur de lis* on the upper limb of the cross.

There is a half-groat and a penny of this coinage, which are of the first rarity.

---

[1] For Henry and Katharine. There are pieces with the initials of his other wives.

GROAT.—C.

16. *Obv.*—HENRIC. VIII. DI. GRA. REX AGL. Z. FR. Profile bust like that on his father's groats.

℞—POSVI, &c. The arms, &c. as on his father's coins.

HALF-GROAT.—C.

17. Differing but slightly from the groats.[1]

PENNY.—R.1.

18. *Obv.*—H. D. G. ROSA SINE SPIN.[2] Full-faced crowned bust, in the royal mantle.

℞—CIVITAS LONDON. Arms and cross.

PENNY.—R.1.

19. *Obv.*—HE. 8. D. G. ROSA. SINE SPINE. Bust as No. 18.

℞—CIVITAS BRISTOLIE. Arms and cross.

HALFPENNY.—R.3.

20. *Obv*—H. D. G. ROSA SIN. SP. Full-faced bust. Mint mark, bolt.

℞—CIVITAS CANTOR. Cross and pellets.

FARTHING.—R.8.

21. *Obv.*—HENRIC. R. DI. . . . . A portcullis.

℞— . . . . Cross with a rose in the centre.

22. *Obv.*—+RVT . . . . ROSA. Portcullis.

℞—H. D. GRATI. Cross and pellets.

23. *Obv.*—HE. D. G. . AG. Cross fourchy, with a rose in the centre.

℞—RVTILANS. . . . .A. A portcullis. Mint mark, a bolt.

These are the only three known.

EDWARD THE SIXTH.

A.D. 1546-7 TO A.D. 1553.

(*Gold.*)

TREBLE-SOVEREIGN.—R.8.

1. *Obv.*—EDWARD VI. DEI GRA. AGL. FRAN. ET HIBER REX. The king seated in a chair of state, holding a drawn sword and the orb. Mint mark, on both sides, Y.

℞—IHS AVTEM, &c. The royal arms supported, as on his father's coins; underneath, E. R.

---

[1] The half-groats of the archiepiscopal mints are marked with the initials of the prelates. Wolsey not only placed these on his coins, but also the *Cardinal's hat*. See p. 280.

[2] A penny in the writer's cabinet reads SPINIS.

Double-Sovereign.—R.8.

2. *Obv.*—EDWARD VI. D. G. ANGLIE. FRANCIE Z. HIBERNIE REX. Type as the sovereign of his father. Mint mark, dragon's head.

℞—IHESVS AVTEM, &c. As that of his father's sovereign.

Sovereign.—R.7.

3. Obverse and reverse, as the preceding.

Sovereign.—R.2.

4. *Obv.*—EDWARD VI. D. G. AGL. FRA. Z. HIBER REX. Profile portrait of the king to the waist, crowned and in armour, holding in his right hand a drawn sword, and in his left the orb. Mint mark, on both sides, a tun.

℞—IHS. AVTE, &c. Type as the treble sovereign.

Half-Sovereign.—R.6.

5. *Obv.*—Type, &c. as the preceding.

℞—IHS. AVTEM, &c. Plain shield, crowned between the letters E.R.

Half-Sovereign.—R.6.

6. *Obv.*—LVCERNA PEDIBVS MEIS VERBVM TVVM. Bust in armour, bare-headed.

℞—EDOVARD VI. D. G. ANGL. FRA. Z. HIB. REX. Shield between the letters E.R. A crescent after every word, both on obverse and reverse.

Half-Sovereign.—C.

7. *Obv.*—SCVTVM FIDEI PROTEGIT EVM MDXLVIII.

℞—EDWARD VI. D. G. ANGL. FRA. Z. HIBER. REX. Oval shield between the letters E.R.

Angel.—R.8.

8. *Obv.*—EDWARD VI. D. G. AGL. FRA. Z. HIB. REX. The usual type. Mint mark, dragon's head. ?

℞—PER CRVCE, &c. Usual type; the mast between the letter E and a rose.

Angelet. ?

Type as the angel. (*Ruding.*)

This piece is not known.

Crown.—R.6.

9. *Obv.*—Legend and type as the sovereign, No. 4.

℞—As the treble-sovereign.

Half-Crown.—R.6.

10. Obverse and reverse, as the crown.

(*Silver.*)

CROWN.—C.

11. *Obv.*—EDWARD VI. D. G. AGL. FRA. Z. HIBE. REX. The king crowned and in armour, with his sword drawn and held upright, mounted on a horse caparisoned and curvetting; beneath, the date 1551. Mint mark, the letter Y on each side.

℞—POSVI DEVM ADIVTORE' MEV'. Royal arms on a plain shield, over which, a cross fourchy.

HALF-CROWN.—C.

12. *Obv.*—As the preceding, but the horse ambling, and a plume of feathers on its head.

℞—As that of the crown.

Another is without the plume, and with the date 1553. Mint mark, a tun, on both sides.

SHILLING.—C.

13. *Obv.*—TIMOR DOMINI FONS. VITE MDXL7. Crowned bust in profile.

℞—EDWARD VI. REX AGL. FRA. HIB. &c. Royal arms in a garnished oval shield, between the letters E. R. Mint mark, on both sides, a rose.

SHILLING.—R.3.

14. *Obv.*—INIMICOS EIVS INDVAM CONFVSIONE. Bust as the preceding.

℞—EDWARD VI. D. G. ANGL. FRA. Z. HIB. REX. Type as the preceding. Mint mark, on each side, a bow.

Some of these shillings (of which there are several varieties) are countermarked with a *greyhound* or a *portcullis* behind the head. See the plate of obverse types of English coins. Side-faced shillings in fine silver, 1547, 1548, are of extreme rarity.

SHILLING (*with full-faced bust*).[1]—C.

15. *Obv.*—EDWARD VI. D. G. AGL. FRA. Z. HIB. REX. Full-faced crowned bust, in parliament robes, with chain of the order, between a double rose, and the numerals XII. to denote the value. Mint mark, on each side, a tun.

℞—POSVI DEVM ADIVTORE' MEV'. Arms in a plain shield, over which, a cross fourchy.

---

[1] The following entry occurs in this king's journal:—"Agreed that the stamp of the shilling and sixpence should be on one side, a king painted to the shoulders in parliament robes, with a chain of the order; five shillings of silver, and half-five shillings, should be a king on horseback, armed with a naked sword hard to his breast. Also that York's mint, Throgmorton's in the Tower, should go and work the fine standard. In the city of York and Canterbury should the small money be wrought of a baser sort," &c. These shillings and sixpences are at this day common to excess.

SIXPENCE (*with full-faced bust*).—C.

16. *Obv.*—EDWARD VI. D. G. AGL. FRA. Z. HIBER. REX. Type as the preceding; VI. for the value. Mint mark, on both sides, Y.

℞—As the shilling.

Another sixpence has CIVITAS EBORACI instead of POSVI.—R.2.

GROAT.—R.6.

17. *Obv.*—EDWARD 6. D. G. AG. FR. Z. HI. REX. Bust crowned in profile. Mint mark, on each side, a bolt.

℞—POSVI, &c. Royal arms, over which a cross fleury.

Another groat has CIVITAS LONDON, instead of POSVI.

THREEPENCE (*with full-faced bust*).—R.2.

18. Obverse and reverse similar to the others of this coinage, with III. for the value.

HALF-GROAT.—R.5.

19. Obverse and reverse similar to that of the groat, with side-faced portrait.

Another half-groat reads EDOARD and CIVITAS CANTOR.

PENNY.—R.6.

20. *Obv.*—E. D. G. ROSA SINE SPI. Crowned profile bust.

℞—CIVITAS LONDON. Royal arms, over which, a cross.

Another has CIVITAS BRISTOLIE.

21. *Obv.*—E. D. G. ROSA SINE SPINA. Full-blown rose. R.1.

℞—CIVITAS LONDON. Arms and cross.

22. *Obv.*—E. D. G. ROSA SPINA. Full-blown rose. Mint mark, mullet.

℞—CIVITAS EBORACI. Arms and cross.

SOVEREIGN-PENNY.—R.8.

23. *Obv.*—E. D. G. ROSA SINE SP. The crowned figure of the king seated on a throne, holding the sceptre and orb. Mint mark, on both sides, a tun.

℞—CIVITAS LONDON. Arms and cross.

FARTHING.—R.8.

24. *Obv.*—E. D. G. ROSA SINE SP. A portcullis.

℞—CIVITAS LONDON. Cross and pellets.

MARY.

A.D. 1553 TO A.D. 1558.

(*Gold.*)

SOVEREIGN.—R.3.

1. *Obv.*—MARIA D. G. ANG. FRA. Z HIB. REGINA M. D. LIII. The queen on her throne, as on the sovereign of her brother. Mint mark, a pomegranate.

   ℞—A DNO. FACTV. EST ISTV. Z EST MIRA. IN OCVL. NRIS. Double rose and royal arms.

RIAL.—R.8.

2. *Obv.*—Legend as the foregoing. The queen crowned and wearing the ribbon of the order standing in a ship; a rose on one side of the mast, and a square flag at the head, bearing the letter M.

   ℞—Legend as the foregoing. In a tressure of eight arches, with the lion of England under a crown, and a *fleur de lis* alternately, a sun of sixteen rays, four of which are pointed fleury; in the centre, a rose.

ANGEL.—R.2.

3. *Obv.*—MARIA D. G. ANG. FRA. Z HIB. REGIN. The usual type of the angel and dragon. Mint mark, a pomegranate.

   ℞—A. DNO. FACTV. EST ISTVD Z EST MIRABI. The usual type of the ship and arms; M. on the right side of the mast, and a rose on the left.

ANGELET.—R.8.

Legend and type similar to the angel.

(*Silver.*)

GROAT.—C.

4. *Obv.*—MARIA D. G. ANG. FRA. Z HIB. REGI. Crowned bust with flowing hair, and necklace with cross of pearls. Mint mark, a pomegranate after the first word of the legend.

   ℞—VERITAS TEMPORIS FILIA. Royal arms and cross.

HALF-GROAT.—R.8.

Obverse and reverse as the groat.

PENNY.—R.7.

5. *Obv.*—M. D. G. ROSA SINE SPINA. Similar bust to that of the groat.

   ℞—CIVITAS LONDON. As the groat; no inner circle.

6. *Obv.*—M. D. G. ROS. . . . . SPINA. A full-blown rose.
R—As that of the preceding, but no inner circle on either side.

This penny is given by Ruding, but it is not known to our collectors.

PHILIP AND MARY.

(*Gold.*)

ANGEL.—R.2.

1. *Obv.*—PHILIP. Z MARIA D. G. REX Z REGINA. Usual type.
R—A DNO. FACTVM EST ISTVD Z EST MIRABILE. The usual type of the ship, with the letters P.M.

HALF-ANGEL.—R.8.

Legend and type similar to those of the angel.

(*Silver.*)

HALF-CROWN.—R.8.

2. *Obv.*—PHILIP ET MARIA D. G. REX ET REGINA ANG. Profile busts of the king and queen, face to face;[1] above, the crown of England between the date 1555. The king bare-headed, and wearing the order of the golden fleece. The queen in her ordinary habit.
R—POSVIMVS DEVM ADIVTOREM NOSTRVM. A crowned shield, charged with the arms of Philip and Mary impaled.

SHILLING.—R.2.

3. *Obv.*—PHILIP ET MARIA D. G. R. ANG. FR. NEAP. PR. HISP. Type similar to that of the half-crown. Date, 1554.
R—Legend and type as the half-crown; above the shield, XII. for the value; no inner circle.

Another shilling has the inner circle. One has the date 1554 in the exergue of the obverse. These pieces are rarely in good condition.

SIXPENCE.—R.3.

4. Legend and types similar to those of the shilling, but with VI. for the value, and with inner circle.

---

[1] These coins were in imitation of those of Ferdinand and Isabella. Butler alludes to the busts in *Hudibras*, p. 3, Canto I.

"Still amorous and fond and billing,
Like Philip and Mary on a shilling."

GROAT.—C.

5. *Obv.*—PHILIP ET MARIA D. G. REX[1] ET REGINA. Bust of the queen only, as on her penny. Mint mark, *fleur de lis.*

℞—POSVIMVS DEVM ADIVTO NOS. Shield and cross.

TWOPENCE.—R.6.

6. *Obv.*—P. Z M. D. G. ROSA SINE SPINE. As the preceding.

℞—CIVITAS LONDON. Shield and cross.

PENNY.—R.1.

7. *Obv.*—P. Z M. D. G. ROSA SINE SPINA. Full-blown rose.

℞—CIVITAS LONDON. Arms and cross.

PENNY.—R.6.

8. *Obv.*—P. Z M. D. G. ROSA SINE SPINA. Crowned bust.

℞—CIVITAS LON. Arms and cross; no inner circle. Mint mark, on both sides a *fleur de lis.*

ELIZABETH.

A.D. 1558 TO A.D. 1603.

(*Gold.*)

SOVEREIGN.—R.2.

1. *Obv.*—ELIZAB. D. G. ANG. FR. ET HIB. REGINA. Type similar to that of the sovereign of her sister. Mint mark, on each side a tun.

℞—A DNO. FACTV. EST ISTVD ET EST MIRAB. IN OCVL. NRS. Type as her sister's sovereign.

SOVEREIGN.—R.1.

2. *Obv.*—ELIZABETH, &c. Bust in profile, with high-arched crown. Mint mark, on each side, a woolpack.

℞—SCVTVM, &c. The royal arms, surmounted by a crown.

---

[1] Philip, upon his marriage with the queen, on the 25th July 1554, took the title of king, according to the marriage articles.

SOVEREIGN.—R.8.

3. *Obv.*—ELIZABETH, &c. Bust in a mantle ermine, touching the inner circle only at the breast. Mint mark, rose.

℞—IHS. AVTEM, &c. Type similar to the foregoing, and differing merely in the crown and the size of the letters E. R.

HALF-SOVEREIGN.—C.

4. *Obv.*—ELIZABETH. D. G. ANG. FRA. ET HI. REGINA. Crowned bust in profile to the right; the hair flowing, and a ruff about the neck. Mint mark, cross crosslet.

℞—SCVTVM FIDEI PROTEGET EAM. Royal arms in a plain shield crowned, between the letters E. R.

RIAL.—R.4.

5. *Obv.*—ELIZAB. D. G. ANG. FR. ET HIB. REGINA. The queen in a large ruff, crowned, holding the sceptre and the orb, standing in a three-decked ship, with the guns out. Square flag, with the letter E.

℞—IHS. AVTEM, &c. Type as the rial of Mary. Mint mark, A.

ANGEL.—C.

6. *Obv.*—ELIZABETH. D. G. ANG. FR. ET HIB. REGINA. Usual type of the angel.

℞—A DNO. &c. Usual type, with E. and a rose. Mint mark, cross crosslet.

ANGELET.—R.2.

7. Legend and types as the angel. Mint mark, an escalop shell.

QUARTER-ANGEL.—R.2.

8. *Obv.*—As the angel and angelet. Mint mark, an acorn.

℞—ET HIBERNIE REGINA FIDEI. As the former.

CROWN.—R.1.

9. *Obv.*—ELIZAB. D. G. ANG. FRA. ET HIB. REG. Crowned bust.

℞—SCVTVM FIDEI, &c. Royal arms, surmounted by a crown between the letters E. R.

HALF-CROWN.—R.1.

10. Legend and types nearly resembling those of the crown.

The *milled* half-sovereign, with *ingrailed edges*, is R.3; the quarter, or crown, of the same coinage, R.7. The half-crown is not known. The milled half-sovereign, *with plain* edges, is R.2. The crown of the same coinage, R.6.; and the half-crown, R.4.

(*Silver.*)

CROWN.—R.2.

11. *Obv.*—ELIZABETH. D. G. ANG. FRA. ET HIBER. REGINA. Crowned bust, holding a sceptre fleury and the orb. Mint mark, on both sides, the figure 1.[1]

℞—POSVI, &c. Garnished shield upon a cross fourchy.

HALF-CROWN.—R.3.

12. Obverse and reverse as the crown.

SHILLING.—C.

13. *Obv.*—ELIZABETH. D. G. ANG. FR. &c. Crowned bust with ruff.

℞—POSVI, &c. The shield of arms and cross. Mint mark, a martlet.[2]

SHILLING (*milled*).—R.2. to R.6.

14. *Obv.*—ELIZABETH. D. G. ANG. &c. Bust, crowned.

℞—POSVI, &c. Arms and cross. Mint mark, on both sides a mullet of six points.

SIXPENCE.—C.

The milled shilling, with the key mint mark and garnished shield, is very rare: that with the date in the field has been altered by creating the date.

15. *Obv.*—ELIZABETH. D. G., &c. Bust crowned, &c.; a *rose* behind.[3]

℞—POSVI, &c. Arms and cross.

The broad cross sixpence, milled, is R.6.

THREEPENCE.—C.

16. Types similar to the former.

The broad cross threepence, milled, is R.8.

THREE-HALFPENCE.—R.2.

17. Types similar to the former.

THREE-FARTHINGS.—R.2.

18. Types similar to the former.

The milled three-farthing piece, with the broad cross, is R.7.

GROAT.—R.2.

19. Types very similar to the foregoing, but without the *rose*.

---

[1] Another crown resembles this in every respect, except that it has the figure 2 for mint mark.

[2] The arms of Sir Richard Martin, master of the mint, but commonly called at that period a *Drake*, in compliment to the great navigator.

[3] The sixpence, threepence, three-halfpence, and three-farthings, were distinguished by the rose. See the Introductory Account, p. 287.

HALF-GROAT.—C.

20. Type similar to the groat.

HALF-GROAT.—C.

21. *Obv.*—E. D. G. ROSA SINE SPINA. Crowned bust; behind the neck, two pellets. Mint mark, on both sides, A.

℞—CIVITAS LONDON. Arms and cross.

PENNY.—C.

22. Type similar to the half-groat.

HALFPENNY.—C.

23. *Obv.*—A portcullis. Mint mark, a key, an anchor, or the figure 1.

℞—A cross moline, with three pellets in each quarter, as on the earlier English coins.

The milled pieces are all of them, except the sixpence, very uncommon, especially the penny. Groat, R.4., threepence, R.2., twopence, R.3., penny, R.8. There are "pledges" of a penny, halfpenny, and farthing; the first bearing on the obverse a three-quarter-faced portrait, and the legend, THE PLEDGE OF; reverse, a monogram of Elizabeth, crowned, with the legend, A PENNY. The halfpenny has a full-blown rose, crowned; reverse, a portcullis, and over it, 1601. The farthing has the usual crowned bust; reverse, her monogram, crowned. See the Plates of English Types.

JAMES THE FIRST.

A.D. 1603 TO A.D. 1625.

ROSE RIAL.—R.2.

1. *Obv.*—IACOBVS D. G. MAG. BRIT. FRAN. ET HIBER. REX. The king crowned, seated on a throne, holding the sceptre and a globe, the portcullis under his feet. Mint mark, on both sides of the coin, a rose.

℞—A DNO. FACTVM EST ISTVD ET EST MIRABILE IN OCVLIS NRIS. Royal arms in the centre of a double rose.

THIRTY-SHILLINGS PIECE.—R.2.

2. *Obv.*—IACOBVS D. G. MA. BRI. FR. ET HIB. REX. The king seated in a chair of state, crowned, and holding the sceptre and orb, his feet resting upon the portcullis; the ground diapered with roses and *fleurs de lis*, the back of the chair with *fleurs de lis* only. Mint mark, thistle blossom.

℞—A DOMINO FACTVM EST ISTVD ET EST MIRAB. IN OC. NRIS. A large escutcheon of arms on a cross fleury, the ends of which divide a broad circle, in each quarter of which an English lion between a *fleur de lis* and a rose. Above the arms, the numerals XXX.

FIFTEEN SHILLINGS.—R.6.

3. *Obv.*—IACOBVS D. G. MAG. BRIT. FRA. ET HI. REX. The Scotch lion sejant, crowned, holding in his right paw a sceptre, and supporting with his left the royal arms between the numerals X and V. Mint mark, on both sides, a mullet of six points.

℞—A DNO. FACTVM, &c. Type as the rial of Elizabeth.

SOVEREIGN.—R.3.

4. *Obv.*—IACOBVS D. G. ANG. SCO. FRAN. ET HIB. REX. Crowned bust, in profile, to the right, holding a sceptre and the orb. Mint mark, on both sides of the coin, a thistle blossom.

℞—EXVRGAT DEVS DISSIPENTVR INIMICI. Royal arms in a garnished shield, between the letters I. R.

Another sovereign has FACIAM EOS IN GENTEM VNAM for the legend of the reverse.

HALF-SOVEREIGN.—R.2.

5. Type similar to that of the sovereign, but the shield plain.

SPUR RIAL.—R.4.

6. *Obv.*—IACOBVS D. G. MAG. BRIT. FRAN. ET HIB. REX. The king crowned and in armour, standing between the fore and mizen mast of a three-decker, with the ports open, holding in his right hand a sword, and on his left arm a shield bearing the royal arms. At the head, a flag charged with the letter I. Mint mark, on both sides of the coin, a rose.

℞—A DNO. FACTVM EST ISTVD, &c. Type as the fifteen-shilling piece.

UNIT. C.

7. *Obv.*—IACOBVS D. G. MAG. BRI. FRAN. ET HIB. Profile bust to the left, laureated, with mantle on the shoulder; behind, the numerals XX, for the value. Mint mark, on both sides of the coin, a spur-rowel.

℞—FACIAM EOS IN GENTEM VNAM. Arms on plain shield, crowned, on the ancient cross fleury.

ANGEL.—R.2.

8. *Obv.*—IACOBVS D. G. MAG. BRIT. FRA. ET. HI. REX. The angel Michael standing behind the dragon, which he pierces. Mint mark, on both sides, a coronet.

℞—A DNO., &c. Ship with royal arms; above, I. and a rose.

9. *Obv.*—IACOBVS, &c. The angel with both feet on the dragon. Mint mark, on both sides, a rose.

℞—A DNO., &c. A three-masted ship, at the head and stern a lion rampant holding a sword; the mainsail charged with the royal arms, and a lion rampant on a broad pennant.

ANGELET.—R.4.

10. Types very similar to that of the angel, except that the saint stands before the dragon. Mint mark, on both sides, a plain cross.

DOUBLE CROWN.—C.

11. *Obv.*—IACOBVS D. G. MAG. BRIT. FRAN. ET HIB. REX. Type as the half-sovereign, but mint mark, a rose.

℞—HENRICVS ROSAS REGNA IACOBVS. Type as the half-crown.

CROWN.—C.

12. Legends and type as the double-crown.[1] No mint mark.

HALF-CROWN.—C.

13. *Obv.*—I. D. G. ROSA SINE SPINA. Bust as above.

℞—As the crown.

(*Silver.*)

CROWN.—R.1.

14. *Obv.*—IACOBVS D. G. ANG. SCO. FRAN. ET HIB. REX. The king on horseback, crowned and in armour, holding a drawn sword, the horse ambling; on the housing, a rose crowned. Mint mark, on both sides, a thistle.

℞—EXVRGAT DEVS DISSIPENTVR INIMICI.[2] The royal arms on an ornamented escutcheon.

HALF-CROWN.—R.6.

15. Type as the crown.

SHILLING.—R.1.

16. *Obv.*—Legend as that of the crown. Crowned and armed bust in profile; behind the head, XII., for the value. Mint mark, on both sides, a thistle.

℞—Legend and type as the crown, but the shield plain.

SIXPENCE.—R.2.

17. Legends and types as the shilling, except the value, VI., and the date over the shield.

---

[1] Another crown has TVEATVR VNITA DEVS, and differs somewhat in type.

[2] Another crown has QVÆ DEVS CONIVNXIT NEMO SEPARET. C.

TWOPENCE.—C.

18. *Obv.*—I. D. G. ROSA SINE SPINA. Bust as on the larger coins; II. behind the head.

℞—No legend. The royal arms. Mint mark, thistle or *fleur de lis.*

19. *Obv.*—Legend as the preceding. Full-blown rose, crowned. Mint mark, a spur-rowel.

℞—TVEATVR VNITA DEVS.[1] Thistle flower, crowned. Mint mark, a trefoil.

PENNY.—C.

20. Similar to the twopence. Mint mark, on both sides, a trefoil.

HALFPENNY.—C.

21. *Obv.*—Portcullis.

℞—Cross moline and pellets.

22. *Obv.*—A rose. Mint mark, *fleur de lis.*

℞—A thistle flower. Mint mark, rose.

There are two coinages: the first has ANG. SCO., all R.; the other, MAG. BRIT., all C.

(*Copper.*)

FARTHING TOKEN.—C.

23. *Obv.*—IACO. D. G. MAG. BRI. Two sceptres crossed in saltire, one surmounted by a cross, the other by a *fleur de lis;* above, a crown.

℞—FRA. ET HIB. REX. Irish harp crowned.

CHARLES THE FIRST.

A.D. 1625 TO A.D. 1649.

THREE-POUND PIECE.—R.2.[2]

1. *Obv.*—CAROLVS D. G. MAG. BRIT. FRAN. ET HI. REX. Crowned profile bust in armour, holding a drawn sword and an olive branch; feathers in the legends and behind the head

℞—EXVRGAT DEVS DISSIPENTVR INIMICI; and in three lines across the field of the coin, RELIG. PROT. LEG. ANG. LIBER. PAR., a plume of three feathers above, and the numerals III., and 1642 below.

---

[1] There are half-groats and pennies with TVEATVR, &c., on *both* sides, which are R.6.

[2] That with OX is R.4.

TWENTY-SHILLING PIECE.—R.2.[1]

2. *Obv.*—Resembling the three-pound piece; the numerals XX. behind the head instead of plume.

℞—The whole legend of the three-pound piece joined together in one scroll; above, plume of three feathers; below, 1644. OX.

TEN-SHILLING PIECE.—R.3.

3. Legend and type similar to those of the preceding, but with the date 1643.

UNIT, or BROAD.—C.

4. *Obv.*—CAROLVS D. G. MAG. BRI. FR. ET HIB. REX. Crowned bust in profile; behind, XX., for the value. Mint mark, on both sides, *fleur de lis.*

℞—FLORENT CONCORDIA REGNVM. The royal arms, surmounted by a crown.

UNIT, or BROAD.—C.

5. *Obv.*—CAROLVS D. G. MAG. BRIT. FR. ET HIB. REX. Bust in armour, with short hair, falling ruff, and scarf tied in a knot on the shoulder; behind the head, XX. Mint mark, on both sides, plume.

℞—FLORENT CONCORDIA REGNA. Oval shield, garnished and crowned, between the letters C. R.

UNIT, or BROAD.—C.

6. Another, with long hair and broad laced band. Mint mark, on both sides, a harp. The letters C. R. on the reverse crowned.

ANGEL.—R.3.[2]

7. *Obv.*—CAROLVS, &c. Type similar to the usual one of the angel, with the value, X., in the area. Mint mark, on both sides, a bell.

℞— AMOR POPVLI PRÆSIDIVM REGIS. Type as the angel of James, with a large *fleur de lis* on the ship.

DOUBLE-CROWN.—C.

8. *Obv.*—Similar to that of the unit. Mint mark, a bell.

℞—CVLTORES SVI DEVS PROTEGIT. As the unit.

CROWN.—C.

9. Similar to the double crown. Mint mark, both sides, a tun.

---

[1] There are also very elegant pieces by Briot. The twenty-shillings, R.2.; ten shillings, R.3.; five shillings, R.8.

[2] The angels of Charles I. are generally disfigured by a hole bored through them, having been used as *touch pieces,* and hung about the necks of those who had been touched for the king's evil.

(*Silver.*)

TWENTY-SHILLING PIECE.—R.1. to 6.

10. *Obv.*—CAROLVS D. G. MAGNI (*sic*) BRITANI. FRAN. ET HIB. REX. The king on horseback, crowned, holding a drawn sword; armour and weapons under the horse's feet; behind, plume of feathers. Mint mark, plume.

℞—EXVRGAT DEVS DISSIPENTVR INIMICI, and, in two lines across the field, RELIG. PROT. LEG. ANG. LIBER. PAR.; above, plume of three feathers and the numerals XX.; beneath, 1642.

There are varieties of these pieces. Some are without the armour, &c. under the horse's feet; others have the inscription in a compartment, and OX. (*Oxford*). It was at one time supposed that all these pieces were coined at Oxford, but some of them were struck at Exeter, and perhaps in other mints. A *ten*-shilling piece bears EX.

TEN-SHILLINGS.—R.1 to 8.

11. Similar to the pieces of twenty-shillings, differing in the numerals of value.

FIVE-SHILLINGS or CROWN.—R.2.

12. Similar to the former, and differing merely in the numerals, &c.

Of this coinage there is also the shilling, R.2., sixpence, R.2., groat, R.2., threepence, R.2., twopence, R.4., and penny, R.8.

CROWN.—R.1.

13. *Obv.*—CAROLVS D. G. MAG. BRIT. FRA. ET HIB. REX. The king on horseback, crowned and in armour; a drawn sword in his right hand, raised as if about to strike. A plume of feathers on the head of the horse, and also on the crupper. Mint mark, on both sides, a *fleur de lis*.

℞—CHRISTO AVSPICE REGNO. The royal arms on a garnished shield, over a cross fourchy.

There are many varieties of these pieces.

CROWN.—R.1.

14. *Obv.*—CAROLVS, &c. The king on horseback, but the horse not caparisoned. Mint mark, on both sides, a portcullis.

℞—CHRISTO, &c. Oval shield of arms; above, a plume.

There are varieties also of these pieces, some having the shield between C.R.

"OXFORD CROWN."—R.8.

15. *Obv.*—CAROLVS D. G. MAG. BRIT. FRAN. ET HIBER. REX.' The king on horseback, as usual; underneath, a view of the city of Oxford, with OXON above it. Mint mark, a quatrefoil.?

℞—EXVRGAT DEVS DISSIPENTVR INIMICI, with a branch of olive after each word. In the area, enclosed by scrolls and similar branches, RELIG. PROT. LEG. ANG. LIBER. PARL. in two lines; above, three plumes and V; underneath, 1644, OXON.

This is one of the finest and most remarkable coins in the English series. It is the work of Rawlins, whose initial appears on the wall of the city.

HALF-CROWN (*York*).—R.3.

16. *Obv.*—Legend and type similar to those of the crown. Under the horse, EBOR. Mint mark, on both sides, a lion passant guardant.

℞—CHRISTO AVSPICE REGNO. The royal arms on a plain shield, between the letters C. R. all crowned.

There are several varieties of this half-crown—that with the *square* shield, is R.4; another, with *round* shield, R.4.

HALF-CROWN (*Briot's pattern*).—R.8.

17. *Obv.*—CAR. D. G. MAGN. BRITAN. FR. ET HIB. REX. Profile bust bare-headed, in armour, with the ribbon of the order.

℞—AVSPICIIS REX MAGNE TVIS. The royal arms on a garnished square shield, between the letters C.R. all crowned. Date above the crown, 1630, between a small B. and George and dragon as mint mark.

HALF-CROWN (*Briot's pattern*).—R.5.

18. *Obv.*—O. REX DA. FACILEM CVRSVM. The king on horseback, the sword resting on his shoulder; plume on the horse's head; below, N. BRIOT. F. Mint mark, an anemone.

℞—ATQVE AVDACIBVS ANNVE COEPTIS. The royal arms on an oval garnished shield, surmounted by a crown; on the sides, 16-28.

HALF-CROWN.—R.1.

19. *Obv.*—CAROLVS, &c. The king on horseback, as on the crowns; over the point of the sword a small B. Mint mark, a rose. ?

℞—CHRISTO, &c. Small garnished oval shield between the letters, C. R., all crowned.

HALF-CROWN (*Chester*).—R.6.

20. *Obv.*—CAROLVS, &c. The king on horseback, as before; behind, a plume; under the horse, CHST. Mint mark on both sides, three garbs (wheatsheaves), the arms of Chester.

℞—CHRISTO, &c. The royal arms in a richly garnished shield.

HALF-CROWN (*Worcester*).—R.6.

21. *Obv.*—CAROLVS, &c. The king on horseback, as usual. Mint mark, a pear.

℞—CHRISTO, &c. The royal arms on garnished shield. Mint mark, three pears, the arms of Worcester.

SHILLING.—R.1.

22. *Obv.*—CAROLVS D. G. MAG. BRI. FRA. ET HIB. REX. Crowned bust, in parliament robes, with the collar of the order; short hair; behind the head the numerals XII., for the value. Mint mark, on both sides, a *fleur de lis*.

℞—CHRISTO, &c. Plain square shield, and cross fourchy.

SHILLING.—R.2.

23. *Obv.*—CAROLVS, &c. Crowned bust, in plain dress; short hair. Mint mark, on both sides, a blackamoor's head.

℞—As the preceding.

Another, with the mint mark of a castle, has a plain square shield, without the cross; over it, a plume of feathers.

SHILLING.—C.

24. *Obv.*—CAROLVS, &c. Bust crowned and in armour; long hair. Mint mark, on both sides, an anchor.

℞—CHRISTO, &c. Royal arms on a plain square shield, and cross fleury, terminating at the inner circle.

SHILLING.—R.1.

25. *Obv.*—CAROLVS, &c. Bust, with short hair, large ruff and ribbon of the order. Mint mark, on both sides, a plume.

℞—CHRISTO, &c. Garnished oval shield; between, C. R.; above the shield, a plume.

SHILLING.—R.6.

26. *Obv.*—CAROLVS, &c. Profile bust; behind the head, XII. Mint mark, a martlet.

℞—CHRISTO, &c. Plain square shield, supported by lions' paws. Mint mark, boar's head, between a coronet and two small crosses.

SHILLING.—R.1.

27. *Obv.*—CAROLVS, &c. Profile bust; behind the head, XII. Mint mark, on both sides, a lion passant guardant.

℞—CHRISTO, &c. Plain shield, over which a cross fourchy; above it, EBOR.

Another shilling differs from this, and has the word EBOR under the shield.

SIXPENCE.—R.2.

28. Types very similar to those of the shillings, with VI. for the value.

GROAT.—R.1.

29. *Obv.*—Type as the shilling, No. 24; behind the bust, IIII. Mint mark, *fleur de lis.*

℞—Round shield. Mint mark, lion passant guardant.

GROAT.—R.1.

30. *Obv.*—CAROLVS, &c. 1644. The usual bust; behind, IIII. Mint mark, on both sides, a rose.

℞—CHRISTO, &c.

THREEPENCE.—R.5.

31. *Obv.*—CAROLVS D. G. MA. BR. FR. ET H. REX. Usual bust, with rose behind the head. No inner circle. Mint mark, a bell.

℞—SALVS REI PVBLICÆ SVPREMA LEX. Garnished oval shield; above, 1634.

THREEPENCE.—R.6.

32. *Obv.*—CAR. D. G. MAG. BRIT. FR. ET H. R. Bust extending to the edge of the coin; behind, III.; a rose above and D. below.

℞—Same legend as the above. Plain shield and cross; 1634.

TWOPENCE.—C.

33. *Obv.*—C. D. G. ROSA SINE SPINA. Full-blown rose, crowned.

℞—IVS THRONVM FIRMAT. Full-blown rose, crowned.

There are also the penny of this coinage, same legend, with full-blown rose on each side, C.; and the halfpenny with a full-blown rose on each side, and without legend, C.

TWOPENCE.—C.

34. *Obv.*—CAROLVS D. G. MAG. BRIT. FR. ET HIB. R. Bust not touching the inner circle; behind, II., below, B.

℞—IVSTITIA THRONVM FIRMAT. Plain shield and cross.

35. *Obv.*—CAR. D. G. ANG. SCO. FR. ET HIB. REX. Profile bust, with large ruff.

℞—FLOREBIT IN AEVVM. A full-blown rose irradiated. Mint mark, a small rose. R.5.

36. *Obv.*—As the preceding.

℞—REGIT VNVS VTROQVE. A sceptre and trident united by a triple knot. R.5.

37. Another half-groat has for reverse FIDEI DEFENSOR. Two C's interlinked and crowned; underneath, the letter B.—C.

38. *Obv.*—CAROLVS D. G. MA. BR. ET HI. REX. Crowned bust; behind, II.

℞—IVSTITIA THRONVM FIRMAT. Large plume and coronet; beneath, on a scroll, ICH DIEN. Mint mark, crown.—R.8.

There is a twopence R.1, and a penny R.4, of similar type, but without the ICH DIEN on the scroll.

PENNY.—C.

39. *Obv.*—CAR. D. G. MAG. BRIT. FR. ET. HI. Type as the two-pence, but the bust touching the circle; behind the head, I.

℞—FIRMAT IVSTITIA THRONVM. Type as the twopence.

40. *Obv.*—CAROLVS, &c. Bust in profile, &c.

℞—IVSTITIA THRO. FIRMAT. Large plume.

HALFPENNY.—R.4.

41. *Obv.*—A rose.

R—A plume.

(*Copper.*)

FARTHING-TOKEN.—C.

42. *Obv.*—CAROLVS D. G. MA. BRI. As the token of James I. Mint mark, on both sides, a rose.

℞—FRA. ET HI. REX. A rose, crowned.

These coins had a piece of brass in the centre, to render the counterfeiting of them more difficult. There were others of this denomination, resembling those of his father, James I. See the Introductory Account, pp. 292-3.

SIEGE COINS.

(*Silver.*)

CROWN.—R.2.

1. An irregular shaped piece, stamped on each side, 19 dwts. 8 grs.

There are the half-crown, shilling, ninepence, sixpence, and groat, of this coinage, stamped with their respective weights, and others with the weight on one side, and annulets on the other for the denomination. The sixpence has six annulets, the groat four, threepence three.[1]

CROWN.—R.4.

2. Another, stamped on each side Vs.

There is also a half-crown of this description with IIs. VId.—R.4.

CROWN.—R.1.

3. *Obv.*—The letters C. R., surmounted by a large crown.

℞—The numeral Vs.

There is also the half-crown, R.1., shilling, R.1., sixpence, R.1., groat R.1., threepence, R.1., and twopence, R.1. The *penny* has also been engraved, but it is believed that there was no such coin.

These coins were struck in the year 1643. They are called the Ormond money, having been made current by proclamation of the Duke of Ormond, then Lord-Lieutenant of Ireland.

THREE SHILLINGS (*Carlisle*).—R.4.

4. *Obv.*—The letters C. R. and IIIs., between two anemones, surmounted by a crown.[2]

℞—OBS. CARL. 1645, between two anemones.

THREE SHILLINGS.—R.6.

5. *Obv.*—The letters C. R. between two anemones, surmounted by a crown; below, IIIs.

℞—OB^s. CARL, 1645; beneath a large anemone.[2]

---

[1] Half-crown, R.3., shilling, R.4., sixpence, R.6., with annulets, R.8., groat, R.8., threepence, R.8. *There are modern forgeries of these coins*, especially of the smaller pieces.

[2] These pieces were struck by Sir Thomas Glenham, when he held out Carlisle for Charles the First.

SHILLING.—R.4.

Two varieties, differing but slightly from the three-shilling piece.

HALF-CROWN (*Newark*).—R.2.

6. *Obv.*—A crown between the letters C. R.; below, XXX.

℞—OBS. NEWARK, 1646. (*Lozenge-shaped*).

Of this coinage there are the shilling, R.2., ninepence, R.2. and sixpence, R.2.

SHILLING (*Cork*).—R.6.

7. *Obv.*—CORK, 1647.

℞—XII. (*Octagon shaped*).

There is also the sixpence of this coinage, R.2.

SHILLING (*Pontefract*).—R.3.

8. *Obv.*—A castle, with a streamer flying on the highest tower; above the castle, P. C.;[1] on the right side, OBS.; and a hand with a sword erect issuing out of the left; below, 1648.

℞.—DVM SPIRO SPERO. In the area, C. R. surmounted by a crown. (*Octangular*).

SHILLING (*Pontefract*).—R.3.

9. *Obv.*—A similar castle to that on the preceding coin: on the right side, OBS.; on the left XII., with P. above, and C. beneath. Under the castle, 1648.

℞—Type as the preceding. (*Lozenge*).

There are several other coins of this period formed out of pieces of plate, and stamped with the value. Some have also the rudely drawn figure of a castle. A piece for *fourteen pence* bears the inscription *Carolj fortvna resvrgam*, and is supposed to have been struck at Colchester.

---

[1] In a newspaper of the day, entitled, "The Kingdome's Faithfull and Impartial Scout," Feb. 2 to 9, 1648, there is a notice of this money to the following effect:—" Munday, Feb. 5. The intelligence from Pontefract is this: the besieged have lately made two sallies forth, but repulsed without any great losse to us; in the last they killed but one man of ours, and we took two of theirs prisoners, one of which had a small parcel of silver in his pocket, somewhat square, on the one side thereof was stampt a castle, with PO. for Pontefract; on the other side was the crown, with C. R. on each side of it. These pieces they make of plate which they get out of the country, and pass among them for coyn." The PO. here described is doubtless misread for P. C., the form of the latter letter, from bad striking, resembling an O. See a Note by Sir Henry Ellis to the Numismatic Society, printed in the Numismatic Journal, Vol. I., p. 273.

COMMONWEALTH.

A.D. 1649. TO A.D. 1660.

(Gold.)

TWENTY SHILLINGS.—R.1.

1 *Obv.*—THE COMMONWEALTH OF ENGLAND. Saint George's cross between a branch of palm and laurel. Mint mark, the sun.

℞—GOD WITH VS, 1656. Two escutcheons, side by side; the first charged with Saint George's cross, the other with the Irish harp; over the shields, XX.

TEN SHILLINGS.—R.2.

2. Legends and types as the former, with X. for the value. Date, 1649. Mint mark, sun.

FIVE SHILLINGS.—R.2.

3. Legends and types as the former; date, 1651. Mint mark, sun.

Pieces with the *anchor* mint mark are all rare.

(Silver).

The types of the silver of the Commonwealth resemble those of the gold coins. The denominations are the crown, half-crown, shilling, sixpence, twopence, penny, and halfpenny. Those with *sun* mint mark are C.; with the *anchor*, rare.

4. PATTERN HALF-CROWN, by Blondeau.[1] R.4.

5. ———— SHILLING, by ditto. R.6.

6 .———— SIXPENCE, by ditto. R.4.

7. PATTERN HALF-CROWN, by Ramage, R.8.

Obv.—THE COMMONWEALTH OF ENGLAND. The English shield between two branches of laurel. Mint mark, on both sides, a mullet of five points.

℞—GVARDED WITH ANGELES, 1651. The shields of England and Ireland, supported by an angel.

---

[1] Some of the half-crowns are inscribed on the edge, TRVTH AND PEACE, 1651. PETRVS BLONDAEVS INVENTOR FECIT: others have, IN THE THIRD YEAR OF FREEDOME BY GOD'S BLESSING RESTORED. The shillings and sixpences are grained on the edges.

PATTERN SHILLING, by Ramage.—R.8.

8. As the preceding.

PATTERN SIXPENCE, by Ramage.—R.8.

9. *Obv.*—TRVTH AND PEACE. A mullet of five points between the words.

℞—Same legend. The Irish harp.

(*Pewter and Copper.*)

FARTHING.[1]—R.3.

10. *Obv.*—¼ OVNCE OF FINE PEWT^R. A plain shield, charged with a cross fourchy; above, T. K., surrounded by a wreath of roses.

℞—FOR NECESSARY CHANGE. A radiated shield, with the Irish harp; above, a wreath of laurel.

FARTHING.—R.5.

11. *Obv.*—FARTHING TOKENS OF ENGLAND. The English shield and cross. Mint mark, on both sides, a mullet of five points.

℞—FOR NECESSITY OF CHANGE, 1649. The Irish shield and harp.

FARTHINGS.—R.6.

12. *Obv.*—THE FARTHING TOKENS FOR. Type and mint mark as the preceding.

℞—THE RELEFE OF THE PORE. Type and mint mark as the preceding.

FARTHING.—R.4.

13. *Obv.*—ENGLAND'S FARTHING. The English shield and cross crowned with laurel.

℞—FOR NECESSARY CHANG. The Irish shield and harp crowned in a like manner.

---

[1] Snelling thought that these pieces were issued by some tradesman, and that the letters T. K. were his initials; but in a newspaper of the day is the following: "This night are come out new farthings, weighing a quarter of an ounce of fine pewter, which is but the price of new pewter, that so the people may never hereafter fear to lose much by them, with the harp on one side, and a cross on the other, with T. K. above it." See a Communication by Sir Henry Ellis to the Numismatic Society. (Num. Journal, Vol. I.)

OLIVER CROMWELL.

(*Silver.*)[1]

CROWN.[2]—R.4.

1. *Obv.*—OLIVAR D. G. R. P. ANG. SCO. HIB., &c. PRO. Bust of Cromwell laureated, in Roman habit.

   ℞—PAX QVÆRITVR BELLO, 1658. A shield surmounted by an imperial crown, charged as follows: first and fourth, Saint George's cross, for England; second, Saint Andrew's cross, for Scotland; third, the harp, for Ireland. On an escutcheon of pretence, a lion rampant. On the edge, HAS NISI PERITVRVS MIHI ADIMAT NEMO.

HALF-CROWN.—R.3.

2. Obverse and reverse as the crown.
3. Another with obverse legend, OLIVAR D. G. R. P. ANG. SCO. HIB. PRO.—R.8.

Ruding says of the half-crown No. 3, "As this coin wants, '&c.' after 'HIB.,' I suspect that it was struck from a die which still remains in the Tower, and which Dr. Combe supposes to have been intended for a shilling, but to have been laid aside on account of that omission. * * * There is also in the Tower another die. which is often called the *ninepence.*" Pieces struck from this are sometimes admitted as a substitute for the sixpence, which is *exceedingly scarce.*" No 3 is in all probability a pattern for a shilling, though called a two-shilling piece.

SHILLING.—R.3.

4. Types as the crown.

SIXPENCE.—R.8.

5. Types as the crown. Only two are known.

(*Copper.*)

FARTHING.—R.6.

6. *Obv.*—OLIVAR PRO. ENG. SC. IRL. Bust, as on his silver coins.

   ℞—CHARITIE AND CHANGE. The arms, &c. as on his silver coins.

---

[1] There are gold pieces of Cromwell resembling in legend and types those of his silver coin, but the portrait appears to the neck only, and is not draped, and the shield on reverse is plain at the edges. They consist of the fifty-shilling-piece, R.8., twenty shillings, or Broad, R.3., and ten shillings, R.8. The fifty-shilling piece bears on the edge PROTECTOR LITERIS LITERAE NVMMIS CORONA ET SALVS. They are supposed not to have been current.

[2] "There dined with us to-day Mr. Slingsby, of the Mint, who showed us all the new pieces, both gold and silver (examples of them all), that were made for the king by Blondeau's way, and compared them with those made for Oliver. The pictures of the latter, made by Symons, and of the king, by one *Rotyr*, a German, I think, that dined with us also. He extols those of Rotyr above the others; and indeed, I think they are the better, because the sweeter of the two;

FARTHING.—R.6.

7. *Obv.*—OLIVER PRO. ENG. SCO. & IRE. Bust as No. 6. No inner circle. Mint mark, mullet of five points.

℞—CONVENIENT CHANGE, 1651. The arms as usual.

FARTHING.—R.6.

8. *Obv.*—As No. 6.

℞—THVS VNITED, INVINCIBLE. The English cross, Irish harp, and Scotch thistle, on three pillars lashed together. Mint mark, a mullet of five points.

CHARLES II.

A.D. 1649 TO A.D. 1685.

(*Gold.*)

TWENTY SHILLING PIECE.—R.4.

1. *Obv.*—CAR. II. D. G. M. BR. FR. ET HI. REX. Profile laureated bust, in the Roman habit.

℞—FLORENT. CONCORDIA REGNA, 1662. Plain shield of arms, crowned. (*Milled*).

TWENTY SHILLINGS.—C.

2. *Obv.*—CAROLVS II., &c. Type as the preceding; behind the head, XX., for the value. Mint mark, a crown.

℞—FLORENT, &c. Crowned garnished oval shield, between the letters C. R.

TEN SHILLINGS.—R.1.

3. Legends and types as the preceding, but with X, for the value.

FIVE SHILLINGS.—R.2.

4. Legends and types as the preceding, but with V, for the value.

5. Another, without the numeral.—R.2.

FIVE POUNDS.—C.

6. *Obv.*—CAROLVS II. DEI GRATIA. Laureated profile bust with the neck bare; under the bust an elephant.[1]

℞—MAG. BR. FRA. ET HIB. REX, 1664. Four crowned shields of England, Ireland, Scotland, and France. In the centre, four C's interlinked. In the quarters, four sceptres, surmounted respectively by a cross for England, harp for Ireland, thistle for Scotland, and *fleur de lis* for France.

---

but, upon my word, those of the Protector are more like in my mind than the king's, but both well worth seeing. The crownes of Cromwell are now sold, it seems, for 25*s.* and 30*s.* a-piece."—*Pepys' Memoirs.*

[1] Some are without this symbol. These pieces were coined out of gold imported by the African company, who were permitted by their charter to stamp the elephant, which sometimes has a castle on its back.

Two Pounds.—C.

7. As the five pound piece.

Guinea.—C.

8. As the former.

Half Guinea.—R.2.

9. As the former.

(*Silver.*)

Simon's Petition Crown.—R.7.

10. *Obv.*—Legend and type similar to the foregoing, but with a lock on the left shoulder, and the button of the mantle omitted. Below, SIMON.

℞—MAG. BRI. FR. ET HIB. REX, 1663. Four escutcheons crowned with interlinked C's between them. In the first shield, England; in the second, Ireland; in the third, Scotland; in the fourth, France. The George and garter in the centre, with the motto, HONI SOIT, &c. Upon the edge of the coin, in two lines, with two linked C's, and two branches of palm, THOMAS SIMON MOST HVMBLY PRAYS YOVR MAIESTY TO COMPARE THIS HIS TRYAL-PIECE WITH THE DVTCH, AND IF MORE TRVLY DRAWN AND EMBOSSED, MORE GRACEFVLLY ORDER'D, AND MORE ACCVRATELY ENGRAVEN, TO RELIEVE HIM.

11. Another, with REDITE QVAE CÆSARIS CÆSARI, etc. POST, and the sun appearing from behind a cloud to express NVBILA PHOEBVS, in the place of the petition on the reverse.—R.7.

12. Another, with RENDER TO CÆSAR THE THINGS WHICH ARE CÆSAR'S.—R.8.

No. 12. occurs only in pewter.

Crown.—C.

13. *Obv.*—CAROLVS II. DEI. GRA. Laureated profile bust in the Roman habit; below, a rose.

℞—MAG. BR. FRA. ET HIB. REX, 1662. Four escutcheons crowned; in the first and fourth, France and England quarterly; in the second, Ireland; in the third, Scotland. Two C.'s interlinked, between the shields. In the centre, the star of the order of the garter. On the edge of the coin, DECVS ET TVTAMEN.

Some are without the *rose* under the bust; and some have the *elephant*, being coined of silver imported by the African Company. See the five-pound pieces described above.

Of this coinage there are the half-crown, shilling, and sixpence, resembling the crown, and also the groat, with four C.'s, interlinked and crowned; the threepence, with three C.'s; the twopence, with two C.'s; and the penny, with one C. There is a half-crown with a plume under the bust, R.8., and a shilling with the same symbol, R.3. Some have also the feathers in the centre of the cross.

CROWN.—R.5.

14. *Obv.*—CAR. II. D. G. MAG. BRIT. A large crown; roses between the words. Mint mark, on both sides, a *fleur de lis.*

℞— FRA. ET HYB. REX. F. D., &c. In the field, Vs.

This and the two following pieces are said by Folkes to have been coined before the restoration of Charles. Snelling thinks they were struck in Ireland.

HALF-CROWN.—R.6.

15. *Obv.*—Legend, type, and mint mark, as No. 5.; but with *fleurs de lis* between the words on each side.

℞—Legend as the crown. In the field, IIs. VId.

16. *Obv.*—Legend and type as No. 1. Mint mark, a quatrefoil, and the same symbol between the words on both sides.

℞—Legend as the preceding. In the field, IIs. VId.

HALF-CROWN.—R.4.

17. *Obv.*—CAROLVS II. D. G. MAG. BRIT. FRAN. ET HIB. REX. Profile bust, crowned and in armour, with long flowing hair, and broad laced band. *No inner circle,* nor numerals for the value. Mint mark, a crown.

℞—CHRISTO AVSPICE REGNO. The royal arms quarterly in a plain shield. In the first and fourth England and France quartered; in the second Scotland; and in the third Ireland.

There is a shilling R.2, sixpence, R.4, twopence, C. and penny, C. of this coinage.

HALF-CROWN.—R.6.

18. Types as the preceding, but with the numerals XXX. for the value.

Of this coinage there are the shilling, R.4, sixpence, R.4, twopence, and penny.—C.

HALF-CROWN.—R.1.

19. Types as the preceding, but *with an inner circle.*

Of this coinage there are the shilling, R.4, sixpence, R.4, groat, R.1, threepence, R.1, twopence, R.1, penny, R.1.

The half-crown, *well struck up and fine,* is R.6, shilling, R.4, sixpence, R.6.

FARTHING?—R.2.

20. *Obv.*—Two C's linked and crowned.

℞—A full-blown rose.

This is supposed to be a pattern piece; it is of mixed metal.

SIEGE PIECES.

(*Silver.*)

PONTEFRACT SHILLING.—R.3.

1. *Obv.*—CAROLVS SECVNDVS 1648. A castle, with a streamer flying on the highest tower; OBS. on one side, and a cannon issuing from the wall on the other; above, P.C.

   ℞—DVM SPIRO SPERO. In the centre, C.R., surmounted by a crown.

PONTEFRACT SHILLING.—R.4.

2. *Obv.*—CAROL. II. D. G. MAG. B. F. ET H. REX. Across the field, HANC DEVS DEDIT 1648. Below, a crown.

   ℞—POST MORTEM PATRIS PRO FILIO. Type as the preceding.

There is a gold coin of this type, R.8.

MONEY OF THE PLANTATIONS.

(*Silver.*)

SHILLING.—R.1.

1. A circular piece, with NE. near the edge.[1]

   ℞—XII.

SIXPENCE.—R.8.

2. Resembling the shilling, but with the value VI.

SHILLING.—R.4.

3. *Obv.*—CAECILIVS DNS. TERRAE MARIÆ, &c. Profile bust of Lord Baltimore; bare head and neck. Mint mark, a cross patée.

   ℞—CRESCITE ET MVLTIPLICAMINI. Arms under the crown of his palatinate; on the sides, XII.

SIXPENCE.—R.2.

4. Differing only in the value VI.

GROAT.—R.6.

5. Differing only in the value IV.

---

[1] See Introductory Account, p. 297.

SHILLING.—C.

6. *Obv.*—MASATHVSETS IN. The American pine. Mint mark, on both sides, a rose composed of dots.

℞—NEWE ENGLAND AN. DOM. In the field, 1652; below, XII.

There are the sixpence, threepence, and twopence of similar type, all C. The *penny* is not authenticated.

SHILLING (*Unique*).

7. *Obv.*—MASSATHVSETS IN. Group of the good Samaritan. Above, FAC SIMILE.

No reverse. *Pembroke, pl.* iv.)

(*Copper.*)[1]

PENNY (*Unique*).?

8. *Obv.*—CÆCILIVS DNS. TERRÆ MARIÆ &c. Bust and mint mark, as on the shilling.

℞—DENARIVM TERRÆ MARIÆ. Two flags out of a ducal coronet; the Baltimore crest.

HALFPENNY.[2]—R.1.

9. *Obv.*—CAROLVS A CAROLO. Laureated bust.

℞—BRITANNIA. Britannia seated with her attributes.

FARTHING.—C.

10. As the halfpenny.

JAMES THE SECOND.

A.D. 1685 TO A.D. 1689.

(*Gold.*)

FIVE-POUNDS.—C.

1. *Obv.*—IACOBVS II. DEI GRATIA. Profile bust, laureated; the hair falling on the shoulder.

℞—As the five-pound piece of Charles I., but without the interlinked C.'s in the centre of the reverse.

Some of these pieces have the elephant under the bust.

---

[1] There is a very singular piece in brass, bearing the legend SOMMER ISLAND, with the type of a hog; above which, the numerals XII.; Reverse, a ship under sail, firing a gun. It is said to have been struck for the Sumner Islands, about the year 1612, when the Virginia Company endeavoured to establish a colony there. Vide Ruding, Supp. Pt. II. Pl. VII. No. 14.

[2] See the Introductory Account, p. 299. Money was also coined at Bombay in this reign.

Two-Pounds.—R.5.

2. *Obv.*—As the five-pound piece.

℞—As the five-pound piece.

Guinea.—R.1.

3. Resembling the two-pound piece.

Half-Guinea.—R.3.

4. Resembling the others.

(*Silver.*)

Crown.—C.

5. *Obv.*—IACOBVS II. DEI GRATIA. Laureated profile bust, clothed.

℞—MAG. BR. FRA. ET HIB. REX, 1686. Four shields, as on the coins of his predecessor, but without any symbol in the angles.

Half-Crown.—R.1.

6. Similar to the crown.

Shilling.—R.1.

7. Similar to the former.

Sixpence.—R.2.

8. Similar to the former.

The Maundy money, consisting of the groat, threepence, twopence, and penny, have the respective values, IIII. III. II. I. crowned. The neck of the bust is bare.

(*Tin.*)[1]

Halfpenny.—R.2.

9. *Obv.*—IACOBVS SECVNDVS. Laureated profile bust, in the Roman habit.

℞—BRITANNIA. The usual seated figure of Britannia.

Farthing.—R. 2.

10. As the halfpenny.

WILLIAM AND MARY.

A.D. 1689 to A.D. 1694.

(*Gold.*)

Five-Pounds.—C.

1. *Obv.*—GVLIELMVS ET MARIA DEI GRATIA. Their heads side by side in profile—his laureated; the necks bare.

Some of these pieces have an elephant under the busts.

---

[1] Snelling, pl. iv. 24, gives a piece in this metal, with name and titles, and the king in armour, laureated, and on horseback. Reverse, VAL. 24. PART REAL HISPAN. The arms of England, Ireland, Scotland, and France on four shields, crowned and chained.

Two-Pounds.—R.2.

2. *Obv.*—As the five-pound piece.

℞—MAG. BR. FR. ET HIB. REX ET REGINA, 1694. On a shield garnished and crowned: first and fourth, France and England quarterly; second, Scotland; third, Ireland. Nassau on an escutcheon of pretence.

Guinea.—R.2.

3. Resembling the preceding.

Half-Guinea.—R.3.

4. Resembling the preceding.

(*Silver.*)

Crown.—R.2.

5. *Obv.*—GVLIELMVS ET MARIA DEI GRATIA. Profile busts side by side.

℞—MAG. BR. FR. ET HI. REX ET REGINA. The letters W. and M., interlinked, in the angles formed by the four shields. In the centre, the escutcheon of Nassau. Date, 1692.

Half-Crown.—C.

6. As the crown.

Half-Crown.—C.

7. Reverse only. Date, 1689. A plain shield, crowned, with the arms of France and England quarterly in the first and fourth; Scotland in the second, and Ireland in the third. The arms of Nassau on an escutcheon of pretence.

Half-Crown.—C.

8. Reverse only. Date, 1689. A plain shield crowned. The arms of England in the first quarter; Scotland in the second; Ireland in the third; and France in the fourth.

Shilling.—R.2.[1]

9. As the crown No. 1.

Sixpence.—R.4.

10. As the former.

The maundy money, consisting of the groat, threepence, twopence, and penny, have the Arabic numerals of their respective value, crowned.

---

[1] A *fine* shilling, R.8.

(*Copper.*)[1]

HALFPENNY.—C,

11. *Obv.*—GVLIELMVS ET MARIA. Profile busts, side by side.

℞—BRITANNIA. Britannia seated with a spear and shield, holding an olive branch in her right hand. Date, 1694.

FARTHING.—C.

.12 Obverse and reverse resembling the halfpenny.

WILLIAM THE THIRD.

A.D. 1694 TO A.D. 1702.

(*Gold.*)

FIVE-POUNDS.—C.

1. *Obv.*—GVLIELMVS III. DEI GRA. Profile bust.

Some have an elephant and castle beneath the bust.

TWO-POUNDS.—R.2.

2. *Obv.*—As the five-pound piece.

℞—MAG. BR. FRA. ET HIB. REX, 1701. As the two-pound piece of Charles II. with the arms of Nassau in the centre.

GUINEA.—C.

3. As the two-pound piece.

HALF-GUINEA.—R.2.

4. As the former.

(*Silver*).

The recoinage of all the hammered money was effected in this reign, as previously noticed in the Introductory Account, p. 301; and the coins of the different mints are distinguished by letters under the bust. A particular account of all the varieties, which are numerous, will be found in Marshall's "View of the Silver Coin and Coinage of Great Britain, from the year 1662 to 1837," 8vo. London, 1837. Those pieces, with the *feathers* under the head and between quarters of the arms on the reverse, were struck from Welsh silver, from the mines of Sir Carberry Price and Sir Humphrey Mackworth. Those with the *roses* were coined from silver of the west of England, but were found too expensive, and discontinued. Shilling and sixpence, with feathers under the head, R.8.; shilling and sixpence, with feathers on reverse, R.4; shilling and sixpence, with roses (rarely found well preserved), R.5; half-crown, with feathers, R.4, with elephant, R.7. Well preserved pieces are of course much valued.

[1] There is a copper piece of this reign, having an elephant on the obverse, and on the reverse the inscription, GOD PRESERVE NEW ENGLAND, 1694. It is R.

(*Copper.*)

HALFPENNY.—R.2.

5. *Obv.*—GVLIELMVS TERTIVS. Profile bust, laureated.
℞—BRITANNIA. Britannia seated. Date, 1699.

FARTHING.—R.2.

6. As the halfpenny.

ANNE.

A.D. 1702 TO A.D. 1714.

(*Gold.*)

FIVE-POUNDS.—R.1.

1. *Obv.*—ANNA DEI GRATIA. Profile bust; the hair tied up behind.
℞—MAG. BRI. &c. The four shields of arms, &c.

Some of these pieces have VIGO under the bust, having been struck from gold taken at that place. There is also the guinea and half-guinea. They are all R.7.

TWO-POUNDS.—R.2.

2. Resembling the former, but without VIGO.

GUINEA.—C.

3. Resembling the former.

HALF-GUINEA.—R.1.

4. Resembling the former.

All the gold money of Anne before the Union has a *rose* in the centre of the reverse; that struck after the Union has a *star*.

(*Silver.*)

CROWN.—C.

5. *Obv.*—ANNA DEI GRATIA. Profile bust.
℞—MAG. BRI. FRA. ET HIB. REG., 1708. In the upper and lower shields, England and Scotland impaled (to denote the union of the two kingdoms); on the dexter side, Ireland; on the sinister side, France. A plume of feathers in each angle formed by the cross.

HALF-CROWN.—C.

6. As the crown.

SHILLING.—C.

7. As the crown.

SIXPENCE.—C.

8. As the crown.[1]

(Copper).[2]

HALFPENNY.—R.6.

9. *Obv.*—ANNA D. G. MAG. BR. FR. ET HIB. REG. Profile bust.

℞—Britannia, with shield and spear, sitting beneath a crown, and holding a rose and thistle on one stalk in her right hand.

There is another, on which Britannia holds the olive branch, R.6.; another having a rose and a thistle only on reverse, R.6.; and a fourth with the rose and a thistle crowned, R.6. These are all patterns, and were never circulated.

FARTHING.—R.6.

10. *Obv.*—ANNA DEI GRATIA. Profile bust, as usual.

℞—BRITANNIA. Britannia, with her attributes, seated under a portal; 1713.

FARTHING.—R.6.

11. *Obv.*—ANNA AVGVSTA. Bust as the former.

℞—PAX MISSA PER ORBEM. Peace, in a car; 1713.

FARTHING.—R.2.

12. *Obv.*—ANNA DEI GRATIA. Usual bust.

℞—BRITANNIA. Britannia seated, with her attributes; 1714.

This is the only current farthing of Anne; the others are patterns.

FARTHING.—R.8.

13. *Obv.*—ANNA DEI GRATIA. Usual bust, but with an inner circle, and a scroll beneath.

℞—BELLO ET PACE (*the letters incuse*). Britannia standing, holding a spear and an olive branch. Date, 1715.

---

[1] The coins which have the feathers between the shields were struck from Welsh silver, but as it frequently happened that the silver from the Principality was brought to the Mint at the same time as that from the mines in the West of England, the coins struck from this mixed silver have the feathers and roses alternately in the angles of the cross formed by the four shields, a practice continued till the reign of George II. All the coins struck before the Union are much less common than those minted afterwards.

[2] See page 302.

LIST OF MINT MARKS.

FROM HENRY THE THIRD TO CHARLES THE SECOND.

HENRY III.

Crescent and star.
Star only.

EDWARD I.

Cross moline.

EDWARD II.

Cross moline.
Lion rampant.
Lion rampant and fleur de lis.
Lion rampant between two fleurs de lis.

EDWARD III.

Crown or coronet.
Star.
Cross crosslet.
Rose.
Mullet of six points.
Cross, each bar of which is terminated by a pellet.

RICHARD II.

Gold.

Rose.
Coronet or crown.

HENRY IV.

Cross crosslet.
Cross pierced.
Fleur de lis.
Mullet.

HENRY V.

Gold.

Fleur de lis.

HENRY VI.

First Coinage.

Cross crosslet.—℞ cross patée.
Cross patée fitchée.
Martlet.[1]

Last Coinage.

Fleur de lis.
Rose.

Gold.

Fleur de lis.
Fleur de lis between three trefoils.
Rose.
Three quatrefoils.
Quatrefoil.—℞ fleur de lis.
Cross patée.

EDWARD IV.

First Coinage.

Cross crosslet.
Rose.
Cinquefoil.

Second Coinage.

Crown or coronet.
Crown.—℞ star.
Star.—℞ crown.
Rose.
Star.
Cross patée fitchée.—℞ star.
Cross, with a pellet in each quarter.—℞ plain cross.
Cinquefoil.—Rev. plain cross.
Cinquefoil.
Annulet.
Annulet inclosing a pellet.
Annulet surmounted by a cross.
Y.
Y.—℞ rose.
Fleur de lis.
Plain cross.—℞ star.
Sun.
Sun.—℞ annulet.
Cross Calvary.—℞ star.

---

[1] Query, of Henry VII.?

Rose.—℞ star.
Annulet.—℞ trefoil.
Y.—℞ star of six rays.
Y.—℞ star of eight rays.

Gold.

Crown or coronet.
Rose.
Sun.
Sword.
Circle or annulet.

RICHARD III.

Boar's head.
Boar's head.—℞ rose.
Rose.
Fleur de lis.

Gold.

Boar's head.
Rose.

HENRY VII.

First Coinage.

Crown with single arch.

Greyhound's head.
Cross crosslet.

Crown with double arch.

Greyhound's head.
Cinquefoil.
Cinquefoil.—℞ anchor.
Anchor.
Escallop shell.
Cross crosslet.
Leopard's face crowned.
Fleur de lis.
Portcullis.
Tun.
Tun.—℞ fleur de lis.
Martlet.
Key.
Double fleur de lis.

Second Coinage.

Cross crosslet.
Fleur de lis.
Fleur de lis.—℞ Pheon.
Pheon.
Greyhound's head.
Cinquefoil.
Martlet.
Fleur de lis and rose united.

Gold.

Plain cross.
Cross crosslet.
Portcullis.
Greyhound's head.
Dragon.
Cross patée fitchée.
Pheon.
Fleur de lis.
Cinquefoil.
Quatrefoil.
Castle.
Rose.
Sword.

Ecclesiastical.

Fleur de lis. Durham.
Rose.—℞ martlet. York.
Martlet. York.

HENRY VIII.

First Coinage. His Father's face.

Bolt.
Portcullis.
Castle.
Martlet.
Poppy head.
Long cross.
Cinquefoil.
Escallop.
Pheon.
Bird's head.

Second Coinage. His own side face.

Rose.
Bolt.
Pheon.—℞ fleur de lis.
Fleur de lis.
Sun shining through a cloud.
Plain-cross.
Key.
Cross fleury.
Cross fleury and T.
Cross fleury and V.
Catharine wheel.
Star.
Sun, crescent, and star.
Crescent.

Third Coinage. Full face.
Fine Silver.

Fleur de lis.

Fourth Coinage. Full face.
Base silver.

Fleur de lis.
Fleur de lis, plain cross, and annulet, inclosing a pellet.
Picklock.
Bolt.
K.
Plain cross.
Martlet.
E.
Є.
W.
Ꞇ. Tau.

Fifth Coinage.

Bow.
E.
VY.
Saltire.—℞ lozenge pierced.

Gold.

Fleur de lis.—℞ cross crosslet.
Fleur de lis.—℞ bolt.
Castle.
Lion passant guardant.
Pheon.
VY. on reverse.
S.
Annulet.
Bolt.
VY and cross.
Portcullis crowned.
Rose.
Fleur de lis.
E.
Quatrefoil. — ℞ VY. and quatrefoil.
Annulet and fleur de lis.
Circle or annulet.
A shield with St. George's cross.
Glory.

Ecclesiastical.

Canterbury:
Martlet.
Flower.
T. Tau.
Catherine wheel.
Martlet.—℞ fleur de lis.
Cross crosslet.

Durham:
Crescent. — ℞ trefoil.
Star.
Trefoil.

York:
Flower.
Key.
Fleur de lis.
Plain cross.
Star.
Cross patée.
Acorn. — ℞ cross patée.
Thistle ?—℞ bell ?

EDWARD VI.

First Coinage.

Bolt, on both sides.
Square.

Testoons.

Cinquefoil.
Bolt.
Rose.
Rose.—℞ picklock.
Picklock.
T.—℞ T.
t.
Ꞇ.—℞ star.
Bow.
V.
y.
Bow.
Rose on reverse.
Plain cross.
Fleur de lis.
Harp.
Swan.
Lion.
Key.
T.G. in a cipher.

Rose.—℞ square and rose.
Flower like a marigold.—℞ cinquefoil.

Last Coinage.

Tun. 1551, 2, 3.
Y. 1551.
Mullet on both sides.
Mullet pierced.

Gold.

Y.
Y.—℞ Y and rose.
Rose.—℞ Y.
Arrow or bolt.
Bow.
Tun.
Cinquefoil.
Eagle's head.
Rose.
Swan.
Picklock.

MARY.

Small pomegranate.
Rose.

Gold.

Small pomegranate.

PHILIP AND MARY.

Fleur de lis.
Annulet.
Trefoil.

Gold.

Fleur de lis.
Fetterlock.

ELIZABETH.

First Coinage.

Martlet.
Cross crosslet.
Fleur de lis.

Second Coinage.

Pheon. 1561, 2, 3, 4, 5.
Rose. 1565.
Portcullis. 1566.
Lion. 1566, 7.
Crown or coronet. 1567, 8, 9, 70.
Castle. 1569, 70, 71.

Third Coinage.

Ermine spot. 1572, 3.
Acorn. 1573, 4.
Cinquefoil. 1574, 5, 6, 7.
Plain cross. 1578, 9.
Long cross. 1580, 1, 2.
Sword on both sides. 1581, 2.

Fourth Coinage.

Bell. 1582, 3.
A. 1582, 3, 4.
Escallop. 1584, 5, 6.
Crescent. 1587, 8, 9.
Hand. 1590, 1, 2.
Tun. 1592, 3, 4, 5.
Woolpack. 1594, 5, 6.
Key. 1595, 6, 7, 8.
Anchor. 1597, 8, 9, 1600.
Annulet. 1600.

Fifth Coinage.

Emony.
1. 1601.
1. 1602.

Milled Money.

Star. 1561, 2, 3, 4, 5, 6, 1570.
Fleur de lis. 1567, 8, 70.
Castle. 1571.
Star of five points. 1574, 5.

Portcullis Money.

Annulet.

Gold.

Portcullis.
Rose.
Crown or coronet.
Fleur de lis.
Lion.
Eglantine flower.
Cross.
Long cross.
1.

2.
A.
Tun.
Cross crosslet.
Escallop shell.
Acorn.
Woolpack.
Mullet or star.
Crescent.
Cinquefoil.
Sword.
Ermine spot.
Cross.
Bell.
Hand.
Key.
Anchor.
Lion and tun.
Coronet.
Fleur de lis.

JAMES I.

First Coinage. Angl. Scot.

Thistle. 1603, 4.
Fleur de lis. 1604.

Second Coinage. Mag. Brit.

Fleur de lis. 1604, 5.
Rose. 1605, 6.
Escallop shell. 1606, 7.
Bunch of grapes. 1607, 8, 9.
Coronet. 1609.
Key. 1609, 10.
Bell. 1610.
Bell.—℞ mullet. 1610.
Mullet. 1611.
Castle. 1612.
Trefoil. 1613.
Cinquefoil. 1615.
Tun. 1615.
Book. 1616.
Crescent. 1617.
Cross patée. 1618.
Saltire. 1619.
Spur rowel. 1619.
Rose. 1620.
Thistle. 1621, 2.
Fleur de lis. 1623.
Trefoil. 1624.
Fleur de lis.—℞ trefoil.
Thistle.—℞ trefoil.

Gold.

All the mint marks above occur upon the gold coins.

Copper.

Thistle.
Trefoil.
Pellet.
Three fleurs de lis, two and one.
A.
Rose.
Plain cross.
Lozenge.
Lion.
Rose of dots.
St. George's cross surmounting St. Andrew's.
Diamond.
Coronet.
Bunch of grapes.
Annulet.
Triangle.
Key.
Fleur de lis.
Martlet.
Cinquefoil.
Lozenge surmounted by St. Andrew's cross.
Tun.
Tower.
Dagger.

Gold.

Thistle.
Rose.
Rose.—℞ thistle.

CHARLES I.

First Coinage. Square Shield.

Fleur de lis.
Long cross.

Second Coinage. Bust in Robes.

Fleur de lis. 1625.

Cross on two steps.
Castle.
Blackamoor's head.
Anchor.
Helmet.
Long cross.
Heart.
Feathers.
Full-blown rose.
Anchor, in the middle of legend. ℞ an anchor.
No mint mark on obv.; a rose on reverse.

Third Coinage. Long Bust.

Long cross. 1626.
Blackamoor's head. 1626, 7.
Castle. 1627.
Anchor. 1628.
Heart. 1629, 30.
Fleur de lis. 1630.
St. George. 1630.
Harp.
Portcullis.
Bell.
Crown.
Triangle.
Star of six points.
Triangle within a circle.
P. within two semi-circles.
R. within two semi-circles.
Eye.
Full-blown rose.
Triangle within two semi-circles.—℞ P. within two semi-circles.

Fourth Coinage. Oval Shield.

Feathers. 1630.
Rose. 1631.

Fifth Coinage. Short Bust.

Harp. 1632.
Portcullis. 1633.

Sixth Coinage.

Bell. 1634.
Crown. 1635.
Tun. 1636.

Seventh Coinage.

Tun. 1638.
Anchor. 1638.
Triangle or delta. 1639.
Star. 1640.
Triangle in a circle. 1641.
P. within two semi-circles. 1643.
R. within two semi-circles. 1644.
Eye. 1645.
Sun. 1645.
Sceptre. 1646.
Bugle horn.

Briot's Works.

Anchor.
Rose.
Anchor and small star.
Anemone flower and small B.
Small B.
Anemone flower and small B.—℞ small B.

Aberistwith Mint.

Open book.
Fleur de lis.
Crown.
Cross.

York Mint.

Lion.
Rose.
Fleur de lis.—℞ lion.

Oxford Mint.

Fleur de lis. 1644, 5, 6.
Trefoil. 1644.
B. and R. in a cypher. 1643, 4, 5.
A. 1645.
B. 1646.
Open book.
Rose.

SECTION IV.

ANGLO-GALLIC COINS.

ANGLO-GALLIC COINS.

THE series of Anglo-Gallic coins, or coins of our English princes struck in their French territories, though not extensive, is of great interest, and some pieces are extremely rare. On this account they are not collected by many persons, who despair of forming anything like a perfect series, and content themselves with a few pieces as specimens. In England, they appear to have been first treated of by Ducarel, in 1757, and afterwards by Snelling, in 1769. Some plates were also executed at the cost of Sir Charles Frederick, who was himself a collector of these coins; but these, as well as the before-mentioned works, are so inaccurate, that they serve only to embarrass and mislead those who may refer to them.

In 1826, a description of the Anglo-Gallic coins in the British Museum was drawn up by Mr. Edward Hawkins, and printed by order of the Trustees. This work is illustrated by beautiful plates, and is a valuable book of reference to the collector of these interesting coins.

In 1830, another work appeared, under the title of "Illustrations of the Anglo-French Coinage." This is also enriched by engravings of much beauty and fidelity. The author of this volume was for many years an indefatigable collector, and left no means untried to perfect his valuable cabinet, travelling through those provinces of France which had once been in possession of the English, and frequently enriching his collection by the acquisition of some rare piece previously unknown to the numismatists of England and the continent.[1] This gentleman, notwithstanding his care and diligence, has, however, ventured to assert, that particular coins which escaped

---

[1] The whole collection is about to be brought to the hammer.

his researches do not exist, while certain pieces, of which he could obtain no authentic account, have come to light since the publication of his elegant work: the list which follows is therefore a more extensive one than has ever yet been published, several new pieces appearing for the first time.

It should be remarked that several Anglo-Gallic coins, which were of great rarity a few years since, are much less so now; especially the Poitou penny of Richard I., a considerable number having been recently discovered in France.

It may be as well to observe, that the earliest Anglo-Gallic coin is of Henry II., and that those given by Ducarel cannot be classed with this series, having been struck before the Norman conquest. That engraved in Plate VI. of Ducarel's work is more than suspected to be a modern forgery. The coins of Henry II. must have been struck previous to the year 1168, in which Aquitaine was given by that monarch to his son, Richard Cœur de Lion. This prince is said by Le Blanc to have coined money in Normandy, Tours, Anjou, and Maine, but only some of these are at present known.[1] His Aquitaine penny has descended to us, and is a scarce coin. Some of them bear his name without the title of king, from which circumstance it is conjectured they were struck previous to his accession to the crown of England. It has been supposed that John, his successor, did not coin money in France; but, as hereafter noticed, there appear some grounds for believing that he did.

Of Henry the Third no Anglo-Gallic coins are known, although an order dated in his twelfth year directs the Seneschal of Gascogny to coin his money of Bordeaux of the same weight and fineness as that of Tours. The piece given by Ducarel,[2] Duby,[3] and Ruding,[4] is suspected to belong to Henry the Fourth.

The lion passant guardant occurs on the coins of Edward the First. This animal was the heraldic bearing of Aquitaine,

---

[1] See page 372. [2] Plate XIII. fig. 4.
[3] Pl. XXXVII. fig. 10. [4] Supp. Pt. II. Pl. X. fig. 10.

and was incorporated by Henry the Second with two lions passant guardant, the arms of Normandy, thus forming the coat since borne by the kings of England.

Edward the Third was the first English monarch who coined *gold* in his French territories. The denominations are the *guiennois, leopard, chaise, and mouton*. Mr. Hawkins, in his "*Description of the Anglo-Gallic coins in the British Museum*," observes, in reference to the name and type of the "leopard," that modern heralds do not admit the explanation of Nisbet, who says that the distinction between a lion and a leopard depends upon the position of the animal, and that Edward the Third is styled upon his monument in Westminster Abbey "*Invictus pardus.*" With respect to the term *chaise*, it was given because the prince is seated on a chair of state, without attending to the circumstance of his holding a shield (*escu*), or of his not doing so, as on the coins of Edward the Black Prince. The *mouton* was first struck by Louis IX. of France, and was named, from its type of the holy lamb, *aignel*, afterwards changed to *mouton*. The *guiennois* is supposed to have received its name from the country in which it was struck. Edward the Black Prince coined both gold and silver, which is interesting from the circumstance of its bearing an attempt at his portrait: at any rate the costume, arms, and decorations are those of the time. The denominations of this gold coinage are the guiennois, leopard, chaise, hardi, and pavilion. The demi-chaise is also given by Duby, and we should be disposed to question its authenticity, if we were not aware that the existence of the guiennois of this prince was doubted by the author of the "*Illustrations of the Anglo-French Coinage*," &c., and that a specimen has since been procured for the collection of the British Museum.

Henry, duke of Lancaster, the grandfather of Henry the Fourth, as a reward for the services rendered by the capture of Bergerac, in Guienne, had the city and castle given to him and his heirs by Edward the Third, with the privilege of striking money. The two pieces hereafter described are erroneously given by Ruding to Henry IV. Richard the Second struck gold and silver of the denominations noticed in the list which follows. Of his successor, as well as of Henry VI., there are gold and silver coins.

It may be here observed that the Calais groats and their divisions with the name of Henry, are not with certainty appropriated rightly to the three monarchs of that name. In type, weight, and standard, they agree with the coins of the same denomination struck in England.

The last of the series of Anglo-Gallic coins, are the Tournay groats of Henry the Eighth. It does not appear that among the many rare and singular pieces obtained by the author of the "*Illustrations of the Anglo-French Coinage*" on the Continent, he procured a single piece of this coinage, although one type is not of great rarity.

ANGLO-GALLIC COINS.

HENRY THE SECOND.

DENIER.—R.6.

1. *Obv.*—+HENRICVS REX. A plain cross, reaching to the inner circle.

   ℞—AQVITANIE. In four lines across the field; the last letter between two annulets.[1]

HALF-DENIER.—R.8.

2. *Obv.*—+ENRICVS. A plain cross, reaching to the inner circle; in the first and fourth quarter, an annulet.

   ℞—Ꝏ. REX +, in three lines across the field.

ALEONOR.

DENIER.—R.5.

1. *Obv.*—+DVCISIA. In the field, Ꝏ. Λ. perpendicularly; on each side, a cross patée.

   ℞—+AQVITANIE. In the centre, a plain cross, reaching to the inner circle.

HALF-DENIER.—R.8.

2. Same legends and type. (*Cabinet of Mr. J. D. Cuff.*)

There is a coin of Aleonor, on which her name occurs jointly with that of her first husband, Louis, king of France; but this is, of course, not ranged with the series of Anglo-Gallic coins.

---

[1] The author of the "*Illustrations of the Anglo-French Coinage,*" gives a denier with this type, but differing from the above in weight and style of fabric, and conjectures that it may have been struck by the son of Henry while master of Bordeaux.

RICHARD THE FIRST.

DENIER.—R.2.

1. *Obv.*—+RICARDVS ω. in four lines across the field.

℞—+AQVITANIE. In the centre, a plain cross, within the inner circle.

HALF-DENIER.—R.4.

2. Same legend and type on obverse and reverse as the denier.

DENIER.—R.1.

3. *Obv.*—+RICARDVS REX. A plain cross within the inner circle; in the third quarter, an annulet.

℞—PICTAVIENSIS, in three lines across the field.

The coins with an annulet on the reverse are more rare than those without it.

HALF-DENIER.—R.7.

4. Same as the denier.

There is also a coin termed the "Norman penny," with RODVMDVCO, for RODOMACO, on the reverse, which resembles the money of Aleonor; and another, with EXELDVNI for Issoudun. They are both of the first rarity, and are assigned to this king.

JOHN.

The author of the "*Illustrations of the Anglo-French Coinage*" observes, that no Anglo French coins of this prince and of Henry III. are preserved, and that "it does not appear that the first ever struck money." It would seem, however, from an entry on the patent roll of the 17th John, A.D. 1215, that it is probable he coined money in Poictou. Emerius was an hereditary moneyer there, and had the right of coinage in Poictou confirmed to him.[1] In a charter, granted by Henry III. in 1226, to Hugh, viscount of Thouars, mention is made of Monetæ Pictaviæ ut quod æqualiter currat in Pictaviâ cum nostrâ.

EDWARD I.

(*As Prince.*)

LION. BILLON.—R.2.

1. *Obv.*—EDWARD' FILI' A lion passant guardant, to the right.

℞—H. REGIS ANGLIE. In the field, a cross patée, reaching to the inner circle.

HALF-LION. BILLON.—R.6.

2. Similar types and legend.

The first of these coins was erroneously given, by the late Mr. Taylor Combe, to Edward, the Black Prince. Mr. Hawkins modestly defers to this opinion, in opposition to his own judgment, which rightly assigned it to the first Edward.[2]

---

[1] See a notice, by Sir Henry Ellis, Numismatic Journal, Vol. II. p. 254.

[2] Description of the Anglo-Gallic Coins in the British Museum, 4to. 1826, printed by order of the Trustees.

(*As King.*)

LION. BILLON.—R.6.

1. *Obv.*—EDVVARDVS REX. A lion passant, as on the preceding coins.

℞—DVX. AQVITANIE. A cross patée.

HALF-LION. BILLON.—R.8.

2. Similar types and legends.

LION. BILLON.—R.3.

3. *Obv.*—EDVARDVS REX. The field consisting of three divisions: the first having within it a lion passant; the second, the letters AGL.; and the last, the letter E.

℞—DVX. AGIT. BVRD.[1] A cross patée, reaching to the inner circle; in the first quarter, the letter E.

LION. BILLON.—R.3.

4. A coin with similar types, but with a G in the first quarter of the cross on the reverse.[2]

LION. BILLON.—R.3.

5. Another with "a rose of six leaves" in the third division of the field of the obverse.

LION. BILLON.—R.3.

6. Another with the letter G in the first division, and E in the third, and the addition of a small cross between the letters A and N in *Agitanie*.

PONTHIEU PENNY.—R.4.

7. *Obv.*—+EDOARDVS REX. A cross patée, reaching to the inner circle; an annulet in the first and fourth quarter.

℞—MONETA PONTI, in two lines across the field, which is divided into four compartments; above and below, a cross saltier between two annulets.

The author of the "Illustrations" says he is acquainted with but three of these rare coins. Two are in his own collection, and the third is in the French cabinet. More are now known.

HALFPENNY.—R.8.

8. Similar types and legends.

---

[1] For Burdegale—Bourdeaux.

[2] Supposed by the author of the "Illustrations" to be intended for "Guessin, a castle near Bayonne, where Edward the First had a mint," p. 59.

EDWARD I. II. III.

GROS. BILLON—R.8.

1. EDOVARDVS REX. A cross patée, extending through the inner legend to the second of three concentric circles; in the outer circle +BNDICTV : SIT : NOME : DNI : NRI : DEI :

℟—+DVX*AQVITANIE. A lion rampant guardant; the outer circle or border composed of twelve double arches, in each of which is a trefoil.

A rare piece, in the cabinet of the author of the "Illustrations of the Anglo-French Coinage," who observes, that it closely resembles a gros of Louis, the first or second, Count of Flanders.

EDWARD THE THIRD.

GOLD FLORIN.—R.8.

1. *Obv.*—IOHANNES B. The full length figure of Saint John the Baptist; the right arm extended, the left holding a staff, which is directed towards the small cross preceding the legend, at the beginning and end of which is a small open crown of the period.

℟—+DVX AQITANIE. In the field the flower of the white lily, or *fleur de lis*, as on the coins of Florence.

This piece is in the cabinet of the author of the "Illustrations," at pp. 1, 2, 3 of which will be found his reasons for assigning it to Edward the Third, to whom it probably belongs. The well-known type of the Florin was at this time copied by nearly all the states and petty princes of Europe; but in France, about the year 1364, it was no longer used, as, according to Leblanc, it was considered "derogatory to the dignity of the crown, being borrowed."

LEOPARD.—R.3. to R.8.[1]

2. *Obv.*—EDWARDVS : DEI : GRA : ANGLIE : FRANCIE : REX : A crowned lion (*leopardé*) guardant passant to the right, his recurved tail terminating in three points, within a compartment of ten arches; between the arches and the inner circle, nine quatrefoils and a star of five points (the presumed mint mark for Poictiers) a trefoil at each point.

℟—XPC : VINCIT : XPC : REGNAT : XPC : IMPERAT : An elaborately ornamented cross, within a compartment formed of four semi-circles and as many angles; in each angle of the cross, a lion passant guardant.

---

[1] Those weighing from sixty-five to seventy grains are R.8.

GUIENNOIS.—R.6.

3. *Obv.*—ED : D : GRA : REX : AGLE : DO : AQVITAIE. The king walking, to the right, completely armed, a drawn sword in his right hand, and a shield bearing the arms of France and England quarterly on his left arm, beneath a gothic porch ; near the pinnacles of the porch, to the right, the letter P. ; beneath the king's feet, two lions couchant guardant.

℞—GLIA : IN : EXELCIS : DEO : ET : IN : TERRA : PAX : HOBVS : A large ornamented cross, within a compartment formed by sixteen arches. In the angles of the cross, a *fleur de lis* and a lion passant guardant alternately.

ECU.—R.2.

4. *Obv.*—EDVVARDVS : DEI : GRA : AGL : Z : FRANCIE : REX : Within a compartment formed of twelve arches, the king seated in a gothic chair of state, crowned, a drawn sword in his right hand, his left resting on a shield semé with *fleurs de lis.*

℞—XPC : VINCIT : XPC : REGNAT : XPC : IMPERAT. Within a compartment formed by four arches, the points ending in strawberry leaves ; a cross filleted, trefoiled, with a quatrefoil in the centre, and another at the end of each limb of the cross.

MOUTON.—R.8.

5. *Obv.*—+AGN : DEI : QVI TOLL PECCA : MVNDI : MISERE : NOB. Within a compartment of fourteen arches, the holy lamb, the head encircled by the *nimbus* enclosing a cross, turned back towards a staff surmounted by a cross crosslet pierced in the centre, and having a banner of three tails ; beneath the feet of the lamb, EDVARD.

℞+XPC : VINCIT : XPC : REGNAT : XPC : IMPERAT. Within a compartment formed of four arches and as many angles ; a cross fluted and ornamented with a cinquefoil in the centre, the ends terminating in an acorn between two oak leaves ; a *fleur de lis* in each angle of the cross, and eight *fleurs de lis* in the outer angles formed by the compartment.

The author of the "Illustrations" (p. 9), supposes Snelling was in error in describing a mouton of Edward the Third, an opinion which is refuted by the existence of this piece in the French cabinet, politely communicated by M. de Longpérier.

GROS. BILLON.—R.8.

6. *Obv.*—ED' REX : ANGLIE, in the inner circle; in the outer circle, B . . . OMI : NRI : D : A cross Calvary, the lower limb passing to the outer legend.

℞—+DVX . AQITANIE, within a border of double arches and strawberry leaves; a large crown in the field; below the small cross preceding DVX, and on the T in AQITANIE, an annulet.

BILLON ———?—R.8.

7 *Obv.*—+ED' : REX. ANGLIE, in the inner circle; in the outer circle, +BNDICTV : SIT : NOME : DNI : NRI : DE : In the centre, a plain cross.

℞—DVX : AGITANIE, within a border of thirteen arches, with a strawberry leaf in each; in the centre, an object described as a building, resembling a church, with a spire placed between two towers; in the foreground, the ground plan.?

This piece, which is of base metal and of the size of the gros, is supposed not to have been current money, but a sort of ticket or pass. Another, somewhat similar, is given by the author of the "Illustrations."[1]

HALF GROS. SILVER.—R.5.

8. *Obv.*—ED' : REX : ANGL+IE,[2] in the inner circle; in the outer circle, BNDICTV : SIT : NOME : DNI : NRI : D : in the centre, a plain cross patée.

℞—DVX : AGITANIE, within a border of nine arches, having a strawberry leaf in each; in the centre, an ill-defined representation of a building; above, a lion passant guardant.

HALF GROS. SILVER—R.4.

9. *Obv.*—Same type and legend.

℞—DNS . HIBERNIE . A similar type to that of the reverse of the previous coin, but without the lion above the building.

This coin is considered by the possessor as a numismatic enigma. It is given by the author of the "Illustrations," who observes, that it could not have been struck in Ireland. We do not see why it should be supposed to have anything to do with that country: the type is in every respect Anglo-French, and the words DNS. HIBERNIE may be considered merely as a continuation of the style from the obverse side.

---

[1] Groats of this type have, however, since been discovered.

[2] The cross between the L and I, in ANGLIE, is supposed to be the private mark of the moneyer.

HALF GROS. SILVER.—R.8.

10. *Obv.*—EDVARD DEI : GRA : REX : ANGLE, within a compartment of ten arches; the side-faced half-length figure of the king, crowned with an open crown; in his right hand a drawn sword, resting against his shoulder.

℞—DNS. AQVITANIE in the inner circle; in the outer circle, . . . DO : ET : INT'RA : PAX. . . . . A plain cross patée at the end, reaching to the edge of the coin; in each angle, three pellets, as on his English money.

A very rare piece in the cabinet of the author of the "Illustrations," who supposes that the groat of this coinage has disappeared in consequence of its fineness.

LIGHT BILLON GROAT.—R.6.

11. *Obv.*—+ED : REX : ANGL+IE in the inner circle; in the outer circle, BNDICTV : SIT : NOME : DNI : NRI : D : in the centre, a plain cross patée, reaching to the inner circle, with a fourchée in one of the angles.

℞—DVX : AQITANIE, within an outer border of eleven compartments, each containing a strawberry leaf; in the centre, an open ducal crown above a lion passant guardant; a cinquefoil between his fore and hind legs.

HALF-GROAT. BILLON.—R.4.

12. *Obv.*—ED : REX : ANGL°IE, in the inner circle; in the outer circle, BNDICTV : SIT : NOME : DNI : NRI : D : A similar type to that of the former coin, with a *fleur de lis* in the angle of the cross.

℞—DVX. AQITANIE. A similar type to that of the former coin, but with a pellet beneath the lion.

There are varieties of this half-groat.

AQUITAINE STERLING, OR PENNY.—R.2.

13. *Obv.*—EDVARD' REX ANGL+. The royal bust, nearly full-faced, crowned, with an open crown fleury; on the breast, a lion passant guardant.

℞—DVX AQITANIE. A cross patée cleft at the extremities; between each cleft, a minute cross; in each angle of the cross, an open crown fleury.

There are others with slight variations from this type.

AQUITAINE HALFPENNY.—R.7.

14. Similar types and legends.

HALFPENNY. BILLON.—R.4.

15. *Obv.*—+ED' REX ANGLIE. In the centre, a lion passant guardant; below, a mullet.

℞—DVX AQITANIE. A plain cross, reaching to the inner circle; in the first quarter, an open crown.

DENIER. BILLON.—R.4.

16. *Obv.*—+ED': REX ∘ ANGLIE. In the field, a lion passant guardant; below, the letters M. B.', for "Moneta *Burdigalensis*" (Bordeaux); beneath the lion, a mullet of six blunt points.

℞—+DVX: A . . . BVRD. In the centre, a plain cross, reaching to the inner circle; in the second quarter, an open crown.

On another denier the crown is placed in the first quarter of the cross.

STERLING.—R.8.

17. *Obv.*—+CIVITAS BVRDEGALE. A lion's? head, full-faced, crowned with an open crown fleury.

℞—ED': REX: ANGLIE. A plain cross, reaching nearly to the edge of the coin; in the first and fourth quarter, three pellets; in the second quarter, the bud of the lily; in the third quarter, an open crown.

DOUBLE-DENIER. BILLON.—R.5.

18. *Obv.*—+EDVVARDVS REX. No inner circle. In the centre, a large open crown.

℞—+MONETA DVPLEX. "A cross calvary patée, imperfectly flurt barred at the lower limb, which extends through the inner circle almost to the edge of the coin." Ill. pl. iv. 33.

This piece is supposed by the author of the "Illustrations" to have been an imitation of the double tournois of Philip VI. king of France, p. 76.

DOUBLE-DENIER. BILLON.—R.4.

19. *Obv.*—+ED': REX: ANGLIE. In the centre, a lion passant guardant; above, A.; below, GI.

℞—+MONETA DVPLEX. A plain cross, with an open crown at the extremity of each limb.

DOUBLE-DENIER. BILLON.—R.3.

20. *Obv.*—+ED' REX ANGLIE. In the centre, a large open crown, resting on the head and tail of a lion passant guardant; beneath the lion, a mullet (or a rose of six leaves).

℞—+ MONETA DVPLEX. A plain cross, reaching to the inner circle; in the first and fourth quarter, an open crown.

LION. BILLON.—R.4.

21. *Obv.*—+ED' : REX : ANGLIE. In the centre, a lion couchant guardant, his tail ending in a large bush; beneath the lion, the letter B.

℞—DNS. AQITANIE. A plain cross, reaching to the inner circle.

LION. BILLON.—R.3.

22. *Obv.*—+ED' REX ANGLIE. A lion to the left, passant guardant; beneath, B.

℞—A similar type and legend to those of the preceding coin.

The B. beneath the lion indicates the place of mintage, which the author of the "Illustrations" conjectures to be Bayonne. There are varieties of these coins.

HALF-LION. BILLON.—R.5.

23. *Obv.*—∘+∘ED' REX ANGLIE. A plain cross, reaching to the inner circle.

℞—+DVX. AGITANIE. A lion passant guardant on a horizontal line, below which is the letter G., supposed to indicate the place of mintage, Guissen, a castle near Bayonne.

STERLING.—R.6.

24. *Obv.*—+EDVVART[1] REX ANGLIE. Half-length crowned bust of the king to the right. In his right hand a drawn sword, resting against his shoulder; his left hand raised in an admonitory attitude.

℞—DNS. AGITANIE. A plain cross, reaching almost to the edge of the coin; in each quarter, three pellets, as on the English money.

There are varieties of this coin.

DOUBLE-DENIER. SILVER.—R.8.

25. *Obv.*—+CIVITAS BVRDEGALE. Crowned bust of the king, to the left; on each side, an open crown fleury.

℞—ED' REX ANGLIE. A plain cross, reaching to the edge of the coin. In the first and fourth quarters, three pellets; in the second and third, an open crown.

---

[1] The T. is supposed to stand for *Tertius;* but this is mere conjecture. It is much more likely to be the blunder of a foreign moneyer but imperfectly acquainted with our language.

DENIER. BILLON.—R.7.

26. *Obv.*—+EDWARDVS REX. A plain cross, reaching to the inner circle; an annulet in each quarter.

℞—MONETA POTIVI, in two lines across the field; between them, a lion passant guardant on a compartment; above the word "Moneta," a cross patée; between two annulets, and below the word POTIVI, three annulets, the centre one being larger than the others.

GROAT OF CALAIS.—R.3.

27. *Obv.*—+EDWARD⁝DEI⁝G⁝REX⁝ANGL⁝DNS⁝HYB. ∘S° AQT. The king's head, full-faced, as on his English groats, within a compartment of nine arches, each terminating in a trefoil, except that over the neck, which has an annulet.

℞—+POSVI ⁑ DEVM ⁑ ADIVTOREM ⁑ MEV.—VILLA · CALESIE, in two concentric circles. A plain cross, reaching to the edge of the coin; in each quarter, three pellets.

HALF-GROAT.—R.6.

28. *Obv.*—+EDWARDVS⁝REX⁝ANGL⁝DNS⁝HYB. A similar type to that of the preceding coin.

℞—+POSVI ⁑ DEVM ⁑ADIVTORE ⁑ MEV —VILLA · CALESIE, in two circles. Type same as the preceding.

PENNY OF CALAIS.—R.8.

29. *Obv.*—+EDWARD ⁝ ANGL ⁝ R ⁝ DNS ⁝ HYB. The king's head, full-faced, crowned as on his English coins.

℞—VILLA ∘ CALISIE. A plain cross, reaching to the edge of the coin, with three pellets in each angle, as on his English coins.

EDWARD THE BLACK PRINCE.

HARDI.[1] GOLD.—R.4.

1. *Obv.*—ED : PO : GNS : REGIS : ANGLI : PNS : AQVITA : Within a compartment, formed of twelve small arches, the three-quarter length figure of the prince; the ducal mantle on his shoulders, and his head crowned by a fillet of roses; in his right hand a drawn sword, to which he points with the fore-finger of his left.

---

[1] A name derived from a small coin struck by Philip l'Hardi, king of France, now represented by the *liard*, a corruption of the Gascon "*li ardito*."

℞—AVXILIVM : MEVM : A : DOMINO : R : [1] A similar compartment to that of the obverse, within which a cross, the ends terminating in an acorn between two oak leaves; in the angles of the cross, a lily and lion passant guardant alternately.

LEOPARD. GOLD.—R.6.

2. *Obv.*—+ED : PMO : GNS : REGIS : ANGLIE : PNCEPS : AQITANIE : A lion léopardé, crowned, his tail terminating in three points, within a compartment of eleven arches, the points terminating in quatrefoils; between each of the arches and the inner circle, a quatrefoil.

℞—+XPC : VINCIT : XPC : REGNAT : XPC : IMPERAT : An elaborately ornamented cross, within a compartment formed of four arches and as many angles; between the compartment and the inner circle, eight quatrefoils. In each quarter of the cross, a lion passant guardant.

CHAISE. GOLD.—R.6.

3. *Obv.*—ED : PO : GNS : REGIS : PNS : AQITANIE. The prince, seated in a gothic chair of state, with four pinnacles. A fillet of roses round his head. In his right hand, the ducal bâton, surmounted by a lily; his left resting on his knee.

℞—DEVS : IVDEX : IVSTVS : FORTIS : PACIENS : B : [2] A type very similar to that of the preceding coin.

PAVILLION. GOLD.—R.2.

4. *Obv.*—+ED : PO : GNS : REG : ANGL : PNPS : AQIT : The prince, standing beneath a canopy, crowned with a fillet of roses, and a robe of state; in his right hand, a drawn sword, held perpendicularly, to which he points significantly with his left. Two lions couchant guardant at his feet. On each side of the prince, two ostrich's feathers.

℞—+DNS : AIVTO : PTECIO : ME : IIPO : SPAVIT : COR : MEVM : B : Within an ornamented compartment, a cross, in the centre of which is a figure of a diamond or lozenge, containing the letter E., each limb of the cross terminating in an acorn slip. In the first and fourth quarter, a *fleur de lis*; in second and third, a lion.

---

[1] Indicating the mint, *La Rochelle*.
[2] For Bayonne or Bordeaux.

GUIENNOIS.—R.8.

5. *Obv.*—ED. PGNS. REGIS ANGLIE P'INCPS AQITANIE. Typè very similar to the Guiennois of his father.

℞—GLIA : IN : EXCELCIS : DEO : ET : IN : TRA : PAX : HOMINIBVS. Type very similar to that of the Guiennois of his father; but with a B in the centre of the cross.

The author of the "Illustrations" doubts the existence of a Guiennois of this prince; but a fine specimen has recently been obtained for the British Museum.

GROAT. SILVER.—R.6 to R.8.

6. *Obv.*—+EDVVARDVS PRIMO GNS. REGIS T.[1] Half-length bust of the prince, to the right, within a compartment of twelve (or fourteen) arches; in his right hand, a drawn sword; his left arm extended, the fore-finger being raised, and the rest closed.

℞—+PRINCEPS AQITANIE, in the inner circle. In the outer circle, GLIA : IN : EXCELCIS : DEO : ET : IN : TRA : PAX : A cross patée, reaching to the edge of the coin, with three pellets in each quarter, as on the English coins of the period.

HALF-GROAT. SILVER.—C.

7. *Obv.*—+ED'. PO' GENIT' REGIS. ANGLIE. A similar type to that of the preceding.

℞—PRNCPS. AQVTAE, in the inner circle; in the outer circle, GLA IN E . . . . . TRA PAX : R. A similar type to that of the preceding.

The letter R. indicates the place of mintage, Rochelle. Others have an L., for Limoges, or P., for Poictiers. The varieties of these coins differ principally in the contractions of the legends.

HARDIT. SILVER.—C.

8. *Obv.*—ED. PO. GNS. REG. AGL. B. A half-length figure of the prince, full-faced, beneath a gothic arch. His head bound with a fillet, and the mantle on his shoulders; in his right hand a drawn sword, to which he points significantly with his right.

℞—PRNCPS. AQITANIE. A Greek cross patée coralino, reaching to the edge of the coin; in the first and fourth quarters, a *fleur de lis;* in the second and third, a lion passant guardant.

There are several varieties of these coins: the above is of the Bordeaux mint, as indicated by the letter B. at the end of the legend on the obverse.

---

[1] Supposed to indicate *Tarbes*. Others have R or A, for *Rochelle* and *Auch.*

Those of Poictiers have a small P between the letters Q and I in *Aquitan.* Those of Limoges have an L at the end of the legend of the obverse. Rochelle and Auch, or Aquae Tarbellicæ, as well as Tarbes, have also the initial letter at the end of the legend. Some are without the canopy, and are otherwise slightly distinguished in the legends.

STERLING.—R. 1.

9. *Obv.*—+ ⁝ ED' ⁝ PO ⁝ GNS ⁝ REGIS ⁝ B.[1] Half-length figure of the prince, to the right, *in profile ;* a drawn sword in his right hand, his left raised, and the fore-finger pointing upward.

℞— ⁝PRNCPS AQITAN. A plain cross and pellets, as on the English penny of this period.

BLACK MONEY.[2]—R. 6.

10. *Obv.*—+ED' : PRIMO : GENITVS. A lion couchant guardant, crowned, the tail elevated; beneath, the letter B, for Bordeaux.

℞—+PRINCEPS AQITANIE. A plain cross, reaching to the inner circle.

The varieties of this coin differ principally in the contractions of the legend.

BLACK MONEY.—R. 5. to R. 7.

11. *Obv.*—...D' PO : GN∘S : REGI NGL. The field of the coin divided into four quarters; in the first and fourth quarter, a *fleur de lis ;* in the second and third a lion passant guardant.

℞—. . . . NCPS. AQITANI. A plain cross, reaching to the inner circle.

Another specimen of this black money, given in the "Illustrations," has an L at the end of the obverse legend, for *Lectoure,* the place of mintage for this description of coin. They are very rarely found even in fair condition.

JOHN OF GHENT.

The money of this prince, the fourth son of Edward the Third, Duke of Lancaster and Aquitaine, King of Castille and Leon, is ranged with this series, though not strictly Anglo-Gallic coins. The right of coining money was granted to him by his father, and confirmed by his nephew, Richard the Second.

DENIER. ?—R. 8.

1. *Obv.*—IOHANIs REX, divided into two parts by the king's head, crowned and in profile, to the left; four roses appear

---

[1] For Bordeaux or Bayonne: others of this type have an L., for Limoges.

[2] *Of two parts silver and ten parts alloy.*

on the band of the crown, and a collar of roses hangs on the shoulders; the bust is beardless, and the hair is long and flowing.

℞—+CASTELLE. E : LEGIONIS : A building with three towers, the centre one being much higher than the others, above which are the letters P : S, and in the exergue B. (for *Pelegrinus Serius*, *Bayonnæ*, the mint-master of Bayonne).

Both sides of this rare coin are without the inner circle. See the "Illustrations of the Anglo-French Coinage," p. 107-8.

HENRY DUKE OF LANCASTER.

GROS. BILLON.—R.8.

1. *Obv.*—In the inner circle, +.EN ⁑ DNS : BRAGII. E[1]. In the outer circle, part of which is lost, ... NOME* DNI* ....; a plain cross reaching to the inner circle;

℞—·DVX LANCAIE· A building with two towers and a spire; in front, the ground plan?; above, a lion passant guardant; the whole within a border of circles, each enclosing a strawberry leaf.

GROS. BILLON.—R.8.

2. *Obv.*—+·EN : DNS : BRAGIIE*, in the inner circle; in the outer circle, +BNDI ... NOME . DNI.; a cross Calvary patée at the ends, the lower limb reaching through the inner circle, and a pellet beneath.

℞—LANCAI IЄ : DVX., in two lines across the field; beneath, a lion couchant guardant, crowned; the whole within a border of circles, each containing a strawberry leaf.

These coins are in the collection of the British Museum.

In the catalogue of the collection of the author of the "Illustrations," now announced for sale, are a groat and a half-groat, the former weighing 43½ grains, and having the legend HEN. COMES. LAN.—Reverse, DNS. BRAGAIRAC; the latter 28¼ grains, legend, EN. COMES. LA.—Reverse DNS. BRAGAIRA. The groat resembles that given above; the half-groat differs from the others.

---

[1] For *Henricus, Dominus Brageriaci*, Henry Lord of Bergerac.

RICHARD THE SECOND.

HARDIT. GOLD.—R.7.

1. *Obv.*—+RICARD' : D' : GRA : AGLE : FRACIE : RX : D' : A. A full-faced half-length figure of the king, within a compartment of nine arches, crowned with an open crown, and holding in his right hand a drawn sword perpendicularly, to which he points significantly with his left.

℞—+AVXILIVM : MEVM : A : DOMINO : B : within a similar compartment to that of the obverse; an ornamented cross, with an acorn between two oak-leaves at the extremity of each limb; in the first and fourth quarter, a lion passant guardant; in the second and third, a *fleur de lis*.

HALF-HARDIT. GOLD.—R.8.

2. *Obv.*—RICARD : RX : ANGLIE : FRACI. Crowned full-faced bust to the shoulders, within a compartment of nine arches.

℞—+AVXILIVM : MEVM : A : DNO : B. Type similar to that of the hardit, but with the *fleur de lis* in the first and fourth quarter, and the lion in the second and third.

The author of the " Illustrations" (pp. 9 and 19) doubts the existence of this rare piece, and suspects Snelling's account (p. 18) " is mere hearsay." The coin, however, is authentic, and is no doubt that which Snelling saw in 1756, in the French cabinet, and where it is now preserved. M. de Longpérier, to whom I am indebted for a tracing, observes that he is unable to account for this error, as the well-known politeness of M. Oberlin, forbids any suspicion that the information sought by the author of the " Illustrations" was purposely withheld.

DOUBLE-HARDIT. SILVER.—R.8.[1]

3. *Obv.*—RICARDVS : REX : ANGLIIE. Type similar to the hardit.

℞—FRANCIE : DNS : AQVITANIE. Type similar to the hardit.

---

[1] Cabinet of J. D. Cuff, Esq. This piece has only recently been brought to light, and was unknown to the author of the " Illustrations."

HARDIT.—R.4.

4. *Obv.*—RICARD RX : AGL. Beneath a gothic canopy, the half length full-faced figure of the king, crowned with an open crown fleury; in his right hand a drawn sword, to which he points with the forefinger of his left hand.

℞—FRACIE : DNS : AQITANE. A cross patée filleted, reaching to the edge of the coin (which has no inner circle on the reverse); in the first and fourth quarter, a lion passant guardant; in the second and third, a *fleur de lis*.

The varieties of this coin are insignificant.

DENIER. BILLON.—R.6.

5. *Obv.*—RICARD. RX. ANGLIE. FRACIE. The field of the coin divided into four quarters; in the first and fourth quarter, a *fleur de lis;* in the second and third, a lion passant guardant.

℞—DOMINVS. AQITANIE. A plain cross, reaching to the inner circle.

HENRY THE FOURTH.

GOLD HARDI.—R.8.

1. *Obv.*—+HENRIC : DEI : GRA : R : ANGLIE : F : D : AQVT. The king, nearly to the knees, crowned, and wearing a mantle, holding in his right hand a sword erect, to which he points with his left; on his right shoulder, a lion; on his left, a bear. (?)

℞—+ : AVXILIVM · MEVM · A · DOMINO : B : Cross with a quatrefoil in the centre; the limbs terminating in an acorn between two leaves of oak; in the angles, alternately, a lion passant guardant and a *fleur de lis*.

The author of the "Illustrations" considered this piece "imaginary" (p. 19). It exists in the French cabinet, and we have been favoured by M. de Longpérier with a drawing. See Ruding, Supp. Part ii. Pl. xiii. No. 9.

DENIER. BILLON.—R.6.

2. *Obv.*—ENRICVS : REX : ANGLE. The field of the coin divided into four quarters; in the first and fourth, a *fleur de lis;* in the second and third a lion passant guardant.

℞—DOMINVS : AQITANIE. A plain cross, reaching to the inner circle.

The varieties of this coin are unimportant.

HARDIT. SILVER.—R.2.

3. *Obv.*—ENRIC : R : ANGLE. Half-length figure of the king, crowned, in the same attitude as the figure on the hardit of the Black Prince.

℞—FRACIE . DNS : AQI. A plain open cross patée at the ends; in the first and fourth quarter, a lion passant guardant; in the second and third, a *fleur de lis,* at the stalk of which a pellet.

On other coins of this denomination the king stands beneath a gothic canopy.

HENRY THE FIFTH.

AIGNEL, or MOUTON.—R.8.

1. *Obv.*—+AGN : DEI : QVI : TOL : PECA : MVDI : MISE : NOBIS : Within a compartment of twelve arches, the holy lamb, the head radiated, the rays bounded by a nimbus, turned backwards to a swallow-tailed banner, the staff of which is surmounted by a cross crosslet, pierced in the centre; on one side the staff, HF, on the other RX (*Henricus Francorum Rex*).

℞+XPS : VINCIT : XPS : REGNAT : XPS : IMPERAT : Within a compartment of four arches and as many salient angles, an ornamented cross, the extremities having a trefoil between two leaves; in the first and fourth quarters, a *fleur de lis;* in the second and third, a lion passant guardant; on the outside of the compartment, eight *fleurs de lis.*

SALUTE.—R.7.

2. *Obv.*—+HENR : DEI : GRA : REX : ANGL : HERES : FRANCI : A shield bearing the arms of France and England quarterly, and surmounted by a large open crown; on the sinister side, the Virgin Mary, full-faced, with the nimbus encircling her head, and with her arms extended; on the dexter side, an angel in profile; above the crown which surmounts the shield, a scroll, inscribed AVE, and in the upper part of the field, nine rays.

℞—+XPC : VINCIT : XPC : REGNAT : XPC : IMPERAT : within a compartment of ten arches, the points ending in *fleurs de lis;* a cross calvary between a *fleur de lis* and a lion passant guardant; beneath the foot of the cross, the letter H.

ROUEN GROS.—R.3.

3. *Obv.*—+HENRICVS : FRANCORV : REX : Three *fleurs de lis,* "two and one," surmounted by a large open crown; between the two first, a pellet.

℞+SIT : NOME : DNI : BENEDICT. A plain cross patée; at the extremity of each limb, a *fleur de lis;* in the first quarter a crescent, surmounted by an open crown; in the fourth, a lion passant guardant.

4. A similar type, but with two lions supporting the large open crown, and with an H in the centre of the cross on the reverse.[1] This, instead of a pellet between the three *fleurs de lis,* has an annulet above the N in *benedictum.*

ROUEN GROS. BILLON.—R.3.

5. Another with H : REX : ANGLIE Z HERES FRANCIE, with an annulet under the first letter, and another annulet below the I in SIT.

LION GROS. BILLON.—C.

6. *Obv.* +H : REX : ANGL : HERES : FRANC : A crowned lion passant guardant to the left; above, a *fleur de lis;* a pellet under the first H.

℞ +SIT : NOME : DNI : BENEDICTV : A plain cross patée, reaching to the inner circle; in each angle, a trefoil; in the centre of the cross, the letter H; a pellet under the S in SIT.

LION GROS. SILVER.—R.8.

7. *Obv.* Same legend as No. 6. A crowned lion passant guardant to the left; above, two *fleurs de lis,* surmounted by a large open crown; between them a pellet; and below the lion, another *fleur de lis.*

℞—+SIT : NOMEN : DOMINI : BENEDICTVM : An ornamented cross fleury, with a compartment in the centre containing the letter H.

GROS BLANC. BILLON.—R.6.

8. *After a flaming star,* FRANCORVM : ET : ANGLIE : REX : and in the field, HERICVS, above two shields side by side, the first charged with the arms of France;

---

[1] By an ordonnance dated Gisors, September 25, 1419, this king directs that all his gold, silver, and billon money shall be distinguished by the letter H in the centre of the cross on the reverse. A *mouton* in the British Museum is without this letter; and is, therefore, supposed by Mr. Hawkins to have been struck prior to this date.

the second with the arms of France and England quarterly; the inner circle forming the outside edge of the shield.

℞—After a flaming star, SIT NOMEN : DNI : BENEDICTVM. A cross calvary between a *fleur de lis* and a lion, the top of the cross reaching to the inner circle; across the field, at the foot of the cross, HERICVS, with a line drawn beneath.

This gros is assigned to Henry V., and is supposed to have been struck by that king at Rouen.

HENRY THE SIXTH.

SALUTE. GOLD.—C. to R.4.

1. *Obv.*—HENRICVS :. DEI : GRA : FRA'CORV : Z : AGLIE : REX. A similar type to that of the salute of Henry Vth.

℞—Legend and type similar to the salute of Henry Vth.

The mint marks of the salutes of this king, in the collection of the British Museum, are a lion, a crown, a crown of thorns, and a *fleur de lis*. The author of the "Illustrations" has salutes with the mint marks of a star of six points, and the holy lamb.

ANGELOT. GOLD.—R.6.

2. After a small open crown, HENRICVS : FRACORV : ET ANGLIE : REX. An angel, crowned with a chaplet of flowers, and with wings expanded, full-faced, behind, and supporting two shields, one bearing the arms of France, the other the arms of France and England quarterly.

℞—After a small open crown, XPC : VINCIT : XPC : REGNAT : XPC : IMPERAT : in the field a cross calvary between a *fleur de lis* and a lion passant guardant.

GROS BLANC. BILLON.—C.

3. *Obv.*—After a lion passant guardant, to the left, FRANCORVM : ET : ANGLIE : REX : and across the field, HĒRICVS, above the two shields, as on that of Henry Vth.

℞—A similar type to that of the gros, attributed to Henry the Fifth, but with a lion passant guardant preceding the legend.

There are varieties of this gros.

PETIT BLANC.—R.3.

4. *Obv.*—After a lion passant guardant, HENRICVS REX. The shields of France and England, the outer edges extending over the inner circle.

℞—After a lion passant guardant, SIT : NOME : DNI : BENEDICTV. In the field, a cross calvary between the letters H. R.

DENIER. BILLON.—R.7.

5. *Obv.*—FRACORV. Z AGL. REX. In the field, HERI, surmounted by a large crown; below, a *fleur de lis* and a lion passant guardant.

℞—After an open crown, PARISIVS · CIVIS. A plain cross patée, with a *fleur de lis* at the extremity of each limb.

DENIER TOURNOIS. BILLON.—R.4.

6. *Obv.*—After a cross moline, HENRICVS REX. In the field, a *fleur de lis* and a lion passant guardant.

℞—After a cross moline pierced, TVRONVS. FRANCIE. A plain cross patée, reaching to the inner circle.

FARTHING. BILLON.—R.8.

7. *Obv.*—HENRICVS REX, after a large cross, which extends almost to the centre of the field; below, a lion passant guardant.

℞—OBOLVS CIVIS, after a large cross, which, like that of the obverse, reaches almost to the centre of the field, and touches the upper part of a *fleur de lis*, the base of which encroaches upon the legendary circle; a pellet beneath the right limb of the lis.

HENRY IV., V., VI.

GROAT C.

1. *Obv.*—HENRIC' * DI' * GRA' * REX * ANGL' * Z * FRANC. The king's head, crowned and full-faced, as on the English groats of the period; an annulet on each side of the neck.

℞—POSVI ∘ DEVM ⁑ ADIVTORE' * MEVM—VILLA ⁑ CALISIE ⁑. A similar type to that of the English groat of the period, but with an annulet conjoining the pellets in the second and third quarter.

The half-groat, penny, halfpenny, and farthing of this coinage are of similar type and character as the preceding, the legends on the smaller pieces being of course contracted. Some are without the annulets on each side the bust, and also without the annulets in the second and third quarters of the cross on the reverse. They are all common, except the farthing, which is R.8.

PERKIN WARBECK?

GROS.—R.7.

1. *Obv.*—DOMINE * SALVVM * FAC REGEM ⁑. In the field, a shield charged with the arms of France and England quarterly, and surmounted by a large arched crown; on the dexter side of the crown, a *fleur de lis*, surmounted by a crown; on the sinister side, a rose, also surmounted by a crown; a lion passant guardant, as mint mark.

   ℞—MANI ⁑ TECHEL ⁑ PHARES ⁑ 1494 ⁑. Within a compartment of four large and four small arches, formed of three lines, the inner one being beaded, a *fleur de lis* and lion passant guardant; above, an arched crown; below, a rose; a lion passant guardant, for mint mark.

Folkes, in his *Table of English Silver Coins*, was the first to notice this piece. "We may further," says he, "take notice of a very uncommon and singular coin, charged with the royal arms, but without a name, &c. It is, by the make and size, a French *gros*, and is supposed to have been coined by the Duchess of Burgundy for Perkin Warbeck, when he set out to invade England." Mr. Hawkins observes, in his "Description of the Anglo-Gallic Coins in the British Museum," (p. 37), that "the legend of the reverse is taken from the denunciation against Belshazzar; and as it was originally directed against a monarch in possession of the throne, it was supposed that in the instance of this piece it pointed to King Henry the Seventh, and the date of 1494 indicates the then intended invasion, as the power by which he was to be removed. That this piece has reference to the circumstances of the country produced by the claims of Warbeck, is probable; it is also probable that it is a small medal, and not a coin. If a coin, it would surely have borne the name as well as the title of the king de jure or de facto, who issued them. If Henry struck them, they would have borne his usual titles; if the Pretender, he would assuredly have expressed his titles in terms at least as strong as those of the reigning monarch. The weaker the claim, the stronger would be the terms of its assertion."

HENRY THE EIGHTH.

TOURNAY GROAT.—R.8.

1. *Obv.*—HENRIC' 8. DI. GRA. FRANCIE : ET : ANGLIE : REX : A large shield, charged with the arms of France and England quarterly, and surmounted by a large arched crown; a *fleur de lis* on the dexter side, and a lion passant guardant on the left.

   ℞—CIVITAS TORNACENSIS, .1.5:1:3. A voided cross, extending to the edge of the coin, each limb crossed with three short lines, and a quartrefoil in the centre, within which is the letter ℌ; in the first and fourth quarter, a *fleur de lis;* in the second and third, a lion passant guardant.

TOURNAY GROAT.—R.2.

2. *Obv.*—HENRIC' x DI' x GRA' x REX x FRANC x Z x AGLIE x. Profile head with arched crown, to the right.

℞—CIVITAS ⁙ ⁙ TORNACENS. A cross patée extending nearly to the edge of the coin, over a shield charged with the arms of France and England quarterly. A crowned ꞇ preceding the legend, as a mint mark.

TOURNAY GROAT.—R.8.

3. *Obv.*—HENRIC. 8 DI. GRA. FRANC. Z. ANGLIE. R. Plain shield of arms crowned.

℞—CIVITAS TORNACENSIS. 1·5·1·3. Within a tressure of nine arches, a cross patée, extending to the edge of the coin; in the centre, a full-blown (guelder?) rose.

Vide Snelling's Coins of English Princes struck in France, Pl. 11, No. 27.

SECTION V.

IRISH AND SCOTCH COINS.

IRISH COINS.

Mr. Lindsay, in his recently published work,[1] has appropriated to the early Irish princes several rude coins, hitherto considered uncertain by English collectors; but as this gentleman has for many years past paid great attention to this subject, his appropriations are entitled to our consideration. From one of the appendices to his work, the following list is taken.

	A.D.		A.D.		
Ifars I.?	870	to	872.—	Penny ?—	R.3.
Anlaf IV.	962	to	981.	,,	R.8.
Sihtric III.	989	to	1029.	,,	R.3 to R.8.
Ifars II.	993	to	994.	,,	R.6 to R.8.
Anlaf V.?	1029	to	1034.	,,	R.8.
Sihtric IV.	1034	to	1041.	,,	R.3 to R.8.
Anlaf VI.	1041	to	1050.	,,	R.7.
Ifars III.	1051	to	1054.	,,	R.3 to R.8.

Uncertain; supposed to have been struck by Irish princes.—R.2. to R.8.

Ethelred		R.4 to R.7.
Cnut		R.8.
John, *as Lord of Ireland*.—	Penny (Dublin.)—R.4.[2]	
	Ditto (Waterford).—R.6.	
	Farthing (ditto).—R. 7.	
,, *as King* ,,	Penny (Dublin).—R.3 to R.4.	
	Ditto (Limerick).—R.4.	
	Ditto (Waterford).—R.8.	
	Halfpenny (Dublin).—R.4.	
	Ditto (Limerick).—R.7.	
	Farthing (ditto).—R.8.	

---

[1] "A View of the Coinage of Ireland, from the invasion of the Danes to the reign of George IV." Cork, 4to. 1839.

[2] The English princes appear to have coined in Dublin, Cork, Drogheda, Limerick, Trim, Waterford, Wexford, and Youghal.

HENRY III. . . .	Penny (Dublin ?).—R.2 to R.8.
	Halfpenny (ditto).—R.8.
EDWARD I. II. III. .	Penny (Dublin).—R.1 to R.8.
	Ditto, without triangle.—R.8.
	Ditto (Waterford).—R.1 to R.4.
	Ditto (Cork).—R.6.
	Halfpenny (Dublin).—R.3 to R.8.
	Ditto (Waterford).—R.4.
	Ditto (Cork).—R.8.
	Farthing (Dublin).—R.5.
	Ditto (Waterford).—R.5.
HENRY VI. . . .	Groat (ditto).—R.6.
	Penny (ditto).—R.7.
	Groat (Dublin).—R.4.
	Ditto (Waterford).—R.8.
	Penny (Dublin).—R.8.
EDWARD IV. . . .	Groat. ℞ cross.—R.7.
	Penny (Waterford).—R.8.
	Ditto (Dublin).—R.7.
	Ditto (Waterford).—R.8.
	Ditto (Dublin).—R.8.
	Groat. ℞ sun.—R.8.
	Penny, ditto.—R.8.
	Groat. Rose and sun.—R.6.
	Half-Groat, ditto.—R.7.
	Ditto (Trim).—R.8.
	Penny (Dublin).—R.8.
	Groat, ditto.—R.2.
	Ditto. Rose.—R.3.
	Ditto (Waterford).—R.3.
	Ditto (Trim).—R.4.
	Ditto (Drogheda).—R.4.
	Ditto. Rose.—R.5.
	Ditto (Limerick).—R.7.
	Ditto (Cork).—R.8.
	Ditto (Wexford).—R.8.
	Half-Groat (Dublin).—R.7.
	Ditto (Limerick).—R.8.
	Penny (Dublin w. head).—R.4.
	Ditto (Drogheda).—R.6.

EDWARD IV. (*continued*). Penny (Waterford).—R.7.
Ditto (Limerick).—R.8.
Halfpenny (Dublin).—R.4.
Ditto (Drogheda).—R.6.
Penny (Waterford).—R.7.
Ditto (Limerick).—R.8.
Halfpenny (Dublin).—R.8.
Groat. With three crowns.—R.1.
Ditto. EDWAR. &c.—R.4.
Ditto. DOMINVS on both sides.—R.3.
Ditto. With REX.—R.7.
Half-Groat (Dublin).—R.5.
Ditto. DOMINVS.—R.4.
Ditto. Arms of Kildare.—R.8.
Penny. Ditto.—R.7.
Farthing. Ditto.—R.8.
Patrick, two varieties.—R.8.
Brass. Three crowns.—R.8.
Ditto. King's head.—R.8.

RICHARD III. . . . Groat (Drogheda).—R.8.
Penny (ditto).—R.8.
Ditto (Waterford).—R.8.
Groat. Three crowns.—R.7.

HENRY VII. . . . . Groat. Without tressure.—R.4.
Ditto. With tressure.—R.7.
Ditto. Arched crown.—R.4.
Half-Groat Ditto.—R.8.
Penny. ꝧ crowned.—R.8.
Groat. Three crowns.—R.7.
Ditto (Waterford).—R.2.
Groat. REX ANGLIE.—R.3.
Ditto. DOMINVS HYB, on each side.—R.6.
Half-groat (Dublin).—R.6.
Ditto. REX ANGLIE.—R.6.
Penny.—R.8.

HENRY VIII. . . . . Groat.—R.1.
Ditto, with REX.—R.2.
Half-groat. H. A.[1]—R.2.

---

[1] These initials are for Henry and his queens.

HENRY VIII. (*continued*).	Half-groat. H. K.—R.7.
	Ditto. H. I.—R.8.
	Sixpence, full-face.—R.2.
	Threepence, ditto.—R.4.
	Three-halfpenny piece.—R.8.
	Three-farthing piece.—R.8.
EDWARD VI. . . .	No coins known.
MARY	Shilling.—R.6.
	Groat.—R.7.
	Half-groat.—R.8.
	Penny.—R.8.
PHILIP AND MARY .	Shilling.—R.4.
	Groat.—R.2.
ELIZABETH . . .	Base shilling, with head.—R.3.
	,, groat.—R.3.
	Fine shilling (three harps).—R.3.
	Groat (ditto).—R.6.
	Base shilling, without head.—R.3.
	,, sixpence.—R.3.
	,, threepence.—R.6.
	Penny (copper).—R.2.
	Halfpenny.—R.5.
JAMES I.	Shilling (1st coinage).—R.2.
	Ditto (2nd ditto).—R.1.
	Sixpence (1st ditto).—R.2.
	Ditto (2nd ditto).—R.1.
	Farthing.—R.2.
CHARLES I. . . .	Farthing.—R.1.
	Inchinquin crown.—R.4.
	Ditto, with Vs.—R.5.
	Half-crown, Inchinquin.—R.4.
	Ditto, with IIs. VId.—R.5.
	Shilling.—R.6.
	Ninepence.—R.8.
	Sixpence, with weight.—R.7.
	Ditto, annulets.—R.8.
	Groat.—R.7.
	Ditto, annulets.—R.8.
	Threepence, ditto.—R.8.
	Ormond crown.—R.2.

CHARLES I. (*continued*).	Half-crown.—R.2.
	Shilling.—R.2.
	Sixpence.—R.2.
	Groat.—R.4.
	Threepence.—R.5.
	Twopence.—R.5.
	Penny. ?[1]
	Rebel crown.—R.7.
	„ half-crown.—R.8.
CHARLES I.	St. Patrick's halfpenny.—R.6.
	Ditto farthing.—R.2.
	Cork shilling.—R.7.
	Ditto sixpence.—R.4.
	Ditto (brass).—R.8.
	Ditto (ditto square).—R.8.
	Youghal (square brass).—R.7.
COMMONWEALTH .	Cork farthing.—R.8.
CHARLES II. . . .	Crown.—R.7.
	Half-crown.—R.8.
	Copper Siege P.—R.8.
	Farthing.—R.4.
	Halfpenny.—R.1.
JAMES II.	Halfpenny, A.D. 1685 to A.D. 1688.—R.1.
„ *Gun Money.*[2]	Crown.—R.2.
	Half-crown.—R.1.
	Ditto, with various dates.—R.2. to R.8.
	Crown, Aug. 1689.—R.8.
	Ditto.—R.1.
	Brass halfpenny, 1690.—R.7.
	White metal crown.—R.7.
	„ groat.—R.8.
	„ penny.—R.6.
WILLIAM & MARY .	Halfpenny.—R.2.
WILLIAM III. . .	Halfpenny.—R.4.
ANNE	No coins.

[1] Mr. Lindsay quotes this coin, but it is not known to our collectors.

[2] The pieces termed "gun money" were principally struck from metal, the produce of old cannon, and are remarkable for their bearing the date, not only of the year, but also of the day and month. The reverses bear two sceptres in saltire, through a crown, between the letters I and R. Proofs exist, both in silver and gold, of these coins.

SCOTCH COINS.

ESTIMATE OF THE RARITY OF SCOTCH COINS FROM DAVID THE FIRST TO MARY.

For the estimations of these coins I am indebted to Mr. Cuff. It is a reproach to Scottish antiquaries that we have no work of recent date on the coins of that country. The volume of Cardonnel is so imperfect, and the plates are so execrably engraved, that little use can be made of them. Mr. Cuff has for some years past made collections in this series, and it is to be hoped that he may be induced to publish an account of such undescribed pieces as have come under his notice, or that he will hand his interleaved and annotated copies of Snelling and Cardonnel to some numismatist competent to undertake a work on Scotch coins. It may be proper to notice, that many of the pieces described in this list are distinguished merely by the names conventionally bestowed on them by collectors, the public acts in which they are mentioned being unknown to antiquaries.

Alexander I. .	Penny. ?
David I. . . .	Penny.—R.8. (Cab. of J. D. Cuff, Esq.)
Malcolm IV. .	Penny.—R.8.
William I. . .	Penny.—C. to R.6.
Alexander II. .	Penny.—R.5.
Alexander III.	Penny.—C. to R.6.
	Halfpenny.—R.2.
	Farthing.—R.6.
John Baliol . .	Penny.—C.
	Halfpenny.—R.2. to R.6.

The halfpenny with *four mullets* is R.8.

ROBERT I.	Penny.—R.2.
	Halfpenny.—R.3.
	Farthing.—R.6.
DAVID II. . . .	Noble.—R.8.
	Groat.—C.
	Half-groat.—R.1.
	Penny.—R.2.
	Halfpenny.—R.5.
	Farthing.—R.8.
EDWARD BALIOL.	No authentic coins.
ROBERT II. . .	Lion.—R.4. to R.8.
	St. Andrew.—R.6.
	Groat.—C.
	Half-groat.—R.2.
	Penny.—R.3.
	Farthing.—R.6.
ROBERT III. . .	St. Andrew.—R.2.
	Half St. Andrew.—R.8.
	Groat.—C.
	Half-groat.—R.3.
	Penny.—R.5.
	Halfpenny.—R.7.
JAMES I. . . .	St. Andrew.—R.4.
	Half St. Andrew.—R.7.
	Groat.—C. to R.4.
	Half-groat (not known).
	Penny (not known).
	Halfpenny (not known).
	Farthing (not known).
JAMES II. . . .	St. Andrew, side-face.—R.8.
	Lion.—C.
	Half-lion.—R.7.
	Groat.—R.2.
	Half-groat.—R.6.
	Penny.—R.6.
	Halfpenny (not known).
	Farthing (not known).
JAMES III.	Unicorn.—C.
	Half-unicorn.—R.2. to R.8.
	Groat.—C.

JAMES III. (*continued*). Half-groat.—R.4. to R.7.
Penny.—R.2.
Billon pieces.—R.1. to R.5.

JAMES IV. . . . Four-angel piece.—R.8. (British Museum.)
Unicorn.—R.7.
Half-unicorn (unknown).
St. Andrew.—R.8.
Half-St. Andrew.—R.8.
Rider.—R.2. to R.8.
Two-thirds of Rider.—R.8.
One-third ditto.—R.6.
Groat.—R.4.
Half-Groat.—R.6 to R.7.
Penny.—Uncertain.
Billon.—R.2.

JAMES V. . . . . Bonnet piece.[1]—R.2 to R.6.
Gold piece, with crowned portrait.—R.8.
Half-bonnet piece.—R.7.
Quarter-Bonnet piece.—R.7.
Gold piece.—St. Andrew's cross through a crown.—R.8.
Gold Ecu.—C.
Double Ecu.—R.8.
Groat.—C. to R.4.
Half-Groat.—R.4 to R.6.
Billon piece.—C. to R.3.

MARY . . . . . Ecu —R.1.
Lion.—R.2 to R.8.
Half-Lion.—R.3 to R.8.
Rial.—R.4.
Half-Rial.—R.7.
Testoon, without head.—C.
Half-Testoon, without head.—R.2 to R.4.
Testoon, with head, before her marriage.—R.6.
Half-Testoon, with head, before her marriage.—R.8.[2]

---

[1] So called from its bearing the profile bust of the king wearing his bonnet. These coins are of remarkably bold workmanship, and were probably executed by some French or Italian artist.

[2] This piece is described as Unique in the Trattle Catalogue, No. 1252.

MARY (*continued*).

Gold Rial of Francis and Mary, with the arms of France and Scotland impaled.—R.8.

Testoon, with heads of Francis and Mary face to face.—R.8.

Testoon, without their heads.—C.

Half-Testoon, without heads.—R.4.

Testoon, with her portrait.—R.4.

Half-Testoon, with portrait.—R.8.

Rial of Mary and Henry, with portraits.—R.8.

Rial of the same, without portraits.—R.1.

Two-thirds of the Rial, without portraits.—R.2.

One-third of Rial, without portraits.—R.4.

Rial of Mary, as widow, without portrait.—R.1.

Two-thirds Rial.—R.2.

One-third.—R.6.

Copper penny, without head.—R.4 to R.8.

Copper pieces, without head.—C.

Billon pieces, without head.—C. to R.3.

Billon of Francis and Mary.—C.

ABBREVIATIONS.

AV. . . . . Gold.
EL. . . . . Electrum.
Æ. . . . . Silver.
Æ. . . . . Copper or Brass.
POT. . . . . Potin.
BIL. . . . . Billon.

C. . . . . Common.
R.1. the lowest degree of rarity.
R.2. the next degree of rarity, and so on up to R.8., which denotes the highest degree.

Plate 1.

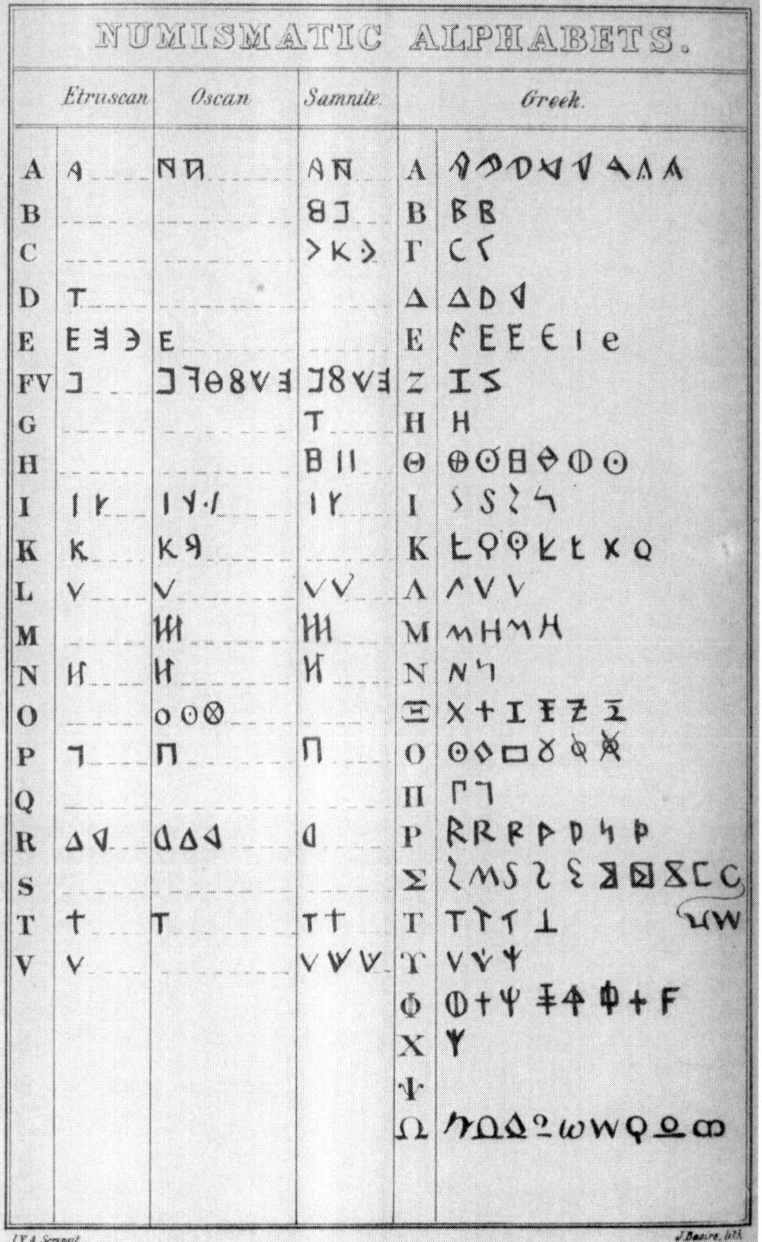

I.Y.A. Scripsit.

J. Basire, lith.

London. Taylor and Walton, Upper Gower Street.

Plate II.

NUMISMATIC ALPHABETS.

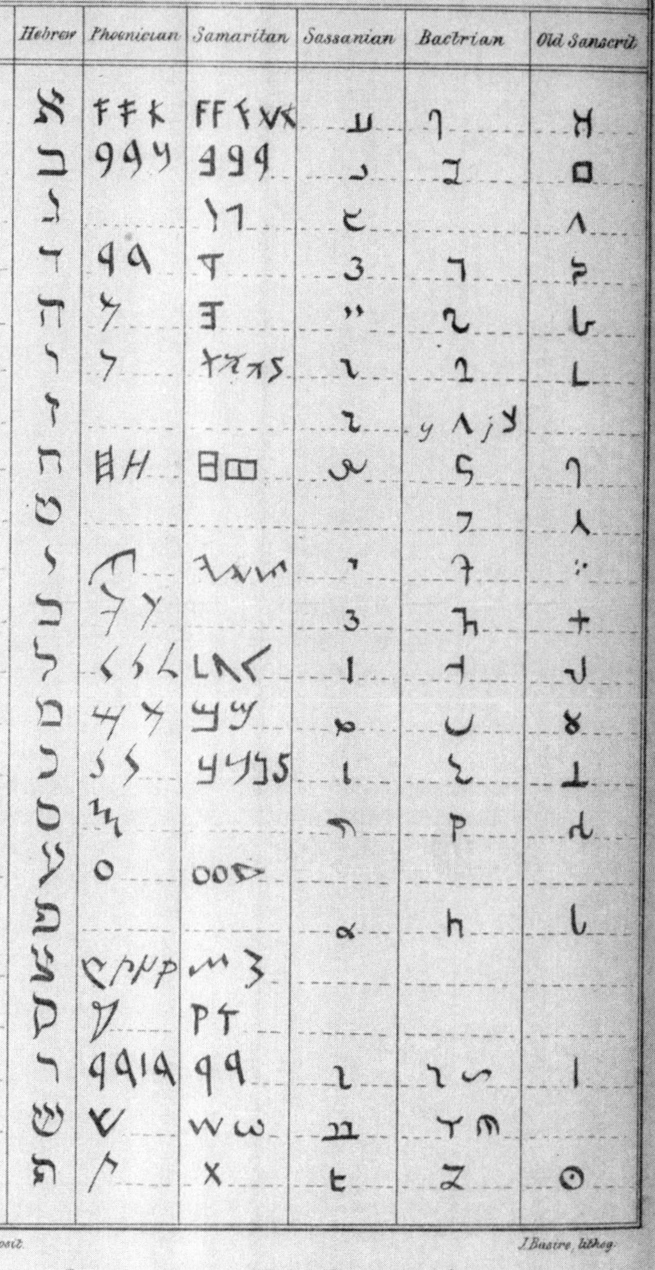

I.Y.A. scripsit. J.Basire, lithog.

London. Taylor and Walton, Upper Gower Street.

Plate III.

NUMISMATIC ALPHABETS.

ARCHAIC LEGENDS.

Examples of Legends on Early Greek Coins

ϘΡΟΤΟΝ. ΟꟼϘ		*Croton, Bruttiorum.*
RECINON		*Rhegium, Bruttiorum.*
ƧΙVVΤƧΙ8		*Phistelia, in Campania*
ΥΑꓘ		*Caulonia, Bruttiorum*
ΚVΜΑΙΟΝ		*Cumae in Campania*
ΑΚΡΑϹ / ƐΟΤИΑ	*(Boustrophedon)*	*Agrigentum in Sicily*
ΓΟΜΕƧDΑ		*Posidonia in Lucania*
HΙΠVVΥ. ΑЯƎΜΙΝ		*Himera in Sicily*
ƩΕ<ΕƩΤΑ		*Segesta in Sicily*
ΓΑΝΔΟƩΙƩ		*Pandosia in Bruttium*
ΙϽΟΑ⅃Ǝꟻ		*(Felathri) Volaterrae*
ƎDƎ†V†		*Tuder in Umbria*
ΕИΙΟИ / ƧƧƎΜ	*(Boustrophedon.)*	*Messana, Sicily*
ИΑꓘ. ΚΑИ		*Camars in Etruria*
ƧΝΙ⅃VΚΙ		*Iguvium in Umbria*
UƧ⅃Ǝꟻ		*Velia in Lucania*

J.Y.A. Scripsit — J. Basire. lith.

London. Taylor and Walton, Upper Gower Street.

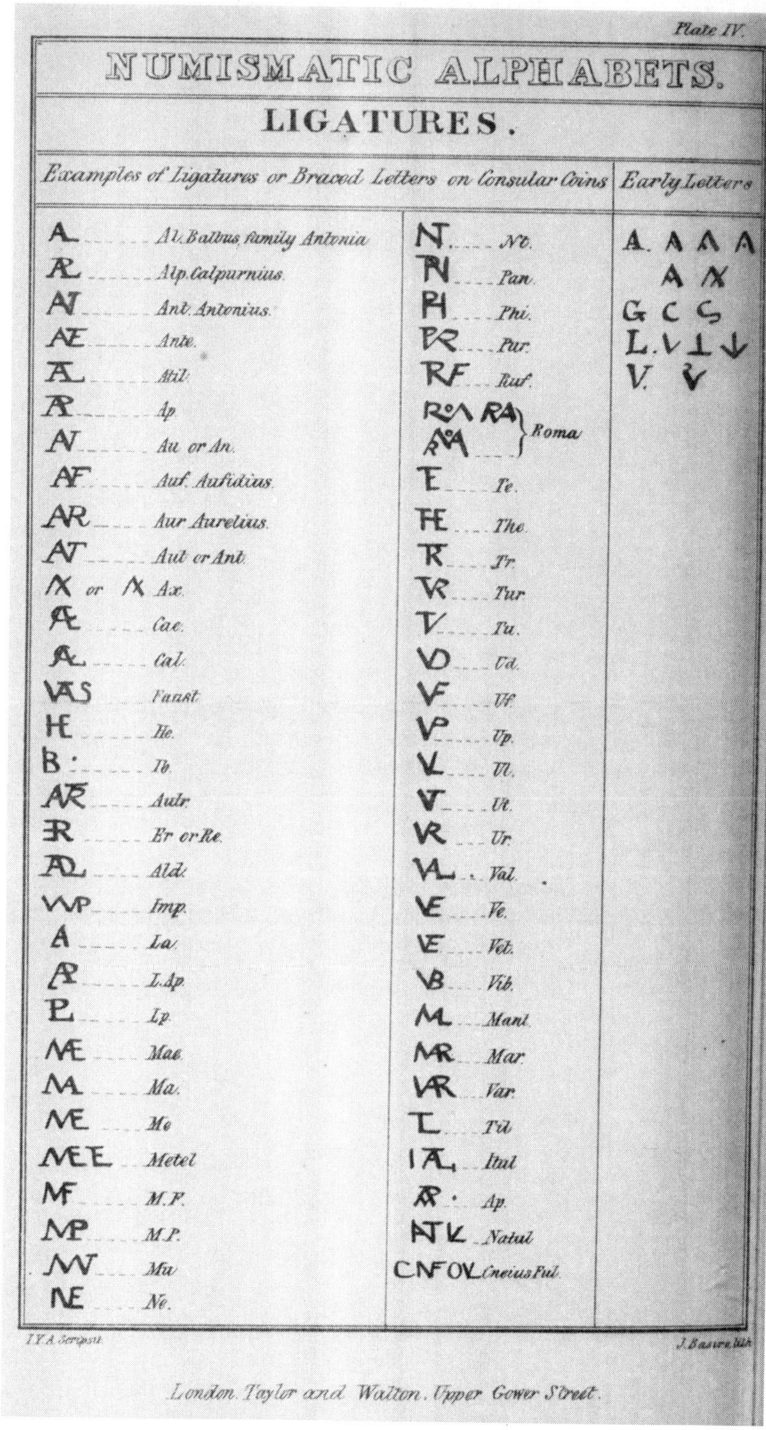
Plate IV.
NUMISMATIC ALPHABETS.
LIGATURES.
Examples of Ligatures or Braced Letters on Consular Coins
Early Letters
Al. Balbus, family Antonia
Alp. Calpurnius.
Ant. Antonius.
Ante.
Atil.
Ap.
Au or An.
Auf. Aufidius.
Aur. Aurelius.
Aut or Ant.
or
Ax.
Cae.
Cal.
Faust.
He.
Ib.
Audr.
Er or Re.
Ald.
Imp.
La.
L. Ap.
Lp.
Mae.
Ma.
Me
Metel
M.F.
M.P.
Mu
Ne.
Nt.
Pan.
Phi.
Pur.
Ruf.
Roma
Te.
The.
Tr.
Tur
Tu.
Ud.
Uf.
Up.
Ul.
Ut.
Ur.
Val.
Ve.
Vet.
Vib.
Mant.
Mar.
Var.
Til
Ital
Ap.
Natal
Cneius Ful.
I.Y.A. Scripsit.
J. Basire lith.
London. Taylor and Walton. Upper Gower Street.

DESCRIPTION OF THE PLATES.

PLATE I.

This plate contains the Etruscan, Oscan, Samnite, and early Greek alphabets, as they are found on coins.

PLATE II.

Contains the Phœnician, Samaritan, Sassanian, Bactrian, and old Sanscrit alphabets.

PLATE III.

Examples of legends in the early Greek character, as they appear on the coins of Sicily and Magna Græcia. Some of these are retrograde, others boustrophedon, or alternately right and left (see page 19). The limits of an elementary work, like the present, afford no room for observations in detail upon the various examples here given, but the legend which stands first, and which occurs on the coins of *Croton*, deserves especial notice. The *point* in the centre of the early character, *koph* (a letter which is perpetually found on the very common coins of Corinth, with the Pegasus), is also placed within the centre of both the omicrons. It is easy to account for the *omission* of portions of a letter in early inscriptions; but it is difficult to explain why these marks are thus used superfluously in the legends of coins which must be referred to a very ancient date, when, as is generally supposed by the learned, the use of points was not known. Nevertheless, that some such meaning is intended, may be conjectured from the fact, that a coin, in the collection of the late M. de Cadalvene, is inscribed Ξ⊙ИΑΧΛƎ⊐[1]

PLATE IV.

The names on consular coins are very frequently given in a contracted form, and several letters are often linked together, as represented in this plate; which contains every variety which has come under my notice, or that of my numismatic friends.

---

[1] Vide Recueil de Médailles Grecques, 4to. Paris, 1828. Par M. Dumersan.

PLATE V.

This plate contains examples of letters on Byzantine, Saxon, and English coins. In the first will be found that mixed character from which the second was in all probability derived. At foot are the contractions so frequently occurring on Byzantine and Saxon coins.

PLATE VI.[1]

TYPES OF AUTONOMOUS GREEK COINS.

1. Abdera.—2. Acanthus.—3. Achaia.—4. Aegina.—5. Aenus. —6. Aetolia.—7. Agrigentum.—8. Agrigentium.—9. Amisus (the parazonium).—10. Amphipolis.—11. Antioch.—12. Arcadia (Pan seated on a rock, on which are some of the letters of a magistrate's name, OΛYM).—13. Athens, early type.—14. Athens, more modern type.—15. Bœotia in genere.—16. Cales, a type found also on the coins of other Campanian cities.—17. Campania in genere. A common type of Neapolis.—18. Camarina.—19. Camarina.—20. Carthage.—21. Carthage.—22. Centuripa—bird perched on ploughshare.—23. Chalcis.—24.—Chalcis.—25. Chios.—26. Cnidus. —27. Cnossus (labyrinth).—28. Corinth.—29. Corcyra.—30. Croton. —31. Cyme.—32. Cyrene. Silphium. —33. Cyzicus.—34. Dyracchium, the gardens of Alcinous.—35. Ephesus.—36. Elis (thunderbolt).—37. Faleria.—38. Gelas.—39. Gortyna.—40. Gortyna.—41. Heraclea.—42. Histiæa.—43. Larissa.—44. Lita.—45. Lyttus. 46. Melita.—47. Messina.—48. Metapontum.—49. Methymnia. 50. Miletus.—51. Naxus.—52. Neapolis in Macedonia.—53. Opuntii. —54. Pantacapeum.—55. Pelinna.—56. Pergamus in Mysia.—57. Phocis in genere.—58. Posidonia.—59. Rhodes Insula.—60. Segesta.—61. Selge in Pisidia.—62. Selinus.—63. Seleucia.—64. Side in Pamphilia. — 65. Side. — 66. Sidon. — 67. Sinope in Paphlagonia. — 68. Sicyon. — 69. Smyrna. — 70. Stymphalus.—71. Syracuse.—72.—Syracuse.—73. Tarentum.—74. Tarentum.—75. Tenedos.—76. Thasus.—77. Tauromenium.—78. Tralles.—79. Velia.—80. Zacynthus.—81. Zancle.

---

[1] Plates VI. to XVII. inclusive are drawn and engraved by Mr. Ogg, to whom my acknowledgements are due for the pains he has taken to assist me in this respect, by examining various collections for specimens best suited for illustration, as well as for general attention not usually considered within the province of the artist. It should be mentioned that all the drawings have been made from actual coins.

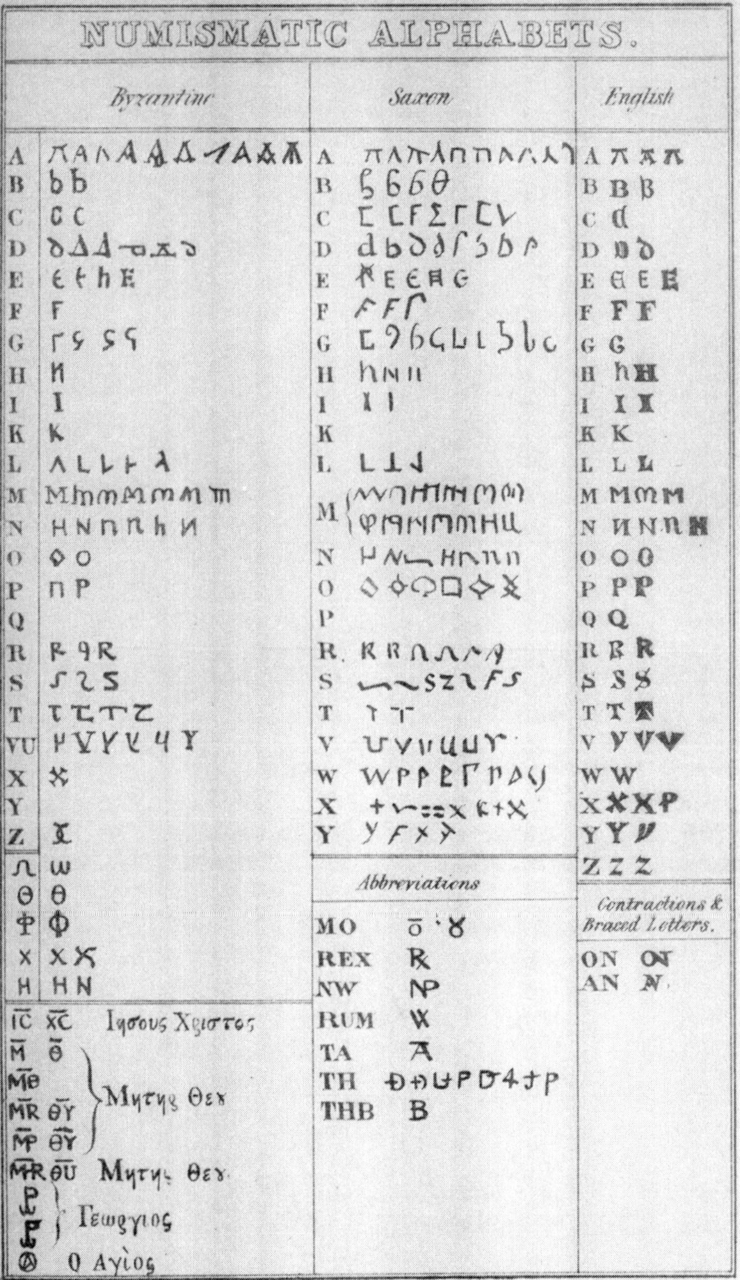

I. Y. A. Scripsit. J. Basire lith.

London. Taylor and Walton, Upper Gower Street.

Plate VI.

EXAMPLES OF GREEK AUTONOMOUS TYPES.

H.A. Ogg. — Bel et Sculp.

London, Taylor & Walton, Upper Gower Street.

EXAMPLES OF GREEK AUTONOMOUS & IMPERIAL TYPES.

H. A. Ogg. Del. et Sculp.

PLATE VII.

AUTONOMOUS TYPES CONTINUED.

82. Melita Insula.—83, 84, 85. Judæa in genere.—86. Rhodes. 87. Tyre.—88. Zacynthus.

TYPES OF IMPERIAL GREEK AND COLONIAL COINS.

1. A very common reverse of the small brass of Alexandria, of the age of Diocletian.—2. Antioch. The city personified seated on a rock, the Orontes figured swimming at her feet, the usual representation of a city on the banks of a river.—3. Ascalon. Astarte, standing on the prow of a galley, holding the Acrostolium, between an altar and a dove.—4. Beroea. BЄPOAIѠN. B. (*of the people of Beroea, year* 2), a common reverse of the coins of Trajan.—5. Berytus, a common reverse.—6. The same.—7. Byblus. Astarte, in a temple of peculiar structure, her foot on the prow of a vessel; before her, a Victory, placed on a pedestal, presenting a garland.—8. Another representation of the same deity in a different temple, also of Byblus.—9. Byzantium. A dolphin between two tunny fish.—10. Byzantium. The helmet of Byzas, the reputed founder of the city.—11. Cæsarea in Cappadocia. Mount Argæus placed on an altar, inscribed with the date.—12. Corinth. Bellerophon combating the Chimæra.—13. The usual reverse of the coins of the Roman Emperors struck at Antioch, Δ. Є. Δημαρχικῆς Ἐξουσίας, i.e. *Tribunitia Potestate*, and S. C. *Senatus Consulto*[1].—14. 15. Two different representations of the far-famed temple of Venus, on the coins of Cyprus.—16. Cyrrhestica. The common type of that city bearing the legend ΔΙΟC KATAIBATOY.—17. The head of Abgarus, king of Edessa, from the reverse of a coin of Gordian III.—18. Emerita, in Spain. The gate of the city inscribed AVGVSTA EMERITA.—19. Emisa. A representation of the stone called El Gabal, on which an eagle is standing.—20. Emisa. The same deity on an altar placed within a temple[2].—21. Ephesus. The usual representation of "the Great Diana."—22. Ierapolis. Cybele seated on a lion.—23. Macedonia. The Macedonian shield, the type of the province.—24. Nemausus. Crocodile changed to a palm tree,

---

[1] These coins are extremely common, except those of Otho, which are of the first rarity.

[2] Roman coins of Elagabalus also bear representations of this deity.

symbolical of the subjugation of Egypt, from an extremely common colonial coin, with the heads of Augustus and Agrippa.—25. Nisibi in Mesopotamia.—26. Perga in Pamphilia. The object worshipped as Diana Pergæa.—27. Samos. The deity known as the Samian Juno.—28. Seleucia. A representation of Jupiter as ZEYC KACIOC.—29. Sidon. Europa.—30. Tripolis, in Phœnicia.—31. Tyre. The representation of the anointed rocks.—32. Viminacium in Mœsia.—33. Zeugma in Commagene.

PLATE VIII.

PORTRAITS ON ROMAN COINS.

CONSULAR SERIES.

1. Balbus.
2. Caldus.
3. Sylla.
4. Brutus the Elder.
5. Ahenobarbus.
6. Ahala.
7. Postumius.
8. Ancus.
9. Quirinus.
10. Numonius.
11. Rufus.
12. Tatius.

IMPERIAL SERIES.

13. Pompey, from his denarius.
14. Julius Cæsar, from large brass.
15. The same, veiled head. Denarius.
16. Cn. Pompey, the son.
17. Sextus Pompey.
18. Marcus Brutus.
19. Lepidus.
20. Marc. Antony.
21. The same.
22. Cleopatra.
23. Lucius Antony. Denarius.
24. Augustus. Denarius.
25. The same. Large brass.
26. Agrippa. Middle brass.
27. Tiberius.
28. Drusus, Junior.
29. Drusus, Senior.
30. Germanicus.
31. Agrippina.
32. Caligula. Denarius.
33. Claudius. Large brass.
34. Agrippina the Younger.
35. Britannicus.
36. Nero. Youthful head.
37. Nero. Large brass.
38. Antonia.
39. Galba. Large brass.
40. Otho. Denarius.
41. Vitellius. Large brass.
42. Vitellius Pater. Silver.
43. Vespasian.
44. Domitilla.
45. Titus.
46. Domitian.
47. The same.
48. Julia Titi.
49. Domitia.
50. Nerva. Large brass.
51. Trajanus. Crowned head.
52. The same. Laureated.
53. Trajanus, the father. Denarius.
54. Plotina.
55. Marciana.
56. Matidia.
57. Hadrianus. Bare head. Gold.
58. The same. Laureated. Denarius.
59. The same. Crowned.
60. Sabina.
61. Lucius Aelius.
62. Antoninus Pius. Bare head.
63. The same. Laureated.
64. The same. Crowned.
65. Faustina, the Elder.

Plate VIII.

PORTRAITS ON ROMAN COINS.

PORTRAITS ON ROMAN COINS.

H. A. Ogg. Del. et Sculp.

66. Faustina, the Elder. Veiled.
67. Marcus Aurelius. Youthful head.
68. The same. Laureated.
69. Faustina, the Younger.
70. The same. Veiled head.
71. Lucius Verus.
72. Lucilla.
73. Commodus. Youthful head.
74. The same. Laureated.
75. The same. The head covered with the lion's skin.
76. Crispina.
77. Pertinax.
78. Didius Julianus.
79. Manlia Scantilla.
80. Didia Clara.
81. Pescennius Niger.
82. Clodius Albinus.
83. Septimius Severus.
84. Julia Domna.
85. Caracalla. Youthful head.
86. The same. Laureated.
87. The same. Crowned.
88. Plautilla.
89. Geta.
90. The same.

PLATE IX.

PORTRAITS ON ROMAN COINS.

91. Macrinus.
92. Diadumenianus.
93. Elagabalus. Laureated.
94. Elagabalus. Crowned.
95. Julia Paula.
96. Julia Aq. Severa.
97. Annia Faustina.
98. Julia Soaemias.
99. Julia Maesa.
100. Severus Alexander.
101. Barbia Orbiana.
102. Julia Mamaca.
103. Maximinus. Large brass.
104. Paulina. Large brass.
105. Maximus Cæsar. Large brass.
106. Gordianus Africanus, the Elder.
107. Gordianus Africanus, the Younger.
108. Balbinus.
109. Pupienus.
110. Gordianus III.
111. Tranquillina.
112. Philippus.
113. Philippus, the Younger.
114. Otacilia.
115. Trajanus Decius.
116. Etruscilla.
117. Herennius Etruscus.
118. Hostilianus.
119. Trebonianus Gallus.
120. Volusianus.
121. Aemilianus.
122. Cornelia Supera.
123. Valerianus.
124. Mariuiana.
125. Gallienus.
126. Salonina.
127. V. Saloninus.
128. Postumus.
129. The same.
130. Laelianus.
131. Victorinus.
132. Victorinus.
133. Marius.
134. Tetricus, the Younger.
135. Tetricus, the Elder.
136. Macrianus.
137. Quietus.
138. Claudius Gothicus.
139. The same. Crowned.
140. Quintillus.
141. Aurelianus.
142. The same.
143. Severina.
144. Vabalathus.
145. Tacitus.
146. Florianus.
147. Probus.
148. The same.
149. Carus.
150. Carinus.

151. Numerianus.
152. Magnia Urbica.
153. Nigrinianus.
154. Julianus Tyrannus. 3 B.
155. Diocletianus.
156. The same.
157. Maximianus Hercules. 3 B. Crowned.
158. The same. Laureated.
159. Carausius, from his gold coin in the British Museum.
160. The same. 3 B.
161. The same. 3 B.
162. Allectus. Gold.
163. Domitius Domitianus. 2 B.
164. Constantius Chlorus.
165. Helena.
166. Theodora.
167. Galerius Maximianus.
168. Valeria.
169. Severus Cæsar.
170. Maximinus Daza.
171. Maxentius. Silver.
172. Romulus. 2 B.
173. Licinius.
174. Licinius, the Younger.
175. Valens.
176. Martinianus.
177. Constantinus Magnus.
178. Constantinus Magnus.
179. Fausta.
180. Crispus. Gold.
181. Helena.
182. Delmatius.
183. Constantinus, the Younger.
184. Constans.
185. Constantius, Chlorus.[1]
186. Jovianus.

PLATE X.

ROMAN COINS. REVERSES.

1. Adlocutio, from 1 B. of Hadrian.
2. Adventus ,, Gold of Aurelian.
3. Aegyptus ,, 1 B. of Hadrian.
4. Aeternitas ,, 1 B. ,,
5. Aeternitas ,, 1 B. Ant. Pius.
6. Aesculapius and Telesphorus. 1 B. Caracalla.
7. Aequitas. 1 B.
8. Alexandria. 1 B.
9. Annona[2]. 1 B.
10. Ancilia. 2 B. Ant. Pius.
11. Apollo. 1 B.
12. Apollo, in female habit. Silver.
13. Apollo, idem.
14. Arabia. The emperor and the province sacrificing.
15. Bonus Eventus.
16. Britannia. 2 B. Hadrian.
17. Cappadocia. 1 B. Hadrian.
18. Ceres, seated. Gold of A. Pius.
19. Ceres, standing.
20. Clementia Temporum. 1 B. Ant. Pius.
21. }
22. } Consecration types of an Emperor.[3]
23. }
24. }
25. } Consecration types of an Empress.[4]
26. Concordia.
27. The same. From a gold coin of Ant. Pius and Faustina.
28. Concordia. The Emperor and Empress joining hands, from a coin of Tranquillina.
29. Concordia. Aurelius and Verus joining hands.[5]

---

[1] This portrait is drawn out of order. It is taken from his 2 B. coin, and is evidently more correct than that of No. 164.
[2] Annona is sometimes represented seated.
[3] There is another type of an eagle standing on an altar. No. 23 is the funeral pile.
[4] No. 25. The throne, sceptre, and peacock of Juno.
[5] A favourite type at this period. It appears even on some Imperial Greek coins.

Plate X.

TYPES OF ROMAN COINS.

H. A. Ogg. REVERSES. Del. et Sculp.

Plate XI.

TYPES OF ROMAN COINS.

H. A. Ogg. Del. et Sculp.

REVERSES.

30. Concordia Militum. Woman holding two standards.
31. Concordia. Woman holding a standard, and a small figure of Victory. From 1 B. of Ant. Pius.
32. Concordia Militum. From 3 B. of Marius.[1]
33. Conservator. Aug. From gold of Elagabalus.[2]
34. Jovi Conservatori. The Emperor standing, under the protection of Jupiter.
35. Cybele. From 1 B. of Ant. Pius.
36. Dacia.
37. Dacia. Figure holding the military lituus. From gold of T. Decius.
38. Dacia Capta. Silver, Trajan.
39. Decursio. 1 B. Nero.
40. Diana Venatrix. Silver.
41. Diana Lucifera. 1 B. A. Pius.
42. Exercitus. 1 B. Nero.
43. Fecunditas. 1 B. Faustina.
44. The Tiberian Sow. 1 B. A. Pius.
45. Felicitas. 1 B. Hadrian.
46. Fides Exercitus. Gold.
47. Fides Militum. 1 B.
48. Fortuna. Usual type.
49. Fortuna.
50. Genuis Exercitus. Decius.
51. Genio Populi Romani. Brass, Diocletian.
52. Hercules. Gold. Diocletian.
53. Hercules Pacifer. Brass.
54. Hercules Musagetes. From Consular silver.
55. Hilaritas. Usual type.
56. Honos.
57. Indulgentia. 1 B. A. Pius.
58. Invictus.
59. Italia. 1 B. Hadrian.
60. Isis Faria. 3 B. Julian the Apostate.
61. Jupiter Stator. Usual type.
62. Jupiter Victor. „
63. Jovi Tutatori. „
64. Jupiter Axur. From Consular silver.
65. Jovi Ultori.
66. Jupiter Custos.
67. Jovi Crescenti. Silver, Gallienus.
68. Judæa Capta. 1 B. Vespasian.
69. Juno Lucina. Gold, Faustina.
70. Juno Regina. „
71. Juno Sospita.[3] 1 B. of A. Pius.
72. Laetitia. Gold. Pertinax.

PLATE XI.

ROMAN COINS. REVERSES.

73. Libertas.
74. Legionary standards. From the denarii of Antony.
75. Leg. IIII. Silver of Carausius.[4]
76. Liberalitas. Gold. Macrinus.[5]
77. Liberality.[6]
78. Mauretania. 1 B. Hadrian.
79. Mars. 1 B. Vespasian.
80. Mars Pacifer. 1 B. Sev. Alexander.
81. Mars Victor.

---

[1] This type is sometimes used with other legends, as on the coins of Domitian, Balbinus, &c.

[2] The figure represented in the chariot is the famous deity of Elagabalus, *El Gabal.*

[3] Juno Sospita is also represented on Consular coins.

[4] Other legionary badges will be found on the coins of Gallienus.

[5] The Emperor is represented on a tribune, attended by the Prætorian præfect, Liberality holding a tessera and cornucopia, standing before; below, a figure holding up his robe to receive the gift.

[6] A repetition of the figure in the preceding group.

82. Mater Castrorum. 1 B. Faustina.
83. Mercury. 2 B. M. Aurelius.
84. Minerva. Silver, Severus.
85. Minerva. Silver, Domitian.
86. Moneta. Usual type.
87. "Moneta Augustorum," 1 B. Gallienus.
88. Neptune. 1 B. Hadrian.
89. Nilus. 1 B. Hadrian.
90. Ops. 1 B. Ant. Pius.
91. Oriens. 3 B. Aurelian, &c.
92. Pax. 1 B. Vitellius.
93. Pax.[1] 2 B. Galba.
94. Pannonia. Silver, Treb. Gallus.
95. Pietas. Gold, Aelius.
96. Pietas. 1 B. Matidia.
97. Pietas. Pontifical instruments. A rev. of Maximus.
98. Princeps Juventutis. Silver.
99. The same. Silver.
100. Profectio. M. Aurelius.
101. Providentia.
102. The same. 1 B. Hadrian.
103. The same. 1 B. „
104. Gate of the Prætorian camp, with "Providentia," &c. From small brass of Constantine.
105. Pudicitia. Gold, Faustina.
106. The same. Gold, Etruscilla.
107. Rector Orbis. 1 B. D. Julianus.
108. Restitutor Achaiæ. 1 B. Hadrian.
109. Roma. 1 B.
110. Roma. 1 B.
111. Roma Resurges. 1 B. Vespasian.
112. Restitutor Urbis. 3 B.
113. Saeculares Aug. Silver, Philip.
114. Salus. Usual type.
115. The same.
116. The same.
117. Salus Reipublicæ. Gold, Galla Placidia.
118. Securitas. Silver, Otho.
119. Securitas. 1 B. Ant. Pius.
120. Securitas. 1 B.
121. Securitas Reipublicæ. The Bull Apis. 2 B. Julian the Apostate.
122. Soli Invicto Comiti. The sun standing. A common reverse of the lower empire.
123. Soli Invicto. The same.
124. Spes. The usual type.
125. Temporum Felicitas. The four seasons. Commodus.
126. The same. Aelianus.
127. Triumphal arch, with "De Britann." Gold and silver of Claudius.
128. Trophy. Common type of the lower empire.
129. Venus Victrix.
130. Venus Genetrix.
131. Venus Victrix.
132. Victoria.
133. Victory, with trophy.
134. Victory, marching.
135. Victory. Silver, Caracalla.
136. Victory, on a globe. 1 B. Ant. Pius.
137. Victory, bearing a shield, inscribed "BRITAN." 2 B. Hadrian.
138. Victoria Navalis. 2 B. Vespasian.
139. Victoria. Silver, Constantine.
140. Virtus. Silver, Gordian.
141. Virtus. 3 B. Allectus.
142. Vota Publica, a sacrifice. Gold, Hadrian.
143. VOT. V.[2] within a garland. Silver, Procopius.
144. Wolf and twins. 1 B. A. Pius.
145. The same. 3 B. Temp. Constantine.
146. Uberitas. Silver, Carausius.
147. Monogram of Christ, composed of the letters X and P, between the letters Alpha and Omega. Brass of Magnentius.

---

[1] The common pax type is Peace, holding an olive branch and the hasta.
[2] Vide page 160.

Plate XII

TYPES OF SAXON COINS.

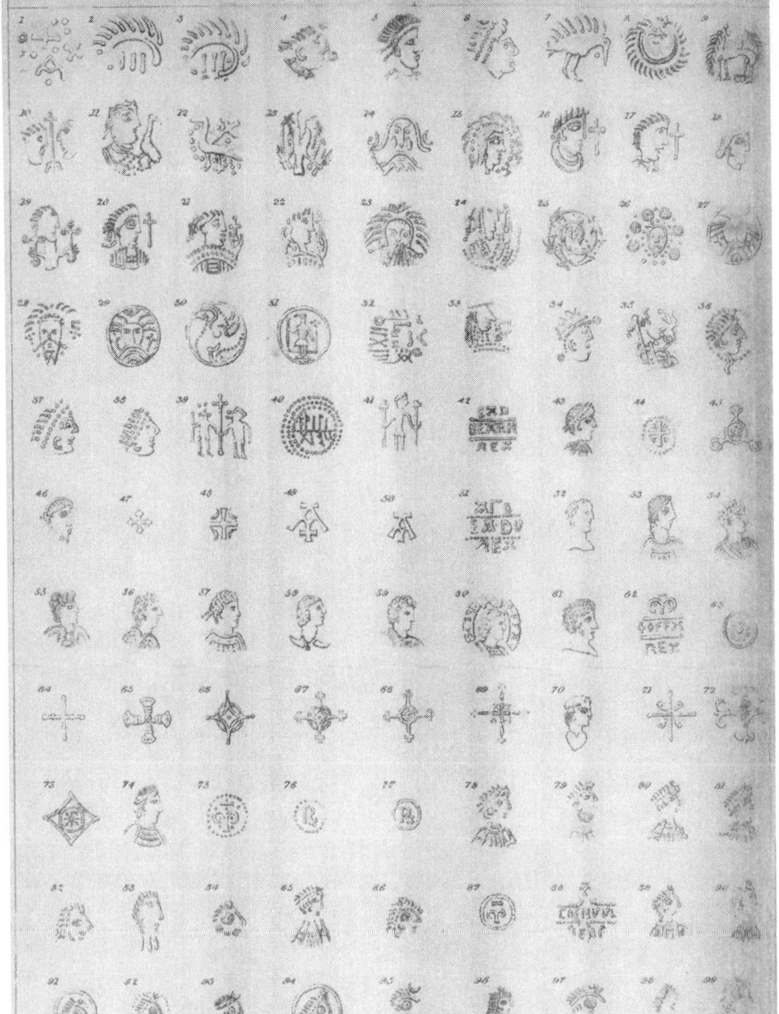

H. A. Ogg. OBVERSES. Del. et Sculp.

TYPES OF SAXON AND ENGLISH COINS.

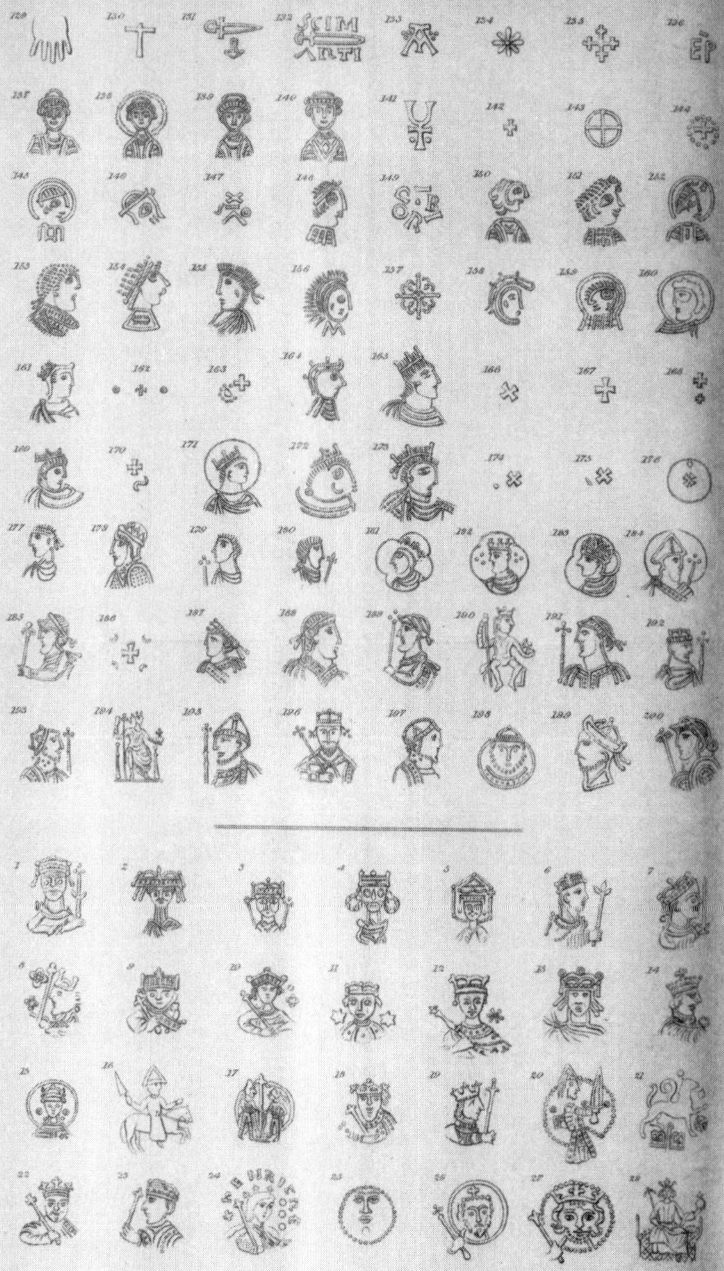

H.A. Ogg. Del. et Sc.

OBVERSES.

London. Taylor & Walton, Upper Gower Street.

PLATE XII.

SAXON COINS. OBVERSE TYPES.

1 to 39. Examples of the Types of unappropriated Sceattas.
40. Ethelbert.
41. Ecgberht.
42. Eadberht.
43. Cuthred.
44. „
45. „
46. Beldred.
47. „
48. „
49. Aethelweard.
50. „
51. Eadvald.
52 to 73. Offa.
74. Cenethreth.
75. „
76. Ecgberht.
77. „
78 to 88. Coenwulf.
89. Ciolvulf.
90. Ciolvulf
91. Beornvulf.
92. Ludica.
93. Berhtulf.
94. „
95. to 98. Burgred.
99. Ciolvulf II.
100. „
101. Beonna.
102 to 105. Eadmund.
106 to 108. Ethelstan.
109 to 114. Eanred.
115 to 120.
121. Regnald.
122. Anlaf.
123. „
124. „
125. „
126. Eric.
127. Ethelred.
128 „

PLATE XIII.

SAXON AND ENGLISH COINS. OBVERSE TYPES.

SAXON.

129 to 131. Saint Peter.
132. St. Martin.
133. St. Edmund.
134. Iaenberht, Archb.
135, 136. Ethelweard, Archb.
137. Vulfred „
138 to 140. Cialnoth „
141. Plegmund „
142 to 144. Vulfhere „
145 to 147. Ecgberht.
148, 149. Ethelvulf.
150, 151. Ethelberht.
152 to 154. Alfred.
155 to 157. Edward.
158 to 163. Ethelstan.
164 to 168. Edmund.
169 to 170. Eadred.
171. Eadwig.
172 to 176. Eadgar.
177. Edward II.
178 to 180. Ethelred II.
181 to 186. Cnut.
187. Harold I.
188, 189. Harthacnut.
190 to 198. Edw. Confessor.
199. Harold II.
200. „

ENGLISH.

1 to 7. William the First.
8 to 15. Henry the First.
16. Robert.
17. Stephen and Henry?
18, 19. Stephen.
20, 21. Eustace.
22 to 24. Henry II.
25. John (Irish).
26, 27. Henry III. *Long cross.*
28. Henry III. Gold penny.

PLATE XIV.

ENGLISH COINS. OBVERSE TYPES.

29. Henry III. Groat ?[1]
30. 31. Edward I.
32. Edward I. *Proof Groat.*
33. Edward III. Quarter-Noble.
34. „ Groat.
35. „ Noble.
36. „ Halfpenny.
37. „ Quarter-Florin. (See p. 311).
38. „ Half-Florin.
39. Richard II. Groat.
40. „ „
41. Henry IV. „
42. „ Halfpenny.
43. Henry V. Groat.
44. Edward IV. „
45. Henry V. or VI. Penny.
46. Edward IV. Norwich Groat.
47. „ Penny.
48. „ Groat.
49. „ *Bristol Groat.*
50. „ Rose Noble.
51. „ Durham Penny.
52. „ Angel.
53. Richard III. Groat.
54. Henry VII. Groat, *arched crown.*
55. „ Shilling, *side face.*
56. „ Half-Groat.
57. „ Sovereign.
58. „ Sovereign Penny.
59. „ Rose rial.
60. Henry VIII. Testoon.
61. „ Side-faced Groat.
62. Henry VIII. Crown ?
63. „ Half-Groat.
64. „ Groat.
65. „ Gold Crown.
66. „ Irish Groat.
67. „ George Noble.
68. „ PortcullisFarthing.
69. Edward IV. Sixpence.
70. „ Base Shilling.
71. „ „
72. „ Half-Sovereign.
73. „ Crown.
74. „ Sovereign.
75. „ Shilling, with countermark of a greyhound.
76. „ Base Shilling.
77. „ Farthing.
78. „ Penny.
79. „ Probably a pattern for a Half-Sovereign.
80. Mary. Groat.
81. Philip and Mary. Shilling.
82. „ Half-Crown.
83. Elizabeth. Shilling.
84. „ Sixpence (p. 333.)
85. „ Shilling.
86. „ Crown.
87. „ Shilling.
88. „ Sixpence.
89. „ Penny Pledge (p. 333).
90. „ Halfpenny. Anchor. mint mark.
91. „ Portcullis money (p. 290.)

PLATE XV.

SAXON COINS. REVERSE TYPES.

1 to 41. Unappropriated Sceattas.
42. Ethilberht.
43. Ecgberht.
44. „
45. Eadbearht.
46. Eadbearht.
47. Cuthred.
48. „
49. „
50. Beldred.

---

[1] An unknown piece given by Ruding, the type resembling the penny of this king.

TYPES OF ENGLISH COINS.

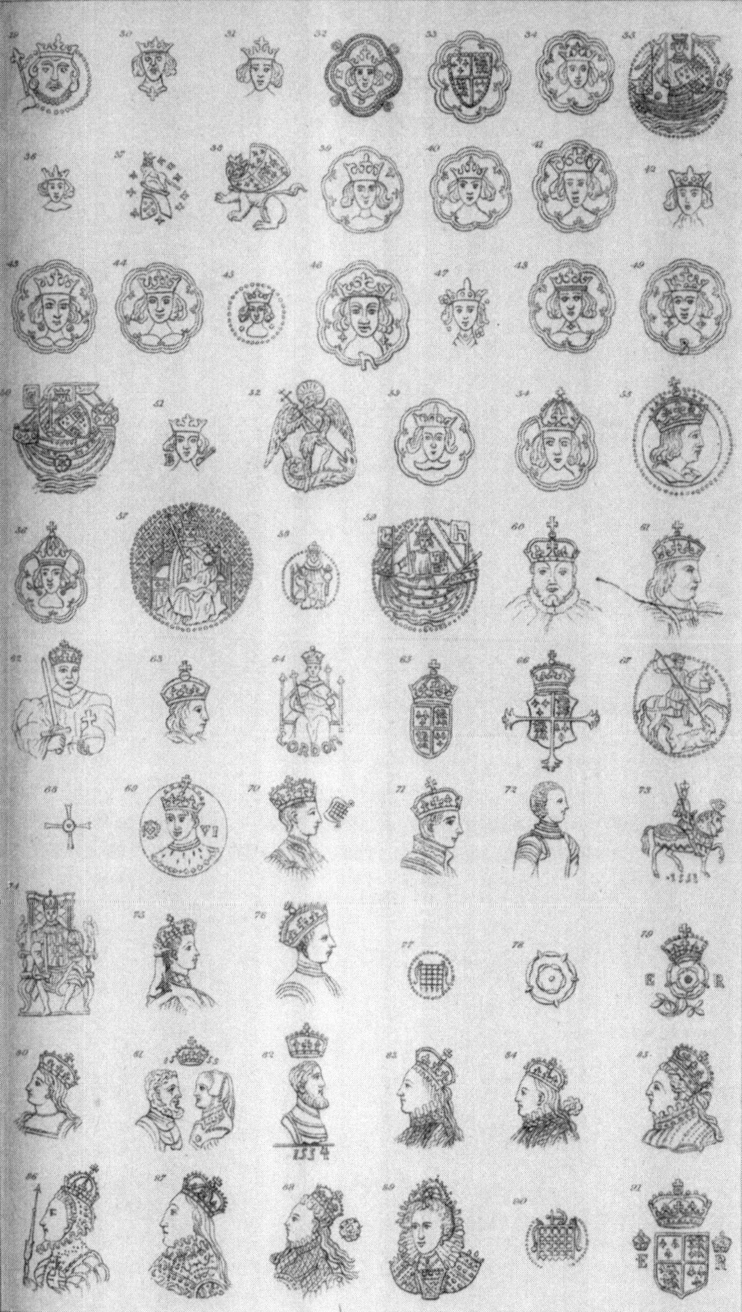

H.A. Ogg. Del. et Sculp.

OBVERSES.

TYPES OF SAXON COINS.

F.L.A. Ogg, Del. et Sculp.

REVERSES.

51. Beldred.
52. Aethelweard.
53. „
54. Eadvald.
55. Offa.
56. „
57. „
58. „
59. „
60. „
61. „
62. „
63. „
64. „
65. „
66. „
67. „
68. „
69. „
70. „
71. „
72. „
73. „
74. „
75. „
76. „
77. „
78. „
79. Cenethreth.
80. „
81. Ecgberht.
82. „
83. Coenvulf.
84. „
85. „
85. „
86. „
87. „
88. „
89. „
90. „
91. „
92. „
93. Coenvulf.
94. „
95. „
96. Ciolvulf I.
97. „
98. Ludica.
99. Berhtulf.
100. „
101. „
102. Burgred.
103. „
104. „
105. „
106. „
107. „
108. Ceolvulf II.
109. „
110. Beonna.
111. Eadmund.
112. „
113. „
114. Ethelstan.
115. „
116. „
117. „
118. Eanred.
119. „
120. „
121. „
122. „
123. Ethelred.
124. „
125. „
126. „
127. „
128. „
129. „
130. Anlaf.
131. „
132. „
133. Eric.
134.
135. Ecgfrith.

PLATE XVI.

SAXON AND ENGLISH COINS. REVERSE TYPES.

SAXON.

136. St. Peter.
137. „
138. „
139. St. Martin.
140. „
141. St. Eadmund.
142. Offa and Archbishop Ianberht.
143. Offa and Archbishop Aethilheard.
144. „ „ „
145. Vulfred.
146. Ceolnoth.
147. „
148. „
149. „
150. Vigmund.
151. „
152. Vulfhere.
153. Ecgbeorht.
154. „
155. Ethelvulf.
156. „
157. Aethelbearht.
158. Aethilred.
159. Aelfred.
160. „
161. „
162. Eadweard I.
163. „
164. „
165. „
166. „
167. „
168. „
169. „
170. „
171. „
172. „
173. „
174. Aethelstan.
175. „
176. „
177. „
178. Eadmund.
179. „
180. „
181. „
182. Eadred.
183. Eadwig.
184. „
185. Eadgar.
186. „
187. „
188. „
189. Eadweard II.
190. Aethilred II.
191. „
192. „
193. Cnut.
194. „
195. „
196. „
197. „
198. Harold I.
192. Harthacnut.
200. Edward Confessor.
201. „
202. „
203. „
204. „
205. „
206. „
207. Harold II.
208. „

ENGLISH.

1. William I. and II.
2. „
3. „
4. „
5. „
6. „
7. „
8. Henry I.
9. „
10. „

Plate XVI.

TYPES OF SAXON AND ENGLISH COINS.

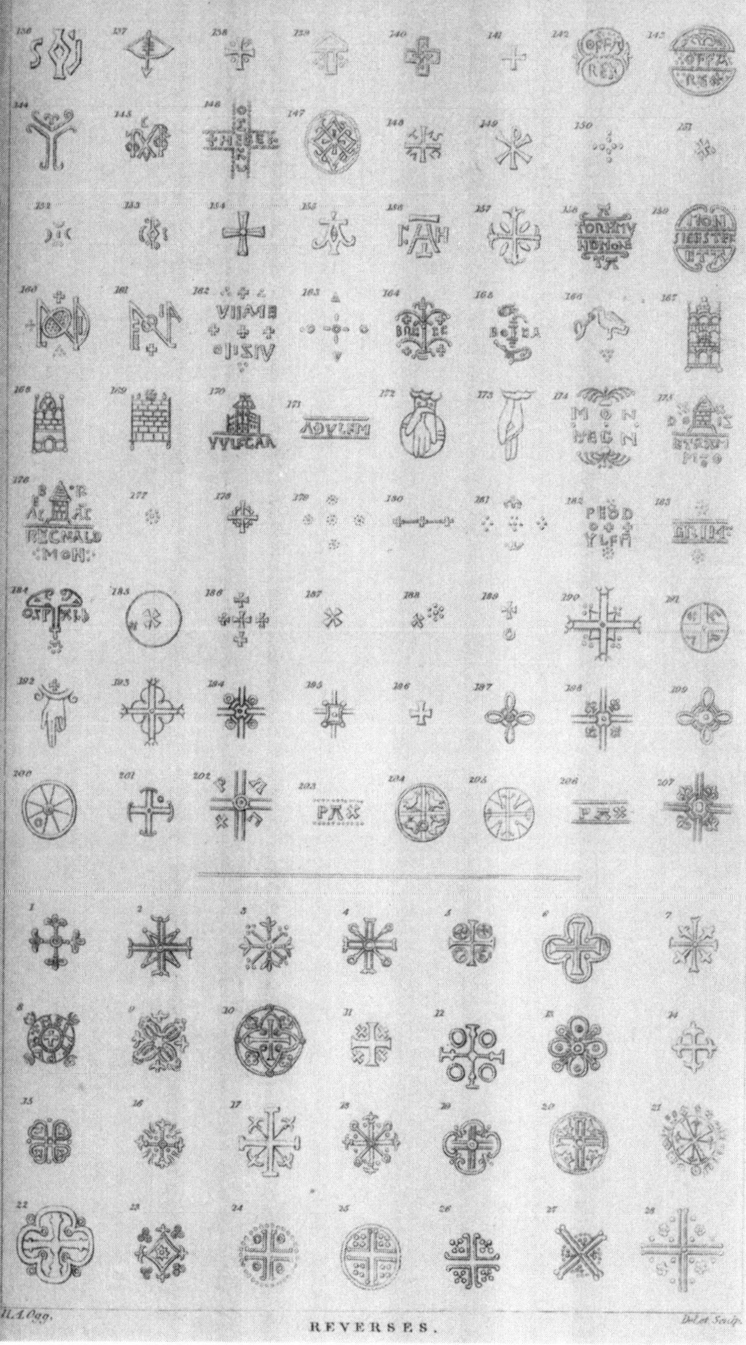

H. A. Ogg. REVERSES. Del. et Sculp.

TYPES OF ENGLISH COINS.

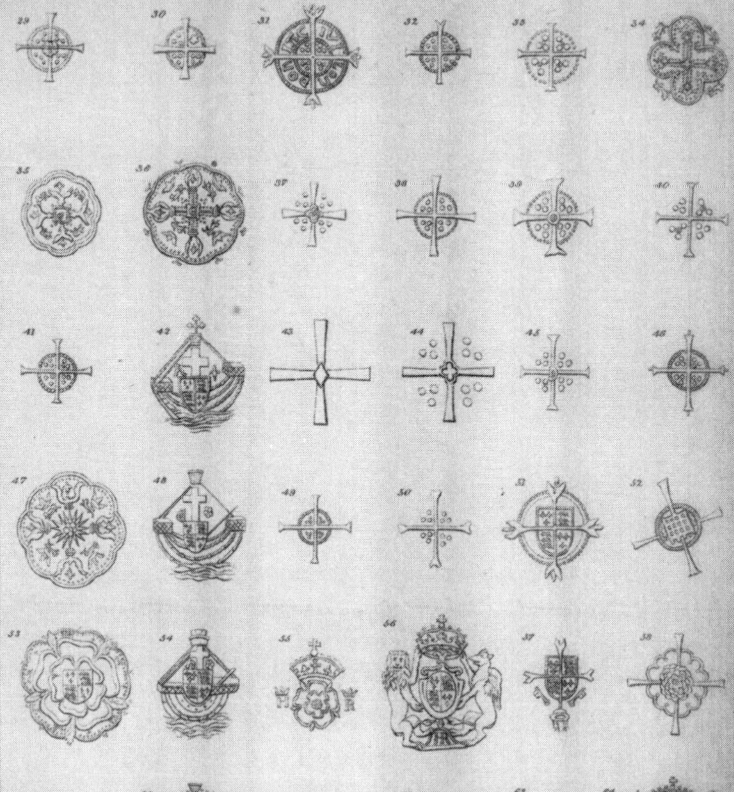

H. A. Ogg. Bri Lt Sculp.

REVERSES.

London, Taylor & Walton, Upper Gower Street.

11. Henry II.[1]
12. Henry I.
13. „
14. „
15. „
16. „
17. Robert.
18. Stephen and Henry.
19. Stephen.
20. Stephen.
21. „
22. Eustace.
23. Henry II?
24. John (Irish).
25. Henry III., Short Cross.
26. „
27. „ Long Cross.
28. „ Gold Penny.

PLATE XVII.

ENGLISH COINS. REVERSE TYPES.

29. Edward I. Penny.
30. „ Reading Penny.
31. Edward I.? Proof Groat.
32. Edward II. Penny.
33. Edward III. Penny.
34. „ Florin.
35. „ Quarter Noble.
36. „ Noble.
37. Richard II. Penny.
38. „ Groat, &c.
39. Henry IV., V., VI. Durham Penny.
40. „ Groat, &c.
41. „ Penny, &c.
42. Henry. Angel.
43. „ Groat.
44. Henry VI. York Penny.
45. Edward IV. Durham Penny.
46. „
47. Edward IV. Rose Noble.
48. „ Angel.
49. „ Penny, &c.
50. Henry VII. Groat, with arched crown
51. „ Groat, with "Septim."
52. „ London Groat.
53. „ Sovereign.
54. Henry VII. Angel.
55. Henry VIII. Testoon.
56. „ Crown?
57. Half-Groat of Wolsey with the Cardinal's hat.
58. Henry VIII. Tournay Groat.
59. „ London Penny.
60. „ Angel.
61. „ Portcullis Farthing.
62. Edward VI. Groat, fine silver, side face.
63. „ Base Shilling.
64. „ Sovereign.
65. „ Fine Shilling.
66. Philip and Mary. Shilling.
67. „ Half-Crown.
68. „ Angel.
69. Elizabeth. Shilling, &c.
70. „ Pledge.
71. „ Crown and Halfcrown.
72. „
73. „ Sixpence, &c. broad cross.
74. „ Pledge.
75. „ „
76. „ Halfpenny.

---

[1] This type is drawn out of order.

WOOD CUTS.

The Vignette on the title-page is copied from the reverse of a rare and beautiful silver coin of Camarina, in the collection of Lord Northwick. The original is under the usual size of the Tetradrachm. The following observations have been obligingly communicated by Mr. Burgon.

"It appears to me that the true meaning of this beautiful composition has never yet been perceived. The older Numismatists, as cited by Eckhel (Doct. Num. Vet., Vol. I. p. 200), seem to think that it represents Venus or Leda. This latter opinion is adopted by Noehden (Coins of Magna Græcia and Sicily, p. 12), who is the last that has given any explanation of the subject.

"A careful consideration, however, of the inscription KAMAPINA around the representation in question, taken in connexion with the subject of the obverse of the coin (see Noehden Loc. Cit.), leads me to look upon this graceful and unusual type as no other than a personified and symbolical representation of *the lake itself*, which is well known to have been called *Camarina*, and to have been situated close to the Sicilian city of the same name.

"Eckhel observes (Doct. Num. Vet., Vol, I., p. 185), that 'the Sicilians were fond of introducing on their coins the names and representations of their rivers;' and we have a remarkable example of this in the obverse of the coin before us, which is no doubt to be considered as a symbolical personification of the river Hipparis. We have therefore the river on one side of the coin, and on the other, the lake Camarina. It may be added in proof of this assertion, that there exists another coin of the city of Camarina (Mionnet, Vol. I., p. 222, No. 119), bearing types very analogous to those on the coin in question: on one side of which, around the personified head of the river is the inscription IΠΠΑΡΙΣ, and on the other, around the female on the swan, the word KAMAPINA; leaving no doubt in this instance, that the inscriptions refer to the representations, and that KAMAPINA is not to be regarded as forming a part of the truncated word KAMAPINAIΩN, as, at first sight, it might appear to do."

Page.

1. Silver of Aegina, from a specimen in the British Museum.
2. Another of more recent period, with the letters AIΓ in one of the compartments.
7. Representation of the Temple of Venus at Paphos, on a coin of Cyprus, with the legend ΚΟΙΝΟΝ ΚΥΠΡΙΩΝ. The Community of the Cyprians.
11. Tetradrachm of Alexander the Great, ΑΛΕΞΑΝΔΡΟΥ. Jupiter seated; in the field, a symbol, probably the representation of some ancient deity under the form of a cone-shaped stone, surmounted by a star; below, ×.
12. Silver of Antiochus, of Syria, ΒΑΣΙΛΕΩΣ . ΑΝΤΙΟΧΟΥ . ΝΙΚΗΦΟΡΟΥ . ΘΕΟΥ . ΕΠΙΦΑΝΟΥΣ. In the British Museum.
16. Shekel, in the cabinet of Doctor John Lee.
17. Brass of Antony and Cleopatra, in the cabinet of the Chevalier de Horta.—*Obv.*—BACIΛ . . . ΘЄΑ · ΝЄ . the Queen (Cleopatra) *the new goddess.*—℞. ΑΝΤ . ΥΠ . Γ. *Antonius, thrice Consul.*[1]
32. Second brass of Caligula, struck in the colony of Cæsar Augusta, in Spain.
36. Unique brass of Lebadia in Bœotia, in the collection of the Chevalier de Horta [2]
39. Brass, probably of Pergamus, an unique coin, in the collection of Thomas Burgon, Esq.; legend, ΕΠ(Ι) . ΑΝ . ΑΥ . Ι . ΚΟΥΑΔΡΑΤΟΥ under the Prætor? Aurelius Julius Quadratus. A river-god seated, typifying the river ΚΑΙΚΟC.
54. The obverse of the exquisite piece termed the Syracusan Medallion.
55. Silver of Zacynthus Insula (Ζ)ΑΚΥΝΘΟΣ. In the cabinet of the Chevalier de Horta.
83. Brass of the Bosphorus.—*Obv.* The head of the Emperor Claudius; legend, ΤΙ . ΚΛΑΥΔΙΟΥ . ΚΑΙΣΑΡΟΣ . ΙΒ. *In the twelfth year of Tiberius Claudius Cæsar.*—℞. The head of the Empress Agrippina; legend, ΙΟΥΛΙΑΝ . ΑΓΡΙΠΠΙΝΑΝ ΣΕΒΑΣΤΗΝ and ΒΑ ΚΩ *in monogram* (the people worship); *the Empress Julia Agrippina. King Kotys.* [3] The names and titles of the emperor and empress are here given at length,

[1] Num. Chronicle, Vol. I. p. 198. [2] Ibid, p. 48. [3] Vide p. 29, n. 3.

Page.

while those of the king, Cotys, are expressed by the monogram in the field.

104. Remarkable coin of the Magnesians of Lydia, with the head of Cicero. *Obv.* The head of Cicero, legend, ΜΑΡΚΟΣ ΤΥΛΛΙΟΣ ΚΙΚΕΡΩΝ.—℞. ΜΑΓΝΗΤΩΝ. ΑΠΟ. ΣΙΠΥΛΟΥ. ΘΕΟΔΩΡΟ(Υ), of the Magnesians under (mount) Sipulus, in the Prætorship of Theodorus.

162. The rare large brass of Matidia, in the cabinet of Capt. Smyth. *Obv.* MATIDIAE. AVG. DIVAE. MARCIANAE. F. Matidia Augusta, daughter of the divine Marciana. ℞. PIETAS. AVGVSTA(E). S. C.

213. Gold British coin of the age of Cunobeline, or perhaps earlier.

215. Silver Gaulish coin (see p. 215).

217. Metal Wheels of Gaulish origin, from the Revue Numismatique.

218. Rings found in Ireland.

218. Gold British coin, similar to that at p. 213, but with the letters VER. on the reverse.

221. Gold coin of Cunobeline. *Obv.* CAMVI.—℞. CVNOBHI.

225. Early uninscribed Saxon skeatta, found by Mr. Burgon in the Isle of Sheppy (Num. Chronicle, Vol. I.)

240. Skeatta of Aldfrid (cabinet of Mr. Loscombe).

258. Penny of Henry the Third, with short cross. ℞. TER. RI. ON. LVND.

339. Half-Crown of Charles the First, in the cabinet of Mr. Cuff. From the letters : SA : conjectured to have been struck at Salisbury. In rudeness of workmanship it resembles many of the half-crowns of this stormy period.

J. Wertheimer & Co., Printers, Finsbury Circus.